DAMAGES AND COMPENSATION CULTURE

The focus of the essays in this book is on the relationship between compensation culture, social values and tort damages for personal injuries. A central concern of the public and political perception of personal injuries claims is the high cost of tort claims to society, reflected in insurance premiums, often accompanied by an assumption that tort law and practice is flawed and improperly raising such costs. The aims of this collection are to first clarify the relationship between tort damages for personal injuries and the social values that the law seeks to reflect and to balance, then to critically assess tort reforms, including both proposals for reform and actual implemented reforms, in light of how they advance or hinder those values. Reforms of substantive and procedural law in respect of personal injury damages are analysed, with perspectives from England and Wales, Canada, Australia, Ireland and continental Europe. The essays offer valuable insights to anyone interested in the reform of tort law or the tort process in respect of personal injuries.

Damages and Compensation Culture

Comparative Perspectives

Edited by
Eoin Quill and Raymond J Friel

• HART •
OXFORD • LONDON • NEW YORK • NEW DELHI • SYDNEY

HART PUBLISHING
Bloomsbury Publishing Plc
Kemp House, Chawley Park, Cumnor Hill, Oxford, OX2 9PH, UK

HART PUBLISHING, the Hart/Stag logo, BLOOMSBURY and the Diana logo are trademarks of Bloomsbury Publishing Plc
First published in Great Britain 2016

First published in hardback, 2016
Paperback edition, 2019

A catalogue record for this book is available from the British Library.

Library of Congress Cataloging-in-Publication Data

Names: "Compensation Culture—Comparative Tort Law Reform in the 21st Century" (Conference) (2014 : University of Limerick) | Quill, Eoin, editor. | Friel, Raymond, editor.

Title: Damages and compensation culture : comparative perspectives / edited by Eoin Quill and Raymond J. Friel.

Description: Oxford ; Portland, Oregon : Hart Publishing, 2016. | "This book presents a collection of papers from a conference entitled 'Compensation Culture—Comparative Tort Law Reform in the 21st Century' held at the University of Limerick on 23–24 May 2014"—Introduction. | Includes bibliographical references and index.

Identifiers: LCCN 2016028882 (print) | LCCN 2016029537 (ebook) | ISBN 9781849467971 (hardback) | ISBN 9781509902057 (Epub)

Subjects: LCSH: Personal injuries—Congresses. | Damages—Congresses. | Compensation (Law)—Congresses. | Torts—Social aspects—Congresses.

Classification: lCC K925 .C664 2014 (print) | lCC K925 (ebook) | DDC 346.03—dc23

LC record available at https://lccn.loc.gov/2016028882

ISBN: HB: 978-1-84946-797-1
PB: 978-1-50992-793-7
ePDF: 978-1-50990-204-0
ePub: 978-1-50990-205-7

Typeset by Compuscript Ltd, Shannon

To find out more about our authors and books visit www.hartpublishing.co.uk. Here you will find extracts, author information, details of forthcoming events and the option to sign up for our newsletters.

PREFACE

It is now two years since the University of Limerick hosted the conference that gave rise to this collection of thought-provoking essays on damages and compensation culture. We would like to firstly thank all of those who made the conference itself a success—the International Commercial and Economic Law Group at the School of Law in the University of Limerick and the Faculty of Arts, Humanities and Social Sciences at the University of Limerick, both of whom provided funding for the event; Michelle Hyland, who provided the administrative support that led to the smooth running of the conference and, of course, the participants who provided such a lively debate.

We are also greatly indebted to those who helped us to transform the conference into a book—the authors, whose painstaking efforts put further flesh on the bones of the papers delivered at the conference and the staff at Hart for their support in getting the concept off the ground and in transforming the raw manuscript into the finished production; in particular we would like to thank Bill Asquith, the Commissioning Editor, for all his assistance in getting the book proposal approved; Mel Hamill, the Managing Editor and her team for copy editing and Emma Platt, the Marketing Manager, for promoting the book. Special thanks are also due to Séamus Haughey, research librarian in the Oireachtas (Irish Parliament) library for providing material sought for John Kleefeld's chapter.

Eoin Quill
Raymond J Friel
23 May 2016

TABLE OF CONTENTS

Part IV: Compensation and Personal Responsibility

LIST OF CONTRIBUTORS

Denise Amram, Avv, Solicitor (Italy), postdoctoral researcher at Scuola Superiore Sant' Anna, Pisa, Italy. Scientific Collaborator of the International Observatory on Personal Injuries (www.osservatoriodannoallapersona.org).

Jeff Berryman, LLB (Hons), MJur, LLM, Professor, Faculty of Law, University of Windsor Ontario; (Formerly Dean of the Faculty). Fractional Chair as Professor of Law, Faculty of Law, University of Auckland.

Dorothea Dowling, LLB (Hons), LLM, FCII, FCIArb, FCIS, MIRM, Cert IoD, Chartered Insurer, Accredited Mediator. Former non-executive Chairperson of the Personal Injuries Assessment Board [PIAB] October 2002–April 2014 and prior to that of the Motor Insurance Advisory Board [MIAB] 1998–2004 statutory investigation into insurance costs. Executive positions as Group Liability Manager of the self-insured national transport company in Ireland for 20 years until 2013 and previously a decade as an insurance company Claims Manager in Dublin and in London.

Raymond J Friel, BCL, LLM, BL, Senior Lecturer, School of Law, University of Limerick; Director of the International Commercial and Economic Law Group, UL.

James Goudkamp, BSc, LLB, MA, BCL, MPhil, DPhil, Fellow, Keble College, Oxford; Associate Professor, Oxford Law Faculty; Academic Fellow, Inner Temple; Honorary Senior Research Fellow, Faculty of Law, University of Western Australia; Honorary Professorial Fellow, Law School, University of Wollongong; Barrister, 7 King's Bench Walk.

John C Kleefeld, BA, LLB, LLM, Associate Professor, University of Saskatchewan; member of the British Columbia and Saskatchewan bars.

Erik S Knutsen, BA(Hons), JD, LLM (Harvard), Associate Professor, Faculty of Law, Queen's University, Kingston, Ontario.

Richard Lewis, MA (Oxon), LLD (Cardiff), DCL (Oxon), Professor of Law, Cardiff University.

Annette Morris, LLB, LLM, PGDip (non-practising barrister), Reader, School of Law and Politics, Cardiff University.

Carol A Newlands, Forensic Psychiatrist, Masters Degrees in Forensic Psychology and in Health and Medical Law. Past Chair of the Victoria Branch of the RANZCP Faculty of Forensic Psychiatry; PhD Candidate, Deakin University, Geelong, Victoria.

Tim O'Connor, BL, BCL, LLM, is a practising barrister.

Ken Oliphant, BA, BCL, Professor, University of Bristol Law School. Former Director, Institute for European Tort Law; former Vice-Director, European Centre of Tort and Insurance Law, Vienna.

Eoin Quill, BCL, LLB, LLM, Senior Lecturer, School of Law, University of Limerick; Fellow of the European Centre of Tort and Insurance Law; member of the International Commercial and Economic Law Group, UL.

Desmond Ryan, LLB, BCL, MA (Oxon), PhD, Associate Professor, Trinity College Dublin.

Introduction

EOIN QUILL AND RAYMOND J FRIEL

Background

This book presents a collection of papers from a conference entitled 'Compensation Culture: Comparative Tort Law Reform in the 21st Century' held at the University of Limerick on 23–24 May 2014. Its focus is on damages in personal injury claims; this was not a planned feature of the original idea, but rather the result of the organic emergence of a theme from the papers offered. The conference was timed to mark the tenth anniversary of the introduction of the Personal Injuries Assessment Board (PIAB) in Ireland. The original call for papers focused on Ireland, England and Wales, and Australia because all three had some experience of a perception of an emerging compensation culture in public debate. Ireland and Australia had implemented significant reforms early in the century, while England and Wales had also engaged in reform and further reform was still being contemplated. Also, the jurisdictions covered have a similar common law basis for their tort laws, so it was felt that some useful comparisons might emerge. While there is a wealth of US literature in this area, there are significant idiosyncrasies in US tort that differentiate it from the jurisdictions originally targeted; much of the US literature is focused on jury trials (which are not generally used elsewhere for personal injuries) and on punitive damages (which are employed and assessed very differently in the US compared with the targeted jurisdictions). As a result, many of the lessons from the US were felt to be of only marginal relevance to scholars and reformers in the jurisdictions targeted. Australian interest was not as strong as hoped for, but a significant level of interest came from Canadian scholars; while those scholars did not perceive compensation culture to be a significant factor in Canada, they did highlight numerous aspects of tort reform being debated there.[1] Some continental European comparisons also emerged in the papers offered.

The chapters compiled in this book address aspects of tort law and practice for the determination and delivery of personal injury damages in England and Wales, Canada, Australia, Ireland and continental Europe. The first three are often considered together in tort literature because of the similarities between England and the Commonwealth countries.

[1] Although the use of juries in personal injuries cases in Canada gives rise to some differences from the other jurisdictions, comparisons between Australia, England and Canada are sufficiently well established in tort literature to justify the inclusion of the Canadian perspectives in this collection.

While Irish tort law rarely features in leading works from these countries, it does receive the occasional mention and has significant similarities with them in the main structure of its tort principles; furthermore, procedural reforms in Ireland may be of interest to those interested in tort reform in those jurisdictions. Because of EU membership and the embryonic development of European harmonisation in private law,[2] a continental European perspective is both useful and necessary for those in the UK and Ireland with an interest in tort reform.

Compensation Culture and Tort Reform

The idea of a compensation culture as a social problem has been prominent in public debate in Ireland and the UK for more than three decades; the phenomenon is also evident, though less prevalent in Australia.[3] While much of the use of the term in a pejorative sense has taken place in the media and in political speech, it can also frequently be seen in judicial analysis.[4] Concerns with the social problems that would be associated with more expansive tort principles are not, however, an entirely modern phenomenon, as examples of judicial concern can readily be found in nineteenth-century cases rejecting claims for fear of the deleterious social effects that the developments sought by claimants might bring by way of a growth in litigation.[5]

The term is notoriously difficult to define, being associated with a variety of concerns: it may be a basic concern that there are simply too many claims, eating up valuable resources or it may be a concern that damages levels and legal costs are too high (again causing concerns with the overall cost to society); sometimes it is a concern over the level of fraudulent or exaggerated claims and the ease with which these can be pursued (often successfully); in other instances it is the fact that too many trivial cases are pursued and that it reflects a general decline in moral fibre—that we are greater whingers than past generations who

[2] In respect of tort harmonisation, see P Giliker, *The Europeanisation of English Tort Law* (Oxford, Hart Publishing, 2014).

[3] EW Wright, 'National Trends in Personal Injury Litigation: Before and after "Ipp"' (2006) 14 *Torts Law Journal* 233.

[4] Prominent judicial examples include decisions on capping general damages for non-pecuniary losses, the continuing cautious approach to claims for negligently inflicted psychiatric harm and claims against public authorities. On capping, note the similarity of reasoning in the Irish decision in *Sinnott v Quinnsworth* [1984] ILRM 523 and the Canadian decision in *Andrews v Grand and Toy Alberta Ltd* [1978] 2 SCR 229. In respect of psychiatric injury, see H Teff, *Causing Psychiatric and Emotional Harm* (Oxford, Hart Publishing, 2009) 10–20. In respect of public authorities, see the cases discussed by R Mullender, 'Negligence Law and Blame Culture: A Critical Response to a Possible Problem' (2006) 22 *Journal of Professional Negligence* 2, 5–7; also the Irish cases discussed by R Ryan, 'Impact of the Act on the "Compensation Culture": Big or Small?' in C Craven and W Binchy (eds), *Civil Liability and Courts Act 2004: Implications for Personal Injuries Litigation* (Dublin, FirstLaw, 2005) 144–46.

[5] *Winterbottom v Wright* (1842) 10 M & W 109 (Exch) 113–14 (Lord Abinger CB) 115 (Alderson B) (both emphasising a fear of the scale of claims being uncontrollable); *Brinsmead v Harrison* (1872) LR 7 CP 547 (Ex Ch) 551 (Kelly CB) (focusing on unscrupulous lawyers bringing multiple claims to get more costs).

stoically accepted misfortune without complaint.[6] In some instances even the perception of a problem is regarded as a basis for concern and a driver for reform.[7]

Whatever the precise variant, a central concern of the public and political perception of personal injuries claims (and a key motivation for reform) is the high cost of tort claims to society, reflected in insurance premiums; this is often accompanied by an assumption that tort law and practice is flawed and improperly raising such costs and is further accompanied by a depiction of both claimants and their lawyers as motivated more by greed than justice. It is ironic that many of those bemoaning the monetarist motivations of claimants and lawyers are themselves almost exclusively concerned with insurance costs rather than a serious examination of the justice issues raised; it is implicit in the criticisms of those complaining of compensation culture that increases in claims (either in number or value) are bad and decreases in insurance costs are good, yet there is little (if any) consideration of the underlying factors involved in any such changes to determine whether useful social goals are being advanced or retarded.[8] The socially beneficial goals of tort, such as vindication of victim's rights, the accountability of those that inflict injury and the deterrence of wrongful behaviour, are generally confined to academic commentary and are often absent from much of the media and political commentary.

While statistical evidence can disclose a certain amount about growth or decline in a given activity, such as tort claims, or its cost in terms of insurance prices (provided reliable statistics are available), it cannot tell us whether the values underlying the change are socially desirable. The evaluation of the merits or otherwise of changes is not amenable to a clear objective answer; it is a matter of judgement and perspective. As Lewis and Morris succinctly observe those complaining 'that claiming represents a decline in personal responsibility choose to privilege anecdotal critical accounts: long-term increases in claiming could equally be presented as a desirable increase in access to justice and defendant accountability'.[9]

A second difficulty with the idea of compensation culture as a social problem is that while it is frequently blamed on tort, discussion often also includes non-tort sources of compensation and it can be difficult to disentangle the contribution of tort from the other systems. A further problem is that the contribution of tort to a claims culture, whether good

[6] For detailed consideration of the variety of supposed ills addressed by the term, see K Williams, 'State of Fear: Britain's "Compensation Culture" Reviewed' (2005) 25 *Legal Studies* 499, 500–03; Ryan (n 4) 140–42; Wright (n 3) 237–38; R Lewis, A Morris and K Oliphant, 'Tort Personal Injury Claim Statistics: Is there a Compensation Culture in the United Kingdom?' (2006) 2 *Journal of Personal Injury Law* 87, 88; A Morris, 'Spiralling or Stabilising? The Compensation Culture and Our Propensity to Claim Damages for Personal Injury' (2007) 70 *MLR* 349, 350; A Morris, '"Common Sense Common Safety": The Compensation Culture Perspective' (2011) *27 Journal of Professional Negligence* 82, 85.

[7] Williams (n 6) 508–09 discusses potential defendants taking excessive risk-avoidance measures, though Morris, '"Common Sense Common Safety"' (n 6) 86–87 notes a lack of evidence to substantiate claims of greater risk aversion; Mullender, 'Negligence Law and Blame Culture' (n 4) 4–7, 29 gives examples of judges rejecting plausible or even meritorious claims. See Ryan (n 4) 138–39 on the perception of a problem as a basis for change.

[8] On the problem of distinguishing 'good' and 'bad' claims, see Williams (n 6) 504–05; Ryan (n 4) 157–59; S Hedley, 'The Rise and Rise of Personal Injury Liability—A Temporary Difficulty or a Permanent Crisis?' in C Craven and W Binchy (eds), *Civil Liability and Courts Act 2004: Implications for Personal Injuries Litigation* (Dublin, FirstLaw, 2005); Morris, 'Spiralling or Stabilising?' (n 6) 363–64; R Mullender, 'Blame Culture and Political Debate: Finding Our Way Through the Fog' (2011) 27 *Professional Negligence* 64, fn 9 and accompanying text and the table on 81.

[9] R Lewis and A Morris, 'Tort Law Culture: Image and Reality' (2012) 39 *Journal of Law and Society* 562, 585.

or bad, must distinguish between tort law and the tort process; the former refers to the substantive rules theoretically governing claims, while the latter refers to the actual practices involved in resolving claims.[10]

The original call for papers was put out under the title 'Compensation Culture or Accident Culture? Comparative Tort Law Reform in the 21st Century'. The question of whether there is an accident culture—ie, that the number and cost of tort claims is contributed to by a lack of adherence to appropriate standards in the conduct of many daily activities—has not yet become a point of focus in the literature. No papers were offered to address this question, so it was dropped from the conference title. An examination of that question will have to wait until another day.

A Synopsis of the Book

Theme

The focus of the chapters is on the relationship between compensation culture, social values and tort damages for personal injuries. The aims of this collection are to first clarify the relationship between tort damages for personal injuries and the social values that the law seeks to reflect and to balance, then to critically assess tort reforms (both proposals for reform and actual implemented reforms) in light of how they advance or hinder those values. The role (or lack of role) of perceptions of compensation culture in actual or proposed developments also features in many of the contributions.

Part I

General Features of the Relationship between Damages and Compensation Culture

These chapters raise a variety of issues in respect of damages reform which may, at first sight, appear specific to the particular jurisdictions discussed; however, the insights they provide are of general relevance to any jurisdiction with a tort system considering reform of the measure or delivery of damages. They also provide useful tools for the design and evaluation of reform processes that reformers and commentators would be well advised to take note of.

The opening chapter by Ken Oliphant explores whiplash claims in the UK and provides a microcosm of wider issues in the compensation culture debate. Whiplash provides a clear example of how a high volume of low-value claims can make a large contribution to

[10] On the relationship between substantive tort law and compensation culture, see Mullender, 'Negligence Law and Blame Culture' (n 4) 1–29; Hedley (n 8) 209. On the relationship between tort practice and compensation culture, see ES Knutsen, 'The Cost of Costs: The Unfortunate Deterrence of Everyday Civil Litigation in Canada' (2010) 36 *Queen's Law Journal* 113; Wright (n 3) 238; Williams (n 6) 508 (both of the latter two focus on insurance practices, emphasising flawed risk assessment practices and investment decisions, coupled with historic under-pricing).

the overall cost of the tort system. The manner in which the issue has been addressed in the UK is representative of many of the key features of the broader compensation culture debate. The chapter opens with an examination of the changing perception of the whiplash issue within the insurance sector from a health and safety focus to a compensation culture problem. The chapter also examines the role of the press and politicians in fostering the presentation of the issue as a major compensation culture problem.

The various proposals for reform that have been mooted and those that have been implemented are explored; these include using restrictive criteria to define what qualifies as an injury, medical examination and reporting processes, anti-fraud measures and other legal process reforms to bring about a significant reduction in costs. All of the measures considered are also either vaunted or utilised in other areas of the compensation debate, so this chapter provides an incisive introduction to matters which are taken up in more detail in later chapters.

The chapter also demonstrates the risks associated with the manipulation and misuse of statistics to portray a false image, which can mask the real issues at stake. It compares several aspects of the statistics on whiplash claims in several jurisdictions, including the UK, Italy and France and demonstrates how a focus on different elements of the data can create very different pictures of which jurisdiction is 'best' or 'worst'. The chapter also analyses the research design and methodology behind the statistics, identifying significant shortfalls in both. Oliphant's analysis highlights the gap between the perception of a UK whiplash compensation culture and the evidence offered in support. He warns that rhetoric can distract from access to justice concerns and a proper evaluation of the impact of reforms is lacking.

The second chapter by Richard Lewis focuses, as its title suggests, on two issues central to the compensation culture debate as it is unfolding in Britain—the number of personal injury claims and the value of those claims—and it examines the factors that have contributed to modern developments in these areas.

On the first issue, he summarises the data from available sources on trends in the rate of claiming in Britain, providing updates on what can be found in the established literature; the analysis shows a long-term rise in the total number of claims, but with dramatic variations in the types of claims brought—motor accident claims growing dramatically, public liability claims stabilising and employers' liability claims falling (though with significant fluctuations in the past 15 years). He then examines the institutional and personal factors impacting on claims' rates. On the institutional side, he identifies trade unions as being strongly associated with assisting in bringing workplace claims and notes a significant fall in trade union membership over the years—the area with a dramatic fall in claims. Next he looks at liability insurers who pay not only the damages, but also much of the costs associated with claims; while their association with the defence of claims is well known, this chapter emphasises that through BTE insurance they provide for much of the plaintiffs' representation too, with nearly three in five adults covered.[11] Counter-intuitively, he notes insurers' practices have encouraged increases in certain types of unmeritorious claims. He then examines the role of claims management companies and claimant personal injury law firms and the complex interaction between their practices and the regulation of fees, costs

[11] BTE is 'before-the-event insurance', also referred to as 'legal expenses insurance'.

and commercial strategies. On the personal side, changes in attitude and social values are suggested as making people more assertive and willing to see claiming as acceptable, while the personal response to the institutional factors creates a belief that claims are a routine matter of administration, free of stress or risk and virtually anonymised.

On the second issue, a number of factors tending to increase the value of claims are identified—the replacement of lump sum awards with periodical payment orders in cases of serious injury, the increased reimbursement of the state for benefits provided to victims, changes to the way pain and suffering is measured, greater sophistication in expert evidence on pecuniary losses and changes to discount rates for the financial return on investing awards.

The overall conclusions are, first on the negative side, that institutional problems and a 'dysfunctional insurance market' have contributed to motor claims increasing significantly; but, more positively, much of the increase in the cost per claim is based on getting a more accurate measure of the plaintiff's loss and so actually pursues the central aim of tort compensation—returning the plaintiff to his or her pre-accident position.

In the closing chapter of the section Erik Knutsen engages in a thought-provoking examination of the balance between process goals and justice concerns in personal injury tort reform, using mainly Canadian and Irish reforms to illuminate the general questions posed. Though focused on different jurisdictions from Lewis' chapter, this chapter also highlights the interconnectedness of tort law, insurance and the civil litigation process. Furthermore, even though compensation culture has not been prominent in Canadian tort reform discourse, he opens by noting the similarity in motivation for Canadian reform to that in other jurisdictions—controlling the cost of litigation, reducing insurance premiums, reducing delay in processing claims and concerns over fraud.

The two points of focus for the examination of these interconnected matters are 'damages limiters' and 'public dispute resolution mediaries'. The first of these involves an examination of the various judicial and legislative constraints placed on the recovery of damages, such as caps, threshold requirements for eligibility, deductibles and scales of damages for particular categories of injury.[12] He highlights a variety of potential unintended negative effects that can flow from such limiters and notes that judicially imposed limits are more likely to give consideration to justice goals as well as process goals, while legislative reform is likely to be focused almost exclusively on the latter and the political process militates against rectifying any damage inflicted on justice goals.

The second point of focus examines the use of various public administrative entities as an alternative or adjunct to the judicial process to resolve tort claims. Knutsen notes that these are exclusively targeted at process goals—to deliver 'justice that is faster, cheaper, and more accessible to the lay person', creating a variety of risks of undermining justice goals. He notes that great care is needed in the design and evaluation of such processes if justice goals are to be properly pursued and a fair balance between the two sets of goals is to be achieved.

Overall, it is suggested that reflexive evaluation of reform measures is essential to ensuring a proper balance between justice goals and process goals so as to avoid or at least reduce

[12] These different limiting factors may in turn be subdivided in quantitative limits (specifying specific monetary values) or verbal limits (descriptors of thresholds, scales or other qualifying criteria).

the potentially detrimental side effects identified in respect of the popular methods chosen for limiting tort damages and the cost of their delivery.

Part II

Damages Reform in Various Jurisdictions

This section explores a mixture of existing examples of damages reform and further possibilities for reform. It provides a range of insights into the relationship between the quantification of damages and the social values promoted or inhibited by particular approaches.

James Goudkamp opens this section; while not advocating widespread reform of tort in the UK, he begins with the premise that such reform is likely. He also suggests that the 'need principle' is likely to resonate with politicians reforming tort.[13] Noting that both recent UK legislation and UK tort reform proposals have been at least partially influenced by developments in Australia, he uses the Australian provisions as lessons, good and bad, for the reform of UK tort. Much of the chapter is focused on aspects of the measurement of damages, though some aspects of eligibility for damages are also touched on.

A cap on the level of recovery for lost income, based broadly on the Australian variants, is recommended on the basis that full income recovery for wealthy victims goes beyond need and drains resources that could be better deployed elsewhere. It is noted that care must be taken to pitch the cap at a level sufficient to meet objective need, but low enough to give meaningful savings in the system. Goudkamp then suggests that minimum thresholds could be considered for some or all heads of damages and compensation for those exceeding the threshold could be based on set sliding scales (rather than being left simply to judicial discretion); some Australian examples are provided, but he notes that some of the terminology employed in them is unduly vague and advises that more care be taken in devising thresholds were this option to be pursued. It is argued that a carefully set threshold will only exclude those whose injuries are sufficiently slight that their ability to meet their needs will not be unduly prejudiced. He then suggests that both exemplary damages and aggravated damages could be abolished, as neither addresses any pressing need on the part of claimants, though he notes that the systemic savings would be limited. He then moves to contributory negligence; while noting that the entire concept is conceptually incompatible with the need principle, he accepts it is too ingrained to be ripe for abolition. He recommends the introduction of fixed and minimum reductions, modelled loosely on the Australian provisions, as a means of fettering judicial discretion so as to provide fair and sensible systemic savings; though he warns that the provisions permitting an allocation of 100 per cent contributory negligence to a claimant should not be followed.

He then turns to examples of Australian reforms that would be distinctly unhelpful to follow, including the raising of the discount rate on awards to unrealistic levels in present

[13] The principle prioritises compensation to the most in need, giving greater preference in the allocation of scarce resources to those with more severe injuries. It would provide a substantive justice-orientated basis for change.

market conditions; illusory reforms where statutory provisions restate the common law; new statutory illegality defences; immunities for Good Samaritans and volunteers; and, finally, the creation of a multitude of liability schemes which generate undue complexity and inconsistency. The first of these runs contrary to the need principle, while the others are regarded as objectionable for a variety of other reasons.

Next, Jeff Berryman explores Canada's approach to non-pecuniary loss for personal injury. He opens by noting the lack of a 'compensation culture' in Canada, but points out that there have been occasional periods of concern over insurance costs. He discusses the triumvirate of leading cases from the Supreme Court of Canada (SCC) in 1978 which introduced controls over damages for non-pecuniary loss for personal injury based on an underlying social policy of containing tort awards in order to limit the social cost. He then examines subsequent cases and finds that, although fidelity to the SCC's principles is formally expressed, the substance of what is happening is at odds with their spirit. Two problems emerge—the cap on such damages is argued to be at too high a level and, secondly, there is a lack of consistency between awards. Contributing factors identified are the limited instructions provided to juries, the standard of appellate review and lack of guidelines on quantification coupled with a lack of coordinated reporting of awards.

He then examines non-pecuniary damages under the various statutory automobile insurance schemes across Canada, where the goal of containing the social cost of compensation is even more prevalent; a significant divergence in the manner of control and levels of damages is noted. A brief contrast with the limits in workers' compensation is provided, where non-pecuniary damages are generally significantly lower than in personal injury cases and again there is a wide variation across provinces. He then engages in a comparison with non-pecuniary loss in other categories of cases, once again noting different approaches across the provinces as to whether the cap has a role to play in the other categories. There are numerous examples where the cap has no application as the underlying policy reason for the cap is seen not to be in play and the head of damages performs different functions in such cases from those in personal injury cases.

The chapter concludes by suggesting it is time to recognise that the basis for awards has shifted to a new conceptual basis from the 1978 cases and the highlighted problems of inconsistency both within personal injury awards and between different systems of compensation need to be addressed. After examining the pros and cons of having a non-pecuniary loss award at all, he suggests the balance is in favour of retention. The cap for personal injuries cases in tort is suggested to be too high and either the SCC or legislature should lower it to reduce the inconsistency between different compensation schemes. Beyond the cap, for consistency in lesser awards, better jury instructions are required; a fair scale can only emerge if juries are informed of the policy reasons underlying the award. The key to attaining the goal of containing the cost of the system lies in controlling lower level awards, where most claims are located. He also favours retaining a distinction between personal injury cases and other categories of cases because of the different functions of the awards.

In the last chapter of this section the focus switches to an EU perspective. Denise Amram engages in a comparative analysis of the definition and calculation of damages for non-pecuniary loss in personal injury cases in Ireland, Italy, France and Belgium. The object is to increase the dialogue between practitioners, judges and scholars and to find the most efficient tools to collect and deliver data, with the aim of encouraging harmonisation of this area of compensation across Europe.

With respect to France and Belgium, it is noted that charts drawn up by unofficial groups classifying heads of loss and scales of assessment are widely used by the courts, despite a lack of formal legal basis. In Italy the heads of damage have been set by the Supreme Court and the scale of assessment often follows charts draw up by judicial tribunals (most notably that of Milan). By contrast, the Personal Injuries Assessment Board's Book of Quantum in Ireland has a clear legislative basis, but the Board has a greater discretion in each case in selecting the value of award within the bands in the Book than continental courts and tribunals have when following charts.

Amram highlights divergences in both the definition of non-pecuniary losses and in their valuation across the chosen jurisdictions. She further emphasises the lack of detailed data on awards made, especially by lower courts and tribunals. She then offers the model of the database developed and maintained by the International Observatory on Personal Injuries Damages in Pisa as a means of facilitating greater understanding of what is actually taking place across Europe in order to better inform a dialogue between the legal actors.[14]

Part III

The Process for Delivery of Damages

This section analyses three different types of reform to the tort system from three different jurisdictions, each aimed at systemic cost reduction. The chapters explore how the reform processes unfolded and note the social values advanced and impeded by the reforms.

Annette Morris opens the section with an incisive analysis of the reform of civil procedure in England and Wales; such reform being for the express purpose of reducing legal costs for personal injury claims. She examines the reforms brought about as a result of the reports of both Lord Woolf and Lord Justice Jackson, which are focused on ensuring proportionality of legal costs, and notes that they have raised concerns about both access to justice and the quality of substantive justice (as accuracy of outcome may be reduced). Her central thesis is that there is no objectively correct balance between costs, access to justice and legal accuracy of outcomes in cases and, therefore, no objectively demonstrable problem and no objectively right approach (such as proportionality) to resolving the problem. Rather, there is a socially constructed perception of a problem and the social construct drives the policy direction and underlying values that are engaged to resolve the problem. She then engages in a detailed examination of the role of three major institutional players in shaping the idea of personal injury litigation costs as a problem and the drive for proportionality as the preferred solution—insurers, senior members of the judiciary and politicians.

Insurers' strategies examined include challenging costs through litigation, administrative practices to streamline claims, political lobbying and media campaigns. Their object is to improve insurers' commercial circumstances. Some considerable success on their part in altering the civil justice process is noted. Apart from the obvious judicial contribution of the two major reports, a range of other extrajudicial comments by senior judges are identified on the issue of costs as a problem and proportionality as the solution; the driving

[14] Of course such information would also be very useful for other stakeholders in the debate on personal injury compensation.

factor is the fair distribution of scarce resources. Morris notes that these add support to the prioritisation of access to justice and efficiency, which are posited as the good social values, while the values promoted by greater accuracy in delivering substantive justice are played down. On the political front, she notes that while Labour had to be persuaded of the need for reform, their successors (principally the Conservatives) are more willing reformers, locating procedural reform in a wider agenda of deregulation. The combination of these diverse factors coalesces in procedural reform and cost reduction, widening the gap between tort law and tort practice and favouring particular values over others.

This is followed by Dorothea Dowling's fascinating inside perspective on the Personal Injuries Assessment Board (PIAB) in Ireland. It opens with a concise summary of the benefits delivered by the new system—a significantly reduced number of claims, speedier resolution of claims, dramatically reduced delivery costs and considerably lower insurance premiums. Dowling then explains the background to the establishment of the PIAB—a concern over high insurance costs (particularly the contribution of litigation costs) and a second concern over the time taken to resolve cases through the legal system. There was some political concern about the rate of claims, but neither this nor the legal rules used to determine such claims were considered for reform. Thus, the focus was on economic efficiency rather than a concern with principles of liability, levels of damages or rates of claim.[15]

The chapter then provides a detailed description of the PIAB process and addresses the criticisms levelled at it by commentators. The chapter identifies the relative stability of personal injury claims rates in Ireland over the first decade of the Board's operation, counter to public perceptions of a spiralling compensation culture. One suggested item of reform to existing tort rules is the introduction of a system of structured settlements instead of a single lump sum payment for those suffering from long-term injuries; this is focused more on the internal logic of the system, looking for greater equity in the quantum and delivery of damages than on any concern with a compensation culture.

The last chapter of the section by Carol Newlands explores the role of Medical Panels in personal injury compensation in Victoria, Australia. She notes that the Panels were initially introduced in the field of workers' compensation to reduce the cost of proceedings by replacing the parties' medical experts with a single neutral panel as part of a range of measures aimed at, inter alia, reducing systemic costs and cutting out exploitation of the system by professionals and claimants. They were extended to all personal injury claims disputes in Victoria in the reforms following the Ipp Report.

Newlands provides a history of the functioning and cost of the Panels, providing a fascinating insight into the political debates surrounding the many reforms of the Panels' role and the system within which they function. She emphasises that overall the Panels have been successful at contributing to reduced costs in processing personal injury claims and in reducing the level of legal disputes over the matters within the Panels' remit. However, she also raises a number of potential concerns for any reformers considering the Victorian model. First, the system clearly sets process goals to the fore and has been influenced by a compensation culture debate similar to that in Britain; she highlights some of the criticisms

[15] Though reduced claims levels have actually resulted in practice.

raised in respect of justice goals being adversely affected and some of the design problems that impeded the attainment of the process goals at various points in the evolution of the panels. Second, she notes that there have been numerous judicial review applications brought in respect of the Medical Panels' activities; any would-be reformer should recognise the need for careful design to avoid replacing one type of expensive legal dispute process (tort disputes over medical evidence) with another (judicial review of Medical Panel Opinions and Determinations).

Part IV

Compensation and Personal Responsibility

The final part of the book looks at personal responsibility—a key feature of the compensation culture debates; to the extent that reformers suggest that plaintiffs are part of the problem—whether as whingers, fraudsters, malingerers or opportunists—the solutions they offer usually seek to have victims take greater responsibility for their condition. These chapters examine some key social values involved in setting the balance between the personal responsibility of victims and the responsibility of third parties that contribute to injuries.

John Kleefeld's chapter examines two central aspects of the relationship between tort damages and personal responsibility—contributory negligence and concurrent wrongdoers—both grouped under the composite title of concurrent fault. The primary focus is on Canadian law, but with substantial use of English law as a comparison, with occasional comparisons to Ireland and the US (and a brief reference to Tasmania). The chapter (the longest in the book by a significant margin) provides an engaging and compelling history of the law in these areas. It examines the myriad legal moves from traditional common law exclusionary rules to modern statutory allocation provisions and explores the reasons underlying the changes wrought and the values reflected in those changes.

The exclusionary rules achieved a number of the goals sought by modern reformers, such as a high level of victim responsibility, protection of insurers from fraudulent claims, curbing floodgates fears and inhibiting growth in the number of claims; Kleefeld emphasises that they did so by crude measures which generated significant substantive injustices, as they often excluded victims entirely from access to damages despite the fact that they had been wrongfully injured and they also exculpated wrongdoers often entirely by reason of chance rather than reason. The various reforms gradually reduced these injustices, though not without producing problems of their own in the various formats attempted over the years. He draws out key principles for a just allocation of responsibility between multiple wrongdoers and notes the tension between those principles is such that no a priori correct balance between them can be said to exist. He then posits how current reform proposals from British Columbia and Manitoba would strike the balance between them.

He finishes with some recommendations for reform, suggesting the removal of misleading or pejorative terminology and the enactment of an 'Apportionment of Liability Act'. Overall the chapter highlights how compensation principles can be debated on the internal logic of law reform, focused on justice considerations between the parties. The debate can be informed by appropriate public values, with input from stakeholders in making decisions within the range of supportable just solutions; this can reduce the level of injustice to either plaintiffs or defendants that can result from rules which are narrowly focused on a specific goal without due consideration for their wider implications.

The final two chapters are not directly aimed at the topic of damages, but explore aspects of spillover—how concerns about the (potential) high cost of tort damages and their delivery can lead to avoidance measures such as reform of eligibility for tort compensation or defensive practices by potential defendants. Both strategies are aimed at circumventing exposure to damages and costs liabilities and raise significant questions about the balance of responsibility between victims and potential defendants. Each of the chapters looks at a specific manifestation of spillover in particular contexts, providing a microcosm of a potentially broad ranging problem. The first examines a judicial rebalancing of responsibility in occupiers' liability in light of compensation culture fears, while the other examines how potential defendants in a sporting context interpret their responsibility in response to perceived liability exposure.

In the first of the two chapters on the spillover phenomenon Desmond Ryan examines occupiers' liability decisions in England and Wales and Ireland since the turn of the millennium, exploring the way in which the values of individual autonomy and personal responsibility have been espoused by the judiciary. Ryan explores whether and to what extent there is a relationship between the coming to prominence of this theme in the cases and the more general compensation culture debate, prompted by concerns over the perceived cost (or potential cost) of claims. The analysis raises questions as to whether there is a risk of worthy claimants being entirely excluded from access to damages because of an interweaving of similar but distinct issues in the cases and the broader debate. Ryan calls for a clearer demarcation between how autonomy and responsibility are addressed in setting the liability threshold in the cases and how they are employed in the compensation culture debate.

In the final chapter of the book Tim O'Connor examines the relationship between compensation culture concerns and the reform of safety measures in Irish rugby. He first examines the law on the liability of sporting bodies generally and notes that although a potential for liability exists, it is very difficult to establish such liability and there is very little personal injury litigation in sport.

O'Connor then contrasts the approach to safety reform in two distinct areas of risk—scrummaging and concussion injuries—to demonstrate how the governing body is misinterpreting its legal obligations because it is driven by false perceptions of litigation risks. He notes that scrummaging rules in Ireland were rapidly reformed in light of a fear of high costs associated with an anticipated proliferation of claims, based on two high-profile cases in England and Wales; he proceeds to note that, in a classic example of misguided defensive practice, the measures adopted are counterproductive as they damage the sporting culture that gives social value to the sport and may actually reduce player safety.

O'Connor observes that the second area received little attention from the governing bodies in many jurisdictions (including Ireland) for many years, despite clear medical evidence of avoidable risk and a very clear possibility of being in breach of legal obligations. He suggests that the absence of any perception of a likelihood of litigation reduced the impetus for reform and it has only been some prominent examples of injury and the recent emergence of concussion litigation in the US that has spurred belated consideration of rule changes in Ireland.

Part I

General Features of the Relationship between Damages and Compensation Culture

1

'The Whiplash Capital of the World': Genealogy of a Compensation Myth

KEN OLIPHANT

One of the most persistent refrains in the current debate about the so-called compensation culture[1] is that the UK has become 'the whiplash capital of Europe'—or even, on some accounts, 'the world'. This chapter explores the origins of the claim subjects it to critical analysis and provides some wider reflections on the rhetoric employed. But it begins by placing the claim in the context of the wider debate and the UK's ongoing civil justice reforms.

Context: The Road to Whiplash Reform

Whiplash Becomes an Issue

In retrospect, it is remarkable how recent a phenomenon the *problematisation* of whiplash has been, notwithstanding the recognition of its *prevalence* for quite some time. In 2002, when the Association of British Insurers (ABI) responded to an Insurance Europe questionnaire on 'minor cervical trauma claims',[2] it reported that these made up 76% of all motor bodily injury claims in the UK,[3] but the focus of the measures it described as

[1] See generally K Williams, 'State of Fear: Britain's "Compensation Culture" Reviewed' (2005) 25 *Legal Studies* 499; R Lewis, A Morris and K Oliphant, 'Tort Personal Injury Claims Statistics: Is there a Compensation Culture in the United Kingdom?' (2006) 14 *Torts Law Journal* 158; A Morris, 'Spiralling or Stabilising? The Compensation Culture and Our Propensity to Claim Damages for Personal Injury' (2007) 70 *MLR* 349; R Lewis and A Morris, 'Tort Law Culture in the United Kingdom: Image and Reality in Personal Injury Compensation' (2012) 3 *Journal of European Tort Law* 230; R Lewis and A Morris, 'Tort Law Culture: Image and Reality' (2012) 39 *Journal of Law and Society* 562; A Morris, 'The "Compensation Culture" and the Politics of Tort' in TT Arvind and J Steele (eds), *Tort Law and the Legislature: Common Law, Statute and the Dynamics of Legal Change* (Oxford, Hart Publishing, 2013); R Lewis, 'Compensation Culture Reviewed: Incentives to Claim and Damages Levels' [2014] *Journal of Personal Injury Law* 209.

[2] The results were published as Comité Européen des Assurances (CEA), *Minor Cervical Trauma Claims: Comparative Study* (Brussels, 2004) (hereafter *CEA Study*). The document no longer appears to be available on the CEA website but is available online at www.svv.ch/sites/default/files/document/file/CEA_HWS-Studie_englisch.pdf. Insurance Europe is the current English name for the organisation then known as the Comité Européen des Assurances.

[3] *CEA Study* (n 2) 6.

having been taken by insurers was on injury avoidance (more efficient head-rest systems) and the prevention of long-term complications,[4] rather than on problems associated with routine, low-value claims, which have been the main focus of the current debate. In 2003 and 2004, the market intelligence firm Datamonitor reported that whiplash was the most common type of motor personal injury claim, with between 80 and 90 % of all motor personal injury claims being for whiplash-related injuries, mostly for relatively low amounts of compensation.[5] But this information was presented purely descriptively, without any indication that whiplash as such was a problem. More strikingly still, in 2005, when the ABI presented a set of proposals for reforms to improve the compensation system, there was no mention of whiplash at all.[6] And even Lord Justice Jackson's *Final Report* into the costs of civil litigation, published in December 2009, contains just a single reference to whiplash and that only in evidence presented to the judge[7] and not in his own analysis of issues of concern.

It was only around this time that insurers came to problematise whiplash claims as a category. In 2008, the ABI published a dedicated report on the issues raised: *Tackling Whiplash: Prevention, Care, Compensation*.[8] The report highlighted that the number of whiplash claims was rising even though the Government's road casualty statistics suggested that British roads were getting safer.[9] This was followed by further news releases by the ABI,[10] reinforced by media interventions by its officers. Under the headline, '[t]he UK's pain in the neck culture must end', James Dalton, the ABI's then Head of Motor and Liability, was quoted as saying: '[i]f whiplash was an Olympic sport, the UK would be gold medallists'.[11] In a BBC interview, the ABI's Rob Cummings referred to 'a whiplash epidemic' gripping the UK.[12]

The ABI's membership took up the same refrain—most notably in a significant 'Whiplash Report' published by AXA Insurance in July 2013,[13] which explicitly sought to identify 'lessons from overseas' with a view to reforming UK law on the basis of best practice from elsewhere in Europe.[14] In a report by Aviva the following year, whiplash—and specifically

[4] Ibid, 23.

[5] Datamonitor, UK Personal Injury Litigation 2003—Where Does the Industry Go From Here? (London, 2003) 45; ibid, UK Personal Injury Litigation 2004: Trial and Error (November 2004) 38.

[6] ABI, Care and Compensation: Delivering a Fair and Efficient Compensation System (December 2005).

[7] R Jackson LJ, *Review of Civil Litigation Costs: Final Report* (London, Judiciary of England and Wales, January 2010) (hereafter Jackson Report) ch 21, para 3.12.

[8] ABI, Tackling Whiplash: Prevention, Care, Compensation (November 2008) (hereafter Tackling Whiplash).

[9] Ibid, 1.

[10] ABI news release, 19 May 2011 ('Britain's Pain in the Neck Culture Must be Reduced Says the ABI') available at: www.abi.org.uk/News/News-releases/2011/05/Britains-pain-in-the-neck-culture-must-be-reduced-says-the-AB ('the UK's pain in the neck culture ... has made the UK the whiplash capital of Europe' I; ABI news release, 13 March 2013 ('Fair, Independent, Objective—ABI Publishes Proposals to Curb the UK's Whiplash Epidemic') available at: www.abi.org.uk/News/News-releases/2013/03/Fair-Independent-Objective--Abi-Publishes-Proposals-To-Curb-The-Uks-Whiplash-Epidemic ('UK Must Lose its Title of Whiplash Capital of Europe'); ABI news release, 22 April 2013 ('Brace yourself—UK is the Biggest Pain in the Neck in Europe') available at www.abi.org.uk/News/News-releases/2013/04/Brace-Yourself--UK-Is-The-Biggest-Pain-In-The-Neck-In-Europe.

[11] James Dalton, ABI's Head of Motor and Liability, quoted in ABI news release, 'The UK's pain in the neck culture must end says the ABI' (24 April 2012).

[12] Rob Cummings (ABI) interviewed for *BBC Television News*: 'Is the UK in a Whiplash Claim Epidemic?', available at: www.bbc.co.uk/news/business-21769907 (13 March 2013).

[13] AXA, 'The AXA Whiplash Report' (July 2013) available at www.publications.parliament.uk/pa/cm201314/cmselect/cmtran/117/117vw56.htm.

[14] Ibid, 16 ff.

claims for minor, short-term whiplash injury—was identified as the main reason why the UK's system for dealing with motor bodily injury claims needed reform.[15] The Aviva report summarised the outcomes of research the insurer had commissioned which again highlighted the prevalence of whiplash and soft tissue injury claims as the main driver of increases in the number of road traffic accident (RTA) personal injury pay-outs.[16]

Shaping the Political Debate

These interventions decisively shaped the political debate. In October 2010, the House of Commons Transport Committee launched an investigation into the cost of motor insurance in the light of reported rises in average premiums in the preceding year (estimated to be 29.9% by the Automobile Association, AA) at a time when the number of road accident casualties was decreasing.[17] In its written evidence to the Committee,[18] the ABI highlighted whiplash claims as a significant factor in the cost rises, claiming that 20% of motor premiums was paid out against such claims every year[19] and urging the adoption of measures to address the problem by improving driver awareness of the risk and practical precautions such as adjusting car head restraints properly and keeping a safe distance.[20] This constituted only one of a set of seven proposals advanced with a view to the better controlling of motor insurance costs: others included the implementation of the recommendations of the Jackson Report on civil litigation costs, measures to reduce the incidence of uninsured driving, and facilitating greater data sharing between the insurance industry and the public sector in order to tackle fraud.[21] It was only in oral evidence provided by ABI Director Nick Starling that the ABI suggested that the problems of whiplash and fraud were interrelated, Starling saying: '[w]hiplash … is a soft tissue injury. There is no physiological evidence, as I understand it, that you've got that injury. I think people are put in temptation's way to a large extent and people are encouraging them to make these claims'.[22] Others giving evidence to the Committee linked whiplash and fraud more explicitly, especially in connection with so-called 'cash for crash' scams.[23] The Committee itself noted these concerns without expressly endorsing them[24] but perhaps had them in mind when stating that the wider access to justice that was a welcome consequence of the introduction of conditional

[15] Aviva, *Road to Reform: Tackling the UK's Compensation Culture* (July 2014) 3, 'The main reason we need these changes is to reduce the impact of minor, short-term whiplash claims'.

[16] Frontier Economics, Motor Insurance Compensation Systems with a Focus on Whiplash and Soft Tissue Injuries: A Report for Aviva (March 2015).

[17] House of Commons Transport Committee, *The Cost of Motor Insurance*, Fourth Report of Session 2010–12 (HC, 591) (two volumes) (hereafter *Cost of Motor Insurance*) vol 1, paras 1 and 7. The Report noted (para 6) that there were 163,554 road accidents involving personal injury in 2009, the most recent year for which figures were available, which was 31% fewer than the average figure for the years from 1994 to 1998; this was part of a longer-term trend, the number of casualties per 100 million vehicle kilometres having fallen by 75% since 1967.

[18] *Cost of Motor Insurance* (n 17) vol 1, Ev 50 ff.

[19] Ibid, vol 1, Ev 52, para 3.14.

[20] Ibid, vol 1, Ev 50, para 2.1.

[21] Ibid.

[22] Ibid, vol 1, Ev 14, Q100.

[23] See, eg, *Cost of Motor Insurance* (n 17) vol 1, Ev 1, Q2 (oral evidence of AA President, Edmund King) vol 2, Ev w20 (written evidence of RBS Insurance).

[24] *Cost of Motor Insurance* (n 17) vol 1, paras 14 and 16.

fee agreements (CFAs) 'should not provide an opportunity for people to make fraudulent claims for compensation for non-existent or pre-existing aches and pains'.[25]

After the Committee's report was published on 11 March 2011, a number of discrete threads of development became intertwined. In September 2011, the Government published its Response to the Report,[26] without a single reference to whiplash or soft tissue injuries or problems created by claims for such injuries. Instead, the Government's main focus was on the implementation of the Jackson proposals to reform CFAs and other measures to reduce the cost of civil litigation generally,[27] though it also endorsed the Committee's recommendations about the tackling of fraud through joint initiatives with the insurance sector.[28]

Proposals for Targeted Whiplash Reform

Parliament's attention was drawn back to whiplash claims by a ten minute rule Bill introduced by Jack Straw MP in September 2011.[29] Introducing the Bill, Straw described whiplash as 'not so much an injury, more a profitable invention of the human imagination—undiagnosable except by third-rate doctors in the pay of the claims management companies or personal injury lawyers'.[30] Clause 2 of the Bill, entitled 'Whiplash', accordingly sought to introduce two limitations on the ability to recover damages for whiplash injuries: first, a requirement for 'independent, objective evidence' of the injury, and not merely the claimant's 'subjective description of symptoms'; second, a rebuttable presumption that no whiplash injury has been suffered in the absence of musculoskeletal indications or if the relative speed of the collision giving rise to the accident was 15 miles per hour or less. In full, the clause read:

(1) This section applies to any personal injury claim for whiplash.
(2) The onus shall be on the claimant to satisfy the court that there is independent, objective evidence that the claimant has suffered harm, and of the extent of that harm.
(3) No damages shall be recoverable if the only evidence is the subjective description of symptoms by, or behalf of [sic], the claimant.
(4) There shall be a rebuttable presumption that no harm or injury to the claimant has been suffered where either or both of the following conditions applies—
  (a) the collision giving rise to the accident took place at a relative speed of 15 miles per hour or less;
  (b) there are no musculoskeletal signs of any injury, including fracture and dislocation.
(3) In this section 'whiplash' means a neck injury caused by a sudden movement of the head forwards, backwards or sideways.

[25] Ibid, vol 1, para 22.

[26] House of Commons Transport Committee, The Cost of Motor Insurance: Government Response to the Committee's Fourth Report of Session 2010–12, Fifth Special Report of Session 2010–12 (HC 1466).

[27] Ibid, 3–4. One possible measure was the banning of referral fees which were seen to increase costs undesirably.

[28] Ibid, 4–5.

[29] Motor Insurance Regulation Bill 2010–12, Bill 229. Ten Minute Rule Bills are a mechanism whereby a backbench MP is able to introduce a Private Member's Bill to the House of Commons and to make a case for it in a speech lasting up to ten minutes: www.parliament.uk/site-information/glossary/ten-minute-rule-bill/.

[30] HC Deb 13 September 2011, col 897.

Other proposals in the Bill to clean up the 'extensive and grubby industry'[31] that had grown up around whiplash claims were the abolition of referral fees and the cutting in half (from £1,200 to £600) of the fixed fee that lawyers were entitled to recover as costs for their work on low-value road traffic claims.

The Bill did not receive a second reading and failed to complete its passage through Parliament before the end of the session, consequently making no further progress.[32] However, even before Straw had formally introduced the Bill, the Government had indicated its support for his proposal to abolish referral fees,[33] as previously recommended in the Jackson Report.[34] A set of provisions on referral fees was accordingly introduced to the Legal Aid, Sentencing and Punishment of Offenders (LASPO) Bill that was brought to the House of Lords from the Commons in November 2011.[35] It fell to the House of Commons Transport Committee to pick up Straw's proposals relating specifically to whiplash. In a follow-up to its report on *The Cost of Motor Insurance*,[36] it indicated its support for an 'objective evidence' requirement should the Jackson reforms prove ineffective in reducing the number of whiplash claims:

> [I]n relation to whiplash, we are not convinced that a diagnosis unsupported by any further evidence of injury or personal inconvenience arising from the injury should be sufficient for a claim to be settled. In our view, the bar to receiving compensation in whiplash cases should be raised … We note the Government's argument that its legal reforms should reduce the money in the system and encourage insurers to defend claims more vigorously. If the number of whiplash claims does not fall significantly once these changes are implemented there would in our view be a strong case to consider primary legislation to require objective evidence of a whiplash injury, or of the injury having a significant effect on the claimant's life, before compensation was paid.[37]

Though the LASPO Act did not receive Royal Assent until 1 May 2012, and though its reforms to the CFA regime and referral fees did not come into effect until 1 April 2013,[38] the Government continued to press on with measures to address the problem of whiplash claims without waiting to evaluate the impact of the LASPO reforms. After a summit with insurance industry, consumer and business groups in February 2012, David Cameron made a personal commitment that the Government would take action to 'tackle the compensation culture' and reduce legal costs.[39] One of the measures agreed was for the Government

[31] Ibid.

[32] services.parliament.uk/bills/2010-12/motorinsuranceregulation.html.

[33] HC Deb 13 September 2011, col 896.

[34] Jackson Report (n 7) para 5.1.

[35] Legal Aid, Sentencing and Punishment of Offenders Bill 2010–12, HL Bill 109, brought from the Commons on 3 November 2011, cls 54–58, available at: services.parliament.uk/bills/2010-12/legalaidsentencingandpunishmentofoffenders/documents.html. The provisions had not been included in the Bill that was given its first reading in the Commons on 21 June 2011.

[36] House of Commons Transport Committee, *Cost of Motor Insurance: Follow Up*, Twelfth Report of Session 2010–12 (HC 1451).

[37] Ibid, para 8.

[38] Legal Aid, Sentencing and Punishment of Offenders Act 2012, ss 44 and 46 (CFAs) ss 56–60 (referral fees); Legal Aid, Sentencing and Punishment of Offenders Act 2012 (Commencement No 5 and Saving Provision) Order 2013/77, art 3 (CFAs); Legal Aid, Sentencing and Punishment of Offenders Act 2012 (Commencement No 6) Order 2013/453, art 3 (referral fees).

[39] Prime Minister's Office news story, 14 February 2012 ('Statement on Outcomes Following Downing Street Insurance Summit').

and insurance industry 'to work together to identify effective ways to reduce the number and cost of whiplash claims'.[40] This commitment was reiterated in April of the same year in the Government's response to the House of Commons Transport Committee's second, follow-up report on the cost of motor insurance.[41] The outcome, in December 2012, was a Ministry of Justice consultation paper specifically focused on reducing the number and costs of whiplash claims.[42]

The consultation paper highlighted the Government's concern that the growth in whiplash claims arising from road traffic accidents could be linked to an increase in fraudulent and/or exaggerated claims[43] and identified four key areas in which the Government wished to make progress: improving diagnosis, the development of standards for diagnosis, challenging questionable claims and tackling the perception that exaggerated claims are acceptable.[44] The difficulty in diagnosing soft tissue injuries, the consultation paper suggested, might be addressed by the delivery of better Government guidance and, in particular, by the creation of a register of independent medical practitioners subject to assured standards of training and audit.[45] Greater scope for challenging questionable claims might be allowed if the limit for small personal injury claims were raised from £1,000 to £5,000 for whiplash claims or road traffic accident claims generally, bearing in mind the strict limitations on recoverable costs in such proceedings: this would take away an economic incentive for insurers to pay out on questionable claims rather than see them tested in court.[46] The consultation paper also noted insurance industry efforts to combat fraud, including the creation of a cross-industry fraud database to enable insurers to share data about fraudulent claims; describing this as a positive step, the Government encouraged that the data be shared with all those who could help deter potential fraudsters from making claims,[47] and not just within the insurance sector.

The Ministry of Justice's proposals met with a mixed reaction from the House of Commons Transport Committee in July 2013, in its third report on the cost of motor insurance, on this occasion with a specific focus on whiplash.[48] The Committee expressed its broad support for the proposals to improve medical reports,[49] but opposed the suggested increase in the financial limit for small claims, fearing that this might impair access to justice, inadvertently fuel a boom for claims management companies in cases solicitors were unwilling to take on and, insofar as expert evidence is not generally submitted in small claims, be

[40] Ibid.

[41] House of Commons Transport Committee, The Cost of Motor Insurance: Follow-Up: Government Response to the Committee's Twelfth Report of Session 2010–12, Thirteenth Special Report of Session 2010–12 (HC 1934) 2.

[42] Ministry of Justice, Reducing the Number and Costs of Whiplash Claims: A Consultation on Arrangements Concerning Whiplash Injuries in England and Wales, Consultation Paper CP17/2012 (Cm 8425, 2012) (hereafter Whiplash Consultation).

[43] Ibid, para 22.

[44] Ibid, para 24.

[45] Ibid, para 24 and Part Two.

[46] Ibid, Part Three (especially para 58).

[47] Ibid, para 86. Presumably the 'all' was meant to include claimant lawyers, though they were not mentioned expressly.

[48] House of Commons Transport Committee, *The Cost of Motor Insurance: Whiplash*, Fourth Report of Session 2013–14 (HC 117) (2 volumes) (hereafter *Cost of Motor Insurance: Whiplash*).

[49] Ibid, Summary and para 37.

counterproductive in countering fraudulent and exaggerated claims.[50] But the Committee urged the Government to consider an issue not addressed in the consultation, namely, reducing the normal three-year limitation period for personal injury claims in whiplash cases, bearing in mind that the symptoms of a whiplash injury generally emerge within seven days and do not usually last for more than one year.[51]

The Government's Programme of Whiplash Reforms

In October 2013, the Ministry of Justice announced the Government's plan to press ahead with the introduction of independent medical panels, backed up by an accreditation scheme, to establish a more robust system of medical reporting and scrutiny for whiplash claims.[52] The Government also proposed to take further steps to tackle the problem of fraudulent and exaggerated claims by working with stakeholders to prevent claims from proceeding before a medical examination and report has been completed, thereby stopping insurers from making 'pre-medical offers to settle', and by encouraging the insurance industry to share its data on known fraudsters so as to facilitate 'know your client' checks by claimant solicitors.[53] However, although continuing to believe that increasing the small claims threshold would be beneficial in providing a low-cost route for bringing a claim through the courts, the Government decided that it would be better to consider the combined impact of other reforms before embarking on any further change, bearing in mind the possible detriment to genuine accident victims and the risk that unscrupulous claims management companies might enter the market to offer advice that might not be in claimants' best interests.[54] The Government also rejected the House of Commons Transport Committee's suggestion to reduce the limitation period for road traffic accident claims, noting that this would create complexity in the law and might only serve to increase the number of cases in the short term while front-loading the expenses into a shorter period with cost implications for the courts and the parties.[55]

Following a further exchange of views and information with the Transport Committee,[56] the Government proceeded with the implementation of its reforms relating to medical

[50] Ibid, paras 50–52.

[51] Ibid, para 40.

[52] Ministry of Justice, Reducing the Number and Costs of Whiplash Claims: A Government Response to Consultation on Arrangements Concerning Whiplash Injuries in England and Wales/Cost of Motor Insurance—Whiplash: A Government Response to the House of Commons Transport Committee (Cm 8738, 2013) (hereafter Government Response) 6 (ministerial foreword) and para 8 ff.

[53] Ibid, 6 (ministerial foreword) and paras 24–28. The Government also 'invite[d]' the insurance industry to collect and publish robust data on case volumes, case injury types, initial claim values and final case settlements, together with information on suspected exaggerated and fraudulent claims and on claims which were withdrawn: ibid, para 50. It remains to be seen whether this invitation will be taken up.

[54] Ibid, 6 (ministerial foreword) and paras 38–45. The Government reiterated its position in October 2014 in its response to another Transport Committee report: House of Commons Transport Committee, *Driving Premiums Down: Fraud and the Cost of Motor Insurance: Government and Association of British Insurers Responses to the Committee's First Report of Session 2014–15*, Fifth Special Report of Session 2014–15 (HC 716) para 11 f.

[55] Government Response (n 52) para 18.

[56] House of Commons Transport Committee, *Cost of Motor Insurance: Whiplash: Further Government Response to the Committee's Fourth Report of Session 2013–14*, Eleventh Special Report of Session 2013–14 (HC 902).

reports, establishing working groups to consider improvements to the medical examination and reporting process[57] and launching a further mini consultation with stakeholders in May 2014 to consider proposals for a regime of fixed costs for medical examinations in whiplash claims.[58] The outcome was the announcement in August 2014 of a set of proposals to introduce special rules on soft tissue injury claims into the Civil Procedure Rules (CPR) and the Pre-Action Protocol for Low Value Personal Injury Claims in Road Traffic Accidents (the RTA Protocol), effective for claims brought on or after 1 October 2014.[59] The key changes were the fixing of the cost of medical reports for soft tissue injuries at £180;[60] a presumption that no claim for disbursements shall be allowed for such a report where the medical expert or an associated person has provided treatment to the claimant or proposes or recommends treatment that they then provide;[61] a presumption in soft tissue injury claims that the court will give permission only for one expert medical report, which must be a fixed cost medical report;[62] and changes to the regime of offers to settle under Part 36 of the CPR so as to discourage pre-medical offers.[63]

A further follow-up consultation was conducted in September 2014, addressing the independence of medical experts and their accreditation.[64] The Government announced that a centrepiece of the new system for medical reports would be an internet hub known as 'MedCo', to be funded and built by the ABI, which would provide a list of relevant experts for every soft tissue injury claim, using filters to prevent there being any financial link between the expert and the person commissioning the report. The MedCo system ultimately went live on 6 April 2015,[65] and from then on experts providing a fixed cost medical report for a soft tissue injury claim have had to be registered with MedCo and from 1 February 2016 must be accredited by it.[66]

The Government was also supporting cross-industry efforts by the ABI, the Law Society and claimant solicitors representatives to negotiate a data sharing process in an effort to

[57] Letter from Chris Grayling MP to Louise Ellman MP regarding '[p]roposals to reduce the number and cost of whiplash claims' (12 March 2014) available at: www.parliament.uk/business/committees/committees-a-z/commons-select/transport-committee/publications/?type=&session=1&sort=false&inquiry=1375.

[58] Lord Faulks, Letters to all interested stakeholders, 'Whiplash Reform: Proposals on Fixed Costs for Medical Examinations/Reports and Related Issues' (2 May 2014). See further Keogh's Client Alert, 'Whiplash Reform: Proposals on Fixed Costs for Medical Examinations/Reports and Related Issues', 6 May 2014, available at: www.keoghs.co.uk/Publications/Client-Alert--Whiplash-Reform-Proposals-on-fixed-costs-for-medical-examinationsreports. The Ministry of Justice initially failed to respond to the author's emails asking for the actual consultation materials and the account in the text was written on the basis of the secondary sources cited. The Ministry ultimately supplied relevant materials in response to the author's freedom of information request.

[59] Lord Faulks, Letters to all interested stakeholders, 'Whiplash Reform: Proposals on Fixed Costs for Medical Examinations/Reports and Related Issues' (4 August 2014). See further Keogh's Client Alert, 'MoJ Announcements on Fixing Costs of Medical Reports and Limiting Evidence for RTA Soft Tissue Injury Claims', 4 August 2014, available at: www.keoghs.co.uk/Publications/Client-Alert--MoJ-announcements-on-fixing-costs-of-medical-reports-and-limiting-medical-evidence-.

[60] CPR rule 45.19(2A)(a).

[61] CPR rule 45.19(2B).

[62] CPR rule 35.4(3B).

[63] CPR rule 36.21(4). Broadly speaking, this provides for the deferral until the date the defendant receives the medical report of the normal 21-day period within which the claimant must decide whether to accept a Part 36 offer or run the risk of having to bear the defendant's cost from that date onwards if the judgment is no more advantageous than the offer.

[64] Keogh's Client Alert, 'Whiplash Consultation—Independence and Accreditation', 4 September 2014, available at: www.keoghs.co.uk/Publications/Client-Alert-Whiplash-consultation--independence-and-accreditation.

[65] www.medco.org.uk/.

[66] RTA Protocol, paras 1.1(A1) and 7.8A(1).

prevent fraudulent personal injury claims.[67] This led to the construction of a new internet platform known as 'askCUE PI', allowing approved organisations to check records held on a database of reported incidents of personal injury or industrial illness before they submit a personal injury claim.[68] From 1 June 2015, before submitting a claim notification form, the claimant's legal representative must undertake a search of askCUE PI and must provide in the form an access code enabling the defendant to retrieve the search results.[69]

Additional Measures

As noted, the programme of whiplash reforms described above overlapped with multiple other efforts to reduce the costs of civil litigation and to counter fraudulent and exaggerated claims. The introduction of a new system of medical reports and mandatory 'know your client' checks must therefore be seen in the context of a variety of other initiatives which were intended to deter unmeritorious claiming. The following may be noted as among the most important: the implementation of the Jackson recommendations relating to CFAs and referral fees,[70] with effect from 1 April 2013 (as detailed above); the introduction in 2010 of a new special procedure for the resolution of low-value road traffic accident claims where liability is not in dispute and no contributory negligence is alleged, based on fixed recoverable costs and the use of an online 'claims portal'[71] for communication between the parties;[72] and a series of rule changes strengthening the regulatory regime applying to claims management companies (CMCs) under Part 2 of the Compensation Act 2006. These included banning CMCs from offering cash inducements for making a claim[73] and preventing CMCs from acting for claimants based on a phone call alone by requiring them to have a signed contract before they can take any fees.[74] CMCs were also exposed to the possibility of complaint to the Legal Ombudsman, who has the legal power to award compensation

[67] Letter from Lord Faulks QC regarding '[w]hiplash reform: cross-industry data sharing' (7 April 2014) available at: www.parliament.uk/business/committees/committees-a-z/commons-select/transport-committee/publications/?type=&session=1&sort=false&inquiry=1375.

[68] www.askCUE.co.uk.

[69] RTA Protocol, para 6.3A. See further J Hyde, 'Insurers Open Data to Claimant Solicitors in Fraud Crackdown' [2015] *Law Society Gazette*, 27 April.

[70] Legal Aid, Sentencing and Punishment of Offenders Act 2012, ss 44 and 46 (CFAs), ss 56–60 (referral fees). See further, in addition to the Jackson Report itself, Ministry of Justice, *Proposals for Reform of Civil Litigation Funding and Costs in England and Wales: Implementation of Lord Justice Jackson's Recommendations*, Consultation Paper CP13/10 (Cm 7947, 2010); ibid, *Reforming Civil Litigation Funding and Costs in England and Wales—Implementation of Lord Justice Jackson's Recommendations: The Government Response* (Cm 8041, 2011).

[71] www.claimsportal.org.uk.

[72] Under the RTA Protocol. The procedure applies to claims valued at up to £25,000 (raised from £10,000 in July 2013).

[73] Ministry of Justice, Claims Management Regulation: Annual Report 2012/2013 (hereafter CMR Annual Report 2012/2013) ch 8, para 2; Ministry of Justice, Claims Management Regulation: Annual Report 2013/2014 (hereafter CMR Annual Report 2013/2014) ch 6, para 24.

[74] *CMR Annual Report 2012/2013* (n 73) ch 8, para 1; Ministry of Justice (MOJ), press release, 8 July 2014, available at: www.gov.uk/government/news/new-rules-to-protect-customers-from-rogue-claims-firms. This followed a consultation on proposals for amendments to the Claims Management Regulation rules on the Conduct of Authorised Persons, available at: consult.justice.gov.uk/digital-communications/cmr-rules-consultation-cp15-2012. See further MOJ, press release, 8 April 2013, available at: www.gov.uk/government/news/new-rules-for-cmcs.

for poor service where appropriate.[75] In addition, separate statutory provision was made in 2013 for CMCs to be liable to fines by the Claims Management Regulator for breaches of applicable regulations,[76] and the new financial penalties scheme came into force in December 2014.[77] These changes accompanied a 'clampdown' on 'rogue' claims firms by the Ministry of Justice's Claims Management Regulation Unit,[78] which revoked 514 licences in the three years from April 2012 to March 2015, contributing significantly to the fall in the number of CMCs in the personal injury sector from 1,902 in 2013 to 979 in 2015.[79]

These changes to the CMC regime had knock-on effects for other claimant representatives. In April 2015, the ban on offering cash inducements for making a claim was extended to all 'regulated persons', including solicitors and barristers.[80]

A final set of developments that undoubtedly reflected concerns arising in relation to whiplash claims, though not limited to them, was directed at countering fraudulent claims. In April 2015, a statutory requirement was introduced that a court must dismiss any claim for damages in respect of personal injury in which it finds that, although the claim would otherwise have succeeded, the claimant was fundamentally dishonest, unless it is satisfied that the claimant would suffer substantial injustice if the claim were dismissed.[81] The passage of the legislation overlapped with determined action by police and prosecutors in combination with insurance companies to bring the weight of the criminal law to bear on dishonest claimants and representatives, which has now resulted in some high-profile convictions for fraud in connection with personal injury claims.[82] A further development

[75] CMR Annual Report 2012/2013 (n 73) ch 8, para 1; CMR Annual Report 2013/2014 (n 73) ch 9, paras 8–10; Ministry of Justice, Claims Management Regulation Annual Report 2014/2015 (hereafter CMR Annual Report 2014/2015) ch 9, paras 9–12. The Legal Ombudsman's CMC complaints service was launched in January 2015 and accepted 648 complaints for investigation in its first six months: Legal Ombudsman, Complaints in Focus: Claims Management Companies (November 2015) 1.

[76] Financial Services (Banking Reform) Act 2013, s 139.

[77] Ministry of Justice, *Claims Management Regulation Financial Penalties Guidance* (December 2014); *CMR Annual Report 2014/2015* (n 75) ch 9 paras 5–8. In August 2015, claims management company The Hearing Clinic became the first CMC to be fined (£220,000) by the Claims Management Regulator following hundreds of complaints from members of the public who had received speculative calls about claims for Noise Induced Hearing Loss: MOJ, press release, 5 August 2015, available at: www.gov.uk/government/news/first-fine-issued-against-rogue-claims-management-company. The decision is available at www.claimsregulation.gov.uk/details.aspx/31218. Further information about the Regulator's recent enforcement actions and investigations is available at www.claimsregulation.gov.uk/enforcement.aspx.

[78] MOJ, press release, 21 February 2014, available at: www.gov.uk/government/news/clampdown-on-rogue-claims-firms.

[79] *CMR Annual Report 2014/2015* (n 75) ch 3, para 10 (table) and ch 4, para 5 (table).

[80] Criminal Justice and Courts Act 2015, ss 58–61, effective 13 April 2015 (Criminal Justice and Courts Act 2015 (Commencement No 1, Saving and Transitional Provisions) Order 2015/778, art 3 and Sch 1, paras 48–51). The relevant clauses were inserted in the Bill during the Committee stage of its progress through the House of Lords: see HL Deb 23 July 2014, col 1271 (Lord Faulks).

[81] Criminal Justice and Courts Act 2015, s 57, effective 13 April 2015 (Criminal Justice and Courts Act 2015 (Commencement No 1, Saving and Transitional Provisions) Order 2015/778, art 3 and Sch 1, para 47). The relevant clause was inserted in the Bill at the end of its consideration by the House of Commons: see HC Deb 17 June 2014, col 1066 (Chris Grayling MP). The provision seems to have been inspired by s 26 of the Civil Liability and Courts Act 2004 (Ireland) but differs from it in requiring that the dishonesty be 'fundamental', while limiting the court's power to allow the claim despite the dishonesty to cases where dismissing it would cause *substantial* injustice.

[82] Most notably, in March 2015, John Smith of Cheshire-based Swift Accident Solutions, a claims management company, was found guilty of fraud and conspiracy to defraud at Manchester Crown Court in respect of a serial bus crash scam; nine other defendants were also guilty of conspiracy to defraud, four more having pleaded guilty

in this context was the Government's creation in January 2015 of a new Insurance Fraud Taskforce, whose terms of reference stated its aim as '[t]o investigate the causes of fraudulent behaviour and recommend solutions to reduce the level of insurance fraud in order to ultimately lower costs and protect the interests of honest consumers'.[83]

The 'Whiplash Capital' Claim

A persistent refrain in the problematisation of whiplash and the introduction of the reforms outlined above has been that the UK is the 'whiplash capital' of Europe or even the world. As the claim has been a key aspect of the rhetoric employed by those pushing for reform, it seems useful to trace its origins and to subject it to critical analysis. As noted above, the claim dates back at least as far as 2008, when the ABI published its report *Tackling Whiplash: Prevention, Care, Compensation*,[84] which claimed: '[w]hiplash claims form a much higher proportion of personal injury claims in the UK than elsewhere in the EU'.[85] It was left to the accompanying news release, entitled 'ABI reveals whiplash epidemic', to anoint the UK as Europe's 'whiplash capital': 'The UK is the whiplash capital of Europe', read the ABI statement, '75% of motor personal injury claims are for whiplash, compared to an average of 40% throughout the rest of Europe'.[86] This 'whiplash capital' claim was repeated in further news releases by the ABI,[87] endorsed by other players in the insurance sector,[88] and picked

to the same offence. It was reported that the fraud involved a series of stage-managed crashes in which cars and vans were driven into the side of First Group buses so that passengers—who were mainly friends and relatives complicit in the scam—could falsely claim damages for soft tissue injuries. In each case, the owner of the car or van admitted full liability, exposing the insurer to the claims. Smith made an illicit profit of £159,000 by referring 218 claims to law firms, receiving £960 each time. Most of the claims were settled out of court by the insurers without independent verification of the claimants' injuries. It was estimated that, had all the bogus claims been successful, the total cost would have been over £1 million. See S Cockcroft and T Burrows, 'Moment Audi Deliberately Crashed into Side of Bus as Part of £1Million No Win No Fee Scam Which Led to Hundreds of Fake Whiplash Claims' *Mail Online* (1 April 2015). In April 2015, Smith, the ringleader, was sentenced to six years' imprisonment: Hyde, 'Insurers Open Data to Claimant Solicitors in Fraud Crackdown' (n 69).

83 www.gov.uk/government/groups/insurance-fraud-taskforce.

84 *Tackling Whiplash* (n 8).

85 Ibid, 6.

86 ABI news release, 8 November 2008 ('ABI reveals whiplash epidemic') available at: www.abi.org.uk/News/News-releases/2008/11/ABI-reveals-whiplash-epidemic.

87 ABI news release, 19 May 2011 ('Britain's Pain in the Neck Culture Must be Reduced Says the ABI') available at: www.abi.org.uk/News/News-releases/2011/05/Britains-pain-in-the-neck-culture-must-be-reduced-says-the-AB ('the UK's pain in the neck culture … has made the UK the whiplash capital of Europe' I; ABI news release, 13 March 2013 ('Fair, Independent, Objective—ABI Publishes Proposals to Curb the UK's Whiplash Epidemic') available at www.abi.org.uk/News/News-releases/2013/03/Fair-Independent-Objective--Abi-Publishes-Proposals-To-Curb-The-Uks-Whiplash-Epidemic ('UK Must Lose its Title of Whiplash Capital of Europe'); ABI news release, 22 April 2013 ('Brace Yourself—UK is the Biggest Pain in the Neck in Europe') available at: www.abi.org.uk/News/News-releases/2013/04/Brace-Yourself--UK-Is-The-Biggest-Pain-In-The-Neck-In-Europe; 31 July 2013 ('ABI Responds to Transport Select Committee, Cost of Motor Insurance: Whiplash Report') available at: www.abi.org.uk/News/News-releases/2013/07/ABI-responds-to-Transport-Select-Committee-Cost-of-Motor-Insurance-Whiplash-report ('Facts … The UK is the Whiplash Capital of Europe').

88 See, eg, British Insurance Brokers' Association news release, 23 October 2013 ('British Insurance Brokers' Association Support Government Whiplash Move') available at: biba.org.uk/MediaCenterContentDetails.aspx?ContentID=3466.

up by a number of media outlets.[89] A *Daily Mail* headline from April 2013 read: 'Europe's whiplash capital: Compensation culture makes British twice as likely to claim, adding £90 to premiums'.[90] The *Telegraph* looked to explain '[w]hy Britain is the whiplash capital of Europe'.[91] And the *Times* told us that '[b]eing the "whiplash capital" of Europe costs us dear'.[92] Government ministers were also quick to adopt the claim: writing in the *Mail on Sunday* in 2013, Transport Secretary Justine Greening regretted that '[s]adly, Britain is now the whiplash capital of Europe' and vowed to end that state of affairs.[93] In her foreword to the Ministry of Justice's whiplash consultation, launched in December 2012, Helen Grant MP, the Parliamentary Under-Secretary of State for Justice, had gone even further, inflating the claim to be that the UK is 'the whiplash capital of *the world*'.[94] (emphasis added)

In launching its own inquiry into the effect of whiplash claims on the cost of motor insurance in March 2013, the House of Commons Transport Committee set out to probe this claim, asking specifically '[w]hether the Government is correct in describing Great Britain as the "whiplash capital of the world"'.[95] As might well have been expected, the answers it received in the evidence submitted to it varied significantly. The claim was endorsed by the ABI and others in the insurance sector,[96] but rejected by the Law Society and claimant representatives.[97] The Committee's conclusion was that the claim 'cannot be conclusively proved or disproved from the information available'.[98] It observed acidly that '[i]t is surprising that the Government has brought forward measures to reduce the number of fraudulent or exaggerated whiplash claims without giving even an estimate of the comparative scale of the problem'.[99]

To assess the adequacy of the evidence base for ourselves, we need to go back to the original source of the 'whiplash capital' claim. As noted, it was in the news release accompanying the ABI's report on whiplash in 2008 that the 'whiplash capital' terminology seems first to have been used. The evidence purporting to substantiate the contention that whiplash claims form a much higher proportion of personal injury claims in the UK than elsewhere

[89] See, eg, in addition to the items highlighted in the text: www.express.co.uk/news/uk/298630/6mph-the-whiplash-limit; www.thesun.co.uk/sol/homepage/features/6365758/Whiplash-scams-costing-Brit-drivers-25billion-a-year.html.

[90] *Mail Online* (20 April 2013).

[91] D Hyde, Comment: 'Why Britain is the Whiplash Capital of Europe' *Daily Telegraph*, online edn (18 July 2013) available at www.telegraph.co.uk/finance/personalfinance/insurance/10185382/Why-Britain-is-the-whiplash-capital-of-Europe.html.

[92] A Brown, 'Being the "Whiplash Capital" of Europe Costs Us Dear' *The Times* (7 May 2012) available at: www.thetimes.co.uk/tto/business/columnists/article3406600 (paywall).

[93] J Greening, 'Britain is the Whiplash Capital of Europe—And I'm Going To Stop It' *Mail on Sunday* (4 February 2013) available at www.dailymail.co.uk/news/article-2096597/Justine-Greening-Britain-whiplash-capital-Europe--Im-going-stop-it.html

[94] *Whiplash Consultation* (n 42) 3.

[95] Cost of Motor Insurance: Whiplash (n 48) vol 1, para 7.

[96] Ibid, vol 1, Ev 7, Q53 (David Brown, Chair of the Third Party Working Group, Institute and Faculty of Actuaries, IFoA); Ev 47, para A1 (Thatcham Research) ('Whiplash Capital of Europe'); Ev 53, para 6 (IFoA); Ev 58, para 2.1 (Lloyd's Market Association); Ev 66, para 5 (ABI); Ev 78, para 3.2 (AXA Insurance). Thatcham Research is a motor vehicle research centre funding by UK motor insurers.

[97] *Cost of Motor Insurance: Whiplash* (n 48) vol 1, Ev 27, Q228 (Andrew Ritchie QC); Ev 27 Q231 and Ev 29 Q246 (Desmond Hudson, Chief Executive, Law Society); Ev 88 (Association of Personal Injury Lawyers, APIL); Ev 97, para 17 (Motor Accident Solicitors Society, MASS) (claim not based on reliable, current data).

[98] *Cost of Motor Insurance: Whiplash* (n 48) vol 1, 3 (summary) and para 28.

[99] Ibid, para 28.

in the EU was a study by Insurance Europe, the Comité Européen des Assurances (CEA), published in 2004 (*CEA Study*). The same research was also the basis for the 'whiplash capital' claim made in the Government's *Whiplash Consultation* of 2012. Having noted Compensation Recovery Unit (CRU) data that showed that whiplash injury claims formed 70% of total RTA personal injury claims, the consultation document stated: 'An international comparison study carried out in 2004 showed that this figure is significantly higher in the UK than in other European jurisdictions, such as Spain, Germany or France'.[100] It thus seems worthwhile to see precisely what the *CEA Study* said and how its data was collected.

The *CEA Study*

The *CEA Study* was based on responses provided by national insurance associations to a common questionnaire circulated in July 2002. Ten country associations replied to the questionnaire. The focus was 'minor cervical trauma', defined as 'a lesion of the cervical spine, caused by acceleration-deceleration mechanisms … without neurological complications and without affecting the osseous, nervous or ligamentary-disc structures'.[101] Respondents were asked, inter alia, about the total number of motor liability claims, the number of bodily injuries, the number of claims linked to minor cervical trauma, the cost of bodily injuries claims, the cost of claims linked to cervical trauma, and the average cost per claim linked to cervical trauma.

In terms of claims numbers (Table 1), by far the most were made in Italy (4,700,000) and Germany (3,960,000) if bodily injury and material damage claims are combined; the UK's figure was 2,900,000. The UK overtakes Germany if one looks at bodily injury alone, with 493,000 recorded claims as compared with Germany's 424,000; however, Italy remained out in front, both in absolute and percentage terms (846,000 or 18% of the combined number of bodily injury and material damage claims). Italy also remained at the top of the list if one looks at the total number of cervical trauma claims (558,000) but this was a lower percentage of all bodily injury claims (66%) than in the UK (76%). It was that 76% figure ('twice the average')[102] that was seized on by those claiming the UK to be Europe's 'whiplash capital'.

A quick look at the CEA data on the cost of claims (Table 2) provides a further measure according to which the UK leaves the rest of Europe behind: the cost of cervical trauma claims as a percentage of total bodily injury claims costs. At 50%, the UK was ahead of a group of countries on 40%, comprising the Netherlands, Norway and Switzerland. But the total cost of cervical trauma claims in the UK (€1,080 million) was well below the total cost in Italy (€2,393 million), even though that accounted for only 32.6% of the total cost of Italian bodily injury claims. The superficial disparity is explained when one looks at the average cost per claim linked to cervical trauma, which was €4,288 in Italy but only €2,878

[100] Whiplash Consultation (n 42) para 18.

[101] *CEA Study* (n 2) 4. The definition does not refer specifically to whiplash injuries but these were acknowledged to be its focus: G Chappuis and B Soltermann, 'Number and Cost of Claims Linked to Minor Cervical Trauma in Europe: Results from the Comparative Study by CEA, AREDOC and CEREDOC' (2008) 17 *European Spine Journal* 1350, 1352.

[102] Tackling Whiplash (n 8) 4.

Table 1: Number of Claims: In Total, for Bodily Injury and for Cervical Trauma (CEA, 2004)[103]

Country	Number of claims (bodily + material)	Bodily injury	Cervical trauma (compared with BI)
Belgium	420,000	12% or 50,000	No data available
Switzerland	300,000	10% or 30,000	33% or 10,000
Germany	3,960,000	10.7% or 424,000	47% or 200,000
Spain	2,320,000	10.8% or 250,000	32% or 80,000
Finland	88,839	13% or 11,574	8.5% or 1,000
France	2,500,000	9% or 225,000	3% or 6,750
Italy	4,700,000	18% or 846,000	66% or 558,000
Netherlands	600,000	8% or 48,000	40% or 19,200
Norway	165,378	9.1% or 15,000	53% or 8,000
UK	2,900,000	17% or 493,000	76% or 375,000

Table 2: Cost of Claims: Bodily Injury (Total), Cervical Trauma (Total/Average) (CEA, 2004)[104]

Country	Cost of bodily injury	Cervical trauma (compared with BI)	Cervical trauma: average cost/claim
Belgium	+/– €1,400 million	no data available	no data
Switzerland	€860 million	40% or 350 million	€35,000
Germany	€5,346 million	9% or 500 million	€2,500
Spain	€2,199 million	No data	no data
Finland	€190 million	0.78% or 1.5 million	€1,500
France	€3,950 million	0.5% of 19.75 million	€2,625
Italy	€7,480 million	32.6% or 2,393 million	€4,288
Netherlands	€800 million	40% or 320 million	€16,500
Norway	€121 million	40% or 48 million	€6,050
UK	€2,159 million	50% or 1,080 million	€2,878

in the UK. In fact, both these figures were well behind the average costs of cervical trauma claims in Switzerland (€35,000) and the Netherlands (€16,500).

It will be clear from the summary provided here of the CEA data that the support it provides for the 'whiplash capital' claim is somewhat fragile. Two particular criticisms can be made: first, that the 'whiplash capital' claim relies very selectively on the CEA data, which might plausibly be interpreted as identifying a number of alternative 'claims capitals'; second, that the research design and methodology are simply inadequate for the production of reliable data sufficient for the making of any claim of that nature.

[103] Reproducing the table in the *CEA Study* (n 2) 6 (with very minor amendments for presentational purposes).
[104] Reproducing the table in the *CEA Study* (n 2) 7 (with very minor amendments for presentational purposes).

Selective Use of the CEA Data

It is apparent that the 'whiplash capital' claim as applied to the UK is dependent on a selective use of the CEA data that leaves out details that do not fit the agenda being pursued. In fact, the same data provide equal support for a number of alternative 'claims capital' statements:

— **'Italy and Germany are the motor claims capitals of Europe'**, with respectively 4.7 million and 3.96 million motor claims per year, well ahead of the UK with 2.9 million claims per year.
— **'Italy is the bodily injury claims capital of Europe'**: 18% of all claims (846,000) are for bodily injury and their overall value is €7.48 billion, ahead of Germany (€5.346 billion), France (€3.95 billion) and Spain (€2.199 billion). The UK ranks only in mid-table with an overall cost for bodily injury claims of €2.159 billion (paid out in 493,000 claims, comprising 17% of all motor claims).
— **'Italy is also the *whiplash* capital of Europe'**, with 558,000 claims for minor cervical trauma (as compared with only 375,000 in the UK) at a total cost of €2,393 billion (more than double the €1,080 billion in the UK).
— **Alternatively: 'Switzerland is the whiplash capital of Europe'**: the average cost per claim linked to cervical trauma is €35,000, massively higher than the €2,878 average reported for the UK—which was also behind the Netherlands (€16,500), Norway (€6,050) and Italy (€4,288) and perhaps other countries, like Spain, for which no data were available.

Compounding this selectivity in the use of the CEA data has been the drawing of some very dubious inferences from it. In particular, the claim that the proportion of cervical trauma claims in the UK to bodily injury claims is 'twice the [European] average'[105] seems simply to be based on the aggregation of the national data from nine countries and then the calculation of an average without any regard to population size or numbers of vehicles.[106]

Flaws in the CEA Research Design and Methodology

Additionally, the *CEA Study* barely hints at the considerations that were considered relevant in designing the research and the methodology employed in it. The use of a common questionnaire is mentioned in the Study's foreword[107] but nothing is said about the choice of countries for comparison. A plausible, even likely, inference is that the questionnaire was sent to all the national insurance associations that constitute the CEA's membership[108] and the 10 featured in the Study were simply those that responded. Though these include the EU's five largest countries by population and size of economy (France, Germany, Italy,

[105] Tackling Whiplash (n 8) 4.
[106] Figures for numbers of inhabitants and number of vehicles were stated in a table in the *CEA Study* (n 2) 5; that is not reproduced here.
[107] *CEA Study* (n 2) 2.
[108] At the date of writing, the Insurance Europe website (www.insuranceeurope.eu) lists 34 member countries.

Spain and the UK), the data for one of these countries (Spain) are incomplete. No country in Central or Eastern Europe is included and, even if one assumes (plausibly) that claims markets in Western Europe are rather more developed, there are still quite a few countries in that region that are omitted (including Austria, Luxembourg and Portugal). For the purposes of comparison in respect of the key indicator of cervical trauma as a proportion of bodily injury it is immaterial that these countries are rather small in terms of population or economic power: the figure used for comparison purposes is a percentage, not the total number of claims.

Further, the Study is entirely silent on how the national insurance associations compiled the data they supplied. The disparities between some of the findings—notably between the 78% of bodily injury claims said to be linked to cervical trauma in the UK and the corresponding figure of just 3% in France (see Table 1 above)—is strongly suggestive that the questions posed, and/or the underlying data, may have been interpreted in divergent ways.[109] For example, the definition of 'minor cervical trauma' as 'a lesion of the cervical spine, caused by acceleration-deceleration mechanisms … without neurological complications and without affecting the osseous, nervous or ligamentary-disc structures'[110] seems to leave it open whether or not cases of neurological injury, bone fracture and nerve or ligament damage should be excluded from the data provided. (Was the qualification introduced by the word 'without' intended only to ensure that cases of minor trauma should be counted *as well*, even if they did not involve such sequelae?) The Study also gives us no idea of what other classifications of injury were used by the national associations, which leaves open the possibility that some national associations may have classified as, for example, back or neck injuries what in the UK was counted as cervical trauma. We also have no way of knowing what national associations did if they simply did not know the nature of the injury involved in a proportion of claims received: did they have a large category of 'unknowns' which might have included additional cervical trauma cases?

The ABI's Further Research

In 2013, the ABI claimed to have conducted new research which substantiated its 'whiplash capital' claim, updating its 2008 news release to read: 'The UK is the whiplash capital of Europe: 78% of low value motor personal injury claims are for whiplash, compared to an average of 48% throughout the rest of Europe'.[111] This further research by the ABI has not, to my knowledge, been published but data from it were submitted as written evidence to the House of Commons Transport Committee in connection with its inquiry *Cost of Motor Insurance: Whiplash*. This is what the ABI wrote:

> The ABI has carried out further research with a number of insurance federations across the EU and the overall position has changed little since 2004. The UK (78%) still has [a] substantially higher

[109] That the French figure should rise to 30% when a second survey was attempted (see below) suggests this even more powerfully, as it seems very unlikely that there should be a ten-fold growth in such claims in just a few years.

[110] *CEA Study* (n 2) 4.

[111] ABI news release, 31 July 2013.

than average percentage of whiplash claims as a proportion of personal injury claims, than our EU counterparts (48%).[112]

The following information was then appended in chart form:

Table 3: ABI's Revised Data on Whiplash Claims (2013)[113]

Country	Cervical trauma (compared with BI)*
UK	78% *(76%)*
Italy	68% *(66%)*
Sweden	61% *(–)*
Netherlands	35% *(40%)*
Spain	31% *(32%)*
Denmark	30% *(–)*
France	30% *(3%)*

** 2004 CEA Study figures in brackets*

Unfortunately, this research appears to share the methodological flaws of the *CEA Study* of 2004 (including a failure to disclose the research methods adopted). It is based on a very narrow set of comparator countries (only seven, including the UK), which differ to some extent from the comparators used in the *CEA Study*, preventing straightforward comparison of the two data sets. A footnote in the ABI's written evidence notes that the information was collected from national insurance associations, but states that the German, Austrian and Hungarian insurance bodies were unable to supply data as they did not collect such information (any more) because whiplash 'is not seen to be a problem in their countries'.[114] This really is quite remarkable when it is recalled that the 2004 Study showed that Germany had a well above average percentage of cervical trauma claims (47%).

Nevertheless, it is still possible to compare the ABI's 2013 data with that in the *CEA Study* for the five countries included in both, and this reveals that the proportion of RTA PI claims involving cervical trauma is reported to have risen not just in the UK (from 76% to 78%), but also in Italy (from 66% to 68%) and—most strikingly—in France, from the suspiciously low 3% reported in the 2004 Study, to 30%. This large disparity regarding the French figures in the two studies lends weight to the contention that the studies are methodologically flawed and so may well have actually been counting different things. It also prompts the thought that a new 'whiplash capital' might be anointed: **'*France* is the new whiplash capital of Europe'**, with proportionally ten times as many whiplash claims in 2013 than in 2004, a rate of growth massively in excess of that in any other country for which data are available.

112 Cost of Motor Insurance: Whiplash (n 48) vol 1, Ev 66, para 6.
113 Ibid, vol 1, Ev 66, Chart 1 (reproduced in amended format, 2004 *CEA Study* figures added in brackets).
114 Ibid, vol 1, Ev 66, fn 5.

The 'World Capital' Claim

Not content with calling the UK the whiplash capital of Europe, Helen Grant (Parliamentary Under-Secretary of State for Justice) raised the bar in her Foreword to the Ministry of Justice's *Whiplash Consultation* of 2012: Britain,' she said, 'has become the whiplash capital *of the world*'[115] (emphasis added). The basis for this 'claim inflation' is not stated and is far from clear. The only international comparison referred to in the consultation document is the *CEA Study* of 2004.[116] There is no reference at all to experience with whiplash claims in any country outside Europe. So, what was the evidence (if any) on which this new assertion was based?

One possible explanation is that Grant had been given advance notice of calculations by the Institute and Faculty of Advocates (IFoA) which were subsequently included in the IFoA's written evidence to the House of Commons Transport Committee for its *Cost of Motor Insurance: Whiplash* report of 2013. Finding that it was 'likely' that the UK was the whiplash capital of the world,[117] the IFoA explained that this conclusion was based on a comparison between the UK and the United States, relying on 'an assumption that, given the high litigiousness which we see demonstrated in the USA as observed in other insurance products, we would have expected the USA to show more whiplash claiming than any other country all else being equal'.[118] Moreoever, data in respect of the US was '[t]he most ready source of overseas data' that was available.[119] The IFoA admitted, however: 'We have not been able to confirm the comparability of this data or otherwise, either in terms of the structure of motor insurance products, their use, or on the structure of the data'.[120]

Proceeding despite these acknowledged issues to compare data from the UK and the US, the IFoA specified that the basis for comparison would be the ratio of the number of third-party personal injury (TPI) claims made to the number of insured accidents, as measured by the number of third-party property damage (TPD) claims which are made largely in respect of damage to third-party vehicles. It believed that this provided a measure of the scale of whiplash 'given that personal injury claim numbers are dominated by small whiplash type claims'.[121] The IFoA's figure for the UK, 30%, exceeded by a significant margin the equivalent figure for the US, 23%, and hence the UK could reasonably be considered the whiplash capital of the world.[122]

It will be immediately apparent that this analysis is deeply flawed. The conclusion that the UK is the whiplash capital of the world is based on a comparison with just one other country, the US, and it is simply assumed that any country that has a higher number of

[115] See above (n 94).

[116] *Whiplash Consultation* (n 42) 18. In fact, the *CEA Study* is not mentioned by name, but a link is provided to it in a footnote (fn 9).

[117] Cost of Motor Insurance: Whiplash (n 48) vol 1, Ev 53, para 6.

[118] Ibid, vol 1, Ev 52, para 4. This was reiterated in oral evidence provided by David Brown, Chair of the IfoA's Third Party Working Group: 'the US leads the world in terms of matters of liability, in terms of being more litigious and so on' (ibid, Ev 7, Q53).

[119] Ibid, vol 1, Ev 52, para 4.

[120] Ibid.

[121] Ibid, vol 1, para 5.

[122] Ibid, vol 1, Ev 53, para 6. The US figure was provided by the Independent Statistical Service (ISS), a subsidiary of the American insurance trade association, the Property Casualty Insurers Association of America. See further www.pciaa.net/.

whiplash claims than the US must have the highest number in the world. Further, the IFoA itself admitted that it was unable to confirm the comparability of the data from the two countries. Perhaps most remarkably, the data used as the basis of the claim that the UK is (likely) the whiplash capital of the world did not include data about whiplash claims at all; instead, data about *all RTA personal injury claims* were used as a proxy. Indeed, the IFoA's 'whiplash capital' claim was based on no evidence at all about the incidence of whiplash claims in the US, the only other country taken for comparison.

Lastly, one might note a subtle sleight of hand in the IFoA's conclusion that '*the UK shows more whiplash claiming per insured third party accident than the US*'.[123] Measuring the prevalence of whiplash claims with reference to *all accident claims*, including claims for property damage only, may well be a reasonable approach. But it was not this measure that the ABI and the Government relied upon for evidence that whiplash claims were more prevalent in the UK than in the rest of Europe. That contention took data from the 2004 *CEA Study* that considered the ratio of whiplash (more accurately: minor cervical trauma) claims to bodily injury claims, not the ratio of bodily injury claims to all accident claims (bodily injury and property damage). Actually, if the latter measure had been highlighted, Italy would have been placed at the top of the European comparison, with bodily injury claims making up 18% of all accident claims, while the comparable figure for the UK was only 17%.[124] So, perhaps we should say that **'Italy is the whiplash capital of the world'.**

Wider Reflections on the 'Whiplash Capital' Rhetoric

The evidence to support the claim that the UK is the whiplash capital of the world is, for all the above-stated reasons, entirely lacking in substance. The claim may well be justifiable, but the evidence base presented provides inadequate support for it. Nevertheless, the way it has been adopted as a slogan in the wider debate about compensation culture, encapsulating a specific view of whiplash injury as a problem that needs to be addressed, is an interesting phenomenon in its own right and warrants further reflection.[125]

The UK's ongoing programme of whiplash reforms is premised on the view that whiplash injury is a category that is ripe for exploitation by those willing to engage in fraud and exaggeration. The 'whiplash capital' slogan projects the UK as peculiarly susceptible to such conduct and serves as a shorthand reminder of various features of the UK's civil litigation landscape that were conditions of possibility for it, in particular by inducing various professional actors in the civil justice system to become complicit with dishonest claimants. Thus, lawyers were provided with financial incentives through the CFA regime to take on routine whiplash claims despite their low value—and to do so without looking too closely at the veracity of their clients and the reality of the injury alleged or its effects.

[123] *Cost of Motor Insurance: Whiplash* (n 48) vol 1, Ev 53, para 6.

[124] See Table 1 above. Of course, both figures are lower than the IFoA's 2013 estimate of 30% for the UK, but they come from quite different data sets which cannot meaningfully be compared.

[125] The following analysis adopts, albeit somewhat loosely, the approach advanced by C Bacchi in *Analysing Policy: What's the Problem Represented to Be?* (Frenchs Forest, Pearson Australia, 2009).

A claims economy developed in which CMCs acted as intermediaries between the lawyers and potential clients, whose claims were seen as commodities to be traded for financial gain through the mechanism of referral fees.[126] Doctors compliantly certified whiplash injuries out of sympathy for their own patients or, when acting as independent experts, to ensure their continued engagement in that role. And insurers were willing to settle claims without adequate evidence of the injuries alleged or their effects, or even before any medical evidence had been submitted at all, because they saw economic advantage in closing their files as quickly as possible.

The insurers, with the ABI in the lead, were the main proponents of reform, and decisively shaped the surrounding discourse with their 'whiplash capital' rhetoric. Their own complicity in the claims 'epidemic' (to use another favoured metaphor) was largely passed over and attracted little by way of consequence: only the relatively small tweaking of Part 36 of the CPR to reduce the temptation to make 'pre-med' offers can be seen as specifically directed at them. But each of the other parties who were deemed to bear responsibility for the failures of the system was individually targeted as the programme of reforms unfolded. Even before the *Whiplash Consultation* of 2012, the Government had introduced fixed fees for low-value motor claims (via the Claims Portal) and resolved to further reduce the financial incentives for lawyers to bring personal injury claims by reconfiguring the system of CFAs so that success fees were no longer recoverable from the insurer on the other side. The main focus of the subsequent whiplash reforms so far as lawyers were concerned was the introduction of mandatory 'know your client' checks (via askCUE PI) so as to enlist claimant solicitors as gatekeepers against fraud. At the same time, the Government targeted CMCs through the aggressive use of its regulatory powers and a series of extensions to the regulations, exposing CMCs (inter alia) to fines for regulatory violations and to compensation awards in respect of complaints upheld by the Legal Ombudsman. There was also a sustained effort to dismantle the whole 'claims economy' by banning cash inducements to claimants and referral fees for those selling on their claims. And concerns about the partiality of medical experts were addressed by a new system of accreditation and allocation (MedCo), combined with revisions to the rules on recoverable costs which sought—in combination with the MedCo scheme—to ensure the expert's independence from the claimant and the claimant's representatives. Lastly, potential claimants were given clear warning that fraudulent and exaggerated claims might result in criminal prosecution and conviction, while a new statutory provision provided for the complete loss of any entitlement to damages in 'fundamentally dishonest' claims, even where partly well founded.

Though there is undoubtedly some truth in the above representation of the problem, the manner of its representation is troublesome in a number of respects. The focus on fraudulent and exaggerated claims diverts attention from those who have genuine claims and the possible effects on them of the various reforms; the need to uphold access to justice for the deserving is routinely affirmed but, in the absence of any serious effort to gauge how it may have been affected by the reforms, it remains an empty platitude. Further, the coupling of fraud with exaggeration blurs the line between what is criminal and what may only be

[126] As to commoditisation generally, see further J Ilan, 'The Commodification of Compensation? Personal Injuries Claims in an Age of Consumption' (2011) 20 *Social & Legal Studies* 39.

an optimistic estimate based on the resolution of all remaining doubts in the claimant's favour, used as an opening salvo in a bargaining process in which both sides are expected to compromise. One may now expect such estimates to be met with a threat from the insurer that, if the claimant holds out for even near to the amount claimed, an application will be made to the court to dismiss the entire claim for fundamental dishonesty. Even if this might only be bluff, it seems likely that some claimants will be pressured into settling for much less than their claim is worth, especially if they are litigants in person—which will become more frequent if the limit for small claims, in which legal representation is discouraged, is raised from £1,000 to £5,000. It may also be noted in this context that there is no equivalent sanction for a defendant or insurer who knowingly defends a claim on a basis for which there exists inadequate evidence.

More generally, the repeated recycling of the 'whiplash capital' rhetoric testifies to the power of simple slogans to colonise public debate about tort law, coined by those pursuing an agenda of tort reform and enthusiastically taken up by conservative commentators because they reinforce and provide tantalising new examples to illustrate more general narratives about declining standards of personal conduct and individual responsibility.[127] As demonstrated above, the evidence base for the claims made can be exceptionally flimsy, but mud sticks even if the justification for flinging it is dubious. Purported rebuttals never gain the same currency[128] and do nothing to stop the slogan's repetition until the point that it becomes a habit of speech and then a habit of thought. Attempts to counter the claim with 'real facts' are doomed when all the data are in the hands of the claim's proponents, who can selectively release whatever seems likely to strengthen the claim, while ignoring awkward questions about its reliability or representative nature.

None of this is to suggest that there has not been a problem in the UK with claims for whiplash injury. Indeed, there is convincing evidence that such claims have in fact been exploited for fraudulent gain in some instances.[129] It may also be the case that lawyers and other actors in the civil justice system have culpably failed to prevent or even facilitated such conduct. But it is hard to believe that fraud is involved in anything other than a very small proportion of claims that are made, so it seems an unwarranted overreaction to allow the whole reform agenda to be driven by the perceived need to prevent such fraud and counter complicity in it by professional actors in the system. That representation of the problem pushes into the shadows other narratives that see the real issues as lying elsewhere, especially in the adoption of commercial rather than professional models for the delivery of legal services and a reliance upon market forces to ensure access to justice after the abolition of legal aid. How access to justice is to be achieved if the claims economy is dismantled—precisely because innovative market-based solutions that have emerged are deemed unacceptable—is just one of the pressing social questions that the 'whiplash capital' rhetoric has encouraged us to ignore.

[127] See generally W Haltom and M McCann, *Distorting the Law: Politics, Media, and the Litigation Crisis* (Chicago IL, University of Chicago Press, 2004) especially 54–56.

[128] Ibid, ch 3.

[129] See above (n 82).

Update: In November 2015, in what was seen as a surprise move, it was announced in the Chancellor of the Exchequer's Autumn Statement[130] that the Government would bring forward measures to raise the small claims limit to £5,000 for personal injury claims and, following a consultation on the details in 2016, to remove the right to claim general damages for minor whiplash injuries.[131] The announcement followed an early review of the MedCo system[132] in the light of concerns that new business practices had developed that had the potential to undermine the Government's policy objectives and public confidence in the system.[133]

130 www.gov.uk/government/publications/spending-review-and-autumn-statement-2015-documents/spending-review-and-autumn-statement-2015.

131 See further J Hyde, 'Spending Review: Osborne Raises Small Claims Limit to £5k and Scraps Whiplash Compensation' [2015] *Law Society Gazette*, 25 November.

132 Ministry of Justice, 'MedCo Framework Review: Call for Evidence' (July 2015).

133 Ibid, Foreword (Edward Faulks QC, Minister of State for Justice) 3.

2

Structural Factors Affecting the Number and Cost of Personal Injury Claims in the Tort System

RICHARD LEWIS*

This chapter examines Britain's 'compensation culture'. This is one of the terms most frequently used by the media today when discussing claims for damages for personal injury.[1] The expression has a variety of meanings but here we focus upon the allegation that society has had to bear an increasing burden as a result of the rising number and cost of these claims. Rather than celebrating greater access to the legal system whereby the needs of those injured are more likely to be met, the predominant view of the culture is a negative one: it is alleged that unwarranted claims have been generated for which ultimately we all must pay.[2] This chapter examines the key factors which have contributed to what has

* For their comments on an earlier and shorter draft published as 'Compensation Culture Reviewed' [2014] *Journal of Personal Injury Law* 209 I wish to thank Kevin Williams and the participants at the conference organised at the University of Limerick which stimulated the production of this book.

[1] For discussion of compensation culture in academic publications, see J Spencer, 'An Unethical Personal Injury Sector' [2014] *Journal of Personal Injury Law* 226; L O'Sullivan, 'Money for Nothing and Cheques for Free? Negligence and the Perceived "Compensation Culture"' (2014) 2(1) *UK Law Student Review* 74; A Morris, 'The "Compensation Culture" and the Politics of Tort' in TT Arvind and J Steele (eds), *Tort Law and the Legislature: Common Law, Statute and the Dynamics of Legal Change* (Oxford, Hart Publishing, 2013); R Lewis and A Morris, 'Tort Law Culture: Image and Reality' (2012) 39 *Journal of Law and Society* 562; J Ilan 'The Commodification of Compensation? Personal Injury Claims in an Age of Consumption' (2011) 20 *Social & Legal Studies* 39; J Hand, 'The Compensation Culture: Cliché or Cause for Concern?' (2010) 37 *Journal of Law and Society* 569; A Morris, 'Spiralling or Stabilising? The Compensation Culture and Our Propensity to Claim Damages for Personal Injury' (2007) 70 *MLR* 349; R Lewis, A Morris and K Oliphant, 'Tort Personal Injury Claims Statistics: Is there a Compensation Culture in the United Kingdom?' (2006) 14 *Torts Law Journal* 158 and [2006] *Journal of Personal Injury Law* 87; K Williams, 'State of Fear: Britain's "Compensation Culture" Reviewed' (2005) 25 *Legal Studies* 499; R Mullender, 'Negligence Law and Blame Culture: A Critical Response to a Possible Problem' (2006) 22 *Journal of Professional Negligence* 2; D Lloyd, 'The Compensation Culture: A New Legal Paternalism?' in E Lee (ed), *Compensation Crazy: Do We Blame and Claim Too Much?* (London, Hodder and Stoughton, 2002); F Furedi, *Courting Mistrust: The Hidden Growth of the Culture of Litigation in Britain* (London, Centre for Policy Studies, 1999).

[2] However, among official investigations and reports the conclusion usually reached is that the fear of compensation culture is greater than that warranted by the evidence. See Better Regulation Task Force, *Better Routes to Redress* (London, Cabinet Office Publications, 2004); *Tackling the Compensation Culture. Government Response to the Better Regulation Task Force Report: Better Routes to Redress* (2004); Lord Young, *Common Sense, Common Safety* (London, Cabinet Office Publications, 2010); RE Löfstedt, *Reclaiming Health and Safety for All: An Independent Review of Health and Safety Legislation* (Department for Work and Pensions, Cm 8219, 2011). Despite limited evidence of the damaging effects of compensation culture, the Coalition Government has made significant reforms of the system. For the political background see Morris, 'Politics of Tort' (n 1).

become such a pejorative description of personal injury litigation. The analysis is divided into two parts: the total number of claims brought each year is discussed first, and this is followed by an assessment of the overall cost of disposing of individual actions. The chapter gathers together information from a variety of academic and practitioner sources to produce a novel and up to date perspective upon the compensation culture debate.

With regard to the first section the chapter shows that, although it is indeed true that claims have increased, they have done so only with regard to specific types of injury. What influences our different propensity to claim following one injury as opposed to another? Among the key factors highlighted are the working practices of three institutions which form the bedrock of our claims system: liability insurance companies, claims management organisations and claimant law firms. Criticisms are made here of a 'dysfunctional' insurance industry; this is followed by a description of the rise and fall of an even more criticised claims gathering industry; and finally, attention is focused upon the rapidly changing structure of the legal profession involved in personal injury. All three of these institutions have had a profound effect upon the way that the compensation debate has developed.

When we turn to consider the rising cost of individual claims we ask to what extent are insurers and health authorities, among others, justified in their complaints that much more money now has to be paid out in damages and costs in order to dispose of each claim. The key changes to tort damages awards are summarised. Reforms have been made not only of the method by which compensation is calculated, but also of the form in which the money is to be paid: periodical payments are now common in cases involving serious injury. Damages for pain and suffering have been raised substantially without appreciating the full policy implications, whilst compensation for financial loss has had to be revised to match the realities of the wider financial world. These reforms are placed in a broader context which sees the increasing cost of claims as an inevitable result of closer adherence to the principle of restoring the claimant to the financial position that was enjoyed before the injury took place. Following proposals to reinforce that principle still further, one of the conclusions drawn in the final section is that the structural factors identified here will continue to generate concern about 'compensation culture' for some time to come.

Compensation Culture Disease: The Dangers of New Diagnosis

As the medical profession is aware, merely giving a name to an abnormal condition, whether physical or mental, can be a very significant event. It can help patients accept and come to terms with their illness. However, official recognition may also encourage doctors, patients and others to attribute symptoms too readily to the newly recognised condition. For example, it may be that children are prematurely labelled as suffering from attention deficit hyperactive disorder or dyslexia. The naming process makes some individuals too prepared to place the illness or disability into the new category. Examples especially relevant to personal injury litigation include whiplash injury and various states of mental upset, including post-traumatic stress disorder.[3] Claimants may be presumed to be suffering from these conditions as a result of an accident without there always being sufficient foundation for this belief. Both the condition itself and the risk of developing it may have both been found too easily. This constitutes one of many 'compensation culture' concerns.

If we examine the term 'compensation culture' itself we can make a similar analysis. The phrase has a wide range of meanings. It has come to be used as a broad catch-all term to encompass a variety of concerns including many which are based upon misinformation about the litigation system and prejudice about lawyers.[4] At its heart, as we shall see, there is indeed evidence which supports the need for careful monitoring of what actually happens in our tort system; there should especially be concern about certain features which have developed in recent years. However, the identification of potential and actual problems in that system has enabled all sorts of accusations to be levelled, many of them without empirical foundation. The ills have been too easily laid at the door of exploitative lawyers, fraudulent claimants or unscrupulous claims companies. One of those ills is that an increased burden has been placed upon society from the rising cost of personal injury litigation and this is the meaning associated with compensation culture that will be examined in the two parts which comprise this chapter.

The Number of Claims

Trends in the Rate of Claiming

A claim in tort is now made each year by about one person in every 64 in the UK. The total number of claims in 2015 is just short of a million, having exceeded that figure in the three years immediately preceding. As revealed in the table below which is derived from the official statistics,[5] road and work accidents predominate. They loom large over the practice of tort even though they constitute, at best, only about a half of all accidents.[6]

[3] There is a marked difference in the practical importance of these two injuries. Whereas PTSD is a factor in less than 5,000 claims a year, whiplash accounts for about 480,000 claims and neck injury is a factor in 87% of all motor claims. See the House of Commons Transport Committee, *Cost of Motor Insurance: Whiplash: Further Government Response to the Committee's Fourth Report of Session 2013–14*, Eleventh Special Report of Session 2013–14 (HC 902) 4 and Annex B. Despite its lesser importance, mental injury receives extensive discussion in tort textbooks whereas the effects of whiplash claims upon various aspects of the system are hardly considered.

[4] W Haltom and M McCann, *Distorting the Law: Politics, Media, and the Litigation Crisis* (Chicago IL, University of Chicago Press, 2004); P Almond, 'The Dangers of Hanging Baskets: "Regulatory Myths" and Media Representations of Health and Safety Regulations' (2009) 36 *Journal of Law and Society* 352.

[5] In 1989 the Compensation Recovery Unit was set up by government in order to recover from damages certain social security benefits that the claimant receives as a result of his injury. Reliable data has been generated on the number of claims, no matter whether successful or unsuccessful, and irrespective of whether the claim was settled or disposed of by a court hearing. See Department for Work & Pensions, *Compensation Recovery Unit—Performance Statistics*: www.dwp.gov.uk/other-specialists/compensation-recovery-unit/performance-and-statistics/performance-statistics. The reliability of the figures is discussed in Lewis, Morris and Oliphant (n 1). For more detail on the current figures see Lewis and Morris (n 1).

[6] *Report of the Royal Commission on Civil Liability and Compensation for Personal Injury* (Cmnd 7054, 1978) vol 2, table 57 (Pearson Commission). In Australia road and work accidents are less than a fifth of the total. H Luntz and D Hambly, *Torts: Cases and Commentary* 5th edn (Sydney, LexisNexis, 2002) 4.

Table 1: Claims 2014–15: The Type of Injury

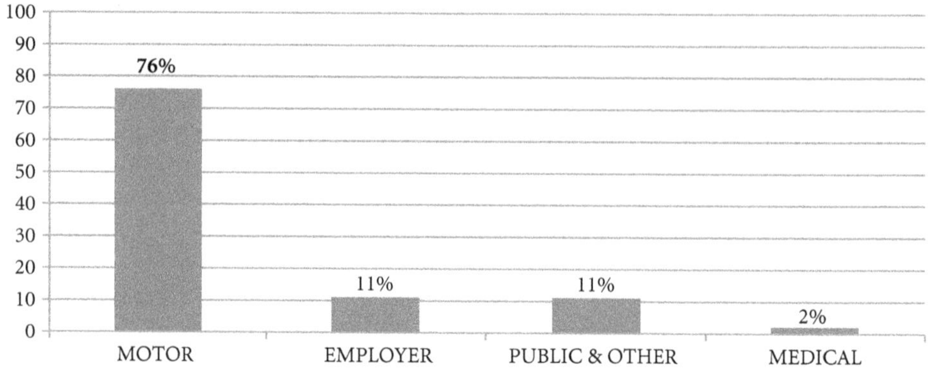

Whilst historical data are in short supply, those which are available support the view that over the long term there has been a very substantial increase in claims. They appear to have risen four-fold since the 1970s. In 1973 the Pearson Commission estimated that there were about 250,000 claims.[7] In 1988 it was thought that claims had grown to around 340,000.[8] This figure then doubled by the new millennium. Now claims are a third more than they were at the start of the millennium, the figure of a million being exceeded in 2012 and it has continued around that level since.[9]

Table 2: The Rise in Claims over 40 years

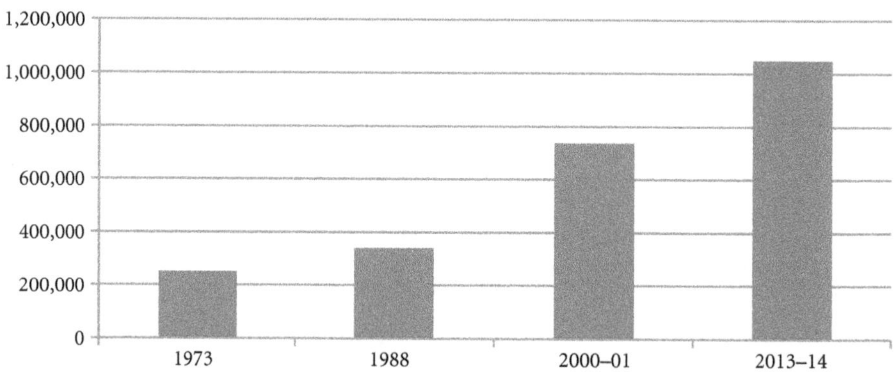

[7] Pearson Commission (n 6) vol 2, para 59.

[8] Lord Chancellor's Department, *Report of the Review Body on Civil Justice* (Cm 394, 1988) para 391. This estimate is given with no indication of the facts upon which it is based and seems not to be derived from the research from Inbucon Management Consultants, *Civil Justice Review: Study of Personal Injury Litigation* (Lord Chancellor's Department, 1986).

[9] Compensation Recovery Unit figures (n 5). For more detail see Lewis and Morris (n 1).

This rising trend in claims has not been a consistent one. Indeed the total number of claims actually fell slightly between 1998 and 2006 although it has risen in each year since. However, overall claims figures disguise major changes which have taken place in relation to particular kinds of injuries. These are revealed in Table 3.[10]

Table 3: Trends in the number of claims 2000–2015 (biennial figures)

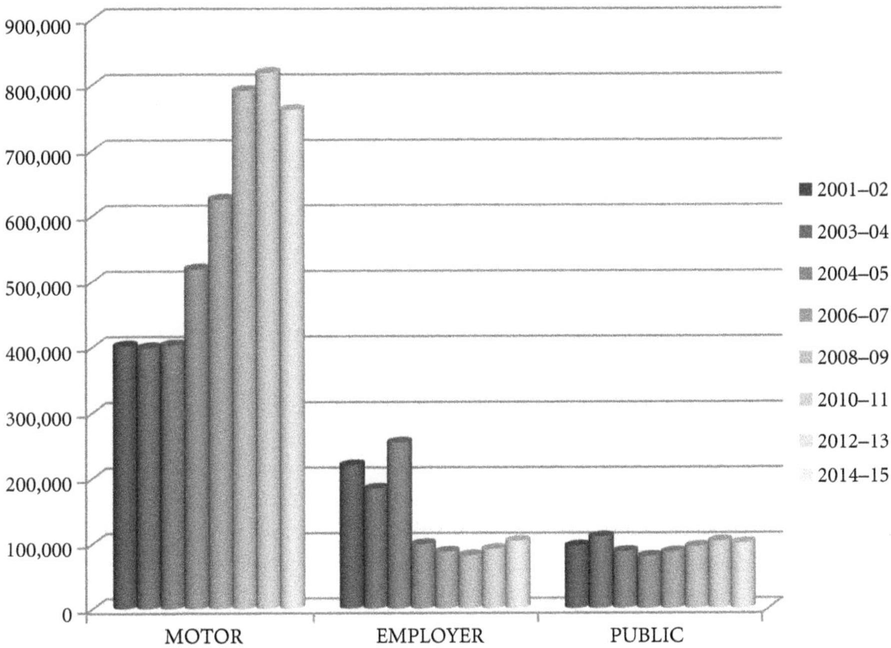

As can be seen, public liability claims in recent years have remained fairly constant, hovering around 100,000 a year. By contrast between 2000 and 2007 the number of employers' liability claims fluctuated considerably, reaching a peak of 291,000 in 2004. This was largely due to the creation of temporary special schemes of compensation for coalmining diseases.[11] These schemes closed in 2004 and since then the annual number of employers' liability claims has fallen by almost two-thirds to around 100,000. Although in the last four years claims have increased by a third, there are still fewer today than there were in 1973. They have declined in relative importance to such an extent that they now account for only 11% of all claims whereas in 1973 they represented 45%.[12]

[10] The table has been compiled by the author using the annual statistics published by the Compensation Recovery Unit (n 5).

[11] The claims of miners in respect of, firstly, respiratory disease, and secondly, the use of vibrating tools led to settlement schemes which were called 'the biggest personal injury schemes in British legal history and possibly the world'. From 1999–2004 about 760,000 claims were registered. Department of Trade and Industry, *Coal Health Claims*: www.dti.gov.uk/coalhealth/01.htm.

[12] Only one in seven workers suffering disease or injury make a claim according to the Trades Union Council and the Association of Personal Injury Lawyers, *The Compensation Myth: Seven Myths about the 'Compensation Culture* (2014).

In stark contrast to the other types of claim, there has been both a long-term and short-term increase in the number of road traffic accident (RTA) claims involving personal injury. Between 2000 and 2004 such claims actually fell but since 2004 there has been an increase every year except for the last two with the result that the total over the last ten years has doubled to 761,000. This increase is largely responsible for the long-term rise in the total of all personal injury claims. In 1973 RTAs constituted 41% of all personal injury claims. By 2001 this had increased to 54% and by 2014 RTAs constituted 76% of all claims. A notable feature has been the growth of claims involving whiplash injuries which now constitute well over half of all claims made.[13] Supposedly, by 2004 the UK had substantially more whiplash cases than any other European country and since then the number of claims has doubled.[14]

This rapid expansion in the overall number of claims can be explained by a combination of factors that relate, first, to the institutions which play a leading part in personal injury practice, and second, to the individual who makes the claim. The following account does not seek to deal with these factors in detail, but does highlight some of the more recent developments.

Institutional and Personal Factors Encouraging Claims

Our propensity to claim is very much affected by the institutions involved in personal injury practice. A major example is the role that trade unions have played in encouraging and facilitating claims for work accidents and diseases.[15] Following injury, members have been able to gain access to union counselling and free legal advice. The organised referral of these assisted claims to particular law firms led to the first specialised personal injury representation for injured claimants. This made a considerable difference to whether a claim was brought and for how much it was settled; the reputation of certain trade union lawyers as hard negotiators and aggressive litigators continues to this day. However, union membership has declined from a peak of about 13 million in 1979 to half of that figure today.[16] This still means that about a quarter of the workforce is covered, although there is a much greater concentration in public as opposed to private employment where there is only 14% membership. Apart from trade unions, in recent years three other institutions have significantly affected our propensity to claim damages: liability insurers, claims management companies and claimant law firms.

[13] There were 480,000 whiplash claims in 2012–13 constituting 58% of all motor personal injury claims. However, the increase in motor personal injury claims has also been driven by claims with a description of 'neck or back' injuries. Over the last five years, these claims have almost trebled to around 270,000. Claims which would have previously been labelled as 'whiplash' are now instead being labelled as 'back or neck' injuries. This means that neck injuries which include whiplash account for 87% of all road traffic claims. Transport Committee, Eleventh Special Report (n 3) 4.

[14] European Insurance and Reinsurance Federation (Comité Européen des Assurances) (CEA), *Minor Cervical Trauma Claims: Comparative Study* (Brussels, 2004) 4. In its response to the Ministry of Justice Consultation Paper CP17/2012 APIL emphasised the European data is unreliable and outdated, and in its response the Law Society similarly doubts the insurers' figures. For more detail see K Oliphant, ch 1 of this book.

[15] G Latta and R Lewis, 'Trade Union Legal Services' (1974) *12 British Journal of Industrial Relations* 56. For an engaging account of the emergence of the former leading trade union law firm see S Allen, *Thompsons: A Personal History of the Firm and its Founder* (London, Merlin Press, 2012).

[16] Department for Business, Innovation & Skills, *Trade Union Membership 2013: Statistical Bulletin*.

Liability Insurers

A fact which has always been well known to practitioners has begun to attract more attention from academics recently: it is increasingly appreciated that insurance companies are fundamental to tort and the operation of the personal injury system.[17] They are its 'lifeblood'. What they do very much affects whether a claim is made, how it is processed and the amount of damages paid. Liability insurance is not merely an ancillary device to protect the insured, but is the 'primary medium for the payment of compensation, and tort law [is] a subsidiary part of the process'.[18]

Although the great majority of claims are brought against defendants who are individual people, they almost all are insured. In nine out of ten cases the real defendants are insurance companies, with the remainder comprising large self-insured organisations or public bodies such as local authorities.[19] A handful of insurers dominate the market so that in motor claims four companies only are responsible for over half the premiums collected, these being Direct Line, Admiral, Aviva and AXA.[20] Insurers are the real paymasters for the tort system for they are responsible for 94% of the compensation paid out for personal injury.[21] They fund not only the damages award itself but also most of the administrative and legal costs of the system. They provide legal representation not only for most defendants but also many claimants. The reason for this lies in the rapid expansion in recent years of before-the-event (BTE) insurance. This form of legal expenses insurance covers almost three in five adults.[22]

The influence of insurers inevitably permeates the system. Intuitively we might expect that out of self-interest insurers would act as the system's gatekeepers and policemen. This might involve them discouraging certain claims being made in the first place, carefully examining those that are brought and paying up only when evidence of legal liability is clear. However, the reality has been far from this. In recent years insurers have actually encouraged claims in a number of ways and they have very readily made payments, albeit usually of low amounts.

An insurer's desire to defend a case has always had to be tempered by cost considerations. A heroic defence denying that a driver has been negligent in a marginal case may prove not only to be a risky but also a very expensive tactic. This is especially the case where the

[17] R Merkin and J Steele, *Insurance and the Law of Obligations* (Oxford, Oxford University Press, 2013); R Lewis, 'Insurance and the Tort System' (2005) 25 *Legal Studies* 85; R Lewis, 'Insurers and Personal Injury Litigation: Acknowledging "The Elephant in the Living Room"' [2005] *Journal of Personal Injury Law* 1; J Morgan, 'Tort, Insurance and Incoherence' (2004) 67 *MLR* 384; and G Wagner (ed), *Tort Law and Liability Insurance* (New York, Springer Publishers, 2005).

[18] P Cane, *Atiyah's Accidents, Compensation and the Law*, 6th edn (Cambridge, CUP, 1999) 191.

[19] Even where local authorities fund damages awards directly, they may still employ private insurance company personnel to handle the claims made against them. S Halliday, J Ilan and C Scott, 'Street-Level Tort Law: The Bureaucratic Justice of Liability Decision-Making' (2012) 75 *MLR* 347, 356.

[20] This is based on market share in 2012. See the evidence of Thompsons Solicitors to the House of Commons Transport Committee, *Driving Premiums Down: Fraud and the Cost of Motor Insurance* (2014) First Report of Session 2014–15 (HC 285).

[21] Pearson Commission (n 6) vol 2, para 509.

[22] R Lewis, 'Litigation Costs and Before-The-Event Insurance: The Key to Access to Justice?' (2011) 74 *MLR* 272; FWD Group, *The Market for 'BTE' Legal Expenses Insurance* (Ministry of Justice, 2007) para 3.3.

damages claimed are small. Legal costs then can easily exceed the sum being claimed.[23] This danger is present in the majority of cases because the average payment of damages is less than £5,000.[24] As a result, it is unusual for insurers to contest liability: one study of insurers' files revealed that they 'contained remarkably little discussion of liability', finding it initially denied in only 20% of cases.[25] In fact claimants succeed in more than nine out of 10 cases.[26] Because insurers make some payment in this great majority of cases, in effect, they encourage claims to be made.

Insurers also encourage claims by giving claimants ready access to a lawyer: they provide legal expenses insurance as an extra benefit in the motor and home policies they sell. Not only do insurers profit from this by including an additional cost in the premiums charged, but they also used to receive a referral fee from solicitors for each personal injury case they forwarded to their associated law firm. Referrals earned insurers about £700 per case[27] and constituted a substantial income. For example, Admiral insurance company received over £18 million in referrals in 2012. This was about £6 for each vehicle it insured and constituted 6% of its profit.[28] A related practice of insurers was to collect information about all potential claimants in an accident and again sell those details to law firms. The result was the development of an ultimately flawed business practice: profit was sought from these individual cases but in doing so a more febrile claims atmosphere resulted. Both insurers and premium payers at large eventually suffered.[29]

Gradually insurers became increasingly concerned about the problems which they had in part created. These included not only the rising number of claims, but also the increasing legal costs to which they became subject. Legal aid for personal injury was largely abolished in 2000 and this stimulated the widespread use of conditional fee agreements.[30] Under these agreements claimant lawyers could secure an increase in their fees in each case they won.

[23] Lord Justice Jackson found evidence of disproportionately high costs in his *Review of Civil Litigation Costs: Final Report* (London, Judiciary of England and Wales, January, 2010). Data collected for one survey showed that for 280 cases which had come before the District Court the claimant costs alone amounted to £1.80p for every £1 of damages paid. On average, costs exceeded damages for cases settled up to £15,000 in the 'fast track' procedure. Previously insurers had stated that overall they paid an additional 38p in legal costs for every £1 recovered by the claimant but that this rose to 90p for claims below £5,000. See *The ABI Response to the Government's Consultation on Case Track Limits and the Claims Process for Personal Injury* (2007).

[24] In a survey of conditional fee claimants in 2011 half of them received less than £5,000. Insight Delivery Consultancy, *No Win No Fee Usage in the UK* appendix 5 of the Access to Justice Action Group, *Comments on Reforming Civil Litigation Funding*: www.accesstojusticeactiongroup.co.uk/home/wp-content/uploads/2011/05/NWNF-research.pdf. P Fenn and N Rickman, *Costs of Low Value Employers' Liability Claims 1997–2002* (London, Department for Constitutional Affairs, 2003) record average damages of only £3,000 for employers' liability accident claims.

[25] T Goriely, R Moorhead and P Abrams, *More Civil Justice? The Impact of the Woolf Reforms on Pre-Action Behaviour* (London, Law Society and Civil Justice Council, 2002) 103.

[26] As a rough estimate, based on Compensation Recovery Unit figures (n 5), the average ratio of RTA settlements to claims made for the last six years is 90%. There is a time lag between claims and settlements which, given the steep recent rise in claims, makes the actual success rate somewhat higher than 9 out of 10 despite the suspected growth of unmeritorious actions which are likely to be unsuccessful.

[27] Otterburn Legal Consulting, *Personal Injury Marketing and Referral Fees*, Report for the Association of Personal Injury Lawyers (2012); Jackson, *Review of Civil Litigation Costs: Final Report* (n 23) 202.

[28] Admiral Annual Accounts 2013. J Hyde, 'Admiral still cashing in on PI referral fees' [2013] *Law Society Gazette*, 4 March. It had long been recognised that referral fees constituted a major part of the profits from providing BTE. See FWD Group (n 22) 4A II 4.

[29] J Straw, 'Dirty secret that drives up motor insurance; Companies are selling drivers' details to claims firms exploiting no-win no-fee system' *The Times* (27 June 2011).

[30] The Access to Justice Act 1999, s 27 and s 29.

They could recover up to double their costs if successful. In seeking to avoid or reduce these costs insurers adopted practices which again in the longer term had the opposite effect of that originally intended. For example, one tactic still used today is 'third-party capture'. This is where the insurer makes a direct approach to any injured party who is not their own insured. They may do so either before or after they have contacted a solicitor. Insurers seek a quick settlement of the potential claim before any legal costs can be incurred. This has resulted in many people with only very minor injury from the accident in which they were involved (or often no injury at all) being offered sums to settle cases which they had no previous intention of bringing! Claimants' solicitors have been especially upset by a small minority of insurers who have approached their clients directly even after they have engaged legal help. A test case against one insurer alleging that claimants have been induced to break their contracts with their solicitors could mean that hundreds of settlements which have been agreed since 2009 will be reopened.[31]

A similar insurer tactic employed to reduce legal costs which has also had the unintended effect of encouraging claims has been for insurers to make 'pre-med offers'. These are offers made to the claimants' solicitors very early in the proceedings, often immediately on receiving notice of a claim, and before any medical report has been obtained. They are pitched at a low level, usually less than £1,500, and are aimed at removing the nuisance value of a small claim together with its potentially disproportionate legal and disbursement costs. For example, until recently a quick offer could save an insurer paying up to £700 (now reduced to a maximum of £180) for the cost of a medical report even though these are often standard form and can be produced by a mere GP.[32] Commonly made in whiplash cases, these pre-med offers have been heavily criticised on the one hand as attempts to buy off claims for derisory amounts[33] and, on the other hand, as encouraging claims where injury is non-existent and thus feeding the compensation culture.[34] There have been proposals that a medical examination and report should be made compulsory before settlement.[35] Although the Ministry of Justice wants to discourage pre-med offers it has opted against making such a ban.[36]

Criticism of insurers making very ready offers was voiced by a solicitor interviewed as part of the author's forthcoming contribution to an empirical project investigating personal injury practice in several European countries and funded by the European Centre of Tort and Insurance Law. He said:

> [I]f it becomes known, as I think it did with whiplash, that all you have to do is say: 'I was in a car accident' and really the insurers just pay you some money, I'm not sure that's necessarily a good

[31] *Gavin Edmondson Solicitors v Haven Insurance* [2014] EWHC 3062 QB is to be appealed. See 'Insurer in line of fire over client capture' [2014] *Law Society Gazette*, 17 November.

[32] Ministry of Justice, Press release: www.gov.uk/government/news/fee-cut-for-whiplash-medical-reports.

[33] eg, J Spencer, 'Pre-med offers result in injustices' [2014] *Law Society Gazette*, 11 March; and S Rigby (2014) 158 (7) *Solicitors Journal* 15.

[34] Ministry of Justice, Reducing the Number and Cost of Whiplash Claims: A Government Response to Consultation on Arrangements Concerning Whiplash Injuries in England and Wales/Cost of Motor Insurance—Whiplash: A Government Response to the House of Commons Transport Committee (Cm 8738, 2013).

[35] See the recommendation in the House of Commons Transport Committee, *The Cost of Motor Insurance: Whiplash*, Fourth Report of Session 2013–14 (HC 117) and especially the evidence of the Motor Accidents Solicitors Society. The Association of Personal Injury Lawyers has similarly opposed such offers.

[36] Ministry of Justice, press release (n 32).

> message to be sending out to the public. I think that insurers have got caught … If they're going to make those sort of offers, they can expect people just to have a go all the time.

The conclusion of a parliamentary committee was that 'a highly dysfunctional market' has been created 'in which the pursuit of profit by the different firms involved has led to higher prices for consumers and, in some cases, business practices which are not in the consumer interest'.[37] Overall it is clear that certain routine institutional practices of insurers in processing claims have significantly contributed to some of the problems now identified as part of compensation culture.

Claims Management Companies

Claims management companies (CMCs) first emerged about twenty years ago. They made money by trawling for accident victims and seeking quick settlements from which they extracted high fees from claimants. Alternatively, they passed on their clients to solicitors and received a referral fee in return. Today they also offer services such as vehicle repair and credit hire, and some can arrange accident reports and evidence from medical experts. To recruit clients, CMCs have used a variety of tactics from mass media advertising to direct approaches to individuals in the street.[38] Over three-quarters of the population have reported being contacted about making a claim.[39]

The growth of CMCs was fuelled especially by the removal of legal aid in 2000 which led to the more extensive use of conditional fee agreements. Under these agreements claimant lawyers could secure an increase in their fees in each case that they won. They could recover up to double their costs if successful but nothing at all if they lost. This potential for increased profit added to the incentives to obtain referrals. One problem solicitors faced was that conduct rules prevented them from paying CMCs for these claims. However, these rules were flouted on such a regular basis that the ban on referral payments was eventually lifted in 2004.[40] The development of an efficient, high volume claims department founded upon referrals and advertising proved to be a successful business strategy for a number of law firms.

However, there was growing concern about the abuses that resulted from CMCs being given such a free rein. The press, in particular, used CMC 'to describe anything and anyone who is perceived as promoting "compensation culture", ripping off consumers, stealing from them and ultimately "mugging" the most vulnerable in our society'.[41] There continues to be foundation for such stories: only recently CMCs have been found guilty of a range of misdemeanours from helping to arrange 'crash-for-cash' scams to bribing policemen to steal details of accident victims from a police computer.[42] To combat some of the more extreme practices, the Government began to regulate the operation of CMCs in 2007.[43]

[37] The House of Commons Transport Committee (HC 285, 2014) (n 20) para 38.

[38] National Association of Citizens Advice Bureaux, *Door to Door: CAB Clients' Experiences of Doorstep Selling* (2002).

[39] ABI news release 29/12 (19 June 2012).

[40] A Higgins, 'Referral Fees—The Business of Access to Justice' (2012) 32 *Legal Studies* 109.

[41] A Wigmore, 'The Death of Claims Management Companies' [2013] *Journal of Personal Injury Law* 248.

[42] Ministry of Justice, *Enforcement Actions Carried Out by CMR* (The Stationery Office, June 2014).

[43] The Compensation Act 2006, s 4 and the Compensation (Claims Management Services) Regulations 2006 (SI No 3322).

In response to attempts to prevent them making approaches in person, the companies adapted by sending unsolicited text messages and making unsolicited phone calls.[44] Although these practices were later banned, other tactics continued to prove successful as evidenced by the fact that the largest increases in claims are found in areas where CMCs are concentrated.[45] By 2010 the turnover of CMCs from personal injury work was almost a fifth of that of solicitors' firms.[46] The number of CMCs continued to grow, reaching a peak in late 2011 when there were 2,553 companies operating in the personal injury claims sector. However, following increased regulation and, in particular, the banning of referral fees in 2013[47] they have been halved in number to around 1,125. This resulted in a similar reduction in their turnover which fell from £455 million to £238 million.[48]

As discussed under the next heading, this decline in CMCs does not necessarily indicate a commensurate reduction in marketing and the aggressive pursuit of potential claimants. At the same time that referral fees were banned, claimant law firms also found that they were no longer able to recover their success fee from insurers.[49] These two changes are having a major effect upon the structure of personal injury law firms and the business models they now adopt. It is to these changes that we now turn.

Claimant Personal Injury Law Firms

Initially solicitors' firms were very reluctant to become involved with what was considered the distasteful business of claims gathering. By the late 1990s, however, following the relaxation of the rules on advertising, specialist personal injury firms were actively seeking clients.[50] They still avoided the brash techniques of CMCs but many were prepared to pay referral fees to these companies; they were content to 'turn a blind eye' in order to secure a regular flow of work.[51] Eventually more law firms recognised that the work being done by CMCs could be replicated by them. A few firms even adopted certain tactics which matched some of the excesses of the CMCs. For example, some offered inducements to sue including free iPads, shopping vouchers or cash promises of up to £2,000.[52] CMCs were banned from

[44] M Boleat (2010), Ministry of Justice, *Claims Management Regulation Annual Report 2010/2011* (2011). Despite later being banned, unsolicited approaches continue. In 2014 the Information Commissioner's Office reported that 2,355 complaints concerning calls or texts concerning accidents were made for the month of November alone. J Hyde, 'PI Nuisance Calls still Plaguing Consumers' [2014] *Law Society Gazette*, 14 December.

[45] Especially Manchester, Liverpool and Birmingham. D Brown and S MacDonnell, *Update from the Third Party and PPO Working Parties* (Faculty of Actuaries, 2012). 'Liverpool is whiplash capital of Britain' *Financial Times* (27 May 2012).

[46] It amounted to £377 million compared with about £2 billion received by solicitors. London Economics, *Access to Justice: Learning from Long Term Experiences in the Personal Injury Legal Services Market* (Report for the Legal Services Board, 2014) 4 and 59.

[47] The Legal Aid, Sentencing and Punishment of Offenders Act 2012, s 56 prevents the payment of referral fees. However, the Claims Management Regulator has continued to issue warnings about the companies failing to comply.

[48] As at March 2014. Ministry of Justice, Claims Management Regulation: Annual Report 2013–14.

[49] The Legal Aid, Sentencing and Punishment of Offenders Act 2012, s 44 makes claimants liable to pay the uplift in fees out of their damages.

[50] R Abel, *English Lawyers between Market and State: The Politics of Professionalism* (New York, Oxford University Press, 2003); and H Kritzer, 'The Fracturing Legal Profession: The Case of Plaintiffs' Personal Injury Lawyers' (2001) 8 *International Journal of the Legal Profession* 225.

[51] For more details see Wigmore (n 41).

[52] C Budsworth, 'Should solicitors be able to offer financial inducements to claimants?' (2014) 158 (17) *Solicitors Journal*.

making such gifts but solicitors continued to be able to do so until 2015.[53] Although only a minority offered such inducements, the aggressive claims gathering of the profession has now resulted in solicitors supplanting many CMCs. According to the policy director of the Claims Standards Council:

> In 2013, over 90 per cent of law firms now practice what they used to criticise. They market and advertise very efficiently spending over £60 million a year, which is double the spend of two years ago. They have marginalised the traditional CMC to such an extent that less than 70,000 claims from a total of 600,000 claims are generated by traditional CMC activity. That figure will decline and so will CMCs.[54]

Further changes have occurred following the relaxation of the rules relating to the ability of law firms to form business relationships with other enterprises. Since 2011 non-lawyers have been able to own and manage legal practices as part of an 'alternative business structure' (ABS) which can involve a multidisciplinary partnership. Over 240 licences for such arrangements have been granted by the Solicitors Regulation Authority in the last two years. The ABS is a particularly attractive vehicle for conducting personal injury work. The wider organisation can include within it, for example, a medical reporting agency that is able to give evidence on claims, or a financial department that gives advice on how a damages award should be invested. For present purposes, however, the significant advantage of an ABS is that it enables personal injury firms to avoid the difficulties caused by the prohibition of referral fees by making such payments 'in house'. As a result we have seen leading personal injury firms merge with CMCs or insurance companies. For example, Admiral Insurance has taken over the legal firms of Lyons Davidson and Cordner Lewis whilst Ageas insurance is now in partnership with New Law Solicitors. Similarly, trade unions have also entered into associations with law firms.[55]

The growth of ABS practices has been dramatic. Perhaps the best example involves the prominent trade union linked firm of Russell, Jones and Walker which acquired the notorious CMC, Claims Direct, only for it then to be merged with the very large international ABS firm of Slater & Gordon. This took place in 2012 and was the first U.K. acquisition of that ABS firm, which originates from and has its shares listed in Australia. Attracting some controversy, the firm is the only one in the world to be publicly listed on the Stock Exchange and to derive its capital base from shareholders in this way. Slater & Gordon has aggressively expanded in this country since making its first acquisition here two years ago. Its share price and profits have risen sharply following its takeover of other key claimant firms such as Fentons and Pannone. It now has almost 2,000 UK employees spread around 18 locations. ABS firms accounted for a fifth of the turnover of personal injury solicitors' firms in 2012–13. That figure will rise sharply as more alternative practices are established. Their expansion continues apace, especially that of Slater & Gordon whose turnover doubled in

[53] Inducements to claim were banned by the Criminal Justice and Courts Act 2015, s 58. This measure was strongly supported by the House of Commons Transport Committee (HC 285) (n 20).

[54] Wigmore (n 41) 252.

[55] Morrish has formed an association with the Transport Salaried Staffs' Association. Thompsons, the best known trade union firm, became an ABS in 2012 but its refusal to enter into an arrangement with the GMB trade union resulted in it being dropped from its panel of solicitors in 2014. J Hyde, 'Trade union to partner law firm' [2013] *Law Society Gazette*, 23 December.

the last financial year to over £100 million, with over 80% of its total revenue being derived from personal injury work.[56]

To secure economies of scale there have also been a series of mergers of traditional personal injury firms outside the ABS umbrella. Mergers of whatever kind have been accompanied by a drive for efficiency in order to deal with the mass of small claims which dominate the system. Largely because of funding constraints, much of the work involving smaller run-of-the-mill claims in these firms is now being carried out by unqualified or paralegal personnel.[57] They are working in what has been identified in the US as 'settlement mills' where the assembly line resolution of claims 'represents quite a departure from the intimate, individualized, and fact-intensive process thought to underlie the traditional process of tort'.[58] The legal process has been de-skilled and de-personalised in these factories which have direct comparators in the UK.

The funding reforms and new business opportunities have convinced a former President of the Association of Personal Injury Lawyers that firms must now 'get big, get niche or get out'.[59] In other words, they need to either become larger and more efficient or develop specialist skills in order to deal with the minority of claims where more serious injury is suffered. Otherwise they will fail. These views are echoed by the head of Slater & Gordon who predicts that in the near future just three firms will control up to 40% of personal injury claims.[60] Some may think this a dramatic claim, but there have been more firms closing their doors than ever before and 'run off' insurance is now a favoured topic for professional development seminars. In 2013 a book was published giving advice on developing a personal injury practice for the future under the more limited costs regime. A year later the author's law firm went into administration.[61]

All this cost cutting and consolidation in the market is matched by the continued aggressive searching for potential clients and the further encouragement of claims in tort, albeit in a regime which now has reduced funding because of the loss of the ability to reclaim success fees and insurance premiums. It is a time of very rapid change. The focus of attention has been upon how claims are funded and what rules of civil procedure should apply. However, it is perhaps even more important to appreciate the changes that are taking

[56] Slater & Gordon's turnover in the UK increased by 119% during the 2013–14 financial year: [2014] *The Lawyer*, 25 September. Its acquisition of the Cardiff based firm of Leo Abse in 2015 was its seventh in just over a year. It then made its most significant acquisition to date by acquiring a division of Quindell for £677 million, more than doubling the 2,000 staff it employs. It thus raised its share of the UK personal injury market to 12%, twice that of its nearest competitor, Irwin Mitchell. According to their managing director, the deal allowed it 'to penetrate the highly fragmented £2.5 billion UK personal injury market'. For its rationale in securing finance by publicly offering shares, see A Grech and K Morrison, 'Slater & Gordon: The Listing Experience' (2009) 22 *Georgetown Journal of Legal Ethics* 535.

[57] Association of Personal Injury Lawyers, *The Impact of the Jackson Reforms on Costs and Case Management* (Evidence to the Civil Justice Council, 2014); D Evans, 'Shifting Strategy in the Personal Injury Market' [2014] *Journal of Personal Injury Law* 85.

[58] N Engstrom, 'Sunlight and Settlement Mills' (2011) 86 *New York University Law Review* 805, 810 and by the same author, 'Run-of-the-mill Justice' (2009) 22 *Georgetown Journal of Legal Ethics* 1485.

[59] D Marshall (2013) 157 *Solicitors Journal*, October 16.

[60] J Hyde, 'Slater Chief Predicts Rapid Consolidation in PI Market' [2014] *Law Society Gazette*, 1 May. A year later, the three leading firms controlled an estimated 22% of the market. N Rose, 'Slater & Gordon strikes £677 million deal to buy Quindell's professional services division' *Legal Futures*, 30 March 2015.

[61] 'Surviving Jackson Author Closes Firm' [2014] *Law Society Gazette*, 15 December; J Zindani and D Regan, *Surviving Jackson—Developing a Personal Injury Practice for the Future* (Birmingham, Sun Legal Publishing, 2013).

place in the structure of the legal profession and the personnel now involved in personal injury litigation. The reforms are thus having a considerable effect upon how tort actually operates in practice; they will help determine how compensation culture is perceived in the future.

Personal Factors Encouraging Claims

Apart from these institutional influences, there are factors which are personal to the individual claimant which can account for the increase in claims. These are not discussed in detail here partly because the analysis of 'naming, blaming and claiming' is well known.[62] That is, the individual first has to recognise that he has suffered an injury; then he needs to attribute responsibility; and only finally does he seek formal recompense for his loss.[63] The increase in claims is the result of a complex mix of changing personal factors which affect all three parts of this analysis.

It is certainly the case that we are less prepared to put up with misfortune than in the past. Today we are more likely to recognise that we have suffered from wrongdoing. We are better able to identify, for example, the work-related factors that are the cause of our injury or disease, and we are also more willing to sue our employer. To an extent this may be because we have less fear of recrimination although many workers are still concerned about discrimination after being labelled an 'awkward' employee. The seriousness of the injury is also a major factor in determining whether a claim is made for it is clear that it is much more likely that recompense will be sought if substantial financial loss is suffered.

This last fact may make it appear that tort compensation follows where the need is greatest. However, in fact the reverse is true. This is because the vast majority of claims brought today are for relatively minor road traffic injuries which have little effect on the pocket and no long-lasting consequences. The increase in these types of claims reflects a significant change in social mores. Even though the injury is minor, we have been encouraged to seek compensation as if it were a consumer right. Artful advertising can make lawyers appear not just accessible but even friendly and their hourly charges do not hold the fears they once did. The claim appears risk-free, stress-free and involving merely an administrative process. It is legitimised by the routine, de-personalised and non-adversarial nature of the mass of litigation for minor injury. The message is that you hardly need to get directly involved and that you will certainly not end up in court; your claim will be dealt with as merely a private transactional exercise arranged between anonymous bureaucratic organisations.

When the individual weighs up the pros and cons of claiming, a major element will be the risk of incurring legal costs against the level of potential reward. The fear of being out of pocket should the claim fail has been largely removed by the 'no win, no fee' mantra supplemented by the availability of insurance against potential liability to pay the defendant's costs. The possibility of getting nothing from the process seems remote. The utility of claiming therefore seems high. This is accentuated by the increasing levels of damages on

[62] W Felstiner, R Abel and A Sarat, 'The Emergence and Transformation of Disputes: Naming, Blaming and Claiming' (1981) 15 *Law and Society Review* 631.

[63] See Morris, 'Spiralling or Stabilising?' (n 1) 372–77.

offer. This brings us to consider the second part of this chapter which focuses upon the rising cost of individual claims.

The Rising Cost of Claims

The Changing Form of Payment: Periodical Payment Orders

A significant cause of the increased cost of claims has been the change made in the way in which damages may now be paid: periodical payments have replaced lump sums in many cases where serious injury is involved. The lump sum system survived almost intact until about 25 years ago. Damages almost always took the form of one large payment made on a once and for all basis. However, that system imposed upon claimants an enormous responsibility for their future: they had to manage the lump sum in order to ensure that it would continue to meet their needs for the rest of their life. Unfortunately, inflation and the vagaries of the returns upon investment often resulted in the rapid erosion of the compensation. In addition, the damages were bound to be insufficient where losses continued for a longer period of time than that forecast in the settlement or in the court judgement. This frequently happened where the compensation depended upon an assessment of life expectancy for then the money was bound to run out if the claimant lived longer than forecast. Recipients of damages awards thus not only had the risk of investment thrust upon them but also the risk presented by their own mortality. Accident victims who did not die prematurely inevitably found that their compensation eventually would prove too little.

To counter these criticisms the concept of a structured settlement was developed.[64] It enabled seriously injured claimants to receive regular annuity-based payments which could be guaranteed to last for their lifetime. In addition, the payments were free of tax and could be protected against inflation in prices. Claimants receiving structured payments were relieved from the stress of having to invest and be responsible for a lump sum far greater than most people encounter in their lifetime. In spite of these benefits, expansion of structured settlements was hindered by a variety of factors, including the refusal of many professionals to give proper consideration to the merits of the alternative form of payment. This was aided by the fact that either of the parties unilaterally could veto any proposed settlement based on periodical payments. The result was that, largely through inertia, the lump sum retained its dominance.

However, this was changed by legislation which came into force in 2005. The Courts Act removed the parties' veto and gave judges the power to impose a periodical payments order (PPO) even if it was against the wishes of either, or both, of the parties.[65] A former President of the Association of Personal Injury Lawyers concluded that the legislation was

[64] R Lewis, *Structured Settlements: The Law and Practice* (London, Sweet & Maxwell, 1993); N Bevan, T Huckle and S Ellis, *Future Loss in Practice: Periodical Payments and Lump Sums* (London, Butterworths, 2007); and the International Underwriting Association of London, *Periodical Payments Order Study* (2011): www.iua.co.uk/IUA_Test/Documents/Circulars_2010/Circulars_2011/Periodical_Payment_Orders__PPO__Study.aspx.

[65] Courts Act 2003, s 100 and s 101 amending the Damages Act 1996. R Lewis, 'The Politics and Economics of Tort Law: Judicially Imposed Periodical Payments of Damages' (2006) 69 *MLR* 418.

'the most important development ever relating to the law of damages'.[66] Judges are now required to consider making a PPO in any personal injury case which comes to court if it involves future pecuniary loss. Although only a small percentage of cases involve such future loss, these claims are responsible for a substantial amount of the overall damages bill: insurers have estimated that the top 1% of cases account for 32% of total monies paid to claimants.[67]

Defendants and their insurers are now faced with a much higher bill in these periodical payment cases. There are two reasons for this. The first relates to the way in which most of these arrangements are funded. To safely guarantee the lifetime payments liability insurers usually purchase annuities from life offices. This can prove much more expensive than paying lump sum damages partly because of lack of competition in supplying the annuities required. Arranging for PPOs could be costing liability insurers up to a third more than under the lump sum regime.

The second reason for the increased bill relates to the radical changes made to the way in which periodical payment damages are now assessed. Claimants have been given considerable incentives to choose PPOs over lump sums. The advantages derive from the fact that there is now no need to calculate what lump sum would be required in order to work out the value of the periodical payments to be made. Instead, using a 'bottom-up' approach, the court must assess the claimant's needs for the future and then order that periodical payments matching those needs be paid irrespective of their capital cost. These annual payments do not have to be adjusted to take account of speculative estimates of the claimant's life expectancy. Nor do returns have to be forecast of the income that arises upon investment of the damages because the lump sum is simply not there to invest. Instead, the defendant must comply with the order to make the specified regular payments no matter how the market performs and even if the claimant lives longer than forecast. In contrast to the traditional lump sum system, therefore, it is the defendant rather than the claimant who is now exposed to an uncertain financial future by being burdened with the twin risks of investment return and mortality.

This can be explained further by noting that in the calculations needed for a PPO there is no place for the 'Ogden Tables'.[68] That is, multipliers and discount rates are not used: no multiplier is required to reflect the period of years of the loss in order to convert it into an immediate capital amount; and no discount rate is needed to convert the future stream of financial losses into a capital sum representing present day values. As considered under a later heading, the discount rate continues to operate very harshly against claimants if they seek a lump sum. The rate has been set far too high and expects claimants to obtain an unrealistic return on their damages. By contrast, for PPOs defendants cannot take advantage of the artificially high estimate of investment return embedded in the discount rate for lump sums. Instead they can be ordered to provide annual payments irrespective of what this might cost as an equivalent capital sum. Furthermore, the order extends for an uncertain period—the rest of the claimant's life. The risks that arise which relate to both

[66] C Ettinger (2005) 155 *New Law Journal* 525.

[67] Lord Chancellor's Department, *Courts Bill: Regulatory Impact Assessment* (November, 2002) table 1.

[68] Government Actuary's Department, *Actuarial Tables for Use In Personal Injury And Fatal Accident Cases*, 7th edn (London, The Stationery Office, 2011 and subsequent updates).

the investment return and the longevity of the claimant are thus entirely transferred to the defendant and this carries with it a substantial additional cost.

The final advantage of a PPO over a lump sum is that, following a key appellate decision, periodical payments can now be inflation proofed by being tied not just to the future rise in prices but to the rise in earnings.[69] This is of considerable importance in ensuring that a claimant's care costs will continue to be met. This is because, in general, the wages of carers over time will significantly exceed price inflation and will considerably increase the bill for future care. As a result of the case which allowed for this wage inflation the number of cases involving PPOs has increased substantially. The additional care costs which defendants must now bear, together with those costs arising from the new investment and mortality risks described above, account for the considerable rise in the true value of damages in these serious injury cases.

Recovery of State Benefits from Damages

Since 1990 defendants and their insurers have had to pay more for claims because they have had to reimburse the state for certain benefits received by the claimant as a result of the injury suffered.[70] The state has been able to recover some of the cost of its social security expenditure and healthcare costs: public finances have thus been replenished. There are limits on the amounts that can be recovered. For example, money can only be sought for benefits received up to the date that a case settles; social security and NHS treatment provided later are at public expense. Another limit is that there is a maximum sum payable for health treatment. However, over the years the recovery scheme has proven effective in clawing back increasing amounts of money, especially following the inclusion of health service charges in 1999. By the new millennium the amount of social security recovered had risen steadily and had reached £201 million a year. Since then, caused partly by a marked decline in work accidents, the amounts recovered have fallen by a third so that in 2013–14 only £134 million was recouped.[71] However, to this must also be added the health service charges recovered for that year of £223 million so that in total £357 million was repaid to the public purse. Unlike social security, these health service costs have increased year on year and now constitute the more important source of revenue. Even so, they represent but a tiny fraction of the actual expenditure on the NHS.

The recovery scheme has clearly increased the cost of claims, added to the premiums charged by insurers and thus contributed to one of the concerns about compensation culture. However, its effect upon the number of claims brought varies. Because the NHS is freely available, claimants are not directly affected by charges made to compensators for health costs. By contrast, the recovery of social security benefit has affected them. This is because the scheme enables compensators to reduce the damages that claimants can

[69] *Thompstone v Tameside and Glossop Acute Services NHS Trust* [2008] EWCA Civ 5, [2008] 2 All ER 553. R Lewis, 'The Indexation of Future Payments in Tort: The Future Assured?' (2010) 30 *Legal Studies* 391.

[70] R Lewis, 'Recovery of State Benefits from Tort Damages: Legislating For or Against the Welfare State?' in TT Arvind and J Steele (eds), *Tort Law and the Legislature: Common Law, Statute and the Dynamics of Legal Change* (Oxford, Hart Publishing, 2013) 285; R Lewis, *Deducting Benefits from Damages for Personal Injury* (Oxford, Oxford University Press, 2000).

[71] Compensation Recovery Unit (n 5).

obtain from them by the amount of social security benefit that has to be repaid to the state. Damages have thus been reduced and, as a consequence, the incentive to claim.

However, the incentive was restored somewhat when the scheme was changed to exempt the claimant from any reduction in that part of the damages award which is paid for non-pecuniary loss. This means that no reduction in damages is to be made, even if a claimant receives benefits, provided that no financial loss has been suffered because, for example, earnings have been unaffected and there has been no need to pay for treatment or care. The compensation then is for pain and suffering alone and there can be no reduction. This is so even though the compensator remains liable to repay the social security benefits the claimant has received. In effect, such claimants have the whip hand in negotiations and can force advantageous settlements. They can emphasise that the longer the claim remains unpaid the larger will be the bill for benefits even though this will not reduce the amount of damages to be paid. The result is that insurers are encouraged to settle certain claims promptly and at the higher end of the potential scale of payment. Predominantly these claims involve minor injury such as whiplash where it is often the case that the only compensation to be awarded is for pain and suffering. The recovery of benefits scheme can thus affect aspects of compensation culture.

Non-Pecuniary Loss and Increasing the Price of Pain

In practice, it is the compensation paid for pain and suffering that often provides the financial incentive to claim. In many cases it is the only head of personal injury damage that is sought. In recent years this compensation has increased significantly. There are a number of reasons for this, the most important being the changes made as a result of the test case of *Heil v Rankin*.[72] The judges in that case took the opportunity to raise awards for pain, suffering and loss of amenity in two ways: first, they increased payments for more serious injuries by up to a third; and second, they tied all awards in future to the rise in the Retail Price Index. This second measure has accounted for a further rise in damages of about quarter since the test case was decided. Irrespective of whether the policy reasons given in the case justified these increases,[73] it is clear that damages for non-pecuniary loss have risen substantially as a result. For example, at the top end of the scale, damages for severe brain damage or tetraplegia have increased from £150,000 at the turn of the century to about £330,000 today.

Damages have also risen as a result of the introduction and extensive use of the Judicial College's *Guidelines for the Assessment of Damages in Personal Injury Cases*.[74] This is a book to be 'packed in every judge's lunch bag'[75] for it provides the parameters within which awards for pain and suffering are to be assessed. It is a two-way process in as much as it informally guides courts but also tries to reflect their most recent decisions on quantum.

[72] *Heil v Rankin* [2000] EWCA Civ 84, [2001] QB 272.

[73] R Lewis, 'Increasing the Price of Pain: Damages, the Law Commission and *Heil v Rankin*' (2001) 64 *MLR* 100.

[74] Judicial College, *Guidelines for the Assessment of Damages in Personal Injury Cases*, 12th edn (Oxford, Oxford University Press, 2013).

[75] T Weir, *A Casebook on Tort*, 9th edn (London, Sweet & Maxwell, 2000) 637.

First issued in 1991, it has been revised almost every two years and is now in its twelfth edition. It has become increasingly detailed. The booklet has been very helpful to practitioners and has removed some of the uncertainty that traditionally clouds the negotiation process. However, there can still be major disputes on the facts of cases, for example, in deciding which of the nine specified levels of neck injury the claimant has actually suffered. Subject to notable exceptions the regular revision of the booklet has generally resulted in a real increase in the scale of awards for particular injuries. In addition, the inflation update has ensured that practitioners have recent figures ready to hand which was not always the case in the past. On the whole, claimants have benefited. To counteract this, insurers now want practitioners to be forced to assess pain and suffering by using computer software which values claims by incorporating information about the mass of settled claims instead of only the few that are adjudicated in court.[76] Despite the successful political lobbying by insurers in recent years, the prospect of displacing the Judicial *Guidelines* with a calibration tool that insurers have devised seems very remote.

A final cause of increasing damages in this area relates to the changes in funding introduced as a result of the Jackson reforms.[77] Claimants have been compensated for no longer being able to recover from defendants two items of expenditure: first, the success fee charged by their solicitor; and second, the premium that was paid for after the event insurance which was bought to protect against the risk of costs should the case be lost. In return for claimants bearing these extra pecuniary costs themselves, their damages for non-pecuniary loss have been increased by 10%.[78] On the surface this seems an odd method of compensation for it substitutes apples for the loss of pears: that is, it increases the pain and suffering award when it is a financial loss that has been suffered. Even though the rough justice involved in devising this equivalent has some empirical support, it emphasises the peculiar prominence that pain and suffering now occupies within the tort system.

Let us take this point further. The overall increase in this head of claim is especially significant because the largest component of damages for personal injury is the payment made for pain and suffering: two-thirds of the total damages awarded by the system are for non-pecuniary loss.[79] The reason for this dominance lies in the fact that the tort system overwhelmingly deals with small claims, the great majority leading to damages of less than £5,000.[80] In these cases claimants suffer very little, if any, financial loss from their bodily injury. They make a full recovery and have no continuing ill effects. The typical injury involves a whiplash, neck injuries of some sort accounting for four out of five claims in the

[76] Association of British Insurers, *Evidence to Transport Committee* in Transport Committee, Eleventh Special Report (n 3). Similarly in its evidence the Forum of Insurance Lawyers wanted to limit the rise in low value claims in the *Guidelines*.

[77] Jackson, Review of Civil Litigation Costs: Final Report (n 23) and R Jackson LJ, Civil Litigation Costs Review—Preliminary Report by Lord Justice Jackson (London, Judiciary of England and Wales, May 2009).

[78] Confirmed by *Simmons v Castle* [2012] EWCA Civ 1039.

[79] Pearson Commission (n 6) vol 2, table 107. The Health and Safety Executive similarly estimated that the cost of including pain and suffering would increase payroll costs from 1% to 2.5% in an integrated compensation scheme for work injury. Greenstreet Berman, *Changing Business Behaviour—Would Bearing the True Cost of Poor Health and Safety Performance Make a Difference?* (2002).

[80] In a survey of conditional fee claimants in 2011 half of them received less than £5,000. Insight Delivery Consultancy, *No Win No Fee Usage in the UK* (n 24). The average payment for non-pecuniary loss for cases settled within the claims portal was reported as £2,300 in January 2014.

system.[81] Apart from recovering the cost of damage to the vehicle, the claim is usually only brought to recover the compensation for pain and suffering. In many cases, therefore, non-pecuniary loss provides the only incentive to sue for personal injury. It is the engine that drives the tort system. By contrast, it also accounts for much of the disproportionate cost of the litigation system and it provides opportunities for exaggeration of losses and fraudulent claims. As such, it is the root cause of many of the concerns about compensation culture.

Pecuniary Loss, Discount Rates and the Real Financial World

The final reason accounting for a rise in the level of damages is that the tort award is wedded to the principle of returning the claimant to the position enjoyed before the injury took place insofar as it is possible to do so.[82] In trying to give practical effect to this often merely rhetorical aim, judges have been forced in recent years to confront the realities of the financial world. This has led to a substantial increase in damages especially in cases of serious injury. Various examples of this are given below.

One of the most notable ways in which the practice of personal injury litigation differs from that of a generation ago is in the extensive use of expert evidence. In serious injury cases experts have been employed in areas which extend far beyond the traditional medical fields. They now consider all aspects of the injured person's life and future needs. This relates to a second change in litigation practice: claim schedules are now much more comprehensive than they once were, partly because of the involvement of these experts. Lawyers have been able to specify in considerable detail what the claimant will require in the future. With expert help, they have been able to place more precise monetary figures on what it costs to meet these needs. This level of detail and accounting, prompted by the avowed aim of making full reparation, has inevitably led to an increase in the value of claims.[83]

One group of experts who have been crucial in the construction of these detailed schedules are the financial analysts. Actuarial evidence is now accepted in courts in ways not thought possible years ago.[84] It was not by accident that forensic accountants proved more important in establishing and developing structured settlements than lawyers or judges.[85] Very recently labour market economists have been added to the personal injury financial team. Their role has been pivotal, for example, in establishing that periodical payments can be tied not merely to the rise in prices but to wages, thus adding considerably to the value of such an award.[86]

[81] Transport Committee, Eleventh Special Report (n 3).

[82] 'The only principle of law is that the claimant should receive full compensation for the loss he has suffered as a result of the defendant's tort, not a penny more but not a penny less' (Lady Hale, *Simon v Helmot* [2012] UKPC 5, para 60).

[83] Ipsos Mori Research Institute, *Personal Injury Discount Rate Research* (Ministry of Justice Analytical Series, 2013) 24. The author was the consultant for this research.

[84] Such evidence was made admissible by the Civil Evidence Act 1995. Contrast *Auty v National Coal Board* [1985] 1 WLR 784 where Oliver LJ stated that 'the predictions of an actuary could be only a little more likely to be accurate (and would almost certainly be less entertaining) than those of an astrologer'.

[85] R Lewis, 'Structured Settlements: An Emergent Study' (1994) 13 *Civil Justice Quarterly* 18.

[86] Lewis, 'The Indexation of Future Payments in Tort' (n 69).

A major contribution of these financial experts has been to refine the 'Ogden Tables',[87] the actuarial tables devised especially for personal injury cases in order to compute pecuniary losses. Two recent examples will suffice to illustrate how changes to these tables have led to further increases in damages. First, successive reforms have been made to allow for projected increases in mortality. We now live significantly longer than our forebears and this improvement is expected to continue into the future. Future mortality figures rather than those based on historic mortality are now used and these substantially increase damages, for example, for loss of pension rights especially where the claimant is young. These life expectancy gains can have a considerable effect in certain serious injury cases. Advances in medicine and support services have been such that paraplegics, for example, can today generally expect only a small reduction in their life expectancy. As a result, lifetime awards of damages have had to be increased to continue to allow for such matters as the length of time that future care will be needed.

A second change made to the tables relates to the allowance made for the prospective potential earning capacity of a disabled claimant. Research has demonstrated that people with disabilities spend more time out of employment than previously thought.[88] As a result a higher discount is now applied to increase their damages so as to account for their particular difficulties in the labour market. Acceptance of the value of such economic and social science data has been an important factor in raising damages awards.

In spite of the increase in damages which has taken place this century, it remains the case that claimants are very unlikely to receive 'full' compensation; they are not returned to the position they were in before the accident. The experience of past decades has proven that, for those who need long-term care and support, the lump sum will prove insufficient. Few claimants injured in their youth have any compensation left when they enter old age today. There are several reasons for this but perhaps the most important is that too much allowance has been made for the potential return which can be obtained by a claimant by investing the damages. A discount rate is used to allow for the fact that the claimant receives compensation earlier than he would have had done so, for example, if he had been required to work for the wages now lost. The discount recognises that investment income can be obtained from this accelerated receipt of money. However, the rate used to calculate the damages has consistently been wrongly set; the figure has never reflected the true investment return that the claimant can actually achieve.[89]

For 30 years, until 1998, the discount rate was fixed at 4.5% in spite of a myriad of changes which took place in the financial world during that time. No matter when claimants invested, it was nearly always impossible to obtain the set return. Net interest and

[87] Ogden Tables (n 68).

[88] R Lewis, R McNabb, H Robinson and V Wass, 'Court Awards of Damages for Loss of Future Earnings: An Empirical Study and an Alternative Method of Calculation' (2002) 29 *Journal of Law and Society* 406; and R Lewis, R McNabb, H Robinson and V Wass, 'Loss of Earnings Following Personal Injury: Do the Courts Adequately Compensate Injured Parties?' (2003) 113 *Economic Journal* 568. These publications eventually led to the revision of the Ogden Tables (n 68), in order to take more account of the impact of disability on future employment.

[89] See also the above discussion of periodical payment orders. The introduction to the Government Actuary's Department, *Actuarial Tables for use in Personal Injury and Fatal Accident Cases*, 5th edn (2004) para 15 noted that the set discount rate had never been within 0.5% of the correct rate of return. The resulting substantial under-compensation is illustrated in the introduction to R de Wilde et al, *Facts and Figures*, 13th edn (London, Sweet & Maxwell, 2008–09). See also the comments of the former Government Chief Actuary, Chris Daykin, 'Fair Compensation Needs Actuaries' [2009] *Journal of Personal Injury Law* 48.

capital gain fell well short of what was required and this led to rapid depletion of the long-term value of the compensation. Today the legal system expects a claimant to achieve a real rate of return above inflation and after taxation of 2.5%. With inflation at 2% and taxation costs at a further 1%, in effect the claimant must obtain a return of 5.5% at a time when the best secure savings rate is far below that figure. It is inevitable that any lump sum awarded will be eroded much more quickly than the court presumes.

The present discount rate was set by the Lord Chancellor in 2001 and was based on the return on index linked government stocks (ILGS). Since then there has been a severe decline in the return from these gilt investments. Despite this, the 2.5% discount rate has remained unchanged and has become increasingly anachronistic. The real rate of return after inflation is traced in the below table. Even making no allowance for liability to tax, the returns have been far below 2.5%.

Table 4:

Year	ILGS % Yield after inflation	Real Yield after tax & inflation
2001	2.4	2.11
2003	1.7	1.33
2007	1.6	
2009	1.4	
2011	0.6	
2013	0.0	

To illustrate the dramatic effect a change in the discount rate can have upon an award of damages let us take the case of injury to a young person and an earning loss calculated to last for 40 years:

— Applying the old 4.5% rate the multiplier for the annual loss would be 18.4.
— For the present 2.5% rate it is 24.85, an increase in damages of 35%.
— If the discount rate is reduced to nil so as to reflect the real investment return today on ILGS the multiplier is 38.85, an increase in damages of 111% since the 4.5% rate was last used in 1998.[90]

For many years claimant lawyers lobbied for the discount rate to be revised but they had little success. However, in 2012 the Ministry of Justice issued a consultation paper asking how the rate should be set.[91] Insurers were particularly alarmed by the prospect of a change

[90] *Simon v Helmot* [2012] UKPC 5 dramatically illustrates the potential effect of lowering the discount rate. It concerned the long-term care of a young victim of a Guernsey road accident. Because of the jurisdiction, the Court was not bound by the specified 2.5% discount rate and instead based the decision upon common law principles. As a result the total award was almost £14 million and the difference between the cost of future care using a 2.5% discount rate and the minus 1.5% rate actually used was £5.25 million. See A Lewis, 'Discount Rates' [2012] *Journal of Personal Injury Law* 40.

[91] Ministry of Justice, Damages Act 1996: The Discount Rate—How Should it be Set? Consultation Paper CP12/2012.

in the discount rate and emphasised that in practice claimants did not actually invest in ILGS. After effective lobbying, the Ministry was persuaded that further investigation was required and a second consultation paper was issued dealing with the legal framework.[92] Although this may have the effect of limiting any downward pressure upon the discount rate, it is the change threatened in this area that could potentially have the greatest effect on defendants and the overall cost of the tort system.[93] The Ministry at present is sitting on its hands and two years after consultation closed it has yet to respond.[94]

Conclusion

In reviewing compensation culture this chapter has focused upon the number of claims and the cost of claims. Although motor claims have doubled this century, largely because of institutional factors and a 'dysfunctional insurance market', other claims have remained relatively stable. By contrast the cost of claims has continued to increase, albeit for reasons which many supporters of the tort system would support. Much of the increase in compensation can be attributed to the overall aim of returning the claimant, as far as possible, to the position enjoyed before personal injury was suffered. As that principle is developed further, with courts increasingly using financial expertise to assist in the calculations, it can be anticipated that levels of damages in serious injury cases will continue to rise. As a result, current compensation culture issues, together with the reforms in the legal profession which much influence them, will continue to be debated for some time to come.

[92] Ministry of Justice, Damages Act 1996: The Discount Rate—Review of the Legal Framework Consultation Paper CP3/2013.

[93] For the most recent analysis see E Tomlinson, 'The Discount Rate: What Options Does the Lord Chancellor Have?' [2014] *Journal of Personal Injury Law* 255.

[94] In a letter to the Association of Personal Injury Lawyers in August 2014 the Justice Secretary, Chris Grayling, saw no reason to publish a timetable setting out when the decision might be taken.

3

A Reflexive Approach to Accident Law Reform

ERIK S KNUTSEN

The Canadian accident law system has been a microcosm of social experiments in legal reform. The chief concerns motivating any accident law system reform efforts in Canada have been the perennial issues that prompt accident law reform in any country: litigation cost containment, insurance cost containment, processing delay, and concerns about fraud.

Many Canadian initiatives to address personal injury compensation processes have mirrored the recent Irish reform approaches, and with varying successes and failures. There are two important aspects about the comparative value in examining what both countries have separately done to address the issue of compensation for personal injury. The first lies in learning how different legal cultures, different national identities, and different political and industry pressure points lead to remarkably similar institutional creations. The second lies in how each country's failures and gains realised from these reform efforts may also track each other in parallel fashion. What does this mean?

For Canada and for Ireland, it means that for realising gains in creating a fair, efficient accident law system, assessment of any reform efforts must proceed in a holistic and systemic fashion by keeping three distinct though not separate legal structures in mind: tort and liability law, insurance law and the law and behaviour surrounding civil litigation. Each of these structures must, in turn, somehow be tempered by a fourth overarching structure: justice. This chapter examines how accident law reform can most wisely proceed by adopting a reflexive approach to ensure reform accountability that considers the effects of any reform on liability law, insurance law, civil litigation, and justice concerns. It uses two common accident law reform mechanisms as examples of this approach: the damages limiter and the public dispute resolution mediary.

Accident Law Reform Aims: Process Goals versus Justice Goals

The standard set of goals touted when reforming accident law share one thing in common—they are all 'process' goals. They are all aimed at streamlining the process in the accident law system. Whether it is to eject unmeritorious claims from the system, contain ballooning costs of lawyers or insurance premiums, stamp out costly fraud, or simply speed up claims processing, each of these goals squarely targets the machinery behind the accident law system. That machinery includes regimes about how lawyers charge fees, about the court process and about liability insurance premium rate setting.

What is conspicuously absent in any accident law system reform efforts in Canada (and arguably in Ireland as well) has been a focus on justice as a goal. Reforms are not typically driven by the quest to ensure a more fair, equitable, fulsome, holistic and reliable outcome to an accident scenario. Reforms are not typically driven to help the system do a qualitatively better job in assessing and adjudicating an accident claim. Rather, reforms target the quantitative masses of claims and attempt to direct the flow, the process.

Some may argue that, part and parcel of justice is the process for accessing the justice system. Unfairness in cost, delay and fraud can impinge on dispensing justice. That is certainly true. But justice is not a by-product of efficiency. Justice is not about efficiency, it is about justice. Yet in Canada, and perhaps in Ireland, we have unwittingly slipped into making 'justice' merely a meme for 'efficiency'. One is challenged to find these justice goals motivating any accident law reform efforts.

Justice Goals Through a Reflexive Approach to Accident Law Reform

Accident law system reforms are in direct response to serious, expensive social problems. How, then, could justice goals ever be realised when the weight of cost, delay, insurance premiums and fraud press down upon an over-burdened system? Doing a better job of dispensing justice often appears to be the more expensive option. The answer to incorporating justice goals in accident law reform lies in evaluating the reform solutions in a realistic and reflexive way.

First, any reform efforts need to account for the reflexive nature of the accident law system. The accident law system is not merely about the legal rules of tort or the concepts of damages. It is not merely about liability law. It impinges on, and is impinged upon by, the insurance system and insurance law. At the same time, liability law and insurance law are also mediated in a dynamic fashion by the civil litigation system in which both liability law and insurance law must operate. Liability law, insurance law and civil litigation exist in a symbiotic fashion. They are reflexive of each other. Reforms to one area necessarily impact the operation of the other two. The accident law system is like a web—pull one strand of the web and the other areas of law are affected as well. Therefore, this reflexive nature must be kept in mind and carefully plotted before any changes to the accident law system take place.

There is enough evidence in today's Canadian accident law system (and likely Ireland's) that the desire for reform is not about tort law alone—the insurance network and the fragmented litigation behaviour surrounding tort and insurance are equally important in shaping the system.[1] The interests of the insurance industry drive much of the landscape. Canada's socialised medicare system, for example, recoups losses to the system by chasing

[1] See, eg, ES Knutsen, 'Five Things Wrong With Personal Injury Litigation (And What To Do About It)' (2013) 40 *Advocates Quarterly* 492; KS Abraham, *The Liability Century: Insurance and Tort Law from the Progressive Era to 9/11* (Cambridge MA, Cambridge University Press, 2008); T Baker, 'Liability Insurance as Tort Regulation: Six Ways That Liability Insurance Shapes Tort Law In Action' (2006) 12 *Connecticut Insurance Law Journal* 1; JM Feinman, *Delay, Deny, Defend: Why Insurance Companies Don't Pay Claims and What You Can Do About It* (Penguin, 2010).

the tortfeasor for reimbursement.[2] Liability insurance is also mandatory for all motor vehicle operation in Canada and is thus the collateral in the greatest number of accident compensation disputes. Insurance policy limits act as de facto caps on tort damages.[3] The litigation pathways behind the lawsuits themselves are purposefully crafted in pleadings to tag liability insurance coverage.[4] Settlement behaviour and settlement information (both formal and informal), including concerns about how lawyers will get paid also drive the success or failure of the victim's quest for compensation.[5] The real or illusory impact of insurers as institutional repeat-players in the tort system is also a consideration.

Academic 'silo-ing' of tort, insurance and civil litigation from law school training onwards is one root cause of the muted or reverse effects of many personal injury law reform efforts. Whatever particular account about tort and accident compensation is in fancy, greater attention than before must be given to the complex interrelationship between tort and insurance and civil litigation. Only then will an account of the accident law system, as a system, be able to advance. Tort, insurance and civil litigation impact the other in a dynamic, tripartite and reflexive fashion.

Second, reforms must be accompanied by palpable accountability measures that include justice as a measurement indicator in order to ensure that the process goals do not unreasonably eclipse justice goals. How one measures 'justice' is admittedly a challenge. But how can any responsible legal system ignore that challenge? Surely the reform goal cannot solely be 'how can we push more claims out of the accident law system?'. The logical corollary of that goal is: 'at what cost to justice?'. Justice here also includes process concerns like cost and delay, of course, but in a different fashion. Cost here is injury cost, borne by the injured victim and perhaps eventually by society.[6] For the costs of an under-compensated injury do not simply disappear if a claim goes uncompensated or under-compensated by the tort system. Its cost must be taken up elsewhere, perhaps in the public sphere through social welfare benefits. Cost here is also the cost of the deterrent effect of liability. Part of the justice in the accident law system is that it has some public effect—however minor—on safety.

Damages Limiters

What is a Damages Limiter?

The damages limiter concept, or damages 'cap', as it is most often called, is most commonly enacted to mediate the value range of non-pecuniary damages, such as damages for pain

[2] See, eg, the subrogated rights of the Ontario Health Insurance Plan to all personal injury actions save automobile accidents, under s 30 of the Health Insurance Act, RSO 1990, c H-6.

[3] Baker, 'Liability Insurance as Tort Regulation' (n 1).

[4] T Baker, 'Constructing the Insurance Relationship: Sales Stories, Claims Stories, and Insurance Contract Damages' (1994) 72 *Texas Law Review* 1395; ES Pryor, 'The Stories We Tell: Intentional Harm and the Quest for Insurance Funding' (1997) 75 *Texas Law Review* 1721.

[5] ES Knutsen, 'The Cost of Costs: The Unfortunate Deterrence of Everyday Civil Litigation in Canada' (2010) 36 *Queen's Law Journal* 113; Feinman (n 1); Baker, 'Liability Insurance as Tort Regulation' (n 1).

[6] In terms of workplace accommodations or cost of state welfare benefits. For an exploration of the interconnected costs of injury beyond those borne by liability insurance alone, see ES Pryor, 'Part of the Whole: Tort Law's Compensatory Failures Through a Wider Lens' (2008) 27 *Review of Litigation* 307; Knutsen, 'Five Things Wrong With Personal Injury Litigation' (n 1).

and suffering. Damages limiter regimes are almost universally designed with pure process goals in mind: contain the cost of personal injury damages to regulate the price of liability insurance premiums. The damages limiter aims to provide an objective threshold for injury cost-containment purposes.

These limiters can exist in a variety of formats. At its simplest, a damages limiter could be a quantitative monetary limit on the upper end of a personal injury damages claim, such as a dollar value limit for non-pecuniary losses.[7] The limiter could also be a verbal threshold that acts as a qualitative descriptor gatekeeper for certain accident law processes. An accident victim is allowed to claim certain damages or access a certain process if their injuries exceed the seriousness as described in the threshold.[8] The reasoning behind a threshold is that only serious, high-value claims merit certain benefits or procedural processes (such as full access to the civil justice system as opposed to being funnelled into an administrative processing body or barred entirely by operation of a no-fault regime).

The damages limiter could also be a deductible whereby only claims of a certain dollar value are dealt with by the accident law system. These deductibles can be staggered or slide in order to target certain dollar value ranges.[9] The limiter could also come in the form of a defined injury guideline or 'meat chart' concept that delineates defined benefits ranges for certain predetermined injury constellations.[10]

A Reflexive Account of Damages Limiters

Damages assessments in the personal injury context are typically qualitative assessments based on highly subjective information from the injured accident victim.[11] They include considerations of severity, age, the victim's pre- and post-injury employment capacity, and the impact on the victim's daily life. Because the common law of damages relies on a subjective, qualitative assessment, justice concerns inherently trump process concerns.

[7] See, eg, the Supreme Court of Canada's judicially created damages cap for non-pecuniary losses in *Andrews v Grand and Toy Alberta Ltd* [1978] 2 SCR 229, which was set at $100,000 in 1978 for the worst injury imaginable: a young person quadriplegic and completely reliant on others. Today, this amount equates to about $357,000 in 2015 Canadian dollars. Damages caps may or may not be indexed to inflation or reviewable over time.

[8] In Ontario's hybrid tort/no-fault automobile accident regime, for example, a motor vehicle accident victim is entitled only to receive limited first party no-fault accident benefits as compensation unless she suffers an injury to a significant degree, in which case she is entitled to pursue a third-party liability claim in the traditional tort system by launching a civil lawsuit for her non-pecuniary general damages. See, eg, ES Knutsen, 'Auto Insurance as Social Contract: Solving Automobile Insurance Coverage Disputes through a Public Regulatory Framework' (2011) 48 *Alberta Law Review* 715, 717–23. The qualitative descriptors for determining an accident victim's entitlement to sue in tort include 'death' or the victim's injury must be a 'permanent serious disfigurement' or a 'permanent serious impairment of an important physical, mental, or psychological function': see Ontario, Insurance Act, RSO 1990 c I-8, s 267.5; Court Proceedings for Automobile Accidents that Occur on or After November 1, 1996, O Reg 461/96.

[9] In Ontario, for example, there are sliding statutory deductibles for non-pecuniary damages claims in motor vehicle accidents as claimed by victims and a separate deductible for claims for affected family members. For injured accident victims, there is a deductible of $30,000 unless the non-pecuniary damages are deemed to be greater than $100,000, in which case the deductible disappears. For family members of accident victims, the deductible is $15,000 unless the non-pecuniary damages are deemed to be greater than $50,000, in which case the deductible disappears. See Ontario's Statutory Accidents Benefits Schedule, O Reg 34/10, ss 32–46.

[10] See, eg, Ontario's no-fault accident benefits that include pre-approved, set benefits frameworks for whiplash injuries: Ontario's Statutory Accidents Benefits Schedule, O Reg 403/96. Ireland's Book of Quantum (Injuries Board) is also an example of a defined injury guideline. This book is sectioned by various body parts and includes monetary ranges for injuries to a victim's body part.

[11] See, eg, K Cooper-Stephenson, *Personal Injury Damages in Canada*, 2nd edn (Toronto, Carswell, 1996).

When viewed in a reflexive fashion, keeping in mind the effects in liability, insurance and civil litigation spheres, damages limiters quickly become touchstones for subverting justice goals in favour of pure process goals.

First, over time, any limiter or cap on a subjective, qualitative assessment acts not as much as a limiter but as an incentive for claimants to test the limiter. This 'limiter loop-back' phenomenon is often foreseeable with the inception of the limiter. It is a 'loop-back' because the limiter was created for distinct process goals in the first place: claims cost containment. However, those goals are turned on their head by the very existence of the limiter. If a limit is set to contain costs but every case is then striving to meet that limit and expending time and cost in doing so, the limit is thus working against itself to some degree. The cost savings can loop back on themselves and become redundant.

It is the litigator's job to advocate for the most optimum level of damages for their client. Because a hard limit has been set, it becomes a litigation goal to put a case as close to that limit as possible. The limiter loop-back phenomenon is an effect of litigation behaviour and, secondarily, of the desire to contain insurance pay-outs. It is not an effect of liability law. Injured accident victims and at-fault defendants (and their insurers) are incentivised to either strike as close to, or as far from, the applicable damages limit as possible, depending on their clients' position.

The limiter loop-back phenomenon creates all sorts of inefficient litigation behaviour, from over-pleading one's case to devising new ways to claim harms which may be more evidence-intensive, time-consuming and ultimately expensive. For example, in *To v Toronto Board of Education*,[12] the Court of Appeal for Ontario greatly increased the typically modest non-pecuniary damages award for a child fatality when the surviving parents' counsel were able to prove that the child played an important cultural and economic role in that particular family, akin to a parent or spouse, because of the cultural traditions and language barriers of the family itself. Since that case, other cases have attempted to align with those qualitative factors to also increase similar non-pecuniary damage awards for family members.[13] The result has actually been a gradual ratcheting up of the value of these types of awards over time in instances less and less analogous to the facts in *To*. In the same vein, the boundaries of the verbal threshold for allowing accident victims the right to sue in tort for non-pecuniary damages in automobile accidents have been one of the most consistently litigated issues in the province of Ontario. On an almost cyclical basis, the threshold is judicially watered down to allow less severe injuries to pass the threshold.[14] This is followed shortly by parallel legislative rampings up of the threshold in response.[15]

[12] To v Toronto Board of Education (2001) 55 OR (3d) 641 (CA).

[13] See, eg, *Fiddler v Chiavetti*, 2010 ONCA 210 (where a $200,000 non-pecuniary damages awarded by a jury, based on an analogy to *To*, was reduced on appeal to $125,000); *Osman v 629256 Ontario Ltd*, 2005 CarswellOnt 2728 (where the plaintiff's counsel argued for non-pecuniary damages of $100,000 for the parents, based on an analogy to *To*, and the plaintiff's parents were each awarded $80,000).

[14] See, eg, the gradual weakening of the interpretation of Ontario's legislated verbal threshold for automobile accidents which restricts victims' rights to sue in tort for non-pecuniary damages, as explained above (n 8): Ontario's Insurance Act, s 267.5. What began in 1993 in *Meyer v Bright* (1993) 119 DLR (4th) 354 (Ont CA) as a difficult test to meet has now been watered down significantly. See, eg, *Whilby v Redhead*, 2010 ONSC 2420; *Golab v Schmidt*, 2007 CarswellOnt 2190 (SCJ); *Sasso v Copeland* (2005) 78 OR (3d) 263 (SCJ).

[15] See, eg, the specific regulatory amendments to repeatedly strengthen the wording of the verbal threshold in s 267.5(5) of Ontario's Insurance Act, RSO 1990, c I-8 to make it more difficult for motor vehicle accident victims to bring a claim for non-pecuniary damages in the tort system: Ontario's O Reg 461/96, amended by O Reg 381/03.

Perhaps, in the end, this judicial 'damages creep' is a more just response to inherently qualitative, subjective damages awards. But it certainly goes in the opposite direction to the process goal behind the damages limiter in the first place. What used to be a rather perfunctory claims assessment (for better or for worse) became a more nuanced, contextual and expensive process as the *To* case moved the bar higher. What typically happens is that the limiter may require further readjustment after litigation experience. That also has an administrative cost to revision, whether on a case by case basis for a judicially created limiter or through the legislative process for a politically created limiter.

A corollary to this incentive problem is that the costs of testing these damages limiters in litigation are borne by injured accident victims conducting private litigation, and not through some other public process. Because the damages limiters are aimed at claims cost containment, it falls to victims to sort out, through litigation, what is the damages continuum leading towards that limiter. Testing the damages limiter's limit has a cost in terms of legal expenses and delay in a case. This is especially so in the case of injury guidelines or 'meat charts' that have ranges. The cost of litigating to explore the actual range continuum falls to the injured accident victim to bankroll. What this does, of course, is fuel more litigation behaviour—precisely what these guidelines and charts are trying to avoid.

Setting a damages limiter can be an arbitrary exercise in line-drawing. While the line must be drawn somewhere, it is important to understand who is affected by that line. To answer this question, one must look past private insurance law to the larger compensatory web within society to understand the broader effect of some of these reform efforts.

For traditional damages caps, the most severely injured accident victims are the ones who are most affected by the caps. Only those with a potential damages award that hits near or past the proposed cap would feel its effect. A policymaker would have to seriously think if such a cap is therefore performing a social good or is a social expense, the cost of which may outweigh any insurance premium savings. While such a cap may apparently have a positive effect on private liability insurance premiums, is there an effect on the social benefits system that may be called upon to respond to the excess amount of the claim that extends past the cap? Where do those uncompensated costs go? Furthermore, are those severely injured individuals' cases the ones that are creating the particular process problem that is attempting to be fixed by the damages limiter? Or is it instead low-value claims of questionable merit?

At the opposite end of the spectrum, cases that have thresholds or deductibles are aimed at removing lower value claims from the system. A policymaker would also have to ask where the costs for those cases go if they are removed from the tort system (and thus the private liability insurance system). What is the social safety net cost of weeding out lower value claims from an accident compensation system? Might those accident victims then have to partake of social welfare benefits, lost work time, or workplace accommodation costs borne by their employers? More importantly, one would want an idea of how many claims will be redirected away from the liability compensation regime to some other compensatory regime. The cost of 'lumping it' can bleed out in unsuspecting ways.

It is important to examine where the cost of the damages limiter is borne. It is not proper to assume that the cost disappears if the limiter removes the claim (or part of it) from the private liability insurance system. One must look beyond that system and ask whose money is paying for the losses in the end. If the aggregate number of low-level claims deterred or the number of high-level claims capped is eclipsing the savings generated by the cap, then the limiter is self-defeating.

Finally, because liability law is not static over time but is litigated in the common law on a case-by-case basis, personal injury law will advance. Can the damages limiter stand the tests of time, the economy and public sentiment? A damages limiter enacted to solve a particular insurance financial crisis at a particular time may be of limited value when viewed across a temporal continuum. Monetary damages caps and deductibles diminish in value over time due to the time value of money unless an inflationary factor is built in. This leads to administrative costs in maintaining the limiter or a risk in the limiter's effectiveness being eroded over time as the cost of things rises.

More importantly, the monetary value of some damages limiters may quickly be out of touch with public sentiment about the nature of a particular injury's expected financial value. What may have once seemed like a generous sum for a particular injury can, in a few years, feel like an insultingly insufficient amount. Credibility of the justice system can be at stake when a damages limiter is of a fixed amount and the public finds it abhorrently low for what it is. There is a certain justice goal being subverted by that sort of happenstance.

A damages limiter could be a judicial creation but is more often a product of legislation. A judicially created damages cap is responding to justice goals as well as process goals. The judicial process for controlling the effects of a damages limiter on accident compensation is far different from the legislative process attempting to do the same thing. The judicial process is necessarily set within the context of an individual case yet in a fashion that is mindful of the effect of such a cap on future cases. This precedential mindfulness is important. A judicially created damages limiter can be revisited and can be responsive to legal developments and case law, advancement of medical and scientific knowledge, and developing societal trends about injury. Over time, with litigation, the damages limiter and its effects can be honed.

If the damages limiter is a legislated creation, it is almost certainly in response to process goals. The legislature is not viewing a situation in a qualitative fashion, on a case-by-case scenario. It is viewing accident claims as populations to be managed. Furthermore, legislatures are not in the business of dispensing justice: courts are. More importantly, once set, legislated damages limiters have a way of becoming immutable fixtures over time. It is necessary to invoke the political process to effect change. Few political actors are motivated to again wade into the accident reform thicket. Indeed, the incentive is probably to run as far away from it as possible. This leads to stagnation and ossification of the damages limiter. It can quickly become out of touch with the value of money, the law, scientific and social understandings about injuries, and societal values. Any changes that do come about can be subject to political pressure from interest groups and stakeholders. This has the tendency to push any justice goals far to the background.

Evaluating Damages Limiters

The damages limiter cannot be viewed as having a singular effect with a singular process purpose. It is just not that simple. Only through a reflexive lens can the real effects of damages limiters be assessed. Damages limiters can change litigation behaviour and injury claims processes in often unintended and inefficient ways. They can have unintended effects on often the most vulnerable in society. They may add to, and not reduce, litigation and insurance costs as a result. They may also increase the overall cost of injury to society. Damages limiters can have real justice costs, too.

The key to evaluating any damages limiter, in whatever form it takes, is to maintain this reflexive approach by being mindful of the effects of the liability, insurance and litigation regimes at play. These tripartite concerns must inform the design of accountability measures to determine whether or not the damages limiter is doing what it is really supposed to be doing, while also not offsetting any process gains with other process losses or, at worst, other justice losses.

A policymaker should undertake at least the following considerations:

a. What is the value of the aggregate claims affected by the damages limiter and where does that cost truly go?
b. What is the cost of the 'limiter loop-back' phenomenon, when litigants are incentivised to test the damages limiter?
c. What mechanisms are built into any proposed damages limiter to avoid problems with respect to issues of the time value of money, the economy and public sentiment?
d. Does the damages limiter achieve any justice goals, or merely a few process goals?
e. How will the above be monitored over time, to ensure accountability that the damages limiter is actually achieving its stated process goals without eclipsing its own purpose at the cost of other process goals or justice goals?

Public Dispute Resolution Mediaries

What are Public Dispute Resolution Mediaries?

Resolution of injury claims through a public mediary instead of through the court system is another reform effort that requires not only a reflexive approach to design and assessment but also some safeguard to allow justice goals to thrive alongside process goals. Personal injury reform efforts often turn to alternatives to private litigation in the public court system as one option to solve certain pressing issues. These pressing issues are, again, predominantly process goals, not justice goals. They include reductions in lawyer costs for all parties involved. This aim is tied to the hope that such a reduction will also correspondingly reduce liability insurance premiums, a portion of which typically go to funding insurance defence litigation. Reducing costs to the perennially over-burdened public justice system is another process goal. Another process goal includes reducing the delay that adversarial litigation brings. This, too, goes directly to litigation, court and insurance costs. Rarely, if ever, is the pursuit of greater justice a primary goal for creating an entirely new public regime for solving injury claims.

Models of Public Dispute Resolution Mediaries

Various models of alternative, public non-court dispute resolution mechanisms exist. Common among them is that they are set up by the political process in response to some concern about injury compensation (typically process concerns of cost and delay related to the slow chug of the court system and the costly involvement of lawyers). These public dispute resolution mediaries (PDRMs) are often creatures of statute that exist as some board or government entity charged with running an administrative claims processing scheme.[16] Their members may include appointees from various stakeholder groups who may or may not be lawyers. The PDRM will hold some variation of assessment or hearing for a claim that may or may not be binding upon the claimant and defendants. It will have its own set of procedures. It may or may not apply its own law or have reference to the relevant common law. Its results may or may not be appealable or reviewable by an adjudicative body. While lawyers may represent some claimants, the PDRM process is most typically designed with the intent to foster lay claimant participation without the assistance of a lawyer (hence a savings in time and cost).

The PDRM can be charged with managing a wide or narrow scope of injury class, from workers compensation or automobile claims to the entire panoply of personal injuries suffered in any modality. In Ontario, for example, a PDRM called the Financial Services Commission of Ontario administers mandatory mediation for those no-fault accident benefits claims on behalf of motor vehicle accident victims.[17] In Ireland, the Injury Board provides a non-binding assessment of non-medical malpractice personal injury claims.[18] New Zealand has perhaps the widest scope of a PDRM in that there is a countrywide administrative no-fault public injury compensation system.[19] Some American states have pre-trial screening panels for medical malpractice cases.[20]

What is most important for this discussion is that PDRMs:

a. Operate outside the court system as an administrative body.
b. Are set up by government as part of a political process.
c. Are set up in response to a particular concern about the court system's processing of injury claims.
d. Are almost always designed to encourage lay claimants to participate without the assistance of a lawyer.
e. Are always set up in response to concerns about litigation costs, delay and insurance claims costs.

[16] Such as Ireland's Injuries Board, as set up by the Personal Injuries Assessment Board Act 2003, Ontario's arbitration system operated by the Financial Services Commission of Ontario for accident benefits claims arising from motor vehicle accidents, as set up by Ontario's Insurance Act, RSO 1990, c I-8, ss 279–83 or Ontario's Workplace Safety and Insurance Board which runs a no-fault workplace accident compensation scheme, as set up by the Workplace Safety and Insurance Act 1997, SO 1997, cl 6, Sch A.

[17] Ibid.

[18] Above (n 16).

[19] Since 1974 New Zealand has maintained an administrative no-fault system for injury compensation. This system resulted from the Woodhouse Report: New Zealand Royal Commission of Inquiry into Compensation for Personal Injury, *Compensation for Personal Injury in New Zealand: Report of the Royal Commission of Inquiry* (Wellington, Government Printer, 1967). See also S Todd, 'Negligence Liability for Personal Injury: A Perspective from New Zealand' (2002) 25 *University of New South Wales Law Journal* 895; C Brown, 'Deterrence in Tort and No-Fault: The New Zealand Experience' (1985) 73 *California Law Review* 976.

[20] See, eg, Alaska (Alaska Stat § 09.55.536); Delaware (Del Code tit 18, § 6803 to § 6814); Florida (Fla Stat § 766.106); Idaho (Idaho Code § 6-1001 to § 6-1011); Indiana (Ind Code § 34-18-8-4); Kansas (Kan Stat § 65-4901 to § 65-4908); Louisiana (La Rev Stat § 40:1299.47); Maine (Me Rev Stat tit 24, § 2851 to § 2859; Maryland (Md Code, Cts & Jud Proc § 3-2A-01 to 3-06B; Massachusetts (Mass Gen Laws, ch 231, § 60B); Michigan (Mich Comp Laws § 600.4901–4923; Montana (Mont Code § 27-6-101 to 27-6-704); Nebraska (Neb Rev Stat § 44-2840 to 44-2847); New Hampshire (NH Rev Stat § 519-B:1 to 519-B:14); New Mexico (NM Stat § 41-5-14); Utah (Utah Code § 78B-3-416 to 3-420); Virginia (Va Code § 8.01-581.1 to.11:1); and Wisconsin (Wis Stat § 655.42 to § 655.58).

A Reflexive Account of Public Dispute Resolution Mediaries

Inherent in the very nature of public dispute resolution mediaries is the fact that they are aimed at process goals. They attempt to deliver what the public court system cannot: justice that is faster, cheaper and more accessible to the lay person. To that end, the process goals very often eclipse the justice goals when a public dispute resolution mediary supplants the full-blown court system.

This imbalance occurs because the public dispute resolution mediary model brings with it the bureaucratic systematisation of accidents.[21] Accidents are treated as a population to be administratively managed, despite the legal system stressing a largely subjective, qualitative treatment of a single injured individual. The problems with the bureaucratic systematisation of accidents bleed out in all sorts of ways, skewing justice goals.

First, the PDRM system typically becomes more complex than the litigation system it was designed to supplant. More processing steps are added in the trajectory of resolution for an accident claim. There are more administrative layers, making dispute resolution more complex a process as a result. There is necessarily more procedure and more law specific to the new forum. The PDRM system can create unexpected cottage industries, such as private centres specialising in claims processing (which eventually becomes necessary as the 'simple' system gets more complex) or even an entire assessment industry offering services from medical to vocational assessment, for use by claimants and defendants. Lawyers and legal assistance can quickly become more necessary for claimants to employ as the system balloons to become too complex for the average layperson to navigate or, instead, as the advantage of having skilled, repeat-player legal expertise becomes clear to the point that it is unwise to represent oneself. As the system ripens, there can be unexpectedly large administrative costs to maintain the administrative machinery of the PDRM—from staffing resources required as a result of increasing complexity, to legal assistance for the PDRM, to additional help in processing the sheer volume of claims if the complexity bogs down claims processing altogether (a frequent concern for many PDRM systems). All of this, over time, typically requires more reforms to manage the system as it grows. Most challenging is that revisions to the PDRM system must be made through the partisan political process, making incentives to change skewed by political pressure. The result is often that a PDRM monster is created that one never thinks of at inception. It simply becomes one more expensive 'process' on the way to court, and not the panacea for bureaucratic claims management one thinks it will be.

Second, one must query whether lawyer-free zones are actually appropriate in personal injury cases in the first place.[22] Removing legal counsel for injured accident victims in an inherently adversarial process raises serious justice concerns, regardless of the design of the PDRM. There are few more adversarial disputes in the private law system where interests are so opposite as personal injury. The plaintiff alleges that something the defendant did

[21] Knutsen, 'Five Things Wrong With Personal Injury Litigation' (n 1) (introducing the problems with the 'bureaucratic systematization of accidents' as has happened in Ontario's no-fault automobile insurance system).

[22] See, eg, A Zuckerman, 'No Justice Without Lawyers—The Myth of the Inquisitorial Approach' (2014) 33 *Civil Justice Quarterly* 355 (arguing that the adversarial nature of the civil justice system necessarily requires some legal assistance or litigants face a dire 'justice deficit').

somehow injured or killed her. The defendant either believes such is not the case or, at the very least, is incentivised to keep the damages payable to a minimum.

The defendants in a personal injury claim are typically repeat-player insurers or large institutional defendants. They are well funded and well lawyered. They have more than just the victim's case to worry about. For predictability reasons alone, defendants would prefer a system in which the bureaucratic systematisation of accidents leads to stable and expected dispute resolution results. The victim, however, is a one-shot player whose life compensation may be on the line. They may be jobless, having difficulty with finances, unsophisticated and most certainly desperate. They may have no idea beyond urban myth as to what they may be entitled to in terms of compensation.

The PDRM can also serve as a free 'look-see' for institutional defendants, all to the detriment of the injured accident victim. Defendants can get a case evaluation in a PDRM process with often little downside risk, as the result may not be binding on other procedures (including traditional court avenues). This evaluation can then serve to beat down the injured plaintiff's expectations. If the evaluation is low, a defendant can pressure the plaintiff to accept the evaluation by touting the costs risk of proceeding in court. If the evaluation is too high, the defendant can often ignore it and continue on in the regular civil justice system with the claim.

An often unplanned but serious by-product of the PDRM is a sort of public legitimacy conundrum that occurs, especially with personal injury cases and the inherent power imbalance embedded within. Having a PDRM gives the process an air of legitimacy when claims are removed from the court-based adversary system and then put into a government-blessed public dispute resolution system. Especially in the context of lay parties, the PDRM can be seen to be dishing out general legal advice with the cloak of government blessing. Query whether this is right or just. There are often no checks and balances to the results of a public dispute resolution mediary's session. These are sacrificed for process goals of cost and timeliness. There are few, if any, safeguards for claimants that their assessment or the institution's assessment is legitimate in law. How is a layperson, or even a defendant, to know that the PDRM's assessment of the case is in line with the courts? Nevertheless, the fact that it is a government-sanctioned PDRM carries with it some legitimacy—intended or otherwise—that can be a powerful force in swaying an otherwise very adversarial, complex system in which an injured accident victim must navigate.

This problem is compounded for lay victims representing themselves in a PDRM system due to the lay victim 'evaluation downside'. Lay victims may not be in a position to evaluate the value of their claims without legal and medical assistance. In designing a PDRM system, architects must assume the mediary will get the lowest common denominator as claimants—the people with the most difficulty due to injuries who also simultaneously have no claims evaluation assistance. A PDRM system is essentially asking these claimants not to acquire legal assistance and instead 'trust' the PDRM process in what is otherwise an inherently adversarial system.

The PDRM system therefore has the danger of supplanting justice goals with process goals in a particularly insidious way: by legitimising the supplantation through government-sanctioned processes. A PDRM system often is not designed in a reflexive fashion. Its effect on, and relation to, the liability law regime is minimised or ignored. Its necessary interaction with the insurance and compensation systems is eclipsed by its aims to affect litigation behaviour by providing a fast, cheap system that bureaucratises the processing of accident claims. Justice concerns are the collateral that fall by the wayside.

Evaluating Public Dispute Resolution Mediaries

Therefore, great care must be taken at inception when designing a PDRM system to avoid some of these important justice trade-offs. Even greater care must be taken when evaluating the efficacy of a PDRM system over time because, as mentioned above, these systems tend to grow and multiply, overshadowing the court system in complexity, delay and cost.

To ensure a reasonable balance between process and justice goals, oversight of a PDRM system should consider two fundamental aspects to any review. First, in addition to any quantitative data collection, there should be a qualitative follow-up with claimants who used the PDRM. This qualitative data should be sampled at a sensible interval two, five and ten years after the claimant accessed the PDRM system. Only then would the claimant-side story come out. Quantitative data immediately post-claim about claims handling, cost savings and timing of claims resolutions do not get at justice goals. No one knows if the resolution was just and sensible until some time passes. Was the resolution 'enough' for the claimant and, if not, how so? Therefore, a qualitative measure taken by examining what happened with claimants who used the system at two, five and ten years post-resolution would provide a window into how just—or not—the resolution with the PDRM actually was.

Second, although 'justice' is difficult to measure, it is likely possible to measure the results obtained for lay claimants accessing the PDRM system against an independent claims assessment by lawyers and medical professionals of the value of the claim. Such could be done on an anonymous basis for data collection purposes only, not to reopen any settlements or affect the PDRM process on an individual basis. In this way, the PDRM results for lay claimants can at least be evaluated as against another professional opinion. This would go a long way to cementing the legitimacy of the results of any PDRM system and ensuring that litigation process goals are not trumping justice goals. It would also ensure that the valid operation of liability law (ie, damages) is being tracked by the results from the PDRM. Any variance between the independent assessments and the PDRM results should somehow then be accounted for in the PDRM system through reforms. In this way, the PDRM can be reflexive to not only litigation but liability and insurance concerns, thereby achieving more just results for claimants over time.

Conclusion

Accident system reforms need to be evaluated in a reflexive fashion by considering the symbiotic effects of liability law, insurance law and litigation behaviour on the proposed reforms. Whether reforms take the shape of damages limiters or public dispute resolution mediaries or something else, both accident claimants and defendants to claims (be they insurers or institutions) need to be assured that process goals are being fairly balanced with justice goals. The reformed system cannot self-justify by counting only claims processing 'outputs'. There needs to be meaningful evaluative criteria that include making claims evaluation more 'just', and 'better', not just faster and cheaper. Whether in Canada or Ireland or elsewhere, in designing reforms to the accident law system, justice goals cannot simply be assumed or ignored.

Part II

Damages Reform in Various Jurisdictions

4

Reforming English Tort Law: Lessons from Australia

JAMES GOUDKAMP

Introduction

The rise of legislation has profoundly affected all areas of the law in the major common law jurisdictions. Tort law was arguably the last major stronghold of judge-made law.[1] However, even this common law citadel has crumbled in recent years, unable to withstand the relentless onslaught of statutory law. Unsurprisingly, the extent of statutory alterations to tort law vary very considerably from jurisdiction to jurisdiction. New Zealand famously underwent by far the most far-reaching legislative changes. As a result of recommendations made by a Royal Commission chaired by Sir Owen Woodhouse,[2] the New Zealand Parliament provided for a comprehensive accident compensation scheme.[3] This scheme, which came into force in 1974, provides for benefits to be paid to accident victims on a no-fault basis. It leaves tort law with a relatively minor role to play. Tort law throughout Australia has also been changed very extensively by statute. The most significant modifications were made in 2002 and 2003[4] in response to hikes in the price of liability insurance premiums.[5]

[1] In 1997, Stephen Sugarman wrote that 'torts remains, of all the law school courses we offer, the queen of the common law subjects': S Sugarman, 'Assumption of Risk' (1997) 31 *Valparaiso University Law Review* 833, 833, fn 1.

[2] New Zealand Royal Commission of Inquiry into Compensation for Personal Injury in New Zealand, *Report of the Royal Commission of Inquiry* (Wellington, Government Printer, 1967).

[3] The original legislation was the Accident Compensation Act 1972 (NZ). The scheme is now governed by the Accident Compensation Act 2001 (NZ).

[4] Civil Liability Act 2002 (NSW); Civil Liability Act 2003 (Qld); Wrongs (Liability and Damages for Personal Injury) Amendment Act 2002 (SA), amending the Wrongs Act 1936 (SA) and renaming it the Civil Liability Act 1936 (SA); Civil Liability Act 2002 (Tas); Wrongs and Other Acts (Public Liability Insurance Reform) Act 2002 (Vic), amending the Wrongs Act 1958 (Vic); Civil Liability Act 2002 (WA); Civil Law (Wrongs) Act 2002 (ACT); Personal Injuries (Liabilities and Damages) Act 2003 (NT). Many of the provisions of these statutes are based on recommendations made in an important report commissioned by the federal government: Commonwealth of Australia, *Review of the Law of Negligence: Final Report* (Canberra, Canprint, 2002). This report is widely known as the 'Ipp Report' after its Chairperson, the Hon Justice David Ipp.

[5] The catalysts for the Australian changes are described in P Cane, 'Reforming Tort Law in Australia: A Personal Perspective' (2003) 27 *Melbourne University Law Review* 649; J Goudkamp, 'The Young Report: An Australian Perspective of the Latest Response to Britain's "Compensation Culture"' (2012) 28 *Journal of Professional Negligence* 4; B McDonald, 'Legislative Intervention in the Law of Negligence: The Common Law, Statutory Interpretation and Tort Reform in Australia' (2005) 27 *Sydney Law Review* 443.

These changes did not go as far as those made in New Zealand. The essence of the tort system was retained. However, extensive restrictions were placed both on the circumstances in which liability arises and on the damages that are recoverable. The United Kingdom lacks tort reform legislation that is comparable to that which exists in Australia and New Zealand. It does not have a New Zealand-style accident compensation scheme or the type of sweeping legislation that exists in Australia. The Parliament at Westminster has nevertheless intervened very extensively in tort law. Fields in which it has legislated include occupiers' liability,[6] defamation,[7] animals,[8] contributory negligence,[9] contribution,[10] product liability,[11] defective premises[12] and fatal accidents.[13]

Given the regularity with which the Parliament of the United Kingdom has legislated with respect to tort law and the fact that tort law is often attributed with responsibility for all manner of evils in British society,[14] it is not unlikely that Parliament will soon put more wide-ranging changes on its agenda.[15] If and when this happens, British legislators may well look to developments in other jurisdictions for inspiration and guidance. The New Zealand changes are likely to be seen as too radical to form the basis of tort reform in the United Kingdom. Although the New Zealand no-fault scheme is now more than 40 years old, it has not been replicated in any other major common law jurisdiction.[16] More fundamentally, the creation of a large and expensive government-funded scheme is not a serious possibility in the economic and political climate that currently prevails in the United Kingdom. The present age of austerity is simply incompatible with the introduction of a scheme along the lines of that in New Zealand. As Peter Cane aptly put it in the preface to the latest edition of *Atiyah's Accidents, Compensation and the Law*, '[t]ort law and the tort system are (it seems) here to stay … Whatever the defects of tort law and the tort system as mechanisms for dealing with personal injury and disability, in the world of *realpolitik* the burning question is not how to get rid of tort law but how to live with it'.[17]

[6] Occupiers' Liability Act 1957 (UK); Occupiers' Liability Act 1984 (UK).

[7] Defamation Act 1952 (UK); Defamation Act 1996 (UK); Defamation Act 2013 (UK).

[8] Animals Act 1971 (UK).

[9] Law Reform (Contributory Negligence) Act 1945 (UK).

[10] Civil Liability (Contribution) Act 1978 (UK).

[11] Consumer Protection Act 1987 (UK).

[12] Defective Premises Act 1972 (UK).

[13] Fatal Accidents Act 1976 (UK).

[14] See, eg, Ministry of Justice, press release, 1 May 2013, 'Turning the Tide on Compensation Culture'; Ministry of Justice, press release, 31 July 2013, 'Action on Compensation Claims for Slips and Trips'; Ministry of Justice and Chris Grayling MP, press release, 2 June 2014, 'Grayling: Law Must Protect Everyday Heroes'.

[15] Steve Hedley writes: 'Personal injury liability … has powerful enemies, and we might for that reason expect it to decline' (S Hedley, 'Tort and Personal Injuries, 1850 to the Present' in TT Arvind and J Steele (eds), *Tort Law and the Legislature: Common Law, Statute and the Dynamics of Change* (Oxford, Hart Publishing, 2013) 249. See also at 252.

[16] In 1975, Australia came close to emulating the New Zealand model. Sir Owen Woodhouse, the architect of the New Zealand scheme, chaired an inquiry into the possibility of introducing an even more extensive no-fault compensation system in Australia: Australian National Rehabilitation and Compensation Committee of Inquiry Compensation and Rehabilitation in Australia, *Report of the National Committee of Inquiry* (Australian Government Publishing Service, Canberra, 1974). A Bill to implement the inquiry's recommendations was introduced into the Commonwealth Parliament but this reform effort was defeated with the fall of the Whitlam Government in 1975. These developments are masterfully described in H Luntz, 'Looking Back at Accident Compensation: An Australian Perspective' (2003) 34 *Victoria University of Wellington University Law Review* 279. No-fault compensation schemes have since been introduced in some Australian jurisdictions in certain contexts (see, eg, the Workers Compensation Act 1987 (NSW)), and various recommendations have been made since 1975 for the creation of a federal no-fault compensation scheme: see, eg, Productivity Commission, *Disability Care and Support*, Report 54 (Productivity Commission, 2011).

[17] P Cane, *Atiyah's Accidents, Compensation and the Law* 8th edn (Cambridge, Cambridge University Press, 2013) xvi.

If British legislators look to other jurisdictions for ideas, it is more likely that attention will be turned to Australia than New Zealand. It is notable in this connection that consideration was given by the Parliament at Westminster to the Australian statutes in the course of enacting the Compensation Act 2006 (UK).[18] It seems that the Australian reforms may also have influenced the Young Report,[19] which spawned some reasonably significant statutory changes to tort law (mainly in relation to the procedural apparatus by which tort law is administered).[20] Some of the language used in the Young Report is strikingly similar to, or reminiscent of, that used in Australia at the height of the insurance crisis, and several proposals made in the Young Report mirror, to a degree, certain of the changes made in Australia. It is also worth mentioning the Social Action, Responsibility and Heroism Act 2015 (UK) (SARAH).[21] The provisions of this recent addition to the corpus of tort law in England and Wales[22] have clear parallels with the Australian legislation. Although the Australian statutes were not mentioned in parliamentary debates concerning the Bill that became SARAH, SARAH's provisions track roughly certain of the stipulations in the Australian statutes.[23] It is not unlikely, therefore, that architects of SARAH were conscious of, and were perhaps influenced by, the Australian legislation. All of this suggests an awareness of, and an interest in, the Australian statutes on the part of British legislators.

The purpose of this chapter is, therefore, to reflect upon what might be learned by British lawmakers from the Australian tort reform experience.[24] It is hoped that this analysis might, in particular, assist legislators in the United Kingdom to understand, if they conclude that British tort law requires wider-scale statutory reforms than has occurred to date, which provisions in the Australian legislation might usefully be replicated or which at least deserve to be given serious consideration as a model for reform in the United Kingdom. It is also hoped that the analysis will help British legislators to appreciate which of the Australian provisions stand as nothing but warnings. Due to the small amount of space available only a handful of the Australian changes can be addressed. The analysis centres, therefore, on the most significant or interesting changes or those that seem to have the greatest prospect of being copied in the United Kingdom.

It is stressed that nothing in this chapter should be read as advocating for statutory intervention in tort law in the United Kingdom, and certainly not for sweeping legislation of the kind that exists in Australia. That is not its burden. The chapter remains agnostic on the

[18] See, eg, HL Deb 20 Dec 2005, vol 676, cols GC 258–71.

[19] Lord Young, *Common Sense, Common Safety* (London, HM Government, 2010).

[20] The Young Report and the Australian changes are compared in Goudkamp, 'The Young Report' (n 5).

[21] The provisions of SARAH that did not come into force on the date on which it received Royal Assent (12 February 2015) came into force on 14 April 2015: the Social Action, Responsibility and Heroism Act 2015 (Commencement and Transition Provision) Regulations 2015 (UK) r 2. SARAH is discussed in J Goudkamp, 'Restating the Common Law? The Social Action, Responsibility and Heroism Act 2015 (UK)' (2017) *Legal Studies* (forthcoming).

[22] SARAH does not apply to Scotland: s 5(1).

[23] Compare, eg, s 2 of SARAH with s 5B(2)(d) of the Civil Liability Act 2002 (NSW). The former provides: 'The court must have regard to whether the alleged negligence or breach of statutory duty occurred when the person was acting for the benefit of society or any of its members'. The latter states: 'In determining whether a reasonable person would have taken precautions against a risk of harm, the court is to consider the following (amongst other relevant things): … the social utility of the activity that creates the risk of harm'.

[24] The Australia statutes have been very extensively discussed. This chapter skates over most of the detail. Excellent treatments can be found in Cane, 'Reforming Tort Law in Australia' (n 5); McDonald, 'Legislative Intervention in the Law of Negligence' (n 5); JJ Spigelman, 'Tort Law Reform: An Overview' (2006) 14 *Tort Law Review* 5; B McDonald, 'The Impact of the Civil Liability Legislation on Fundamental Policies and Principles of the Common Law of Negligence' (2006) 14 *Torts Law Journal* 268.

desirability of statutory reforms, which is an issue that cannot sensibly be addressed within the confines of this chapter. The entire analysis is premised on the assumption that more far-reaching legislative intervention in tort law than has happened to date is reasonably likely to occur in the United Kingdom in the foreseeable future. It also assumes that if such intervention occurs, it is likely to be carried out with one eye on the Australian experience. Proceeding on the basis of these assumptions, the chapter asks what should be made of the Australian reforms. Which of the provisions in the Australian legislation might sensibly serve as a template for reforms in the United Kingdom, and which of them should be dismissed as ill conceived?

The Need Principle

One idea that features regularly in the analysis and which is hence worth mentioning at the outset is the notion that tort law should give priority to those claimants who are most in need of compensation (the 'need principle'). This principle was powerfully developed by Patrick Atiyah in his groundbreaking *The Damages Lottery*.[25] Atiyah convincingly showed that tort law in the United Kingdom fails spectacularly to comply with it.[26] Although *The Damages Lottery* was published nearly two decades ago, and despite the fact that it was written principally for a lay audience, the arguments in it were, and remain, highly relevant to lawyers. The need principle will be used in this chapter in order to support and criticise certain of the Australian changes, although it will not be the sole criterion for assessing those changes.

It is neither feasible nor necessary to explore here in any detail what is meant by 'need'. It is difficult to define that concept without circularity. However, the basic idea is simple enough. (Atiyah himself did not find it necessary to develop it in *The Damages Lottery*.[27]) The gist of the notion is that the limited funds that are available to provide redress to accident victims should be allocated so as to give preferential treatment to those who, by virtue of the severity of their injuries, will in all probability be most seriously affected if they are denied compensation. Rules that prioritise or give equal preference to less seriously injured claimants, or which award damages in order to advance some end other than satisfying a need for compensation, such as to punish or deter wrongdoing, are incompatible with the need principle.

Is the need principle justified? It is flatly rejected by many theorists. For example, Ernest Weinrib condemns it on, inter alia, the ground that it explains only why the claimant should be compensated but does not account for why the defendant must pay.[28] It is possible, however, for the purposes of this chapter, to bypass the theoretical objections that have

[25] PS Atiyah, *The Damages Lottery* (Oxford, Hart Publishing, 1997).

[26] Ibid, 143–49.

[27] Some comments regarding the idea are offered in Cane, *Atiyah's Accidents* (n 17) 470–72.

[28] 'From the standpoint of the compensation rationale, the plaintiff's loss lacks bipolar significance. At most, the loss justifies improving the plaintiff's situation; it does not state a ground for taking something from the defendant. Accordingly, the compensation rationale does not support the *defendant's* liability to the plaintiff': EJ Weinrib, *The Idea of Private Law* (Cambridge MA, Harvard University Press, 1995) 121 (emphasis in original). Consider also R Stevens, *Torts and Rights* (Oxford, Oxford University Press, 2007) (arguing that tort law can be rendered coherent only if it is understood as a system for vindicating rights).

been or might be levelled at the need principle. It is deployed in this chapter solely for the pragmatic reason that it is likely to resonate, at least to some degree, with a government that is bent on changing tort law. Whenever tort law comes onto the government's radar, an important concern is often to reduce its tremendous cost and hence the cost of insurance premiums. Votes are often seen in laws that reduce the cost of premiums. The need principle is a readily intelligible guide as to how legislators who have the objective of cutting costs in view should proceed. Making savings while still delivering services to critical areas is a notion that will be intimately familiar to legislators. Conversely, the theoretical objections that have or might be put against the need principle, however compelling they may be, will simply be lost on them.

Positive Changes

This part of the chapter catalogues a series of changes made by the Australian statutes that are defensible according to the need principle or certain other bases.

Caps

Caps are ceilings on the recoverable damages. The most prominent and important type of cap in Australia is a cap on damages for a loss of earnings.[29] In New South Wales, for example, the most that can be awarded in respect of a loss of earnings is three times average weekly earnings.[30] Similar provisions exist in some other Australian jurisdictions.[31] If the British tort system is thought to be too expensive, the introduction of caps is a reasonably sensible reform. Caps save money by restraining what might be regarded as excesses in the tort system, and they do so without running a significant risk of seriously impairing the ability of claimants to meet their basic needs provided that they are not set too low. Caps are consistent with the need principle.

Damages for a loss of income are uncapped in the United Kingdom. The British tort system is, as a result, presently committed to providing full income replacement. Consequently, if a Premier League footballer is run over by a negligent motorist and unable to play football again because of the injuries suffered in the accident, he is entitled to recover damages in respect of the full extent of his lost earnings. It is irrelevant that this would see the footballer recovering far in excess of what the average member of society might need in order to maintain themselves in reasonable comfort. The absence of a cap on claims for lost earnings is arguably unjustified given that very high income earners may be able

[29] Caps also exist in relation to damages for gratuitous care and damages for what in Australia is generally called 'non-economic loss', which comprises damages for pain and suffering, loss of amenity, loss of expectation of life and disfigurement. See, eg, Civil Liability Act 2002 (NSW) ss 15(4) and (5) (capping damages for gratuitous care) and 16(2) (capping damages for non-economic loss).

[30] Civil Liability Act 2002 (NSW) s 12.

[31] See, eg, Civil Liability Act 2003 (Qld) s 54; Civil Liability Act 1936 (SA) s 54; Civil Liability Act 2002 (Tas) s 26; Wrongs Act 1958 (Vic) s 28F; Civil Liability Act 2002 (WA) s 11; Personal Injuries (Liabilities and Damages) Act 2003 (NT) s 20.

to provide amply for themselves without having recourse to the tort system at all, even if their injuries are catastrophic, due to the financial reserves that they may have been able to accumulate.[32] The absence of a cap is also difficult to defend given that income above a certain level is not required in order to meet any basic need.

The introduction in the United Kingdom of a cap on damages for a loss of income would not be a wholly novel development considering that a cap of sorts has long existed in relation to damages for non-pecuniary loss. The maximum that may be awarded in respect of non-pecuniary loss is currently around £265,000. This cap is prescribed in the *Guidelines for the Assessment of General Damages in Personal Injury Cases*, which is published by the Judicial College.[33] The *Guidelines* endeavour 'to assist judges by setting out what the authors consider to be the current levels of awards that have been and are being made by judges up and down the country'.[34] The courts have described the *Guidelines* as 'valuable'[35] and a 'welcome development'.[36] The *Guidelines* are not, strictly speaking, binding.[37] They are '"soft law" rather than "hard law"' but 'judges will tend to follow them'.[38]

To summarise the argument that has been made so far in this section, caps on damages comply with the need principle. Provided that they are fixed at an appropriate level, caps can ensure that claimants who do not really have a pressing need for compensation above a particular figure cannot recover damages under the relevant head in excess of the applicable figure. Thus, if the tort system in the United Kingdom is thought to be too expensive, capping damages for a loss of earnings, as has happened in many Australian jurisdictions, would be one of the more sensible ways available of controlling costs.

There are a few additional points that should be noted in this connection. First, it only makes sense to cap certain heads of damages, such as damages for a loss of earnings. It would be a mistake to cap damages that are calculated in accordance with some need. For example, it would be inappropriate to cap damages for future out-of-pocket expenses (which, in the case of a catastrophically injured claimant, encompass damages in respect of care, home modification costs, the cost of special equipment and so on). Such a cap would be inconsistent with the need principle as it would tend to impact most severely upon more seriously injured claimants, such claimants being, of course, precisely the types of claimant who would be more likely to suffer losses relevant to this head.

Second, while capping a given head of damages may be justifiable in the abstract according to the need principle, the precise level at which a certain cap is set may not be. For example, caps that are pitched at such a high level that they will hardly ever be relevant are unjustifiable, such as a cap on damages of loss of earnings of £10 million. Such a cap would complicate the law without conferring any corresponding advantage. Very low caps would also be unjustifiable. For example, capping damages for a loss of earnings at £100 per week

[32] An excellent discussion of tort law's commitment to income replacement is offered in Cane, *Atiyah's Accidents* (n 17) 151–56.

[33] Judicial College, *Guidelines for the Assessment of General Damages in Personal Injury Cases*, 11th edn (Oxford, Oxford University Press, 2012).

[34] *Ball v Secretary of State for Energy and Climate Change* [2012] EWHC 145 (QB), [16].

[35] *Simmons v Castle* [2012] EWCA Civ 1039, [2013] 1 WLR 1239, 1241 [10].

[36] *Heil v Rankin* [2001] QB 272 (CA) 294 [25].

[37] *Choudhary v Martins* [2007] EWCA Civ 1379, [2008] 1 WLR 617, 621 [10]; *Proctor v City Facilities Management Ltd* [2012] NIQB 99, [31].

[38] *Wall v Hutuelle de Poitiers Assurances* [2014] EWCA Civ 138, [24].

would be inconsistent with the need principle. Such a low cap would result in people who have been left unable to work as a result of a tort, which is an event that would leave most people in dire straits financially, receiving next to nothing by way of compensation for that loss. Very low caps also beg the question of whether the head of damages concerned should actually be recognised.

Thresholds and Sliding Scales

Thresholds prevent damages from being awarded under a certain head unless the damage suffered by the claimant for the purposes of that head is sufficiently great. Thresholds are the inverse of caps. Some Australian legislatures have placed thresholds on certain heads of damages. For example, in New South Wales damages for gratuitous care are withheld unless the claimant has received such care for at least six hours per week for six months.[39] In the same jurisdiction, damages may not be awarded for non-economic loss[40] 'unless the severity of the non-economic loss is at least 15% of a most extreme case'.[41] If the tort system in the United Kingdom is thought to be too expensive, introducing thresholds is a defensible way of addressing that problem. Thresholds are consistent with the need principle as they prioritise more seriously injured claimants. Claimants whose injuries are insufficiently serious to exceed a certain threshold are more likely to be able to get by without the support of the tort system than claimants whose damage is more extensive.[42]

It is interesting to note that the threshold on damages for non-economic loss in New South Wales is combined with a rule that tapers damages awarded for such loss in the case of loss that does not significantly exceed the threshold.[43] If the threshold is exceeded, damages awarded in respect of non-economic loss increase exponentially rather than linearly depending on the extent by which the claimant exceeds the threshold. For example, a claimant who is deemed to be 15% of a most extreme case is entitled only to 1% of the maximum award that can be made in respect of non-economic loss[44] while a claimant who is found to be 30% of a most extreme case can recover 23% of the maximum award.[45] Such tapering is also consistent with the need principle as it prioritises more seriously injured claimants.

[39] Civil Liability Act 2002 (NSW) s 15(3).

[40] Regarding this concept, see above (n 29).

[41] Civil Liability Act 2002 (NSW) s 16(1).

[42] More radically, it might be contended that some of the heads of damages in Australia that are subject to thresholds, including damages for gratuitous care and non-economic loss, which have been discussed here, should simply be abolished on the ground that damages awarded under them do not fulfil any need. In both Australia and the United Kingdom, it is doubtful that damages for non-economic loss (or non-pecuniary loss, according to the British terminology) meet any need. For discussion of this and other objections to such damages, see Cane, *Atiyah's Accidents* (n 17) 160–70. In Australia, awarding damages for gratuitous care is justified according to the need principle as such damages reflect a need for care: *Griffiths v Kerkemeyer* (1977) 139 CLR 161 (HCA). The courts in the United Kingdom have failed to develop a coherent theory (or, indeed, any theory) as to why these damages are awarded, but the latest indications suggest that they are granted in order to compensate the loss of the carer rather than the claimant: see E Peel and J Goudkamp, *Winfield & Jolowicz on Tort*, 19th edn (London, Sweet & Maxwell, 2014) [23-081].

[43] Civil Liability Act 2002 (NSW) s 16(3).

[44] Damages for non-economic loss are capped in New South Wales: see above (n 29).

[45] The maximum award is fixed by s 16(2) of the Civil Liability Act 2002 (NSW) at $350,000. This figure is indexed annually (Civil Liability (Non-Economic Loss) Order 2010 (NSW) r 3) and it presently stands at $572,200 (which converts to around £300,000).

It is stressed that it has merely been suggested that thresholds and sliding scales are in principle a respectable way of reining in the cost of the tort system. The precise way in which a given threshold or sliding scale is formulated might leave a lot to be desired. For example, it is arguable that the concept of 'a most extreme case', which is used in one of the thresholds in New South Wales, is too vague.[46] A further point that is worth noting is that thresholds differ from caps in that there is no reason, according to the need principle, why *all* heads of damages should not be subject to thresholds. Unlike the situation in relation to caps, no objection could validly be made by reference to the need principle to a proposal to impose a threshold on damages for out-of-pocket expenses.

The imposition of thresholds may also be consistent with the need principle for a further reason. It is well known that most tort claims are relatively low value and that such claims tend to consume a disproportionately large amount of resources.[47] Thresholds, especially if combined with sliding scales, would have the added advantage of removing at least some low-value claims from the tort system altogether by making the recoverable damages so low that claiming is not worthwhile. Eliminating low-value claims would ease delays in the tort system so that other claims involving more needy claimants can be processed more expeditiously. Of course, the gains that stand to be made in terms of processing times are likely to be fairly limited given that claims in the United Kingdom are already steered into different procedural channels depending (principally) on their quantum.[48]

Exemplary and Aggravated Damages

Most of the Australian statutes abolished exemplary and aggravated damages[49] or eliminated them from certain types of case, such as in claims in respect of negligently caused personal injury.[50] Exemplary damages are awarded in order to punish the defendant for the contumelious violation of the claimant's rights and to deter similar behaviour from being committed in the future. Given their purpose, it is clear that the Australian restrictions on the award of exemplary damages are justified according to the need principle. Awarding damages to punish and deter is incompatible with the idea that the resources of the tort system should be spent on delivering compensation to the neediest claimants. It follows that the award of exemplary damages should arguably be sacrificed in the United Kingdom. Of course, the savings that can be made by taking this step are minimal given the rarity with which exemplary damages are awarded[51] and the principle that, when they are awarded, the award should be the minimum necessary to meet the goals of punishment and deterrence.[52]

[46] As to the meaning of this phase (which features in several Australian statutes), see *Matthews v Dean* (1990) 11 MVR 455 (NSWSC); *Dell v Dalton* (1991) 23 NSWLR 528 (CA); *Kurrie v Azouri* (1998) 28 MVR 406 (NSWCA).

[47] See Cane, *Atiyah's Accidents* (n 17) 155.

[48] See Civil Procedure Rules, rr 27, 28 and 29.

[49] See, eg, Personal Injuries (Liabilities and Damages) Act 2003 (NT) s 19.

[50] See, eg, Civil Liability Act 2002 (NSW) s 21; Civil Liability Act 2003 (Qld) s 52.

[51] They are 'a remedy of last resort': *Kuddus v Chief Constable of Leicestershire Constabulary* [2001] UKHL 29, [2002] 2 AC 122, 145 [63].

[52] *Rookes v Barnard* [1964] AC 1129 (HL) 1227. See further, J Goudkamp, 'Exemplary Damages' in G Virgo and S Worthington (eds), *Commercial Remedies* (Cambridge, Cambridge University Press, 2016) (forthcoming).

The purpose of awarding aggravated damages is a matter of some debate.[53] However, according to the dominant view, aggravated damages are compensatory. Their function is to provide the claimant with redress for the mental distress and hurt feelings that he suffered on account of the manner in which the defendant committed the tort.[54] Even if, however, aggravated damages are compensatory, it does not necessarily follow that they are consistent with the need principle. This is because it is doubtful whether, when awarded, aggravated damages compensate any pressing need. Certainly, aggravated damages are a far cry in this regard from, for example, damages that are awarded in respect of a loss of income. Accordingly, even if aggravated damages are compensatory, they should arguably be sacrificed along with exemplary damages.

Judicial Discretion and Contributory Negligence

The provision for apportionment in Australia[55] and the United Kingdom[56] confers judges with significant discretion to determine the extent by which damages should be discounted for contributory negligence. The provision permits judges to reduce damages by any amount that they consider to be 'just and equitable'.[57] The discretion conferred is enormous. It is true that judges must, in applying the apportionment provision, take into account the causal potency of the parties' acts and their relative blameworthiness.[58] Judges must of course also, by virtue of their office, act judicially, and this requires them to respect the fundamental principle of justice that like cases should be treated alike and that different cases should be treated differently. It follows that the apportionment provision does not allow judges to pluck discounts out of the air.[59] Judges must try to achieve discounts that correspond with the discounts applied in other like cases, and which are different from discounts imposed in factually different cases. But despite these controls, the discretion that the apportionment provision confers on judges is extremely wide. The width of this discretion is reflected in the principle that appellate courts will only interfere with a trial judge's apportionment of damages where the trial judge's holding is 'plainly',[60] 'fundamentally'[61] or 'clearly'[62] incorrect.

[53] See J Murphy, 'The Nature and Domain of Aggravated Damages' (2010) 69 *CLJ* 353.

[54] See, eg, *Rookes v Barnard* [1964] AC 1129 (HL) 1221; *Cassell & Co Ltd v Broome* [1972] AC 1027 (HL) 1124.

[55] See, eg, Law Reform (Miscellaneous Provisions) Act 1965 (NSW) s 9.

[56] Law Reform (Contributory Negligence) Act 1945 (UK) s 1; Law Reform (Miscellaneous Provisions) Act (NI) 1948 s 2.

[57] For empirical investigation of how this discretion is applied in practice, see J Goudkamp and D Nolan, 'Contributory Negligence in the Twenty-First Century: An Empirical Study of First Instance Decisions' (2016) 79 *Modern Law Review* 575.

[58] *Stapley v Gypsum Mines Ltd* [1953] AC 663 (HL) 682; *Podredersek v Australian Iron and Steel Pty Ltd* (1985) 59 ALJR 492 (HCA) 494. As to these criteria, see J Goudkamp, 'Apportionment of Damages for Contributory Negligence: Appellate Review, Relative Blameworthiness and Causal Potency' (2015) *Edinburgh Law Review* 367; J Goudkamp and L Klar, 'Apportionment of Damages for Contributory Negligence: the Causal Potency Criterion' (2016) 53 *Alberta Law Review* 1.

[59] As HLA Hart observed in his 'lost' essay on discretion (HLA Hart, 'Discretion' (2013) 127 *Harvard Law Review* 652, 657): 'When we are considering the use of discretion in the Law we are considering its use by officials who are holding a responsible public office. It is therefore understood that if what officials are to do is not rigidly determined by specific rules but a choice is left to them, they will choose responsibly having regard to their office and not indulge in fancy or mere whim'.

[60] *Phethean-Hubble v Coles* [2012] EWCA Civ 349, [86].

[61] *Dixon v Clement Jones Solicitors (a firm)* [2004] EWCA Civ 1005, [51].

[62] *Kerry v Carter* [1969] 1 WLR 1372 (CA) 1376.

The discretion that the apportionment provision affords to judges is fettered in several Australian jurisdictions by rules that provide that the court must, in certain contexts, reduce the claimant's damages by a fixed or minimum amount.[63] For example, in the Northern Territory[64] and South Australia[65] legislation provides that damages must be reduced by 25% for failing to wear a seat belt.[66] Such rules will be called 'fixed reduction rules' as they define precisely the amount by which damages must be diminished on account of a given act of contributory negligence. Many examples can be found of provisions that require minimum reductions in damages ('minimum reduction rules'). For instance, in Tasmania a failure to wear a seat belt attracts a minimum reduction in the damages awarded of 15%.[67] In several states, damages must be diminished by at least 25% where the claimant is intoxicated[68] or where he negligently 'relied' on an intoxicated defendant to exercise skill and care.[69] In some jurisdictions, the minimum discount is increased to 50% where the claimant's contributory negligence is thought to be 'aggravated', such as where the claimant was a driver,[70] or where the person on whom the claimant relied to take care of him was a driver.[71] Fixed and minimum reduction rules diminish to different degrees the discretion that the apportionment provision confers on judges. Fixed reduction rules eliminate completely the discretion. Once the judge has found that a fixed reduction rule applies, he has no choice but to cut the damages back by the prescribed amount. Minimum reduction rules fetter the discretion afforded by the apportionment provision to a more limited extent by preventing the judge from reducing damages by an amount that falls below the minimum amount.

It is strongly arguable that the apportionment provision gives judges far too much discretion and that matters would be considerably improved in the United Kingdom if that discretion was more limited. This could be accomplished by introducing rules along the lines of the Australian fixed and minimum reduction rules that have been mentioned. Reducing judicial discretion in relation to apportionment would have several benefits. First, it would make the outcome of litigation more certain. If, for example, a fixed reduction rule applies to a given case, the parties will know in advance the percentage by which the damages will be discounted for contributory negligence. All other things being equal, the more predictable the outcome of litigation the more likely it is that litigants will settle their dispute. Second, limiting judges' discretion would reduce the cost of litigation. Fixed reduction rules, for instance, leave much less room for evidence to be called and for submissions to be made in relation to the issue of apportionment than the apportionment provision. By limiting the scope for evidence to be called and submissions to be made, trials would be conducted more expeditiously and economically than is presently the case.

[63] Regarding rules that limit the discretion of judges to determine the discount of damages for contributory negligence, see J Goudkamp 'Apportionment of Damages for Contributory Negligence: A Fixed or Discretionary Approach?' (2015) 35 *Legal Studies* 621.

[64] Motor Accidents (Compensation) Act (NT) s 11(1).

[65] Civil Liability Act 1936 (SA) s 49(3).

[66] The Northern Territory and South Australian legislation extends to a failure to wear a safety helmet. The legislation in South Australia applies also if the claimant travelled in a compartment of a vehicle other than the passenger compartment.

[67] Motor Accidents (Liabilities and Compensation) Act 1973 (Tas) s 22(4).

[68] Civil Liability Act 2002 (NSW) s 50; Civil Liability Act 2003 (Qld) s 47; Civil Liability Act 1936 (SA) s 46.

[69] Civil Liability Act 2003 (Qld) s 48(4).

[70] Ibid, s 47(5); Civil Liability Act 1936 (SA) s 46(4).

[71] Civil Liability Act 2003 (Qld) ss 48–49; Civil Liability Act 1936 (SA) s 47.

Third, restricting judges' discretion is likely to promote consistency in the way that cases are decided. The highly discretionary system established by the apportionment provision creates a great danger that similar cases will be treated differently and that different cases will be handled in a like manner. The danger of disparate outcomes is particularly acute given that the vast majority of cases in which apportionment is in issue are decided by courts the decisions of which are not available to the public. The lack of transparency in this regard means that there are only very limited opportunities for judges to refer to each other's decisions on apportionment with a view to achieving a degree of consistency in the discount applied. The difficulty with this situation is aggravated by an apparent lack of appellate oversight of decisions on apportionment. As mentioned above,[72] conventional learning holds that appellate courts will rarely review decisions regarding apportionment. They will intervene only exceptionally and where it is clear that the first-instance decision is flawed. Fourth, restricting discretion would promote the rule of law. In an ideal world, every possible situation would be catered for by a rule that is settled ex ante. The development of a comprehensive set of rules by which we are to be governed is one of the demands made by the rule of law.[73] Of course, because we are not omniscient, and because our language is imprecise, it is impossible to comply absolutely with this goal. The use of discretion by judges to deal with disputes the resolution of which cannot be justly provided for in advance is, therefore, inevitable. But it is very doubtful that the apportionment provision is as close to the ideal as can be achieved.

For the foregoing reasons, the apportionment provision confers judges with too much discretion. The Australian fixed and minimum reduction provisions, which fetter that discretion, therefore merit serious attention as models for reform. It is not of course being suggested that those provisions should be replicated *verbatim* in the United Kingdom. It has merely been argued that, in principle, judicial discretion in the area of apportionment for contributory negligence should be more limited than it is at present. It is true that some fixed apportionment rules already exist in England and Wales. In the famous case of *Froom v Butcher*[74] Lord Denning MR (with whom Lawton and Scarman LJJ agreed) laid down fixed reduction rules in the seat belt context. According to these rules, a failure to wear a seat belt will attract either a 15% or 25% reduction in damages depending on whether the damage would have been partly or completely prevented had the claimant worn a seat belt.[75] These rules have been extended to closely related acts of contributory negligence, such as a failure of motorcyclists[76] and bicyclists[77] to wear crash helmets.[78] However, despite the *Froom* rules, it is clear that most cases in the United Kingdom in which apportionment is in question will be determined by the unfettered application of the

[72] See the text accompanying nn 59–61.

[73] See the classic discussion in LL Fuller, *The Morality of Law* (New Haven CT, Yale University Press, revised edn, 1969) ch 2.

[74] *Froom v Butcher* [1976] QB 286 (CA).

[75] Ibid, 296.

[76] *Capps v Miller* [1989] 2 All ER 333, [1989] 1 WLR 839 (CA).

[77] *Smith v Finch* [2009] EWHC 53 (QB).

[78] For discussion, see J Fulbrook, 'Cycle Helmets and Contributory Negligence' [2004] *Journal of Personal Injury Law* 171. The rules were not extended to riding in the boot of a car: *Gleeson v Court* [2007] EWHC 2397 (QB), [2008] RTR 10, [25] (30%).

apportionment provision. There is much scope, therefore, for more widespread restrictions on the discretion that the apportionment provision confers on judges.

Before leaving the topic of apportionment, it is worth noting the intersection between it and the need principle. According to that principle, the entire doctrine of contributory negligence is misconceived. If what matters is delivering compensation to those claimants who need it the most, why should contributory negligence be relevant? The fact that a claimant was guilty of contributory negligence has nothing to do with his need for compensation. It was essentially this logic that led Patrick Atiyah to call for the abolition of the doctrine of contributory negligence.[79] It is neither feasible nor necessary to engage with this proposition here. It is simply observed that the argument that has been offered in this part of the chapter assumes that the doctrine of contributory negligence is here to stay, which is surely a realistic assumption. Although other scholars have also voiced objections to it,[80] there is simply no prospect of Parliament repealing legislation that is plainly regarded as working reasonably well. On the basis of this assumption, it has merely been contended that the highly discretionary regime that exists under the apportionment provision should be modified. Judicial discretion in the apportionment of damages should be more limited.

Negative Changes

This part of the chapter explores changes made by the Australian statutes that are incompatible with the need principle or which are otherwise objectionable.

Discount Rates

Arguably the most catastrophic provisions in the Australian statutes are those that increase the discount rates that are used to calculate damages for future losses. Because courts generally award damages for all losses, past and future, at the date judgment,[81] the component of the award that relates to future economic loss needs to be adjusted given that the claimant will have the enjoyment of the money before the losses to which it relates will be incurred. Discount rates are used in order to arrive at the present value of damages awarded in respect of future economic losses. The theoretical aim of this process is to ascertain the sum of money which, when invested, corresponds to the claimant's future economic loss.[82] Lawyers

[79] Cane, *Atiyah's Accidents* (n 17) 50–58. Atiyah's analysis is much more nuanced than this description suggests and justice cannot be done to his sophisticated arguments within the confines of this chapter. Briefly, however, Atiyah also emphasised the fact that the doctrine of contributory negligence is unfair in the sense that claimants who are found guilty of contributory negligence suffer personally on account of the reduction in their damages since they are typically uninsured whereas defendants, who are usually insured, do not have to put their hands into their own pockets to pay the share of the loss for which they are responsible.

[80] See, eg, R Stevens, 'Should Contributory Fault be Analogue or Digital?' in A Dyson, J Goudkamp and F Wilmot-Smith (eds), *Defences in Tort* (Oxford, Hart Publishing, 2015) (arguing that the doctrine of contributory negligence should be abolished on the ground that it is incompatible with understanding tort law as being about the vindication of rights).

[81] See Peel and Goudkamp (n 42) [23-005].

[82] *Simon v Helmot* [2012] UKPC 5, [2012] Med LR 394, [11].

traditionally speak of 'discount rates' because it is usually assumed that a return can be made on the damages which at least offsets the impact of inflation and taxation. When such returns can be achieved, the award needs to be diminished to prevent overcompensation. But in economic environments in which returns on investments that offset the effect of inflation and taxation cannot safely be achieved, it may be necessary to augment the award by applying a negative rate,[83] in which case the language of 'discount' rates is not really appropriate.

The discount rate at common law in Australia is 3%.[84] This rate has been significantly increased by several Australian legislatures, generally to 5%.[85] The difficulty with these increases is that it is crystal clear that the returns that these types of rates assume can be realised simply cannot be realistically achieved (especially given that many claimants cannot afford to take significant risks with their award). In the current investment climate, a discount rate of 5% is excessive. It results in significant under-compensation. Moreover, the most seriously injured claimants, and hence the neediest, are likely to be disproportionately affected by the increase in the rate. Seriously injured claimants are, of course, much more likely than less seriously injured claimants to suffer economic losses into the distant future. A proportionality greater percentage of their awards are likely to comprise damages in respect of future economic losses. By increasing the discount rate, these claimants are therefore affected to a greater degree than other claimants. A simple hypothetical illustrates the momentous effect that the discount rate can have on the size of awards in catastrophic injury cases. Suppose that X, an infant, suffers catastrophic injuries. His loss of earnings over his working life (47 years) is found to be $5 million. If a 3% discount rate is applied to that sum, X's damages for his loss of earnings will be $2,711,334. A 5% discount rate slashes those damages to $1,967,062. For the foregoing reasons, the Australian provisions that increase the discount rate should be condemned.[86] They should not be replicated in the United Kingdom. Fortunately, it seems that there is little prospect of this happening. The discount rate in the United Kingdom is 2.5%.[87] There appears to be a general awareness on the part of the government that even this rate, which is very low in light of the Australian experience, requires claimants to achieve returns on their awards that cannot safely be obtained.[88] There seems to be no appetite for increasing it. Indeed, the general sentiment appears to be that it may need to be lowered.

[83] Ibid, [14].

[84] *Todorovic v Waller* (1981) 150 CLR 402 (HCA).

[85] Civil Liability Act 2002 (NSW) s 14 (5%); Civil Liability Act 2003 (Qld) s 57 (5%); Civil Liability Act 1936 (SA) ss 3, 55 (5%); Civil Liability Act 2002 (Tas) s 28A (5%); Wrongs Act 1958 (Vic) s 28I (5%); Law Reform (Miscellaneous Provisions) Act 1941 (WA) s 5 (6%); Personal Injuries (Liabilities and Damages) Act 2003 (NT) s 22 (5%). The common law rate applies in the Australian Capital Territory.

[86] The authors of the Ipp Report, unsurprisingly, recommended against increasing the discount rate: Recommendation 53.

[87] Damages (Personal Injury) Order 2001 (SI 2001/2301) r 2. See also Damages (Personal Injury) (Scotland) Order 2002 (SSI 2002/46) r 3. The courts can deviate from this rate although they must take it into account in setting a different rate: Damages Act 1996 (UK) s 1.

[88] In a recent Ministry of Justice consultation paper concerning the discount rate, it was stated: 'Yields on [Index-Linked Government Gilts] have been declining for some time and there is a risk that the present [discount] rate may now be too high. In the light of this possibility the Lord Chancellor, the Scottish Ministers and the Department of Justice in Northern Ireland have each decided that the discount rate ought to be reviewed to ensure that it is still set at an appropriate rate' (Ministry of Justice, *Damages Act 1996: The Discount Rate—How Should it be Set?* (CP 12, 2012) 4). In 2013, the Ministry of Justice published a fairly detailed research paper concerning the discount rate: Ministry of Justice, *Personal Injury Discount Rate Research* (2013).

Provisions that Restate or Appear to Restate the Common Law

Several provisions in the Australian statutes restate or appear to restate the common law. A good example is section 5I of the Civil Liability Act 2002 (NSW).[89] This provision states:

(1) A person is not liable in negligence for harm suffered by another person as a result of the materialisation of an inherent risk.
(2) An inherent risk is something occurring that cannot be avoided by the exercise of reasonable care and skill.
(3) This section does not operate to exclude liability in connection with a duty to warn.

This provision does not alter the common law in New South Wales.[90] This is because the reasonable person would not attempt to eliminate ineliminable risks. Accordingly, proceeding in the face of such risks will not constitute a falling short of the standard of the reasonable person, which is required in order for the breach element of the action in negligence to be satisfied. Provisions that merely repeat the common law, such as section 5I, should probably not be used as inspiration for reform in the United Kingdom. That is because such provisions are liable to provoke barren arguments about whether the legislature intended merely to restate the common law or whether, in view of the principle that the legislature should not be assumed to act in vain,[91] intended to change the law in some respect. In other words, enacting provisions such as section 5I will simply tend to stimulate litigation. Legislation that restates the common law is also generally undesirable as it increases the size and complexity of the law without providing a corresponding benefit. This is not to say that enacting legislation that repeats the common law is never justified. For example, the legislature may want to increase the visibility of a certain rule to the public and putting it on a legislative footing may be a sensible way of doing that. The legislature may also want to dispel doubts about whether the rule in question actually exists. However, usually, for the reasons that have been given, legislation that restates the common law, especially in a piecemeal way, as has occurred in the case of the Australian statutes, is undesirable.

Illegality Defences

Most of the Australian statutes contain potent illegality defences.[92] It seems that these defences were created mainly in response to a decision of the New South Wales District Court to award damages to a teenage intruder who sustained severe injuries when he was

[89] Other examples include the Civil Liability Act 2002 (NSW) ss 5E (stating that the claimant carries the onus of proof in relation to causation) and 5R (stating that the same rules that apply for the purpose of determining whether the defendant was in breach of his duty of care apply also for the purpose of ascertaining whether the claimant failed to take reasonable precautions for his own safety). See further, McDonald, 'Legislative Intervention in the Law of Negligence' (n 5) 460–63.

[90] See further, McDonald, 'Legislative Intervention in the Law of Negligence' (n 5) 461–2.

[91] Lex nil frustra facit.

[92] Civil Liability Act 2002 (NSW) ss 54–54A; Civil Liability Act 2003 (Qld) s 45; Civil Liability Act 1936 (SA) s 43; Civil Law (Wrongs) Act 2002 (ACT) s 94; Personal Injuries (Liabilities and Damages) Act 2003 (NT) s 10. No precise counterpart to these provisions exists in Victoria or Western Australia. However, s 14G(2) of the Wrongs Act 1958 (Vic) provides: 'In determining whether the plaintiff has established a breach of the duty of care owed by the defendant, the court must consider … whether the plaintiff was engaged in an illegal activity'. This provision

beaten by an occupier.[93] The details underpinning these defences are unimportant for present purposes. Analysis of their fine points has been supplied elsewhere.[94] It suffices for current purposes to say that the defences apply if the claimant was injured while committing an offence of sufficient seriousness and the commission of that offence was causally related to the damage that the claimant suffered. These defences are a stain on Australian tort law. Not only are they probably unnecessary given that the common law recognised (and still recognises) a fairly robust illegality defence,[95] but it is doubtful that they accomplish anything worthwhile. For obvious reasons, they cannot, contrary to what has sometimes been suggested, be justified on the ground that they punish wrongdoers where punishment is deserved. This is primarily because the amount of punishment handed out by denying a remedy will often bear no relationship to the gravity of the claimant's wrongdoing. It is fanciful to think that the defences deter wrongdoing. It is unlikely that defences are well known by the public, which is what would be required in order for them to have a deterrent effect. The defences do not stamp out the possibility of offenders profiting from their wrong since damages in tort are usually compensatory and hence do not enable the claimant to improve upon his or her pre-tort position. It cannot justifiably be suggested that the defences prevent the courts from having to condone what the claimant did, since awarding damages does not necessary imply approval of the claimant's behaviour. The message sent by the defences is, ultimately, that offenders' rights are less important than those of other people.[96] That message is strikingly at odds with the fundamental idea that everyone is entitled to equal protection under the law. In summary, the Australian statutory illegality defences are misconceived.

The United Kingdom already has, it is worth noting, a statutory illegality defence. This defence is concealed in section 329 of the Criminal Justice Act 2003 (UK),[97] which is a statute, as its name implies, that is concerned mostly with the criminal law. Section 329 is a relatively harmless provision, at least judged by reference to the Australian illegality defences. In overview, it provides that liability will not arise when: (1) the defendant committed a trespass against the claimant; (2) the claimant was convicted of an imprisonable offence in

does not create a defence in the strict sense. Rather, the claimant's illegal act is merely a consideration to be borne in mind for the purposes of the negligence calculus. It should be noted that statutory illegality defences that pre-date the insurance crisis exist in both Queensland (Criminal Law Amendment Act 1997 (Qld) s 4(2)), amending s 6 of the Criminal Code Act 1899 (Qld)) and Western Australia (Offenders (Legal Action) Act 2000 (WA) s 5.

[93] *Fox v Peakhurst Inn Pty Ltd* (unreported, District Court of New South Wales, McGuire DCJ, 29 August 2002). The case was unremarkable. Had judgment in it not been delivered at the height of the insurance crisis, it likely would have disappeared without trace. Further details on this case are given in H Luntz, 'The Australian Picture' (2004) 35 *Victoria University of Wellington Law Review* 879, 882.

[94] See J Goudkamp, 'A Revival of the Doctrine of Attainder? The Statutory Illegality Defences to Liability in Tort' (2007) 29 *Sydney Law Review* 445; J Goudkamp, 'Self-Defence and Illegality Under the *Civil Liability Act* 2002 (NSW)' (2010) 18 *Torts Law Journal* 61.

[95] The latest word from the High Court on the common law illegality defence is *Miller v Miller* [2011] HCA 9, (2011) 242 CLR 446. The background to the case is given in J Goudkamp, 'The Defence of Joint Illegal Enterprise' (2010) 34 *Melbourne University Law Review* 425.

[96] Consider also Pt 2A of the Civil Liability Act 2002 (NSW), which provides for heighted restrictions on the assessment of damages where the claimant is an offender in custody.

[97] For discussion of s 329, see *Adorian v Commissioner of Police of the Metropolis* [2009] EWCA Civ 18, [2009] 1 WLR 1859; *McDonnell v Commission of Police of the Metropolis* [2015] EWCA Civ 573; JR Spencer, 'Legislate in Haste, Repent at Leisure' (2010) 69 *CLJ* 19. The primary motivation for the creation of this defence was the Tony Martin saga. That saga is addressed in J Goudkamp, 'Statutes and Tort Defences' in TT Arvind and J Steele (eds), *Tort Law and the Legislature: Common Law, Statute and the Dynamics of Change* (Oxford, Hart Publishing, 2013) 40.

respect of conduct committed at the time of the defendant's trespass; (3) the force used by the defendant was not 'grossly disproportionate'; and (4) the defendant committed the trespass because he believed that it was necessary to prevent the claimant from committing an offence, to protect life or property, or to apprehend the claimant. This provision is reasonably innocuous because the conditions that need to be satisfied in order to enliven it will rarely be met. Its scope is miniscule relative to that of its Australian counterparts. It is hoped that the Parliament at Westminster does not feel the need to create a more robust illegality defence along the lines of the Australian defences.

Good Samaritans

The Australian statutes confer Good Samaritans with immunity.[98] A Good Samaritan 'is a person who, in good faith and without expectation of payment or other reward, comes to the assistance of a person who is apparently injured or at risk of being injured'.[99] The lawmakers who created this immunity evidently believed that the common law gave little or no protection to Good Samaritans above and beyond that conferred upon defendants generally. This is clear even from a cursory glance at the *Hansard*.[100] In holding this view the Australian legislators were, of course, badly mistaken. The common law takes a lenient approach when scrutinising the adequacy of the conduct of Good Samaritans.[101] Most notably, the social utility of their behaviour counts in their favour for the purposes of ascertaining how much care the reasonable person in their behaviour would have taken.[102] More fundamental than the fact that this immunity was created on the basis of a mistaken understanding of the law is the fact that it is far from clear that Good Samaritans should be immunised. The upshot of the immunity is that Good Samaritans may avoid liability in negligence despite failing radically to comply with accepted norms of behaviour. Immunities are incompatible with the basic idea that everyone should be accountable under the law.[103] It is for precisely this reason that they have been steadily eroded.[104] If we are to take seriously the idea of accountability under the law, the immunity of Good Samaritans is difficult to defend. This may explain why Australian courts seem to have been extremely reluctant to find that the immunity applies.[105]

What is the prospect of a parallel immunity being introduced in the United Kingdom? The Parliament at Westminster has, of course, recently enacted SARAH, which applies

[98] Civil Liability Act 2002 (NSW) pt 8; Civil Liability Act 2003 (Qld) ss 25–27; Civil Liability Act 2003 (SA) s 74; Civil Liability Act 2002 (Tas) ss 35A–35C; Wrongs Act 1958 (Vic) ss 31A–31C; Civil Liability Act 2002 (WA) ss 5AB–5AE; Civil Law (Wrongs) Act 2002 (ACT) s 5; Personal Injuries (Liabilities and Damages) Act 2003 (NT) s 8.

[99] Civil Liability Act 2002 (NSW) s 56.

[100] See, eg, New South Wales Legislative Assembly, 30 October 2002, 6189 ff.

[101] The details are given in Peel and Goudkamp (n 42) [6-025].

[102] 'The saving of life or limb justifies taking considerable risk': *Watt v Hertfordshire County Council* [1954] 1 WLR 835 (CA) 838.

[103] For discussion, see J Goudkamp, *Tort Law Defences* (Oxford, Hart Publishing, revised edn, 2016) 137–38.

[104] Ibid, 9, 128–30.

[105] It is unsurprising that the authors of the Ipp Report (Commonwealth of Australia (n 4) [7.24]) recommended against creating an immunity for Good Samaritans. The panel wrote: 'A complete exemption from liability for rendering assistance in an emergency would tip the scales of personal responsibility too heavily in favour of interveners and against the interests of those requiring assistance. In our view, there are no compelling arguments for such an exemption'.

whenever a court needs to determine if a person was negligent or in breach of a statutory duty.[106] Section 2 of SARAH states: 'The court must have regard to whether the alleged negligence or breach of statutory duty occurred when the person was acting for the benefit of society or any of its members'.[107] Section 4 provides: 'The court must have regard to whether the alleged negligence or breach of statutory duty occurred when the person was acting heroically by intervening in an emergency to assist an individual in danger'. It is debatable whether these provisions change the law in England and Wales.[108] It is, however, crystal clear that they do not go nearly as far as the Australian provisions that confer immunity on Good Samaritans, despite the clamour in the national press in Britain about the need to give 'have-a-go heroes' robust protection.[109] Given that SARAH has only been put on the statute books in the United Kingdom very recently, it fortunately seems relatively unlikely that a Good Samaritan immunity will be created in the immediate future.

Volunteers

The Australian statutes also granted immunity to 'volunteers'.[110] A volunteer is 'a person who does community work on a voluntary basis'.[111] This immunity is vulnerable to the same objections as the immunity conferred on Good Samaritans.[112] It is unnecessary, therefore, to elaborate on what has been said under the previous heading. In the light of SARAH, there is no realistic prospect, happily, of a similar immunity being crafted any time soon in the United Kingdom.

Overlapping Schemes

One of the most regrettable features of the Australian statutes is that they are not uniform across Australia.[113] A related problem is that they have created a cacophony of systems in

[106] s 1.

[107] *Cf* s 1 of the Compensation Act 2006 (UK).

[108] The authors of *Clerk & Lindsell on Torts* wrote: 'Given that the courts already take into account the utility of the defendant's activity when determining whether he has taken an unreasonable risk … it is difficult to see what s.2 adds to the common law' M Jones and A Dugdale (eds), *Clerk & Lindsell on Torts*, 21st edn (London, Sweet & Maxwell, 2015) [8.174A]. McBride and Bagshaw argue that 's 4 adds nothing to the law: the same principle has long been given effect to by the courts' N McBride and R Bagshaw, *Tort Law*, 5th edn (Harlow, Pearson 2015) 261 (footnote omitted).

[109] ss 2 and 4 of SARAH need to be understood in the context of, among other things, s 76 of the Criminal Justice and Immigration Act 2008 (UK), as amended by s 43 of the Crime and Courts Act 2013 (UK). s 76 augments the defence of self-defence in the criminal law. It was enacted with a view to protecting 'have-a-go heroes'.

[110] Commonwealth Volunteers Protection Act 2003 (Cth); Civil Liability Act 2002 (NSW) s 61; Civil Liability Act 2003 (Qld) s 39; Volunteers Protection Act 2001 (SA) s 47; Wrongs Act 1958 (Vic) s 37; Volunteers and Food and Other Donors (Protection from Liability) Act 2002 (WA) s 6; Civil Law (Wrongs) Act 2002 (ACT) s 8; Personal Injuries (Liabilities and Damages) Act 2003 (NT) s 7. For discussion, see M McGregor-Lowndes and L Nguyen, 'Volunteers and the New Tort Law Reform' (2005) 13 *Torts Law Journal* 44.

[111] Civil Liability Act 2002 (NSW) s 60(1).

[112] The authors of the Ipp Report recommended against creating a volunteers' immunity: (Commonwealth of Australia (n 4) [11.20]–[11.23]). The Report (at [11.21]) states: 'The Panel is not aware of any significant volume of negligence claims against volunteers in relation to voluntary work, or that people are being discouraged from doing voluntary work by the fear of incurring negligence liability. The Panel has decided to make no recommendation to provide volunteers as such with protection against negligence liability'.

[113] Contrary to recommendation 1 of the Ipp Report: Commonwealth of Australia (n 4).

most States and Territories. The Australian statutes generally supplemented pre-existing legislation concerned with motor vehicle[114] and workplace accident[115] cases with the result that there are multiple schemes in force in most jurisdictions. This situation is highly objectionable. Overlapping systems are a threat to the accessibility of the law. They also make the law unnecessarily complicated with the result that litigants and their lawyers are prone to being tripped up. The precedential value of decisions is more limited as cases that address the interpretation of a particular provision in a given system may not apply to the corresponding provision in a different system. Moreover, the differences between the various systems are simply arbitrary. There is no reason why, as is the case in New South Wales, for instance, the rules governing the award damages for non-economic loss should be different in motor vehicle cases from those that apply in public liability cases.[116] Legislators should assiduously avoid creating parallel systems. The disastrous experience in Australia in this regard is a stark warning to lawmakers in the United Kingdom.

One Hundred Per Cent Contributory Negligence

The Australian statutes, as observed earlier, limit the discretion that the apportionment provision confers upon judges to determine the amount by which damages should be discounted for contributory negligence.[117] The fettering of this discretion is arguably beneficial in principle. However, the same cannot be said of certain other changes that the statutes made to the law in this regard. Take, for example, the provisions in some Australian jurisdictions that authorise the courts to find claimants guilty of 100% contributory negligence.[118] Such provisions changed the law. In *Wynbergen v Hoyts Corp Pty Ltd*[119] the High Court of Australia held that the apportionment legislation did not permit findings of 100% contributory negligence. The Court reached this conclusion, in essence, on the ground that the apportionment legislation is predicated on the existence of fault on both sides, and where there is fault on both sides, it cannot be 'just and equitable' to find 100% contributory negligence.[120] An additional and stronger reason for rejecting the idea of 100% contributory negligence is that a finding of 100% contributory negligence is inconsistent with the holdings that must be made in order for the court to reach the stage where contributory negligence is an issue.[121] A finding of 100% contributory negligence presumably means that the claimant is wholly responsible for the damage about which he complains.

[114] See, eg, the Motor Accidents Compensation Act 1999 (NSW).

[115] See, eg, Workers Compensation Act 1987 (NSW).

[116] Compare Pt 2 Div 3 of the Civil Liability Act 2002 (NSW) with ch 5.3 of the Motor Accidents Compensation Act 1999 (NSW).

[117] See the text accompanying n 55.

[118] Civil Law (Wrongs) Act 2002 (ACT) s 47; Civil Liability Act 2002 (NSW) s 5S; Civil Liability Act 2003 (Qld) s 24; Wrongs Act 1954 (Tas) s 4(1); Wrongs Act 1958 (Vic) s 63. These provisions are based on recommendations made in the Ipp Report: Commonwealth of Australia (n 4) 128. The New South Wales provision, which is representative, provides: 'In determining the extent of a reduction in damages by reason of contributory negligence, a court may determine a reduction of 100% if the court thinks it just and equitable to do so, with the result that the claim for damages is defeated'.

[119] *Wynbergen v Hoyts Corp Pty Ltd* (1998) 72 ALJR 65 (HCA).

[120] Ibid, 68–69.

[121] See further, J Goudkamp, 'Rethinking Contributory Negligence' in S Pitel, J Neyers and E Chamberlain (eds), *Tort Law: Challenging Orthodoxy* (Oxford, Hart Publishing, 2013) 344–46.

But if the claimant is wholly responsible for his or her damage, it is difficult to see how a tort could have been committed. Because the doctrine of contributory negligence only falls for consideration once a tort has been committed,[122] a court that is minded to find that the claimant is guilty of 100% contributory negligence ought to enter a verdict for the defendant without reaching the issue of contributory negligence. Based on this logic, one Australian court suggested that the provisions in the Australian statutes authorising the courts to find 100% contributory negligence accomplish nothing.[123] In other words, on this view, the provisions are simply without effect. It is perhaps because of the inconsistency inherent in the idea of 100% contributory negligence that the provisions authorising the courts to find 100% contributory negligence have rarely been used.[124]

Happily, there is little prospect of the Australian provisions that permit the courts to find 100% contributory negligence being copied in the United Kingdom. After a long period of uncertainty the courts in the United Kingdom confirmed that damages cannot be reduced for contributory negligence by 100%,[125] for reasons including those given above. When the Bill that became the Compensation Act 2006 (UK) was being debated in Parliament, it was proposed that it should have added to it a clause that mirrored the Australian provisions regarding 100% contributory negligence.[126] Fortunately, that motion was withdrawn. It was noted that a finding of 100% contributory negligence was nonsensical. In view of the foregoing, it is unlikely that the United Kingdom is in any real danger of being lumbered with a rule akin to the Australian provisions regarding 100% contributory negligence. There seems to be an understanding in the United Kingdom that these provisions are incoherent.

Conclusion

This chapter has addressed the legislation that was enacted in Australia in response to the insurance crisis that occurred in that country at the start of the twenty-first century. This was done with a view to determining which provisions the Parliament at Westminster might want to use as a model for reform in the United Kingdom, in the event that it decides that reform is needed, and which provisions it should disregard. Provisions in the Australian legislation that are worth giving attention to include those that impose (1) caps, (2) thresholds and sliding scales, (3) abolish or confine exemplary and aggravated damages and (4) reduce the discretion of judges in apportioning damages for contributory negligence.

122 '[O]ne does not get to the question of contributory negligence until liability is established': *Sharpe v Addison* [2003] EWCA Civ 1189, [2007] Lloyd's Rep PN 12, [32].

123 *Robbins v Skouboudis* [2013] QSC 101, [54] relying on J Goudkamp, 'Defences to Negligence' in C Sappideen and P Vines (eds), *Fleming on Torts*, 10th edn (Sydney, Lawbook Co, 2011) 324–25.

124 Findings of 100% contributory negligence were made in *Zilio v Lane* [2009] NSWDC 226; *Adams v State of New South Wales* [2008] NSWSC 1257, [131]–[133]. Consider also *Mackenzie v Nominal Defendant* [2005] NSWCA 180, (2005) 43 MVR 315 where the New South Wales Court of Appeal held that the trial judge would not have erred in reducing damages by 100% had the facts as found by him existed: at [99].

125 *Reeves v Commissioner of Police of the Metropolis* [2000] 1 AC 360 (HL) 372, 387; *Anderson v Newham College of Further Education* [2002] EWCA Civ 505, [2003] ICR 212; *Buyukardicli v Hammerson UK Properties plc* [2002] EWCA Civ 683, [7].

126 HL Deb 20 December 2005, vol 676, cols GC 258–67.

Provisions (1), (2) and (3) reduce the cost of the tort system, which is an objective that is bound to rank high on the list of priorities of any government that hopes to reform tort law in the United Kingdom. They do so without doing massive damage to the tort system in the process. They are consistent with the principle that tort law's limited resources should be directed to the neediest claimants, which is an idea the force of which can be readily appreciated by lawmakers. Provision (4) addresses the doctrine of contributory negligence. That doctrine is inconsistent with the need principle. However, because that doctrine has a sturdy foothold in English law and is plainly not vulnerable to being dislodged, attention was focused on improving it. It was argued that the Australian provisions that reduce judicial discretion in apportioning damages might be worth emulating.

On the other side of things, it was contended that the Australia provisions that (1) increase discount rates, (2) restate or appear to restate common law rules, (3) create illegality defences, confer immunity on (4) Good Samaritans and (5) volunteers, (6) result in overlapping schemes and (7) authorise courts to find 100% contributory negligence are retrograde provisions. Provision (1) is one of the most nonsensical ways imaginable of cutting the cost of the tort system. The cuts that it imposes fall disproportionately on the neediest claimants. Provision (1) is hence inconsistent with the need principle. Provision (2) is prone to stimulate litigation and therefore increase the cost of the tort system. These outcomes are diametrically opposed to those that any government that gives scrutiny to the tort system would hope to achieve. Provisions (3), (4) and (5) are objectionable because there is no good reason in support of these defences. Provision (6) renders the law unnecessarily complex and therefore probably more costly to administer. It also results in arbitrary distinctions being drawn in the law and is hence liable to reduce public confidence in the law. Provision (7) permits the courts to make a finding that is not logically open to them to make in the first place. None of these Australian provisions should be replicated in the United Kingdom. They stand only as a warning of the consequences to rushing head first into tort reform, as the Australian legislatures did, without giving proper consideration to the merits and demerits of particular rules. It is because of provisions such as these that the Australian statutes have properly been described as 'heart-rending',[127] 'unprincipled'[128] and 'hastily drafted and ... unclear'.[129]

[127] R Stevens, 'The Divergence of the Australian and English Law of Torts' in S Degeling, J Edelman and J Goudkamp (eds), *Torts in Commercial Law* (Sydney, Thomson, 2011) 40.

[128] Luntz, 'The Australian Picture' (n 93) 903.

[129] McDonald, 'The Impact of the Civil Liability Legislation' (n 24) 270.

5

Non-Pecuniary Damages for Personal Injury: A Reflection on the Canadian Experience

JEFF BERRYMAN*

Introduction

The pejorative term 'compensation culture', over which much printers' ink has been spilt in Great Britain,[1] has no broad currency in Canada. In fact, Canadians appear to have embraced litigation to deal with society's ills as witnessed by the burgeoning resort to class actions. Nevertheless, there have been sporadic outbursts of a 'litigation crisis', particularly over the rising cost of automobile insurance. Such crises occurred throughout the 1980s and 1990s, and continue sporadically into the twenty-first century.[2] Interestingly, these crises have usually generated piecemeal reforms that qualify rights to pursue litigation, but never towards a universal scheme such as that adopted in New Zealand. One aspect of these crises has been the treatment of damages for non-pecuniary losses. As will be discussed below, starting in 1990, Ontario, and then followed by other provinces, imposed limits on either the right to sue for non-pecuniary loss, or restricted the amounts recoverable for certain types of non-pecuniary losses arising from automobile accidents, largely in response to perceived insurance crises.

With respect to non-pecuniary damages, the most significant development that allayed the development of a 'compensation culture' in Canada was a series of cases, which later became known as the 'Supreme Court Trilogy' (hereafter Trilogy), in which the Supreme Court of Canada embarked on a new direction for the quantification of non-pecuniary loss arising from personal injury.[3] The impetus for change was a fear of importing developments from the United States and the perception of runaway costs.[4]

* I wish to thank my research student, Juliene Cawthorne-Hwang, who was funded by the Law Foundation of Ontario, for her assistance in preparing this chapter.

[1] K Williams, 'State of Fear: Britain's "Compensation Culture" Reviewed' (2005) 25 *Legal Studies* 499.

[2] See C Brown and B Feldthusen, 'The Osborne Inquiry into Motor Vehicle Accident Compensation in Ontario' (1988) 8 *Windsor Yearbook of Access to Justice* 318.

[3] *Andrews v Grand and Toy Alberta Ltd* [1978] 2 SCR 229; *Thornton v Board of Trustees (Prince George)* [1978] 2 SCR 267; and *Teno v Arnold* [1978] 2 SCR 287.

[4] In *Andrews* (n 3) at 261 Dickson J justified limiting non-pecuniary damages because '[i]t is in this area that awards in the United States have soared to dramatically high levels in recent years. Statistically, it is the area where

The arguments that framed the debate 36 years ago in 1978 have changed little in the ensuing years, although, and, as I will explore later, some changes in our understanding of how these losses are felt by victims may cause us to rethink, once again, the level and utility of these awards.

The Supreme Court Trilogy

In a carefully reasoned judgment, Dickson J set out three principles and policies that anchored the approach in the Trilogy:

(1) **Incommensurability**. Realising that there is no market for pain and suffering, loss of expectation in life and loss of amenities means that any damages award is *ipso facto* arbitrary or conventional. These labels, although convenient, mask a myriad of individual subjective experiences. Pain and suffering is readily understood by analogy to our own experiences, and, yet, we readily recognise the subjective individuality of personal experience. This loss covers both sensate (ie, the physical discomfort experienced by the burn victim) and insensate experiences (ie, the feelings of loss experienced by a victim who because of injury is no longer able to bear children). Some aspects can be converted into pecuniary losses, as in where medication is given to deal with pain, or professional counselling is given to deal with grief, psychological, or other psychiatric manifestations of suffering.

Loss of amenities deals with sensate experiences, the inability to respond emotionally to those things that give us pleasure or meaning to our lives. But here again, the magnitude of this type of loss changes over a person's life. For example, in the course of a life one is more likely to be engaged in physical pursuits when young than later in life, such, that to compensate a quadriplegic for this loss should reflect the changing nature of intensity experienced over the victim's life.

Loss of expectation seeks to compensate for the fact that a person who has suffered serious injury will, actuarially speaking, have a shortened life. But again, the magnitude of this loss is also constantly changing in response to medical advancements that extend actuarial tables for this cohort.[5] On these categories, Dickson J reminded us that they are not 'analytically distinct' and thus justified a composite award.

the danger of excessive burden of expense is greatest'. See also R Sharpe and K Roach, *Brian Dickson: A Judge's Journey* (Toronto, Osgoode Society for Canadian Legal History, 2003) 195. Incidentally, the British Columbia Law Reform Commission doubted the correlation between rising damages for non-pecuniary losses and their impact on creating an insurance crisis. See *Report on Compensation for Non-pecuniary Loss* (LRC 76, September 1984) 17.

[5] This head of non-pecuniary loss has been abolished in the UK. See Administration of Justice Act (UK) 1982, s 1(1)(a). In a request to Statistics Canada to determine whether there were separate mortality tables for paraplegics and quadriplegics so that a comparison with mortality tables for the general population could be made, I was informed that Stats Canada does not keep such statistics. The current mortality rate of the general population for males at birth is 79 and females 83 (2009). For comparative date on change in life expectancy as a result of paraplegia see the Annual Report for the Spinal Cord Injury Model Systems published by the National Spinal Cord Injury Statistical Center (Birmingham, Alabama, 2009) Tables 12 and 13: www.nscisc.uab.edu/PublicDocuments/reports/pdf/2009%20NSCISC%20Annual%20Statistical%20Report%20%20Complete%20Public%20Version.pdf. The tables show a loss of life expectancy of around 20% depending upon age of the victim at the time of the injury.

(2) **Any award must be fair and reasonable.** By this, Dickson J was addressing the need for consistency between decisions involving similar injuries and across provincial jurisdictions. An important step in implementing this policy was the imposition of an upper limit or 'cap' on non-pecuniary damages.[6]

(3) **The principle of 'paramountcy of care'** concerning pecuniary loss allowed a court to consider other social policy factors with respect to non-pecuniary damages, and in particular, the economic burden large awards impose on society and insurance costs. The Trilogy also made dramatic changes in the way pecuniary loss was determined, engaging two major heads, compensation for loss of working capacity and future health care costs; later, a tax gross-up was added to deal with the issue of taxation from the interest income on the other two substantive heads of compensatory damages. These changes provided real levels of pecuniary compensation and weakened the need to use non-pecuniary damages to top up an award.[7]

Applying these principles, and inspired by the analytical framework used by Ogus,[8] Dickson J set Canadian law on the path of a 'functional approach' to compensation for non-pecuniary loss. Dickson J described the functional approach as

> attempts to assess the compensation required to provide the injured person 'with reasonable solace for his misfortune'. 'Solace' in this sense is taken to mean physical arrangements which can make his life more endurable rather than 'solace' in the sense of sympathy.[9]

And later in the judgment:

> Money is awarded because it will serve a useful function in making up for what has been lost in the only way possible, accepting that what has been lost is incapable of being replaced in any direct way.
>
> ......
>
> If damages for non-pecuniary loss are viewed from a functional perspective, it is reasonable that large amounts should not be awarded once a person is properly provided for in terms of future care for his injuries and disabilities. The money for future care is to provide physical arrangements for assistance, equipment and facilities directly related to the injuries. Additional money to make life more endurable should then be seen as providing more general physical arrangements above and beyond those relating directly to the injuries.[10]

In a later case in which the Supreme Court of Canada was asked to rule on the appropriateness of its upper limit on damages for non-pecuniary loss set in the Trilogy, Dickson J expanded on his adoption of the functional approach. In *Lindal v Lindal*[11] he reiterated the view that 'money is awarded, not because lost faculties have a dollar value, but because money can be used to substitute other enjoyments and pleasures for those that have been lost'.[12] However, he now added that an award should not be dependent upon the seriousness

[6] Dickson J did not actually use the term 'cap'; this entered the non-pecuniary damages lexicon later in remarks made by Sopinka J in *ter Neuzen v Korn* [1995] 3 SCR 674.

[7] *Watkins v Olafson* [1989] 2 SCR 750.

[8] AI Ogus, 'Damages for Lost Amenities: A Foot, a Feeling or a Function?' (1972) 35 *MLR* 1.

[9] *Andrews v Grand and Toy Alberta Ltd* (n 3) 262.

[10] Ibid.

[11] *Lindal v Lindal* [1981] 2 SCR 629.

[12] Ibid, 636.

of the injury, but rather on the uses to which the award can be put. Similarly, because the assessment depended upon individual circumstances of the claimant, it was impossible to develop a tariff approach. Dickson J also accepted that under a functional approach the ways to provide solace are potentially endless, thus it is appropriate to take account of the social costs of the award. In addition, because under the pecuniary head of damages a certain amount goes to provide substitute amenities, it is appropriate to moderate the claim for non-pecuniary damages to avoid overlap. Finally, taking account of the social cost of the award reflects the fact that under the functional approach the damages are not strictly speaking compensatory but are to provide a substitute for loss of amenities. Such an approach is counter to the primary function of the law, which is compensation, and thus justified moderation.

If courts embrace a functional account then in operation one would expect evidence to be adduced on what steps could be taken to provide the claimant with substitute amenities. The range and cost of these substitute amenities would need to be evaluated against the 'fair and reasonable' criteria and the effective cap. Substitute amenities, which had only a marginal impact on quality of life, or, in combination, were extremely expensive and thus could be said not to be cost effective, would be discounted on the 'fair and reasonable' aspect.

Court Awarded Tort Law Personal Injuries Compensation

Jump forward to the present and let us explore how the Supreme Court's aspiration for adoption of a functional approach has turned out in practice.[13] The first point to note is that the Supreme Court of Canada has not waivered in its support for the functional approach as it applies to non-pecuniary loss for personal injury.[14] Second, the cap imposed in the Trilogy, at the time set at $100,000, has subsequently been adjusted for inflation and now sits at around $320,000.[15] I have written elsewhere that the level of damages awarded for non-pecuniary loss puts Canada in the range of similar damages awarded by English and Australian courts, demonstrably below those awarded in the United States, and clearly above those awarded in New Zealand under its comprehensive no-fault scheme.[16]

The quantification of non-pecuniary damages at the trial and provincial appellate court levels adopts a fairly uniform approach across common law Canada. That approach starts with factual findings on the nature of the claimant's injuries and how that impacts on, and has changed, the way the claimant is able to live his or her life. The next step is to identify

[13] My research student surveyed all cases from British Columbia, Alberta, Ontario and Nova Scotia for the last 10 years using the search terms 'non-pecuniary' and 'functional'. This generated over 1,090 cases, half originating in British Columbia.

[14] See *ter Neuzen v Korn* (n 6), although in this case Sopinka J ultimately appeared to take more cognisance of comparator cases and gave little attention to evidence of what could be provided to the claimant to give solace. See also *Gauthier v Beaumont* [1998] 2 SCR 3, and most recently in obiter in *Vancouver (City) v Ward* [2010] 2 SCR 28, [34], the latter case adopting vindicatory damages for Charter violations.

[15] *Morrison v Greig* [2007] OJ No 225 (SC) awarding $310,000; and *Singh v Bains* (2008) Carswell BC 1323 (SC) awarding $325,000. A straight-line adjustment for inflation in 2014 would merit a cap of $350,000.

[16] See J Berryman, 'Rethinking Damages for Personal Injury: Is it Too Late to Take the Facts Seriously?' in R Sharpe and K Roach eds, *Taking Remedies Seriously* (Ottawa, Canadian Institute for the Administration of Justice, 2009) 192.

comparator cases. The courts have rejected comparing the severity of a claimant's injuries to those experienced in the Trilogy because such an approach would be inconsistent with the functional approach, and would blur the line, where a jury is used to assess damages, as to what is within the purview of the jury (ie, questions of fact, which damage assessment constitutes) and judge (ie, question of law, which the cap on non-pecuniary damages constitutes).[17] Nevertheless, what has been termed a 'horizontal comparative approach' requires the court to compare the severity of the claimant's injuries to comparable cases put before the court by both plaintiff's and defendant's counsel, which is then used to create a range of acceptable awards.[18] To make this comparison meaningful, courts in British Columbia have suggested a number of common factors in which to structure the comparative analysis. The list of factors is:

(a) age of the plaintiff
(b) nature of the injury
(c) severity and duration of pain
(d) disability
(e) emotional suffering
(f) loss or impairment of enjoyment of life.[19]

To which the same court in *Stapley v Hejslet*[20] added:

(g) impairment of family, marital and social relationships
(h) impairment of physical and mental abilities
(i) loss of lifestyle
(j) the plaintiff's stoicism (as a factor that should not generally penalise the plaintiff).

Once the claimant's injuries are classified, the matching comparative cases, which most closely align to the claimant's injuries, determine an appropriate range after adjusting for inflation. The court invariably comments that adjustments may be made for the particular circumstances of the claimant and to include the claimant's need for solace. In other provinces, an even less systematic approach is adopted, although the notion of 'horizontal comparisons' has clearly been applied.[21] A more blatant 'horizontal comparison' approach

[17] Discussed in *Boyd v Harris* (2004) 24 BCLR (4th) 155 (CA) [29–30]. See also *Sandhu (Litigation guardian of) v Wellington Place Apartments* (2008) 291 DLR (4th) 220 (Ont. CA) [25].

[18] Ibid, [41] (Smith JA): 'Our first task is to determine whether the decisions cited by the appellant are reasonably comparable to this case and whether they suggest a range of acceptable awards. Then, we must determine whether this award is within that range and, if not, whether it falls so substantially outside the range that it must be adjusted'.

[19] Ibid, [42].

[20] *Stapley v Hejslet* (2006) 263 DLR (4th) 19 (BCCA) [46]. This judgment is now almost universally cited in cases in British Columbia where non-pecuniary damages are mentioned.

[21] Eg, the key case in Ontario is *Padfield v Martin* (2003) 64 OR (3d) 577 (CA) lowering an award of $274,000 (itself having been lowered by the trial judge from a jury award of $500,000) to $150,000, on the basis that other comparable injuries to competitive athletes, as was the claimant, and that the claimant's injuries were far removed from the most catastrophic injuries that justified the maximum under the cap, had resulted in too high an award. Interestingly, the use of the term 'solace' by this court appears more in keeping with the notion of solace as providing comfort; an approach directly refuted by Dickson J in *Andrews.* Similarly, in Nova Scotia, see *Melanson v Robins* (2009) 274 NSR (2d) 331 (SC) [16–24], where after describing what is required in applying the functional approach, the Court immediately cited the comparator cases proffered by counsel and determined a range. In Alberta, see, eg, *Ward v Ward* 2010 ABQB 654, [356]. In Newfoundland, see *Brewer v Hewitt* (2005) 255 DLR (4th) 368 (Nfld CA) [74] actually describing the current system as a tariff system.

occurs when the court simply tabulates the comparison cases with little discussion.[22] In Nova Scotia, a completely new de facto tariff type structure has been created to deal with soft tissue type injuries, commonly known as whiplash.[23] Some, but very few judgments, flirt with applying a functional approach. Thus, in *AT-B v Mah*[24] the Court explicitly suggested that the non-pecuniary damages 'will pay for things which are not related to her care priorities, but which may improve [the claimant's] enjoyment and quality of her life throughout the future world in which she is fated to live'. But then went promptly on to identify case comparators.

Although token reference is repeatedly made to the applicability of the functional approach, I believe, that it is not applied in Canada; certainly not in the spirit in which Dickson J conceived of the approach. In effect, Dickson J's concern with 'fair and reasonable' treatment of similarly placed claimants across the country has supplanted the functional approach as the dominant criteria governing non-pecuniary damages in personal injury suits. The former criterion simply works better with the cap on damage. Procedurally, it is easier for litigants to make an argument. The claimant already faces the evidential hurdle to prove the types of injuries suffered and the consequences on future lost earning capacity and care costs to receive pecuniary damages. Being required to adduce additional evidence on what can be done to provide alternative avenues of enjoyment, particularly where there is an upper limit on what can be recovered, begs the question whether it is a cost-effective litigation strategy. Providing comparators is a simpler approach to quantification.

If the 'fair and reasonable' criterion dominates the issue of quantification, has it attained success in creating consistency across provincial boundaries for similar types of injuries? An answer to this question confronts a number of obstacles, the first of which is how to define consistency. The 'horizontal comparison' approach requires the court to identify an acceptable range of damages. In application the range is quite large. For example, in *AT-B v Mah*[25] the defendant submitted, which the Court accepted, a range between $50,000 and $285,000, and awarded the latter. In *Morin v Korkola*[26] a range between $45,000 and $120,000 was offered, the court awarding $75,000; and in *Stapley v Hejslet*[27] the Court accepted a range from $66,000 to $100,000 and then promptly awarded $175,000. Clearly, apart from the impact of the cap at the upper end, ranges of this magnitude do little to provide consistency.

A second issue in ensuring consistency is how to account for the role of jury trials when compared with judge alone trials. The Supreme Court of Canada in *ter Neuzen v Korn*[28] indicated that a jury should only be instructed on the cap for non-pecuniary damages and the reasons for its imposition when the trial judge, after receiving submissions from counsel and reviewing the nature of the injuries, is of the opinion that the jury may be

[22] eg, see *Morin v Korkola* 2011 ONSC 1393, [89] simply citing eight cases that had similar fractures to a femur and then concluding that $75,000 was fair and reasonable. See also *Jarmson v Jacobsen* 2012 BCSC 64, [80].

[23] First established in *Smith v Stubbert* (1992) 117 NSR (2d) 118 (CA), and most recently applied by the same court in *Hayward v Young* (2013) 330 NSR (2d) 250 (CA) [48].

[24] *AT-B v Mah* (2012) Alta LR (5th) 223 (QB) [557]. See also *Yick v Johnson* 2012 BCSC 1458, [94] suggesting that non-pecuniary damages may be utilised to allow the claimant to travel on cruises as an adaptation to find some enjoyment, and *Ediger (Guardian ad litem of) v Johnston* 2009 BCSC 386, [222].

[25] Above (n 24).

[26] Above (n 22).

[27] Above (n 20).

[28] Above (n 6).

likely to award damages in the range of or in excess of the cap.[29] In addition, regardless of whether the jury has been advised of the cap or not, if a jury returns a verdict in excess of the cap, the trial judge is required to reduce the award to conform to the jurisprudence surrounding the cap. If the jury is instructed on the cap, it should be cautioned not to make a comparison between the claimant's injuries before it and the injuries of the plaintiffs in the cases that gave rise to the creation of the cap, as in a scale of severity of injuries.[30] Rather, the jury should be instructed on the policy reasons for the cap; to restrain the financial burden that would result from excessive awards.[31] It remains controversial whether, and if so, under what circumstances, a judge may provide a jury with a range of damages to guide their deliberations on an award of damages for personal injury including damages for non-pecuniary loss.[32] The grave fear is impinging upon the role assigned to a jury as a trier of facts, of which damage assessment is an assigned function.

That juries will likely grant higher awards of non-pecuniary damages in personal injuries is recognised implicitly in the not infrequent cases in which a trial judge is requested, and required, to lower an award to accord with the cap, and explicitly by appellate courts when asked to exercise review. This, in turn, raises a third variable that impacts upon the goal of consistency, the standard of appellate review.

British Columbian courts have expressed the standard of review for damages in a personal injury suit in the following propositions:

1. Appellate intervention is not justified simply because on the appellate court's view of the facts, it would have come to a different conclusion.
2. Appellate review is justified where there is a palpable and overriding error. In the case of a judge alone trial such an error occurs when the amount awarded is either inordinately low or so inordinately high that it must be a wholly erroneous estimate of the damage.
3. In the case of a jury award, greater deference is accorded the award, and it will only be upset where it is wholly disproportionate or shockingly unreasonable.[33]

Similar standards, although expressed in slightly different language, are applied in other provincial jurisdictions.[34] As a result, greater deference is accorded a jury's assessment of damages for non-pecuniary loss, but the jury is not necessarily given instructions on the cap or a range of damages. Even if given a range, there is a large deviation from any notion

29 Ibid, [125]. In *Boyd v Harris* 2004 BCCA 146, [32], Smith JA analogised the impact of the cap with the governor on an engine, only influencing the speed of the engine when it reaches the point of control, but within that limit giving the driver complete control.

30 *Howes v Crosby* (1984) 45 OR (2d) 449 (CA).

31 *Rizzi v Marvos* 2008 ONCA 172, [32].

32 The respective positions in varying jurisdictions is explained in *Riedle v McCaskill* 2013 MBQB 222; see also *Abbott v Sharpe* 2007 NSCA 6; *Foreman v Foster* (2000) 196 DLR (4th) 11 (BCCA), and what has been described as the Saskatchewan Procedure discussed in *Junek v Ede* [1991] WWR 60 (Sask CA) 69. In Ontario, the power to give guidance is statutorily enshrined in s 118 of the Courts of Justice Act RSO 1990, c C.43, discussed in *Fiddler v Chiavetti* 2010 ONCA 210, [70].

33 See *Moskaleva v Laurie* 2009 BCCA 260, [125–29]; *Traviras v Lovig* 2011 BCCA 200, [32–33]; *McBryde v Womack* 2013 BCCA 260, [96] and *Toneguzzo-Norvell (Guardian ad litem of) v Burnaby Hospital* [1994] 1 SCR 114, [16].

34 eg, in Nova Scotia see *Abbott v Sharpe* 2007 NSCA 6, [109]; in Ontario see *Padfield v Martin* (2003) 64 OR (3d) 577 (CA) [42–43].

of a standard norm, if indeed a norm can be shown for the particular injury suffered. This divergence between jury and judge alone trials was the point of dissent expressed by Finch CJBC in *Stapley v Hejslet*,[35] although the real gravamen of Finch CJBC is the view that the cap is an unjustified fetter on the province of juries.[36] Finch CJBC suggests that rather than judge alone trials being used to set the range of acceptable damage awards downwards, the 'valuable corrective' effect of jury awards should be used to set the range upwards.

A final obstacle to consistency is the lack of coordinated reporting of awards or the provision of guidelines on how they should be quantified.[37]

Automobile Insurance

In contrast to the common law civil suit process just described for personal injuries, the treatment of non-pecuniary loss in statutory auto-insurance schemes in Canada evidences a more pronounced adoption of the underlying policy that motivated Dickson J in the Trilogy, namely the need to contain awards to curtail the social cost.

To varying degrees, the majority of Canada's provinces have introduced ways to limit the level of compensation for non-pecuniary loss incurred as a result of automobile accidents. In Ontario, the no-fault auto insurance scheme is designed to cover the majority of auto accidents, but preserves the right to commence a civil suit above certain verbal thresholds. In the case of claims for non-pecuniary loss the threshold is crossed where the claimant has sustained either a 'permanent serious disfigurement' or a 'permanent impairment of an important physical, mental or psychological function'.[38] Regulations further provide how the claimant must meet the threshold's evidential requirements.[39] The policy behind the legislation was recognised as limiting rights to sue in return for greater no-fault benefits, and to limit the number of automobile related personal injury suits coming before the courts.[40] In effect, the legislation eliminates claims for non-pecuniary loss that are worth less than $30,000.[41]

Alberta also has a threshold no-fault auto-insurance scheme and has enacted a cap on damages for non-pecuniary loss as a result of minor automobile injuries. Minor injuries cover sprains, strains and grade one or two whiplash that do not result in serious impairment.[42] The cap is currently $4,777 ($4,000 adjusted for inflation). A similar provision prevails in Nova Scotia in that it describes 'minor injury' and, if the claimant's injury as a result of an

[35] Above (n 20).

[36] See Finch CJBC's articulation of this position in *Dilello v Montgomery* 2005 BCCA 56.

[37] In contrast, most Australian states have moved to a statutory graduated indexing system, which gives a percentage of a maximum permissible award depending upon severity of the injury. In the United Kingdom, the English Judicial Studies Board publishes guidelines to assist the judiciary. Discussed in Berryman (n 16) 194.

[38] Insurance Act RSO 1990, c I.8 s 267.5(5)(a) and (b).

[39] Ontario Regulation 461/96.

[40] *Meyer v Bright* (1993) 15 OR (3d) 129 (CA).

[41] This is the effect of the deductible contained in Ontario Regulation 461/96 s 5.1 and Insurance Act s 267.5(7). However, if the amount awarded is above $100,000, the deductible is not deducted.

[42] Minor Injury Regulation, Albta Reg 123/2004. The limit is currently set at $4,777. The impact of these provisions was upheld as being constitutional and not violating the Charter in *Morrow v Zhang* 2009 ABCA 215.

automobile accident falls within that definition, they are restricted to an award of $2,500.[43] New Brunswick, Nova Scotia and Prince Edward Island also have a base level of no-fault benefits and maintain access to tort liability above those thresholds. However, in an attempt to rid the system of smaller claims they have imposed a limit on what is recoverable for non-pecuniary loss if the injury falls within the statutory definitions of a 'minor injury', which normally covers strains, sprains and whiplash.[44]

In contrast, Manitoba has a true no-fault auto-insurance scheme and has taken the step of providing a cap of $100,000 on claims for permanent physical or mental impairment and $215,000 on claims for permanent physical or mental impairment of a catastrophic injury.[45] The scheme creates a scale upon which to measure the percentage of impairment.[46]

Saskatchewan has introduced both a no-fault and fault-based auto-insurance scheme, allowing the individual insured to decide under what scheme they wish to insure the risk of automobile accidents. Under the no-fault scheme there is a distinction between permanent impairment and permanent impairment as a result of a catastrophic injury. A similar approach to that of Manitoba is used to determine a percentage of impairment. The current upper limits are $185,266 and $226,277 respectively.[47] If the insured selects the tort-based scheme there are still a number of no-fault benefits which give compensation for permanent injuries of $12,639 and catastrophic injuries $164,313. If you sue for pain and suffering, a $5,000 deductible applies to the claim.[48] As of December 2013, only 6,294 clients had opted for the tort-based scheme as against 1,134,724 clients who had opted for the full no-fault scheme.[49] These figures may well suggest that as citizens we do not place a high value on being able to recover damages for non-pecuniary loss and that the higher benefit levels under full no-fault are sufficiently attractive as against receipt of minimal no-fault benefits which then risk resort to tort action. Under the scheme, the insurance premium levels do not change, only the forms of benefits provided.

Newfoundland simply includes a deductible of $2,500 on any claim for non-pecuniary loss as a result of an automobile accident.[50]

Workers' Compensation Schemes

In contrast to automobile insurance, provincial workers' compensation schemes, which operate on a no-fault basis throughout Canada, offer a range of rates. For example, in Ontario, the amount is described as a 'non-economic loss benefit' and ranges between

[43] Insurance Act RSNS, c 231, s 113B. This provision has also withstood constitutional challenge. *Hartling v Nova Scotia (Attorney General)* 2009 NSCA 130.

[44] In Nova Scotia the limit is set at $7,956—Automobile Accident Minor Injury Regulation NS Reg 94/2010; New Brunswick the limit is set at $7,500—Injury Regulation NB Reg 2003-20.

[45] Manitoba Public Insurance Corporation Act CCSM c P215, s 127(a) and (b).

[46] Permanent Impairments (Universal Bodily Injury Compensation) Regulation, Man Reg 41/94.

[47] Saskatchewan Government Insurance, *Your Guide to No-Fault Coverage* (2014): www.sgi.sk.ca/pdf/guide_nofault_2014.pdf.

[48] Saskatchewan Government Insurance, *Your Guide to Tort Coverage* (2014): www.sgi.sk.ca/pdf/guide_tort_2014.pdf.

[49] Figures supplied to the author by the Saskatchewan Government Insurance Corporation (April 2014).

[50] Automobile Insurance Act RSNL 1990, c A-22, s 39.1; Automobile Insurance Regulations NRL 81/04.

$82,432 (25-year-old—2011 base year) and $31,705 (65-year-old—2011 base year) depending upon the percentage degree of permanent impairment.[51] In Alberta, a lump sum 'non-economic loss payment' is paid depending upon degree of permanent impairment with a maximum of $86,588 (2014). There are similar benefit levels in New Brunswick (maximum $59,500—2013), Saskatchewan ($45,200),[52] Manitoba ($117,700)[53] and Nova Scotia (permanent impairment benefit as a percentage of net average earnings).

Court Awarded Tort Law, Beyond Personal Injuries, for Non-Pecuniary Losses

Recall, under the heading of 'paramountcy', that Dickson J premised his adoption of the functional approach on the fact that the Court was also changing the quantification of pecuniary damages for lost earning capacity and future care costs to truly reflect the real cost of the losses that would be incurred by the claimant. Genuine levels of compensation under the latter justified constraining the former to reflect the social policy desire to avoid excessive damage awards for non-pecuniary losses and the feared consequential raise in insurance rates.

However, not all claims for non-pecuniary losses arise out of personal injury suits or are parasitic on recovery of pecuniary damages for lost earning capacity or future care costs. In such cases, should the same approach to non-pecuniary damages from the Trilogy be adopted? The Supreme Court of Canada has definitively answered this question in the negative on a number of occasions.

For an academic audience, the tale of *Young v Bella*[54] has a poignant message about the evils of plagiarism as well as civil suits. Young was enrolled as a long distance student at Memorial University with hope of eventually getting into the university's social work programme, which was a restricted entry programme. The plaintiff registered for a social work course and wrote an essay for Professor Bella. In that essay the student appended a first-hand account of a person being sexually abused as a child and with the comment that sexual abusers were usually people who had themselves been sexually abused as a child. The account was actually plagiarised from a course book that was included in the bibliography but with no reference to the specific first-hand account. When received by Professor Bella, she took this as being a first-hand account of the student, and thus thought she should inform the head of the department as well as the Child Protection Services (CPS). This set in chain a series of events where the truth of the offending material was never discovered until some two years later when the plaintiff was finally questioned by a CPS worker. In the

[51] Ontario Workplace Safety and Insurance Board: www.wsib.on.ca/en/community/WSIB/230/ArticleDetail/24338?vgnextoid=bb7e16ac58b33310VgnVCM100000469c710aRCRD.

[52] Taken from the benefit summary provided by the Association of Workers' Compensation Boards of Canada, *Permanent Disability Awards and Escalation Benefits—Summary* (2013): awcbc.org/wp-content/uploads/2013/12/Permanent_Disability.pdf.

[53] Interestingly, the Manitoba guide specifically states that the award is for permanent impairment and that the scheme does not compensate for pain and suffering: awcbc.org/wp-content/uploads/2013/12/Permanent_Disability.pdf.

[54] *Young v Bella* [2006] 1 SCR 108.

intervening time, the plaintiff's name was bandied about by some of the university staff, the CPS and other social workers as a possible sex abuser, and her name entered on a child sex abuser registry. In addition, the plaintiff did not get into the social work programme. As a result, her employment prospects were affected and she suffered non-pecuniary loss.

The plaintiff brought an action in negligence alleging that Bella and the university were obligated to exercise reasonable care when discharging their duty under the Child Welfare Act to report information about potential child sexual abuse. Bella had acted on conjecture and speculation, which fell short of the required 'reasonable cause' to make a report to CPS.

The jury awarded $839,000 damages made up of $314,000 and $47,000 for past and future lost wages, as well as $430,000 general non-pecuniary damages. The evidence on damages was unchallenged and had been submitted by the plaintiff's expert who had factored in various contingencies to the calculations. The Supreme Court held that the jury was entitled to have these awards respected, although the Court was of the view that, if tried *de novo*, they would not have awarded these amounts. Thus, the Court deferred to the jury's decision indicating that the test for appellate review had not been met. The defendant argued that the amount for non-pecuniary damages should respect the capped award of this type of damages in personal injury. The Supreme Court did not accept this argument, noting that a similar argument had been rejected in *Hill v Church of Scientology*,[55] a defamation case that awarded $300,000 general damages, $500,000 aggravated damages and $800,000 punitive damages. In the area of personal injury, there was a trade-off between appropriate pecuniary compensation, the adoption of the functional test and the remaining need for non-pecuniary damages, which justified as a policy decision a cap on the award. This case did not raise the same trade-off. However, the Court did indicate that the possibility of a cap in such a case before it may need to be argued in the future when the proper case and argument is before the Court.

Cases based upon sexual assault raise conflicting authority on whether the cap should apply to non-pecuniary damages. The British Columbia Court of Appeal has held that in cases based upon 'intentional torts involving criminal behaviour' the cap does not apply. The Court reasoned that the same policy reasons do not animate these particular torts because there is no 'need to protect the general public from a serious social burden, such as enormous insurance premiums'.[56] Of course, some of these claims are used to support a vicarious liability claim against an employer, often government, in which case the public purse would be engaged.[57] In other provincial jurisdictions the cap has been applied to intentional torts. The decision of the Nova Scotia Court of Appeal in *BMG v Nova Scotia (Attorney General)*[58] is often cited in this regard. Cromwell J indicated that the nature of sexual battery cases, where the non-pecuniary damages are often designed to vindicate the victim's right of autonomy and dignity, as well as bodily integrity (pain and suffering, loss of enjoyment in life), lend themselves to a functional approach and how such damages can

[55] *Hill v Church of Scientology* [1995] 2 SCR 1130. Also followed in *Botiuk v Toronto Free Press* [1995] 3 SCR 3, [106].

[56] *SY v FGC* (1996) 26 BCLR (3d) 155 (CA) [30]. This statement from the Court was specifically endorsed by the Supreme Court of Canada in *Young v Bella* (n 54) [65]. Followed in *CCB (Litigation Guardian of) v IB* 2009 BCSC 1425, [54].

[57] For vicarious liability for intentional tortious conduct, see *Bazley v Curry* [1999] 2 SCR 534.

[58] *BMG v Nova Scotia (Attorney General)* (2006) NSR (2d) 257 (CA).

be used to provide solace.[59] However, he then went on promptly to identify an acceptable range of damages, somewhere between $125,000 and $250,000.[60]

Commentary

Defining what constitutes a non-pecuniary loss is fraught with difficulty. Even within the area of recovery under tort law for personal injury there are difficulties in classification. For example, Canadian courts have accepted that loss of homemaking services is a pecuniary loss; one that is to be quantified by reviewing the catalogue of services provided, and then determining the substitute homemaker costs for those services.[61] However, courts have also recognised that for some homemaking is a locale of enjoyment and thus falls within a claim for non-pecuniary loss under the heading, loss of enjoyment. Having recognised that activities that fall outside the paid economy have real pecuniary value, and thus are entitled to compensation, this invites courts to determine how matters like gardening, participation in hobbies and other civic minded duties such as coaching a sports team, should be treated for compensation purposes, pecuniary or non-pecuniary.[62] If the latter, they become affected by the cap.

The three orthodox heads, loss of expectation in life, pain and suffering and loss of amenities, have been accepted in Canada as heads of recovery for personal injury suits. However, these heads do not define the complete range of non-pecuniary loss recoverable in tort law and, even within these heads, there are obvious gradations of loss and crossovers into pecuniary damages. For example, as mentioned earlier, if we consider pain and suffering, the sensate experience is highly subjective but, with increasing medical developments, is capable of quite sophisticated management with the intervention of an interdisciplinary team of specialists. Thus, pain can be compensated as a pecuniary loss under future care costs.

[59] Ibid, [132]. Cromwell J cited, [134], the Supreme Court of Canada's decision in *Blackwater v Plint* [2005] 3 SCR 3, [89] on factors approved by the Supreme Court to assist in quantifying non-pecuniary damages in sexual assault cases.

[60] In Ontario, the Court of Appeal assumed the cap would apply, see *B(M) v 2014052* (2012) OR (3d) 351 (CA) [77]. In Alberta the Court applied the cap in the case of incest, *Ms R v Mr W* 2003 ABQB 50. In a careful judgment Veit J suggested that any analogy made to *Hill v Church of Scientology* (n 55) and the defamation context was quite misplaced in the situation of sexual assault. In defamation proceedings, the claim is not usually accompanied by a claim for pecuniary damages for lost income, or where any pecuniary damages are capable of easy proof, or where there is any pressing social need to establish predictability of the damage award. All these considerations are present in sexual assault cases. In *AT-B v Mah* (n 24) [550] the Court applied a cap but questioned whether it should be applied in cases involving the intentional infliction of harm. Interestingly, the cap has not been applied in Ontario to claims made pursuant of the Family Law Act for loss of 'care, guidance, and companionship' experienced by a family member upon the death or personal injury of a family member. The claim for care, guidance, and companionship under the Act is generally thought of as paralleling a non-pecuniary loss claim in personal injury suits. See *Fiddler v Chiavetti* (2010) 317 DLR (4th) 385 (Ont CA) [76]. However, the Court went on to create its own range of damages for such loss, and at a lower level, describing $100,000 (in 2001) as the upper level.

[61] *Fobel v Dean* (1991) 83 DLR (4th) 385 (Sask CA), leave to appeal to SCC denied (1992) 87 DLR (4th) vii (note).

[62] Discussed in *Kroeker v Jansen* (1995) 4 BCLR (3d) 178 (CA); *McTavish v MacGillivray* (2000) 74 BCLR (3d) 281 (CA) and recently applied in *Reynolds v Sanghera & Sons Trucking Ltd* 2014 BCSC 212.

A classificatory range of non-pecuniary loss would include the following:

1. Pain and suffering (both sensate and insensate).
2. Loss of amenities in life.
3. Loss of expectation in life.
4. Psychiatric damage.
5. Physical inconvenience and discomfort.
6. Mental and emotional distress.
7. Loss of enjoyment including feelings of disappointment
8. Loss of reputation, including loss of dignity (moral damages).[63]

As discussed above, the first three form the bread and butter of personal injury suits and where the loss is associated with an actual physical injury. The fourth is usually capable of medical diagnosis. Before recovery, Canadian courts have insisted that the level of psychiatric damage should cross some threshold of seriousness to eliminate distress and upset that flows from the vicissitudes of life.[64] The losses under (5), (6) and (7) are of a more transient nature, but are still recoverable as evident in *Young v Bella*,[65] although parasitic on some other pecuniary loss accompanying the claim. Losses under (8) that flow from defamation are 'at large', while damages for loss of dignity and moral damages are far more modest.

Beyond the tort system, comparisons with other compensation schemes also present challenges. For example, as noted above, Manitoba's workers' compensation board specifically states that it does not provide compensation for 'pain and suffering' when making a lump sum payment for permanent impairment, and other schemes simply describe the parameters of the payment as a 'non-economic loss benefit'. Another point of departure is the function served by the damages award. In a personal injury suit the function is compensation, as with lump sum awards under workers' compensation and automobile insurance. However, the damages awarded for non-pecuniary loss in other tort actions admit to a number of other functions. Thus, in the suits for past sexual assault there are elements of vindication and punishment being pursued with compensation.[66] Nevertheless, there are at least two common threads across compensation schemes. One, the claims are incommensurate, there being no market for the type of loss that is being compensated. Two, the claim is personal, subjectively experienced and defy accurate measurement.

The issue of incommensurability has usually driven those who have systematically studied compensation systems to suggest there is negligible reason to make such awards for non-pecuniary losses. Thus, the father of New Zealand's no-fault accident compensation scheme, the late Justice Sir Owen Woodhouse, saw no reason to make such an award in his original report (it called for compensation for pecuniary loss alone) and, again, when asked to review the scheme by the New Zealand Government in 1988, recommended their abolition and the

[63] 'Moral damages' is a term now used to describe the non-pecuniary loss that flows from egregious termination of employment, *Honda Canada Inc v Keays* [2008] 2 SCR 342, [59] and for the tort of intrusion upon seclusion, *Jones v Tsige* (2012) 108 OR (3d) 241, [75].

[64] See *Mustapha v Culligan of Canada Ltd* [2008] 2 SCR 114; and *Healey v Lakeridge Health Corp* (2011) 103 OR (3d) 401 (CA), [65].

[65] Above (n 54). These types of losses are also compensable in contract actions, but where the awards are much more modest. See *Sun Life Assurance Co v Fidler* [2006] 2 SCR 3.

[66] See, eg, the comments of Cromwell J in *BMG v Nova Scotia (Attorney General)* (n 58).

funds used to expand coverage of the scheme to cover sickness.[67] The Ontario Law Reform Commission adopted a similar position,[68] although contradicted itself in a later report on *Compensation for Personal Injuries and Death* where it recommended retention of the then current law.[69]

On the other hand, recognition has also been given to the fact that elements of the loss generating non-pecuniary damages are genuinely experienced by claimants and thus justify an award, even if it defies accurate assessment. This was the approach adopted by the Pearson Commission, which would have abolished compensation for the 'loss of expectation of life' element, but otherwise retain non-pecuniary damages, but, subject to a threshold (no award for the first three months of injury) to eliminate minor and transient claims.[70] In a later report by the UK Law Commission, they recommended retention of non-pecuniary damages and in fact an increase in the levels of damages awarded. This was largely supported on the ground that the public expected such damages to be paid; that they compensated for a real loss experienced by claimants; and, that abolition could be potentially discriminatory on those citizens who do not experience high levels of income replacement compensation.[71] Subsequently, the English courts heeded the advice and arbitrarily increased the levels of compensation.[72] Incidentally, the UK Law Commission specifically declined to adopt Canada's functional approach, arguing that it imposed an unreasonable evidential burden on claimants, failed to cover all the range of losses covered by non-pecuniary damages, and was inimical to the creation of a tariff structure.[73]

For Canada, the time has come to recognise that we do not apply a functional approach to non-pecuniary damages in personal injury suits. Rather, we apply a modified 'conceptual approach' that links payment to a range of damages that depends upon the severity of the loss of bodily faculty and function. This approach is modified to accommodate 'personal' factors that result in increased levels of payment as in, for example, where an avid musician loses the ability to play his or her instrument as a result of the injury. This recognition can only come from the Supreme Court of Canada, which so far has entrenched the functional approach, or provincial legislation.

Once we accept that we are applying a modified conceptual approach we can move to a better way to ensure a fair and reasonable consistency across the country. How will that be shaped?

The Pearson Commission recommended that damages for loss of expectation of life should be abolished; which was adopted by the UK Parliament.[74] The Commission drew support from Ontario, which it asserted had abolished damages for loss of expectation of life as a separate head of damages. This is somewhat inaccurate. Ontario abolished the claim for loss of expectation of life with respect to survivorship claims by the deceased estate[75]

[67] New Zealand Law Commission, *Personal Injury: Prevention and Recovery* (Wellington, NZLC R4, 1988) para 174.

[68] Ontario Law Reform Commission (OLRC), *Report on Motor Vehicle Accident Compensation* (1973).

[69] OLRC, Report on Compensation for Personal Injuries and Death (1987) 105.

[70] Royal Commission on Civil Liability and Compensation for Personal Injury 1978, vol 1, para 359 et seq (Pearson Commission).

[71] Law Commission, *Damages for Personal Injury: Non-Pecuniary Loss* (Law Com No 257, 1999) paras 2.3 and 3.40.

[72] *Heil v Rankin* [2000] EWCA Civ 84, [2001] QB 272 (CA).

[73] Law Commission, *Damages for Personal Injury* (n 71) para 2.5.

[74] Pearson Commission (n 70) para 372. Administration of Justice Act (UK) 1982, s 1(1)(a).

[75] See Trustee Act RSO 1990, c T.23, s 38(1).

but, as *Arnold v Teno*,[76] one of the Trilogy cases on appeal from Ontario attests, such a claim is still part of the claim for damages for non-pecuniary loss in Ontario. Nevertheless, there is merit in the argument that non-pecuniary damages for the actual expected loss in life expectation should not be granted on the grounds that they serve no function whatsoever. This is to be distinguished from the feelings generated by the thought of a loss in expectation of life, and which is part of the claim for pain and suffering and loss of amenities.[77]

If we accept that the majority of the non-pecuniary damages claim is to compensate loss of amenities and pain and suffering, how is that to be quantified? I have already suggested that we should be careful about sensate losses, and for which we may be able to do much more with medical developments in pain management. Nevertheless, we will be left with a core of insensate losses for which we can describe, rationally understand as likely to occur, and empathise with the claimant, albeit recognising that the loss is still incommensurable. Here, the majority of workers' compensation, and some no-fault auto-insurance, schemes use a highly structured conceptual approach, using a scale to measure the degree of permanent impairment or catastrophic injury and applying a cap on the maximum award. Under the schemes I have reviewed, the damage caps applied in workers' compensation do not exceed $120,000; and under true no-fault automobile insurance, do not exceed $226,000. As mentioned earlier, the current cap under the present tort run scheme is around $325,000. This suggests that the current cap under the civil litigation process is too high by a factor of a third, although, as indicated earlier, it is in line with comparable awards made in the United Kingdom and Australia. Here again, any change would have to come from the Supreme Court of Canada, which was responsible for imposing the cap in the first place.

While it would be impossible to create a formal impairment scale as adopted under workers' compensation without legislation, open adoption of a conceptual approach could better focus the acceptable range of damages upon which to determine any particular damages award.[78] Juries should be instructed on the range and the policy reasons for the imposition of the cap. The valuable check performed by the jury is to **validate the policy arguments**, and decide what level of damages is commensurate with those arguments. It can only perpetuate inconsistency if juries are informed of the cap where their award will likely attain it, but decide in ignorance of the policy when they are not.

Recall that the policy argument for imposing the cap was the fear of excessive insurance claims driving up insurance rates. Most studies on the current tort litigation scheme for personal injuries have concluded that a significant cost driver in terms of insurance rates is not at the top level of awards, but at the lower level of smaller claims for non-pecuniary loss, hence the move to control minor injury claims under the compulsory auto-insurance schemes, and which rids the civil litigation scheme of these particular claims. By using a definition of minor injury (eg, Alberta and Nova Scotia) this is, in effect, a partial adoption of a conceptual approach using an injury rated scale system; but with only one defined level on the scale. Ontario achieves a similar result by a deductible of the first $30,000 in any claim that goes before a court where the threshold is crossed in auto-insurance claims.

[76] Above (n 3).

[77] The UK Administration of Justice Act, s 1(1)(b) specifically keeps this aspect of damages alive.

[78] I have suggested elsewhere that better statistics are need in Canada to operationalise a conceptual approach and that Canada could learn from the UK in this regard, Berryman (n 16).

One final argument on why we should be concerned with the levels of compensation for non-pecuniary loss in personal injury suits arises from the emerging research on the psychology of happiness or 'hedonic psychology'. This research is important because it addresses the fundamental issue of how injuries that generate claims for many non-pecuniary losses are actually experienced.

The study of hedonic psychology is still in its infancy.[79] In 1999 the celebrated Nobel economist, Daniel Kahneman, published a collection of essays on 'Well-Being'.[80] Kahneman's essay detailed what happiness is, and how it can be objectively measured. A central point of this research is survey tools that measure an individual's level of happiness with life (life satisfaction),[81] and one of the largest longitudinal surveys measuring happiness is that known as the British Household Panel Survey.[82] There is much to be done in the research on happiness, but three identifiable phenomena should be closely watched and may already justify some judicial attention. The first is the issue of 'focusing' or the 'focusing illusion'. Cass Sunstein has written on this phenomenon.[83] It describes the notion that if our attention is drawn to a particular facet of loss we will elevate its importance to our overall happiness, where, if not fixated, we would say that the particular facet plays little importance to our overall happiness. Studies support this notion,[84] which may have a bearing on how we instruct juries and how people negotiate settlements.[85]

A second phenomenon is the notion of 'resilience'. We all know of the miraculous healing powers of the physical body over time; it should then come as no surprise that the psychic body exhibits similar recuperative powers. Resilience is the phenomenon of the ability of an injured party to 'bounce back', and to record similar levels of happiness after a period of recuperation.[86] Similarly, just as we know that exercise and good health

[79] A very good introduction for legal scholars and jurists is provided by C Essert, 'Tort and Happiness' (2010) 36 *Queen's Law Journal* 1, although I disagree with his conclusion. Essert's argument may support a continuation of tort awards for hedonic loss but that is a different question from how they should be evaluated and quantified, which I address.

[80] D Kahneman, E Diener and N Schwarz eds, *Well-Being: The Foundations of Hedonic Psychology* (New York, Russell Sage Foundation, 1999). At p ix, hedonic psychology is described as 'the study of what makes experiences and life pleasant and unpleasant. It is concerned with feelings of pleasure and pain, of interest and boredom, of joy and sorrow, and of satisfaction and dissatisfaction. It is also concerned with the whole range of circumstances, from the biological to the societal, that occasion suffering and enjoyment'.

[81] For an overview see P Huang, 'Happiness Studies and Legal Policy' (2010) *Annual Review of Law and Social Science* 405.

[82] The survey, results and publications are available at www.iser.essex.ac.uk/bhps.

[83] C Sunstein, 'Illusory Losses' (2008) 37 *Journal of Legal Studies* S157.

[84] D Schkade and D Kahneman, 'Does Living in California Make People Happy? A Focusing Illusion in Judgments of Life Satisfaction' (1998) 9 *Psychological Science* 340; D Kahneman, A Krueger, D Shakade, N Schwarz and A Stone, 'Would You Be Happier If You Were Richer? A Focusing Illusion' (2006) 312 *Science* 19008; D Smith, N Schwarz, T Roberts and P Ubel, 'Why Are You Calling Me? How Study Introductions Change Response Patterns' (2006) 15 *Quality of Life Research* 621.

[85] J Bronsteen, C Buccafusco and J Lasur, 'Adaptation and the Settlement of Civil Lawsuits' (2008) 108 *Columbia Law Review* 1516, particularly 1532.

[86] D Dunn, G Uswatte and T Elliott, 'Happiness, Resilience, and Positive Growth Following Physical Disability: Issues for Understanding, Research, and Therapeutic Intervention' in S Lopez and C Snyder (eds), *Oxford Handbook of Positive Psychology*, 2nd edn (Oxford, Oxford University Press, 2009) ch 62; G Bonanno, 'Loss, Trauma, and Human Resilience: Have We Underestimated the Human Capacity to Thrive After Extremely Aversive Events?' (2004) 59 *American Psychologist* 20.

can moderate physical bodily injury, we can also build capacity to heal the psychic body, particularly in creating personal and community relationships. This is not to gild the lily and suggest that the loss disappears, but it does suggest that our obvious empathy with a person who has experienced traumatic loss may justifiably be tempered when we come to quantify the non-pecuniary damages claim.

A third phenomenon is the notion of 'adaptation'. Adaptation describes the ability of the psychic body to find alternative avenues in pursuit of happiness and wellbeing. Many studies support the notion that following a life changing event leaving some permanent impairment that, after an initial drop in happiness, people do adapt and return to record similar, although not identical, levels of happiness because they have found new ways to make life meaningful and fulfilling.[87] This phenomenon must give us pause to rethink our approach to non-pecuniary loss; certainly, Sunstein draws this conclusion.[88] However, Sunstein also suggests that we need to realise, that what is termed as a 'capability', is lost, and which is separate from any form of compensation for loss of happiness. Thus, it may well be shown that a person who loses a leg may not suffer any long-term decline in happiness; nevertheless, he has lost a capability that reduces options available to achieve a satisfying life, and that holds value to the individual.[89] Sunstein suggests that American courts may wish to move towards civil damages guidelines drawing an analogy to workers' compensation to avoid jury error and mistakes.[90] I share those sentiments and see explicit recognition given to a modified conceptual approach as a way towards establishing appropriate guidelines.

One last observation in the Canadian context concerns the temptation to compare non-pecuniary damages flowing from personal injuries with other tort actions. As discussed above, this has led to sporadic attacks on the cap and arguments to lift it, or to apply it in non-personal injury actions. What needs clarification is the function being performed by the damages award. In personal injury actions the non-pecuniary damages are kept within the compensation function of civil damages. In other tort settings, often the damages awarded under the rubric of non-pecuniary damages are to satisfy other functions, namely vindication, deterrence and punishment. There is no problem in a damages award performing multiple functions, but we should recognise the occurrence when making comparisons.

[87] A Oswald and N Powdthavee, 'Does Happiness Adapt? A Longitudinal Study of Disability with Implications for Economists and Judges' (2008) 92 *Journal of Public Economics* 1061; Bronsteen, Buccafusco and Lasur (n 85) particularly 1527. But *cf* Richard Lucas, 'Long-term Disability Is Associated With Lasting Changes in Substantive Well-Being: Evidence From Two Nationally Representative Longitudinal Studies' (2007) 92 *Journal of Personality and Social Psychology* 717.

[88] Sunstein (n 83) S182.

[89] Ibid. The notion of a capability loss is supported by research on persons who have had a colonoscopy or require dialysis treatment later in life. These studies show that patients do not show a decline in life satisfaction, nevertheless, if asked what they would give up not to have to live with a colostomy bag or ongoing dialysis, the invariable answer is an appreciable amount. See G Loewenstein and P Ubel, 'Hedonic Adaptation and the Role of Decision and Experience Utility in Public Policy' (2008) 92 *Journal of Public Economics* 1795, particularly 1799.

[90] Sunstein (n 83) S184.

Conclusion

Dickson J was correct to impose a cap on damages for non-pecuniary loss arising from personal injuries, and the choice of $100,000 may not have been far from the mark. Dickson J was also correct to make the link between this form of damages award and the social cost to society as evident in insurance rates and subsequent developments in auto-insurance coverage for personal injury.[91] At the time of Dickson J's judgment the fear was of excessive awards. Subsequent developments suggest that it is the heightened frequency of lower level awards, particularly of non-pecuniary losses, that now generate concern over an insurance crisis. Canadian provincial legislatures have demonstrated a willingness to legislate in this area to cap or limit such awards for workers' compensation and automobile accident claims. For claims that do proceed to court and jury adjudication, I have argued that Canada has not developed a sufficient jurisprudence that would achieve the goal of consistency. I have also argued that the cap is probably too high. Like Patrick Atiyah,[92] and others,[93] I have abandoned all hope of seeing meaningful reform in Canada towards a true comprehensive no-fault scheme, despite its obvious merits.[94] Nevertheless, there is still scope for incremental change. Three developments may influence that development; one, the realisation that we have already adopted a de facto modified conceptual approach; two, changes in both workers' compensation and auto-insurance across the country have widened the gap between compensation treatment for like injuries; and three, new studies and research on how non-pecuniary losses are experienced show that these losses may not be as devastating as currently believed.

[91] A recent report of the Ontario Financial Services Commission to the Standing Committee on Finance and Economic Affairs of the Ontario Legislature makes abundantly clear the correlation between changes in legislation and insurance rates concerning automobile insurance. Report published 9 July 2012 and available at: www.fsco.gov.on.ca/en/auto/Documents/submission-SCFEA.pdf.

[92] PS Atiyah, *The Damages Lottery* (Oxford, Hart Publishing, 1997).

[93] S Sugarman, 'Tort Reform Through Damages Law Reform: An American Perspective' (2005) 27 *Sydney Law Review* 507.

[94] G Palmer, 'New Zealand's Accident Compensation Scheme: Twenty Years On' (1994) 44 *University of Toronto Law Review* 223, 227. In 1988, the New Zealand Law Commission report, *Personal Injury: Prevention and Recovery: Report on the Accident Compensation Scheme* (1988) para 75 stated that the cost per New Zealander for comprehensive coverage was 60 cents per day (NZ$1.02 at today's value).

6

Identifying and Calculating Personal Injury Damages in Ireland, Italy, France and Belgium: Recent Debates between Scholars, Judges and Practitioners

DENISE AMRAM

Introduction

Personal injuries claims are one of the most common forms of litigation: in 2011, for example, the Irish Injuries Board made, according to its annual report,[1] more than 9,800 awards in a country of approximately 4.6 million inhabitants; in 2012, the Italian Institute of Statistics reported that there were 264,716 victims of personal injury damages caused by car accidents in a country of approximately 60 million inhabitants.[2]

The evaluation of personal injury damages is often unpredictable as it is difficult to objectively quantify all the non-pecuniary components of the damage. Moreover, many European systems, like the French, the Italian and Irish include several heads of damages relating to either pecuniary or non-pecuniary losses (physical damage, psychological damage, loss of amenity, special damages, aesthetic damage, health expenses etc).

Homogeneous treatment and certainty are the two main emerging needs in the national debates on such matters. Nevertheless, comparing the awards compensated for similar injuries it seems that the criteria adopted in the given systems are evidence of discrimination between European citizens in their fundamental rights protection, since, for example, a French victim may claim for aesthetic damage as a *quid pluris* with respect to pain and suffering, but an Italian victim suffering the same injury may not.

This analysis aims at finding the best solutions to solving issues relating to the identification and calculation of personal injuries damages through a comparative analysis. The choice to

[1] www.injuriesboard.ie. The Board deals with claims where only the value of damages is in dispute. Just over 16,000 new cases were filed in the courts in the same year, see www.courts.ie/; there is likely to be some overlap between the figures, as some cases before the Injuries Board proceed to court.

[2] www.istat.it, Report, 6 November 2013.

compare France, Belgium, Ireland and Italy is due to the praxis developed in recent years: all of them share the necessity to increase the dialogue between practitioners, judges and scholars in order to solve those interpretative issues in personal injuries damages, arising from the existing gap between legislation and law in action.

Analogies and differences between the systems mentioned, emerging from the juxtaposition of the different experiences, will help to identify an assessment of the different tools used to collect and deliver data in order to identify the most efficient formula able to solve the most controversial legal issues arising from the praxis.

In the countries analysed in this chapter, the dialogue between legal formants (scholars, judges and legislators) allowed the elaboration of the French *Barèmes* (charts), the Italian charts and the Irish Book of Quantum to give the interpreter a useful tool to calculate the awards on the basis of their precedents. This phenomenon is really interesting from a theoretical point of view, because it created new equilibriums between the courts and the legislator in civil law tradition systems. For example, in Italy judicial reasoning on personal injury damages comes before legal definitions, while the so-called *Rapport Dintilhac* aimed at reorganising heads of damages is still not binding for French courts.

The chapter first aims at finding out whether 'nominal' distinctions of heads of damages really affect awards (and thus victims' fundamental rights protection) in Ireland, France, Belgium and Italy. Then, it will analyse the approaches to the calculation of non-pecuniary losses in order to find out analogies and differences in the given systems. From the comparison, methodological remarks will lead me to propose the implementation of databases in order to share models and criteria for a more harmonised compensation system in Europe.

Heads of Damages

Difficulties in the identification of different heads of damages are a common issue among the legal systems considered. In order to better understand the terms of comparison, in the next pages we will illustrate the main features of the foreign personal injuries compensation paradigms.

France

As is known, the principle of integral compensation of damages constitutes the main compass of the French tort law rules included in the Napoleonic Civil Code, aiming at compensating '*tout le dommage et rien que le dommage*' (all the damage, and nothing but the damage).[3] However, in case of personal injury damages, its application is often controversial, stimulating both scientific and legislative debates.[4] The necessity to provide a

[3] T Terré, Ph Simpler andt Y Lequette, *Droit Civil, les Obligations*, 10th edn, Collection Précis (Paris, Dalloz, 2009) fn 899; Ch Coutans-Lapalus, *Le Principe de la Réparation Intégrale en Droit Privé* (Aix Marseille, PU, 2002); F Leduc and Ph Pierre (eds), *La Réparation Intégrale en Europe. Etude Comparative des Droits Nationaux* (Bruxelles, Larcier, 2012).

[4] J Flour, JL Aubert and E Savaux, *Droit Civil, Les Obligations* (Paris, Dalloz, 2006) fn 388; H Groutel, 'Réparation Intégrale et Barémisation: L'éternelle Dispute' (2006) *Responsabilité Civile et Assurances* Rep 11.

proper classification of the heads of damages that can be compensated under the mentioned principle is an open issue.

Today, none of the damages classifications—introduced through several reports (*recte rapports*) and elaborated by many scientific committees—have been formally adopted by the French legislator.[5] The most well-known is the *Rapport Dintilhac* (2005),[6] which classified 29 heads of damages, distinguishing first by the effect on the victim (direct or indirect), then by the nature of loss (economic or non-pecuniary) and then by the duration of the sufferance (temporary or permanent).

Even if the proposed classification resulted in real clarity, since it defines unequivocally all the heads of damages, it presents some asymmetric elements, such as the fact that the *préjudice d'agrément*[7] (loss of amenity) as well as the *préjudice sexuel*[8] (sexual impairment) cannot be temporary.

As mentioned, the *Dintilhac* classification never entered into force, even though the French High Court has often referred to and applied its definitions.[9] This is the case, for example, of the *préjudice d'agrément* (loss of amenity),[10] where the Court used definitions given in the *Rapport Dintilhac* to award compensation:

> Attendu que pour l'indemnisation du *préjudice corporel* (emphasis added), la réparation des postes de préjudice dénommés *déficit fonctionnel temporaire* et *déficit fonctionnel permanent* (emphasis added) inclut, le premier, pour la période antérieure à la date de consolidation, ***l'incapacité fonctionnelle totale ou partielle*** (emphasis added) ainsi que le temps d'hospitalisation et les pertes de qualité de vie et des joies usuelles de la vie courante durant la maladie traumatique, le second, pour la période postérieure à cette date, les atteintes aux fonctions physiologiques, la perte de la qualité de vie et les troubles ressentis par la victime dans ses conditions d'existence personnelles, familiales et sociales; qu'il s'ensuit que la réparation d'un poste de préjudice personnel distinct dénommé *préjudice d'agrément* (emphasis added) vise exclusivement à l'indemnisation du préjudice lié à l'impossibilité pour la victime de pratiquer régulièrement une activité spécifique sportive ou de loisirs.

> (To award pain and suffering the heads of damages called temporary functional deficit and permanent functional deficit should be calculated. The first one includes the temporary functional deficit for the period prior to the date of the harm consolidation, the total or partial functional incapacity and the time of hospitalization, the loss of quality of life, and the usual enjoyment of daily life during the traumatic illness. After that date, the second one includes the violation of physiological functions, the loss of quality of life and the troubles experienced by the victim as a person, within the family and in society. As a consequence, to award a different personal injury called loss of amenity aims at exclusively compensating the harm associated with the inability of the victim to regularly practice a specific sport or leisure activity.)

[5] Rapport du Conseil National d'Aide aux Victimes sur l'Indemnisation du Dommage Corporel, June 2003 in www.gouv.fr; Proposition de Réforme du Médiateur de la République, 31 March 2003; Rapport Annuel du Médiateur, both in *La Documentation Française*, 2004.

[6] Rapport du groupe de travail chargé d'élaborer une nomenclature des préjudices corporels in *La Documentation Française*, 2005 and in www.justice.gouv.fr.

[7] The French Supreme Court covered the lack of a temporary head of damages for the loss of amenity by the judgment Cass, 3 June 2010, no 09-13246 in *Gazette du Palais*, 13–16 July 2011, commented by A Renelier.

[8] P Jourdain, *Nomenclature des préjudices corporels*, in B Dubuisson and P. Jourdain (eds), *Le dommage et sa reparation dans la responsabilité contractuelle et extracontractuelle,* (Bruylant: 2015) 567 ff.

[9] Ibid.

[10] Cass Civ, 28 May 2009, no 08-16829 (2009) *Dalloz* 1606, comments by I Gallmeister and (2009) *Revue Trimestrielle de Droit Civil* 534, comments by P Jourdain; Cass Civ, 4 November 2010, no 09-69918 (2011) *Responsabilité Civile et Assurances*, comm 5.

The same happened to the *préjudice sexuel* (sexual impairment),[11] *préjudice d'établissement* (literally loss of settlement),[12] *préjudices permanents exceptionnels* (exceptional permanent losses) etc.[13]

Indeed, in 2007 the Conseil d'Etat refused to apply the *nomenclature Dintilhac* to evaluate damages in the social security system reform[14] opting for the elaboration of a new classification of heads of damages to be used in administrative disputes.[15] The latter includes five heads of damages for economic losses and a generic one for non-pecuniary ones (*préjudices personnels*), whose all-inclusive feature seems to be in contrast with the same reform, which expressly stated the necessity to evaluate damages *poste par poste* (head of damages by head of damages).

Belgium

Personal injuries damages are also not classified by a statute in Belgium. Indeed, two groups of experts led by judges tried to collect case law in order to elaborate two classifications for personal injuries damages.

Since 2001 the Union National des Magistrats has elaborated six indicative charts,[16] while the Union Royale des Juges de Paix et de Police, composed of solicitors, judges, forensic scientists, and professionals from insurance companies have published two reports—in 2004 and in 2009.[17]

From these studies it emerged that the best criterion to classify damages in Belgium was on the basis of the protected right. From this perspective, we could identify three heads of damages: (i) economic and non-pecuniary losses for personal injuries (ie, pain and suffering); (ii) economic losses for damages to the goods (ie, expenses); and (iii) losses caused by the infringement of other rights and liberties (ie, honour, reputation etc).[18]

The Belgian Supreme Court confirmed that these classifications have just a persuasive efficacy and the courts are not obliged to use them. However, in the case of less serious losses, parameters used in the *Tableau indicatif* 2012 (indicative Chart 2012) perfectly match the substantive and procedural Belgian tort law system, since their application would dissipate the risk of arbitrariness that is a common feature in the assessment of minor damages:

> A cet égard, il s'indique de rappeler que le tableau indicatif, lequel ne doit être utilisé qu'à titre supplétif, ne constitue pas une norme contraignante mais bien un outil de référence destiné à éviter

[11] Cass Civ, 17 June 2010, no 09-15842 (2010) *Responsabilité Civile et Assurances*, comm 240 and (2010) *Revue Trimestrielle de Droit Civil* 562, comments by P Jourdain.

[12] Cass Civ, 12 May 2011, no 10-17148 (2012) *Dalloz* 47, comments by Ph Brun.

[13] Cass Civ, 15 December 2011, no 10-16386 (2012) *Responsabilité Civile et Assurances*, comm 52.

[14] Art 25 Loi no 2006-1640, 21 December 2006, Financement de la Sécurité Sociale Pour 2007, La Documentation Francaise.

[15] Cons d'Etat, Opinion, 4 June 2007, *Lagier*, no 303422, 304214 (2007) Semaine *Juridique* 1840, commented by G Vachet and in (2007) *Revue Trimestrielle de Droit Civil* 577, commented by P Jourdain.

[16] VV AA, Nouvelle Approche des Préjudices Corporels. Evolution! Révolution? Résolution (Liège, Anthémis, Editions du jeune barreau, 2009).

[17] VV AA, Le tableau indicatif 2012 in *Les Dossiers du journal des Juges et de Police* (Bruges, Die Keure, 2012).

[18] Ibid. See also B Dubuisson and P Colson, *Nomenclature des Préjudices Réparables*, in B Dubuisson and P. Jourdain (eds), *Le dommage et sa reparation dans la responsabilité contractuelle et extracontractuelle,* (Bruylant: 2015) 595 ff.

> l'écueil de l'arbitraire; s'il est destiné à permettre une évaluation plus aisée du dommage, il laisse toutefois intacte l'appréciation souveraine du juge du fond, en fonction des éléments de fait à faire valoir par les parties.[19]
>
> (In this regard, we reiterate that the indicative chart, which should be applied on a supplementary basis, is not binding, but a reference tool aimed at avoiding the risk of arbitrary awards; it aims at allowing an easier assessment of damages. However it leaves intact the sovereign discretion of the courts, based on facts proved by the parties.)

At the beginning, these classifications were applied only in car accident disputes, while nowadays their field of application has been extended to all torts in order to assure the same parameters for the same types of losses that occurred to the victims in different circumstances.

Italy

The intense dialogue between legal formants has affected the evolution of the personal injuries compensation system in the last 30 years.

In the 1970s and 1980s personal injuries damages were considered an economic loss, connected to the loss of earnings of the victim. In 1986, the Constitutional Court declared this system unconstitutional, since it protected a victim's income rather than his or her health.[20] This change of perspective opened a new trend, which included the development of a new head of damages.

For example, the *danno biologico* (pain and suffering) referred to the corporal damage, the *danno alla vita di relazione* (loss of social life), related to the effects that the injury had to the daily life of the victim, the *danno estetico* (aesthetic damage) concerned the aesthetics effects of the injury, etc.

In addition to these heads of damages, when the wrong also integrated a criminal offence (or could be identified as an offence, as in car accident cases) courts used to award the *danno morale*—ie, sufferance—to compensate the non-economic part of the injury.[21]

This system survived until 2003, when the Supreme Court[22] finally opted for considering the *danno biologico* (pain and suffering), a non-economic loss, which should include the compensation connected to the corporal harm and also its effects on daily routine. However, the aforementioned decisions issued by the Supreme Court stated that not only the violation of health, but also every violation of a fundamental right included in the Constitution could be compensated as a non-economic loss.

From this perspective, beyond the *danno biologico* (pain and suffering) and the *danno morale* (sufferance) some courts started to award the *danno esistenziale* (loss of amenities). This head of damage cannot be determined by forensic science, but it exists as personal damage that affects the victim's non-economic sphere, and in particular his or her habits

[19] Cass, 10 September 2009, n C.08.0031F, in jure.juridat.just.fgov.be.

[20] C Cost, 14 July 1986, n 184 (1986) I *Foro Italiano* 2053.

[21] See FD Busnelli, Il Danno Biologico dal 'Diritto Vivente' al 'Diritto Vigente' (Torino, Giappichelli, 2001).

[22] Cass, 31 May 2003, fns 8827–28 (2003) *Danno e Responsabilità* 939 ff.

and relationships, upsetting his or her daily life and depriving him or her of opportunities for the expression and realisation of his or her personality in the world.[23]

A new jurisprudential trend developed. This included the compensation of non-pecuniary losses due to the forced violation of a fundamental right, such as the violation of personal freedom in the case of overbooking or flight delay; or dignity in the case a of bad haircut, distorting the whole compensation system. The *danno esistenziale* (loss of amenities) theory had many supporters within the courts[24] and among scholars[25] and it is based on the idea that a fundamental right to be happy exists. Some scholars have remarked that the Constitution does not protect happiness; moreover this system would have duplicated the awards, because the three heads of damages de facto referred to the same 'pain and suffering' of the victim.[26]

For this reason, the Supreme Court was asked to decide once and for all whether or not the *danno esistenziale* (loss of amenities) could be compensated in combination with the *danno biologico* (pain and suffering) and *danno morale* (sufferance).

In four combined decisions the Supreme Court stated that personal injury damages could cause pecuniary or non-pecuniary losses.[27] As far as the latter is concerned, no different heads of damages could be awarded since the loss should be considered a unitary loss that should be proved. As a consequence, *danno biologico* (pain and suffering) and *danno morale* (sufferance) etc could be used only for descriptive aims, but their definitions cannot replace the burden of proof. In particular, the victim should file all the elements related to the existence (*an debeatur*) and quantification (*quantum debeatur*) of non-pecuniary losses in all their pleadings, since the past automatism in awarding different heads of damages to compensate personal injury damages has been considered to be in conflict with the Italian tort law system.

From this perspective, the theory of the *danno esistenziale* (loss of amenities) declined, and the courts started to find new methods to assess damages.[28]

Damages Assessment

From the previous paragraphs, we could learn that in the systems of the civil law tradition, the legal tools used to identify and calculate damages are not introduced by statutory law, but by soft law instruments.

[23] 'Ogni pregiudizio che l'illecito datoriale provoca sul fare areddituale del soggetto, alterando le sue abitudini di vita e gli assetti relazionali che gli erano propri, sconvolgendo la sua quotidianità e privandolo di occasioni per la espressione e la realizzazione della sua personalità nel mondo esterno'. (Each loss caused on the victim's non-economic sphere, which modifies his/her habits and relationships, upsets his/her daily routine and the opportunities to realize his/her person within the external world), Cass SS.UU, 24 March 2006, n 6572 (2006) *Danno e Responsabilità* 852 ff.

[24] The trend developed especially among lower courts, see critics included in G Comandé (ed), *Il Danno Nella Giurisprudenza dei Giudici di Pace* (Milano, Ilsole24ore, 2009).

[25] See contributions collected by P Cendon (ed), *Trattato Breve dei Nuovi Danni* (Padova, Cedam, 2003).

[26] See contributions collected by G Ponzanelli (ed), *Il Risarcimento Integrale Senza il Danno Esistenziale* (Padova, Cedam, 2007); ibid, *Critica del Danno Esistenziale* (Padova, Cedam, 2003).

[27] Cass, 11 November 2008, fns 26972–975 (2009) *Danno e Responsabilità* 1 ff.

[28] See contributions included in VV AA, *Il Nuovo Danno Non Patrimoniale* (Padova, Cedam, 2009); E Navarretta (ed), *Il danno non patrimoniale. Principi, Regole e Tabelle per la Liquidazione* (Milan, Giuffré, 2010); A D'Angelo, G Comandé and D Amram (eds), *La Liquidazione del Danno Non Patrimoniale. Riflessioni e Prospettive ad un Anno Dalle SS.UU. 26972-26975/2008* (Milan, Ilsole24ore, 2010).

Contrast the Irish experience where the Personal Injuries Assessment Board Act 2003[29] established the current system to award personal injury damages through a Board which, since 2004, assesses claims for personal injury damages in cases where liability is admitted.[30]

The Board, whose main aim is to 'implement a less adversarial and faster settlement process for personal injury claims where claimants have an entitlement to compensation', provides an independent compensation assessment service for the benefit of both claimants and respondents where legal issues other than quantum are not in dispute.[31]

This system establishes guidelines for personal injuries assessment—the Book of Quantum[32]—which refers to pain and suffering without considering different heads of damages. It seems that the Injuries Board offers a faster settlement of the dispute, through the sacrifice of a more comprehensive assessment of the loss.

In the next sections, we will discuss this issue, considering the concrete mechanism applied in the assessment of personal injuries damages in the given systems.

Range of Values in the Guidelines

In the systems analysed, each guideline identifies a range of monetary values for each head of damage. For instance, the Book of Quantum uses two criteria to assess pain and suffering: first, it divides injuries on the basis of the affected area of the body and then on the basis of its seriousness, including a different range of amounts for each head of damage. The amounts include pain and suffering and the loss of enjoyment of life, while the Injuries Board also calculates the proved medical expenses and loss of profit separately.

In France, the assessment of *pretium doloris* (price of pain) uses a range of values identified in seven increasing levels. For example, a temporary minor suffering from the injury could be calculated between €1,000 and €1,500, while if suffering is considered as level two of seven, an amount between €2,000 and €2,500 will be added to the evaluation of the other heads of damages and so on up to level seven which refers to a moral damage of more than €25,000.

There, *pretium doloris* (price of pain) constitutes something that is added to the *dommage corporel* (pain and suffering) calculated through the medical *barèmes* (charts) based on age and percentage of disability of the victim.

[29] On 1 June 2004 claims in respect of workplace injuries came under the Board's jurisdiction (SI 252/04); other claims covered by the Act came under the Board's jurisdiction on 22 July 2004 (SI 438/04); these include all personal injuries claims except those caused by the provision of medical services, human rights violations and claims by police officers in the course of duty.

[30] E Quill, 'General Damages and Relative Values in Irish Tort Law' (2007) 2(2) *Quarterly Review of Tort Law* 1; DH Erskine, 'Reforming Federal Personal Injury Litigation by Incorporation of the Procedural Innovations of Scotland and Ireland: An Analysis and Proposal' (2007) 15 *Cardozo Journal of International and Comparative Law* 1, 30; BME McMahon and W Binchy, *Casebook on the Irish Law of Torts*, 3rd edn (Haywards Heath, Tottel Publishing, 2005) 1194.

[31] www.injuriesboard.ie/eng/Forms-Guidelines/Book-of-Quantum.pdf.

[32] Ibid, s 22 of the Civil Liability and Courts Act 2004 requires courts to take cognisance of the book when assessing general damages for personal injuries, but they are not bound to follow it.

Scholars have observed that an evaluation of *pretium doloris* (price of pain) as a percentage of the *dommage corporel* (pain and suffering) considering the disability of the victim as a parameter would be more objective.[33] The *préjudice d'agrément* (loss of amenities) is calculated through the same mechanism based on seven different levels and is added to the other heads of damages.

Could this system inadvertently allow for duplication of damages? In this regard, the French Supreme Court has recently stated that the *préjudice d'agrément* (loss of amenities) refers to the impossibility for the victim to engage in sports or recreational activities and not to the loss of quality of life, whose consequences are already included in the definition of another head of damage, the so-called *déficit fonctionnel* (functional deficit) which reflects the dynamic-relational profiles of the physical harm:

> La réparation d'un poste de Préjudice d'Agrément vise exclusivement à l'indemnisation du préjudice lié à l'impossibilité pour la victime de pratiquer régulièrement une activité spécifique sportive ou de loisir quels qu'en soient la nature et le niveau d'intensité, et ne peut se rattacher à la perte de qualité de vie et des joies usuelles de la vie courante, laquelle est déjà indemnisée par l'organisme social au titre du déficit fonctionnel.[34]
>
> (The loss of enjoyment of life compensation covers just the damages connected to the impossibility for the victim to regularly practice specific sports or leisure activities, regardless of the nature and level of intensity. Moreover it cannot be linked to the loss of the quality of life and usual enjoyment of everyday life, which is already compensated by the social security system under the functional deficit.)

The mechanism used to cumulate the heads of damages and grade suffering in seven different levels has also been applied in Belgium. However, the *Tableau indicatif* 2012 included some hints aimed at overcoming the idea of suffering thanks to the introduction of the definition of *incapacité personnelle* (personal incapacity) described as 'l'ensemble des conséquences de l'atteinte à l'intégrité physico-psychique sur les gestes et les actes de la vie courante non économique, y compris les douleurs et la composante psychique' (all the consequences of the damage to the physical and mental integrity on non-economic activities of daily life, including suffering and psychological harm).

Unfortunately, no reference to the criteria for calculation of this head of damage has been introduced, even if some scholars did not hide their preference for a compensation based on *barèmes* (charts).[35]

Non-Pecuniary Losses Compensation *Poste Par Poste* and as a Unique Head of Damage

A general overview of the illustrated debates reminds one of some steps in the evolution of personal injuries compensation in Italy described above. For example, the risk of duplicating damages was really common in Italy. In fact, before 2008 courts divided non-pecuniary

[33] M Dupré, 'La Réparation Proportionelle du Préjudice Corporel' (2011) *Petites Affiches* (25 May 2011) 6, fn 103.
[34] Cass, 23 February 2012, 11-12.493 in légimobile.fr.
[35] M Van Wilderode, 'Le Tableau Indicatif 2012: Indicatif? Directif? Ou Chance Perdue?' (2013) *Circulation, Responsabilité et Assurances* 1.

losses determined by personal injuries damages into three different heads of damages: *danno biologico* (pain and suffering), *danno morale* (sufferance) and *danno esistenziale* (loss of amenities), corresponding to pain and suffering, non-physical suffering and loss of enjoyment of life. *Danno biologico* (pain and suffering) was calculated using a chart, which reflected an inverse relationship between the grade of disability and the age of the victim for his or her injury.

In addition, courts were used to calculate *danno morale* (sufferance) as a percentage (25–50 per cent) of the *danno biologico* (pain and suffering) and then they calculated the loss of enjoyment of life as a percentage of the *danno morale* (sufferance) or as a surplus without parameters.

In November 2008, the Italian Supreme Court stated that all the non-pecuniary losses should be calculated as a unique amount and not *poste par poste* (head by head).[36] This principle avoided the risk of duplication; however it created many difficulties for the courts in the determination of the due amounts. In particular, the *Tabelle* (Charts) elaborated by the Tribunal of Milan for the so called *danno biologico* (pain and suffering) started to include a range of values that should reflect all the suffering that occurred as a consequence of the wrong (ie, *danno morale* and *danno esistenziale*).

According to this system the judge should choose in the range of these values the correct amount to compensate all the losses suffered, but nothing more (*tout le dommage, rien que le dommage*). From this perspective, the proof of the suffering became an important stage of personal injuries disputes, since judges could not add unproven heads of damages any more. The risk of duplicating damages seems to be stemmed by the classification of the *pretium doloris* (price of pain) in different levels and by the determination of a restrained range of values.

By contrast in Ireland, the Board has a wide discretionary power since it can assess general damages through a large range of amounts. Moreover, the principle of binding precedent shared in common law systems as well as the fact that the Board acts outside the courts makes the identification of different heads of damages very difficult. In fact, it is apparently impossible to understand which evaluations have been made to settle each claim, since no specific databases show data on the assessment of damages. However, the risk of failing to entirely compensate the damage is low.

All Roads Lead to … Pisa?!

As observed, the idea to assess personal injuries damages applying a chart built on the basis of a range of values within which courts as well as other boards can choose the amount of compensation is really common in Europe. However, the lack of databases including records on the amounts awarded does not allow a deeper analysis of the criteria adopted to identify the *quantum* of the compensation within the range of values.

From this perspective, a good practice could be identified in the activities pursued by the International Observatory on Personal Injuries Damages in Pisa. Its research focuses on the implementation of a database, which collects published and unpublished decisions of

[36] Cass, 11 November 2008, fns 26972–975 (2009) *Danno e Responsabilità* 19 ff.

lower courts on personal injuries damages, significantly contributing to the national and comparative debate on the issue.

The database includes data on more than 15,000 judgments issued by Italian lower courts such as Justices of the Peace, Tribunals and Courts of Appeals. Lawyers and practitioners analyse each judgment, filling in all the anonymised legal and medical data concerning the personal injury compensation in the database, greatly increasing its potential heuristics and flexibility. This allows data extraction for research purposes[37] as well as the possibility of operating free text searches for external users. The database is mainly accessed by lawyers through the search keywords in specific areas, according to several classification criteria such as the injury, amount awarded, age or features of the victim, heads of damages awarded etc.

The need to identify better criteria to calculate non-pecuniary losses, such as *pretium doloris* (pain price), enjoyment of life, *préjudice d'agrément* (loss of amenities), etc is shared between practitioners, judges and scholars. In all the given systems we showed that it is really difficult to evaluate the level of application of the *nomenclature Dintilhac* or of the *Tableau indicatif* 2012 since data are not collected, analysed and published on a national scale and—except for Italy—we can refer only to those decisions which are commented on in the law journals.

The lack of data inhibits the improvement of the legal tools currently adopted. For example, the Book of Quantum, whose values have never been amended since its introduction, could be improved through a deeper specification of the injury in the daily life of the victim. This would be possible only through the collection and analysis of data on all claims. Therefore, we encourage both a deeper dialogue between scholars, judges and practitioners and a more intense circulation of compensation models through the collection, analysis and sharing of data.

[37] *Ex multis*, VV AA, 'Osservatorio Della Giurisprudenza in Materia di Danno Alla Persona' (2016) *Danno e Responsabilità*, § 6; VV AA, 'Osservatorio Della Giurisprudenza in Materia di Danno Alla Persona' (2013) *Danno e Responsabilità* 1141 ff.

Part III

The Process for Delivery of Damages

7

Deconstructing Policy on Costs and the Compensation Culture

ANNETTE MORRIS

Introduction

In the early 2000s, concerns about the disproportionate cost of resolving personal injury claims escalated in England and Wales, as such costs were thought to have contributed to a damaging compensation culture. Compensation culture is an amorphous term but in this context referred to structural advantages claimants were perceived to have gained within the tort system, which was said to have become dysfunctional.[1] Insurers complained that whilst they were held to ransom by excessive legal fees and forced to settle unworthy claims, claimant lawyers used these fees to generate even more spurious if not fraudulent suits. In April 2013, the Coalition Government introduced a range of civil justice reforms designed to address these concerns. The reforms sought not only to reduce legal costs but to achieve proportionality between costs and damages. Whilst the policy of proportionality was not new, it was pursued with renewed vigour, leaving critics concerned that the reforms would skew the tort system in favour of defendants and their insurers, rather than simply rebalance it. In other words, it was feared that the civil justice reforms were actually tort reforms 'through the back door'.[2]

This chapter examines how this tranche of civil justice reforms came into being and in doing so adopts a social constructionist approach. Policy does not develop in response to problems that 'exist' outside the policymaking process. This is because problems are not objective realities, they are social constructs. Policies give shape to problematisations that have become dominant within the policymaking process.[3] This chapter examines

[1] On the compensation culture generally, see: K Williams, 'State of Fear: Britain's "Compensation Culture" Reviewed' (2005) 25 *Legal Studies* 499; R Lewis, A Morris and K Oliphant, 'Tort Personal Injury Claims Statistics: Is there a Compensation Culture in the United Kingdom?' (2006) 14 *Torts Law Journal* 158; R Mullender, 'Negligence Law and Blame Culture: A Critical Response to a Possible Problem' (2006) 22 *Journal of Professional Negligence* 2; A Morris, 'Spiralling or Stabilising? The Compensation Culture and Our Propensity to Claim Damages for Personal Injury' (2007) *MLR* 349; J Hand, 'The Compensation Culture: Cliché or Cause for Concern?' (2010) 37 *Journal of Law and Society* 569; R Lewis and A Morris, 'Tort Law Culture: Image and Reality' (2012) 39 *Journal of Law and Society* 562 and R Lewis, 'Compensation Culture Reviewed: Incentives to Claim and Damages Levels (2014) 4 *Journal of Personal Injury Law* 209.

[2] A Morris, 'The "Compensation Culture" and the Politics of Tort' in TT Arvind and J Steele (eds), *Tort Law and the Legislature: Common Law, Statute and the Dynamics of Legal Change* (Oxford, Hart Publishing, 2013) 74.

[3] C Bacchi, *Analysing Policy: What's the Problem Represented to Be?* (Frenchs Forest, Pearson Australia, 2009).

how disproportionate legal costs became problematised in recent years and why that problematisation prevailed. In doing so, it examines the role of insurers, the judiciary and government. The aim is not to assess the desirability of the reforms but to deconstruct and expose their underlying dynamics in order to better understand the direction of policy affecting tort. Policymaking is a political rather than a rational process and so an understanding of the politics is fundamental to an understanding of the policy. This chapter also seeks to buck the academic tendency to focus on tort doctrine, as opposed to the tort system, and to consider tort and civil justice separately. In practice, tortious legal principles are mediated through the civil justice system and so it is important to consider them in tandem. There is a direct relationship between the cost of resolving claims, access to the tort system and the extent to which tort law is realised in the context of individual claims. Studying the problematisation of legal costs can, therefore, reveal much about wider attitudes towards the role, importance and desirability of tort law in society and indeed law more generally.

The 'Big Bang': Reform of the Personal Injury Claims Process

The turn of the millennium saw significant changes in the personal injury claims process. In April 1999, a new civil justice system was introduced with the implementation of the Woolf reforms.[4] Lord Woolf had found that litigation was too often seen as a 'battlefield' where no rules applied and where questions of expense and delay had only low priority. Whilst the majority of claims settled, they did so often after the issue of proceedings, if not at the door of the court, and after much expense had been incurred. Parties controlled the conduct and pace of litigation and pursued their claims and defences in isolation, using partisan experts who only added to the problem. Woolf's reforms, implemented through the Civil Procedure Rules 1998 (CPR) were designed to reduce cost, delay and complexity through a reduction of adversarialism and a commitment to the policy of proportionality. In other words, the achievement of the right result was to be balanced against the expenditure of time and money needed to achieve that result.

The reforms sought to achieve proportionality in three main ways. First, the rules encourage parties to settle their claims without the need to issue proceedings, either through negotiation or alternative dispute resolution.[5] Parties follow pre-action protocols which encourage pre-action contact, the early exchange of information and pre-action investigation by both sides. Second, if claims cannot be settled, then they proceed to litigation but

[4] Lord Woolf, *Access to Justice: Interim Report* (1995) and *Access to Justice: Final Report* (1996). For a critique of these reforms, see: AAS Zuckerman and R Cranston (eds), *Reform of Civil Procedure: Essays on 'Access to Justice'* (Oxford, Clarendon Press, 1995); A Ogus, 'Some Reflections on the Woolf Interim Report [1996] 1 *Web Journal of Current Legal Issues*; and AAS Zuckerman, 'Lord Woolf's Access to Justice: Plus ça change …' (1996) 59 *MLR* 773.

[5] Alternative dispute resolution plays only a very minor role in the resolution of personal injury claims: T Goriely, R Moorhead and P Abrams, *More Civil Justice? The Impact of the Woolf Reforms on Pre-Action Behaviour* (London, Law Society and Civil Justice Council, 2002) 156–57. See also, H Genn et al, *Twisting Arms: Court Referred and Court Linked Mediation under Judicial Pressure* (Ministry of Justice, 2007).

are subject to rationed procedures and judicial case management. Claims are allocated to one of three tracks which give parties access to procedure proportionate to the value and complexity of the claim:

— The small claims track applies to personal injury claims below £1,000 and provides a quick and cheap process involving a short, informal hearing where the rules of evidence are relaxed. There is generally no provision for the recovery of costs on the small claims track as it is expected that parties can represent themselves.
— Claims of up to £25,000 are generally allocated to the fast track. Such claims are subject to judicial case management but generally involve standardised directions. Parties are expected to use single joint experts and are subject to fixed timetables. Trials, for example, are expected to take place within 30 weeks of allocation.
— Claims above £25,000 and/or claims involving complex or important issues are allocated to the multi-track. Such claims are allowed access to more procedure but are still subject to judicial management of the timetable for the case, provisions for disclosure and the use of factual and expert evidence.

Finally, successful parties are only able to recover proportionate costs from their opponent under the loser pays principle. This means that unless lawyers charge clients directly, limits are placed on the amount of work that can be undertaken to progress a claim.

Shortly after the introduction of the Woolf reforms, the operation of conditional fee (or so-called 'no win no fee') agreements (CFAs) was reformed. In April 2000, the then Labour Government abolished legal aid for the majority of personal injury claims on the assumption that they could be funded through the CFA market instead. However, it introduced the concept of recoverability as a corollary which operated in conjunction with the loser pays principle. Unsuccessful claimants paid their own lawyer 'no fee' and used an after-the-event (ATE) insurance policy to pay the other side's legal costs whilst successful claimants could recover the success fee payable under the CFA and the cost of the ATE policy in addition to their normal legal costs. In allowing claimants to obtain legal assistance regardless of their financial capacity, recoverability was 'an interesting attempt to squeeze public provision into a private model approach'.[6] It effectively transferred the costs of claiming from claimants and/or the state to the market or rather, as the majority of personal injury claims are successful, to insurers. Lawyers were permitted to charge success fees of up to 100 per cent of the normal legal costs though recoverability was subject to reasonableness. The idea was that CFAs would work on a swings and roundabout basis. Success fees recovered in successful cases would absorb the cost of unsuccessful cases and also help fund other claims until their conclusion. CFAs altered both the economics and dynamics of the claims market. Lawyers reported that the way to make money out of CFAs was to have 'a regular throughput of small, easy cases'.[7] This encouraged claims advertising and aided the proliferation of claims management companies which farmed claims through mass advertising and direct marketing and then sold them on to lawyers for a referral fee.[8]

[6] R Moorhead, 'CFAs: A Weightless Reform of Legal Aid?' (2002) 55 *Northern Ireland Legal Quarterly* 153, 154.

[7] Goriely, Moorhead and Abrams (n 5) 21.

[8] For further information on the development of the claims market, see R Abel, *English Lawyers between Market and State: The Politics of Professionalism* (New York, Oxford University Press, 2003) and Boleat Consulting, *The Claims Standards Council* (December 2005). On referral fees, see: A Higgins, 'Referral Fees—The Business of Access to Justice' (2012) 32 *Legal Studies* 109.

Despite the Woolf reforms, concerns about the cost of resolving claims continued and indeed escalated during the 2000s. Sir Anthony Clarke, then Master of the Rolls, described costs as a 'central failing' of Woolf.[9] The Association of British Insurers (ABI) complained that the claims process was 'riddled'[10] with 'excessive'[11] legal costs which were leading consumers to pay more for their insurance than necessary.[12] The system, it said, was 'dysfunctional',[13] 'broken'[14] and 'in urgent need of fixing'.[15] Government also expressed concern. Towards the end of the Labour administration, Jack Straw, then Lord Chancellor, complained that CFA lawyers were 'ramping up their fees' to 'scandalous' proportions.[16] Lord Young, commissioned by the Conservatives to investigate the compensation culture, condemned the personal injury claims process as a 'cash cow for lawyers'[17] and a 'burden' on society.[18] The Coalition Government, formed in 2010 and led by the Conservatives, stated that legal costs were 'spiralling'[19] and that high payments for the referral of claims were evidence of 'too much money sloshing around the system'.[20] Profits were being ploughed into generating even more and often weak, spurious and fraudulent claims and defendants were said to be held to ransom by high legal costs. 'It cannot be right', stated the Ministry of Justice 'that, regardless of the extreme weakness of a claim, the sensible thing for the defendant to do is settle, and get out before legal costs start running up. This is precisely what has happened and it is one of the worst instances of this country's compensation culture'.[21] In privileging the interests of claimants and their lawyers above the interests of defendants and wider society, the system was seen to have 'got out of kilter'.[22]

Reform was seen to be necessary. In 2008, and with the support of the Ministry of Justice, the Master of the Rolls asked Lord Justice Jackson to undertake a review of civil litigation costs. Jackson published an extensive final report in December 2009 and the majority of his recommendations were accepted by the Coalition.[23] The Coalition quickly set its mind to implementation, indeed going further in some respects, in a range of reforms said to be necessary to 'turn … the tide on the compensation culture'.[24]

[9] Sir Anthony Clarke, 'The Woolf Reforms: A Singular Event or an Ongoing Process?' (speech delivered at the British Academy, London, 2 December 2008).

[10] Association of British Insurers (ABI) news release, 'Calls grow for the Government to act now on reforming personal injury compensation' (25 March 2008).

[11] ABI news release, 'Dysfunctional and Disproportionate—ABI reveals how motorists are being taken for a ride by high legal costs' (27 October 2010).

[12] ABI news release, 'Care and Compensation: ABI launches plans for reform of UK compensation system' (13 December 2013).

[13] ABI news release, 'ABI comments on Government response to Transport Select Committee Inquiry into cost of motor insurance' (9 September 2011).

[14] ABI, Improving the System for All (2011).

[15] ABI, news release (n 10).

[16] N Watt, 'Straw Vows to Act Against "Scandalous" "No Win, No Fee" Lawyers': theguardian.com (21 September 2008).

[17] Lord Young, Common Sense Common Safety (2010) 8.

[18] Ibid, 19.

[19] Ministry of Justice (MoJ), press release, 'Clarke Stamping out Compensation Culture Fears' (29 March 2011).

[20] MoJ news release, 'Curbing Compensation Culture: Government to Ban Referral Fees' (9 September 2011).

[21] MoJ, Reforming Civil Litigation Funding and Costs in England and Wales—Implementation of Lord Justice Jackson's Recommendations: The Government Response (March 2011) 3.

[22] MoJ, press release (n 19).

[23] R Jackson LJ, *Review of Civil Litigation Costs: Final Report* (London, Judiciary of England and Wales, January 2010).

[24] MOJ news release, 'Action on Compensation Claims for Slips and Trips' (31 July 2013).

The reforms were introduced in April 2013 through the Legal Aid, Sentencing and Punishment of Offenders Act 2012 (LASPO) and amendments to the CPR.[25] They were wide-ranging and pursued the policy of proportionality with renewed rigour.[26] The controversial practice of paying for the referral of claims was abolished,[27] as was the concept of recoverability associated with CFAs.[28] Recoverability was seen as a major driver of 'excessive' costs which the claimant, with no financial stake in the claim, had no interest in controlling.[29] The new regime now operates in conjunction with 'qualified one-way costs shifting'.[30] Unsuccessful claimants do not have to pay the defendants' legal costs except in exceptional circumstances. This is intended to remove the need for ATE insurance in the majority of claims.[31] Those wanting ATE insurance must now pay for it themselves. Whilst successful claimants can still recover their legal costs from insurers, they can no longer recover the success fee. This must instead be met directly by claimants, usually from their damages. To ameliorate the effects of this reform for claimants, damages for pain, suffering and loss of amenity have been increased by 10 per cent.[32] Also, whilst lawyers are still permitted to charge success fees of up to 100 per cent, they are not permitted to recover success fees in excess of 25 per cent of claimants' damages, excluding damages for future care and loss.[33] For lawyers, however, the reforms have led to a substantial reduction in their returns on CFA work.

The overriding objective of the CPR has been amended to emphasise that the rules are to enable the court to deal with cases not only justly but at proportionate cost.[34] Costs incurred are proportionate if they bear a reasonable relationship to: the sums in issue in the proceedings; the value of any non-monetary relief in issue in the proceedings; the complexity of the litigation; any additional work generated by the conduct of the paying party; and any wider factors involved in the proceedings, such as reputation or public importance.[35] The amended rules extend procedural rationing. Further controls have been placed on the use of both factual evidence and expert evidence.[36] Parties seeking permission to rely on expert evidence must provide an estimate of the costs involved and a summary of the issues to be addressed to allow the court to undertake a cost–benefit analysis.[37] In addition, the reforms have fortified judicial case management. The rules provide for tougher enforcement of rules, practice directions and orders[38] and also fuse case management with cost management.[39] In relation to multi-track claims, the court must now

[25] For a discussion of some of the main aspects of the reforms, see Special Issue: The Implementation of Sir Rupert Jackson's Review of Civil Litigation Costs (2013) 32(2) *Civil Justice Quarterly* 109.

[26] J Sorabji, 'Prospects or Proportionality: Jackson Implementation' (2013) 2 *Civil Justice Quarterly* 213.

[27] s 56, Legal Aid, Sentencing and Punishment of Offenders Act 2012 (LASPO).

[28] ss 44 and 36 LASPO.

[29] Jackson, Review of Civil Litigation Costs: Final Report (n 23) ch 10.

[30] CPR 44.13. A Higgins, 'A Defence of Qualified One Way Costs Shifting' (2013) 2 *Civil Justice Quarterly* 198.

[31] Jackson, Review of Civil Litigation Costs: Final Report (n 23) ch 9.

[32] *Simmons v Castle* [2012] EWCA Civ 1039.

[33] Art 5, Conditional Fee Agreements Order 2013.

[34] CPR 1.1.

[35] CPR 44.3(5).

[36] CPR 32.3(3).

[37] CPR 35.4.

[38] CPR 3.9. AAS Zuckerman, 'The Revised CPR 3.9: A Coded Message Demanding Articulation' (2013) 2 *Civil Justice Quarterly* 123; I Levy, 'Lightening the Overload of CPR Rule 3.9' (2013) 2 *Civil Justice Quarterly* 139.

[39] CPR 3.12–3.21. See also Practice Direction 3E—Costs Management.

approve a cost budget at the outset of the litigation which will then be used in the assessment of costs at the end. This is to allow judges to ensure that costs remain proportionate and whilst parties can seek to revise their budget during the case they must convince the judge that this is justified.[40]

Significant restrictions have also been placed on the recovery of legal costs. Fast-track claims, which had previously involved some fixed costs, are now subject to a full fixed cost regime.[41] In addition, the rule governing the recovery of costs has been reformulated. Whilst the Woolf reforms required costs to be assessed with reference to proportionality, the decision in *Lownds v Home Office* meant that successful parties could recover costs disproportionate to the damages if they were deemed to be necessary and reasonable.[42] Jackson felt this conflicted with the underlying purpose of the CPR and proposed that, having assessed each item of cost in relation to reasonableness, judges should consider whether the global figure is proportionate and reduce appropriately if not.[43] The result is that successful parties may not be able to recover the actual costs they have incurred in preparing and advancing their claim even if those costs have been reasonably or necessarily incurred.[44]

Alongside the implementation of the Jackson reforms, the Coalition extended the streamlined procedure that had been introduced for road traffic accident (RTA) claims between £1,000 and £10,000 in April 2010.[45] The scheme now applies to RTA, employers' liability (EL) and public liability (PL) claims between £1,000 and £25,000—the majority of all claims. The streamlined procedure, which utilises an online portal, has three stages.[46] The first stage requires early notification of claims with only basic information. Defendants are then given short time frames on which to respond on liability (15 days in RTA claims, 30 in EL claims and 40 in PL claims). If liability is admitted, claims proceed to the second stage where the claimant gathers supporting evidence for the claim and completes a settlement pack with an offer of damages. Defendants then have 15 days in which to accept or reject the offer and, where relevant, to make a counter offer. If the parties cannot settle within 20 days, the claim proceeds to the third stage and is referred to the court for a decision on quantum. The court can assess damages on the papers though the parties may request, or the court may order, a court hearing. Pre-action protocols introduced as part of the Woolf reforms were seen to aid settlement but to lead to the frontloading of costs as both parties investigated liability and quantum before engaging in negotiations.[47] The new process provides a quick and cheap process for claims to be resolved where liability is not in dispute. If the insurer denies liability, admits liability but alleges contributory negligence or does not respond within specified time limits, the claim falls out of the streamlined and into the

[40] Jackson, *Review of Civil Litigation Costs: Final Report* (n 23) ch 40. P Hurst, 'The New Costs Rules and Practice Directions' (2013) 2 *Civil Justice Quarterly* 153.

[41] CPR 45.29 A–L and CPR 45.33–45.36.

[42] *Lownds v Home Office* [2002] EWCA Civ 365.

[43] Jackson, Review of Civil Litigation Costs: Final Report (n 23) ch 3.

[44] CPR 44.3.

[45] Pre-Action Protocol for Low Value Personal Injury Claims in Road Traffic Accidents, Pre-Action Protocol for Low Value Personal Injury (Employers' Liability and Public Liability) Claims and Practice Direction 8B Pre-Action Protocol for Low Value Personal Injury Claims in Road Traffic Accidents—Stage 3 Procedure.

[46] The claims portal is a stakeholder-led secure electronic communication tool for processing low value personal injury claims: www.claimsportal.org.uk/en/.

[47] Goriely, Moorhead and Abrams (n 5) 172.

normal process. Each stage is subject to fixed costs and the fixed costs that were already in place for RTA claims have been significantly reduced.[48]

Unsurprisingly, the reforms proved extremely controversial.[49] Critics have argued that it is wrong in principle that damages, awarded to provide full compensation following wrongdoing, should be used to pay legal costs. In addition, significant concerns have been raised in relation to access. In combination, the abolition of recoverability, the extension of fixed fees and the tighter restrictions placed on the recovery of legal costs in successful claims have significantly reduced the profitability of personal injury work. The concern is that this will tighten the squeeze on the swings and roundabouts principle and make it more difficult for lawyers to take new cases on a CFA basis.[50]

Concerns have also been raised in relation to under-settlement. Claimant lawyers have argued that streamlined procedures are unsuitable for more complex and higher value claims involving issues of law. Fenn conducted an analysis of the streamlined procedure that had been in place for RTAs below £10,000 and found that whilst only 50 per cent had remained within the scheme, there had been a 6 per cent reduction in mean general damages in these cases.[51] This was probably due to a combination of the rationing of procedure within the scheme and the fixed costs applicable to it, which encourage solicitors to reduce their input in any individual claim so that profits can still be made.

In addition, even outside the streamlined procedure, the extension of fixed costs and restrictions on the ability to cover actual costs incurred in pursuing a claim, will constrain lawyers in the amount of work they can undertake on a claim and still make a profit. This will, in turn, constrain their ability to establish liability on behalf of their injured clients and ensure that they recover the compensation to which they are legally entitled. It will also further impede their ability to have their case heard in court. As insurers will not be operating under the same financial constraints, there are concerns about inequality of bargaining power. In sum, it is argued that the reforms will undermine the claims process by reducing both access and justice.[52] Rather than re-balancing the system, it is feared the reforms will skew it in favour of defendants and their insurers.

[48] For RTA claims: CPR 45.9–45.15. For employers' liability and public liability claims: CPR 45.16–45.29.

[49] See, eg, Association of Personal Injury Lawyers (APIL), APIL Response to Ministry of Justice Consultation on Proposals for Reform of Civil Litigation Funding and Costs in England and Wales (2011) and APIL Response to Ministry of Justice Consultation on Solving Disputes in the County Courts (2011); Law Society, Law Society Proposals for Reform of Civil Litigation Funding and Costs: Law Society Response (2011) and Access to Justice Action Group, Access to Justice Action Group Briefing: House of Lords Stages, Legal Aid, Sentencing and Punishment of Offenders Bill (2012). For a selection of press releases, see APIL, 'Perfect Storm to Deny Access to Justice for Most Seriously Injured' (February 2011); Consumer Justice Alliance news release, 'Legal Aid, Sentencing and Punishment of Offenders Bill: "Buried" Proposals will Block Justice for Injured Victims Warns Consumer Justice Alliance' (June 2011); and 'Personal Injury Claimant Lawyers Hit Back at CFA Reforms' Solicitors Journal, 28 March 2011.

[50] The Jackson reforms introduce damages-based agreements (DBAs) as an alternative to CFAs: s 45 LASPO 2012 and the Damages-Based Agreements Regulations 2013. Under a DBA, lawyers charge a straight percentage of any damages recovered subject to a cap of 25%, excluding damages for future loss. Whilst they were intended to increase access to justice, they have not proved popular as yet: 'How DBAs Ended Up as Don't Bother Agreements' (2013) 157(45) *Solicitors Journal* 10; R Mulheron, 'The Damages-Based Agreements Regulations 2013: Some Conundrums in the 'Brave New World' of Funding' (2013) 2 *Civil Justice Quarterly* 241.

[51] P Fenn, *Evaluating the Low Value Road Traffic Accident Process* (Ministry of Justice Research Series 13/12, 2012).

[52] APIL, press release, 'Balance in the Legal System Tipping the Wrong Way, Says APIL President' (February 2010).

The Coalition accepted that access to justice may be affected and that the accuracy of case outcomes could be reduced, but pressed ahead in any event.[53] As it is still early days, the full impact of the reforms remains to be seen.[54] Their introduction has certainly led to a significant reorganisation of the claims market. Legal firms have been required to assess their business models and the market is consolidating.[55] A number of mergers and takeovers have taken place and some firms have gone out of business, closed their personal injury department or withdrawn from certain areas of personal injury work.[56] The ban on referral fees has undermined the traditional model of claims management companies, which had already been in decline, but the market is quickly adapting by taking advantage of alternative business structures.[57] These allow insurers to operate in business with lawyers so that referrals are made in-house.[58] One leading personal injury lawyer advised firms to 'get big, get niche or get out' and so the reforms are likely to cause further stratification within the market.[59] The reforms are said to have encouraged firms to push work down to the most junior level of fee earner so that work remains profitable and also to have led to the growth of 'caseload farmers'—firms that purchase personal injury work-in-progress caseloads.[60] Certainly, at the lower end of the market, the reforms are encouraging the increased use of standardised and routinised procedures for claims handling administered by non-legally qualified personnel.[61] At the higher end of the market, lawyers are seeking to cope with uncertainties surrounding cost budgeting and the enforcement of sanctions.[62] It is little wonder that many refer to the introduction of the reforms as 'the big bang'.

Disproportionate Costs: A Problem or a Problematisation?

As tort is adversarial, fault-based and individuated, it is well known that it is expensive to administer. The Pearson Commission estimated that the operating costs of the system

[53] MoJ, Overarching Jackson Proposals: Impact Assessment (2011); Conditional Fee Agreements: Impact Assessment (2010); Extension of the System for Dealing with Low Value RTA Personal Injury Claims: Impact Assessment (2010); and MoJ, Referral Fees in Personal Injury Claims: Impact Assessment (2011).

[54] In June 2014, the Civil Justice Committee established a working party to assess the impact of the Jackson reforms. For an early assessment, see: J Peysner, 'Impact of the Jackson Reforms: Some Emerging Themes', report prepared for Civil Justice Council Costs Forum (21 March 2014).

[55] J Hyde, 'Slater Chief Predicts Rapid Consolidation in PI Market' [2014] *Law Society Gazette*, 1 May.

[56] APIL, The Impact of the Jackson Reforms on Costs and Case Management (2014).

[57] A Wigmore, 'The Death of Claims Management Companies' (2013) 4 *Journal of Personal Injury Law* 248.

[58] Alternative business structures, introduced by the Legal Services Act 2007, have been allowed since 2011. See further, Lewis, 'Compensation Culture Reviewed' (n 1) 217–18.

[59] '"Get Big, Get Niche or Get Out", Marshall Tells Personal Injury Firms' (2013) *Solicitors Journal*, October 16. See also, H Kritzer, 'The Fracturing Legal Profession: The Case of Plaintiffs' Personal Injury Lawyers' (2001) 8 *International Journal of the Legal Profession* 225.

[60] APIL, press release (n 56) 2–3.

[61] Engstrom calls firms adopting such approaches 'settlement mills' in the US: N Engstrom, 'Sunlight and Settlement Mills' (2011) 86 *New York University Law Review* 805.

[62] APIL, press release (n 56) 9–10. See also, New Law Journal and London Solicitor Litigation Association, 'Litigation Trends Survey: The Jackson Effect' (October 2013); 'Litigation Trends Survey: Jackson One Year On' (April 2014); and 'Litigation Trends post *Mitchell*: The Search for Clarity' (December 2014).

(legal costs and insurers' administrative costs) amounted to about 85 per cent of the value of tort compensation payments.[63] The ABI stated that insurers paid £4.5 billion in compensation and £2 billion in claimant costs each year.[64] Legal costs were thought to amount to approximately 30–40 per cent of the total cost of tort claims, though the proportion was said to be much higher in relation to lower value claims.[65] There was certainly evidence to suggest that the cost of resolving claims had increased since the Woolf reforms.[66] Nevertheless, significant concerns were raised about the evidence underpinning the Jackson reforms. Jackson attached much importance to judicial statistics but, as Genn noted in her preliminary analysis, 'using these figures to make assumptions about average costs is rather like generalizing about war from the most bloody and hard fought battles'.[67] A working party of academics suggested that his report was 'a misleading and partial account of the problems requiring solutions because it too frequently treats anecdote and opinion as if it were fact, and systematically prefers the evidence of the defence lobby over that favouring injured persons'.[68] Claimant lawyers argued vehemently that disproportionate costs were generated not by them but by insurers' unreasonable behaviour in responding to claims.

Jackson uncovered many instances of legal costs far outstripping damages. In CFA cases featured in the surveys on which he relied, claimant costs ranged between 158 per cent and 203 per cent of the damages awarded.[69] However, he concluded:

> A fair overall summary of civil litigation in 2007 may run as follows: approximately 2.1 million civil cases were launched of which at least 95% were brought in the county courts. Approximately 90% of all civil cases were concluded without any prolonged contest and at costs proportionate to the issues at stake. The remaining 10% of cases were contested (whether or not settled before trial) and potentially gave rise to significant costs liabilities.[70]

From this perspective, the reforms seem to have been more far-reaching than the evidence suggested was necessary. It had already been accepted that there was an issue with disproportionate costs in lower value claims.[71] The streamlined procedure for RTA claims had been introduced to address this and the Civil Justice Council (CJC) was reviewing other areas. This led one academic involved in the process to describe Jackson's review as a 'surprise'.[72]

[63] Report of the Royal Commission on Civil Liability and Compensation for Personal Injury (Cmnd 7054, 1978) para 261 (Pearson Commission).

[64] ABI, The ABI's Response to the Government's Consultation on Case Track Limits and the Claims Process for Personal Injury (2007).

[65] For a review of the evidence, see Lewis, Morris and Oliphant (n 1).

[66] Goriely, Moorhead and Abrams (n 5) 172–82; and P Fenn, N Rickman and D Vencappa, 'The Impact of the Woolf Reforms on Cost and Delay' (Nottingham University Business School, CRIS Discussion Paper Series, 2009.I).

[67] H Genn, 'Preliminary Analysis of Costs Data' (Review of Civil Litigation Costs Seminar, Birmingham, 26 June 2009) 2.

[68] K Oliphant et al, *On a Slippery Slope—A Response to the Jackson Report* (2011).

[69] C McIvor, 'The Impact of the Jackson Reforms on Access to Justice in Personal Injury Litigation' (2011) 30 *Civil Justice Quarterly* 411, 423.

[70] Lord Justice Jackson, Review of Civil Litigation Costs: Preliminary Report, vol 1 (2009) 53.

[71] APIL, press release, 'Costs Savings Within Everyone's Grasp, Says APIL' (May 2006); Law Society, *Compensation Fast and Fair* (2006).

[72] Peysner (n 54) 3.

Despite these concerns, it is important to appreciate that even if there had been solid and fully representative evidence of extensive disproportionate costs within the system, that evidence would still need to have been interpreted. There would still have been disagreement about the costs that were legitimate and those that were wasteful. In addition, disproportionate costs are not inherently problematic. Legal costs are related to both access to the system and the legal accuracy of case outcomes. High costs may preclude, whilst low costs may increase, access. High or disproportionate costs may allow for high levels of legal accuracy whilst low costs may constrain the realisation of substantive law in individual cases. Zuckerman argues that '[w]hat matters is not any particular level of accuracy but the correct balance between accuracy of justice and timeliness of justice and between accuracy and affordability'.[73] Opinions on where that balance should lie depend on a variety of factors including attitudes towards the function and importance of tort law and towards the civil justice system more generally.

The policy of proportionality is controversial and has not been accepted in all jurisdictions.[74] For some, it is problematic as it results in only 'rough justice' as in an adversarial fault-based system based on individuated damages, claimants must sometimes incur disproportionate costs in order to establish liability and recover full compensation. Such critics attach importance to the realisation of law and legal entitlements in practice not just for the individuals concerned but for wider society in terms of accountability, the exposure of wrongdoing and the regulation of behaviour.[75]

The point is that the appropriate level of legal costs is a moot issue and to construe disproportionate costs as a problem is a choice not a given. In the context of policymaking, we often assume that problems exist as objective realities and that policies are developed to solve them. However, problems are socially constructed through social forces in ways that reflect particular interests, values and ideas about how society should be organised, which can be contested.[76] In this context, preferred policies may dictate the problematisation of particular issues in the same way as problematisations may implicitly or explicitly include or exclude consideration of certain policy solutions. The result, Bacchi argues, is that we are governed by problematisations rather than policies.[77] In order to understand any particular policy, we need to understand the problematisation underpinning it and why it has become dominant in the policymaking process. In adopting this analysis, the remainder of this chapter examines the social construction of disproportionate legal costs as a problem.

The Problematisation of Legal Costs

The problematisation of legal costs has been driven by insurers, the judiciary and government which will be considered in turn. As outlined below, their 'meeting of minds' on the issue of costs opened a policy window for reform.

[73] AAS Zuckerman, 'A Reform of Civil Procedure—Rationing Procedure Rather Than Access to Justice' (1995) 2 *Journal of Law and Society* 155, 162.

[74] Jackson, Review of Civil Litigation Costs: Final Report (n 23) 27.

[75] For further discussion, see L Kaplow, 'The Value of Accuracy in Adjudication: An Economic Analysis (1994) 23 *Journal of Legal Studies* 307.

[76] V Burr, *Social Constructionism*, 2nd edn (London, Routledge, 2003).

[77] Bacchi (n 3).

The Power of the Insurance Lobby

Insurers have played an active role in the problematisation of legal costs in recent years through both direct action and political lobbying. Insurers clearly have an interest in reducing the cost of resolving claims. Whilst costs can be passed on to consumers and wider society, reducing the costs of claims handling can increase profitability and help keep premiums both affordable and competitive, especially if there is a downturn in investment income and an increase in the cost of reinsurance. However, insurers' interest in cost is not simply about reduction but also about management. The more predictable the claims process, the more insurers are able to set appropriate claims reserves and also manage risk, which is obviously central to their success.

Insurers were galled by the levels of success fees and ATE premiums they were required to pay under the concept of recoverability, which also increased unpredictability within the system.[78] Insurers were not involved in the setting of success fees and ATE premiums at the outset of the claim and whilst insurers could challenge the reasonableness of both additional liabilities, this could only be done at end of claim and at expense. As a result, in the early 2000s, insurers challenged various aspects of the recoverability regime in a series of satellite litigation now known as the 'costs war' as well as raising their concerns in political circles.[79] Large swathes of cases were stayed pending the outcome of appeal court decisions on the issues raised. Whilst some of the challenges were regarded as legitimate, others were regarded as 'destructive'.[80] Nevertheless, the costs war was an effective strategy for the insurers in many respects. It led some, including Lord Phillips, then Master of the Rolls, to call for the abolition of recoverability.[81] Whilst these calls were ignored at the time,[82] the CJC was required to step in to mediate an industry agreement on reasonable and predictable success fees in low-value RTA and employers' liability claims. In addition, it triggered the CJC to undertake a review of costs and so helped to move the issue up the political agenda.[83]

Labour refused to accept that recoverability was causing significant problems. It had reviewed the sharp increases in employers' liability insurance premiums in the early 2000s, which insurers had attributed in part to CFAs, but found that they were largely attributable to factors external to tort, including the under-pricing of insurance, a fall in investment income and the increasing cost of re-insurance following the September 11 attack in 2001.[84] Later that year, Fenn and Rickman's research on the cost of low-value employers' liability

[78] See further M Zander, 'Where Are We Now on Conditional Fees?—Or Why This Emperor Is Wearing Few, If Any, Clothes' (2002) 65 *MLR* 919; M Zander, 'Where Are We Heading With the Funding of Civil Litigation?' (2003) 22 *Civil Justice Quarterly* 23; S Kalish, 'The English Costs War, 2000–2003, and a Moment of Repose' (2004) 83 *Nebraska Law Review* 114; and A Morris, 'Conditional Fee Agreements in Northern Ireland: Gimmick or Godsend?' (2005) 56 *Northern Ireland Legal Quarterly* 38.

[79] This satellite litigation culminated in a number of appeal decisions, including: *Callery v Gray* (No's 1 and 2) [2002] UKHL 28, [2002] 3 All ER 417; *Sarwar v Alam* [2001] EWCA Civ 1401, [2001] 4 All ER 541; *Halloran v Delaney* [2002] EWCA Civ 1258, [2003] 1 WLR 28; and *Sharratt v London Central Bus Co and other cases (No2) (The Accident Group Test Cases)* [2004] EWCA Civ 575, [2004] 3 All ER 325.

[80] Baroness Scotland of Asthal QC, Parliamentary Secretary at the Lord Chancellor's Department at Association of Personal Injury Lawyers' Annual Conference, Brighton, 9 May 2003.

[81] [2002] *Law Society Gazette* 99 (44) 3.

[82] 'Lord Chancellor Rules Out Abolishing Recoverability' (2003) 26 *Litigation Funding* 1.

[83] Civil Justice Council, 'Improved Access to Justice—Funding Options and Proportionate Costs' (2005).

[84] Department for Work and Pensions (DWP), Review of Employers' Liability Compulsory Insurance, First Stage Report (3 June 2003).

claims suggested that recoverability had had little impact.[85] As it was clear Labour was unlikely to move on recoverability, insurers shifted the focus of their political campaign to the process for resolving low-value claims.

During her study of the settlement process in the 1980s, Genn found that in order to avoid or minimise expenditure on claims, insurers would use delay as a tactic to discourage claimants and put pressure on them to settle.[86] Genn also found that despite the volume of claims being dealt with, the approach taken on liability and quantum generally appeared to be tailored to each individual case.[87] She did note that RTAs did not generally involve questions of law and that decisions on liability were made rapidly in relation to common sense knowledge about a range of factual situations, such as rear-end collisions and right-hand turns, and that these were regarded as relatively clear-cut in so far as liability was concerned. The system was not, however, as routinised, simplified or as bureaucratic as Ross had found during his study of RTA settlements in the United States.[88] However, much has changed since then on both the claimant and insurance side of the process.

In relation to the insurance market, there has been much consolidation resulting in fewer but larger claims centres throughout the country.[89] On the claimant side, a specialised and active claims market has developed and the number of personal injury claims has increased significantly—from an estimated 250,000 such claims in 1973 to over a million each year prior to the reforms.[90] This increase is largely attributable to an increase in RTA claims. It is estimated that there were just over 100,000 such claims in 1973 but by 2000/2001 they had grown to just over 400,000 and by 2012/2013 further still to over 800,000. RTA claims now constitute around 80 per cent of all personal injury claims.[91] The rise in RTA claims relates largely to an increase in low-value whiplash claims.[92] The majority of all claims are low value. Ninety per cent are said to be below £5,000.[93]

These developments have led insurers to reassess their approach to claims handling. By the early 2000s, a study by Goriely et al suggested that insurers' mindsets had changed so that speed was now of the essence: a quick claim was a cheap claim.[94] Their focus had shifted to operational efficiency. In relation to low-value claims, the response was to move to a less

[85] P Fenn and N Rickman, *Cost of Low Value Employers' Liability Claims 1997–2002* (London, Department for Constitutional Affairs, 2003).

[86] H Genn, Hard Bargaining: Out of Court Settlements in Personal Injury Cases (Oxford, Clarendon Press, 1987).

[87] Ibid.

[88] HL Ross, Settled Out of Court: The Social Process of Insurance Claims Adjustment, 2nd edn (Chicago, Aldine, 1980).

[89] R Lewis, 'Insurance and the Tort System' (2005) 25 *Legal Studies* 85; and R Lewis, 'Insurers and Personal Injury Litigation: Acknowledging "The Elephant in the Living Room"' (2005) 1 *Journal of Personal Injury Law* 1; R Lewis, 'Compensation Culture Reviewed' (n 1) 213.

[90] Morris, 'Spiralling or Stabilising? (n 1) 355–57. The 1973 estimate is taken from the Pearson Commission report (n 63). The more recent figures are available from the Compensation Recovery Unit (CRU). All claims, whether settled or litigated, successful or unsuccessful must be reported to CRU for the purpose of the recovery of benefits scheme: The Social Security (Recovery of Benefits) Act 1997; the Road Traffic (NHS Charges) Act 1999; and The Health and Social Care (Community Health and Standards) Act 2003.

[91] For discussion of the causes underlying the significant increase in RTA claims, see Lewis and Morris, 'Tort Law Culture' (n 1).

[92] Of RTA claims, 87% arise from injuries to the neck area (including whiplash injuries): House of Commons Transport Committee, *Cost of Motor Insurance: Whiplash: Further Government Response to the Committee's Fourth Report of Session 2013–2014*, Eleventh Special Report of Session 2013–14 (HC 902) 4.

[93] ABI, Improving the Small Claims Track (2006).

[94] Goriely, Moorhead and Abrams (n 5) 33–34.

individuated and more routinised and standardised approach to resolving claims in bulk, utilising claims management software administered by cheap in-house non-legally qualified claims personnel.[95] Software programmes are used not only to facilitate the efficient progress of a claim but also to help assess damages.[96] The claims system is now process driven and accuracy of case outcomes plays second fiddle to cost. Insurers pay out in the vast majority of cases[97] and insurers' efforts to reduce the cost of processing claims are said to 'have contributed to some of the problems now identified as part of the compensation culture'.[98]

However, insurers' efforts to reduce the cost of processing claims internally are hampered by the involvement of claimant lawyers on the other side as they decrease predictability and increase both the time and cost of resolving claims. This led insurers to pursue two avenues of reform which would remove or at least reduce claimant lawyers' involvement in the process. First, insurers have campaigned for an increase in the small claims track limit for personal injury cases. It currently lies at £1,000 but insurers maintain it should increase to £5,000. As the majority of all personal injury claims are below £5,000, such an increase would largely remove lawyers from the process.[99] As outlined above, the small claims track is relatively informal and there is generally no provision for the recovery of legal costs as it is expected that claimants can represent themselves. Insurers argue that personal injury claims below £5,000 are sufficiently straightforward to allow for this. One insurer states that lawyers are unnecessary in *70 per cent* of injury claims, whilst another states:

> Does access to justice have anything to do with personal injury claims or is it simply a commoditised service? In my opinion, the majority of personal injury claims are a commodity needing little legal input. Arguably customer service skills are as important as technical skills and legal knowledge at the low end of the market. That does not mean to say that lawyers should be taken out of the market but any involvement has to be proportionate in terms of cost and time.[100]

Of course, insurers' preference is for claims not to enter the small claims track at all but to negotiate settlements with claimants directly without any legal involvement. They have increasingly been seeking to achieve this in any event through the controversial practice of 'third-party capture'.[101]

Second, insurers have campaigned for the streamlined procedures that have now been introduced. In requiring claimant lawyers to provide early notification of claims, insurers can decide how best to proceed before many costs are incurred. This gives insurers more control over the process and the conduct of the claim. Where liability is not in dispute,

[95] Ibid, 35–37. A recent study has also revealed that local authorities in Scotland adopt a routinised, simplistic and bureaucratic approach to handling claims made against them: S Halliday, J Ilan and C Scott, 'Street-Level Tort Law: The Bureaucratic Justice of Liability Decision-Making' (2012) 75 *MLR* 347.

[96] J Pendle, 'Quantum Assessment Tools—Encouraging Collaboration and Transparency (2012) 1 *Journal of Personal Injury Law* 32.

[97] Insurers suggest that there is no dispute on liability in about 90% of RTA claims and 80% of employers' liability claims: Jackson, *Review of Civil Litigation Costs: Preliminary Report* (n 70) para 8.4.

[98] Lewis, 'Compensation Culture Reviewed' (n 1) 215. Lewis identifies, for example, the practice of 'pre-med' offers where insurers pay out on claims without even consulting claimants' medical records.

[99] The ABI states that 90% of all personal injury claims are below £5,000: ABI, *Improving the Small Claims Track* (2006).

[100] D Fisher, 'The Future of Personal Injury: An Insurers Perspective' (2008) 2 *Journal of Personal Injury Law* 164, 165.

[101] D Fisher, 'Third Party Assistance (Or Should I Say Capture?) (2011) 4 *Journal of Personal Injury Law* 245.

claims can be resolved not only quickly and cheaply but also with predictability as fixed costs apply at each stage. Streamlined procedures are also designed to keep claimant lawyers' work to a minimum. Lawyers reported that the way to make money out of CFAs was to have a regular throughput of quick, small and easy cases.[102] This led them to adopt bulk processing approaches similar to insurers with increased standardisation and reliance on claims management software and non-legally qualified personnel.[103] In lowering the margins on lower value claims, streamlined procedures with fixed cost force claimant lawyers to go even further down this road and so help insurers to achieve operational efficiency on both sides.

Insurers have not yet achieved all they want. Whilst an increase in the small claims limit appears imminent, it has yet to be introduced.[104] Nevertheless, the fact that civil justice policy has moved significantly in the direction sought by insurers suggests that their instrumental efforts have played an important role. Under Labour, insurers were effective not only in ensuring that costs hit the political agenda but, just as importantly, in shaping the policy response. As will be seen later, the dynamics in relation to the Coalition were quite different.

In the early 2000s, the Labour Government resisted concerns about legal costs.[105] However, insurers exploited opportunities to force both the issue and its preferred policies onto the political agenda. When the Better Regulation Task Force reviewed the existence of the compensation culture in 2004, insurers used the opportunity to campaign for an increase in the small claims track. The Task Force recommended that the Government should undertake research and justify any limit lower than £5,000.[106] With a reluctant tone, Labour agreed to consider the issue.[107] Insurers also made strong representations to the House of Commons Constitutional Affairs Committee during its review of small claims which recommended that the limit should be increased to £2,500.[108] When the Committee later reviewed the compensation culture, the ABI's written evidence focused on the issue of legal costs rather than levels of claiming—the predominant concern at the time.[109]

Insurers also persisted independently. Both Norwich Union and the ABI published reports on increasing the small claims limit and streamlining the claims process, which were distributed to the media, MPs and the Lords.[110] The ABI issued several press releases over the years to keep the issue alive.[111] It also published research to show that an increase

[102] Goriely, Moorhead and Abrams (n 5) 21. Such claims minimise risk because they are usually successful, require little investment and are resolved quickly.

[103] Ibid, 47–58.

[104] The Chancellor of the Exchequer announced the Government's intention to increase the small claims limit in 2015: HM Treasury, *Spending Review and Autumn Statement* (2015).

[105] Department for Work and Pensions, Review of Employers' Liability Compulsory Insurance: First Stage Report (2004).

[106] Better Regulation Task Force (BRTF), *Better Routes to Redress* (2004) 25.

[107] Department for Constitutional Affairs (DCA), Tackling the Compensation Culture—Government Response to Better Regulation Task Force Report: Better Routes to Redress (2004).

[108] Constitutional Affairs Committee (CAC), *The Courts: Small Claims, First Report* (HC 519, 2005).

[109] See the written evidence submitted by the ABI to the CAC inquiry on compensation culture: CAC, *Compensation Culture, Third Report* (HC 754-I, 2005).

[110] Norwich Union, A Modern Compensation System: Moving from Concept to Reality (2004); ABI, Care and Compensation (2005); and ABI, Improving the Small Claims Track.

[111] See, eg, 'ABI backs Task Force Call for Reform of Legal Process in Personal Injury Cases' (27 May 2004), 'ABI Research Shows Claimants Will Benefit from Streamlined Personal Injury Claims Process' (11 July 2006).

in the small claims limit would not prejudice claimants as they would be better off without lawyers.[112] From this perspective, insurers were very effective in their framing of the issues as they effectively stacked the debate against claimant representatives.[113]

Insurers argued that both an increase in the small claims limit and the introduction of streamlined procedures would benefit genuine claimants who were then getting stuck in a slow and expensive system and who were achieving compensation despite the system rather than because of it. In painting legal wrangling by overly adversarial and expensive claimant lawyers as the cause of the problems, lawyers were presented as acting not only detrimentally to the interests of their clients but also in their own self-interest. Claimant lawyers fought back, arguing that any unnecessary cost and delays within the system were caused by the unreasonable behaviour of insurers in defending claims. Insurers, they argued, were not seeking to improve the system but simply engaging in a cynical exercise to save money. Nevertheless, claimant lawyers' attempts to frame their role as 'consumer safeguards' protecting the interests of vulnerable injured victims against rich and powerful corporations were undermined by the association of disproportionate legal costs with greedy claimants pursuing spurious if not fraudulent claims. Also, whilst insurers were able to relate their arguments and reform packages to tangible benefits of reduced costs and reduced premiums, claimant lawyers struggled to assert more intangible values of empowerment, the exposure of wrongdoing, accountability and the regulation of behaviour. In sum, frames utilised by insurers portrayed them as detached, pragmatic and acting in the public interest whilst claimant lawyers were simply fighting for their own survival. Arguments that claims required an irreducible amount of work seemed overly technical and struggled to achieve legitimacy in comparison with more ideologically compelling tropes associated with 'fat cat lawyers' and the 'compensation culture'.

By 2006, Labour's position on costs had changed, stating that it was committed to 'find[ing] ways to make the claims process more timely, proportionate and cost effective'.[114] Sensing the Government's interest in reform, and fearing an increase in the small claims limit, claimant representatives started to make concessions on streamlining.[115] By 2007, Labour's line on low-value claims had hardened further with the Lord Chancellor stating that 'the spiralling costs of small value personal injury claims' needed to be addressed.[116] It issued a consultation paper rejecting an increase in the small claims limit but proposing a streamlined

[112] Frontier Economics, *Outcomes for Legally Represented and Unrepresented Claimants in Personal Injury Compensation* (2006). This report was not published in full by the ABI and its findings are heavily contested.

[113] D Scheufele and D Tewksbury, 'Framing, Agenda Setting, and Priming: The Evolution of Three Media Effects' (2007) *Journal of Communication* 9; J Mathes, 'What's in a Frame? A Content Analysis of Media Framing Studies in the World's Leading Communication Journals 1990–2005' (2009) *Journalism and Mass Communication Quarterly* 349; G Lakoff, *Don't Think of an Elephant: Know Your Values and Frame the Debate* (Vermont, Chelsea Green Publishing, 2004). For discussion of how tort reformers stacked the debate against plaintiffs in the US, see: W Haltom and M McCann, *Distorting the Law: Politics, Media, and the Litigation Crisis* (Chicago IL, University of Chicago Press, 2004).

[114] DCA, The Courts: Small Claims—Government Response to the Constitutional Affairs Select Committee's Report (Cm 6754, 2006) 8.

[115] The TUC said it would consider the early notification of claims: TUC, '*Personal Injury Claims: Proposals for Change*' (2006). Most significantly, however, the Law Society proposed a streamlined procedure for all personal injury claims under £10,000: Law Society, *Compensation Fast and Fair* (2006). See also, APIL, press release, 'Costs savings within everyone's grasp, says APIL' (May 2006).

[116] Lord Falconer, Speech to APIL annual conference (April 2007).

claims process for all personal injury claims up to £25,000.[117] Claimant representatives lobbied hard to keep the impending reforms to a minimum and sensing Labour's hesitancy, insurers maintained pressure to ensure the reforms were driven through.[118] To their disappointment, the scheme eventually announced applied only to RTAs up to £10,000.[119]

Nevertheless, the commission of Jackson's review in 2008 presented a fresh opportunity to campaign. Insurers supported Jackson's recommendations and unsurprisingly particularly welcomed his proposal to abolish recoverability.[120] They lobbied the Coalition to implement the recommendations but found quite different dynamics from those under Labour. As outlined below, the Coalition was keen to act in any event and told insurers that they were 'pushing an open door on costs'.[121]

Insurers are a formidable lobby group. The ABI represents 300 companies which together control assets equivalent to a quarter of the UK's capital.[122] As the paymasters of the tort system, they are difficult to ignore and are well resourced and much more experienced in lobbying than their counterpart, the Association of Personal Injury Lawyers, established in 1990. As revealed by documents obtained under the Freedom of Information Act 2000, insurers have close links not only with ministers but also with civil servants and they were heavily involved in the implementation of the Jackson reforms through LASPO.[123] As the paymasters of the tort system, insurers have made significant efforts to shape the tort system around their own commercial demands and with some success. They have played an instrumental role in getting the issue of legal costs onto the political agenda and in keeping it there. Just as importantly, they have shaped the policies adopted. Insurers worked hard to convince Labour to act and whilst the Coalition was willing to act in any event, it still relied on insurers' policy suggestions when it came to reform. The extension of the streamlined procedure is a clear example.

The Senior Judiciary's Commitment to Proportionate Justice

Just as the Labour Government had turned its attention to the issue of legal costs, the Master of the Rolls asked Lord Justice Jackson to undertake his review. The senior judiciary has, therefore, played an instrumental role in the problematisation of costs. As they deal with the disputed claims which reach court, judges see only a small proportion of all claims but the most expensive proportion.[124] Regardless of whether disproportionate

[117] MoJ, Case Track Limits and the Claims Process for Personal Injury Claims (2007).

[118] ABI, Adding Insult to Injury: The Need for Reform of the Personal Injury Claims Process (2008).

[119] MoJ, Case Track Limits and the Claims Process for Personal Injury Claims: Response to Consultation (2008).

[120] ABI, Ministry of Justice's Consultation Paper—Proposals for Reform of Civil Litigation Funding and Costs in England and Wales—A Response from the Association of British Insurers (December 2010).

[121] Freedom of information documents obtained by shadow justice minister Andy Slaughter revealed meetings between insurers and the MoJ, in which insurers were allegedly told they were 'pushing at an open door' over civil justice reforms: R Rothwell, 'Collision Course' [2011] *Law Society Gazette*, 17 November.

[122] www.abi.org.uk/About.

[123] R Ramesh, 'Insurance Lobbyists were Briefed by Mandarins Over Legal Reform' *The Guardian* (30 January 2012).

[124] Research suggests that in 2003 proceedings were issued in only 15% of personal injury claims and that only 10,000 such claims are tried (1% of all personal injury claims): P Fenn and N Rickman, *Calculating Reasonable Success Fees for RTA Claims* (2003) (report for the Civil Justice Council). This is consistent with the finding of the Pearson Commission that 99% of cases were settled out of court (n 63).

costs were extensive throughout the system or not, the fact that they were a feature at all signalled that the policy of proportionality underlying the Woolf reforms had not been properly implemented. Jackson was not asked to undertake an open review of costs but to put forward recommendations to achieve 'access to justice at proportionate cost'.[125] Sir Anthony May, President of the Queen's Bench Division stated that costs were assessed 'with nodding respect only to proportionality'.[126] Jackson was, therefore, a second attempt to achieve Woolf's ideal. Lord Dyson stated that 'it should come as no surprise that the philosophy underlying the Jackson reforms is the same philosophy that underpinned the Woolf reforms'.[127] However, as Jackson himself acknowledged, proportionality is an open-textured concept and his proposals marked a clear hardening of its interpretation.[128] Indeed, Lord Woolf had been part of the judicial committee in *Lownds*, which Jackson felt had caused some of the problem.

For the senior judiciary, the problematisation of disproportionate costs is driven by two factors: access to justice and inefficiency. Disproportionate costs are said to impede access to justice in two respects.[129] First, they deter or prevent individuals from pursuing legitimate claims or defences. Second, they result in an unfair and undesirable distribution of limited resources. The traditional view is that the civil justice system should seek to attain substantive justice as this is seen to promote access to justice. Access to justice in this context means that claims should be dealt with on their merits in accordance with the law. For example, as leading civil proceduralist, Sir Jack Jacob has stated:

> On the one hand, the system of civil procedural law breathes life into the substantive law of the land, gives it reality and effectiveness and brings it into being … and on the other hand, the members of the community are enabled to have their substantive legal rights recognised and transformed into actual judicial remedies, without which their theoretical legal rights would be diminished or denuded of any real value and would be but a snare and a delusion.[130]

From this perspective, Jacob describes civil justice as a 'major responsibility of the machinery of good government, as an instrument of social justice, and as the tool in the age-long quest for justice'.[131] In this paradigm, value is attached to the realisation of law in practice as it is seen to have benefits beyond the individual parties involved through the public enforcement of values underlying the law and through the regulation of behaviour.

This ideal has certainly not been achieved in practice. Many socio-legal academics have been committed to demonstrating the significant gap between law in action and law in the books, and tort is no exception.[132] Genn's study of the settlement process in the 1980s identified a range of non-legal factors affecting the outcome of many claims, including

[125] Jackson, Review of Civil Litigation Costs: Final Report (n 23) 1–2.

[126] Ibid, 34–35.

[127] Lord Dyson, 'The Application of the Amendments to the Civil Procedure Rules' (18th lecture in the Implementation Programme, 22 March 2013).

[128] Jackson, Review of Civil Litigation Costs: Final Report (n 23) 36.

[129] See further, J Sorabji, *English Civil Justice after the Woolf and Jackson Reforms* (Cambridge, Cambridge University Press, 2014).

[130] J Jacob, 'The Administration of Civil Justice' in J Jacob, *The Reform of Civil Procedural Law and Other Essays in Civil Procedure* (London, Sweet & Maxwell, 1982) 59–60.

[131] Ibid.

[132] See, eg, D Harris et al, *Compensation and Support for Illness and Injury* (Oxford, Clarendon Press, 1984); Genn, *Hard Bargaining* (n 86) and Lewis and Morris, 'Tort Law Culture' (n 1).

inequality of bargaining power.[133] In addition, the cost of civil justice has been a constant concern. By the time of Woolf there had already been over 60 reviews of the civil justice system though the main aim of the resulting reforms was to reduce the cost of delivering substantive justice.[134]

Pursuing substantive justice within a fault-based adversarial and individuated system is expensive and slow. Cost and delay may well secure higher levels of accuracy but reduce access by deterring people from bringing or defending claims. As was once said, 'justice is open to all, like the Ritz hotel'.[135] Faced with a choice between high rates of accuracy and access for the few and lower rates of accuracy but higher rates of access for the many, proponents of proportionality prefer the latter. As Lord Devlin said:

> The fallacy inherent in our High Court procedure of civil litigation is just that—that where justice is concerned, time and money are no object. We think of British justice as an ideal into which such sordid considerations ought not to enter. We refuse to associate with it such homely maxims as that half a loaf is better than no bread. But is it right to cling to a system that offers perfection for the few and nothing at all for the many? Perhaps: if we could really be sure that our existing system was perfect. But of course it is not. We delude ourselves if we think that it always produces the right judgment. Every system contains a percentage of error; and if by slightly increasing the percentage of error, we can substantially reduce the percentage of cost, it is only the idealist who will revolt.[136]

The underlying philosophy is that it is better to ration process than access.[137] The result is that proponents of proportionality focus on access to dispute resolution procedures rather than on access to substantive legal rights and entitlements, and speed and inexpense in resolving disputes are central to their understanding of 'justice'.

In addition, proportionality is seen as a pragmatic response to the tension between increased demand for law and the limited budgets devoted to civil justice. Proponents of proportionality argue that limited resources available for civil justice must be distributed fairly. As Lord Dyson MR has stated:

> Dealing with a case justly does not simply mean ensuring that a decision is reached on the merits. It is a mistake to assume that it does … The court has to consider three things: the claimant's perspective, the defendant's perspective and, importantly, the perspective of other court-users. It is not enough to consider the need to secure justice between the parties … Doing the proper administration of justice goes beyond the immediate parties to litigation. It requires the court to consider the needs of all litigants, of all court-users.[138]

From this perspective, proportionality is seen to give effect to distributive justice.[139] The ideal of substantive justice for all is not possible and so compromises must be made.

[133] Genn, *Hard Bargaining* (n 86).

[134] Woolf, *Access to Justice: Interim Report* (n 4) ch 2, para 2.

[135] This quote is attributed to Sir James Matthews, an Irish judge in the late Victorian era.

[136] Lord Devlin was speaking to the BBC in 1970 for a programme entitled 'What's Wrong with the Law', quoted in Woolf, *Access to Justice: Interim Report* (n 4) ch 4, para 5.

[137] Zuckerman, 'A Reform of Civil Procedure' (n 73). Of course, as outlined above, claimant representatives argue that the reforms reduce rather than increase levels of access.

[138] 'The Application of the Amendments to the Civil Procedure Rules' (18th lecture in the Implementation Programme, District Judges' Annual Seminar, 22 March 2013).

[139] For further discussion, see Sorabji, *English Civil Justice* (n 129) chs 5–6.

Sceptics argue that proportionality is not a means to an end but an end in itself.[140] In other words, it is suggested that proportionality is simply about achieving reduced costs and increased efficiency. There is certainly a strong element of this. During the Woolf reforms, APIL sought to argue that many of the access to justice arguments advanced in favour of proportionality did not apply in the context of personal injury claims. As most such claims are successful, the majority of claims costs are met by insurers.[141] In this sense, personal injury claims were not subject to a fixed budget and so the pressure to ration procedure rather than access was not the same as in other areas. However, Lord Woolf noted that 'even where the individual litigants received back the full cost of achieving their compensation, that cost had to be borne in the first place by the insurers, in the second place by the insured and in the third place by society generally'.[142] He argued that it was 'incorrect to assume that high costs are not a problem merely because they are met out of a relatively deep pocket or are passed on in insignificant amounts to individual consumers. Unnecessary costs to the economy as a whole are not acceptable, however they are distributed'.[143] In addition, he stated that a system which usually paid those who litigated cases as much as, and sometimes more than, the victims received in compensation simply failed to command public confidence.[144]

More recently, in discussing recoverable costs, Jackson stated:

> Most civil litigation is a form of business project in which the parties invest substantial sums in order to achieve a just outcome. Even justice must have a price. It is not rational to spend £1,000 to recover a £100 debt, however strong or virtuous your claim. Outside litigation, no normal business project is conducted on an open-ended basis, with costs simply being added up at the end. The time has now come to apply sensible budgetary control to the recoverable costs of litigation.[145]

In justifying his proposal that disproportionate costs should not be assumed to be recoverable just because they were necessarily incurred, he further noted:

> The policy which underlies the proposed new rule is that cost benefit analysis has a part to play, even in the realm of civil justice. If parties wish to pursue claims or defences at disproportionate cost, they must do so, at least in part, at their own expense.[146]

These statements suggest that the problematisation of disproportionate costs is driven, in part, by a perception that they reflect inefficient practices, which may well be the case in some circumstances but not necessarily so. In addition, they reflect the view that it is simply undesirable to expend disproportionate amounts of money on processing claims. Reduced cost and increased efficiency add more value to society than higher levels of accuracy and substantive justice. Whether for access to justice or efficiency reasons, therefore, disproportionate costs are problematised because they are not seen to serve the public interest. The

[140] T Farrow, *Civil Justice, Privatization and Democracy* (Toronto, University of Toronoto Press, 2014) 298–306; C Hanycz, 'More Access to Less Justice: Efficiency, Proportionality and Costs in Canadian Civil Justice Reform' (2008) 27(1) *Civil Justice Quarterly* 98.

[141] Insurers suggest that there is no dispute on liability in about 90% of RTA claims and 80% of employers' liability claims: Jackson, *Review of Civil Litigation Costs: Preliminary Report* (n 70) para 8.4.

[142] Woolf, Access to Justice: Final Report (n 4), ch 25.

[143] Ibid, para 2.

[144] Ibid.

[145] R Jackson LJ, 'Lord Justice Jackson's paper for the Civil Justice Council conference on 21 March 2014' (2014), 8.

[146] Jackson, Review of Civil Litigation Costs: Final Report (n 23) 38.

value that substantive justice might bring to individuals and to wider society in the form of accountability, the exposure of wrongdoing and the regulation of behaviour is either not prized or not seen as a priority.

Deregulation Politics

The problematisation of legal costs also has a clear political dimension.[147] Whilst Labour was eventually convinced to act on legal costs, the Coalition, driven by the Conservatives, seized on the issue of its own volition. In the run up to the election, the Conservatives expressed their concern that the United Kingdom had 'become simultaneously and dangerously under-regulated in some areas (particularly systemic risks in the banking sector) but chronically over-regulated elsewhere'.[148] They promised to 'sweep away Labour's ineffective system of bureaucracy' and this became a central aspiration of the Coalition.[149] Tort law received some attention in this regard. Section 69 of the Enterprise and Regulatory Reform Act 2013 now prevents civil liability from attaching to breach of health and safety regulations. This removed the strict liability that attached to some breach of statutory duty actions in this context. Employees must now prove that their employers were at fault through common law negligence.[150]

However, the Conservatives' main concern related to the tort system and the development of the claims market. In the run up to the election, the Conservatives seized on the issue of compensation culture in what has been described as a bid to 'win back traditional Tory voters' alienated by an otherwise reforming agenda.[151] David Cameron bemoaned over-the-top health and safety practices which he attributed in large part to the compensation culture. He asked Lord Young to review the matter. The Better Regulation Task Force had reported in 2004 that the compensation culture was perceived rather than real, largely on the basis that claims were not increasing at that time but simply fluctuating.[152] By the time of Lord Young's review, claims had increased by 12 per cent though propensity to claim still remained low outside the RTA context.[153] Both Cameron and Lord Young acknowledged this to an extent but nevertheless continued to use the compensation culture mantra.[154] First, they were concerned that the emergence of a visible and active no win no fee claims market led business to fear being sued and to 'invent lots of their own rules on top of the regulations that already exist'.[155] In response, Lord Young recommended that payments for the referral of claims should be restrained and that claims advertising should

[147] In relation to the US, see DS Reda, 'The Cost-and-Delay Narrative in Civil Justice Reform: Its Fallacies and Functions (2012) 90 *Oregon Law Review* 1085.

[148] Conservative Party Green Paper, Regulation in the Post-Bureaucratic Age: How to get Rid of Red Tape and Reform Quangos—Policy Paper on Better Regulation (2009) 5.

[149] Ibid.

[150] APIL has dubbed section 69 'a charter for rogue bosses': APIL news release, 'Prove It or Lose It—Now Injured Workers Must Turn Detective' (30 September 2013).

[151] C Brown, 'Compensation Culture Targeted in Shift to Right' *The Independent* (1 October 2007).

[152] BRTF (n 106).

[153] Lewis and Morris, 'Tort Law Culture' (n 1).

[154] Young (n 17) 19.

[155] David Cameron MP, 'Reducing the Burden and Impact of Health and Safety' (speech at Policy Exchange, 1 December 2009).

be further controlled.[156] Second, they were concerned that legal costs were too high. Lord Young recommended the implementation of Jackson's proposals and the extension of the streamlined procedure in place for low-value RTAs so as to 'free businesses from unnecessary bureaucratic burdens and the fear of having to pay out unjustified damages claims and legal fees'.[157]

It is clear that the drive to reduce legal costs was intended to ease the burden of tort on businesses, including insurers, both in terms of restraining the claims market that had flourished under Labour and in terms of reducing the cost of resolving claims. In this sense, civil justice reform is one mode of deregulation politics: '[m]uch hoopla about litigation costs may be traceable to those whose real complaint is that they or their clients are exposed to liabilities that they would prefer to avoid'.[158] Sugarman notes, in relation to the United States, that 'conservative political entrepreneurs simultaneously seek both to reduce and stabilise the exposure faced by their business and insurer allies while remaining committed to the basic idea of private law as society's core mechanism for accident regulation and victim compensation'.[159] In England and Wales, the Conservatives have focused on reducing and stabilising that exposure by reforming the tort system more than tort law.[160]

Sensationalist rhetoric surrounding the compensation culture was no doubt used by the Coalition to oil the wheels of reform but it also reflected deep-seated concerns held by the Conservatives about the place of tort law in society, and indeed law more generally. The Coalition argued that its efforts to reduce legal costs were part of a wider package of legal system reforms which included significant reductions in the availability of state-funded legal aid and the further promotion of alternative dispute resolution (ADR), particularly mediation.[161] These policies are not new. For some time governments have sought to reduce the cost of legal aid and civil legal aid has been squeezed by the prioritisation of criminal legal aid.[162] In addition, the ADR movement has gathered apace in recent years. Since the implementation of the Woolf reforms, both litigants and judges have been expected to consider mediation as an alternative to court.[163] Academics have expressed their concern about the resulting privatisation of justice and the state's withdrawal from the civil justice system both of which are seen to mark a declining commitment to private law and civil justice.[164]

156 In addition to the ban on referrals, the Government has also banned the offering of financial inducements to claim: Criminal Justice and Courts Act 2014. This was already banned for claims management companies. See further, C Budsworth, 'Should Solicitors be Able to Offer Financial Inducements to Claim?' (2014) 158(17) *Solicitors Journal Supplementary (Personal Injury Focus)* ix.

157 Young (n 17) 8.

158 PD Carrington, 'Renovating Discovery' (1997) 49 *Alabama Law Review* 51, 53. See also PD Carrington, 'Politics and Civil Procedure Rulemaking: Reflections on Experience (2010) 60 *Duke Law Journal* 597.

159 S Sugarman, 'Ideological Flip-Flop: American Liberals Are Now the Primary Supporters of Tort Law' in *Essays on Tort, Insurance, Law and Society in Honour of Bill W Dufwa* (Stockholm, Jure Forlag AB, 2006).

160 JB Weinstein, 'Procedural Reform as a Surrogate for Substantive Law Revision' (1993) 59 *Brooklyn Law Review* 827.

161 The legal aid reforms were implemented by LASPO 2012. Legal aid has, for example, been removed from family cases (except those involving domestic violence, forced marriage or child abduction) and from areas of immigration, employment, education, debt and housing law. For a discussion of current policy on mediation, see: H Genn, *Judging Civil Justice: The Hamlyn Lectures 2008* (Cambridge, Cambridge University Press, 2010).

162 Ibid, 38–45.

163 CPR 1.4(2)(e).

164 Genn, *Judging Civil Justice* (n 161); R Dingwall and E Cloatre, 'Vanishing Trials: An English Perspective (2006) 1 *Journal of Dispute Resolution* Article 7.

Damaska's work demonstrates the link between procedural arrangements and political ideology.[165] He contrasts active states whose procedural rules focus on implementing policy (ie, giving effect to the letter of the law) with reactive states whose procedural rules focus on conflict resolution. In 1979, Sir Jack Jacob stated that the administration of civil justice 'manifests the political will of the State that ... civil wrongs ... be made good, so far as practicable, by compensation and satisfaction'.[166] Whilst the expense of litigation meant that this was not a reality for many individuals, the political will to implement policy underlying the law has also dwindled because of the expense to the state of providing a court-based civil justice system. England and Wales have, therefore, drifted further towards a privatised model of conflict resolution, involving settlement and ADR, which prioritises compromise of legal rights over substantive justice.

The Coalition reforms pursued the privatised conflict resolution model with deliberate and renewed vigour. The reforms were said to be united by an

> ambition to equip people with the knowledge and tools required to enable them to resolve their own disputes, by working problems through in a non-adversarial manner ... What we are ultimately aiming for is a shift in culture where we look to the law to resolve conflicts to one where we take more responsibility for addressing them ourselves in the first instance.[167]

From this viewpoint, the system is to focus on 'dispute resolution ... for the majority of its users rather than the loftier ideals of justice that cause many to pursue their cases beyond the point that it is economic to do so'.[168] Citizens are expected to resolve disputes quickly and cheaply rather than to assert rights and pursue legal entitlements. In this context tort law is about ordering private affairs and not about substantive justice, accountability and the regulation of behaviour. It is not about preventing the abuse of private power or redressing the imbalance of power between vulnerable individuals and rich corporations, as some personal injury lawyers and academics would argue.[169] Conservative policy, achieved through the Coalition policy, was imbued with anti-law, anti-litigation and anti-lawyer rhetoric.[170] It was driven by an ideology that prefers limited state involvement and a reliance on individual responsibility. This marks a 'turn against law'.[171] Whilst legal frameworks are necessary for the ordering of affairs, too much law jeopardises rather than enhances social and economic relations. Law, litigation and lawyers are seen as a social and financial drain. If a balance is to be struck in the claims process between cost, access and accuracy, cost considerations should prevail.

[165] MR Damaska, *The Faces of Justice and State Authority: A Comparative Approach to the Legal Process* (New Haven CT, Yale University Press, 1986). See also, KE Scott, 'Two Models of the Civil Process' (1975) 27 *Stanford Law Review* 937. Scott contrasts what he calls the 'conflict resolution model' with the 'behaviour modification model'.

[166] Jacob (n 130) 1.

[167] MOJ, Solving Disputes in the County Courts: Creating a Simpler, Quicker and More Proportionate System—A consultation on reforming civil justice in England and Wales (2011) 6.

[168] Ibid, 7.

[169] West argues that the rule of law is important not just in constraining the abuse of state power but also in preventing the abuse of private power: R West, 'The Limits of Process' in JE Fleming, *Getting to the Rule of Law* (New York, New York University Press, 2011).

[170] E Thornberg, 'Reaping What We Sow: Anti-Litigation Rhetoric, Limited Budgets, and Declining Support for Civil Courts' (2011) 30 *Civil Justice Quarterly* 74.

[171] M Galanter, 'The Turn Against Law: The Recoil Against Expanding Accountability' (2002) 81 *Texas Law Review* 285.

Conclusion

This chapter has not evaluated whether there was a problem with disproportionate costs. Instead it has examined how and why disproportionate costs became problematised in recent years. In doing so, it has adopted a social constructionist approach which sees problems not as objective realities but as the products of social forces. As legal academics we tend to ignore costs, funding and procedure but each dictate the extent to which and the way in which tort law in the books is translated into tort law in action. There has been little interest in the reform of tort law in England and Wales. Instead, the compensation culture debate has been focused on the tort system and the structural advantages it is seen to have lent to claimants in recent years. It is the issue of legal costs not liability that has become deeply politicised. The reinvigorated drive for proportionate costs is having a significant impact on the organisation and operation of the tort system. The cost of resolving claims, the legal accuracy of case outcomes and access to the tort system are integrally linked and there are concerns that the reforms will impede the ability of some injured claimants to pursue compensation and also lead to under-settlement. Deconstructing the problematisation of legal costs has exposed the dynamics underlying the reforms and provided a deeper understanding of why policy affecting tort has moved in the direction it has.

The reforms have been motivated by commercial, legal and political considerations, some of which stretch beyond tort. Insurers, as the paymasters of the system, have been concerned to shape the claims process around their commercial requirements. The senior judiciary has been concerned with the distribution of resources. The Conservatives have been concerned about the regulatory impact of the aggressive claims market and the encroachment of law more generally. Their meeting of minds on the issue of disproportionate costs opened a policy window. The reforms have not developed on the basis of rational analysis of the evidence and arguments but are the product of a political process. For different reasons, the social actors examined prioritise cost and process over substantive law. The result is that we remain committed to the ideological and legal framework of tort law but our commitment to its realisation in practice continues to decline. Whilst students learn that tort is about corrective justice, deterrence and accountability, the reality is clearly much more complex.

8

Personal Injuries Assessment Board: A Decade of Delivery?

DOROTHEA DOWLING

My personal perspective is that of the non-executive founding, and now former, Chairperson of the Personal Injuries Assessment Board (PIAB) in Ireland. That body trades as injuriesboard.ie but I will refer to PIAB throughout as my involvement was at the governance rather than the operational level.

The primary purpose of this chapter is to provide a factual account of how the PIAB operates and to give some background on its establishment as part of the insurance reform programme in Ireland.

First, A Few Simple Facts

PIAB commenced operations in July 2004 dealing with all injury claims arising from employers' liability, public liability and motor accidents with the first full year of operations being 2006. It now makes c 12,000 statutory awards per annum compared with c 1,500 in the courts throughout the country.[1] PIAB deals with injuries across the severity range, the largest award to date being €1.6 million, and saved the Irish economy over €1 billion in litigation costs over the first decade of its operations.[2] During 2014 PIAB awards totalled €281 million and the Irish courts during the same period awarded €169 million. The court awards in 2014 included cases outside the PIAB remit, such as medical negligence, and oral hearings were down 10 per cent on the previous year.[3]

The decade of delivery of which PIAB was a part can really be summed up quite simply—personal injury litigation volumes halved; the cost of insurance reduced by 40 per cent in

[1] Data from Courts Service annual reports on www.courts.ie.

[2] The basis of this calculation of savings is set out in the 2014 Annual Report of PIAB available at www.injuriesboard.ie.

[3] Oral hearings in 2014 at 1,527 as between jurisdictions were High Court 509 and Circuit Court 1,018. Courts awards of €169m with 56 cases at over €500,000 each and include medical negligence cases many of which involve multi-million awards for future care. In 2013 courts awards totalled €147m when 27 cases were over €1m each. In 2012 awards amounted to €112m and 15 were over €1m each but that higher level breakdown is not provided in the 2014 report. Annual Report Courts Service available at www.courts.ie.

real terms; and injured parties receive their compensation in an average of seven months compared with three years under the old system, with a delivery overhead in PIAB averaging 7 per cent compared with 58 per cent in the litigation culture which had previously dominated.

Some of the statements in the sentence above have already been challenged by a couple of commentators so it is necessary to state the content of sources briefly in this text rather than merely consign them to footnotes.

Some Simple Statistics

During 2014[4] a total of 16,832 new personal injury summonses were issued compared with c 35,000 annually prior to the reform programme.[5] In the annual reports from the Courts Service it can be seen that there is a significant increase in recent years of actions for medical negligence which are currently excluded from the PIAB remit.[6] For the years 2006 to 2014 total PIAB awards amounted to €1.8 billion on 77,000 formal assessments. In an apparent effort to circumvent the reforms, lawyers seemed to issue proceedings on every potential case before the PIAB commencement date in July 2004. As a result the years 2005 and 2006 in court data must be considered as statistical outliers with issued proceedings at 3,746 and 7,673 respectively. A newspaper article in July 2008 which cited a 700 per cent increase in the number of High Court summonses issued in 2007 (compared with 746 in 2005) as being evidence of the failure of PIAB was obviously not statistically robust although the same source was frequently cited by a couple of commentators.[7] In 2002, before PIAB, there were 33,242 personal injury cases commenced in the litigation system, 12,242 in the High Court and 21,000 in the Circuit Court.[8] Over the entire period of the years 2002 to 2014 inclusive there were 235,127 personal injury summonses issued and 18,590 court awards made. Consistently since records became available, data demonstrates that only 8 per cent of cases made it as far as the courtroom.[9] In the face of such facts we need to abandon the fiction that the primary purpose of tort is bringing defendants to account in

[4] Excluding medical negligence, of which 931 actions issued in 2014. Comparative history—942 in 2013; 1,040 in 2012 and 783 in 2011—from Courts Services Annual Reports at www.courts.ie. New personal injuries summons issued in 2014 were down by 2% on the previous year at High Court 7,047; Circuit Court 9,852; District Court 864.

[5] A feature of the Irish system was that litigation proceedings were issued in almost every case of any significance. 'A feature of our litigation process, which was not one which you will be familiar with in the UK, is that barristers were used in almost all such cases .... In order for proceedings to be issued a barrister was asked to draft them. If any settlements were taking place the majority of them would take place involving a barrister who would be paid a negotiation fee'. From S Gilhooly, 'PI changes in Ireland—Implications for England and Wales?' [2006] *Journal of Personal Injury Law* 104.

[6] In England, the latest NHS Litigation Authority Annual Report shows new clinical claims rose by 10.8% to 10,129 during 2012/13 and had increased by 66% over four years.

[7] www.independent.ie/irish-news/injury-claims-board-fails-to-halt-rise-in-court-cases-26462601.html.

[8] The monetary limit of the Circuit Court over this period was €38,000 but was increased to €60,000 in February 2014.

[9] The 8% of litigation cases which do proceed to trial may involve actual disputes about issues of justice, including what Hart called those at the penumbra of the law where novel issues need to be adjudicated. Hart, H. L. A. (1958). 'Positivism and the Separation of Law and Morals', 71 *Harvard Law Review* 593 71 (4): 593–629.

public hearings or that all such claims facilitate the promulgation of court precedents that influence behaviour by acting as a deterrence to negligence.[10]

The Central Statistics Office Index for motor insurance stood at 108.7 in April 2002 when the first report was published on the statutory investigation into insurance costs undertaken by the Motor Insurance Advisory Board (MIAB).[11] This index had reduced to 74 by year end 2013. To this reduction of 32 per cent must be factored in the Consumer Price Index (CPI) which increased over the same period by 25 per cent making for a reduction in real terms of 40 per cent.[12]

The average finalisation period for personal injury claims was four years at the time of the 1996 Deloitte & Touche report.[13] According to the McAuley Report[14] in 1997 Irish lawyers took six times longer (17.4 months) to initiate a settlement than their English counterparts (2.9 months) once proceedings were issued. From accident to trial, a settlement took an average of 40 months in Ireland compared with 11 months in England. This may be explained by the fact that barristers were used in 77 per cent of claims in Ireland compared with 3 per cent in England.[15] The PIAB annual reports provide data on the average finalisation period under the new system which is currently seven months but assessors will not conclude an assessment until there is a stable medical prognosis. In litigation, plaintiffs' advisers will equally not set a case down for hearing until their client's condition is relatively clear. Statistics from the courts do not provide data on the time taken from issuing of proceedings, which could be considered equivalent to registration with PIAB, to final determination either by trial or Notice of Discontinuance so a robust comparison cannot currently be undertaken.

Details of the delivery overhead at 7 per cent are provided in the annual financial accounts of PIAB which are published on their website.[16] In England at the time of the Pearson Report in 1978 it was said that the operating costs of the tort system was 87 per cent of the value of awards.[17] This was contrasted with the Accident Compensation Corporation in New Zealand where the comparable proportion was 12 per cent at that time.[18] It is interesting to note that Pearson is still widely cited despite being described at the time by one academic as 'a confused and intellectually undistinguished report'.[19]

[10] At the time of the Pearson Commission in England in 1978 it was estimated that 99% of injury claims settled without court adjudication. In Ireland, c75% of injury claims arise from motor accidents where liability is based on duties that are relatively straightforward.

[11] The Central Statistics Office Index on the mid-December 2001 Based Series.

[12] The Central Statistics Office Index also reflects the fact that insurers had already commenced reducing prices from October 2002 once the Interim Board of PIAB was appointed and there was evidence of reforms actually being implemented so there was a positive influence on insurance costs even before the commencement date of July 2004.

[13] *The Economic Evaluation of Insurance Costs in Ireland* (Dublin, Department of Enterprise, Trade & Employment, 1996) (Deloitte Report).

[14] According to research for *First Report of the Special Working Group on a Personal Injuries Tribunal* (Dublin, Stationery Office, 1997) no 1/239—Table 12, 121 (McAuley Report): www.worldcat.org/title/first-report-of-special-working-group-on-a-personal-injuries-tribunal-dan-mcauley/oclc/37801824.

[15] McAuley Report (n 14) 117–18, tables 5 and 6.

[16] www.injuriesboard.ie.

[17] The annual cost of the tort system in England during the 1970s was said to be £202m of which the delivery overhead was £175 million and the number of claims was estimated at 250,000.

[18] Report of the Royal Commission on Civil Liability and Compensation for Personal Injury (Cmnd 7054, 1978) vol 1; vol II, Statistics and Costings; vol III, Overseas Systems of Compensation.

[19] RA Hasson, 'The Pearson Report—Something for Everyone?' (1979) 6 *British Journal of Law & Society* 119.

Current levels of litigation overheads are not known for Ireland as there has been no updated survey since that published in the 2004 MIAB Report when it was 46 per cent.[20] However, other studies on the cost of doing business in Ireland examined trends in legal costs which would indicate a current level in the region of 58 per cent.[21] In England, a paper which studied the period from 1991 to 2000 found that legal costs accounted for 30 per cent of total motor personal injury payments.[22] In a more recent article by an insurer published in 2008, figures are quoted from the Association of British Insurers indicating that for every £1 spent on injury claims across motor and liability, 43p is spent on legal costs.[23] Dr Vincent Hogan of University College Dublin in his 2006 cost–benefit analysis of PIAB recorded (at p 8) that 'Solicitors' Instruction fees increased by 4 per cent in real terms (ie in excess of the CPI) every year for 20 years (1984–2004). Barristers' brief fees grew by 3 per cent in real terms'.[24]

In financial terms, PIAB results are better than those which were said could be delivered by the introduction of a 'no-fault' system for motor insurance in England as espoused in the Pearson Report. At that time it was estimated that such a reform would have cost £130 million according to the parliamentary debates in the House of Commons on 16 March 1978.[25] The reductions in premium charges in Ireland are also well in excess of what might have been delivered by a government proposal in 1994 to cap damages.[26] This was a reform idea which was abandoned after the 1996 Deloitte Report[27] and probably would, in any event, have been unconstitutional.

In a nutshell, until early 2014 the seemingly incompatible objectives of speeding up settlements while reducing insurance costs were achieved by the reform programme.[28] Back in 1992 Irish motorists were paying the highest average premium in Europe.[29] By 2012 an Irish Automobile Association survey demonstrated that the average motor premium in Ireland was half of that in the UK market—which was the exact opposite of the situation a decade earlier.[30]

[20] Department of Enterprise, Trade and Employment, *Motor Insurance Advisory Board Final Report* (2004) 57, s 20 (MIAB Report).

[21] Annual Reports of the the National Competitive Council.

[22] R Lewis, A Morris and K Oliphant, 'Tort Personal Injury Claims Statistics: Is there a Compensation Culture in the United Kingdom?' (2006) 14 *Torts Law Journal* 158 and (2006) 2 *Journal of Personal Injury Law* 87.

[23] D Fisher, 'The Future of Personal Injury: An Insurer's Perspective' (2008) 2 *Journal of Personal Injury Law* 164.

[24] www.justice.ie/en/JELR/legalcosts.pdf/Files/legalcosts.pdf, 8.

[25] Hansard: hansard.millbanksystems.com/commons/1978/mar/16/civil-liability-royal-commissions-report.

[26] A Bill was proposed by the then Minister for Enterprise and Employment, Mr Ruari Quinn, in 1994. The Dáil Debates 13 October 1994, col 1981; and *The Irish Times* (21 October 1994).

[27] Deloitte Report (n 13).

[28] In Ireland, motor insurers are also considerably more profitable than their counterparts in England where the combined operating ratio of claims and expenses compared with premium income has been negative every year since 1996 with policyholders experiencing significant price inflation.

[29] Survey published by the Belgian Consumer group Test, Achat, and the EC consumer group BEUC as debated in the Irish Parliament 29 April 1992: www.oireachtasdebates.oireachtas.ie/debates%20authoring/debateswebpack.nsf/takes/dail1992042900013?opendocument.

[30] In a similar period since the 1999 Woolf reforms were launched in England the number of motor claims doubled from 400,000 in 2000 to 800,000 in 2013.

A Couple of Subversive Thoughts

First, insurers never pay claims, policyholders do—as do all consumers of goods and services. This means that the most financially vulnerable in our society may pay disproportionately more for inefficiencies in the tort redress system. The loudest calls for reform in Ireland came not from the insurance industry itself but from premium payers.[31]

Second, longitudinal statistical analysis indicates that a trend of increasing claims costs can sometimes make more money for insurers, so reducing claims costs may actually pressurise their profits.[32] I will return to my challenges to the orthodoxy of law and economics after I present a factual account of the Irish insurance reform programme which commenced in 1998.

The Great Match: Ireland versus England

At this point it may be necessary to explain to an international readership that Ireland has a slightly different tort environment from England. While these countries are the two main common law jurisdictions in the European Union,[33] a comparative study highlights some important variances in the current context of redress for personal injuries that are (allegedly) negligently caused. A few pertinent examples are summarised below:

1. Motor insurance is compulsory under EU directives but employers' liability cover is not compulsory in Ireland as it has been in England since 1969.[34]
2. General damages in Ireland are many multiples of amounts awarded for similar injuries in England being 12 times higher overall in motor, employers' liability and public liability.[35]
3. Unlike in England,[36] in Ireland levels of general damage awarded by the courts are not increased annually. There are no Judicial Studies Board guidelines on general damages, as first published in England in 1992 and of which the thirteenth edition was released in 2013. The first similar publication in Ireland was the PIAB Book of Quantum compiled in 2004.[37]

[31] Young motorists who were finding cover unaffordable established a lobbying group called MIJAG—motor insurance justice action group. Some businesses established AIR which stood for the Alliance for Insurance Reform.

[32] The MIAB 2002 Report found that over the period from 1983 to 1999 Irish motor insurers made 11 times the total post-tax profit earned by their UK counterparts and only recorded losses in three years compared with eight out of 17 years in the UK.

[33] Northern Ireland was established as a separate jurisdiction within the UK in 1921. Malta has a mixed common and civil law system.

[34] Not having a strong history of heavy industry, Ireland has not had to introduce schemes for coalminers or asbestosis sufferers as has been a feature of the trend in claims volumes in the UK.

[35] McAuley Report (n 14) 128, table 24. More recent preliminary high-level analysis in 2015 indicates that in England at an overall level the average injury claim vale is £5,000 compared with €38,000 in Ireland—the relevant raw data is contained in an as yet unpublished paper by this author.

[36] Following the English test case of *Heil v Rankin* [2000] EWCA Civ 84, [2001] QB 272 future awards were linked to the Retail Price Index, and as part of the Jackson reforms in 2012 were increased by a further 10%.

[37] www.google.ie/?gws_rd=ssl#q=piab+book+of+quantum.

4. There is no legislative provision in Ireland setting the discount rate for actuarial future loss claims.[38] This contrasts with the Ogden Tables or equivalent in England where a rate of 2.5 per cent was established by the Lord Chancellor in 2001 in the face of the issues tried in House of Lords test case of *Wells v Wells*.[39]
5. There is no system of structured settlements or periodic payment orders (PPOs)[40] as there has been in England since 2005. However, one such case was concluded on that basis by means of an interim settlement by Irish Rail in July 2010 pending the introduction of a statutory scheme.[41]
6. Ireland has never had extensive legal aid for civil cases so the need to abolish it did not arise as it did in England.[42]
7. For seriously injured plaintiffs whose sole source of future income is from their lump sum settlement the interest earned is tax free in Ireland.[43] In contrast, this exemption from taxation on future interest only applies to PPOs in England.[44]
8. Unlike the system in operation in England since 1990, the recovery by the state of social welfare benefits paid as a result of negligence actions has not been a part of the Irish system.[45]
9. With a less sophisticated National Health System of more limited coverage than in England, half of Irish citizens have private health insurance.[46] This is provided on the basis of 'community rating' and lifetime open coverage under a risk equalisation scheme between underwriters.[47]
10. For personal injury cases, Ireland does not have a system of active case management of negligence claims in the courts. There is little in the way of effective pre-action protocols nor provision for preliminary applications to dismiss cases of no merit at an early stage.

[38] While such a provision was included in the Civil Liability and Courts Act 2004 that s 24 was never commenced. A discount rate of 3% was established in *Boyne v Dublin Bus* [2002] IEHC 135, [2003] 4 IR 47.

[39] *Wells v Wells* [1999] 1 AC 345. In November 2015 in *Gill Russell (a minor) v HSE* [2015] IECA 236 the (newly established) Court of Appeal upheld a High Court decision of the previous year to apply a discount rate of 1.5% instead of the 3% which had previously been applied since 2002 as established by the High Court in *Boyne v Dublin Bus* (n 38).

[40] Proposals were published in Ireland during July 2015 for PPOs in clinical negligence cases and possibly in other injury actions against the state sector. It is planned that the index used to calculate the revision shall be the annual rate of Irish Harmonised Index of Consumer Prices (HICP) as published by the Central Statistics Office rather than the index of average household earnings—Civil Liability (Amendment) Bill 2015.

[41] 'Historic Structured Settlement Approved' *Irish Times* (29 July 2010); 'Irish Rail to Pay Injured Man's Care Costs for Life' *Irish Independent* (30 July 2010).

[42] The 1999 Woolf reforms included removal of legal aid and the introduction of conditional fee agreements (CFAs).

[43] Irish Tax Consolidation Act 1997, s 613.

[44] The receipt of general damages compensation and restitutionary special damages to date is tax exempt in both jurisdictions.

[45] With effect from 1 August 2014 a measure has been introduced which obliges defendants to repay to the state up to five years' social welfare benefits that were caused to be paid as a result of negligent accidents, but as the effective date relates to the date of settlement rather than the accrual of the cause of action this retrospectively imposes an additional liability which may raise Constitutional issues. At the time of writing such payments would not be reflected in the data analysed so this development is not relevant for historical comparison purposes.

[46] In 2012 data from the Health Insurance Authority reflected a reduction in coverage to 46% of the population from 51% in 2008. The fall-off is largely attributed to the economic crisis in the intervening period.

[47] See C Barrington, D Dowling and S Creedon, *A Business Appraisal of Private Medical Insurance in Ireland* (Dublin, Department of Health, 2007)—a review for the Minister of Health: health.gov.ie/blog/press-release/government-approves-reform-measures-for-private-health-insurance-market/.

11. Claims management companies,[48] which appear to have been such a source of difficulty in England,[49] have not been a feature of the Irish environment[50] nor has legal expenses insurance, either before or after the event.[51] Similarly, Conditional Fee Arrangements (CFAs) introduced in England, under which lawyers could double their fees, have not been a feature of the Irish system nor have referral fees which were banned in England during 2013.[52]
12. The Irish legal professions are still largely self-regulated.[53] Accordingly, the country has not experienced the negative fallout which seems to be emerging in England with 'Alternative Business Structures' where some solicitors are now merging into claims management companies.[54]

There have been many other divergences in the development of Irish law and related processes since 1922 when the Republic adopted the (then) existing English system but those are not relevant in the current context.

However, one other significant fact is that Ireland has a written constitution. Article 40.3.2 guarantees the right to bodily integrity and this underpins the entitlement to general damages for 'pain and suffering' negligently caused.[55] Accordingly, the abolition of general damages as in other jurisdictions is not a right that could be reversed unless approved in a referendum (which would not be likely to be passed).[56]

What PIAB Is Not

PIAB is not a species of 'alternative dispute resolution' (ADR) in the sense that such a term is usually understood.[57] The long title of the Personal Injuries Assessment Board Act 2003 makes it clear that it is not an 'alternative' to the courts:

> An Act to enable, in certain situations, the making of assessments, without the need for legal proceedings to be brought in that behalf, of compensation for personal injury (or both such

[48] As referred to by Professor Richard Lewis at the University of Limerick conference in May 2014 and explained further in ch 2 of this book.

[49] Since the introduction of regulatory standards in England, including the banning of referral fees in 2013, the number of CMCs declined from 2,553 in 2012 to 1,125 in March 2014: Lewis (n 48).

[50] However, in the first 2015 edition of the *Law Society of Ireland Gazette* the concept of 'claims-harvesting' is identified as an emerging trend and concerns arise about this unregulated activity which may be contrary to advertising regulations.

[51] Recovery of After the Event (ATE) legal expenses premium payments was abolished in England during 2013.

[52] There are concerns in Ireland that internet searches using key words like 'injury, compensation or claim' have led unsuspecting members of the public to divulge their personal data to unregulated entities in recent years.

[53] In 2011 a Bill to establish an independent Legal Services Regulatory Authority was published but, as at November 2015, it is still the subject of amendment.

[54] On CMCs in the UK, see R Lewis, ch 2 of this book.

[55] *Ryan v AG* [1965] IR 294 (Supreme Court).

[56] Research undertaken in New Zealand and Australia by the author during 2010 indicates that the abolition of general damages in favour of a 'no-fault' scheme has not been an unmitigated success and can bring with it a host of other challenges.

[57] Described as 'alternative dispute resolution' by DH Erskine, 'Reforming Federal Personal Injury Litigation by Incorporation of the Procedural Innovations of Scotland and Ireland: An Analysis and Proposal' (2007) 15 *Cardozo Journal of International and Comparative Law* 1.

> injuries and property damage), in those situations to prohibit, in the interests of the common good, the bringing of legal proceedings unless any of the parties concerned decides not to accept the particular assessment or certain other circumstances apply, to provide for the enforcement of such an assessment, for those purposes to establish a body to be known as The Personal Injuries Assessment Board and to define its functions and to provide for related matters.

PIAB is a mandatory procedure which must be exhausted before any court proceedings are issued.

The introduction of PIAB is not a move towards a 'no-fault' system. It is, however, true that a prospective plaintiff is relieved of the burden of proof in relation to negligence in cases resolved through the non-adversarial process. There is no bargaining within the independent assessment process and this removes many of the unequal power dynamics of negotiation on which much literature focuses.

In deliberations[58] on the Fifth Motor Insurance Directive during 2003 the EU Commission had considered reversing the burden of proof for vulnerable road users.[59] This is, obviously, not consistent with the common law tradition. It is also questionable whether such a proposal by the EU would be compatible with the legal basis of that harmonisation project.[60]

The PIAB procedure does not require an admission of liability on the part of the prospective defendant. I shall return to these points when examining the process in detail.

Transferable Lessons?

Perhaps the most important transferable lesson from the Irish experience is that it is essential in any reform programme to properly define the problem(s) and identify the main cost drivers. Accidents per se were not the main challenge in the Irish situation.[61] Obviously safety was and is a government priority but for reasons more important than mere premium trends.[62] I am also of the view that many tort reform programmes fail to deliver

[58] European Commission, Insurance Committee Newsletter (21 November 2003); MARKT/2538/03-EN Orig.

[59] Defined as cyclists and pedestrians.

[60] Whether the objective is viewed as creating a single insurance market or in aid of the free movement of people throughout the EU.

[61] Here, the first challenge was that of increasing insurance costs and delays in injured parties securing compensation. Road accident rates per 10,000 registered vehicles had fallen for serious injury from 26.73 in 1990 to 9.74 in 2000 and fatals had reduced from 4.1 to 2.15 over the same period, based on data from the National Roads Authority. While only 2.4% of vehicles in 1990 (decreasing to 1.9% by 2000) reported being involved in an accident, the volume of claims in a decade increased from 12% and 14% of registered vehicles according to statutory returns to the Financial Regulator. In England, the standardised index for motor injury claims rose from 98.3 in 1991 to 128.5 in 2000—a shift of 31% (Lewis, Morris and Oliphant (n 22)).

[62] Econometric methodology used by safety agencies to calculate fatal accident costs is based on the 'willingness to pay' method. While this method is well recognised internationally, it has proven to lead to very different results for different countries. Even where a rigorous approach is applied, the estimates can vary quite widely. Statistics from the European Transport Safety Council Study, *Social and Economic Consequences of Road Traffic Injury in Europe* (5) valued road accident deaths by country and showed wide differences between countries. For example, the official monetary valuation of a road accident death in Portugal was as low as €56.8k and as high as €3.19m in the United States. These are not suitable measures in the context of a review of insurance costs. NG Schwab Christe and NC Soguel (eds), *Contingent Valuation, Transport Safety and the Value of Life* (Boston MA, Kluwer Academic Press, 1995).

on cost-cutting goals because they lack a parallel focus on accident prevention which is an objective tort in itself does not serve well.[63] There is a logical inconsistency between an approach that involves individualised remedies but at the same time also pools the liabilities through insurance charged to individuals collectively.[64] Whatever our views about the merits or efficiency of either approach, it involves a fiction of axiomatic correlatives.[65] Perhaps we should fight the fictions to aid clarity about modern tort functions.[66]

In my opinion, the insurance cost crisis in Ireland was brought to a head in the mid-1990s by a series of disjointed reforms. In 1988 Ireland caught up with what England had done in 1933 by abolishing jury trial for personal injury cases. The objectives were to curtail costs and to bring more consistency to awards. Predictability probably matters more to insurers than the level of damages per se.[67] Even from the plaintiff perspective alone, a failure to treat 'like cases alike' makes tort look arbitrary and this risks undermining public confidence in the law. Jury abolition did not work largely because there was no guide to damages in the absence of a Judicial Studies Board and no equivalent of regular publications such as Kemp & Kemp in England.[68]

It was also projected that jury abolition would lower legal costs by shortening trials. The expectation was that barristers would no longer need to 'play to the gallery' with lengthy advocacy designed to secure the sympathy of jurors. Of course that didn't work. The system of two senior and one junior counsel in almost every High Court case persisted. The waiting list for trials grew longer and litigation overheads nearly doubled.

There was such an outcry about restrictive practices in the legal profession that the Fair Trade Commission was asked to investigate.[69] One of the main recommendations in their

[63] As reflected in the literature the assertion that tort performs an effective deterrence function is 'forced and difficult to sustain'—GC Keating, 'Is Tort a Remedial Institution?' University of California Working Paper 117 of 2010: law.bepress.com/usclwps/lewps/art117. In Ireland, regulatory reforms such as through the criminal system have proven to be more effective as demonstrated in road accident data where frequency reduced after the introduction of 'on the spot' penalty points during a time when tort costs, as reflected in premium rates, were reducing rapidly.

[64] The recent literature on civil recourse theory as developed by Goldberg and Zipursky has produced rich debate on some of the fundamentals of tort, but personally I reject its reliance on 'law jobs' as a necessary ingredient in cases at the core of the law which do not involve contested concepts and existing precedents are accepted rather than being extended.

[65] WN Hohfeld, 'Fundamental Legal Conceptions as Applied in Judicial Reasoning' (1917) 26 *Yale Law Journal* 710. The assignment of the nomenclature 'right' reflects a liability, which is commensurate in his contract example, but this is not open to empirical disproof as it is normative rather than material.

[66] In motor insurance, the widespread introduction of 'protected bonuses' often means that no penalty is sustained by the negligent motorist but an adverse claims experience at national level will be the basis for increasing prices for all policyholders.

[67] Getting the pricing right to cover future liabilities is the main challenge for underwriters if insurers are to profitably continue in business and deliver a dividend to their shareholders. For the benefit of consumers, conditions to enhance price competition can be depressed when insurers need to retain reserves for long periods to cover the volatility that can emerge in a long-tailed run-off of liability exposures. The other side of that coin is that maximum severity claimants are not well served by one-off lump sum settlements that are often based on unreliable projections of future care needs.

[68] W Norris (ed), *Kemp & Kemp: Quantum of Damages* (looseleaf) is published four times a year in England as a comprehensive guide to personal injury awards by the courts and other relevant materials of interest to practitioners. It retails at £1,102 from Thomson Reuters.

[69] The Fair Trade Commission was subsequently known as the Competition Authority which examined these issues further as reported in 2006: www.tca.ie/images/uploaded/documents/Solicitors per cent20and per cent20barristers per cent20full per cent20report.pdf.

March 1990 report was to increase the jurisdictions of the lower courts so that more cases would be dealt with in the lower legal costs jurisdiction. Of course that didn't work. That simplistic approach ignored the reality known to practitioners that legal costs in personal injury were largely proportionate to compensation regardless of jurisdiction, or indeed complexity.[70]

The second major recommendation by the Fair Trade Commission was that solicitors should be allowed, indeed encouraged, to advertise.[71] In fairness to the Law Society of Ireland they had always resisted advertising which, of course, in the personal injury context produced none of the benefits espoused by competition theory. What happened in reality was that the cost of insurance increased by 48 per cent in the following eight years, and was up 87 per cent by 2002 as reflected in the Central Statistics Office index.[72] These three reforms had just made matters worse.

Perhaps the reason I was asked by government in 1998 to chair the statutory investigation into the cost of insurance was that, while I had been headhunted into the self-insured sector, my background was in the insurance industry in Dublin and London and there may have been a view that I might know where 'the skeletons were hidden'. But the reason why the MIAB investigation worked so well was because of the 18 dedicated fellow board members and most particularly a statistician, Cyril Connolly.[73] Before most people had even heard the term in Ireland, we were crunching 'big data' and I am talking raw data. Insurers yielded up that detail kicking and screaming—sometimes they seemed not to be great fans of transparency. I am often concerned how financial regulators think they can do their jobs properly without 'getting their hands dirty' by digging into the bases of simple numbers rather than merely relying on mathematical models. As any actuary will tell you, models mean 'rubbish in, rubbish out'. My concerns in this context may be supported by a succession of insurer failures in the British Isles. To quote the statistician George Box: 'The most that can be expected from any model is that it can supply a useful approximation to reality: All models are wrong; some models are useful'.[74]

Based on the robust analyses of extensive raw data and hard facts, the MIAB Report was not one of those which merely sat on a shelf somewhere gathering dust. It took six years of work from 1998 to 2004, all of it on a pro bono basis and most of it spent battling with insurers about data. It concluded with recommendations focused in three distinct areas—accident prevention, the tort system of redress and the operations of the insurance market.[75]

[70] Verified by subsequent independent research by Dr Vincent Hogan for the Legal Costs Working Group 2005 (n 24).

[71] The adverse effects of aggressive advertising and offering inducements to potential claimants can be seen in the claims frequency in England where giving gifts such as iPads and Smartphones was recently banned.

[72] The index rose from 78.5 at year end 1990 to 146.7 at year end 2001.

[73] Mr Connolly was at that time employed by the National Roads Authority but is now a lecturer in statistics at Dublin Institute of Technology.

[74] GEP Box, JS Hunter and WG Hunter, *Statistics for Experimenters: Design, Innovation, and Discovery*, 2nd edn (Hoboken NJ, Wiley, 2005) 440.

[75] In all, there were 67 recommendations in the April 2002 MIAB Report which were adopted in the Agreed Programme for Government in October 2002 after a general election in May 2002 during the campaign for which escalating insurance costs were a major issue raised by voters.

First Steps to Reform

The first MIAB Report was published in April 2002. Two measures were immediately implemented.

First, government introduced a ban on solicitors advertising 'no win, no fee' arrangements.[76] Such inducements were considered misleading—a plaintiff always has an exposure for defendants' costs upon a dismissal. The existence of before (or after) the event legal expenses insurance does not change that legal rule. There is no statutory guarantee of indemnity under such policies. If a plaintiff's credibility is dented at a tort trial there is a high risk that he has also failed in his duty of full disclosure to his legal expenses insurers at proposal stage, so at the end of the day cover may well be denied.[77] Some writers give credit for this reform to the Law Society of Ireland.[78] However, it was by reason of the self-regulatory status of the profession that the regulation was issued under their auspices but the measure arose from a MIAB recommendation which was adopted by government.

The second most immediate measure implemented in 2002 was to empower consumers to search for the best alternative insurance deal by providing them with a minimum of 14 days' notice of renewal terms, along with a statement of their accident free record. This removed one of the barriers to effective competition in the market. Subsequently the EU promulgated a directive of a similar content to facilitate switching of service providers in 2009.[79]

A third step on which this chapter focuses was to set about establishment of the Personal Injuries Assessment Board.[80] Once there is political will to implement brave reforms it need not take long.[81]

There is no need to recite every detail of how PIAB came to be established. Suffice it to say that the Interim Implementation Body was appointed in November 2002. That board included a representative from the Irish Business and Employers' Confederation, two nominees from the Irish Congress of Trade Unions, one from the Irish Insurance Federation, consumer perspectives, plus independent medical and legal experts.[82]

The interim board quickly progressed the logistics to a point where the Heads of Bill were published on 27 May 2003. These were circulated to all government departments for input to ensure 'joined up thinking' across the whole of public administration. This is a step which is often missing from reform proposals.[83] The legislation was drafted by the Attorney General's Office and completed its passage through both Houses of Parliament

[76] s 7 of the Solicitors (Amendment) Act 2002.

[77] ATE insurance was not found acceptable as an alternative to security for costs by the Court of Appeal in *Greenclean Waste Management Ltd v Leahy p/a Maurice Leahy Wade & Company Solicitors* [2015] IECA 97.

[78] J Ilan, 'Four Years of the Personal Injuries Assessment Board: Assessing its Impact' (2009) 1 *Judicial Studies Institute Journal* 54; N Patton, 'Personal Injury Reform: Eight Years On' (2012) *Cork Online Law Review* 65.

[79] The Fifth EU Motor Insurance Directive 2009/103.

[80] Other significant measures commenced in parallel included the area of road safety.

[81] PIAB has been variously described in the academic literature as 'radical', 'innovative', 'unique', 'an oddity' and the 'greatest experiment of all'.

[82] Others were the Director of Consumer Affairs; a representative of the Financial Regulator; Professor Denis Cusack Barrister-at-Law and Head of Forensic Medicine at UCD; the Chairman of the Health and Safety Authority.

[83] The Department of Health sought inclusion of 'med neg' at the outset but that was postponed because of ongoing negotiations with the Medical Defence Union on a new system of Enterprise Liability Indemnity.

on 19 December 2003 before being signed by the President on 28 December 2003.[84] This gestation period of eight months was a record for the establishment of a new statutory body up to that time. In fact, it is also historic because it was the first time the Senate[85] sat on a Monday and the first time the Lower House[86] took a debate on a Friday. Resolving the public outcry about motor and liability insurance was a political priority.[87]

In reality, it had taken nearly 20 years to achieve action on a better low-cost system for straightforward genuine personal injury claimants rather than leaving them no option but the vagaries of the court system.[88] The first mention goes back to at least 1986 in a report from a joint parliamentary committee.[89] At that time litigation overheads accounted for what was considered an 'eye watering' 15 per cent of the cost of insurance. Ten years later in 1996, there was political concern about rising insurance costs for ordinary consumers as well as the negative effect on job security which was being undermined by such overheads. An investigative report by Deloitte & Touche found that litigation overheads had risen to 25 per cent of the cost of insurance.[90] That report contained a proposal from the Irish Congress of Trade Unions for a Personal Injuries Tribunal which would have involved oral hearings, an adversarial process and the awarding of costs. This was vehemently resisted by the legal lobby.[91] By the time of the first MIAB Report in 2002, litigation overheads were found to be adding 42 per cent to every cent paid in compensation.[92] This had risen to 46 per cent by the time of the 2004 MIAB Report, despite the fact that less than 10 per cent of litigation cases ever went near the door of a courtroom.[93] So, litigation overheads rose from 15 per cent to 25 per cent to 42 per cent to 46 per cent—a 207 per cent increase in two decades.[94] Finally there was action in 2002.

Upon publication of the first MIAB Report in April 2002 there was cross-party political support for PIAB. This was unusual, courageous and far seeing—particularly in the face of fierce lobbying by lawyers some of whom fundamentally misrepresented the planned PIAB process. There were also some politicians who had legitimate concerns. For example, 'if we make the claims process easier would there be an explosion of claims frequency'—too much 'access to justice' depending on your viewpoint.[95] The facts now prove such reservations were largely unfounded but it was by reflecting on those risks that they were well managed

[84] P Fenn, A Gray, N Rickman and Y Mansur, *The Funding of Personal Injury Litigation: Comparisons Over Time and Across Jurisdictions* (London, Department for Constitutional Affairs, February 2006—DCA Research Series 2/06) 44, assert that lawyers were not consulted in the process, which is incorrect.

[85] Seanad in Irish—Upper House of Parliament.

[86] Dáil in Irish—Lower House of Parliament.

[87] Trade unions on behalf of their members complained not just about the cost of insurance but also the litigation system, including the delays in compensation.

[88] Or the 'Damages Lottery' as termed by PS Atiyah, *The Damages Lottery* (Oxford, Hart Publishing, 1997).

[89] Joint Oireachtas Committee on Enterprise & Small Business under the chairmanship of Ivan Yates.

[90] Deloitte Report (n 13).

[91] 'Law Society Slams New Personal Injuries Board' (2001) 95(4) *Law Society of Ireland Gazette* 2.

[92] The overall litigation overhead percentages reported in the 2002 MIAB Report varied by class of business: employers' liability 45.9%; public liability 56.4%; and motor 39.5%.

[93] That 46% litigation overhead paid by defendants' insurers obviously does not include solicitor-own-client fees generally deducted at an additional 10% of clients' compensation.

[94] See above (n 24), 8.

[95] Minister Willie O'Dea's article in the *Sunday Business Post* (22 September 2003).

in advance.[96] I will return to this point later in an analysis of the objections by those who were resistant to the establishment of PIAB.[97]

The Objectives

PIAB was not just about tackling litigation costs. The old system was essentially making people more ill.[98] Independent research in 1997 showed that claimants in Ireland waited several years to secure their compensation entitlements and actually waited six times longer than in England for negotiations to even commence on their case.[99] This was probably related to the fact that at that time in England only 4 per cent of claims involved barristers compared with 77 per cent of cases in Ireland. There was a clear need for a quicker and lower cost system for delivering compensation entitlements in straightforward cases.

As I have said at many conferences, to state matters as simply as possible: 'PIAB is for genuine claims where the person who is likely to be sued requires an independent assessment of the 100 per cent value of compensation because they do not wish to dispute legal issues, for whatever reason'. If there are reservations about the genuineness of the claim, new court procedures were introduced for challenge by a potential defendant. It is important to stress that there were changes to the litigation system in parallel with the establishment of PIAB as part of the Government's coordinated insurance reform programme.[100]

A 1995 study by international consultants Datamonitor on five factors in the business attractiveness of 16 EU locations rated Ireland last in terms of legal environment. The country had a negative reputation for fraud and propensity to litigiousness.[101] This required a focus on measures to tackle exaggerated claims. That was implemented under the Civil Liability and Courts Act 2004. The legislation requires the plaintiff to swear an affidavit as to the veracity of their allegations. If any part of their claim is materially overstated they potentially lose all entitlement to compensation, along with fines of up to

[96] In the context of motor claims frequency, the rights of injured parties against the Motor Insurers Bureau where vehicles are uninsured or untraced have been extended on a number of occasions, most recently the 5th Directive EU Motor Insurance Directive 2009/103/EC. In 2008 the English Court of Appeal in *Byrne (A Minor) v MIB & Secretary of State for Transport* [2008] EWCA Civ 574, [2009] QB 66 held that the failure to comply with previous directives was 'sufficiently serious' under the criteria laid down by the European Court of Justice (ECJ) to warrant *Francovich* damages. The principle of equivalence for victims regardless of the insurance status of the vehicle had also been addressed by the ECJ in *Evans v Secretary of State for the Environment, Transport and the Regions* (C63/01) [2005] All ER (EC) 763. This position had already been clarified in Ireland by a 1999 Circuit Court decision of McMahon J in *Dublin Bus v MIBI*, DCA no 199/99 + 120/99 where he held that MIBI were as responsible as the state for improper implementation of an EU Directive, consistent with a number of earlier ECJ decisions. The 2002 MIAB Report records the disagreements between MIBI and the Board on whether Irish law fully complies with the requirements under EU law in a number of contexts.

[97] Under the heading 'Objections & Propaganda' later in this chapter.

[98] Justice Susan Denham, 2004 Report as Chair of the Committee on Court Practice and Procedure.

[99] Research by Professor Brian Greenford of Limerick University for the McAuley Report (n 14).

[100] eg, the Civil Liability and Courts Act 2004—s 14 verifying affidavit, s 25 false evidence, s 26 fraudulent actions—although other measures in that legislation were not introduced.

[101] See C Parsons et al, *Report on the Economics and Regulation of Insurance* (London, Cass Business School, 2004).

€100,000 and imprisonment of up to 10 years.[102] One of the most important aspects of this requirement was that it imposed a retrospective 'obligation to tell the truth' which was not considered repugnant to the Constitution since it has always been a criminal offence to lie under oath.[103] But axiomatically, defendants can no longer just put in a blank defence denying everything and are required to swear an affidavit stating the clear grounds on which the claim is being resisted. As can be appreciated, many defendants dislike having to 'put their cards on the table' at such an early stage. There is now a better, albeit still imperfect balance, in pleadings between parties in litigation.

Unfortunately, many of the other worthwhile measures introduced under the Civil Liability and Courts Act 2004 were not utilised. These include mediation, court appointed neutral experts, pre-trial conferences, focused case management, publication of actuarial tables and the requirement for plaintiffs to make an offer of their minimum terms. These were simply never adopted—nor were the efficiencies in the courts, as proposed in the 2004 Denham Report, advanced in any meaningful way in relation to personal injury actions.

To return our focus to the PIAB process, two points need to be emphasised:

1. There are no oral hearings in the new system which is largely a 'documents only' process, so there is no role for advocacy on behalf of either the claimant or the respondent.
2. There is generally no award of legal costs for or against any party.[104]

Establishment of PIAB did not change anything in relation to how the initial claim is made. The claimant can first seek compensation directly from the person whom they consider responsible for the accident—'naming, blaming and claiming'.[105]

PIAB does not enquire into the circumstances of accidents. The Statutory Assessors are concerned solely with the extent of injury and/or loss. Enforcement of the law on accident prevention is the responsibility of other state agencies such as the police for road accidents and the Health and Safety Authority for workplace occurrences. I will return to the purported deterrence effect of tort in my concluding remarks about legal theory.[106]

[102] To date there has been one known suspended sentence for a conviction under s 29 of the Civil Liability and Courts Act 2004. A number of cases have been dismissed by the High Court under s 25 and s 26 but the numbers which have been withdrawn in the face of evidence is an unknowable.

[103] In 2015 a similar deterrent to an equal mischief was introduced in England but will only apply to litigation pleadings issued after the introduction of new legislation so it is likely to be many years before its effectiveness can be measured. Additionally, the requirement for a defendant to prove 'fundamental dishonesty' in the wording of the Criminal Justice and Courts Act 2015 will require the emergence of an unpredictable set of precedents. Honesty, on the other hand, is a binary concept.

[104] PIAB publishes guidelines on awards of fees and expenses under s 44 to vulnerable and other claimants, as published on their website at www.injuriesboard.ie.

[105] WLF Felstiner, RL Abel and A Sarat, 'Emergence and Transformation of Disputes: Naming, Blaming, Claiming …, The Special Issue on Dispute Processing and Civil Litigation: Part Two—The Civil Litigation Research Project: Some CLRP Contributions to Understanding Disputes and Dispute Transformation' (1980–81) 15 *Law & Society Review* 631; H Kritzer, 'Propensity to Sue in England and the United States of America: Blaming and Claiming in Tort Cases' (1991) 18 *Journal of Law and Society* 400.

[106] Under the heading of 'A Dip into Doctrine' later in this chapter.

How PIAB Works in Practice

With the assistance of the National Adult Literacy Agency, PIAB published a laypersons' guide to explain the process as simply as possible.[107] An outsourced service centre operates a helpline to provide claimants with guidance from 8.0 am to 8.0 pm and will assist them in completing their initial claim submissions on a LoCall number. All the details with 'Frequently Asked Questions' are available on the website at www.injuriesboard.ie. The PIAB itself is staffed by independent public servants, from varying professional backgrounds in a wide range of industries, who provide the statutory assessment service.

In addition to internal expertise, PIAB established an Independent Panel of several hundred medical experts in different specialities throughout the country.[108] But contrary to the impression that some lawyers attempted to create initially, and unlike litigation, the claimant is not faced with a battery of experts on behalf of the respondent or their insurance company. If, in the opinion of PIAB, an examination is necessary then the outcome of an examination by a member of the Independent Medical Panel is the report which is relied upon in the assessment. Such independent examinations are held in the vast majority of cases. Where an assessment is sought too soon by a claimant they are required to wait until a stable medical prognosis is possible. This process is subject to the maximum time frame for finalisation of an assessment, which is nine months, and otherwise the case is released to the courts.[109] Claims which on first notification involve injuries that will obviously take a longer time to stabilise are released to the court system on day one.

To an extent, the difficultly many lawyers seemed to have experienced in understanding the PIAB process appears to have arisen from their training and education in, and thus preference for, an adversarial system, involving at least two sets of competing experts earning increasing fees while the case dragged on for years. The default position of lawyers seemed to be that all cases involve 'essentially contested concepts'.[110] In contrast, the only important parties—the potential plaintiff and potential defendant—do not necessarily view matters in that light. I maintain that 'just settlement' can be 'a just settlement' provided there is an independent expert neutral assessor of entitlements. This is far different from enforced compromise, by mediation or other ADR approaches, about which there are many reservations in the literature.[111]

Obviously, there will always be personal injury cases that involve legal issues that are the sole preserve of the courts. Approximately two-thirds of claims which proceed to full

[107] Web reference for claimant and respondent guide respectively: www.injuriesboard.ie/eng/resources/Forms_and_Publications/Guidelines/Claimant_Guide_2011.pdf; www.injuriesboard.ie/eng/Forms-Guidelines/Respondent-Leaflet-Mon-Fri.pdf.

[108] An announcement in December 2014 by the Secretary of State, Chris Grayling MP, Department of Justice, that only reports from accredited examiners will be acceptable in whiplash claims from April 2015 in England has echoes of the PIAB medical panel established in 2004.

[109] Although that nine months can be extended to 15 months, or longer if the claimant agrees. However, there is a duty on assessors under s 49—*Assessments to be made expeditiously*.

[110] WB Gallie, 'Essentially Contested Concepts' (1955–56) 56 *Proceedings of the Aristotelian Society, New Series* 167.

[111] Such as Dame Hazel Genn, 'Judging Civil Justice' (Hamlyn Lectures, 2008).

formal registration are released by PIAB to the courts at the outset because they involve such disputes.[112] Those litigation cases will involve solicitors, and sometimes barristers, as well as two sets of experts on any potentially contested issue. But these litigation overheads are not necessary in all claims. Most cases do not involve any real legal disputes but are more a matter of how much money is involved. This is evidenced by the fact that historically of all the litigation cases issued in the old system less than 10 per cent ever proceeded to an oral hearing. The only problem with that was, as succinctly commented on by Professor William Binchy, '[t]oo many cases have been settled at too late (and too expensive) a stage'.[113]

How the Layers of Competing Experts have been Taken Out from the Old Process

Whether, and to what extent, an injury has been sustained is a medical question, not a legal one. In that context, PIAB uses the Independent Medical Panel and the report from the claimant's treating doctor.[114]

Whether a claimant was earning the level of wages or other earnings they allege to have lost is a factual question, not a legal one. On this aspect PIAB has direct access to relevant information from the Revenue Commissioners who are the Irish tax authority and from the Department of Social and Family Affairs who administer welfare benefits.

Whether the actuarial multiplier is X or Y for calculation of future losses is a statistical question, not a legal one. There are no published actuarial tables for this purpose in Ireland so PIAB retains independent experts for this purpose.

A fact not often highlighted in discussions on litigation costs, although it was widely covered in the MIAB Report, is the extent to which doctors earned substantial fees in the old litigation system.[115] At the outset of its operations, PIAB had determined to pay a fixed fee of €150 for medical reports—and such payment was subject to an acceptable standard of presentation and appropriate detail in the content.[116] This measure met with considerable resistance from doctors' representative bodies. The Competition Authority also launched an investigation in July 2006 into the system of recommended fees operated by the Irish Medical Organisation during the period from June 2004 to June 2005.[117] That matter was subsequently resolved by way of an undertaking. The professional fees earned by medical

[112] Although only a small proportion of those proceed to trial as evidenced by statistics in the annual reports of the Courts Service: www.courts.ie.

[113] W Binchy, 'The Implications of the [PIAB] Act for Tort Law and Practice' (Conference on PIAB, Trinity College Dublin, March 2004) says 'too many are settled at too late and too expensive a stage' but he largely blames defence lawyers for such delays. In contrast, research for the McAuley Report (n 14) 127, table 23 indicates that claimants' excessive demands play a major part in protracted negotiations.

[114] According to the PIAB template, not a 'medico-legal' report www.injuriesboard.ie/eng/Forms-Guidelines/August-2014-Revised-Form-B-1.docx.

[115] MIAB 2002 at C135–37 on medico-legal reports and court attendance fees.

[116] The initial fixed-fee level was later replaced by variations to reflect market conditions and different medical specialties.

[117] www.tca.ie/ News-Releases/The-Competition-Authority-begins-High-Court-proceedings-against-the-Irish-Medical-Organisation.aspx.

experts from litigation are not as frequently highlighted as lawyers' fees, although the term 'litigation costs' clearly encompasses all such outlay. In medical negligence cases, which are defended by the State Claims Agency in Ireland on the basis of enterprise-wide liability indemnity, there was a 255 per cent increase in their outlay on medical fees between 2008 and 2013.[118]

A Change of Legal Culture?

The biggest surprise was the change in legal culture in the immediate aftermath of the establishment of PIAB. This was manifested by the extent to which parties were able to resolve their disputes within the initial 90-day cooling off period from when a claimant applies for an assessment. Through the facilitation of PIAB, claimants have an opportunity to fairly state their injuries and the respondents are provided with a clear indication of the potential of the claim they face. It has become apparent that at least one-third of cases are settled directly, without a fee having to be paid to PIAB, because there is now an improved symmetry of information on compensation levels with the publication of the Book of Quantum.[119] Mediation experts also agree that when parties can focus on the value at stake in their dispute most other issues can be resolved and an impasse overcome.[120] To ensure the equity of these direct settlements the Financial Regulator[121] undertakes inspections of insurers' files to ensure compliance with the code of conduct.[122] Interestingly, prior to the establishment of PIAB no regulator undertook any auditing of the equity of claims settlements by insurers even though 90 per cent of such cases did not involve any independent adjudication. There is no rival explanation for the change in legal culture since the establishment of PIAB and related reforms.[123] A triangulation of data analyses rules out a null hypothesis.[124]

[118] Analysis contained in C Ó Culáin, 'Opportunity Costs' (2015) 109(1) *Law Society of Ireland Gazette* 32.

[119] The annual reports of PIAB provide data on the volumes of claims settled direct.

[120] Laura Kaster on Impasse: It's the Value, Stupid!: www.mediate.com/articles/KasterLbl20111227.cfm.

[121] Themed inspections by the Central Bank (CB) of 6,672 settled injury files in insurers' offices found that 78% had been finalised without proceedings being issued. As clear from the long title of the PIAB Act 2003 the overall objective is to avoid unnecessary litigation. Where CB analysed litigation cases it was found that delivery overheads added 89% on top of compensation when the case proceeded to trial; 54% when settled 'on the steps' of the court; and 61% at the early stage of proceedings. In comparison, cases concluded with PIAB awards carried an 11% delivery overhead.

[122] Inspections by the Central Bank in 2011 of settled claims found that damages paid in direct settlements were largely in line with the Book of Quantum and that PIAB awards were higher than the insurer's last recorded offer. The 22% of claims involving litigation took between 12 and 60 months to finalise in the files examined and 6% of overall claims were settled on the steps of the court. A subsequent report published in November 2015 by the Central Bank on their inspections of settled injury claims does not provide the same level of detail.

[123] Legal culture refers to the shared values, attitudes, standards and beliefs that characterise members of the legal profession and define its nature. It may also refer to the ideas, values, attitudes and opinions, people in some society hold with regard to law and the legal system. See among others—LM Friedman, 'Legal Culture and Social Development' (1969) 4 *Law & Society Review* 29; JL Mashaw and DL Harfst, 'Regulation and the Legal Culture: The Case of Motor Vehicle Safety' (1986–87) 4 *Yale Journal on Regulation* 257; RE Miller and A Sarat, 'Grievances, Claims and Disputes: Assessing the Adversary Culture (1980–81) 15 *Law & Society Review* 525.

[124] A null hypothesis in case study research addresses the question as to whether the changes would have occurred without the interventions being assessed: RK Yin, *Case Study Research, Design and Methods*, 5th edn (Los Angeles CA, Sage, 2013).

One of the ill-founded objections to the PIAB process was the assertion that the claim would be 'flushed out' at an early stage. This implied that personal injury litigation was to be approached like a game of poker, rather than the serious business of fairness to both plaintiff and defendant. Those who might have been operating previously with 'aces up their sleeves' had to realise that those days were largely over.

The parallel litigation reforms in the Civil Liability and Courts Act 2004 represented a 'new era of honesty and early disclosure'. That quotes a phrase from a report by a committee on deficiencies in the litigation system chaired by the now Chief Justice Mrs Justice Susan Denham.[125]

In line with the 2003 Supreme Court decision in *McGrory v ESB* a person waives their usual right to privacy of medical history when seeking injury compensation.[126] In litigation a claimant is now required to be fulsome in disclosure in the new Injury Summons from the very outset of their legal proceedings if the case is one that must go down the court route.

In contrast to the years it can take for litigation to be finalised, within a matter of months of submission to PIAB both the claimant and the respondent know the amount of the independent assessment of compensation on a 100 per cent liability basis. On average, cases which proceed through the full formal process are concluded by PIAB within seven months. This is in stark contrast to the old litigation system, even though delays in reaching trial have reduced since the Deloitte Report in 1996, but where one still has no idea when a final determination may be reached. This is another 'win-win' aspect of PIAB.[127]

Rehabilitation experts agree that ongoing litigation is not conducive to motivating recovery.[128] A win-win solution for claimants is getting that to which they are entitled, getting it speedily and then getting on with their lives—in some cases, as best they can. Money cannot possibly compensate for injuries of maximum severity when you really just wish you could turn the clock back and be restored to your pre-accident health.[129]

Objections and Propaganda

The level of misinformation from certain quarters about PIAB was quite extraordinary at times. I will now dispense with some of those misconceptions.

Contrary to what was often asserted, adoption of the PIAB process by the respondent is not limited to those cases where liability is admitted. There can be many reasons why potential defendants would agree to an independent body assessing a genuine claimant's

[125] Mrs Justice Susan Denham, 2004 Report as Chair of the Committee on Court Practice and Procedure.

[126] *McGrory v ESB* [2003] IESC 45.

[127] Satisfaction levels of users is reported through feedback channels at 90% in the PIAB annual report 2014 (at 29). The Courts Service in Ireland does not undertake similar surveys. In England a Ministry of Justice research paper in March 2008 reviewed the literature on public and participant satisfaction with courts and tribunals from which the indications are that process is as important as the outcome, but there are many 'perplexing inconsistencies' in those studies: www.law.cf.ac.uk/research/pubs/repository/1854.pdf.

[128] Dr Clem Leech Department of Social Welfare, Ireland; Nick Nevin, Department for Work and Pensions, UK; Gordan Waddell, A Kim Burton, *Concepts of Rehabilitation*: www.gov.uk.

[129] *Sinnott v Quinnsworth* [1984] ILRM 523—Chief Justice O'Higgins stated in the course of his judgement: 'Since money cannot possibly compensate [for quadriplegia], a jury may question whether it matters what sum is

compensation. One such reason is simple mathematics. What is the point of going to court to secure maybe a 20 per cent reduction in compensation for an employee's contributory negligence when an extra 50 per cent must be spent on litigation costs?[130]

Take the example of a case involving contract indemnification. An office worker sustains a fractured arm when a new but defective chair collapses. The employer wants to see that this person is properly compensated but intends to pursue full indemnity from the supplier of the chair and does not want that right of recovery to be prejudiced. Why should the genuine injured employee be caught up for years in that ongoing litigation when his interests would be better served by securing that to which he is entitled and being relieved of the burden of involvement in multiparty litigation?

Other detractors painted a misleading picture of the old litigation system by contrasting the PIAB documentary procedure with 'a requirement for giving oral evidence under oath in the witness box'. There was a fear by some of what may be called the 'expressway principle' that if the claims process was made too easy then too many people would claim. That did not happen. The reality always was that less than 10 per cent of litigation cases ever got to a court trial and many litigation cases settled on a nuisance value basis despite the damage academics assert that this does to the reputation of tort.[131] Over 90 per cent of litigation cases were concluded without an oral hearing. The only problem with that was that they carried an excessive litigation overhead and without a Book of Quantum there was no publicly available guide by which to decide whether an offered settlement was at the appropriate level.[132]

PIAB was also accused of not permitting parties to have independent legal advisers.[133] While PIAB will not award litigation costs for or against any party,[134] there is absolutely no restriction on anyone seeking legal advice. That was very clear in the legislation from the very outset of its drafting.[135] Whether the claimant retained a lawyer or not, it had

awarded … the answer must be that it does matter. It matters to the defendant or his indemnifiers, and would be a ground for legitimate complaint if the sum awarded were so high as to constitute a punishment … rather than … an attempt to compensate the injured. It also matters to contemporary society if, by reason of the amount decided upon and the example which it sets for other determinations of damages by juries, the operation of public policy would be thereby endangered'.

[130] This is not merely a nil sum game—if compensation of 100k is reduced by 20% to 80k and 50% is spent on litigation costs then total outlay is 120k which is 20% cent higher than the full value of compensation which can be assessed through the PIAB process for a fixed fee of €600 and even allowing a similar amount for medical reports means a delivery overhead of €1,200 or 1.2%. The overall delivery overhead in PIAB on awards of €244m was 7.3% in 2013.

[131] eg, Binchy, 'The Implications of the [PIAB] Act for Tort Law and Practice' (n 113): 'An area at present causing much dissatisfaction is where insurance companies settle claims of modest amount when liability is highly questionable simply because it is economically more convenient in the short term to do so. This has the effect of misleading the public into believing that the tort system is based on arbitrary and unfair principles and of encouraging insured people and those who work for them to adopt a timorous or fatalistic attitude to the discharge of their duty of care'.

[132] www.injuriesboard.ie/eng/Forms-Guidelines/Book-of-Quantum.pdf.

[133] Various articles in the *Law Society of Ireland Gazette* and assertions by lawyers reported in the national media.

[134] As confirmed by the High Court in *Plewa v PIAB* [2010] IEHC 516 (High Court, Ryan J, 19 October 2010).

[135] s 7(1) 'Nothing in this Act is to be read as affecting the right of any person to seek legal advice in respect of his or her relevant claim and no rule shall be made under section 46 that affects that right'.

been the intention of PIAB to always communicate directly with the claimant so that the injured party was at the heart of the process and knew exactly how their assessment was progressing. A frequent cause of complaint against solicitors relates to clients not being kept properly informed.[136] PIAB is a user-focused organisation.[137] However, at the first judicial review launched within weeks of PIAB opening its doors, it was held that they could not continue to correspond directly with claimants while sending a copy to their solicitors. PIAB must now communicate with the solicitor but can send a copy of important documents to the claimant.[138] There were a number of judicial reviews initiated against PIAB.[139] Just as in the UK post-Woolf reforms, sometimes there seems to be more litigation about litigation costs than about substantive litigation issues.[140]

Claimants who continue to choose to incur the cost of using solicitors can now avail themselves of lawyers who advertise online to undertake a PIAB case for a fixed fee of €399. What a change from historical practice. Some years ago many solicitors were taking a percentage from the claimants' compensation.[141] This was despite the fact that such a practice has been against the law since 1994.[142] That percentage was taken from victims in addition to the solicitor being paid their full party and party costs by the defendant.[143]

The Question of Damages

According to surveys by Kluwer Law, Ireland has the highest level of injury compensation in EEA countries that operate a lump sum award system.[144] Ireland will likely always be generous to injured parties. An English commentator cites average damages in that jurisdiction at £2,500.[145] This compares with the average PIAB award which is 10 times that amount. In March 2009 the EU Commission, in the context of Rome II, launched a consultation process to examine policy options on harmonising compensation levels between Member States.[146] It seems that national variances were too wide to proceed with

[136] www.independentadjudicator.ie/pdfs/AnnualReportoftheIndependentAdjudicator200708.pdf.

[137] PIAB, 'Strategic Statements & Plans', on website at www.injuriesboard.ie.

[138] O'Brien v Personal Injuries Assessment Board [2008] IESC 71, [2009] 3 IR 243.

[139] The plaintiff's costs sought in the *O'Brien* case amounted to €2.143m. Upon challenge by PIAB that bill was reduced to 18% of the amount sought or €393,472. 'Taxing Master Cut the "Grossly Excessive" Legal Bill by 82 per cent' *Irish Times* (1 July 2010): www.highbeam.com/doc/1P2-25283334.html; 'Legal Fees in Injury Case "Revolting" in the Extreme' *Irish Times* (1 July 2010): www.highbeam.com/doc/1P2-25283343.html.

[140] Satellite litigation in England after the Woolf reforms as in P Fenn, D Vencappa, C O'Brien and S Diacon, 'Is there a "Compensation Culture" in the UK?' (Nottingham University Business School, CRIS Discussion Paper 2005-04).

[141] As detailed in the MIAB Report 2004 (n 20).

[142] Solicitors (Amendment) Act 1994.

[143] Or in addition to costs paid by state compensation schemes such as the Residential Redress Board as reported in 2006: www.independent.ie/irish-news/solicitor-fined-over-double-bill-26363782.html.

[144] D McIntosh and M Holmes (eds), *Personal Injury Awards in EU and EFTA Countries* (The Hague, Kluwer Law International, 2003).

[145] Fisher (n 23) 169.

[146] Regulation (EC) 864/2007 claims arising from cross-border road accidents.

such a project. Its basis in law by the Internal Market and Services Directorate General may also be questionable.[147]

It is important to stress that it was never the role of PIAB to reduce compensation levels. Even from a pragmatic perspective, if PIAB made lower awards than the courts then such amounts would be rejected by claimants who would pursue litigation. Similarly, overly generous awards would simply be rejected by respondents and/or their insurers.

To review the reasonableness of PIAB awards and/or settlement offers, a Book of Quantum was published in 2004. It was the first ever publicly available guide in the Irish jurisdiction on levels of general damages. The process of estimating compensation had previously been described as 'a difficult guessing game', even for solicitors.[148]

The guide shows the range of values for various frequent injuries all along the severity spectrum up to a quadriplegia for which the Irish Supreme Court has set the maximum compensation for pain and suffering. Sadly the severest of cases are sometimes the easiest to assess as such claimants have limited if any prospects of improvement so they are entitled to the limit of general damages and 24/7 care for life. A one-off lump sum is not always, of course, the best way of providing for such tragic cases as MIAB made clear in its 2002 Report.[149]

It is necessary to be clear on a number of points in relation to the Book of Quantum. First, it shows only the compensation amounts for pain and suffering but claimants are also awarded their financial losses such as wages and medical expenses as is made clear in the narrative of the Book of Quantum. It should be noted that actual net wage losses are awarded, in contrast to basic earnings as in the Employment Appeals Tribunal which also has a cap.[150]

Second, the Book of Quantum is not representative of the views of PIAB. It was compiled by an international firm of consultants based on data on court awards as well as data on 100 per cent value settlements which were reviewed by an external expert.[151]

Last, and most important, the Book of Quantum is a guide which gives a range of values. It is not a tariff that says a broken leg is worth 'X' because each person must be assessed on their individual characteristics. For example, a simple fracture for a young person may have very different consequences for an older claimant where there is a risk of arthritis.

The judiciary are also required under the 2004 Civil Liability Act to have regard to the Book of Quantum in cases which come before them for adjudication.[152] Some judges

[147] European Commission Consultation Paper on the Compensation of Victims of Cross-Border Road Traffic Accidents in the European Union (Brussels, 2009); MARKT/H2/RM markt.h.2(2009)61541 FS/050.160/0032.

[148] R Pierce, 'Quantum Leap: General Damages in the 1990s' (1999) 93(4) *Law Society of Ireland Gazette* 20. He was also the author of the leading practitioners' guide—R Pierse, *Quantum of Damages for Personal Injuries 1999* (Dublin, Round Hall Sweet & Maxwell, 1999).

[149] MIAB recommendation no 50: That the system of lump sum compensation payments be reviewed on the basis that the long-term needs of the seriously injured may be better served by guaranteed annual payments.

[150] As does the equivalent in England.

[151] Professor Brian Greenford, University of Limerick.

[152] s 22(1) Civil Liability and Courts Act 2004: The court shall, in assessing damages in a personal injuries action, have regard to the Book of Quantum. (2) Subsection (1) shall not operate to prohibit a court from having regard to matters other than the Book of Quantum when assessing damages in a personal injuries action. (3) In this section 'Book of Quantum' means the Book of Quantum required to be prepared and published by the Personal Injuries Assessment Board under the Act of 2003.

openly acknowledged the usefulness of the Book of Quantum but most significantly a measure of consistency emerged in data on court awards received by PIAB in the post-reform period.

Contrary to the impression that is often created in the literature there is, thankfully, only a small volume of maximum severity claims each year although each is a human tragedy in its own right for the injured party and often for their extended family. The vast majority of claims are for minor injuries. This is a fact supported by analysis of awards both by the courts and by PIAB, as well as analysis undertaken by MIAB of raw data which underpin insurers' statutory returns.

Of the amounts awarded by PIAB in 2014, totalling €281 ml, the proportionality between the three main classes of business in value bands is published in their annual report. That breakdown is set out as below:

Table 8.1: PIAB Awards 2014

		Annual Report 2014		
Value Range €000s	**Motor**	**Employers' Liability**	**Public Liability**	**TOTAL**
>20k	5,930	351	1,073	7,354
20k to 38k	2,679	363	730	3,772
38k to 100k	664	208	338	1,210
>100k	55	19	10	84
ALL	**9,328**	**941**	**2,151**	**12,420**

In PIAB, consistent with previous years 90 per cent of awards in 2014 were for amounts below €38,000. In the context of the type of injury involved, €38,000 would be about the mid-point for a whiplash injury in Ireland as reflected in the Book of Quantum.

During the same period courts throughout the country made awards totalling €169 million between the Circuit Court (monetary limit €60,000) and the High Court (unlimited jurisdiction). It will be noted in the table below that 47 per cent of the 509 awards made by the High Court were for amounts which were within the Circuit Court jurisdiction.[153] Many of these may have been commenced in an inappropriate jurisdiction, for which there is only a minimal costs penalty, but some may have resulted in apportioned liability where the full value sought was in excess of the Circuit Court limit.[154] A breakdown by type of claim in awards as between motor or employer/public liability or medical negligence is not provided by the Courts Service and such information on litigation profiles would be of considerable value in monitoring the outcome of reforms and the consideration of future measures.

[153] The jurisdiction of the Circuit Court was increased from €38,000 to €60,000 for proceedings issued from 3 February 2014 but most cases which reached trial in 2014 would have been issued under the previous limits.

[154] There is little benefit for a defendant to seek to have a case remitted from the High Court to the Circuit Court since it then carries an unlimited jurisdiction.

Table 8.2: Court Awards 2014 Annual Report Courts Service

Circuit Court		
Value Range	No	
€0 to €15,000	654	
€15,000 to €60,000	356	
€60,000+	8	
Sub-total	1,018	
Total Amount		€14ml
High Court		
€0 to €60,000	237	
€60,000 to €199,999	171	
€200,000 to €499,999	45	
€500,000+	56	
Sub-total	509	
Total Amount		€155m
Overall Total Volume and Value	1,527	€169m

In terms of volume, 82 per cent of court awards were for amounts below €60,000. Unfortunately the value bands which were published in previous years' annual reports from the Courts Service were changed in 2014 so a year on year comparison is not readily available. However, from other sources it is known that 33 awards of €1 million and over accounted for 64 per cent of the total value of High Court awards compared with 27 such cases representing 57 per cent of total award value in 2013. These obviously reflect the most serious injuries and many related to medical negligence claims which were widely reported in the media. For statistical robustness the median value of High Court awards is a better measure than a simple average calculation. Removing the four outlier cases where awards were €5 million or more, the median value in 2014 was €63,400 compared to a median of €65,000 in 2013. Motor insurers attempted to publicly justify their price increases during 2015 on bases which included the assertion that the average High Court award had increased by 34 per cent in the previous year.

To curtail the potential for double counting of overall claims volumes, it is necessary to state that all injury claims (bar medical negligence) which appear in the court data were originally registered in the PIAB system. It is not possible to issue proceedings for personal injury without a PIAB authorisation except for the limited classes set out at section 3 of the legislation as interpreted by court precedents.[155]

[155] eg, in July 2014 the Supreme Court overturned a High Court decision to strike out a claim which was to be heard by jury in an action by a sister against her brother for alleged sexual abuse in the 1970s—*Clarke v O'Gorman* [2014] IESC 72.

Back to the PIAB Assessment Process

As a leading tort scholar in Ireland, Professor Binchy has commented that 'the principles on which personal injury claims are adjudicated are well within the understanding of even the simplest soul'.[156] That sentiment was echoed by Mr Justice Sean Ryan of the High Court in October 2010 when dismissing judicial reviews against PIAB for refusing to award legal costs: 'There are many straightforward cases and the mere fact that a solicitor is retained does not necessarily mean that the solicitor's fees will have been reasonably and necessarily incurred for the purposes of s 44 of the Act of 2003'.[157] Set out below is that straightforward process in six steps:

1. If the parties cannot agree a direct settlement after a claim has been made, referral of all such injury cases to PIAB is mandatory. There is no question of parties choosing between the Board and the courts. All personal injury claims must be referred to PIAB before any legal proceedings can be commenced.[158] The claimant submits a very simple form with a medical report from their treating doctor and details of any financial losses or outlays to date.
2. PIAB sends a copy of the application for assessment to the respondent who has 90 days to conclude their investigations and indicate whether they consent to an assessment proceeding or whether this is a case they intend to defend in court.[159]
3. If the case involves legal arguments, PIAB issues a Release Certificate at the outset which authorises proceedings to be commenced should the claimant choose to pursue the matter further.[160] In contrast to the old litigation system where the real issues did not emerge until late in the proceedings, the claimant will now know early on that they face a full defence in court. Pleadings will state the actual basis of that defence and not just a blank denial that anything ever happened as was usually the way in the old system.
4. PIAB operates a documents only procedure. Once the respondent has consented to the assessment proceeding they are essentially out of the process until the award is determined. There is no role for advocacy and therefore no provision for payment of legal fees except in vulnerable cases.[161] The question of whether and to what extent an injury has been sustained is a medical one. At initial application stage, all that the treating doctor is asked to do is summarise the injuries and treatment already detailed on the patient's file, and for which the doctor's treatment fees will be awarded as part of the claim. In contrast, the member of the Independent Medical Panel must undertake a *de novo* examination of the claimant and establish from the medical records what injuries and treatment were actually involved. Once there is a stable prognosis it is the

[156] W Binchy and P Quigley, The Personal Injuries Assessment Board Act 2003: Implications for the Legal Practice (Dublin, FirstLaw, 2004).

[157] *Plewa v PIAB* (n 134).

[158] Currently excludes medical negligence which encompasses not just clinical cases but also public liability in a medical environment.

[159] Failure by the respondent to reply within 90 days results in the case proceeding to assessment against them in default.

[160] Within the period permitted by the Statute of Limitations, plus six months.

[161] eg, infants and fatal injuries where court rulings are required. PIAB publishes guidelines on awards of fees and expenses under s 44 available on their website at www.injuriesboard.ie.

report(s) from members of the Independent Medical Panel, copied to both sides, that forms the basis of the compensation award.

5. The ethos of PIAB is inquisitorial rather than adversarial. The role of the assessors is to get to the heart of the damages claim and ensure that the claimant gets that to which they are entitled. This is done by employing PIAB's own expertise rather than two sets of professional witnesses charging large fees for duplicate actuarial, accounting, taxation and other such calculations. Special damages for wage losses are awarded at levels consistent with declared earnings history. That was a change introduced by the Civil Liability and Courts Act 2004 so that undeclared earnings from the black economy can no longer be recovered.[162] In this context PIAB has relevant information directly from both the Revenue Commissioners[163] and the Department of Social and Family Affairs.[164]

[162] s 28 Civil Liability and Courts Act 2004:

> (1) In a personal injuries action (other than an action under section 48 of the Act of 1961), any income, profit or gain in respect of which—
>
> (a) the plaintiff is making a claim, and
> (b) (i) a return has not been made before the hearing of the action in accordance with the Taxes Consolidation Act 1997, or
> (ii) the plaintiff has not otherwise notified the Revenue Commissioners, shall, for the purposes of assessing damages, be disregarded by the court, unless the court considers that in all the circumstances it would be unjust to disregard such income, profit or gain.
>
> (2) This section does not apply to causes of action accruing before the commencement of this section.

[163] s 28 PIAB Act 2004:

> (1) A claimant, by virtue of his or her having made an application under section 11, shall be deemed to have consented to the Revenue Commissioners complying with the following request.
>
> (2) That request is a request by the assessors (which by virtue of this section they have power to make) of the Revenue Commissioners to furnish to the assessors particulars or other information in their possession or control in relation to the amount of income of the claimant for the purpose, and the purpose only of, the assessors' verifying any item of financial loss that is alleged by the claimant in his or her relevant claim and which relates to that income.
>
> (3) Notwithstanding any enactment, it shall be the duty of the Revenue Commissioners to comply with such a request unless the consent referred to in subsection (1) is deemed to have been revoked by virtue of subsection (4).
>
> (4) That consent shall be deemed to have been revoked if, at the date of the making of the request of the Revenue Commissioners, the application under section 11 of the claimant concerned stands withdrawn by him or her in accordance with section 47.
>
> (5) The particulars or other information that may be the subject of a request under this section include particulars or other information that came into existence, or into the possession of the Revenue Commissioners, before the passing of this Act.

[164] s 26 PIAB Act 2004:

> (1) The assessors may request any person (including a Department of State or any other public body (other than the Revenue Commissioners)) to furnish to them such records, documents or other information in his or her possession or control as they reasonably request for the purpose of—
>
> (a) verifying any item of loss alleged by the claimant in his or her relevant claim, or
> (b) complying with the provisions of any enactment that requires specified amounts to be deducted or specified matters to be taken account of in the making of an assessment of damages, and the records, documents or other information that may be the subject of such a request include records, documents or information that came into existence, or into the possession of the person requested, before the passing of this Act, and it shall be the duty of such person to comply with such request.

6. At the end of the process, the parties are free to reject the PIAB award and the required Release Certificate will be issued for litigation. There are, however, downsides for unreasonable refusals of awards. For example, if a claimant rejects a PIAB award of €30,000 that amount automatically stands as the defendant's tender when proceedings are served—or they can lodge a lower figure since defence costs must now be incurred and allegations of contributory negligence may arise. Just like the long-standing lodgement system in the courts, if that figure of €30,000 is not subsequently exceeded, not only does the plaintiff not receive any award of costs but he or she will also be responsible for the defendant's costs.[165] A PIAB award is not 'an offer of settlement' as some misdescribe it, but is an independent statutory award which is enforceable by the same mechanism as a judicial decree.

So essentially, claimants in assessment cases are now relieved of the burden of proving negligence that would have earned fees for experts but often did little for the injured party except increase the delivery overhead and delay their claim to the steps of the court.

Interestingly, by 2015 most solicitors' websites now provide a factually accurate account of the PIAB process. This demonstrates that the vast majority of the legal profession have embraced the new reality and are operating professionally rather than in a self-serving manner when it comes to educating clients on how the new claims process works. This compares starkly with articles in the *Law Society of Ireland Gazette* resisting reforms with banner headlines such as 'Why we must fight PIAB tooth and nail'.[166] That was from the solicitors' regulatory body's monthly magazine. There are numerous other insightful examples in the monthly publications by the Bar Council of Ireland.

In Summation on PIAB

A respondent, when considering whether to pay PIAB the fixed fee of €600,[167] need only ask themselves some hard questions that are basically mathematical.[168] To take a simple example: there is no financial advantage in an employer spending years defending an employee claim to secure a 20 per cent reduction in the damages award for the contributory negligence of the employee, when that will result in the employer being responsible for litigation costs that will add 50 per cent to the cost of the net award. Contrast that with PIAB where no litigation costs are awarded for or against any party and the assessment will be finalised

[165] Introduced by the Personal Injuries Assessment Board (Amendment) Act 2007.

[166] C O'Toole and W McEllin, 'Why We Should Fight the PIAB Tooth-and-Nail?'(2004) 98(1) *Law Society of Ireland Gazette* 18.

[167] The original fixed fee of €1,000 was reduced in successive years by PIAB as a reflection of continuous improvement in internal efficiencies and process re-engineering. In 2013 the fee was reduced by 30% from the previous year to €600.

[168] Internal efficiencies achieved by PIAB over the years, in addition to successive defences of judicial reviews, facilitated annual reductions in the fixed fee from an original level of €1,050. The nominal fee paid by claimants of €45 is awarded at the end of an assessment provided they have not caused wasted costs such as failure to attend an independent medical examination without good grounds or in the absence of advance notice of cancellation.

in a statutory maximum period of nine months. Some annual reports of the Courts Service show that, in the less than 10 per cent of litigation cases which do proceed to trial, only 3 per cent of that number are successfully defended so there is a 0.3 per cent prospect of a dismissal at hearing.[169]

PIAB represents a win-win solution for the only two interests that it seeks to serve—the interests of genuine victims of negligent accidents and the legitimate interests of defendants, which in a balanced combination serve the common good. As we all know, in the British Isles the mere occurrence of an accident does not entitle a person to compensation, even where there is no question about the genuineness of the injury. That said, it must be recognised that there are many relatively straightforward occurrences that were taking far too long and which were costing far too much to finalise. Thus, the focus was always on the 90 per cent of cases that never progressed to a court hearing and are now dissuaded from entering litigation, with its attendant costs, because they are handled through PIAB either as the facilitator of direct settlements or by formal statutory awards.

The test of success for PIAB is essentially the extent to which it can put itself out of business. The reality is that insurers will not 'behave' unless there is an incentive for them to make early adequate compensation offers in cases that cannot be defended. That incentive now is the choice between low-cost fixed-fee assessments by PIAB, or penal litigation costs. Claimants may cheat unless they or their advisers are reminded of the need to be honest.[170] That incentive is the deterrent to exaggerated claims in the court system.[171] We are not usually talking of 'fraud' here but mostly opportunism.[172] While there are staged accidents, the overwhelming majority of claimants are genuine.[173] However, the perverse incentive of a litigation system that encourages parties to 'put their case at its height' on quantum rather than to seek fair compensation may be considered inconsistent with the

[169] That statistic, of course, ignores the fact that many plaintiffs abandon their litigation in the face of strong defence evidence, even if that is only done 'on the steps of the court' when faced with the prospect of liability for the defendant's costs. Data on dismissals has not been provided in the most recent annual reports of the Courts Service.

[170] Behavioural economist Dan Ariely's book *The Honest Truth about Dishonesty* (New York, HarperCollins, 2012) was on the best seller list for many months in 2014 because he nails the truth that we lie to everybody and most of all we lie to ourselves to maintain our self-image as moral and honest. The book is fascinating because it gives prescriptions on what works to counteract cheating and what does not work. Equally, S Karstedt and S Farrall, 'The Moral Economy Of Everyday Crime: Markets, Consumers and Citizens' (2006) 46 *British Journal of Criminology* 1011 found that nearly two-thirds of people admitted to acts of dishonesty such as paying a builder in cash or buying clothes for a special occasion and returning them afterwards. The worst offenders were the middle classes, with 70% of those in the A and B social brackets admitting to everyday fiddling, deceitfulness and fraud, compared with 53% of those in the D and E brackets. It is all too easy to persuade ourselves that everybody is at it. Ariely concludes that 'if people are regularly reminded of moral codes they are far less likely to misbehave. People want to be good. You just have to remind them'.

[171] Civil Liability and Courts Act 2004 at s 14 verifying affidavit; s 25 false evidence; s 26 fraudulent actions; s 29 civil sanction.

[172] Fisher (n 23) 166 says in respect of the UK 'The Insurance Fraud Bureau report 22,500 staged accidents in the last 12 months. Their work is starting to have an impact, with £5.5m of assets seized under the Proceeds of Crime Act (POCA) as a direct consequence of their work'.

[173] Investigations into fraud are notoriously difficult from a legal perspective and can be so consuming of resources that a very long-term view must be taken to establish a payback. An example of a successful such effort was reported in the *Irish Times* in July 2015: www.irishtimes.com/news/crime-and-law/courts/circuit-court/judge-claims-roma-working-with-travellers-in-insurance-scams-1.2277545?utm_source=lunchtime_digest&utm_medium=email&utm_campaign=news_digest.

goal of equity between the parties.[174] Defendants do have rights too, one of which is not to be blackmailed by excessive litigation costs or a 'vulture culture' as one paper termed it.[175]

However, in this context of 'compo culture' I must share a professional experience. Since CCTV was introduced widely on our national transport system in Ireland I have observed some claimants review footage of their accident and have observed them being amazed at how different what actually happened compares with what they truly believed had happened. For example, is there not a natural inclination to blame the bus driver for severe breaking rather than admit you fell down the stairs because you were not holding the handrail like your Mummy told you to do when you were a child? Most injured parties when they see the evidence that they were 'the authors of their own misfortune' do not pursue unmeritorious actions, but surprisingly a minority do. Such claimants possibly hope for a 'nuisance value' settlement. From a defendant perspective this is only short-term economics being applied to such settlements by insurers and will be reflected in increased premium rates. A long-term view is more likely to be adopted by the self-insured, often operating under more constrained public funding, and concerned about precedents within which their businesses must then operate. There may be different priorities for an insurance company whose policyholders can change on an annual basis at renewal. Crystallising liability exposures out of provisions on live claims and into paid outlay on finalised claims facilitates pricing decisions by underwriters.

The faraway future may be one of Telematics and driverless cars. Such developments will challenge our existing models of compulsory motor insurance and theories of tort, but that may happen sooner than currently anticipated.

How It All Went Wrong in 2014

A repeat of the 'mistake' made in 1991 by increasing the monetary limits of the lower courts, referred to earlier, occurred in February 2014. The Department of Justice increased the limit of the Circuit Court from €38,000 to €60,000 and the limit of the District Court, which traditionally heard very few injury cases, from €5,000 to €20,000.[176] The Regulatory Impact Analysis relied upon by the Department used largely the same argument which was pursued by the then Minister for Justice during parliamentary debates in 1990 at the time of the previous jurisdictional increases—that more cases would be heard in the lower

[174] Irish insurers estimate that policyholders pay an extra €100 per year between 'fraud' and the cost of uninsured driving but their definition of both terms is open to a debate which goes beyond the scope of this chapter: www.independent.ie/business/personal-finance/insurance-fraudsters-add-50-to-average-motorists-premium-30982567.html.

[175] Fisher (n 23) 166 says 'While there may not be a compensation culture, there is a "vulture culture" in respect of legal fees. Figures from the Association of British Insurers (ABI) show that across motoring and liability, for every £1 spent on injury claims, 43p is spent in legal costs'.

[176] www.justice.ie/en/JELR/Regualtory per cent20Impact per cent20Analysis per cent20Courts per cent20Bill per cent202013.pdf.

costs jurisdiction. While it may be too early yet to draw any conclusions, those in the claims business say that very few such cases are being commenced in the District Court since the jurisdictional increases in 2014. The major difference from 1991 is that a Book of Quantum now exists to assist those on the bench who might not have previously had extensive experience of general damages levels for various types of injury. Presumably the next annual report of the Courts Service will include data on the summonses issued and awards made in each of the three levels as their statistics on personal injury awards are currently confined to the High Court and Circuit Court.[177]

In the decade after the last jurisdictional increase, the positive margin for motor insurers between written premium income and claims paid widened which left more scope for absorbing fixed costs and generating profit margins.[178] Insurers did not seem to make very strong efforts in 2013 to argue against the increases in court limits which were also resisted by the Law Society of Ireland which expressed concerns about resources in those venues and that the extra workload would cause delays at District Court level.

An analysis published in November 2015 by the Central Bank as the regulator of insurers reflected an increase between 2012 and 2014 of 8 per cent in the average motor injury claim cost.[179] In contrast, inflation in motor insurance from February 2014 to November 2015 has been many multiples of that percentage. Public and professional debate continues around the causes of price increases but it is clear that many insurers find themselves challenged in advance of the enhanced solvency requirements which will take effect in 2016. Although this change to the prudential regime had been flagged many years in advance, a number of companies have had to seek capital injections from their parent organisations or by the sale of assets.[180] Not surprisingly the representative body of insurance in September 2015 placed the blame for price increases solely on the 'excessive cost of claims'.[181] As was a feature of previous debates on insurance costs a number of assertions made by various parties are not supported by even the published data. For example, acceptance rates of PIAB awards remained constant over the previous five years at 60 per cent and they are concluding an increasing volume of awards annually, up 17 per cent in 2014 on 2013. Without access to detailed raw data held by insurers on all cases it is not possible at this time to arrive at robust conclusions about the dynamics in operation behind the latest trends but there are calls for another MIAB-type investigation.

These are new challenges in 2016 which will need to be monitored for the protection of injured parties and consumers.

[177] Budgetary constraints on the Courts Service have been acute during the financial crisis which commenced in 2008. See *Irish Times* (25 November 2015): www.irishtimes.com/news/crime-and-law/courts-service-boss-fears-collapse-of-it-system-1.2443666#.VlYiiIULlLU.email.

[178] In 1990 Written Premium Income (WPI) for motor insurance at market aggregate level was €452m and Claims Paid amounted to €368m leaving a margin of €84m. That margin between those two figures had grown by 147% to €206m by 1999.

[179] In the other two main injury classes the increases were 27% in employers' liability and 8% in public liability.

[180] eg, Royal Sun Alliance, Liberty and FBD. As reported in the *Sunday Business Post* (15 November 2015): www.businesspost.ie/parent-shores-up-liberty-with-e25m-injection/.

[181] www.insuranceireland.eu/news-and-publications/news-press-release/insurance-ireland-proposes-range-of-measures-to-address-increases-in-the-cost-of-claims.

Finally, A Dip Into Doctrine

Thankfully it does not fall to supporters of PIAB to address the inherent inconsistencies within tort theory as the Board's function relates solely to redress as established by court precedents on quantum. However, in a personal capacity I suspect some would describe me as a contrarian so I will express my challenges to some of the orthodoxy.

In a paper entitled 'Some Reflections on the Process of Tort Reform', Professor Rabin is somewhat dismissive of the role of increasing administrative costs. He states that tackling this is 'not the stuff of breath-taking reform proposals'.[182] I beg to disagree. Tackling the administration costs had an extraordinary result in Ireland over a decade both for injured parties[183] and for the premium paying public.[184]

In my opinion, before anyone contemplates reducing the standard of the duty of care and before there is any tampering with compensation levels for injured parties, by abolition or the capping of damages, I contend the first step should be to optimise the redress system. That approach is consistent with that of the law and economics school theory on efficient investment in accident prevention.[185]

It matters not whether there was ever a snail in the *Donoghue v Stevenson* ginger beer bottle.[186] We needed that case to know who our neighbour was and that litigation needed a sophisticated court system to extend the boundaries of tort law. However, 99 per cent of cases are not in that category so the court system is the last place they should be. If your redress system is court based, get to the bottom of where the money is going and where the inefficiencies are being caused. Rather than 'cherchez la femme', it is a case of follow the euro/pound/dollar. Find out first who are the 'rent sharers' as they would be called in competition theory.[187] Do not allow them, be they insurers or lawyers, to set the agenda in a self-serving manner not just out of self-interest but because they often seem incapable of thinking outside the adversarial box.[188] We need to build new boxes—be revolutionary rather than evolutionary.

There were those who questioned the membership of the Board of PIAB[189] and why none of the representative bodies from the legal professions were involved on the

[182] RL Rabin, 'Some Reflections on the Process of Tort Reform' (1988) 13 *San Diego Law Review* 42.

[183] In terms of faster compensation delivery and relief from the stress of litigation.

[184] In terms of reduced premium charges.

[185] Largely based on the works of RH Coase, 'The Problems of Social Cost' (1960) 3 *Journal of Law and Economics* 1; G Calabresi, *The Costs of Accidents: A Legal and Economic Analysis* (New Haven CT, Yale University Press 1970). As reviewed, for example, by RA Posner, 'The Law and Economics Movement' (Richard T Ely lecture, May 1987) 77(2) *Papers & Proceedings of the 99th Annual meeting of the American Economic Association* 1.

[186] *Donoghue v Stevenson* [1932] AC 562. Lord Macmillan, at 619, stated 'the conception of legal responsibility may develop in adaptation to altering social conditions and standards'.

[187] David Richardo introduced the term 'rent' in economics. It means the payment to a factor of production in excess of what is required to keep that factor in its present use. 'On the Principles of Political Economy and Taxation' in *The Works and Correspondence of David Ricardo*, 11 vols (ed Piero Sraffa, with the collaboration of MH Dobb) (Cambridge, Cambridge University Press, 1951–1973). Available online at: www.econlib.org/library/Ricardo/ricP.html.

[188] RA Posner, 'Can Lawyers Solve the Problems of the Tort System?' (1985) 73 *California Law Review* 747, 748.

[189] The membership of the Board of PIAB was questioned by many—W Binchy, 'The Implications of the [PIAB] Act for Tort Law and Practice' in W Binchy and P Quigley, *The Personal Injuries Assessment Board Act 2003: Implications for the Legal Practice* (Dublin, FirstLaw, 2004); G Hogan, 'Public Law and Constitutional Aspects

Board.[190] That is a more fundamental question than it might first appear. It is a question of perspectives which is widely discussed in the literature. As Llewellyn might term it, lawyers are doing 'law jobs'.[191] In my view, I might provocatively suggest that lawyers should be seen as the servants of the system not its central architects.[192] If tort is not the problem, perhaps the players are—to invoke sporting parlance often favoured by the *Law Society of Ireland Gazette*. The role of independently minded academics in bringing balance to reform programmes is also a worthwhile topic for debate. Such scholars have a particular responsibility. They have what may be described as 'privileged voices' in public discourse and they can also influence the judiciary in the administration of the rule of law, as well as the Law Reform Commission.

PIAB satisfies what I would call the Alexy's 'claim to correctness'.[193] Indeed, this was recognised by Mrs Justice Fidelma Macken in the Supreme Court when saying of PIAB that

> a public policy which aims to reduce legal and associated costs arising in court proceedings, and which has as its basis, *inter alia*, the aim of disposing of claims for personal injuries in a simple straightforward manner, which may also enable a claimant to apply for and benefit from the statutory assessment scheme without legal representation if he/she desires, is a perfectly proper and acceptable public policy aim, and an appropriate basis for a legislative scheme of the type under review here.[194]

That important section of the decision in *O'Brien v Personal Injuries Assessment Board* is rarely cited in critiques of this new successful redress system.

Administrative law actions are essential to protect us all from the potential excesses of executive power but there needs to be a sense of proportion.[195] The plaintiff's costs sought in that case amounted to €2.143 million. Upon challenge at taxation that bill was reduced by 82 per cent to €393,472.[196] The case was launched within weeks of PIAB opening its doors in July 2004 and a final decision was delivered on 19 December 2008, over four years later. The wheels of justice revolve slowly and expensively.

of the PIAB Regime' (Trinity College Dublin Conference on PIAB, March 2004); Gilhooly (n 5); Patton (n 78) although others, even from abroad—Erskine (n 57), were able to readily identify from the legislation that the actual claims were dealt with by statutory assessors and that the function of the Board was governance of the organisation and the setting of policy.

190 MIAB Report 2002, para C.25—The Law Society of Ireland declined the invitation from MIAB by their written response of 27 July 2001 in the following terms: 'It seems to us that the focus of your enquiry is on matters which are internal to the insurance industry and of which the Society has no direct knowledge'.

191 K Llewellyn and EA Hoebel, *The Cheyenne Way: Conflict and Case Law in Primitive Jurisprudence* (Buffalo NY, WS Hein & Co, 1941).

192 R Banakar, 'Whose Experience is the Measure of Justice?' (2008) 10 *Legal Ethics* 378.

193 R Alexy, S Paulson and B Paulson, *The Argument from Injustice—A Reply to Legal Positivism* (Oxford, Oxford University Press, 2002).

194 O'Brien v Personal Injuries Assessment Board (n 138).

195 See Chris Grayling's proposals for changes to judicial review regulations in England—Ministry of Justice, *Proposals for the Reform of Legal Aid in England and Wales* (Consultation Paper CP12/10)—which were challenged by the Public Law Project: www.publiclawproject.org.uk/data/resources/188/Ravi-Low-Beer-Jr-reforms-update.pdf—and rejected by the High Court in 2015 because of adverse effects on legal aid cases: *Ben Hoare Bell Solicitors & Ors, R (On the Application Of) v The Lord Chancellor* [2015] EWHC 523 (Admin), [2015] 1 WLR 4175.

196 'Taxing Master Cuts "Grossly Excessive" Legal Bill by 82 Per Cent' *Irish Times* (1 July 2010): www.highbeam.com/doc/1P2-25283334.html; 'Legal Fees in Injury Case "Revolting" in the Extreme' *Irish Times* (1 July 2010): www.highbeam.com/doc/1P2-25283343.html.

The greatest body of judicial reviews against PIAB related to legal costs. Mr Justice Ryan in his judgment on 18 October 2010 found that the Board acted reasonably at all times and complied with fair procedures.[197] Among the reasons which had been put forward for paying the level of legal fees sought was that the claimants did not have law degrees nor qualified barristers or solicitors. Mr Justice Ryan said that 'a person does not need to have detailed information about the legal system in order to make a claim to the Board'. Mr Justice Sean Ryan also held that the claims were 'straightforward and were the kind of claims intended to be dealt with by the Board and thereby diverted from the courts' burgeoning caseloads'. As Oliver Wendell Holmes remarked in the context of legal education, let us focus on what the 'bad man' needs to know about the law.[198] Tort applies to you too so are you a bad person?

Imagine that you rear-end someone's vehicle in the morning through a momentary lapse in concentration, assuming they have not created an unnecessary emergency or some such contributory factor. I ask you to try Rawls' thought experiment of what we would all like to see happen if we were 'in our original position' and deciding what would be the best way to resolve such situations regardless of our status in life.[199] I doubt your first thoughts would turn to Calabresi's Cathedral which underpins the concept of insurance.[200] Well, certainly not if you knew it would carry a 46 per cent litigation overhead. When I hear Calabresi mentioned I prefer to visualise the Cathedral sculpture by Rodin of the almost clasping hands that threaten to be isolated by adversarial litigation but could instead be reaching out as the helping hands of resolution. The non-adversarial approach worked much better under the IBEC/ICTU voluntary code[201] on Workplace accidents in which I was involved in the mid-1990s where the focus was on prevention while dissuading both parties from turning into litigant mode from the moment of occurrence of an accident.[202]

We are told that insurance is meant to be the most efficient system of sharing the risks of negligent accidents. In the words of Guido Calabresi, general deterrence involves deciding 'what the accident costs of activities are and letting the *market* determine the degree to which, and the ways in which, activities are desired given such costs'.[203] However, nobody seems to have been assigned the role of ensuring that insurers are actually efficient in the interests of the common good. The imperfect market with the imbalance of power between providers and purchasers does not provide us with that service. MIAB called for a better balance by the Financial Regulator between solvency supervision which is their priority, and the other legitimate interests of consumers. That has not happened yet and consumer

[197] *Plewa v PIAB* (n 134).

[198] OW Holmes, 'The Path of the Law' (1897) 10 *Harvard Law Review* 457.

[199] J Rawls, *A Theory of Justice*, rev edn (Cambridge MA, Harvard University Press, 1999).

[200] JL Coleman, 'Doing Away With Tort Law' (2008) *Loyola of Los Angeles Law Review* 1149, referring to the works of Guido Calabresi: 'Torts, the Law of the Mixed Society' (1977) 56 *Texas Law Review* 519; 'Some Thoughts on Risk Distribution and the Law of Torts' (1961) 70 *Yale Law Journal* 499; 'Transaction Costs, Resource Allocation and Liability Rules—A Comment' (1968) 11 *Journal of Law and Economics* 67; *The Costs of Accidents* (n 185).

[201] Irish Business and Employers Confederation/Irish Congress of Trade Unions.

[202] The Deloitte Report (n 13) found that Ireland had the most expensive employer liability premiums in the entire EU and that these costs could represent as much as 8% of payroll for firms with employees of 10 people or fewer.

[203] Calabresi, *The Costs of Accidents* (n 185) 69.

protection continues to be weak.[204] As I mentioned earlier, higher claims costs can make more money for insurers as a simple example demonstrates.[205] A 10 per cent margin on a €400 premium leaves a lot less scope for management expenses and profits than 10 per cent of a €4,000 premium which was the level of cost that was at one time justified in Ireland for a young male driver.[206] The limits of consumer protection by the Regulator seem to be more about process than value for the consumer, especially in the areas of insurance which are compulsory.

We cannot expect to ever hear insurers declare that they are satisfied with improvements introduced by way of government reforms to the injury or safety systems. They will repeatedly draw attention to adverse market developments, even to aid their calls for increases in unrelated classes of business.[207] While price control is not permitted under EU law, the protection of consumer rights to fair pricing of a product which is compulsory has not been abolished but is merely ignored in the main. We cannot rely on market forces to strike that balance because of the asymmetry of information between purchasers and providers, as well as the intangible nature of the product purchased.

In the pricing context, the EU continues to interfere with the purity of the common law system. It is estimated that 50 per cent of our laws now come from Brussels or Luxemburg.[208] One such piece of madness, in my view, is the Gender Directive.[209] This undermines the skills of the prudent underwriter to the detriment of the safest risks on our roads.[210]

From my experience in business, some of the stated objectives of law and economics theory are inherently inconsistent within both the insurance industry and the self-insured sector. If the cost of tort can merely be priced into goods for sale there is no actual net burden on producers but the greatest burden is placed on the poorest of purchasers. In contrast, criminal fines are often not even tax deductible[211] and the reputational risk from

[204] MIAB recommendation no 4: That the unique position of compulsory motor insurance should be adequately reflected in the responsibilities of the new Irish Financial Services Regulatory Authority (IFSRA) as the Board are of the view that there is currently no effective regulatory mechanism to balance the legitimate concerns of consumers with requirements for effective solvency supervision.

[205] Higher premiums also better absorb fixed overheads of insurers such as premises, staff, IT systems etc.

[206] Discrimination on grounds of age per se is contrary to the Equal Status Act 2000 as held by the Equality Tribunal in *Ross v RSA* (2003) DEC-S2003-116. An insurance company refused to provide a quotation for car insurance to Mr Jim Ross aged 77 stating that it did not accept new customers aged over 70.This was deemed to be discriminatory as the insurance company could not provide the required statistical evidence to justify its policy. The Equality Tribunal ordered the insurance company to pay him €2000: www.equality.ie/Files/Annual per cent20Report per cent202003.pdf.

[207] *Sunday Business Post* article (30 November 2014) where insurers cite adverse trends in flood damage to buildings but make no mention of the reduction in average injury claims costs and bemoan the fact that in the decade since 2003 premium income on motor insurance has halved (from €1.9b Net Written Premium to €€1b in 2013) while vehicle volumes have increased (from 1.9m licensed in 2003 to c 2.4m in 2013).

[208] www.telegraph.co.uk/news/worldnews/europe/8067510/Up-to-half-of-British-laws-come-from-Europe-House-of-Commons-Library-claims.html.

[209] Gender Non-Employment Directive 2004/113/EC, as interpreted in Case C-236/09 *Association Belge des Consommateurs Test-Achats ASBL v Conseil des Ministres* [2011] ECR I-773 which became effective from 21 December 2012 in Ireland.

[210] The differentials in the claims cost profiles of motor policyholders aged up to 25 are very significant as between male and female based on the raw data analyses in the 2002 MIAB Report. In October 2015 the Central Bank published private motor statistics which display similar significant margins which vary by gender in Appendix 2 of that report: www.centralbank.ie/polstats/stats/motorins/Documents/Private%20Motor%20Insurance%20Statistics%202013.pdf.

[211] For reasons of moral hazard.

convictions make criminal sanction a much more powerful deterrent than tort. During a period of rapidly reducing insurance prices in Ireland the frequency of accidents decreased which is the exact opposite of what deterrence theory tells us.[212]

In closing, I promised to share some regrets. When the MIAB investigation advertised for public submissions back in 1999 one which really stuck with me was from a mature couple living in a remote part of the countryside who had had to give up their car because of the increasing cost of insurance. Between them they had 90 years of accident free driving experience. Not having access to public transport meant the loss of their independence. They could not go to church nor do their shopping without being beholden to somebody else. That struck me as a real injustice. The 46 per cent litigation overhead, the dysfunctionality of the insurance market, the rent-sharing by experts and all the other factors were not just about big business—they were hurting the most vulnerable and deserving in our society. When the going got tough as Chairperson of PIAB, and it often got very tough, I brought those people to mind to renew my motivation. I regret for their sake that it took us so long to devise an improved and more cost-effective system of redress for injured parties.

I also regret that it was necessary to spend so much time and intellectual energy, as well as cost, defending judicial reviews. Such effort could have been better employed to ensure that a system of structured settlements for maximum severity cases was introduced.[213] In my day job I had the honour of putting in place the first such arrangement by way of an interim settlement contract because an enlightened judge, Mr Justice Quirke, saw that it was the best protection for someone who needed 24/7 care for life. Sadly the subsequent report of the Working Group chaired by Mr Justice Quirke on PPOs is only now being implemented by government.[214] That is a continuing injustice. As we saw in the court data previously, there are thankfully only a couple of dozen awards annually over the €1 million mark. As a society we should be able to find a way to fund the future care of these most vulnerable victims of someone else's negligence. I also repeatedly called upon the ingenuity of the life assurance industry to devise solutions for impaired lives to equitably spread the vagaries of expanding life expectancy which should be a blessing not a burden if we have our social values properly adjusted.

I also regret that the remit of PIAB was not extended as originally planned to straightforward medical negligence cases. I echo the concerns expressed by Mrs Justice Irvine that adversarial litigation is probably the least suitable forum for dealing with many such tragedies.[215]

[212] To quote from the CB private motor statistics published in October 2015 for 2013: 'motor accident frequency trended downwards over the period 2008 to 2013, falling by almost 40 per cent for both comprehensive and third party fire & theft claims … The stable volume of large claims observed between 2006 and 2011 may be explained by the declining number of serious injury accidents reported on Irish roads in recent years. Nevertheless, this trend was interrupted in 2012 when 57 large third party fire & theft claims were recorded, representing the largest such rise in large claims since 1997, when the data series began'.

[213] Although I do not have in mind a mirror image of the English system of PPOs with its inbuilt inflation indices which seem an invitation to increased costs as the years proceed.

[214] Working Group on Medical Negligence and Periodic Payments 2010 Report: www.courts.ie/Courts.ie/library3.nsf/(WebFiles)/5CEEA19C4A5959BC802577DC0055C9F4/$FILE/Medical%20Negligence%201.pdf.

[215] Judge Irvine 'empathises with parents over "cruel and disadvantageous" system' *Irish Times* (22 March 2014): www.irishtimes.com/news/crime-and-law/courts/judge-urges-radical-overhaul-of-clinical-negligence-cases-1.1734166.

While we can debate questions of 'right' policies and effective rules in the abstract, I take a guiding light from the issues raised by Twining:

> In so far as participants in legal processes and other affected people complain that too many of their questions have been left unexplored, and that too many of their questions have been left unanswered by academic lawyers, their complaints are justified. The gist of their complaint is that for their purposes different criteria of relevance are required. A model of legal process developed around the concept of **standpoint**, it is suggested, is likely to provide a more satisfactory theoretical basis for such criteria than that provided by models of legal system as a system of rules (or rules and principles—Dworkin). This is not to reject such theories. It is only to put them in their place.[216]

I leave you with a brief word on the financial model of PIAB. PIAB operates on an entirely self-funded financial basis from its fixed fees levied on respondents to ensure the system is not a drain on either the Exchequer or the taxpayer. This was a self-imposed discipline from the outset and it is not a requirement under the legislation.

PIAB noted with some interest that lawyers' lobbyists projected a need for over 300 staff and annual cost at €38 million for a capacity to deal with 9,700 claims.[217] This compares with the reality of 77 staff at an administrative cost including medical assessments of €10 million per annum for 31,000 claims.[218] Those of you who are quick at maths might spot tjat if those are lawyers' standards they seem to reflect the following:

— one eighth of the productivity
— at four times the cost!

Perhaps those comparisons provide a clue as to why injury cases were taking six times longer in Ireland and why insurance was among the most expensive in Europe.[219]

[216] W Twining, 'The Bad Man Revisited' (1973) 58 *Cornell Law Review* 275, 281–82.

[217] 'Board to Shake Up Insurance Industry Could Cost Eur30m' *Irish Independent* (17 July 2003): www.independent.ie/irish-news/board-to-shake-up-insurance-industry-could-cost-30m-25939276.html. Dr Peter Bacon in a report for the Bar Council asserted that the set-up costs of PIAB would be €30m. The actual set-up costs were €4.5m which PIAB repaid to the Exchequer in December 2011.

[218] Productivity is 403 cases per head compared with 32 annually. Cost is €10m but is recovered in full by fees. Annual cost projected by a consultant, Des Peelo, for the Law Society in October 2001 was based on PIAB running costs at €27m and loss of productivity in the courts of €11m.

[219] Legal costs in Ireland continue to be the subject of wider debate. *Prime Time* on RTÉ Playert: www.rte.ie/player/show/10389063.

9

An Overview of the Role of Medical Panels in Victorian Legislation

DR CAROL A NEWLANDS

Introduction

It is nearly 25 years since Medical Panels started operating in the State of Victoria. Over the intervening years the role and responsibilities of this quite unique entity have been modified by legislated changes and fine tuned following judicial review of opinions and determinations.

Aside from a period of three years in the late 1990s, the publicly underwritten Victorian workers' compensation scheme has, since its inception in 1985, consisted of a 'no-fault' benefits scheme with access to common law limited solely to the provision of damages for non-economic loss. The latter pathway requires the worker to be assessed as having a resulting level of impairment above a given threshold. The Medical Panels undertake these assessments in disputed cases and hence play a role in both the tort and no-tort areas of workers' compensation.

Following amendments to the Wrongs Act 1958 in 2002/03 the role of the Medical Panel was expanded to cover all disputed personal injury claims as it effectively became the 'gatekeeper' to common law access. The need for such reforms to the tort law system has long been debated as has the general perception that one of the main causal factors was that the public had become increasingly litigious with one State Premier on record as saying, 'it's my view that this country is tying itself up in tape because of litigation, a long term trend to see us litigate for everything, to try and settle every problem in our lives … by getting a big cash payment from the courts'.[1] He subsequently added that 'a country as small as ours can't afford to have the American-style culture of litigation'.[2]

It is thus against this backdrop of legislative changes that Medical Panels have come to occupy an important dispute resolution role in the workers' compensation scheme and also in the pre-litigation process required of plaintiffs and respondents seeking access to the common law under the Wrongs Act 1958.

A Medical Panel is deemed to have been convened once the Convenor provides the appointed members with the referral documents and it continues to exist until the required

[1] Laurie Oaks, Interview with Bob Carr, NSW Premier (14 July 2002).
[2] Ibid.

opinion, or determination, has been finalised and signed off by the Presiding Member. A Panel may now be composed of any number of medical practitioners selected from a list of those approved by the Governor in Council to serve in that capacity.[3] In 2013 there were around 180 medical practitioners appointed by the Governor. In addition, there are around 35 consultants in various specialties who are available to be called upon to advise the Panels. The Convenor appoints an appropriate practitioner from amongst those selected to serve on a particular Panel to act as the Presiding Member whose role it is to prepare the Panel's Opinion or Determination, and Reasons for Opinion documents.

The Convenor is appointed by the responsible Minister from amongst the pool of practitioners and has the responsibility of convening each Panel, determining the members required to appropriately address the question(s)[4] and delegating his responsibilities to a Deputy (of which there are currently two) during any absences.[5] In addition, having a Deputy allows for delegation at times when there may be a conflict of interest. The Convenor can only delegate his role of convening Panels to a Deputy Convenor.[6] The position of Deputy was first created in 2000[7] but by 2013 it became possible to appoint 'one or more Deputy Convenors'.[8]

The Convenor is permitted to 'give directions as to the arrangement of the business of the Medical Panels but must not give directions inconsistent with any guidelines made by the Minister'.[9]

The requirements of the Medical Panel are similar under both statutes in that a Panel is 'not bound by rules or practices as to evidence'[10] but 'must act informally, without regard to technicalities, or legal forms and as speedily as a proper consideration of the reference allows'.[11] It is also a requirement of each selected Panel member to ensure that he or she has not previously examined or treated the claimant or worker except in the capacity as a member of a Medical Panel as otherwise he or she would be ineligible to undertake the required role as an independent examiner/assessor.[12] Under current workers' compensation legislation a Medical Panel must provide a written opinion within seven days of forming its opinion and must, in addition, provide a written statement of its reasons for that opinion.[13] The Wrongs Act requires that the Panels provide a determination or certificate within 30 days of last examination of the claimant or receipt of final documentation,[14] but there is no requirement that a statement of reasons be provided, although the Panels routinely provide reasons voluntarily.

[3] Workplace Injury Rehabilitation and Compensation Act 2013 (Vic) s 537(2).
[4] Ibid, s 537(7).
[5] Ibid, s 537(4).
[6] Email from John Malios, Convenor of Medical Panels to Carol Newlands (10 October 2014).
[7] Accident Compensation (Common Law and Benefits) Act 2000 (Vic) s 9.
[8] Workplace Injury Rehabilitation and Compensation Act 2013 (Vic) s 537(3)(a).
[9] Ibid, s 303(6).
[10] Accident Compensation Act 1985 (Vic) s 65(1); Wrongs Act 1958 (Vic) s 28LZ(1).
[11] Accident Compensation Act 1985 (Vic) s 65(2); Wrongs Act 1958 (Vic) s 28LZ(2).
[12] Accident Compensation Act 1985 (Vic) s 63(5).
[13] Workplace Injury Rehabilitation and Compensation Act 2013 (Vic) s 313(2) and (3).
[14] Wrongs Act 1958 (Vic) s 28LZG(3).

Commencement

In 1989 the Treasurer of Victoria introduced a raft of proposed amendments to the Accident Compensation Act 1985 which he explained had become necessary due to 'a number of fundamental problems that have been identified in the WorkCare Scheme',[15] including:

— A level of funding insufficient to ensure the financial viability of the scheme.
— Continuing low rates of return to work.
— A dispute resolution system that has become excessively costly and legalistic with much of the disputation locked around the issue of contested medical opinion.
— Continued rorting of the system by a number of professional groups as well as by workers.[16]

He said that as a result the system was in a poor financial state and it was probable that it would experience a 'negative cash flow in the 1990–91 financial year with a depletion of cash reserves by around 1993'.[17]

Three areas had been earmarked for change including: increasing the average levy so as to increase the revenue base; amendments to the benefit provisions as a means of increasing the incentive for workers to return to employment; and alterations to the procedures for dispute resolution.[18] It was against this backdrop that the Medical Panels were introduced.

Prior to these changes all disputes regarding liability or entitlement under the compensation scheme had been heard by the Accident Compensation Tribunal which employed 14 judges, 21 arbitrators and eight lay persons. It consisted of two tiers and the intention had been that it should settle the majority of disputes informally. However, as Parliament was informed, 'the unintended result has been to end up with both tiers operating in an adversarial and legalistic manner'.[19] Hence, it was decided to create a new and independent body, the WorkCare Appeals Board, to hear matters informally. In the event of a dispute, either party could then appeal to the Accident Compensation Tribunal for a hearing before a judge.

In addition, the proposed Bill made provision for 'expert medical panels which, at the discretion of the board or the tribunal, can be called upon to resolve medical questions relevant to the injured worker's claim'.[20] Thus, at its inception, the Medical Panels were only required to provide an opinion on such medical questions as posed by either of these two bodies. As the first Convenor noted, a 'medical question' could at that time, include matters such as:

— The nature of a worker's medical condition relevant to an injury or alleged injury.
— Whether a worker's employment could possibly have been a contributing factor to an injury or alleged injury, or to a similar injury, other than a question whether the worker's employment was in fact such a contributing factor.

[15] Victoria, *Parliamentary Debates*, Legislative Assembly, 17 August 1989, 519 (Rob Jolly, Treasurer). The proposals were implemented by the Accident Compensation (General Amendment) Act 1989 (Vic).
[16] Victoria, *Parliamentary Debates* (n 15) 520.
[17] Ibid.
[18] Ibid, 521–22.
[19] Ibid, 522.
[20] Ibid, 523.

— The extent of any physical or mental condition resulting from or materially contributed to by the injury.
— The level of impairment of a worker.
— The probable duration or any physical or mental condition resulting from or materially contributed to by the injury.[21]

On the other hand, a Medical Panel was not permitted to consider issues such as:

— Whether an injury or alleged injury arose out of or in the course of a worker's employment.
— Whether a worker's incapacity for work resulted from or was materially contributed to by an injury or alleged injury.
— The extent of any incapacity of a worker for work.[22]

The Panels' opinions at that stage were authoritative in so far as they were binding on the Board or Tribunal, except in limited circumstances.[23]

The restrictions on what questions a Panel was permitted to consider were gradually removed over the years and by 2008 it was reported that the Panels could provide an opinion on 16 different questions including matters such as:

— The nature of the worker's medical condition.
— Issues relating to capacity for work or suitable employment.
— The adequacy, appropriateness or frequency of medical services.
— Whether work was a significant contributing factor or contributing factor to a worker's injury.
— Issues relating to percentage impairment, including permanence and level.
— Medical questions relating to a worker's 'serious injury' application pursuant to section 134AB(16)(b).[24]

The First Decade

During the first 16 months of their operation the Medical Panels received seven referrals to the end of June 1990 and a further 324 in the following 12 months. All were from the WorkCare Appeals Board, there being none from the Tribunal.

It was reported that by the end of the 1990–91 financial year WorkCare had reached the financial targets set out in the 1989 reforms but 'the scheme's medical, legal and common law costs as well as lump sum payments were increasing'.[25] Details provided in the Annual Report of the Accident Compensation Commission 1991–92 demonstrated that there

[21] J Clarebrough, *Medical Panels Annual Report 1990/91* (30 June 1991) 3–4.
[22] Ibid, 4.
[23] Ibid.
[24] P Hanks, *Accident Compensation Act Review. Final Report* (2008) 338 [10.30].
[25] M Stylianou, 'To strike a balance' (Research report No R1-011-018, Monash University, June 2011) 537.

had been total gross claims payments of $856.6 million in 1990–91 and $995.2 million in 1991–92 compared with $717.2 million to the year ending June 1989.[26]

Similarly, the total cost of 'medical and like services' rose from $137.7 million in the 1988–89 financial year to $152.0 million by 30 June 1991 and $168.5 million a year later.[27] In addition, total legal costs increased considerably, particularly those associated with common law settlements which demonstrated an increase of 39.8% from $39.7 million in 1990–91 to $55.5 million just a year later.[28] These figures indicated a rapid increase from the $1.7 million paid in the financial year to 30 June 1989 and the $10.1 million the following year.[29] Other legal costs also demonstrated a similar but less steep rise. The amounts paid in actual common law settlements to injured workers rose from $10.5 million in the year to June 1989 to $57.4 million in 1990–91 and $113.6 million in 1991–92.[30]

A number of external factors were also deemed to have played a role in the increased costs to the system, including the collapse of a group of local building societies and the economic recession which had caused a number of businesses to close or reduce workforce numbers with the result that it became more difficult to return injured workers to employment.[31]

The Government responded to this situation in 1992 by further amending the Accident Compensation Act 1985 with the responsible Minister describing the scheme as it then was as being 'in financial disarray' with 'an unfunded liability of $1.9 billion … this will increase by a further $244 million during 1992–93 if the scheme remains unchanged'.[32] He added that the new legislation would replace 'the current costly system, which is driven by lawyers, with a non-adversarial system which entitles each of the parties to a fair and efficient investigation of the facts of the case'.[33]

The area of dispute resolution was one of those subject to change with Medical Panels to be provided with the power 'to make conclusive findings on all medical questions rather than by legal process'.[34] In addition, the Medical Panel was empowered to consider issues regarding treatment and incapacity for work.[35] The WorkCare Appeals Board and the Accident Compensation Tribunal were both abolished to be replaced by conciliation officers in the case of the former and by the courts and the Administrative Appeals Tribunal in the case of the latter. The reason given for these changes was to reduce legal costs which flowed from lawyers who, it was said, by challenging decisions 'keep clients on benefits and generate legal costs irrespective of the outcome of cases'.[36] At that stage the Panels' opinions on all medical questions were to be binding on the referring agency but not on the claimant.[37] In addition, the Government used its power to vary section 85 of the Constitution Act 1975 (Vic) to

[26] Accident Compensation Commission, *Annual Report 1991–92*, 12.
[27] Ibid, 30.
[28] Ibid, 31.
[29] Ibid.
[30] Ibid, 12.
[31] Stylianou (n 25) 37–38.
[32] Victoria, *Parliamentary Debates*, Legislative Assembly, 30 October 1992, 306 (Phil Gude, Minister for Industry and Employment).
[33] Ibid, 309.
[34] Ibid, 307.
[35] Ibid, 310.
[36] Ibid, 307–08.
[37] H Allan Hunt et al, 'Victorian Workers' Compensation System: Review and Analysis', Volume 1 (Report, W E Upjohn Institute for Employment Research, 29 August 1997) xxiv.

prevent any appeals on the merits of a Panel decision.[38] These changes in role were to mark the beginning of the Medical Panels as a binding decision-making tribunal.

In the same raft of amendments the Government tightened the requirements for compensability for work-related injuries with the introduction of the concept of 'significant contributing factor' with the attendant requirement that 'a worker will now have to establish that the worker's employment has been more than just one of many contributing factors. It must be a significant contributing factor'[39] to the development of the injury. Furthermore, the right to sue for common law damages was restricted to those workers deemed to have suffered a 'serious injury' which was defined as an impairment rating of 30% or more when assessed in accordance with the American Medical Association's (AMA) *Guides to the Evaluation of Permanent Impairment* (second edition), or by successful application for determination of serious injury within the meaning of the Act.[40]

Consequently, under the Accident Compensation (WorkCover) Act 1992 a court could, in accordance with section 45(1)(a), elect to refer a medical question to the Panel if it so wished, but was obliged to do so if a party to the proceedings requested that this be done.[41] The resulting Medical Panel opinion was deemed to be binding on the court.[42]

Not surprisingly, these proposed changes were not popular in some quarters with the Leader of the Opposition complaining that:

> There is an element of unreality when a court, which might be comprised of a judge or a judge and jury, is bound to accept the view of a medical panel, even if contrary medical evidence is available. The court cannot ask the medical panel which can consist of one person, to appear before it to be examined and have its opinion tested.[43]

Nonetheless, the Bill was enacted and the WorkCover scheme was declared to have been 'an outstanding success since it was established by the Government in 1993',[44] with the scheme fully funded by the end of the 1995–96 financial year.[45] Yet despite these positive results, the Treasurer deemed it necessary to introduce the Accident Compensation (Further Amendment) Bill to Parliament on 14 November 1996 as 'the number of workers being classified as having a serious injury has steadily risen due to the assessment of psychological or psychiatric impairment consequential upon an initial physical injury'.[46] To reverse this trend he introduced an amendment which directed that from that time on any psychiatric or psychological injury, impairment or symptoms which had arisen as a consequence or secondary to a physical injury would not be deemed compensable.[47] This change meant that injured workers could no longer summate the impairment ratings for the physical and psychiatric impairments that they received from the assessing independent medical

[38] Victoria, *Parliamentary Debates* (n 32) 311. The proposals were implemented by the Accident Compensation (Workcover) Act 1992 (Vic).

[39] Victoria, *Parliamentary Debates* (n 32) 308.

[40] Ibid, 310.

[41] Accident Compensation (Workcover) Act 1992 (Vic) s 45(1)(b).

[42] Ibid, s 45(1)(c).

[43] Victoria, *Parliamentary Debates*, Legislative Assembly, 11 November 1992, 720 (Jim Kennan, Broadmeadows).

[44] Victoria, *Parliamentary Debates*, Legislative Assembly, 14 November 1996, 1225 (Alan Stockdale, Treasurer).

[45] Ibid.

[46] Ibid, 1226.

[47] Ibid. See the Accident Compensation (Further Amendment) Act 1996 (Vic) s 9(2).

examiners or Medical Panels in the hope of reaching the 30% threshold deemed necessary for acceptance of a serious injury application.

It was just 12 months after these changes were introduced that the same Treasurer described Victoria as having 'the best workers' compensation scheme in Australia'[48] but added that the findings by a review group commissioned by the Government had indicated that:

> [T]he underlying cost of the scheme was now running ahead of premium levels and demanded urgent attention. The issues of common law, serious injury classification, as well as the overall level of disputation emerged as the most serious factors in the cost shift and became the focus of further very detailed and extensive research analysis.[49]

Although he recommended a number of changes, the central plank and that which caused most concern, was the removal of all remaining rights to common law access for injured workers[50] thereby reverting the Victorian scheme to a totally no-fault system albeit with 'generous comprehensive statutory benefits'.[51]

In addition, the role of the Medical Panel was once again expanded with Panel opinions deemed to be 'final and conclusive irrespective of who referred the medical question and must be adopted by the courts as the answer to the medical question'.[52] The stated reason for this was that:

> The government considers that doctors, not lawyers, are the best qualified people to offer medical opinions. Currently the opinion of a medical panel on a medical question is binding only when a court has referred a medical question to the panel. This gives rise to 'duelling experts' which becomes an obstacle to the resolution of disputes, leads to their escalation and drives up costs unnecessarily.
>
> Therefore, and in line with the practice in other jurisdictions, the act will require that the opinion of a medical panel on a medical question be final and conclusive irrespective of who referred the medical question and the opinion must be adopted by the courts as the answer to that question.[53]

The new Convenor of Medical Panels noted that this represented a 'significant increase in the status of Medical Panel opinions'[54] and also presented the Panels with a challenge to 'provide opinions that are of sufficient quality to support their conclusive and binding status'.[55] As a means of meeting this challenge he proposed to develop 'a process for the forming of opinions which is sound with regard to relevant principles of administrative law and natural justice'.[56] In addition, being aware of the new amendments requiring that all practitioners undertaking impairment assessments be trained in the use of the AMA *Guides to the Evaluation of Permanent Impairment* (fourth edition), he arranged for the necessary training of existing and newly appointed members[57] as this was the accepted tool

[48] Victoria, *Parliamentary Debates*, Legislative Assembly, 12 November 1997, 1073 (Alan Stockdale, Treasurer).
[49] Ibid.
[50] Ibid. See the Accident Compensation (Miscellaneous Amendment) Act 1997 (Vic) s 45(1).
[51] Victoria, *Parliamentary Debates* (n 48) 1074.
[52] Ibid, 1075. See the Accident Compensation (Miscellaneous Amendment) Act 1997 (Vic) s 21(4).
[53] Victoria, *Parliamentary Debates* (n 48) 1080.
[54] P Nisselle, 'Victorian WorkCover Authority Annual Report 1997–98' App 8—*Annual Report of the Medical Panels* (1998) 135.
[55] Ibid.
[56] Ibid.
[57] Ibid.

for assessment of physical injuries. The Government had previously accepted advice from psychiatrist members eligible to be appointed to the Medical Panels that a 'revised method for assessing and ascribing permanent impairment percentages to psychiatric conditions'[58] was required, and indeed it fell to them to devise the 'Clinical Guidelines to the Rating of Psychiatric Impairment 1997' which was subsequently adopted for rating all such impairments[59] until it was superseded by the 'Guide to the Evaluation of Psychiatric Impairment for Clinicians' in 2006 which was likewise devised by some of the psychiatrist members eligible, to be appointed to the Medical Panel.[60]

Medical Panels also undertook a drive to recruit new members which was to prove very valuable given that the number of referrals in the 1998–99 financial year was 521, more than double the 252 of the previous 12 months.[61] Over the same time period the maximum number of members which could be appointed to a Panel was raised from three to five.[62] This was the first such increase since Medical Panels came into being in March 1990.

In the early years, despite there being provision for up to three members of a Panel, the majority of cases were assessed by a single person Panel, with 90% of assessments being undertaken by single member Panels in the year to 30 June 1991[63] and 88% in the 1991–92 financial year.[64] The following year saw a swing towards joint Panels with 64% being two-person Panels,[65] though by 1993–94 this was down to 44%,[66] only to increase again the following year to 88%,[67] at which stage there were no single member Panels and 12% of Panel assessments were by three members.[68] However, by the end of the millennium the pattern of Medical Panel service delivery had undergone considerable changes.

In 2013 the only single member Panels constituted were usually for particular specialised assessments such as, for example, by an otolaryngologist. In addition, there has been a move away from Panel members assessing injured workers in their own consulting rooms as used to occur in the early years to these being performed almost universally at the Panel offices in Melbourne CBD. There have been obvious benefits from this practice as Panel members are able to discuss the opinion amongst themselves immediately after the assessment which in turn leads to a more timely delivery of the opinion.[69] There are also benefits for the worker as, wherever possible, all necessary appointments are scheduled on the same day.

[58] Victoria, *Parliamentary Debates* (n 48) 1077. Implemented by the Accident Compensation (Miscellaneous Amendment) Act 1997.

[59] 'Clinical Guidelines to the Rating of Psychiatric Impairment' *Victorian Government Gazette*, No S 87 (28 August 1998).

[60] 'The Guide to the Evaluation of Psychiatric impairment for Clinicians (GEPIC)' *Victorian Government Gazette*, No G 30, 1564–79.

[61] P Nisselle, 'Victorian WorkCover Authority Annual Report 1998–99' App 6—*Annual Report of the Medical Panels* (1999) 105.

[62] Ibid.

[63] Clarebrough, *Medical Panels Annual Report 1990/91* (n 21) 24.

[64] J Clarebrough, *Medical Panels Annual Report 1991/92* (28 September 1992) [8.2].

[65] B McCubbery, 'Victorian WorkCover Authority 1992/1993 Annual Report'—*Medical Panels Annual Report* (Appendix) 97.

[66] B McCubbery, 'Victorian WorkCover Authority 1993/1994 Annual Report'—*Medical Panels Annual Report* (Appendix) 103.

[67] B McCubbery, 'Victorian WorkCover Authority 1994/1995 Annual Report'—*Medical Panels Annual Report* (Appendix) 80.

[68] Ibid.

[69] Nisselle, 'Victorian WorkCover Authority Annual Report 1998–99' (n 61) 105.

The time for return of opinions has also varied over time. Although the available records are not complete, the return times as recorded in the relevant Medical Panel Annual Reports are as given below in Table 1.

Table 1: Time for Opinion Returns

Year	90/91	91/92	92/93	93/94	94/95	95/96	96/97	97/98	98/99	99/00
Days	42	40	N/R	N/R	N/R	165	153	57	42	35

Source: Medical Panel Annual Reports
Prepared by Dr CA Newlands, 21 September 2014
* N/R = not recorded.

The referrals to the Medical Panels over the corresponding period are as shown in Table 2.

Table 2: Total Referrals to Panels by Financial Year

Year	89/90	90/91	91/92	92/93	93/94	94/95	95/96	96/97	97/98	98/99	99/00
Total	7	342	487	117	385	2040	3401	144	252	521	1320

Source: Medical Panel Annual Reports
Prepared by Dr CA Newlands, 21 September 2014

The very large increase in referrals which occurred between 1994 and 1996 was believed to have resulted from legislative changes to section 104 of the Act which related to claims for compensation made under the Table of Maims. According to the Annual Report of 1993/94 prepared by Dr McCubbery, these changes required that a claimant who disputed an offer made by the insurer or Authority, then had to be referred to the Medical Panels for a determination of both the entitlement to compensation and 'the extent of any relevant impairment, disfigurement or pain and suffering'.[70]

The following year he explained that these changes had resulted in 'a ten-fold increase in referrals under the new section 104 which has been designed to minimise court proceedings … [a]s a result the rate of referrals of disputes … has risen from 1 in 33 disputes to 1 in 3 disputes'.[71] He continued, adding that whilst staff had coped with this increase, it had led to delays in scheduling appointments.[72] As shown in Table 1, the turnaround times for release of opinions was also significantly greater from 1995/96 than in the first two years, but as there is a lack of information for the three years from 1992, it is not clear how much of a difference occurred over a year-on-year basis. The situation with regard to the increased workload resulting from the alteration to section 104 was however rectified when such claims were 'diverted to the Conciliation service'[73] rather than to Panels.

It is important to note that at the time Medical Panels commenced their role the Act required that they return opinions to the Board within 28 days unless an extension was

[70] McCubbery, 'Victorian WorkCover Authority 1993/1994 Annual Report' (n 66) 102.
[71] McCubbery, 'Victorian WorkCover Authority 1994/1995 Annual Report' (n 67) 80.
[72] Ibid.
[73] B McCubbery, 'Victorian WorkCover Authority 1996/1997 Annual Report'—*Medical Panels Annual Report* (Appendix) 84.

granted. At that stage of course, the Panel acted merely as a medical advisory body. However, as its responsibilities increased along with its workload, the time allowed for return of opinions was set at 60 days after the reference had been made unless there had been an extension.[74] There had however been some confusion as to exactly what constituted the time at which the reference was made. This was recently clarified under section 313(1) of the recently enacted Workplace Injury Rehabilitation and Compensation Act 2013 (Vic) such that the time frame remained at 60 days but was taken as commencing from the date that the convened Medical Panel received the documents relating to the medical question from the Convenor. The 60 days could be extended if this was agreed to by the referrer.

A New Century: More Changes

The advent of a Labour government in 1999 set in train numerous Bills to amend the Accident Compensation Act 'enacted at a dizzying pace: in 2000, 2001, 2003 and 2004'.[75] The first of these was introduced to honour an election commitment 'to restore access to common-law damages for seriously injured workers to sue employers and recover damages',[76] with the effect backdated to 20 October 1999, this being the date that the government was sworn in.[77] The result of course was that Victoria was back to having a hybrid system of workers' compensation although in actual fact 'the "restored" rights [were] narrower than the common law rights available under the Liberal Kennett Government until they were abolished in 1997'.[78] This was seen as a necessary safeguard since the incoming government was all too aware of the increased costs that had resulted from the rise in serious injury claims in those previous years, even at a time when the overall claim rate had declined.[79]

Thus, the Bill as introduced by the appointed Minister for WorkCover resurrected the 30% threshold required for access to common law damages but added to the definition of serious injury such that the work-related injury also had to be deemed to be permanent. In addition, the requirements of the so-called 'narrative test' were tightened, with the Minister explaining that:

> The former rights which were removed … provided access to common law by a requirement that the compensable injury be a serious injury. The test of serious injury was satisfied by a worker having a 30 per cent or greater permanent impairment as a result of the compensable injury … a worker … deemed to have a serious injury … [was] entitled to bring proceedings for common-law damages.
>
> A worker with a whole-person-impairment … of less than 30% cent had an entitlement to make an application to the Victorian Workcover Authority that the injury was a serious injury or alternatively

[74] Accident Compensation Act 1985 (Vic) s 68(1).

[75] KL Adams, 'Legislative Developments. Here we go again: The Accident Compensation Act 1985 (Vic) and the amendment merry-go-round' (2005) 18 *Australian Journal of Labour Law* 158.

[76] Victoria, *Parliamentary Debates*, Legislative Assembly, 13 April 2000, 1001 (Mr Cameron, Minister for Workcover). See the Accident Compensation (Common Law and Benefits) Act 2000 (Vic) s 1(a).

[77] Ibid.

[78] Adams (n 75) 175.

[79] Stylianou (n 25) 57.

make an application to the court seeking leave to bring proceedings on the basis that the injury satisfied the narrative test of serious injury … section 135A of the Accident Compensation Act contained a definition of 'serious injury' meaning:

(a) serious long-term impairment or loss of a body function; or
(b) permanent serious disfigurement; or
(c) severe long-term mental or severe long-term behavioural disturbance or disorder; or
(d) loss of a foetus.[80]

He then added that under the new legislation the narrative test could only be satisfied if the injury were to be deemed permanent meaning that it was likely to continue indefinitely for the foreseeable future, and the resulting pain and suffering deemed to be 'very considerable'.[81] In addition, the Bill proposed that injured workers would undergo a 'once-only whole-person impairment assessment to determine their entitlement for both statutory lump sum benefits and access to common law under the whole person impairment test'.[82] If the injured worker disputed the determination of impairment then a referral was to be made to the Medical Panel for a binding determination.

Although there were a number of subsequent Bills further amending the Act, there was probably little which impacted on the Panels for some years aside from the Government's response to the case of *Connelly*[83] as detailed in *Hansard* on 16 October 2003.[84] This case was essentially an appeal against a Medical Panel decision not to round up an impairment rating of 29% to 30% thereby placing the injured worker in the serious injury category.[85]

In considering the matter the Supreme Court of Appeal noted that in accordance with section 91(1) of the Accident Compensation Act 1985 a Medical Panel was required to use the AMA *Guides to the Evaluation of Permanent Impairment* (second edition), when undertaking a whole person impairment assessment, the preface of which stated that:

Rating of the whole person: The final step in rating medical impairment takes into account all relevant considerations in order to reach a 'whole person' impairment rating. The final impairment value, whether the result of single or combined impairments, may be expressed in terms of the nearest 5%.

The Court noted that it was therefore 'a matter of judgement for the assessor in each case whether the limited discretion afforded by the rounding provision should be exercised. In some instances the exercise of the discretion will be of advantage to the claimant'.[86] However, the Court further noted that:

It will be recalled that the medical panel … wrongly undertook, of its own volition, the determination of the question whether there was a relevant nexus between the appellant's work-related accident … and his back injury. Its conclusion on that question resulted in it not considering whether the rounding off provision should be applied to an assessment of 29% whole person impairment.[87]

[80] Victoria, *Parliamentary Debates* (n 76) 1001. See the Accident Compensation Act 1985 (Vic) s 134A as it was prior to the amendments by the Accident Compensation (Common Law and Benefits) Act 2000 (Vic).
[81] Victoria, *Parliamentary Debates* (n 76) 1002. See the Accident Compensation (Common Law and Benefits) Act 2000 (Vic) s 18.
[82] Victoria, *Parliamentary Debates* (n 76) 1007. See the Accident Compensation (Common Law and Benefits) Act 2000 (Vic) s 18.
[83] *Connelly v MMI Workers' Compensation (Vic) Ltd* (2003) 6 VR 555.
[84] Victoria, *Parliamentary Debates*, Legislative Assembly, 16 October 2003, 1155.
[85] *Connolly v MMI Workers Compensation (Vic) Ltd* [2002] VSC 247 (21 June 2002) [9].
[86] *Connelly v MMI Workers' Compensation (Vic) Ltd* (2003) 6 VR 555, 566.
[87] Ibid, 567.

The appeal was therefore allowed; the opinion of the Panel was quashed. As is usually the result of successful judicial review, the relevant questions were re-referred for determination by a differently constituted Panel.[88]

This was a cause of concern for the government of the day with the Minister for Workcover pointing to the fact that the question of rounding final impairment values had been debated for some time but that 'because of the impact that even a 1 per cent variation in that value can have in certain cases … rounding to the nearest 5 per cent is not appropriate for the purposes of the Accident Compensation Act' and hence an amendment was introduced to remove this option.[89]

The next step in the evolution of the role of Medical Panels in the workers' compensation system followed from the publication of the Accident Compensation Act Review in August 2008[90] which listed amongst its terms of reference the provision of advice and recommendations with regard to a number of areas including:

— [T]he need to provide fair and effective benefit and premium regimes, having regard to workers' compensation schemes in other jurisdictions and the need to secure long-term positive outcomes for injured workers.
— The fundamental need to protect the operational and financial viability of the scheme.
— Identifying and resolving anomalies in the Accident Compensation Act (AC Act) and in the operation of the scheme.
— Improving employer and employee understanding of the AC Act.
— Reducing the regulatory and administrative burden on employers, including through improved alignment, where appropriate, with related administrative arrangements both within the State of Victoria and with other jurisdictions.
— Improving the usability of the legislation through the removal of inoperative, irrelevant or superfluous provisions.[91]

In the chapter entitled 'Transparency in decision making and the efficient resolution of disputes', the author commented on the establishment of the Medical Panels as a second tier of dispute resolution,[92] referrals to the Panels from conciliation officers and the courts,[93] and the constitution of the Panels.[94] In addition, he noted the high disputation rates in the Victorian WorkCover system,[95] the 'reliance on agent review and specific ADR processes as a precursor to formal litigation, [which] suggests that there are problems inherent with the early stages of the process'[96] and the fact that referral of medical questions to Panels occurred late in the dispute resolution process.[97] He expressed the view that this might be a factor in delaying the resolution of disputes and suggested that, '[i]deally, determination of medical questions should be facilitated early in the process'.[98]

[88] Ibid.
[89] Victoria, *Parliamentary Debates* (n 84) 1155. See the Accident Compensation and Transport Accident Acts (Amendment) 2003 (Vic) s 7.
[90] Hanks (n 24).
[91] Ibid, 8[1].
[92] Ibid, 336 [10.22].
[93] Ibid, 337 [10.23–10.23].
[94] Ibid, [10.26].
[95] Ibid, 345 [10.83].
[96] Ibid, [10.86].
[97] Ibid, 347 [10.105].
[98] Ibid.

The final report contained 151 recommendations, eight of which related to the role or functioning of the Medical Panels. These were identified as the need to:

— Clarify the power of a Medical Panel to return a medical question to the referring body where the referral is unclear or otherwise inadequate. That power should be in addition to the Panel's power to return questions that relate to non-medical matters.
— Amend the definition of 'medical question' to address anomalies identified by stakeholders so as to provide greater clarity and certainty about the matters which may properly be the subject of a referral to a Medical Panel.
— Provide a right of assistance to persons with a disability (including minors) when attending a Medical Panel, similar to those contained in sections 26LZD(2) and (3) of the Wrongs Act 1958.
— Provide the courts with discretion to refuse to refer medical questions to Medical Panels where the proposed question involves non-medical matters, and where the referral would not be in the interests of the proper administration of justice.
— Place a time limit on referral by the courts of medical questions to Medical Panels, with a power to refer after that time limit where 'exceptional circumstances' exist.
— Require Medical Panels to provide written reasons together with their opinions on a medical question.
— Ensure that the Ombudsman has effective oversight of the Medical Panels' Convenor's administrative functions.
— Repeal the restriction in section 63(4) of the Accident Compensation Act on the permitted number of Medical Panel members.[99]

In addition, Medical Panels were seen as the potential model for a further recommendation with the author suggesting that:

> [T]he VWA should consider the feasibility of introducing a 'one-stop shop' for the management of impairment benefits. The 'one-stop shop' could be structured in a manner similar to the Medical Panels, so that there would be a central location where all impairment benefit claims could be processed and where all independent medical assessments could occur.[100]

The Government provided support to all the recommendations with the exception of giving the Ombudsman oversight of the Convenor's administrative functions. The reason cited for this exception was that:

> The Convenor's role is quasi-judicial, disposing of medical questions that would otherwise be determined by the Courts. The Government believes that diminishing the Convenor's protections could undermine the finality of Medical Panel opinions and make retaining quality practitioners as panel members and in the Convenor's role difficult.[101]

The adopted recommendations were presented to Parliament as the Accident Compensation Amendment Bill on 10 December 2009.[102] In his introduction to the House the

[99] Parliament of Victoria, *Government Response to Hanks Report* (17 June 2009) [101–08]: www.compensationreview.vic.gov.au/__data/assets/pdf_file/0003/24672/Government-Response.pdf.
[100] Ibid, [68].
[101] Ibid, [107].
[102] Victoria, *Parliamentary Debates*, Legislative Assembly, 10 December 2009, 4622 (Timothy Holding, Minister for Finance, WorkCover and the Transport Accident Commission). See the Accident Compensation Amendment Act 2010 (Vic).

responsible Minister informed the Members that the Bill aimed to provide 'more transparent decision making and efficient dispute resolution'[103] and a 'number of important amendments to promote the efficiency of the conciliation process'[104] acknowledging that the Accident Compensation Conciliation Service remained the 'primary vehicle for resolving statutory benefits disputes'.[105] In addition, he pointed to the fact that the Bill also proposed a number of changes 'to the current medical panel processes that are designed to improve its efficiency and fairness. The changes focus on improving the quality of referrals of medical questions to the panel by conciliation officers and the courts'.[106]

The Bill was passed unopposed although it was noted by the Shadow Treasurer that the first of the key recommendations of the Hanks Report was not, at that stage, drafted into the legislation.[107] In the Report the first recommendation to the Government was that:

> [T]he entire current accident compensation legislation should be recast (with the caveat that the wording of those sections that have been the subject of regular judicial interpretation through litigation should be retained) into a comprehensive Act, arranged more logically and coherently and expressed in a more accessible fashion in plain language.[108]

This step was finally achieved following the enactment of the Workplace Injury Rehabilitation and Compensation Act 2013 which was assented on 12 November 2013 and commenced on 1 July 2014. Its stated purpose was

> to simplify the provisions applying to the rehabilitation of injured workers and compensation in relation to injuries or deaths arising out of accidents or disease in the workplace on or after 1 July 2014 and streamline provisions of the *Accident Compensation Act 1985* which continue to apply.[109]

When the Bill was read for a second time the Treasurer provided further clarification stating that the proposed statute had 'restructured the legislation, removed or streamlined obsolete and redundant provisions, identified opportunities to streamline compliance requirements and improve readability. Importantly, the rewrite has been undertaken on a "no benefit change" basis'.[110] This had been achieved by re-working the Accident Compensation Act and the Accident Compensation (WorkCover Insurance) Act into a single piece of legislation.[111]

From the point of view of the Medical Panels, the changes were largely cosmetic. For example, clause 313(4) reiterated that the opinion provided by a Medical Panel was to be accepted as final and conclusive by any court thereby preventing an appeal on the merits of the opinion.[112] However, the Government tried to introduce clause 313(5) which was aimed at blocking any proceedings being brought against a Panel on the grounds of inadequacy of the reasons provided.[113] This however proved to be

[103] Victoria, *Parliamentary Debates* (n 102) 4625.
[104] Ibid. See the Accident Compensation Amendment Act 2010 (Vic) Pt 9, ss 76–90.
[105] Victoria, *Parliamentary Debates* (n 102) 4625.
[106] Ibid.
[107] Victoria, *Parliamentary Debates*, Legislative Assembly, 2 February 2010, 33 (Kym Wells).
[108] Hanks (n 24) 40 [1.24].
[109] Workplace Injury Rehabilitation and Compensation Act 2013 (Vic) s 1(a)–1(b).
[110] Victoria, *Parliamentary Debates*, Legislative Assembly, 19 September 2013, 3228 (Michael O'Brien, Treasurer).
[111] Ibid.
[112] Ibid, 3232.
[113] Ibid.

unpopular with the parliamentary Opposition, with one particular Member noting that 'it would undermine the judicial oversight of medical panels and reduce the capacity for injured workers to seek judicial review of medical panel opinions'.[114] She continued, expressing the view that:

> [I]n relation to the issue around medical panels, the government was seeking to undermine a matter before the High Court. The *Kocak v Wingfoot* matter is on appeal. The decision made it clear that medical panel opinions are subject to judicial review. This matter is before the High Court. We believe the Napthine government's attempt to pre-empt the High Court decision in this matter was really inappropriate, and that was something that we sought to resolve.[115]

Consequently, this particular clause was never inserted into the final Act. However, the Government's aim was partly achieved by a High Court decision later that year.

The 'Gatekeeper'

With the dawn of a new millennium came a new and quite different role for the Medical Panels. During the period around 2001/02 the Australian Commonwealth, State and Territory governments became very concerned at the apparent crisis in the availability and affordability of personal injury liability insurance. This had resulted in increased professional indemnity premiums, for example, for medical practitioners, and greatly increased cost of cover for some recreational activities.[116] In reflecting on how such a situation could have occurred it 'was suggested that parts of Australia's legal system were "out of control" while sections of the community began to criticise the "culture of blame" which was said to have become entrenched in Australian society'.[117] Clark and McInnnes noted that '[t]hese opinions were fuelled by a combination of factors including the collapse of both a major insurer and a medical indemnity organisation, spiralling premiums and a number of highly publicised awards of damages'.[118]

The authors went on to suggest five factors which they believed had helped to drive these conditions including:

- **Community attitude**: this being the litigious mindset entrenched in many individuals within the community.
- **The development of the tort of negligence** and the judicial expansion of the concept between the 1960s and 1990s.
- **The downturn in the insurance industry cycle**, although the authors acknowledged that there was a natural cycle in the industry.
- **The emergence of specialist plaintive law firms: legal advertising and 'no win no fee' arrangements**, all of which were seen as being designed to draw more business to the

[114] Victoria, *Parliamentary Debates*, Legislative Council, 31 October 2013, 3443 (Jaala Pulford).

[115] Ibid.

[116] 'Adjusting the Balance: Inquiry into Aspects of the *Wrongs Act 1958*' (Draft Report, Victorian Competition and Efficiency Commission, November 2013) v.

[117] S Clark and R McInnes, 'Unprecedented Reform: The New Tort Law' (2004) 15 *Insurance Law Journal* 99.

[118] Ibid.

legal firms that used these methods, thereby encouraging more (often unmeritorious) claims and ultimately driving up the cost of insurance.

— **The rise of class actions** which the authors believed had had a significant effect on insurance costs and on the community's attitude to justice.[119]

Similar concerns were voiced by politicians at all levels with, for example, Small Business Minister Joe Hockey, himself a former lawyer, stating that. 'I'll be excommunicated from the profession, but I don't mind because I feel very strongly about this, about the concept of no-win, no-fee. I think it has got out of hand'.[120] He then went on to add that:

> The simple fact is that unfortunately the courts are out of control, as far as I am concerned, and small business and the community are paying for it because insurance companies are not only massively increasing premiums, but in a whole lot of cases … they're not providing insurance coverage.[121]

Keeler also noted that there were members of the legal profession who had

> become critical of the operation of the common law, arguing that the standard of care imposed on defendants had become too stringent, the levels of care required of potential plaintiffs for their own safety had been unacceptably reduced, that principles of causation had been stretched to barely tolerable limits and that the principles on which damages are awarded were in at least some respects too generous.[122]

In response to these concerns a meeting of Ministers was held. They in turn sent a communique to the Heads of Treasuries on 5 April 2002 requesting that the latter 'develop practical measures for consideration by Governments regarding these issues'.[123] To this end, the firm of Trowbridge Consulting was engaged to provide an assessment of the situation and develop suitable proposals. The authors set their proposals against a framework of four desirable outcomes:

— Cost reduction
— Cost containment for the future
— Improving certainty and predictability in the insurance system
— Changing social and legal attitudes towards the assumption and liability for risk.[124]

One of the areas reviewed was the law of negligence with the consultants noting that:

> We are satisfied that the evidence indicates a gradual 'drift' or stretching of the interpretation of negligence over several decades so that there are cases succeeding today that would not have succeeded at times in the past. We note that there is some dispute over this conclusion, and there is also evidence that recent High Court decisions may have stopped or reversed this trend.
>
> This issue—and what could be done about it—is beyond both our expertise and the time available for this project. It is, however, a fundamental one. We recommend that Governments engage a specific expert panel to consider it.[125]

[119] Ibid, 100–01.
[120] S Kemp, A Crabb and G Costa, 'Compensation Scheme Comes Under Fire' *The Age* (22 January 2002) News 4.
[121] Ibid.
[122] J Keeler, 'Personal Responsibility and the Reforms Recommended by the Ipp Report: "Time Future Contained in Time Past"' (2006) 14(1) *Torts Law Journal* 48, 49.
[123] G Atkins and E Pearson, 'Public Liability Insurance: Practical Proposals for Reform. Report to the Insurance Issues Working Group of Heads of Treasuries' (Report, Trowbridge Consulting, 30 May 2002) i.
[124] Ibid.
[125] Ibid, iv.

This suggestion was accepted and a Panel of Eminent Persons was appointed on 2 July 2002 under the chairmanship of the Honourable David Ipp to review the law of negligence. This was to be a principles-based review with the remit of providing 'a method for the reform of the common law with the objective of limiting liability and quantum of damages arising from personal injury and death'.[126]

The Panel completed its report and submitted this to the Minister for Revenue and Assistant Treasurer on 30 September 2002. In total the Eminent Persons made 61 recommendations which they believed would meet the stated requirements. The first of these was detailed under the heading, 'A national response' and suggested that: 'the Panel's recommendations should be incorporated … in a single statute … to be enacted in each jurisdiction'.[127] However, although all States and Territories adopted some of the recommendations, there was to be no national response.

In Victoria, the Premier addressed Parliament on 12 September 2002 to present the second reading of the Wrongs and Other Acts (Public Liability Insurance Reform) Bill which he described as part of 'the government's wide-ranging response to problems in the insurance sector that have impacted on all sectors of the Victorian economy and community'.[128] He added that 'without further government tort law reform, there is a risk that the trend in public liability claim costs will remain unchecked. Failure to act now would only continue to create uncertainty'.[129] The Bill, which was subsequently enacted, introduced a number of amendments including a cap on loss of earnings and non-economic losses,[130] and was deemed likely to 'help attack the culture of blame and make insurance more affordable and accessible over the longer term'.[131]

However, it was the second phase of Victoria's tort law reform package which was to impact the Medical Panels as this introduced a medical threshold for access to damages for non-economic loss. Thus, in accordance with the amended section 28LE of the Wrongs Act:

> A person is not entitled to recover damages for non-economic loss in any proceeding in a court in respect of an injury to a person caused by the fault of another person unless the person injured has suffered significant injury.

Furthermore, for an individual to be deemed to have suffered such an injury, he or she would normally have to have been assessed by an appropriately trained medical practitioner as having a whole person impairment which reached the threshold level of greater than 5% whole person impairment in the case of a physical injury or a greater than 10% whole person impairment in the case of a psychiatric injury.[132] However, the Act did make provision for acceptance of a significant injury without the need for such an assessment in situations when, for example, the injury was the loss of a foetus;[133] where an individual

[126] Commonwealth of Australia, *Review of the Law of Negligence: Final Report* (Canberra, Canprint, 2002) ix. Also known as the Ipp Report.

[127] Ibid, 1.

[128] Victoria, *Parliamentary Debates*, Legislative Assembly, 12 September 2002, 140 (Steve Bracks, Premier). The Bill was enacted as the Wrongs and Other Acts (Public Liability Insurance Reform) Act 2002.

[129] Victoria, *Parliamentary Debates* (n 128) 141.

[130] Ibid, 142.

[131] Ibid, 145.

[132] Wrongs Act 1958 (Vic) s 28LB.

[133] Ibid, s 28LF(1)(c).

suffered psychological or psychiatric injury arising from the loss of a child following either injury to the mother or foetus or child before, during or immediately after birth;[134] or where the injury was the loss of a breast.[135]

The Premier explained that it had become necessary to introduce such a threshold as general damages were 'an important factor in the cost of claims, and hence in premiums for claims below the catastrophic level. For small claims—that is, $50 000 or below—half of the damages paid are general damages'.[136] He added that the introduced threshold was merely a 'gateway for a court to determine whether damages for non-economic loss can be awarded to a plaintiff'.[137] It was still necessary for the claimant to prove his case and show that the alleged injury had resulted from the defendant's negligence.[138]

The Medical Panels as constituted under the Accident Compensation Act 1985 were given a pivotal role in the pre-litigation process. In cases where a respondent, on being issued with a statement of claim by a claimant, disputed the impairment assessment of that claimant, the medical question was to be referred to a Medical Panel. The Panel was required to determine only one medical question: that being whether the claimant had suffered a 'significant injury' as defined under the Act. In order to achieve this, the Panel had to determine the claimant's degree of whole person impairment.[139] This was the only role the Panel was permitted under the Wrongs Act which was in marked contrast to the many roles it served under the workers' compensation legislation.

In assigning this role to the Panels the Premier acknowledged that the threshold for access to common law damages under the Wrongs Act was set much lower than the level required to pursue a similar claim under the Accident Compensation Act. He explained the apparent anomaly, noting that as the former was a no-fault scheme it was not necessary for the claimant to prove negligence before receiving compensation payments. In addition, the scheme could provide statutory benefits to an injured worker more quickly than a claimant might receive damages in a common law claim for damages.[140] He thus concluded that the 'level and purposes of the thresholds' under the statutory scheme were not 'directly comparable to those' proposed in the amendments to the Wrongs Act.[141]

Just as a Panel's opinion was binding under the Accident Compensation Act, so it was under the Wrongs Act.[142] However, a Medical Panel had to give its determination of the medical question within 30 days of examining the claimant or after receiving any requested documentation from a health practitioner, whichever was the later occurrence.[143] In providing its opinion the Panel had to state whether the degree of impairment satisfied the threshold level but was not to state the specific degree of impairment.[144]

[134] Ibid, s 28LF(1)(ca).
[135] Ibid, s 28LF(1)(d).
[136] Victoria, *Parliamentary Debates*, Legislative Assembly, 21 May 2003, 1783 (Stephen Bracks, Premier). The reform was introduced in the Wrongs and Limitation of Actions Acts (Insurance Reforms) Act 2003.
[137] Victoria, *Parliamentary Debates* (n 136) 1783.
[138] Ibid.
[139] *Wrongs Act 1958* (Vic) s 28LZG(1)(2).
[140] Victoria, *Parliamentary Debates* (n 136) 1783.
[141] Ibid.
[142] Wrongs Act 1958 (Vic) s 28LZI(1).
[143] Ibid, s 28LZG(3).
[144] Ibid, s 28LZG(4).

It was also noteworthy that the Wrongs Act as amended paid particular attention to liability for mental harm with the entire Part XI devoted to this issue. Mental harm was defined as 'psychological or psychiatric injury'[145] and was divided into pure mental harm and consequential mental harm. The latter was defined as referring to 'mental harm that is a consequence of an injury of any other kind' whereas pure mental harm was distinguished as 'mental harm other than consequential mental harm'.[146] This distinction was an important one as section 28LJ of the Act reminds a medical assessor that 'regard must not be had to any psychiatric or psychological injury, impairment or symptoms arising as a consequence of, or secondary to, a physical injury'. Hence, such consequential (or secondary) psychiatric/psychological injury was not an assessable condition under the Act and did not provide grounds for an award of compensation.

The Act also addressed the issue of emotional distress caused to a 'bystander' as a result of the harm done to another. Thus, where a plaintiff sought redress from the alleged tortfeasor for 'pure mental harm … arising wholly or partly from mental or nervous shock in connection with another person … being killed, injured or put in danger by the act or omission of the defendant',[147] the Act stated that:

> s 73(2) the plaintiff is not entitled to recover damages for pure mental harm unless—
>
> (a) the plaintiff witnessed, at the scene, the victim being killed, injured or put in danger; or
> (b) the plaintiff is or was in a close relationship with the victim.

However, it was not the role of the Panel to enquire into the relationship between the plaintiff and the victim, as it had only the one question to answer. In so doing, the Panel also had to make a determination as to whether the impairment was permanent as described in the AMA *Guides to the Evaluation of Permanent Impairment* as this was required prior to determining that the injury was stable and unlikely to change into the future with or without treatment.[148] The Premier explained that this was a necessary step as otherwise a claimant might be undercompensated if his injury subsequently worsened over time, or conversely, might be overcompensated if it improved.[149] There was however a provision inserted into the Act permitting an approved medical practitioner or a Medical Panel to certify that a claimant's impairment exceeded the necessary threshold at the time of the assessment 'if the injuries that have stabilised are sufficient to determine a degree of impairment that satisfies the threshold level'.[150]

The role of the Medical Panels as the 'gatekeeper' for access to common law damages has continued unchanged for over a decade. However, in May 2013 the State Government arranged that the Victorian Competition and Efficiency Commission inquire into certain aspects of the Act. In setting down the terms of reference for the inquiry the Treasurer requested that it

[145] Ibid, s 67.
[146] Ibid.
[147] Ibid, s 73(1).
[148] Victoria, *Parliamentary Debates* (n 136) 1783. Also introduced in the Wrongs and Limitation of Actions Acts (Insurance Reforms) Act 2003.
[149] Victoria, *Parliamentary Debates* (n 136) 1783.
[150] Wrongs Act 1958 (Vic) s 28LN(3).

inquire into and report on the operation of the Act in relation to personal injuries and related matters, and develop, evaluate and recommend options for the Act to operate more efficiently and equitably consistent with the objective of the tort law reforms of 2002 and 2003.[151]

In addition, the Commission was 'to consult with key interest groups and affected parties, and may hold public hearings'.[152] Furthermore, the Commission was required to produce a draft report for public consultation followed by a final report within nine months of receiving its terms of reference.[153]

The Commission met the required time frames providing the draft report in November 2013 and submitted the final report to the Treasurer on 26 February 2014. This was released on 2 September 2014 as was the Government's response to the recommendations. Among the Commission's recommendations which obtained government support was the proposed reduction of the threshold for psychiatric impairment assessment to the level of greater than or equal to 10%. The recommendation to reduce the impairment threshold for spinal injuries to the level of greater than or equal to 5% was not given unqualified support but was deemed to require further consideration.[154] In a media release of the same day members of the Government stated that:

These reforms are an important correction to the tort law reforms introduced by the Bracks Labor Government in the early 2000s.

The changes will lead to fairer outcomes where people have been injured as a consequence of another's fault.[155]

It remains to be seen if this apparent slight alteration in threshold will result in a greater number of psychiatric referrals to the Medical Panels and what overall impact it might have on the gatekeeper role of the Panels. The advice provided by the Victorian Managed Insurance Authority (VMIA) was that if thresholds 'were to be lowered … it is reasonable to expect that there would be an increase in claims frequency in the lowest claims size bands'[156] with an estimated increase in claims costs of around 3%–5%.[157]

However, the advice with regard to lowering the threshold for psychiatric claims was rather more circumspect as it was stated that:

It was not possible to model the potential impact of the threshold of 10% for psychiatric injuries as it has insufficient data for claims relating solely to psychiatric injuries in the medical indemnity claims data. The impact of such a change would need to take into account not only the number of claimants who would reach the threshold who currently do not, but also the extent to which a reduction in the psychiatric injury threshold might impact upon whether the threshold is an effective gateway at all.[158]

[151] M Butin and B Mountford, 'Adjusting the Balance; Inquiry into Aspects of the *Wrongs Act 1958*' (Final Report, Victorian Competition & Efficiency Commission, February 2014) vii–viii.

[152] Ibid.

[153] Ibid.

[154] www.vcec.vic.gov.au/Inquiries/Completed-inquiries/Wrongs-Act/Government-response.

[155] M O'Brien and R Clark, 'Fairer Compensation Under the Wrongs Act' (media release, 2 September 2014) 1.

[156] 'VMIA advice to the Victorian Competition & Efficiency Commission Inquiry into Aspects of the Wrongs Act 1958 (Vic)' (Report, VMIA, 15 November 2013) 9.

[157] Ibid.

[158] Ibid.

Workload Statistics

Statistics available for the last five years or so indicate that the Medical Panels have been coping with a heavy workload which has been steadily increasing. Figures provided by the Convenor in the Annual Report of 2012/13 demonstrated that there was an average increase in referrals of 6% per year since the 2008/09 financial year.[159] The total referrals in the 2012/13 financial year was 4,327 which was composed of 3,820 under sections of the Accident Compensation Act and 507 under the Wrongs Act.[160] Over the same period the Panels had provided 3,683 Opinions and Reasons under the Accident Compensation Act and 456 Determinations under the Wrongs Act. A further 128 referrals were withdrawn, with presumably the remaining 60 still transiting the system.

Although the year-on-year increase in total referrals under the Accident Compensation Act between 2011/12 and 2012/13 was only 154 or 4.2%, there was a noticeable increase in court referrals over that time with Magistrates' Court referrals in particular increasing by 35% from 192 to 259.[161] Although there has been no indication from the Court as to why this might be so, it appears that either more parties or their legal representatives are requesting referral to Panels or that this is being initiated by the court so as to obtain an independent binding opinion particularly in complex medical cases which might otherwise take up a considerable amount of the court's time and result in considerable legal costs.

If this is indeed the case, then it would appear to indicate that the Medical Panel is seen as providing a useful and cost-effective role within the sphere of dispute resolution. Certainly, in his review of the Accident Compensation scheme, Peter Hanks noted the comments provided by the various stakeholders that:

> Medical Panels currently play an important role in the resolution of disputes in workers' compensation jurisdictions in Australia. Over the past decade, most jurisdictions have moved away from reliance on participant provision of expert testimony before courts or tribunals to using panels of medical experts to rule on medical matters.[162]
>
> The move has had the effect of reducing expert testimony disputes; and medical panels have become valued for their independence, as well as the savings in time and costs that they can deliver.[163]

However, not everyone had shared such a positive view of Medical Panels. In 2008 the South Australian Government was preparing to reintroduce such an entity which was to be styled on the Victorian model. The Law Council urged Parliament to 'ensure that the introduction of Medical Panels does not undermine that accessibility to justice by repeating the mistakes of the Victorian experience with similar Panels'.[164] The Council continued, expressing the view that 'the legislation should be drafted to ensure the serious legal questions affecting both employers' interests and worker's rights remain before the Courts',[165] adding that,

[159] J Malios, 'Office of the Convenor of Medical Panels End of Year Result 2012/13' (2013) 3.
[160] Ibid.
[161] Ibid.
[162] Hanks (n 24) 347 [10.100].
[163] Ibid, [10.101].
[164] Law Council of Australia, 'Submission on Part 6C: Medical Panels of the Workers Rehabilitation and Compensation (Scheme Review) Amendment Bill 2008' (13 May 2008) 2.
[165] Ibid.

'The establishment of Medical Panels in other jurisdictions remains a contentious and difficult legal issue'.[166] Some individual lawyers also cautioned against the introduction of Medical Panels with Margaret Kaukas opining that whilst

> [m]edical practitioners have expertise as to medical matters, they are no more qualified to decide the various factual matters underpinning the medical questions before the Panel, than an ordinary citizen. As to the legal issues which will inevitably arise in questions placed before the Panel, surely these are best decided by legally trained judges?[167]

Judicial Review

It is understandable that the number of referrals to Medical Panels has risen considerably over recent years given its decisive role under both workers' compensation legislation and in the arena of personal injury litigation.

Between 2004 and 2013 the total referrals varied from a low of 3,559 in 2009 to a high of 4,970 in 2004. Over that time there was a year-on-year increase in the number of referrals under the Wrongs Act. As has been indicated, each of the opinions or determinations made by a Panel is binding on the courts and cannot be appealed on the merits of that decision. However, relief is still available in the form of judicial review.

During the 2012/13 financial year there were 19 Panel decisions out of the total of 4,139 where application for judicial review was made to the Supreme Court; a figure which represents less than 0.5% of the total.[168] This percentage has been quite stable over several years and of those cases reviewed, less than a third had a successful outcome.

The Medical Panels do not take an active part in such proceedings except on rare occasions when, for example, the Convenor may attend so as to provide clarification regarding the processes undertaken by the Panel. Otherwise, the Panels adopt the so-called '*Hardiman* position' for the reasons outlined in the written statement provided by the High Court in the case which bears that name:

> In cases of this kind the usual course is for a Tribunal to submit to such order as the court may make … If a tribunal becomes a protagonist in this court there is a risk that by doing so it endangers the impartiality which it is expected to maintain in subsequent proceedings which take place if and when relief is granted. The presentation of a case in this court by a Tribunal should be regarded as exceptional, and, when it occurs, should, in general, be limited to submissions going to the power and procedures of the tribunal.[169]

Consequently the Medical Panels agree to submit to the orders made by the Court in those cases subject to judicial review.

An application for judicial review may be commenced in the Supreme Court pursuant to the Administrative Law Act 1978 or by Order 56 of the Supreme Court

[166] Ibid.

[167] M Kaukas, 'Proposed Medical Review Panels' (2008) 30(5) *Bulletin (Law Society of South Australia)* 6.

[168] Malios, 'Office of the Convenor of Medical Panels End of Year Result 2012/13' (n 159) 5.

[169] *The Queen v The Australian Broadcasting Tribunal; Ex Parte Hardiman* (1990) 144 CLR 13, para 54.

(General Civil Procedure) Rules 2005. If relief is granted it is usually in the form of an order in *certiorari* to quash the Panel opinion or determination and an additional order in the nature of *mandamus* remitting the medical question(s) for redetermination to usually, a differently constituted Panel. Though various grounds may be cited for review, one which has been advanced under both the Accident Compensation Act and the Wrongs Act is that of inadequate reasons being provided by the Panel to explain its opinion or determination.

The first case to consider the reasons provided by Panels was that of *Masters v McCubbery*.[170] This case concerned a worker who sought to ascertain the reasons the assessing Panel arrived at the conclusions it did regarding the questions put to it about his employment-related injury. At that time there was no legislated requirement for the Medical Panels to supply reasons for the opinions they provided. However, the appellant sought the requested information not under the Accident Compensation Act but pursuant to section 8 of the Administrative Law Act 1978 which read as follows:

> 8(1) A tribunal shall, if requested to do so by any person affected by a decision made or to be made by it, furnish him with a statement of its reasons for the decision.
>
> (2) ....
>
> (3) The statement of reasons shall be in writing and furnished within a reasonable time.
>
> (4) The Supreme Court or a Judge thereof, upon being satisfied ... that a reasonable time has elapsed without any such statement of reasons for the decision having been furnished or that the only statement furnished is not adequate to enable a Court to see whether the decision does or does not involve any error of law, may order the tribunal to furnish, within a time specified in the order, a statement or further statement of its reasons and if the order is not complied with the Court ... may make any such order as might have been made if error of law had appeared on the face of the record.
>
> (5) Notwithstanding anything in this section a tribunal shall not be bound to furnish a statement of its reasons, and the Court shall not be bound to order it to do so, where to furnish the reasons would, in the opinion of the Court, be against public policy.

The Convenor responded to the request with a simple acknowledgment and a brief response stating that 'Medical Panels does not consider that it is subject to the Administrative Law Act 1978 and, accordingly, no statement of reasons will be forwarded to you'.[171] Thereafter, proceedings were initiated.

The trial judge noted that the legislation 'invested the medical panel with powers enabling it to interfere prejudicially with the rights and interests of individuals in respect of whom it was required to give opinions',[172] but nonetheless decided that the Medical Panel was not required to afford natural justice in undertaking its required functions and hence, was not a tribunal within the meaning of the Administrative Law Act and was not obliged to accord natural justice in carrying out its statutory functions.[173]

[170] *Masters v McCubbery and Others* [1996] 1 VR 635.

[171] Ibid, 639.

[172] Ibid, 641.

[173] Ibid.

However, the decision was appealed and the Supreme Court of Appeal unanimously decided that the Medical Panel was indeed a tribunal and hence subject to the Act. As Winneke P explained:

> It is my view that the Act does require a medical panel, in forming opinions on 'medical questions' referred to it by a court, to observe the rules of natural justice … Although these critical issues are referred to the medical panel couched in terms of 'medical questions' and the responses of the panel to them are couched in terms of 'opinions', such legislative terminology cannot obscure the fact that the panel is being called upon to decide matters of mixed law and fact which decisions operate by virtue of the provisions of the Act to bind the court and thus to effectively dispose of the issues which have been raised by the worker and placed by him before the court for its determination.[174]

He continued adding that:

> To enable the medical panels to carry out their statutory functions, the Act equips them with a range of powers … In my view it can be seen that the legislature did intend to create the medical panels as an alternative dispute resolution to the court.[175]

He subsequently opined that:

> [I]t is my view that such is the nature of the powers conferred on medical panels that it would be expected that in exercising such powers they would be under a duty to act with fairness … The duty to act with fairness in these circumstances springs from the common law.[176]

He further stated that:

> The intent to exclude appeals from decisions of medical panels 'on the merits' is not … inconsistent with the retention by the courts of its undoubted jurisdiction to review the decisions of such panels for want of jurisdiction or other reviewable error.[177]

As such he concluded that the Medical Panel was required to provide reasons given the circumstances of the particular case but added the caveat that the Panel members

> are required to do no more than to provide a succinct statement of why they came to the conclusions which they did sufficient to enable the parties and the court to see that they have addressed their mind to the relevant matters and have not acted unreasonably.[178]

There have been a number of subsequent cases which have sought relief by citing inadequacy of reasons as a means to quash the Panel opinions. One of particular importance is that of *Sherlock v Lloyd*,[179] which was heard prior to the 2010 amendments to section 68 of the Accident Compensation Act which required that thereafter a Medical Panel was obliged to provide reasons for its opinions. However, at the relevant time there was no statutory obligation for a Medical Panel to provide reasons for its opinions.

The essential facts involved a worker who believed that she had suffered a recurrence of her depressive illness as a result of her employment as a payroll officer. A number of questions relating to her condition were referred to the Medical Panel by the County Court. The plaintiff

174 Ibid, 642.
175 Ibid, 643.
176 Ibid, 644.
177 Ibid, 647.
178 Ibid, 651.
179 *Sherlock v Lloyd* [2010] VSCA 122.

later sought an order for judicial review under Order 56 of the Supreme Court (General Civil Procedure) Rules 2005 citing various grounds including that the assessing Panel had failed to comply with the rules of natural justice and that reasons provided by the Panel were inadequate. In considering the relevant details of the case as provided, Kyrou J first determined that the Panel had not breached the rules of natural justice.[180] He then considered the question of adequacy of reasons. He noted that as a tribunal the Panel was subject to section 8 of the Administrative Law Act but that the applicant had, in fact, not sought review under this legislation but under Order 56. He acknowledged that although there had been cases brought under Order 56 which had resulted in the opinions of Medical Panels being quashed, he believed the basis upon which this had been achieved was unclear,[181] and it was his view that even though 'I have concluded that the panel's reasons are inadequate … this is not a basis upon which I can quash the panel's opinion or any specific answers set out in the opinion in an application for judicial review under Order 56 of the Rules'.[182] On 20 February 2009 the plaintiff was granted leave to appeal the decision to the Supreme Court of Appeal.

The Court of Appeal, in reviewing the background facts, noted that the referral to the Medical Panels had come via the County Court and that the appellant had subsequently submitted a request to the Panel under section 8(1) of the Administrative Law Act for a statement of reasons. As she was dissatisfied with the response, she then commenced proceedings under Order 56 and these were then dismissed by the trial judge.[183]

On appeal the appellant sought relief on two grounds; the first regarding the 'nature and effect of the obligation imposed on a tribunal by s 8(1) … to give reasons for a decision'[184] and the second based on the 'function performed by a medical panel when giving an opinion upon medical questions referred to it'.[185]

Following its deliberations the Court of Appeal determined that 'we respectfully agree with the trial judge that, where a medical panel is requested under s 8(1) of the ALA to provide a statement of reasons for its opinion, the provision of an inadequate statement of reasons is not, by itself, an error of law'.[186] Their Honours further concluded that:

> Since an administrative tribunal has no obligation to provide reasons unless the statute under which the decision was made expressly or impliedly so requires, it cannot be correct to say that in the absence of such a requirement, the tribunal's failure to provide reasons or adequate reasons is of itself an error of law. Accordingly … the failure of a medical panel to provide adequate reasons in response to a request under s 8(1) of the ALA is not in itself an error of law. Those cases which have reached, or relied on, a contrary view must be regarded as having been wrongly decided, and must be overruled.[187]

Although this may have seemed to finally put to rest the issue of whether inadequate reasons might be grounds for quashing a Medical Panel's opinion, the matter took a further turn with the case of *Chubb Security Pty Ltd v Kotzman*.[188] The two grounds for review were

[180] Ibid, [15].
[181] Ibid, [34].
[182] Ibid, [46].
[183] Ibid, [3].
[184] Ibid, [1].
[185] Ibid.
[186] Ibid.
[187] Ibid, [74].
[188] *Chubb Security Pty Ltd v Kotzman & Ors* [2010] VSC 242.

cited as being jurisdictional error[189] and inadequate statement of reasons.[190] Cavanough J found that the complaint of jurisdictional error failed.[191] In deciding the issue regarding the adequacy of reasons he found that 'the Panels reasons are ambiguous and unclear to such an extent that it is not possible to determine whether the Panel did or did not err in law as alleged by the employer'.[192] However, he noted that the Panel's statement of reasons was provided voluntarily and that no request under section 8 of the Administrative Law Act had been submitted within the time period allowed and furthermore, that the employer had not taken up 'the Panel's implied invitation to submit a specific and particularised request for further reasons'.[193] Thus notwithstanding the noted shortcomings, he concluded that he had no power to make any order under the Administrative Law Act section 8(4) requiring the Panel to provide further reasons as there had been no timely request under sections 8(1) and 8(2) of the Act.[194]

He further added that had the statement of reasons actually been provided in response to a request made within the necessary time frame under section 8, then 'strictly speaking, it would not have satisfied the requirements of that section' as it would not have allowed the parties or the Court to determine whether it involved an error of law.[195] Nonetheless, he was of the opinion that even in such circumstances, bearing in mind the decision of the Appeal Court in *Sherlock v Lloyd*, the only 'possible consequence of this kind of deficiency would seem to be that the employer might have a claim for a further and better statement of reasons pursuant to s 8(4) of the *Administrative Law Act 1978*'.[196]

Considering the decisions in these two cases, it appears that at that time, since there was no legislated requirement for Panels to provide reasons for their opinions, the Court took the view that if the voluntarily provided reasons were not adequate the only means by which an aggrieved party might seek relief was by carefully following the steps outlined in section 8 of the Administrative Law Act. However, in the first instance a court could only make an order for improved reasons. Only if the Medical Panels failed to comply with such an order would it then be possible to deem that there had been an error of law on the face of the record which would then allow the Court to be in a position to quash the opinion provided.

The situation altered however in September 2010 when section 68(3) of the Accident Compensation Act was amended such that:

> Within seven days after forming its opinion on a medical question referred to it, a Medical Panel must give the relevant Conciliation Officer or the County Court or the Authority or self-insurer its written opinion and a written statement of reasons for that opinion.

It was under this amended legislation that the reasons provided by a Panel were deemed to be inadequate in the case of *Kocak v Wingfoot Australia Partners Pty Ltd*.[197] The facts

[189] Ibid, [3].
[190] Ibid, [4].
[191] Ibid, [37].
[192] Ibid, [5].
[193] Ibid, [52].
[194] Ibid.
[195] Ibid, [51].
[196] Ibid.
[197] *Kocak v Wingfoot Australia Partners Pty Ltd* [2012] VSCA 259.

of the case were that Eyup Kocak was a man of Turkish extraction who had migrated to Australia in 1973 with his family and schooled to year 9. Thereafter he worked in a number of labouring and unskilled roles. He commenced work with the respondent employer in 1992 undertaking heavy physical roles.[198] He subsequently suffered two separate injuries, the first to his neck on 16 October 1996 following which he was placed on light duties until January 1997.[199]

On 8 May 2000 he suffered a lower back injury in relation to which he submitted a WorkCover claim which was accepted. The worker was again provided with light duties but ceased employment in March 2001 and has not been employed since.[200] In 2007 he instituted a Supreme Court action regarding a serious injury claim regarding his lower back injury. That claim was still pending at the time of the Appeal Court hearing.[201]

On 2 November 2009 Mr Kocak instituted proceedings in the County Court seeking common law damages in respect of the neck injury he had suffered on 16 October 1996.[202] On 11 November 2009, he issued a further County Court proceeding seeking entitlement to medical or like expenses under the Act, again in relation to his neck injury. That proceeding was transferred to the Magistrates' Court[203] which referred three medical questions to the Medical Panels. An Opinion and Reasons for Opinion were provided on 15 August 2010.

On 21 September 2010 the appellant's solicitors consented to orders adopting and applying the opinion of the Medical Panel[204] but at that time they were ignorant of the Appeal Court's decision in *Brumar (Vic) Pty Ltd v Norris; Brown v Maurice Blackburn Cashman* which determined that a Medical Panel opinion was binding in common law serious injury proceedings.[205]

The appellant plaintiff subsequently sought leave to bring proceedings for an order *certiorari* to quash the Panel opinion out of time.[206] The request for an extension of time was granted. The grounds for review included an allegation that the Panel failed to take into account mandatory considerations,[207] and that the Panel 'failed to give any or adequate reasons' regarding certain described matters.[208] However, the trial judge found that the Panel's statement of reasons was not inadequate and as there were no separate arguments raised in relation to the alleged failure to take into account mandatory considerations, that contention also failed.[209]

The Court of Appeal noted that although the appellant sought relief on six separate grounds they all in essence alleged that 'the judge erred in holding that the Medical

[198] Ibid, [3].
[199] Ibid, [4].
[200] Ibid, [5].
[201] Ibid, [6].
[202] Ibid, [9].
[203] Ibid, [10].
[204] G Reinhardt, 'Inadequacy of Reasons for Decisions of Medical Panel—Does This Constitute an Error of Law on the Face of the Record? Is Certiorari Available?' (2013) 87 *Law Institute Journal* 62, 62.
[205] *Brumar (Vic) Pty Ltd v Norris; Brown v Maurice Blackburn Cashman* (2010) 28 VR 665; see Reinhardt (n 204) 62.
[206] Reinhardt (n 204) 62.
[207] *Kocak v Wingfoot Australia Partners Pty Ltd* [2011] VSC 285 (27 June 2011) [81].
[208] Ibid, [83].
[209] Ibid, [155]–[56].

Panel's reasons were adequate'.[210] In considering this issue the Court commented on the fact that:

> Rightly or wrongly, there is a significant history of judicial legislation calculated to spare Medical Panels from the burden of justifying their conclusions to a greater extent than referring to the significant aspects of the evidence and asserting a conclusion.[211]
>
> So long as the binding effect of Medical Panel opinions was confined to the realm of statutory benefits applications, there was perhaps some logic in not requiring much by way of reasons. Even then, however, the low standard demanded of Medical Panel reasons stood out as an anomaly in the realm of reasons jurisprudence. In the case of private disputes, it was and still is generally accepted that, if parties engage an expert to express his or her expert opinion on a point in dispute, neither party is entitled to require much by way of reasons. But, if a statutory decision maker exercising public power is enabled by law to make decisions capable of affecting the rights and liabilities of the subject, more by way or reasons was and is ordinarily required. And the justice of that is obvious. It is one thing for parties to agree to resolve a private dispute on the basis of a mutually agreeable expert's opinion. If they do, then presumably neither of them expects to receive anything more than the opinion. It is quite another thing to expect a claimant for a statutory benefit meekly to accept the *ipse dixit* of a state appointed expert as sufficient reasons for the rejection of his claim.[212]

The Court went on to express the view that:

> Now that Medical Panel Opinions have been held by the High Court to be binding for the purposes of determining any question or matter arising under or for the purposes of the Act, and consequently, as we see it, binding in serious injury application proceedings, the standard of reasons required of Medical Panels must surely be greater. The law is clear that the standard of reasons expected of a statutory decision-maker must accord to the purpose for which the reasons are required. In effect, serious injury applications now stand to be determined on the basis of Medical Panel Opinions which judges are bound to accept. Accordingly, just as judges who decide serious injury applications must give reasons sufficient to explain their path of reasoning—from the evidence to the facts and from the facts to their conclusions—so too we think must Medical Panels, on whose opinions the whole exercise may now rest. Further, if that is the standard to be required for some opinions, then consistency and convenience require that it be so for all of them.[213]

In continuing their consideration of the issue the three justices cited previous authority stating that 'if reasons leave a party to wonder which of a number of possible routes has been taken to a Medical Panel's conclusion, the reasons are likely to be inadequate'.[214] They indicated that the case before them fell into such a category adding that the reasons needed to explain how a conclusion had been arrived at but did not need to be lengthy or discuss all the documentation provided,[215] but summarised the requirements stating that:

> In such cases, a Medical Panel's reasons thus shall include a statement of findings on material questions of fact, some sort of identification of the evidence or other material upon which those findings are based; and an intelligible explanation of the process of reasoning that has led the Panel from the evidence to the findings and from the findings to the Panel's ultimate conclusion.

[210] *Kocak v Wingfoot Australia Partners Pty Ltd* (n 197) [22].

[211] Ibid, [44].

[212] Ibid, [46].

[213] Ibid, [47] (citations omitted).

[214] Ibid, [50] citing: *Re Minister for Immigration and Multicultural Affairs; Ex parte Palme* (2003) 216 CLR 212, 224 [40] (Gleeson, Gummow and Heydon JJ) and 245 [113]–[15] (Kirby J).

[215] *Kocak v Wingfoot Australia Partners Pty Ltd* (n 197) [50].

> In particular … if a party to a dispute relies on expert medical opinion … and the Medical Panel forms an opinion which is inconsistent with that expert opinion, it is not enough for the Medical Panel simply to state that it rejects the opinion … more is required than a statement of conclusion. Reasons are not proper reasons unless they provide a comprehensible explanation for … rejecting expert medical opinion or … for preferring one or more … opinions over others.[216]

The Appeal was thus allowed and an order made in the nature of *certiorari* thereby quashing the original decision and a further order in the nature of *mandamus* made remitting the questions to be determined by a differently constituted Panel. This decision resulted in Medical Panels putting a lot of detailed explanation into their opinions in an attempt to comply with these expressed requirements. It therefore appears somewhat incongruous that around a month after this judgment the Justice Legislation Amendment (Miscellaneous) Act 2012 was assented. This provided for the repeal of section 134AE of the Accident Compensation Act which had required that a court hearing an application for compensation for non-economic loss should provide 'detailed reasons which are as extensive and complete as the court would give on the trial of an action'. This amendment came into operation on 1 January 2013 and so for some months the Medical Panels were in the unusual position of being required to provide 'a higher level of reasoning'[217] when providing reasons for their opinions than were the County Court judges hearing common law cases.

However, the issue did not rest here. The employer sought and was granted an appeal to the High Court with the case heard on 15 August 2013.

In dissecting the issues raised the Court defined the questions before it as including: 'What is the legal effect of an opinion of a Medical Panel? What standard is required of a written statement of reasons? Can the legal effect of the opinion be quashed by an order in the nature of *certiorari* for breach of that standard?'[218] The Court first considered the role of the Medical Panels deciding that:

> [I]t is neither arbitral nor adjunctive: it is neither to choose between competing arguments, nor to opine on the correctness of other opinions on that medical question. The function is in every case to form and to give its own opinion on the medical question referred to it by applying its own medical experience and its own medical expertise.[219]

In so doing the Court emphasised the difference between a Medical Panel and a court of law. The Court then moved on to consider the standard of written reasons required by such a Panel and confirmed that it had to provide sufficient information as to 'explain the actual path of reasoning by which the Medical Panel arrived at the opinion … in sufficient detail to enable a court to see whether the opinion does or does not involve an error of law'.[220] The Court added that if this standard was not met then the failure constituted an error of law under section 10 of the Administrative Law Act which could then be remedied by 'an order in the nature of certiorari … removing the legal effect of the opinion'.[221] This was not dissimilar to the discussion around the same topic in *Masters v McCubbery* which in fact,

[216] Ibid, [48]–[49].
[217] Malios, email (n 6).
[218] *Wingfoot Australia Pty Ltd v Kocak* [2013] HCA 43 [2].
[219] Ibid, [47].
[220] Ibid, [55].
[221] Ibid.

the Court cited.[222] The High Court concluded that in the case before it the reasons as given were in fact, adequate and the appeal was allowed.

Although it might be anticipated that such a clear description would finally settle the question of what constitutes adequate reasons by a Medical Panel, this determination was carefully considered by the Supreme Court of Appeal in Victoria in the hearing of a case in which the trial judge had concluded that: 'Reference to its own experience, knowledge and expertise did not suffice to cure the failure of the reasons [given by the Medical Panel] to explain its reasoning process in the manner described by the High Court in *Wingfoot*'.[223] In denying the appeal the three judge panel confirmed that the trial judge had been correct in concluding that the Reasons provided by the Medical Panel were inadequate,[224] explaining that:

> It is important to bear in mind that the question for the Court when considering whether the medical panel's reasons are adequate is not whether the reasons positively disclose that the panel erred in law, but whether the reasons are sufficient to enable the Court to determine whether the panel's opinion does or does not involve any error of law. If the reasons are such that the Court is left in real doubt about whether the panel correctly performed its statutory functions, the reasons will not comply with … the Act. Such a doubt exists in the present case.[225]

The same grounds for relief were cited in a case brought under the Wrongs Act and dealt with by the High Court which in rejecting leave of appeal, confirmed that there is no common law or statutory requirement for a Medical Panel to provide reasons for its determination under the Wrongs Act 1958 and thus, whilst the Panel may choose to voluntarily provide such reasons, it was under no obligation to do so.[226]

In marked contrast to the issue of adequacy of reasons, the requirement of a Medical Panel to provide its opinion or determination within a specified time frame has been cited as grounds for review only once with a presiding judge confirming that:

> Indeed, the parties and I, have been unable to find any other case, which has come before this Court, in which a medical panel, whether under the *Accident Compensation Act* or under the *Wrongs Act*, has failed to deliver its determination within the prescribed timeframe.[227]

The essential facts of the case were that the plaintiff had been assessed by a Medical Panel on 18 March 2011 under the Wrongs Act. However, the Panel did not sign the necessary certificate and determination until 53 days later on 10 May 2011.[228] The plaintiff thereafter sought relief on two grounds, the first being that the Panel had 'exceeded its jurisdiction by purporting to issue its certificate after the period allowed … namely 30 days after the date'[229] of interview, and second, by failing 'to take into account relevant considerations and/or taking into account irrelevant considerations' as exemplified by aspects of the history which the plaintiff stated were not as she had reported them.[230]

[222] Ibid, [51].
[223] *Bakar v Gruma Oceania Pty Ltd* [2014] VSC 206 [38].
[224] *Gruma Oceania Pty Ltd v Bakar* [2014] VSCA 252 [36].
[225] Ibid, [47].
[226] *Colquhoun v Capitol Radiology Pty Ltd* [2013] HCA Trans 320 [255].
[227] *Mikhman v Royal Victorian Aero Club* [2012] VSC 42 [37].
[228] Ibid, [6].
[229] Ibid, [5].
[230] Ibid.

Justice Kaye noted the time requirements adding that: 'The 30 day time period, which is specified by s 28LZG(3)(a), is not unduly onerous'.[231] In considering the ramifications in a situation where the Panel failed to meet this requirement, he concluded that the time frame was not discretionary but was to be strictly complied with[232] and hence in the case under review, it was beyond the power of the Panel to provide a decision outwith the specified time. He ordered that the determination be set aside.[233] Although it was not then necessary for Kaye J to consider the second ground of appeal he chose to do so but found that the plaintiff had made out her case in regard to that matter.[234]

Thus, although the Court signalled to the Medical Panel that it was essential for it to keep to the prescribed time requirements, it is noteworthy that this appears to be the one and only occasion on which a case has been brought on these grounds; which in and of itself, seems to indicate that as a general rule the Medical Panels meet this condition on the exercise of their power. This attention to detail is not merely to prevent a backlog of cases, but is in fact a vital component under both pieces of legislation for without it Parliament's stated intention that cases should be dealt with 'as speedily as a proper consideration of the reference allows'[235] would fail to be met.

From Here to the Future

Medical Panels were introduced into both the Accident Compensation Act and the Wrongs Act to assist in the speedy resolution of disputes in a cost-effective way and in such a manner as to reduce the input from, and hence the cost of, legal practitioners. From the above discussion it would seem evident that the Panels have consistently managed to complete the reporting requirements within the times allocated and largely to the satisfaction of the parties concerned given the low rate of appeal against the decisions.

In addition, whilst it is always difficult to assess the cost of any common law action since so many are settled out of court, it appears highly likely that the cost of a Panel assessment would be much less than any such action. Each medical member of a Panel is paid an amount not too dissimilar from the scheduled fee paid by the Victorian Workcover Authority to an independent medical examiner requested to assess a worker under the Accident Compensation Act, with the Presiding Members being paid slightly more in recognition of the extra work that role requires. In the case of a Panel convened to decide on a medical question under the Accident Compensation Act, the payments to those medical experts are made by the Victorian Workcover Authority,[236] whereas for Panels convened under the Wrongs Act the payment is the responsibility of the respondent.[237] Given that in both cases the Panels' decisions are binding, it appears reasonable to assume that the result would be

[231] Ibid, [37].
[232] Ibid, [38].
[233] Ibid, [39].
[234] Ibid, [57].
[235] Wrongs Act 1958 (Vic) s 28LZ(2).
[236] Accident Compensation Act 1985 (Vic) s 63(7).
[237] Wrongs Act 1958 (Vic) s 28LX.

less costly than both parties instructing legal counsel and arranging for their own medical experts to assess the individual worker/claimant and for these opinions to be tested in court.

Thus, it would appear that the Medical Panel has demonstrated its ability to adapt to the many changes which have impacted on it over the last two decades and continues to fulfil the roles and responsibilities required of it. Its proven capacity to meet legislative timelines and to provide an alternative dispute resolution process which is both informal and cost-effective indicates that there remains an ongoing role for this unique body in Victorian legislation.

Part IV

Compensation and Personal Responsibility

10

Concurrent Fault at 90: A History of Ontario's Negligence Act and Canada's Uniform Contributory Fault Act

JOHN C KLEEFELD*

The year 2014 marks the ninetieth anniversary of Ontario's Contributory Negligence Act,[1] later renamed the Negligence Act.[2] Almost concurrently, the Uniform Law Conference of Canada[3] adopted its own model statute, the Uniform Contributory Negligence Act (UCNA),[4] eventually superseded by the Uniform Contributory Fault Act (UCFA).[5] These two 1924 statutes—actual and model—comprised the first general legislation in the world to address apportionment of liability based on fault and, through subsequent amendments, the rights of those at fault to seek contribution among themselves for amounts paid to a successful plaintiff. The statutes, which I will also refer to in their various versions as the Ontario Act and the Uniform Act, in turn set the stage for further reforms or reform initiatives in Canada, England and the rest of the common law world.

In human life, 90 is an age to celebrate, reflect on and recount one's life. As in life, so with legislation. What are the vital statistics of the legislation? The factors that gave rise to its birth? How has it fared through youth, adulthood and middle age? What of its prospects for its more mature years? In light of work over the years by law reform bodies, is it time to reform the legislation? If so, what principles should apply, what shape should reform take, who will lose and who will gain? By attempting to answer these questions, we will be heeding a call by scholars Arvind and Steele to redress the dearth of attention paid to legislation

* This chapter is dedicated to Glanville Williams, who made everything clearer. Portions of the chapter also appear in 'The Contributory Negligence Act at Seventy' (2015) 78 *Saskatchewan Law Review* 31. I have attempted to state the law and law reform initiatives as of mid-2015.

[1] The Contributory Negligence Act, SO 1924, c 32.

[2] The Negligence Act 1930, SO 1930, c 27.

[3] The Conference, an initiative of the Canadian Bar Association, assembles government-appointed commissioners to draft, recommend and improve uniform legislation. It has met every year since 1918, except for 1940. Originally called the Conference of Commissioners on Uniformity of Laws throughout Canada, it became the Conference of Commissioners on Uniformity of Legislation in Canada in 1919 and the Uniform Law Conference of Canada in 1974. The annual proceedings of the Conference relevant to this chapter are referred to in these notes as 'ULCC 19xx'. These proceedings are archived at www.ulcc.ca/en/annual-meetings/63-annual-meetings-1918-to-present/898-proceedings-of-the-uniform-law-conference-of-canada-1918-1993.

[4] ULCC 1924, 34.

[5] ULCC 1984, 98.

in tort law—to take up their challenge of seeing statutes not just as 'operating at the margins of the common law [but] as contributing to the pattern of principles to be found in the law'.[6]

To understand what the legislation is about and to consider its prospects, we first need to understand the story behind it. For whenever there is a statute, there is a story—one that usually involves a mischief that the common law has failed to resolve.[7] Here, several mischiefs need explaining and several stories need telling in order to understand the legislative backdrop. But they can be categorised into three broad rules that arise from the cases: the *contributory negligence* rule; the *no-contribution-among-tortfeasors* rule; and a set of concepts called the *judgment-and-release-bar* rules. In the next few sections, I outline these rule-cum-stories and the legislation enacted to respond to them. Along the way, I will also address a number of points relating to terminology, including the word 'concurrent' used in the title of this chapter.

The Contributory Negligence Rule: Fast Horses, Fettered Donkeys and Way Stations on the Road to Apportionment

At common law, a plaintiff's failure to take ordinary care was a complete defence to an action on the case, or what we would now call a negligence action. The contributory negligence rule, as it came to be known, originated in the English case of *Butterfield v Forrester*.[8] It was around 8 pm on an August evening in the early 1800s, and Butterfield was in a hurry to get home from the public house where he had been drinking. Butterfield mounted his horse, and in the words of a witness, rode it 'very hard'[9] down the road. Unfortunately, Forrester, who had been fixing his house on the same road, had left a pole extended partway into the road. Although the same witness testified that there was still enough daylight to see the pole at 100 yards, Butterfield rode straight into it and was badly injured as a result. At trial, Bayley J directed the jury members that if Butterfield had used ordinary care, they should find for Forrester, which they did. Butterfield moved for a retrial based on misdirection. Dismissing the motion, Lord Ellenborough CJ said that '[o]ne person being in fault will not dispense with another's using ordinary care for himself'.[10] And so, 'with the offhand manner of judges who are treading on familiar ground',[11] the contributory negligence rule emerged. While it took time to be entrenched in the common law,[12] courts came to

[6] TT Arvind and J Steele (eds), *Tort Law and the Legislature: Common Law, Statute and the Dynamics of Legal Change* (Oxford, Hart Publishing, 2013) 3.

[7] This is a traditional view of statutes, though not the only one. Arvind and Steele would classify the mischief-correcting function as a 'Type 1' interaction with the common law: Arvind and Steele (n 6) 5–6.

[8] *Butterfield v Forrester* (1809) 11 East 60, 103 ER 926 (KB) (*Butterfield*).

[9] Ibid, ER 927.

[10] Ibid.

[11] F James, 'Contributory Negligence' (1953) 62 *Yale Law Journal* 691, 692.

[12] In the UK, the first reference to *Butterfield* in the citation note of the English Reports is *Bridge v Grand Junction Railway Company* (1838) 3 M&W 248, 150 ER 1134 (Ex Pleas). In Canada, the rule, with or without reference to *Butterfield*, applied well before Confederation: see *Nellis v Wilkes* (1844) 1 UCQB 46 (horse falling in hole in road; *Butterfield* cited in argument but case dismissed based on defective pleadings); *Eberts v Smythe* (1846) 3 UCQB 188 (reversing plaintiff's jury verdict and ordering new trial in inland vessel collision case; court referring (Robinson CJ), to the 'painful degree of responsibility' of those charged with deciding cases in which the whole of the loss must fall on one party); *Ridley v Lamb* (1853) 10 UCQB 354 (in a case like *Butterfield* but with a different result, court upholding a verdict for plaintiff rider because '[t]he fact that the horse ran against the pole

find in it 'a convenient instrument of control over the jury, by which the liabilities of rapidly growing industry were curbed and kept within bounds'.[13]

The instrument also proved harsh in some cases, as where the defendant's fault was great and the plaintiff's slight. Juries got wise, and despite receiving the usual direction that contributory negligence barred recovery, would find that the plaintiff hadn't been at fault or would award a lower sum in damages—with courts sometimes giving the nod to such practices. A case in point is *Raisin v Mitchell*,[14] where damage to a cargo of eggs was proved to exceed £500—a great deal of eggs indeed—yet the jury awarded only £250. When Tindal CJ asked why, the foreman answered: 'there were faults on both sides'.[15] The defendant's counsel submitted that this entitled his client to a verdict, to which the Chief Justice summarily replied: 'No. There may be faults to a certain extent'.[16]

Judges also developed glosses, exceptions or modifications to the rule, the most important of which arose in the celebrated case of *Davies v Mann*.[17] Davies had left a donkey by the roadside to graze, having first fettered its feet; Mann's servant came along driving a wagon 'at a smartish pace',[18] hitting the donkey and killing it. The judge directed the jury that even if the fettering of the donkey's feet had prevented it from getting out of the wagon's way, if they thought that the accident could have been prevented by the driver exercising ordinary care, they could find for the plaintiff. Which they did. On a retrial motion, the full court upheld the direction, giving rise to what came to be called the doctrine of 'last clear chance',[19] 'last opportunity',[20] ultimate negligence',[21] or 'clear line'.[22] The notion was that if you could draw a clear line between the plaintiff's and defendant's negligence, or if you could say that the defendant had the last clear chance of avoiding an accident caused at least in part by the plaintiff's failure to take care of himself, the contributory negligence rule wouldn't apply.

While the doctrine has been characterised as an exception to the rule in *Butterfield*, what *Davies v Mann* arguably announced was a synthesised rule that could account for both fast horse and fettered donkey. In each case, the successful party happened to be there first, with pole or donkey, and the last clear message in both cases was that riders of horses and wagons ought to take ordinary care in using the road. This notion was later to take the form of a statutory reverse onus of proof in favour of non-motorists, widely enacted as part of traffic safety legislation, but in *Davies v Mann*, was cast as a matter of proximate cause.[23] The rule could be as unfair to defendants as to plaintiffs: if the plaintiff's fault was great and the defendant's slight but later in time, there was ample opportunity to argue that the plaintiff should be solely liable. This led to a convoluted history for the doctrine and to its

is a circumstance leading strongly to the conclusion that a person [driving] in that direction was not likely without common care, to avoid it'); and *Campbell v The Great Western Railway Co* (1858) 15 UCQB 498 (plaintiff had negligently allowed his colts to be on the defendant's railway tracks, but defendant still had to use ordinary care to avoid hitting them; defendant held solely liable).

[13] W Prosser, 'Comparative Negligence' (1953) 41 *California Law Review* 1, 4.
[14] *Raisin v Mitchell* (1839) 9 Car & P 613, 173 ER 979 (CP).
[15] Ibid, ER 981.
[16] Ibid.
[17] *Davies v Mann* (1842) 10 M&W 547, 152 ER 588 (Ex Pleas).
[18] Ibid, ER 588.
[19] See MM MacIntyre, 'The Rationale of Last Clear Chance' (1940) 18 *Canadian Bar Review* 665.
[20] See AL Goodhart, 'The "Last Opportunity" Rule' (1949) 65 *LQR* 237.
[21] See, eg, *Koeppel v Colonial Coach Lines Ltd* [1933] SCR 529, 41 CRC 141, [1933] 3 DLR 469.
[22] See *McKee v Malenfant* [1954] SCR 651; *Bruce v McIntyre* [1955] SCR 251; *Brooks v Ward* [1956] SCR 683.
[23] *Davies v Mann* (n 17) 588.

characterisation as 'only a disguised escape, by way of comparative fault, from contributory negligence as an absolute bar'[24] or no more than 'a way station on the road to apportionment of damages'.[25]

Judges sometimes expressed dissatisfaction with this state of affairs,[26] but in an era of judicial conservatism, felt powerless to do much about it absent legislative action. The trigger for change in the general law appears to have been a 1923 Supreme Court of Canada decision arising from a railway accident.[27] The plaintiff, Earl, had been hit by a train while trying to cycle across a level crossing in Edmonton, Alberta. As with many railway cases in this era, there was fault on both sides. The railway had been shunting cars at the crossing during the day, contrary to regulations that restricted such activity mostly to night hours; it had also failed to provide a flagman, which might have helped avoid an accident. But Earl was also found to have been at fault, in that he had seen the train coming and had miscalculated: he had tried to reach a track on which he thought the rail car wouldn't pass, but had collided with the car instead. This miscalculation resulted in Earl losing his case, since he apparently had the last clear chance of avoiding the accident. In Duff J's view, the case was one of those 'that sometimes cause one to turn a rather wistful eye to jurisdictions in which … the burden of the loss can be equitably distributed'.[28] Justice Anglin was less wistful and more emphatic in his denunciation of the English rules, which he saw as inferior to the civil law of continental Europe and Quebec:

> [T]he present case illustrates the harshness of the rule by which, where there is common fault contributing to cause injury to a plaintiff, he is deprived of all redress and the defendant entirely relieved, although the culpability of the former may be comparatively slight and that of the latter distinctly gross. The doctrine of the civil law that in such circumstances the damages should be divided in proportion to the degree of culpability commends itself to my judgment as much more equitable.[29]

Early Reform Efforts: The 1924 Ontario Act and 1924 Uniform Act

Spurred at least in part by these remarks as well as Anglin J's extrajudicial calls for legislative reform,[30] a skeletal Bill was introduced in Ontario.[31] Shortly thereafter, an article by railway

[24] MacIntyre (n 19) 689.

[25] Prosser (n 13) 7.

[26] An early instance is *Eberts v Smythe* (n 12).

[27] *Grand Trunk Pacific Railway Company v Earl* [1923] SCR 397, 29 CRC 383, [1923] 2 DLR 741, [1923] 2 WWR 123.

[28] Ibid, 398.

[29] Ibid, 406. See also Mignault J, in dissent but agreeing on this point at 409 (finding civil law and admiralty law 'much more equitable' but concluding that 'courts are obliged to apply the law however harsh it may seem').

[30] Mr Justice Anglin, 'Some Differences Between the Law of Quebec and the Law as Administered in the Other Provinces of Canada' (1923) 1 *Canadian Bar Review* 33, 48–49. Some impetus may have also come from Ottawa lawyer MJ Gorman KC, who had written two earlier articles calling for reform. See MJ Gorman, 'Negligence—Contributory, "Ultimate" and "Comparative", with a Suggested Statutory Amendment' (1917) 37 *Canadian Law Times* 23 and MJ Gorman, 'Contributory Negligence' (1922) 42 *Canadian Law Times* 425.

[31] Bill 68, An Act to amend the law as to Contributory Negligence, 15th Leg, 4th Sess, Ontario, 1923. The Bill was introduced by Hammett Pinhey Hill, Conservative member for Ottawa West from 1919 to 1923.

lawyer Angus MacMurchy KC appeared in the *Canadian Bar Review*, also making the case for reform.[32] The original Bill was withdrawn for more study at the suggestion of Ontario's Chief Justice, Sir William Meredith,[33] but in the version enacted the following year, any studying that was done yielded only one substantive change. The original Bill had required the jury, or the judge in a juryless action, to calculate the plaintiff's entire damages, but gave only the judge the mandate to find the degree of each party's fault and apportion damages accordingly; the enacted Bill required a jury to do both these things in an action tried by jury.[34] With the enactment of the statute, Ontario thus became the first common law jurisdiction to remove the contributory negligence bar from the general law and replace it with a scheme that apportioned liability for damages according to fault.[35]

The UCNA followed shortly thereafter. Speaking at the annual meeting of the Uniform Law Conference of Canada held on 2 June 1924, Commissioner Francis King, president of the Ontario Bar Association, diplomatically explained that '[y]our committee could not see its way to submit [the Ontario bill] to the Conference as a model, and preferred to follow more closely the broad and general terms of the Maritime Conventions Act'.[36] King was alluding to the fact that the English rule in admiralty law, which had divided losses equally in a collision where two or more ships were at fault, had been superseded in states that ratified the 1910 Brussels Convention for the Unification of Certain Rules of Law with respect to Collisions between Vessels. The Convention followed the more common continental practice of apportioning liability for damage to ships or property in a collision according to the degrees of fault of the ships involved. In the UK and Canada, the ratifications had taken the form of the Maritime Conventions Acts, which enacted a several or proportionate liability regime for damage to ships and property and a regime of joint and several liability for loss of life or personal injury.[37]

32 A MacMurchy, 'Contributory Negligence—Should the Rule in Admiralty and the Civil Law be Adopted?' (1923) 1 *Canadian Bar Review* 844. MacMurchy was solicitor for the Canadian Pacific Railway's Ontario division from the early 1890s until his death on a CPR train on 3 May 1931 (see 'Angus MacMurchy, Lawyer, Dies on Train' *The New York Times* (4 May 1931) 19. That his chief client would have been a beneficiary of the contributory negligence rule was well known to MacMurchy, as he had represented CPR in many cases where contributory negligence was in issue; he was also editor of *Canadian Railway Cases*. However, the rule's all-or-nothing character could also work against corporate defendants like CPR. As already indicated, sympathetic juries might find no contributory negligence where they should have, and a regime that apportioned liability according to fault would actually reduce defendants' overall exposure to liability in such cases. Thus advocating for reform, even if based on MacMurchy's personal views rather than those of his clients, was not necessarily inconsistent with a pro-business agenda. On the involvement of Canadian 'elite' lawyers in the drive for reform in this area of the law, see RB Brown and N Yhard, 'The Harshness and Injustice of the Common Law Rule … Has Frequently Been Commented On': Debating Contributory Negligence in Canada, 1914–1949' (2013) 36 *Dalhousie Law Journal* 137.

33 MacMurchy (n32) 862.

34 MacMurchy (n32) 844 (reproducing text of original Bill) and The Contributory Negligence Act, SO 1924, c 32. In the workplace, employees' contributory negligence as a bar to recovery from employers had been removed 10 years earlier, at least in certain industries. See The Workmen's Compensation Act, SO 1914, c 25, ss 107–08.

35 There is a good argument that this step removed contributory negligence from the realm of defences—even so-called 'partial defences'—and put it in the realm of remedies. See J Goudkamp, *Tort Law Defences* (Oxford, Hart Publishing, 2013) 17.

36 ULCC 1924, 34.

37 In the UK, see the Maritime Conventions Act 1911, 1 and 2 Geo V, c 57 (the relevant portions of which were repealed and replaced by the Merchant Shipping Act 1995, c 21, Pt VII). In Canada, see The Maritime Conventions Act 1914, SC 1914, c 13, s 2 (repealed by the Canada Shipping Act, RSC 1985, c S-9 and in turn repealed by the Canada Shipping Act 2001, SC 2001, c 26). For a summary of how the relevant provisions worked and how law reformers tried to adapt them to collisions on land, see J Steele, 'Law Reform (Contributory Negligence)

Both of the original enactments in 1924 were fairly skeletal. Table 1 presents a side-by-side view of the original Ontario Act and the UCNA.

The key concept in both of the original statutes was that of apportioning liability by degrees of fault, or, in the Ontario wording, 'fault or neglect'. Beyond that commonality, though, the two statutes diverged. The Ontario Act seems to have been premised on a litigation world consisting solely of bilateral disputes and focused on a type of action ('founded upon fault or negligence'). The bilateralism was implicit in the singular 'plaintiff'

Table 1: Side-by-Side Comparison of the 1924 Ontario Act and 1924 Uniform Act

The Contributory Negligence Act, SO 1924, c 103[38]	The Uniform Contributory Negligence Act 1924[39]
1. In this Act 'plaintiff' shall include a defendant counter-claiming, and 'defendant' shall include a plaintiff against whom a counter-claim is brought. 2. In any action or counterclaim for damages, which is founded upon fault or negligence, if a plea of contributory fault or negligence shall be found to have been established, the jury, or the judge in an action tried without a jury, shall find: First: The entire amount of damages to which the plaintiff would have been entitled had there been no such contributory fault or neglect. Secondly: The degree in which each party was in fault and the manner in which the amount of damages found should be apportioned so that the plaintiff shall have judgment only for so much thereof as is proportionate to the degree of fault imputable to the defendant. 3. Where the judge or jury finds that it is not, upon the evidence, practicable to determine the respective degrees of fault the defendant shall be liable for one-half the damages sustained.	1. This Act may be cited as The Contributory Negligence Act. 2. Where by the fault of two or more persons damage or loss is caused to one or more of them, the liability to make good the damage or loss shall be in proportion to the degree in which each person was at fault. Provided that: (a) If, having regard to all the circumstances of the case, it is not possible to establish different degrees of fault, the liability shall be apportioned equally, and (b) Nothing in this section shall operate so as to render any person liable for any loss or damage to which his fault has not contributed. 3. In actions tried with a jury the amount of damage, the fault, if any, and the degrees of fault shall be questions of fact for the jury. 4. Unless the judge otherwise directs the liability for costs of the parties shall be in the same proportion as the liability to make good the loss or damage. 5. This Act shall be so interpreted and construed as to effect its general purpose of making uniform the law of those provinces which enact it.

Act 1945: Collisions of a Different Sort' in TT Arvind and J Steele (eds), *Tort Law and the Legislature: Common Law, Statute and the Dynamics of Legal Change* (Oxford, Hart Publishing, 2013) 159, 169 *et seq*. I discuss the terms 'joint', 'several' and 'joint and several' later in this chapter.

[38] This is actually the version from the 1927 Revised Statutes of Ontario, which incorporates slight changes to the section numbering of the 1924 statute.

[39] ULCC 1924, 36.

and 'defendant', but became explicit with the default apportionment provision in section 3: when impracticable to apportion by degrees, a court was to make the defendant 'liable for one-half' of the damages sustained, which would make no sense were there more than one defendant. In contrast, the UCNA contemplated actions based on 'the fault of two or more persons' and the focus, rather than being on the type of action, was on the 'damage or loss caused' to one or more of the two persons.

In the next couple of years, the UCNA was adopted in New Brunswick,[40] British Columbia[41] and, after a brief fling with the Ontario version, Nova Scotia.[42] But in a New Brunswick case that went to the Supreme Court of Canada in 1927,[43] the statute's legislative intent was thwarted by reference to old doctrines. A 10-year-old boy, riding on the running board of a bakery truck, was injured when the truck plunged off the road. The boy had been told not to ride on the running board, and a jury found him 25 per cent negligent, a result upheld by the New Brunswick Court of Appeal. But the Supreme Court, finding a lack of Latin in the case, reversed on the basis that 'in the courts below the application to a charge of contributory negligence of the maxim, *in lege causa proxima, non remota, spectatur*, was not sufficiently adverted to'.[44] The decision that the boy's riding on the running board was too remote to be considered is all the more remarkable for having been reached by Anglin CJC—the same Anglin, now elevated to Chief Justice, who had been one of the instigators for legislative change only a few years earlier.[45] The decision might have been more defensible had the Court said: '10-year-old boys will be 10-year-old boys, and we won't hold them to the same standards as adults'. Instead, the Court effectively ruled that last clear chance, framed, as Fleming would later say, in the 'cabalistic terminology of causation',[46] survived the model legislation and the provincial statutes based on it.

The Commissioners to the Uniform Law Conference of Canada considered whether the UCNA could be improved to deal with this, but concluded in 1928 that

> it is not reasonably possible to define in terms of general application the point at which negligence prior to the accident passes from the category of extraneous and irrelevant events into the list of things which may fairly be considered to have contributed to the result so as to entail a share of the liability.[47]

Accordingly, they continued to recommend the statute to provincial legislatures.

Over the next decade, the Uniform Law Conference and the Ontario legislature continued to deal on separate tracks with the problems raised by the early legislative attempts and judicial interpretations given to them. The most significant of these efforts was the repeal and replacement of the Contributory Negligence Act with the Negligence Act 1930[48] and

[40] The Contributory Negligence Act, SNB 1925, c 41.

[41] The Contributory Negligence Act, SBC 1925, c 8 (repealed and replaced by the Contributory Negligence Act, SBC 1936, c 12 and now called the Negligence Act, RSBC 1996, c 333).

[42] Contributory Negligence Act, SNS 1925, c 5 (repealed and replaced by the Contributory Negligence Act 1926, SNS 1926, c 3).

[43] *McLaughlin v Long*, 1927 SCR 303.

[44] Ibid, 309.

[45] See nn 29 and 30 and accompanying text.

[46] The phrase is from JG Fleming, 'Foreword: Comparative Negligence at Last—By Judicial Choice' (1976) 64 *California Law Review* 239, 259.

[47] ULCC 1928, 92.

[48] The Negligence Act 1930, SO 1930, c 27.

the adoption of a new version of the UCNA in 1935.[49] Both of these statutes added, for the first time, language that provided for contribution and indemnity among those at fault. And that requires telling another story.

The No-Contribution-Among-Tortfeasors Rule: The Miller's Tale and the Stevedore's Widow's Tale

While the contributory negligence saga was unfolding, another one, beginning 10 years before *Butterfield*, was winding its own tortuous path through the courts. It started with the 1799 English case of *Merryweather v Nixan*,[50] the second of two actions, the first having been brought by one Starkey against Merryweather and Nixan 'for an injury done by them to his reversionary estate in a mill, in which was included a count in trover, for the machinery belonging to the mill'.[51] In other words, Merryweather and Nixan had taken Starkey's milling equipment, or had come into possession of it without colour of right and had refused to return it.[52] Starkey got judgment for £840 against both and levied it all on Merryweather, as he was entitled to do, since Merryweather and Nixan were joint tortfeasors in one of the classic senses of that term: two or more persons acting in concert to commit a wrongful act. Merryweather then sued Nixan for a portion—likely half, though we don't know because the case is so sparsely reported—of what he had paid to Starkey. The action appears to have been based on an implied assumpsit; that is, an implied promise or agreement. Merryweather was nonsuited at trial, a result upheld by Kenyon CJ, who said he had never heard of a case where the first action was for a tort as opposed to a judgment against defendants in an (express) assumpsit or an indemnity case, where one person employs another 'to do acts, not unlawful in themselves, for the purpose of asserting a right [against a third person]'.[53] The headnote is about as scant as the report: 'If *A* recover in tort against two defendants, and levy the whole damages on one, that one cannot recover a moiety against the other for his contribution; *aliter* in assumpsit'.[54]

Rarely has a headnote so overstated a case. A comment in *Smith's Leading Cases* says the decision was founded on the maxim *ex turpi causa non oritur actio*—from a base

[49] ULCC 1935, 14–16, 31–32.

[50] *Merryweather v Nixan* (1799) 8 TR 186, 101 ER 1337 (KB) [*Merryweather*].

[51] Ibid, ER 1337.

[52] The plea of detinue *sur trover* applied where the plaintiff had the right to immediate possession of a chattel from the defendant (for reasons other than the defendant having been the plaintiff's bailee with respect to the chattel, that being a plea of detinue *sur bailment*), and the defendant refused to deliver it to the plaintiff. The plea could be used against a finder, a thief, or an innocent purchaser who had acquired possession without knowledge of the plaintiff's rights. The action had four elements: (i) the plaintiff had possessed the chattel; (ii) the plaintiff had lost it; (iii) the defendant had found it—hence the Anglo-Norman French *trover*, 'to find' (now *trouver*); and (iv) the defendant had refused to return it. Allegations (ii) and (iii) were legal fictions designed to overcome the fact that the plaintiff was not in possession. Over time, (iv) changed to an allegation that the defendant had converted the chattel to his or her own use, giving rise to the tort now called conversion. Although detinue has been abolished in the UK in the Torts (Interference with Goods) Act 1977, it continues to apply in Canada.

[53] *Merryweather* (n 50) ER 1337.

[54] Ibid.

(immoral, unlawful or illegal) cause, no action arises.[55] There is nothing to quibble with that policy, which remains a vital, if rarely invoked, aspect of the law.[56] But what was the implied cause? If it was an *ex ante* agreement for Nixan to indemnify Merryweather for part of the consequences of their joint tort, the maxim would seem to apply; but if it was an *ex post* agreement to reimburse Merryweather for part of the judgment ordered against both but executed only against one, there is nothing terribly base about that. As another commentator has noted, 'a contract to pay half a joint judgment if the other party to the contract will pay the whole, would seem to be a good contract; the past history of the judgment is surely immaterial'.[57] The Court had an interpretive choice here, and it opted for the more unsavoury interpretation. This was perhaps understandable when 'tort' was almost entirely identified with what we would now classify as intentionally caused harm, but the *ex turpi* basis for the no-contribution rule was inapplicable once 'tort' came to include liability for unintentional harm.

Merryweather thus had a distinctly unmerry effect on the growth of the law of apportionment and contribution, which by then was well developed in the areas of general maritime average[58] and co-sureties for debt.[59] The rule was later extended from joint tortfeasors to several concurrent tortfeasors—those whose independent acts had concurred (run together) to cause the same damage—in a case involving the London General Omnibus Company.[60] But as with the contributory negligence bar, courts would sometimes try to find ways around it. In *Adamson v Jarvis*,[61] an auctioneer, Adamson, had sold goods at the behest of Jarvis, who, unbeknownst to Adamson, had no right to them. Adamson was thus a tortfeasor under the strict liability of the law of conversion, and would have been a joint one with Jarvis under the other classic use of that term, denoting the joint liability of an agent and principal for the agent's torts. But Best CJ of the Court of Common Pleas

[55] JW Smith, *A Selection of Leading Cases on Various Branches of the Law with Notes*, 5th American edn, vol 2 (Philadelphia PA, T & JW Johnson, 1855) 457, 459.

[56] For a recent analysis of the *ex turpi* doctrine, see *Joyce v O'Brien* [2013] EWCA Civ 546.

[57] JF Williams, 'The Rule in *Merryweather v Nixan*' (1901) 67 *LQR* 293, 297.

[58] General average is a doctrine of maritime law stipulating that if cargo is jettisoned or expenses are incurred in an emergency, the loss is shared proportionately by all parties with a financial interest in the voyage. The law dates to the Island of Rhodes, c 800 BC, and is now embodied in an international convention, the York–Antwerp Rules, and managed by the Comité Maritime International, based in Antwerp.

[59] See *Deering v Earl of Winchelsea* (1787) 2 Bos & Pul 270, 126 ER 1276 (Ex), the headnote of which reads: 'If *A*, *B*, and *C* become bound as sureties to *D* in three separate bonds, and any one of them be compelled to pay the whole debt of the principal, the two others are compellable to contribute in proportion to the penalties of their respective bonds'. The concept was first developed in equity but was taken up in the common law, especially under the resourcefulness of Lord Mansfield, who, 30 years before *Deering*, had suggested that the money paid out for the first judgment had been done so at the implied request of the others. See *Decker v Pope* (1757); D Keane and CT Smith (eds), *Selwyn's Abridgment of the Law of Nisi Prius*, 13th edn, vol 1 (London, Stevens & Sons, 1869) 91.

[60] *Horwell v London Omnibus Co* (1877) 2 Ex D 365 (CA). The case is a stark example of courts initially failing to embrace new legislation—here, the relatively new Judicature Acts (Supreme Court of Judicature Act 1873 (UK) 36 and 37 Vict c 66 and Supreme Court of Judicature Act 1875 (UK) 38 and 39 Vict c 77) and related rules—due to the sway of prior doctrine. Horwell, a bus passenger, sued the London General Omnibus Company following an accident in which he was injured. The bus company got an order permitting it to add The London Tramways Company as a party, on pleading that the accident had been caused by the tramway not keeping their rails level with the road. The order was overturned on appeal, based in part on the notion that, if both the bus company and the tramway company had been negligent, it would be useless to add the tramway company, since there could be no contribution among wrongdoers (Bramwell LJ, 377; Kelly CB, 379). The dissent of Brett LJ is notable for articulating the rationale for what is now routine third-party procedure in litigation throughout the common law world.

[61] *Adamson v Jarvis* (1827) 4 Bing 66, 130 ER 693 (CP).

thought that *Merryweather* should be confined to cases 'where the person seeking redress must be presumed to have known that he was doing an unlawful act'.[62] In other cases, courts would resort to a robust application of Kenyon CJ's exception, and imply an indemnity arising from a 'not otherwise unlawful act' done at another's instance.[63]

But the rule still worked enough of an injustice that, when asked to find it part of Scottish law after a stevedoring accident at the end of the nineteenth century, the House of Lords declined. Like *Merryweather*, the case was a follow-on action. Brought by the Wick and Pulteneytown Steam Shipping Co,[64] it arose out of two actions started by the widow of a stevedore who had been killed by the fall of a block, part of a ship's tackle. At a trial of the conjoined actions, both the shipping company and the stevedore's employer, one Palmer, were found at fault and held jointly liable. The shipping company paid the widow in full and sought to recover a portion from Palmer. Lord Herschell LC thought the case exemplified what the Court of Common Pleas had contemplated in *Adamson v Jarvis* (about *Merryweather* applying only to knowingly unlawful acts), but in any event, concluded that the rule was 'not … founded on any principle of justice or equity, or even of public policy, which justifies its extension to [Scotland]'.[65] Lord Watson also disapproved, as did Lord Halsbury, acerbically adding that *Merryweather* 'has been so long … part of the English law that even if one's own judgment did not concur with its principle it would be now too late to question its applicability … in England'.[66]

Reforming the Reforms: The 1930 Ontario Act and the 1935 Uniform Act

But the rule was questioned, in England and elsewhere. Again, Ontario was first off the mark to legislate. If there was a single trigger, it was likely *Esten v Rosen*,[67] in which the Court of Appeal quashed a defendant's attempt to manoeuvre around the rule by paying a judgment and then assigning it to a solicitor's clerk to execute against a co-defendant. The case was an automobile accident in which both defendants were insured, and in reading between the lines, one senses that insurer rivalry played a part in the litigation strategy. Though Middleton JA refused to allow the manoeuvre, he remarked on the need to legislatively change the rule, as long as change was not based 'upon any such principle as bringing about an equality of contribution among wrongdoers without regard to the actual degree of fault'.[68] In other words, just as degrees of fault were to be used when apportioning liability between a defendant and a contributorily negligent plaintiff, the same approach

[62] Ibid, ER 696.

[63] *Merryweather* (n 50) ER 1337. For an important case in this regard, see *Betts v Gibbins* (1834) 2 Ad & E, 111 ER 22 (KB).

[64] *Palmer v Wick and Pulteneytown Steam Shipping Co* [1894] AC 318 (HL Scotland).

[65] Ibid, 324.

[66] Ibid, 333. The same we've-been-doing-it-this-way-too-long-to-change reasoning was followed with the adoption of *Merryweather* in Canada: see *Sutton v Dundas (Town)* (1908) 17 OLR 556, 13 OWR 126 (CA).

[67] *Esten v Rosen* [1929] 1 DLR 275, 63 OLR 210 (CA).

[68] Ibid, DLR 278.

should be used when creating a regime that would allow for contribution between negligent defendants.

And this in fact is what happened. On 3 April 1930, the Negligence Act 1930 came into force, replacing the Contributory Negligence Act. Section 3 provided the language for a statutory fault-based entitlement to contribution, as can be seen from the italicised portion of the section:

> In any action founded upon the fault or negligence of two or more persons the court shall determine the degree in which each of such persons is at fault or negligent, and where two or more persons are found liable they shall be jointly and severally liable to the person suffering loss or damage for such fault or negligence, *but as between themselves, in the absence of any contract express or implied, each shall be liable to make contribution and indemnify each other in the degree in which they are found to be at fault or negligent.*

The section thus preserved the common law of joint and several liability (also called liability *in solidum* or *solidary* liability)[69] for indivisible loss or damage, but removed the no-contribution-among-tortfeasors rule. Plaintiffs who succeeded against multiple defendants could still collect from the defendants most able to pay, but the paying defendants could now seek contribution or indemnity[70] from others held liable, up to their respective degrees of fault as found at trial. And under the new section 4, defendants could still raise the defence of contributory negligence as under the previous Act; if successful, the defence would continue to result in a reduction of liability by the plaintiff's degree of fault as found by the court. Section 4 read as follows:

> In any action for damages which is founded upon the fault or negligence of the defendant[,] if fault or negligence is found on the part of the plaintiff which contributed to the damages, the court shall apportion the damages in proportion to the degree of fault or negligence found against the parties respectively.

Section 5 continued the presumption of equal liability between any parties to an action where it was 'not practicable' to determine degrees of fault, and section 6 provided for the addition of a party defendant—though not a third-party defendant; that was to come later—'upon such terms as may be deemed just'. However, some of the language in these sections was still problematic and caused disputes over issues relating to contribution, contributory negligence, or both.

An early example arose in *Lecomte v Bell Telephone Co*.[71] Six days after the new Act came into force, Eugene Lecomte, an employee of the Ottawa fire department, was removing fire alarm wires from a 30-foot telephone pole when the pole broke below ground level. The pole came crashing down, killing Lecomte. His widow and children sued the telephone

[69] Technically, it is wrong to equate 'joint and several liability', a term having procedural connotations, with '*in solidum* liability'. However, this is an area in which precision yields to practicality, as the terms are now considered synonymous throughout most of North America. In Quebec, see Civil Code of Quebec, SQ 1991, c 64, art 1480 (parties who 'have jointly taken part in a wrongful act … are *solidarily* liable for reparation thereof').

[70] The term 'indemnify' as used in the Act denotes full, or 100 per cent, contribution. However, 'indemnify' and 'indemnity' have more specialised meanings, based not on comparative fault, but on party relationships. An insurance policy, for example, is an express contract of indemnity under which the insurer agrees to reimburse the insured for losses covered by the policy, subject to amounts deductible under that policy. An indemnity may also be implied rather than express—again, typically flowing from relationships between the parties.

[71] *Lecomte v Bell Telephone Co* (1932) 41 OWN 117 (HCJ), [1932] 3 DLR 220 (trial decision).

company, which had an agreement with the city regarding the use of its poles for the alarm wires. The company successfully moved to add the city as a party defendant. The plaintiffs amended their statement of claim to formally add the city as a defendant, but refused to make any claim against it. The company tried to force the plaintiffs to include a claim against the city, no doubt with an eye to using this as a basis for a contribution claim, but were rebuffed both by Raney J of the High Court and the Court of Appeal on the basis that plaintiffs should not be compelled to claim anything they don't choose to claim.[72] The case went ahead with the company making no claim against the city in its statement of defence, and the city not filing a defence. Thus, the action did not seem to be 'founded upon the fault or negligence of two or more persons', that being a precondition to apportionment of fault. Justice Raney thought this unjust, particularly as the Act had also repealed the Contributory Negligence Act. That would mean that if Lecomte had contributed to his own death, his family would have been without a remedy, for relief would have been barred under the common law contributory negligence rule.

The Court found a detour around such a result. Reading sections 3 and 4 together, Raney J thought that section 4 was intended to apply not only to cases involving the defendant, but also to those involving two or more persons. Thus '*the* defendant' should be read as though the legislature had meant '*a* defendant',[73] and the legislation should apply to cases involving multiple defendants, some of whom might have been at fault, and some not.[74] The city was 'a defendant of sorts',[75] and in any event was a party. Accordingly, the necessary condition existed to ascertain degrees of fault under section 3. Based on the facts, which included knowledge by each party that the pole was old and likely weakened by rot, Raney J apportioned liability at one-third each for the company, the city and the employee, a result that was not appealed.

Linguistic issues again arose in *Mara v Hartley*.[76] William Mara had taken his father, John Mara, for a drive, and had collided with Dr Hartley. The Maras sued Hartley—the father for his injuries and the son for damage to the son's car. The doctor was uninjured, whether as to person or car. The trial judge, Rose CJ, held the defendant-doctor 60 per cent at fault; the plaintiff-driver, 40 per cent at fault. The father was without fault. He got judgment for his full damages; his son got 60 per cent of his. On appeal, the key issue was whether the doctor had a right of contribution or indemnity against the son in relation to the judgment for the father. The trial judge thought not, on the basis that section 3 seemed to contemplate an action founded on the fault of two or more *defendants*, not on the fault of a defendant and co-plaintiff. On appeal, Middleton JA thought that 'persons' might have a wider meaning, and that he couldn't believe that the legislature intended to make contribution between wrongdoers 'depend upon the election of the plaintiff as to whom he will sue'.[77] However, he found it unnecessary to answer the question because Hartley

[72] *Lecomte v Bell Telephone Co* (1931) 66 OLR 580 (CA), [1931] 2 DLR 241 (interlocutory proceedings). Consistent with this theme, the order adding the telephone company also required the telephone company to be responsible for all the costs to which the plaintiffs would be put as a result of adding the city.

[73] *Lecomte* (note 71), 118.

[74] Indeed, although Raney J never said so, he implicitly interpreted 'the plaintiff' in s 4 to mean 'the plaintiffs', and indirect ones at that, since the plaintiffs under fatal accidents legislation were Lecomte's widow and seven children.

[75] Ibid.

[76] *Mara v Hartley* [1931] OR 69 (CA) [1931] 2 DLR 734.

[77] Ibid, OR 73.

hadn't given notice of the contribution claim either in the pleadings or in the notice of appeal. He dismissed the appeal, but without prejudice to Hartley's right to bring a separate third-party action against William Mara for relief under the Rules of Court.

Both the interlocutory appeal in *Lecomte v Bell Telephone Co* and the appeal in *Mara v Hartley* were decided by a full bench—ie, five members—of the Court of Appeal in early 1931. The issues raised and the attention given to them by the Court must have been brought to the legislature's attention quickly, for on 2 April 1931, a new version of section 3 came into force, repealing the words 'in any action founded upon the fault or negligence of two or more persons' and replacing them with 'where damages have been caused or contributed to by the fault or neglect of two or more persons'.[78] This phrase did not remove all ambiguity, as it would seem to apply to a scenario in which the injured person is one of the two who caused or contributed to the damage. But since an injured person 'cannot be considered to be liable to himself',[79] that interpretation didn't make sense. Rather, the scenario posed must be governed by section 4. Curiously, though, that section was not amended to change the words 'in any action for damages' in a manner similar to the amendment to section 3.

A virtue of the 1931 amendment, though, was that it made sections 3 and 4 more congruent through the linking word *damages*. Was this a studied generality or simply a by-product of the fact that in tort law, damages is the usual remedy? Neither the 1930 Act nor its predecessor used the words 'tort' or 'tortfeasor' and it would seem that the phrase 'where damages have been caused or contributed to by the fault or neglect of two or more persons' (section 3) as well as the phrase 'in any action for damages which is founded upon the fault or negligence of the defendant' (section 4) should cover a range of actions, including those for intentional torts, breaches of contract and statutory causes of action that provide damages as a remedy. But courts were reluctant to take such an expansive view of the legislation, and tended to restrict it to torts or even solely to negligence, perhaps influenced by the Act's title. I will return to this theme later.

An ambiguity that remained in section 3 was whether one who is only vicariously liable for another could be, with that other, the 'two or more persons' required by section 3. This was resolved in *Ponsford v McNeill*,[80] in which the plaintiff-patient alleged malpractice in the administration of x-rays. The defendants were a doctor and hospital, and the hospital had served a third-party notice on the doctor claiming indemnity from him based on his having acted as the hospital's servant. The doctor applied to set aside the notice on the contention that the indemnity right in section 3 of the Act covered the situation. The master who heard the application disagreed, noting that if the trial judge were to find the doctor negligent but not the hospital, the court would lack jurisdiction under the Act to give indemnity over the doctor because only one person was at fault. This decision was upheld by Kerwin J,[81] who noted that the reasoning also applied in cases of statutory vicarious liability, such as that of a vehicle owner for the vehicle driver's negligence. In other words, a person who is liable *solely* on a vicarious basis is not one who has 'caused or contributed' to the plaintiff's damages; the person's share of liability becomes that of the defendant for

[78] The Negligence Act 1931, SO 1931, c 26, s 2. This was the sole amendment made.
[79] D Cheifetz, *Apportionment of Fault in Tort* (Aurora, Canada Law Book, 1981) 16.
[80] *Ponsford v McNeill* [1933] OWN 651 (HCJ).
[81] And later approved in another case, *Ellis v Conklin & Garrett Ltd* [1969] 2 OR 753 (CA).

whom the person is vicariously liable. This makes sense, since vicarious liability is premised on a particular legal relationship between defendants, not on the vicariously liable defendant's 'fault or neglect'. However, *Ponsford v McNeill*, and other cases like it, demonstrated certain problems and pitfalls in the Act's wording, some of which remain to this day.

A further problem with section 3 was with the phrase 'are found liable' in the clause 'where two or more persons *are found liable* they shall be jointly and severally liable'. A person may be at fault yet cannot be found liable for various reasons, including a statutory immunity (Canadian workers' compensation legislation, for example, exempts employers from tort liability to employees for workplace injuries); alternatively, a person may have once been potentially liable but can no longer be (for example, because of the passage of a limitation period), or liability may have been excluded under a contract. Does this mean that contribution and indemnity are unavailable in such cases?

The Supreme Court of Canada considered that question in *Macklin v Young*,[82] which originated in Ontario a few months after the new Act came into force. Fred Macklin was driving north between Brantford and Simcoe and coming out of a curve. James Young, accompanied by his wife Mary Young, was driving south on the same road. The cars collided, there were damages on each side, and a jury found the drivers equally negligent. Macklin was awarded indemnity against James Young for half of Mary Young's damages, and a key issue in the appeal was whether that was correct. At the time, neither a husband nor a wife could sue the other for a tort.[83] Thus, James could not be sued by Mary for damages caused by the accident, and therefore was not and could not be liable with Macklin to her. Therefore, while the Supreme Court upheld the trial judgment in all other respects, it struck out the indemnity award, affirming on this point the conclusion that the Ontario Court of Appeal had reached the year before in a similar case.[84]

The legislative response to this and other cases was a strange amalgam of statutory repair work, codification of the Supreme Court's decision, and insurance company pressure on another issue—that of the so-called 'guest' or 'gratuitous' passenger. In 1935, all of these were combined in a new section 3, this time with three subsections.[85]

Subsection 1 was identical to the previous section 3 except that it replaced 'where two or more persons *are found liable*' with the words 'except as provided by subsection 2, where two or more persons *are found at fault or negligent*'. This change addressed the argument that contribution was unavailable *merely* because a defendant hadn't been found liable or couldn't be found liable. Contribution could still be barred for other reasons, such as an express or implied contract between the parties or because of the operation of the new subsection 2.

Subsection 2 was linked to a section of the Highway Traffic Act, enacted at the same time,[86] putatively put in place to protect insurers from fraudulent claims by injured relatives. The section immunised a motor vehicle's owner or driver from liability to a 'guest' or 'gratuitous' passenger—that is, one getting a free ride. It also required the court to determine the degree of fault of the owner or driver, but stipulated that no contribution or

[82] *Macklin v Young* [1933] SCR 603, [1933] 4 DLR 209.
[83] Married Women's Property Act, RSO 1927, c 182, s 7.
[84] *McDonald v Adams* (1932) 41 OWN 145 (CA).
[85] The Negligence Amendment Act 1935, SO 1935, c 46.
[86] The Highway Traffic Act, RSO 1937, s 47(2), enacted by SO 1935, c 26, s 11.

indemnity would apply in respect of the passenger's damages arising from that fault. In most provinces with similar legislation, the passenger could still sue a driver who had been 'grossly' negligent or guilty of 'wilful and wanton misconduct', and contribution rights would still exist with respect to that type of negligence or conduct. But in the Ontario version, even this exception did not apply. Dean Wright later characterised these sections of the Highway Traffic Act and Negligence Act as 'two of the most vicious pieces of legislation which an active insurance lobby was able to foist on an unsuspecting public',[87] and expressed the hope that the desire to discourage fraud could 'surely be achieved without creating new areas of injustice'.[88]

Subsection 3 embodied the idea that it was unseemly for spouses to sue each other for any kind of negligence, whether gross or ungross. It stipulated that where one spouse was at fault for the other's injury or death, 'no damages, contribution or indemnity' could be recovered for the negligent spouse's share of the fault—though, as with subsection 2, the court was still required to determine that spouse's degree of fault. Thus, the subsection effectively affirmed or codified the result in *Macklin v Young*.[89]

And so a paying taxi passenger could sue the driver for negligence that was a cause of an accident in which she was injured; but if the same passenger was in a car driven by her spouse, she was barred from recovering against him under either subsection 2 or 3. In the name of avoiding marital discord from a lawsuit, wives (as most passenger spouses then were) had no access to their husbands' insurance policies. These subsections also created a kind of statutory identification: plaintiff-passenger with negligent driver, plaintiff-spouse with negligent spouse. The identification also included the negligent driver's or spouse's *contributory* negligence vis-a-vis a third-party defendant. Thus, even though our hypothetical spouse couldn't sue her husband-driver for negligence, she could sue the driver of a car with which he collided, and the Act required the court to calculate the negligent spouse's share of the damages so as to determine how much she could recover from the other driver, assuming he was negligent.

The Amended 1930 Ontario Act and the 1935 Uniform Act

While all these amendments were underway, the Nova Scotia Commissioners to the Uniform Law Conference had been tasked with reporting to the Conference on what the courts were doing with the provincial statutes then in effect, with a view to considering possible amendments to the UCNA. Their report was damning. They concluded that the relevant provincial courts and the Supreme Court of Canada had decided that the statutes didn't apply to cases of sequential negligence, 'in which one party had a later chance than the

[87] CA Wright, 'Case and Comment [on *Harrison v Toronto Motor Car and Krug*]' (1945) 23 *Canadian Bar Review* 344, 347. Wright taught at Osgoode Hall Law School from 1927, where he championed many reforms in legal education. When the Law Society of Upper Canada rejected his proposed reforms in 1949, Wright left Osgoode to become Dean at the University of Toronto, Faculty of Law. Along with a group of other professors, including later Chief Justice Bora Laskin, he shaped Canadian legal education into a professional law school model.

[88] Ibid.

[89] Above (n 82).

other of avoiding the accident and was therefore the Cause of it by his *ultimate negligence*'.[90] The Commissioners noted wide disappointment in this 'unwarranted enervation'[91] of the statutes and called for amendments to make it clear that the statutes applied to 'cases of *successive as well as concurrent negligence*'.[92] Even this language was problematic, for concurrence (Latin for 'running together') needn't refer to time, except insofar as both parties' negligent acts or omissions must precede the damage. Perhaps partly due to framing the problem in this way, and perhaps partly out of deference to the courts, the Commissioners scuppered their trenchant analysis with a bizarre remedy—one that tried to stamp out the practice of finding ultimate negligence or last clear chance while preserving the doctrine:

> What is required is an enactment which will nullify this *practice* of the Courts while still leaving intact the *doctrine* as to the inapplicability of the Acts to ultimate negligence ... Unless it appears to the judge ... that there is such an ample separation in point of time, place and other circumstances between the negligent acts of the parties that the jury ... could find that the plaintiff had a substantially later opportunity of averting the accident than the defendant[,] [the judge] should not allow any question as to the plaintiff's ultimate negligence to go to the jury at all.[93]

The proposed amendment was vetoed after responses from some eminent members of the Ontario and British Columbia legal profession.[94] The next year, in August 1935, the Conference compromised by adding section 5 of the Act, italicising it, and recommending that provinces 'may consider the advisability of embodying [it] in the uniform Act'.[95] The Commissioners also added a contribution section like Ontario's section 3, but without correcting for the 'found liable' phrase, as Ontario had earlier that year.

Let us now take another side-by-side view of the Ontario and Uniform Acts as they stood in the 1930s. In Table 2, I have used the version from the 1937 Revised Statutes of Ontario, which renumbered the sections (so that what I have been citing as sections 3 and 4 became sections 2 and 3) and made a few other housekeeping changes.

Faced with these two statutory models, most of the remaining common law jurisdictions adopted the simpler Uniform Act or a variation of it in the next few years.[96] However, three provinces—Alberta, New Brunswick and Nova Scotia—also enacted separate Tortfeasors Acts[97] based on the UK model that I will come to momentarily, and Manitoba enacted a single Act that combined the ideas behind both types of acts into one.[98] Among the things that these legislative efforts aimed to accomplish was a repeal of the judgment-and-release-bar rules—the subject of our last 'mischief' story.

[90] ULCC 1934, 53.
[91] Ibid, 54.
[92] Ibid.
[93] ULCC 1934, 59.
[94] FJ Hughes, Phelan, Cartwright and McTague (Ontario) and Maitland (British Columbia): ULCC 1935, 15.
[95] Ibid, 15 (quotation) and 31 (italicised section).
[96] In Alberta, The Contributory Negligence Act, SA 1937, c 18; in Prince Edward Island, The Contributory Negligence Act, SPEI 1938; in Saskatchewan, The Contributory Negligence Act 1944, SS 1944, c 23; in the Northwest Territories, Contributory Negligence Ordinance, ONWT 1950, c 17; in Newfoundland, The Contributory Negligence Act 1951, SN 1951, c 48; in Yukon Territory, Contributory Negligence Ordinance, OYT 1955, c 8.
[97] In Alberta, The Tort-Feasors Act, SA 1936, c 22; in New Brunswick, The Tort-Feasors Act, SNB 1942, c 57; in Nova Scotia, The Tort-Feasors Act, SNS 1945, c 19.
[98] The Tortfeasors and Contributory Negligence Act, SM 1939, c 75.

Table 2: Side-by-Side Comparison of 1937 Ontario Act and 1935 Uniform Act

The Negligence Act, RSO 1937, c 115	The Uniform Contributory Negligence Act 1935[99]
1. In this Act, 'Action' shall include counterclaim; 'Defendant' shall include a plaintiff against whom a counterclaim is brought; 'Plaintiff' shall include a defendant who counterclaims. 2. (1) Where damages have been caused or contributed to by the fault or neglect of two or more persons the court shall determine the degree in which each of such persons is at fault or negligent, and, except as provided by subsections 2 and 3, where two or more persons are found at fault or negligent, they shall be jointly and severally liable to the person suffering loss or damage for such fault or negligence, but as between themselves, in the absence of any contract express or implied, each shall be liable to make contribution and indemnify each other in the degree in which they are respectively found to be at fault or negligent. (2) In any action brought for any loss or damage resulting from bodily injury to, or the death of any person being carried in, or upon, or entering, or getting on to, or alighting from a motor vehicle other than a vehicle operated in the business of carrying passengers for compensation, and the owner or driver of the motor vehicle which the injured or deceased person was being carried in, or upon or entering, or getting on to, or alighting from is one of the persons found to be at fault or negligent, no damages, contribution or indemnity shall be recoverable for the portion of the loss or damage caused by the fault or negligence of such owner or driver, and the portion of the loss or damage so caused by the fault or negligence of such owner or driver shall be determined although such owner or driver is not a party to the action.	1. This Act may be cited as *The* Contributory Negligence Act. 2. Where by the fault of two or more persons damage or loss is caused to one or more of them, the liability to make good the damage or loss shall be in proportion to the degree in which each person was at fault. Provided that: (a) If, having regard to all the circumstances of the case, it is not possible to establish different degrees of fault, the liability shall be apportioned equally, and (b) Nothing in this section shall operate so as to render any person liable for any loss or damage to which his fault has not contributed. 3. Where damages have been caused by the fault of two or more persons, the court shall determine the degree in which each was at fault, and where two or more persons are found liable they shall be jointly and severally liable for the fault to the person suffering loss or damage, but as between themselves in the absence of any contract express or implied, they shall be liable to make contribution to and indemnify each other in the degree in which they are respectively found to have been at fault. 4. In any action the amount of damage or loss, the fault, if any, and the degrees of fault shall be questions of fact.

(continued)

[99] ULCC 1935, 31–32.

Table 2: *(Continued)*

The Negligence Act, RSO 1937, c 115	**The Uniform Contributory Negligence Act 1935**
(3) In any action founded upon fault or negligence and brought for loss or damage resulting from bodily injury to, or the death of any married person[,] where one of the persons found to be at fault or negligent is the spouse of such married person, no damages, contribution or indemnity shall be recoverable for the portion of loss or damage caused by the fault or negligence of such spouse, and the portion of the loss or damage so caused by the fault or negligence of such spouse shall be determined although such spouse is not a party to the action. 3. In any action for damages which is founded upon the fault or negligence of the defendant[,] if fault or negligence is found on the part of the plaintiff which contributed to the damages, the court shall apportion the damages in proportion to the degree of fault or negligence found against the parties respectively. 4. If it is not practicable to determine the respective degree of fault or negligence as between any parties to an action, such parties shall be deemed to be equally at fault or negligent. 5. Wherever it appears that any person not already a party to an action is or may be wholly or partly responsible for the damages claimed, such person may be added as a party defendant upon such terms as may be deemed just. 6. In any action tried with a jury, the degree of fault or negligence of the respective parties shall be a question of fact for the jury. 7. Where the damages are occasioned by the fault or negligence of more than one party, the court shall have power to direct that the plaintiff shall bear some portion of the costs if the circumstances render this just.	5. *The Judge shall not submit to the jury any question as to whether notwithstanding the fault of one party, the other could have avoided the consequences thereof unless in his opinion there is evidence upon which the jury could reasonably find that the act or omission of the latter was clearly subsequent to and severable from the act or omission of the former so as not to be substantially contemporaneous with it.* 6. When it appears that person not a party to an action is or may be wholly or partly responsible for the damages claimed, he may be added as a party defendant upon such terms as are deemed just. 7. This Act shall be so interpreted and construed as to effect its general purpose of making uniform the law of those provinces which enact it.

The Judgment-and-Release-Bar Rules: Common Law Bars to Common Sense Outcomes

One of the common law distinctions between joint tortfeasors and several concurrent tortfeasors was procedural: a plaintiff had to sue all joint tortfeasors in the same action, whereas if the tortfeasors were concurrent but several, the plaintiff had to sue them separately. Even the first part of this statement is not quite correct, because, by ancient precedent,[100] joinder was merely permissive rather than compulsory, so that joint tortfeasors could be sued severally in separate actions for the entire damages. But there was a consequence to such a choice: on the act-of-one-is-the-act-of-all theory, a judgment against any one joint tortfeasor discharged all the others, thereby barring any subsequent action, or even continuance of the same action. As the theory went, the cause of action 'merged' in the judgment,[101] and the judgment-bar rule thus also came to be known as the 'merger rule'.

This rule applied even where the first tortfeasor hadn't satisfied the judgment, sometimes working a clear injustice. It came up for review by the Court of Exchequer Chamber in *Brinsmead v Harrison*,[102] a case masterfully summarised by Chief Baron Kelly as being about 'the wrongful detention of a pianoforte'.[103] Brinsmead had pleaded this musical wrong as the joint act of Harrison and Thompson, and had got judgment against Thompson. Unsuccessful in executing the judgment against Thompson, Brinsmead made a pitch to sue Harrison. Despite a lucid and well-researched brief by Brinsmead's counsel—even citing US case law contrary to the English position—the Court's five members[104] were unmoved. Alluding to floodgates fears and compelling authority since the time of James I, the Court blocked Brinsmead from suing Harrison.

On the same indivisibility theory, courts also held that a release of one joint tortfeasor released all. Thus in *Cocke v Jennor*,[105] an early trespass case, Jennor boldly pleaded in defence that, yes, he had broken into Cocke's house and beaten him, but had done so jointly with one Milborne, who had since settled with Cocke and released him in writing. The Court acknowledged that the commission of a joint tort meant that the plaintiff could sue Jennor and Milborne jointly or severally, but concluded that 'when he hath taken one satisfaction, he can take no more'.[106] The result appears to have been reached, somewhat laconically, by analogy to cases involving the discharge of a debt.

As with the judgment-bar rule, the release-bar rule made sense if the release had been given in exchange for full satisfaction of a claim, else the plaintiff could get double, or at least additional, recovery. But the rule could be unjust if the plaintiff had recovered only part of the loss by executing the release. Lawyers wishing to effect a partial settlement soon learned that they could surmount this problem by casting the agreement as a 'covenant not to sue' instead of a release, or by expressly retaining a reservation of rights against other

[100] (1302) 30 and 31 Edward 1, RS 107 (*De Bodreugam v Le Arcedekne*).
[101] *King v Hoare* (1844) 13 M&W 494, 153 ER 206 (Ex) 211.
[102] *Brinsmead v Harrison* (1872) LR 7 CP 547 (Ex Ch).
[103] Ibid, 551.
[104] Kelly CB, Blackburn J, Mellor J, Cleasy B and Lush J.
[105] *Cocke v Jennor* (1614) Hob 66, 80 ER 214 (KB).
[106] Ibid, ER 215.

parties. Thus, where a plaintiff's solicitor received a cheque from one of two defendants in 'full discharge of your personal liability' in connection with a theatrical performance, but added that the settlement was 'without prejudice to my client's claim against [the other defendant]',[107] the letter was interpreted not to operate as a release. The case may be contrasted with a libel claim regarding a letter to the editor published in a newspaper, in which the plaintiff's solicitor had promised that his client would, on payment of a sum of money and publication of an apology, 'release from any further liability [the officers and editor of the newspaper]',[108] but without saying anything about the letter writer. Salmon J commented that the difference between a release and an agreement not to sue was 'highly technical' and 'might be reconsidered with advantage',[109] but felt that on the law as it was, there had been no reservation of rights. Thus, the plaintiff was held to have released both the newspaper and the letter writer.

The 1935 Tortfeasors Act (UK) and Canadian Counterparts

Neither the judgment-bar rule nor the release-bar rule applied to several tortfeasors. A plaintiff who got judgment or granted a release in relation to one several (ie, independent) tortfeasor could still pursue the others. The law needed to be reformed so that plaintiffs could have the same benefit with respect to joint tortfeasors; and this had to be done in such a way as to address the prospect of multiple actions and recoveries, these being the underlying concerns that animated the judgment-and-release-bar rules. The first body to take up the reform call was the Law Revision Committee in the UK, appointed by Lord Chancellor Viscount Sankey in 1934, but chiefly guided in its work by Claud Schuster, the Permanent Secretary.[110] This Committee looked at both contributory negligence and contribution among tortfeasors, and the first result of its labours was the Law Reform (Married Women and Tortfeasors) Act 1935.[111] The Act's curious title—I will refer to it as the 1935 Tortfeasors Act—reflected the fact that it dealt with rights of married women (including their capacity to sue or be sued in tort or otherwise), with contribution among tortfeasors, and with the judgment-bar rule.

Section 6 of that Act stipulated three things, viz: (i) judgment recovered against a tortfeasor did not bar an action against another person 'who would, if sued, have been liable as a joint tort-feasor in respect of the same damage'; (ii) if more than one action was brought in respect of the same damage, the total recovery was limited to 'the amount of the damages awarded by the judgment first given' and the plaintiff was denied costs in a subsequent action unless the court was satisfied that there were reasonable grounds for bringing it; and (iii) a tortfeasor liable in respect of the damage could recover contribution

[107] *Duck v Mayeu* [1892] 2 QB 511 (CA) 512.
[108] *Cutler v McPhail* [1962] 2 QB 292, [1962] 2 WLR 1135, [1962] 2 All ER 474 (QB), QB 294.
[109] QB (n 108) 298.
[110] Steele (n 37) 159, 167.
[111] Law Reform (Married Women and Tortfeasors) Act 1935 (UK) 25 and 26 Geo 5, c 30 (1935 Tortfeasors Act).

from 'any other tort-feasor who is, or would if sued have been, liable in respect of the same damage'. Pursuant to section 6(2), the amount recoverable in contribution proceedings was to be 'such as may be found by the court to be just and equitable having regard to the extent of [the contributing person's] responsibility for damage', and could range from complete liability to a complete exemption. Section 6, which I have simplified here for the purposes of concision, crossed the Atlantic and was adopted in Alberta, Manitoba, New Brunswick and Nova Scotia,[112] as well as in other Commonwealth jurisdictions. Unfortunately, these enactments—I will refer to them as Tortfeasors Acts—addressed only the judgment-bar rule, which meant that, for the time being, the release-bar rule remained intact.

The 1945 Contributory Negligence Act (UK)

In 1945, the second major component of the UK Law Revision Committee's work in this area bore fruit in the Law Reform (Contributory Negligence) Act 1945,[113] which I will refer to as the 1945 Contributory Negligence Act. The Committee had the benefit of seeing how Canadian courts, particularly Ontario ones, had interpreted the provincial statutes, and took that into account in its drafting. For example, the Committee adopted the concept of calculating a claimant's entitlement by first reducing the damages by that person's share of fault. That approach had not been clear in the original provisions of either the Ontario Act or the Uniform Act, which had been modelled on the admiralty law assumption that each ship in a two-ship collision would be damaged, and that the total loss would be divided evenly among the parties. Judges had to use that language but apply it to a very different context. The UK approach differed from the Canadian approach in another way: while the court was to calculate the claimant's share of fault, it need only 'have regard' to it when reducing the damages based on what seemed 'just and equitable'. The key part of section 1 read as follows:

> Where any person suffers damage as the result partly of his own fault and partly of the fault of any other person or persons, a claim in respect of that damage shall not be defeated by reason of the fault of the person suffering the damage, but the damages recoverable in respect thereof shall be reduced to such extent as the court thinks just and equitable having regard to the claimant's share in the responsibility of the damage.

The 1945 Contributory Negligence Act also incorporated by reference section 6 of the 1935 Tortfeasors Act, and in section 4, defined 'fault' to mean 'negligence, breach of statutory duty or other act or omission which gives rise to a liability in tort or would, apart from this Act, give rise to the defence of contributory negligence'. The 1945 Act also had sections on its relationship with other legislation dealing with such things as workers' compensation, fatal accidents, and air and marine transport. Except for a few amendments, mostly dealing with linkages to other Acts, the 1945 Act continues in force to this day.

[112] The Tort-Feasors Act, SA 1936, c 22, s 2; The Tortfeasors and Contributory Negligence Act, SM 1939, c 75, s 3; The Tort-Feasors Act, SNB 1942, c 57, ss 2–3; The Tort-Feasors Act, SNS 1945, c 19, ss 2–3.

[113] Law Reform (Contributory Negligence) Act 1945 (UK) 8 and 9 Geo 6, c 28 (1945 Contributory Negligence Act).

Contribution After Settlement: The 1948 Amendment to the Ontario Act

Section 2 of the Act, since renumbered as section 1,[114] requires the court to determine degrees of 'fault or neglect' and refers to two or more persons being 'found at fault or negligent'. It seems that this language may have caused risk-averse insurers and others to hold off on settlements until courts had made the relevant determinations and findings, lest their rights to seek contribution after settlement be found to be non-existent.[115] This possibility was addressed in a 1948 amendment to the Ontario Act. Initially enacted as section 2a[116] and renumbered in the next statute revision as section 3,[117] the amendment is now found, unaltered in wording, in section 2:[118]

> A tort feasor may recover contribution or indemnity from any other tort feasor who is, or would if sued have been, liable in respect of the damage to any person suffering damage as a result of a tort by settling with the person suffering such damage, and thereafter commencing or continuing action against such other tort feasor, in which event the tort feasor settling the damage shall satisfy the court that the amount of the settlement was reasonable, and in the event that the court finds the amount of the settlement was excessive it may fix the amount at which the claim should have been settled.

Another provision, added as section 8[119] and renumbered in the next statute revision as section 9,[120] extended the limitation period for bringing a contribution claim in a very particular circumstance:

> Where an action is commenced against a tort feasor or where a tort feasor settles with a person who has suffered damage as a result of a tort, within the period of limitation prescribed for the commencement of actions by any relevant statute, no proceedings for contribution or indemnity against any other tort feasor shall be defeated by the operation of any statute limiting the time for the commencement of the action against such tort feasor provided:
>
> (a) such proceedings are commenced within one year of the date of the judgment in the action or the settlement, as the case may be; and
> (b) there has been compliance with any statute requiring notice of claim against such tort feasor.

114 1948 Amendment to the Ontario Act, RSO 1990, c N1.

115 There is little information on the public record about the reasons for the amendment that follows. It was introduced as part of Bill 141 by Attorney General Leslie Blackwell on first reading (6 April 1948); passed second reading (9 April 1948) without debate; was approved in committee without amendment (12 April 1948), passed third reading, also without debate (April 16, 1948), and was assented to the same day (16 April 1948). Bill 141, An Act to Amend the Negligence Act, 4th Sess, 22nd Leg, Ontario, 1948, 688 (first reading) 906 (second reading) 944 (Committee) 1240 (third reading) 1249 (Royal Assent). There was no introductory speech on the Bill's purpose, but an explanatory note says: 'The new section 2*a* permits one of two joint tort feasors to settle with an injured person and then recover contribution and indemnity against the other joint tort feasor'. In fact, the word 'joint' inadequately reflects the purpose of this section, which was clearly intended to cover what would come to be referred to as several concurrent tortfeasors.

116 The Negligence Amendment Act 1948, SO 1948, c 61, s 1.

117 RSO 1950, c 252.

118 RSO 1990, c N 1.

119 The Negligence Amendment Act (n 116), s 1.

120 RSO 1950, c 252.

The particular circumstance addressed here is one in which a plaintiff sues or settles with one tortfeasor, but at a time when the plaintiff's limitation period for suing another tortfeasor has expired. The idea is that the second tortfeasor's right to seek contribution from the first shouldn't be destroyed by the plaintiff's decision of when to sue the first. Section 8 addresses this by giving the first tortfeasor a year from the settlement or judgment to bring contribution proceedings; if the tortfeasor does this and complies with any notice requirements, the second tortfeasor can't defeat the contribution claim merely by saying 'you settled (or were adjudged liable) after the plaintiff's time to sue me had expired'. Apart from this particular circumstance, section 8 was silent on the limitation period for bringing a contribution claim, an aspect of the law that would not be addressed until much later.[121]

The intent of these sections was laudable and accords with the value that society places on settlement. But the laudable intent was coupled with much linguistic awkwardness, like a teenager experimenting with new phrases. One problem was that a contribution right cannot arise merely out of liability or the likelihood of being held liable: it is contingent on the one seeking contribution having made a payment to the plaintiff, whether as a result of a judgment or a settlement. The same principle applies in surety law, where an action for recovery of money from co-sureties arises only when the surety pays more than his share.[122]

Another problem was with the use of the words 'tort' and 'tort feasor' (now 'tortfeasor') for the first time. While tort law was already implicit in the Act, making the reference explicit fettered the ability to expand the Act's scope—for example, to breaches of contract, trust or fiduciary duty. And the Ontario courts were soon troubled over the term 'tort feasor' for another reason. If an alleged tortfeasor settled and was later found not to have been legally at fault, did that preclude seeking contribution from one who actually was at fault?

This issue arose in the early 1950s in *Marschler v G Masser's Garage*.[123] Marschler was driving his truck downhill south of Toronto's St Clair Avenue during a slight drizzle when the truck suddenly slipped to the left and into the path of a car driving uphill. Because Marschler's car was on the wrong side of the road and there was no fault on the part of the northbound driver, Marschler's insurer settled with the injured parties. On further investigation, the insurer concluded that the accident was caused by the mechanic who had

[121] An explanatory note to this section in Bill 141 (n 115) reads as follows: 'An example of the situation sought to be taken care of by this amendment would be as follows:

Under section 480 of The Municipal Act an action against a municipality for the non-repair of a highway must be brought within three months after the time when the damages were sustained. If the driver of a car brings action within the three-month period for damages sustained on a highway against the driver of a second car but does not serve the writ until after the expiration of the three-month period, the driver of the second car would be precluded from proceeding against the municipal corporation because of the lapse of the three-month period. Under the amendment, the driver of the second car would not be so precluded provided he had anticipated the bringing of the action and had served the municipality with the notice in writing of his intention to make a claim as required by the statute.

The same principle applies where the driver of the second car settles with the driver of the first car and then seeks contribution or indemnity from the municipal corporation.

The proceedings against the municipality must be commenced within a year of the judgment of settlement as the case may be.

The new section is, of course, not limited to motor vehicle accidents or municipal corporations but the example serves to illustrate the nature and principle of the amendment'.

[122] See *Hawrish v Peters* [1982] 1 SCR 1083, [1982] 5 WWR 659, 137 DLR (3d) 709. The Court notes, though, that a 'declaratory action *in futuro*' might be possible, with the surety getting a declaration as to his contribution or indemnity rights that would arise upon him making a payment beyond his share.

[123] *Marschler v G Masser's Garage* (1956) 2 DLR (2d) 484, [1956] OR 328 (HC) (*Marschler*).

serviced Marschler's truck. The evidence suggested that he failed to repair the truck's brakes properly, which caused them to malfunction when Marschler stepped on them while going down the hill. The insurer brought a subrogated contribution claim against the garage, and succeeded in proving that the mechanic's negligence was indeed the cause of the accident. Then, one of the main points of contention became whether Marschler could rely on the 1948 amendment because he was not, and could not be, found to have been a 'tort feasor'. According to LeBel J:

> The words 'tort feasor' are troublesome ... and their introduction [into the Negligence Act] is rather puzzling, since the unpopular rule of the common law against contribution between joint tort feasors had been ended by the passage of the Negligence Act without mention of the word. It is possible that the adoption of the word here was influenced by the enactment in England of [the 1935 Tortfeasors Act], as counsel seemed to think. In any event, I trust I do no violence to s 3 [now s 2] when I say that the precise and technical meaning [of tort feasor] should be passed over.
>
> In my view the words 'tort feasor' ... refer not to a person who is held liable or admits liability at a trial, but to a person who impliedly assumes or admits liability when he enters into a settlement. In other words, the important time is the time of the settlement, not the time of the delivery of a judgment. A person does not pay anything in settlement of a claim or of an action unless he feels he is liable or may be held liable in some degree, and in my opinion when he settles he becomes a 'tort feasor' within the meaning of the section ... To conclude otherwise would be to defeat the object of the legislation.[124]

As Cheifetz points out, the result is that section 3 (now section 2) differs from section 2 (now section 1) insofar as section 2 requires actual liability of the person seeking contribution (the 'contribution claimant'), whereas section 3 'does not require even potential liability on the part of the [contribution] claimant to the injured person'.[125] Apart from this, the sections are partly duplicative; they both aim at achieving restitution between actual or alleged wrongdoers. This duplication is not surprising given the approach taken to amending the Act—that is, borrowing from other legislation rather than redrafting the statutory language in a way that would integrate the two possibilities. The phrase 'would, if sued, have been liable' was also problematic, as was its relation to section 8. Scenarios arise in which a person would, if sued, have been liable at *some* point, but has since become immune from liability. For example, different limitation periods might apply to different tortfeasors, as noted above. Despite the problems with the statutory language, the 1948 amendments were adopted in Saskatchewan in 1957[126] and in Nova Scotia in 1961,[127] evidently on the basis that the courts had worked out the issues through judicial construction.[128]

[124] Ibid, DLR 490. Similar conclusions had been reached in *Nesbitt v Beattie* [1955] OR 111 (CA), [1955] 2 DLR 91, and LeBel J applied the reasoning in that case. However, the *Marschler* analysis, particularly of the statutory language, is deeper, and thus it is this case that tends to be cited more than *Nesbitt v Beattie.*

[125] Cheifetz, *Apportionment of Fault in Tort* (n 79) 148.

[126] An Act to amend The Contributory Negligence Act, SS 1957, c 30 (adding s 10).

[127] An Act to Amend The Tort-Feasors Act, SNS 1961, c 49 (adding s 3(2)).

[128] See, eg, Saskatchewan, Legislative Assembly, *Debates and Proceedings*, 13th Leg, First Sess, vol 7 (22 February 1957) 35 (second reading, Hon RA Walker) (expressing a preference for judicially tested wording).

Glanville Williams Writes an Opus

A major contribution to the field in this period was Glanville Williams's *Joint Torts and Contributory Negligence*.[129] It is hard to overstate the importance of this work, which followed closely on the heels of his related treatise, *Joint Obligations*.[130] It surveyed the legislation and case law of Great Britain, Northern Ireland, other common law countries in the British Commonwealth, and the Republic of Ireland. Williams paid particular attention to Canadian case law, which he characterised as 'a rich mine on the subject of apportionment of fault'.[131] He also noted, though, that despite the judicial guidance, there were 'many dark places in this part of the law' which he tried to 'illumine for the reader by arguments drawn from principle and convenience'.[132] Williams clarified and imparted much of the terminology in this area—his section on the distinction between joint and several wrongs, for example, as well as his explanations of joint and several liability and his terms 'concurrent fault' and 'several concurrent wrongdoers' continue to be used and cited to this day. And the appendix to his book, which set out a form of model legislation, inspired the Irish Civil Liability Act 1961 a decade later; many years later it also influenced the final form of the Uniform Act and a draft statute prepared by the Ontario Law Reform Commission.[133]

The 1953 Uniform Act

However, after the 1935 version of the Uniform Act was adopted, the Conference's work on it went into limbo. The inattention may have been partly due to the Second World War and partly to the fact that the Act was just getting taken up by most of the common law provinces at this time. By the early 1950s, work resumed but was preoccupied with drafting guest passenger and spousal provisions like those in the Ontario Act[134] and with considering problems such as the difficulty of distinguishing ordinary and gross negligence of drivers.[135] Remarkably, of the 1935 Tortfeasors Act and its Canadian counterparts there is virtually no mention in the Conference proceedings during this period.

Thus, in the version of the Uniform Act adopted in 1953,[136] the changes were modest in terms of either reform or harmonisation. The first of these, and the most important in terms of a revived effort to abolish last clear chance, was to get rid of the italicised

[129] GL Williams, *Joint Torts and Contributory Negligence: A Study of Concurrent Fault in Great Britain, Ireland and the Common-Law Dominions* (London, Stevens & Sons, 1951).

[130] GL Williams, *Joint Obligations* (London, Butterworths, 1949).

[131] Williams, *Joint Torts and Contributory Negligence* (n 129) v.

[132] Ibid.

[133] Williams later became known for his work in the area of criminal law reform. For a dedication to his career in this and other areas of the law, see RY Jennings, 'Glanville' in PR Glazebrook (ed), *Reshaping the Criminal Law: Essays in Honour of Glanville Williams* (London, Stevens & Sons, 1978) 1.

[134] ULCC 1950, 22–23; ULCC 1951, 24.

[135] ULCC 1952, 38–41.

[136] ULCC 1953, 76–77.

section 5 (see the 1935 version in Table 2).[137] This was done in 1953, and by 2000 (things move ponderously in this area of law reform), British Columbia, Prince Edward Island and Alberta had followed suit, enacting amendments that clearly abolished the 'last clear chance' rule.[138] The second change was the retrogressive move of adding guest passenger and spousal provisions (by now, numbered sections 4 and 5) like the Ontario ones. The third change was to add a section allowing for addition of both party defendants and third parties on such terms as the court deemed just (section 7). This followed an amendment that Ontario had made to its section 5 in 1939 to include third parties.[139] The final change was to add a section dealing with costs (section 8). It followed Ontario's section 7, which gave the court power to charge a portion of the costs to the plaintiff 'if the circumstances render this just'. Williams saw this as a 'platitudinous proposition',[140] given that courts have always had discretion over costs. In contrast, Saskatchewan had enacted a costs provision four years earlier that presumptively ('unless the judge otherwise directs') made 'liability for costs of the parties to every action … in the same proportion as their respective liability to make good the damage or loss' and provided for a set-off where one award exceeded the other.[141] Williams, on the other hand, had advocated that calculating costs in proportion to degrees of fault be reserved for situations in which there is both a claim and counterclaim; otherwise, he had suggested that the normal costs rules should apply.[142] Evidently, the Conference's focus at the time was on Ontario; no consideration, for example, seems to have been given to either the Saskatchewan provision or the Williams approach.

This changed after the 1953 Uniform Act was adopted. The Conference maintained a watching brief on it and on the interpretation of apportionment legislation, including spousal identification cases,[143] retrospectivity of amendments,[144] patterns for awarding costs,[145] operation of the judgment-and release-bar rules,[146] various encounters with 'last clear chance;'[147] and even the potential for a Uniform Tortfeasors Act.[148] By the mid-1970s, calls for further reform had become increasingly frequent, not only among the Uniform Law Commissioners, but in Ontario too. I now turn to that period.

[137] ULCC 1953, 76 (removing s 5 and replacing it with a provision relating to spousal fault).

[138] Contributory Negligence (Amendment) Act, SBC 1970, c 9, s 2 (now Negligence Act, RSBC 1996, c 333, s 8, headed 'Further application'); Contributory Negligence Act, SPEI 1978, c 3 (repealing and replacing previous statute and, in s 4, adding provision headed 'Last clear chance abolished'); Justice Statutes Amendment Act, RSA 2000, c 16 (Supp) s 70 (repealing and replacing ss 5 and 6—by then, renumbered to ss 4 and 5—with s 3.1, headed 'Last clear chance rule not applicable').

[139] The Statute Law Amendment Act 1939, SO 1939, c 47, s 23 (inserting after the word 'defendant' in s 5 the words 'or may be made a third party to the action').

[140] Williams, *Joint Torts and Contributory Negligence* (n 129) 494.

[141] An Act to Amend The Contributory Negligence Act 1944, SS 1949, c 32, s 1.

[142] Williams, *Joint Torts and Contributory Negligence* (n 129) ch 21.

[143] ULCC 1954, 130–132.

[144] ULCC 1956, 50–52.

[145] ULCC 1957, 51.

[146] ULCC 1965, 77–80; ULCC 1966, 53–57.

[147] ULCC 1967, 68–73; ULCC 1969, 144–50.

[148] ULCC 1967, 76–82, 85–86.

From 1975 to 1984: A Fertile Period for Reform Initiatives

In 1975, Ontario declared that married people had legal personalities that were 'independent, separate and distinct'[149] from each other. Manitoba had taken the lead on this reform in 1973. Along with the reform came certain things, such as spouses acquiring the 'like right of action in tort against each other as if they were not married'[150] and the repeal of section 2(4) of the Ontario Act—the provision that identified one spouse with another spouse's fault.[151] The next to be repealed were the guest passenger provisions. They had already been amended in 1966 to accord with the 'gross negligence' exception elsewhere—meaning that a guest passenger injured in part because of her driver's fault could only hope that the driver would be found not merely contributorily negligent, but grossly so, so that she could recover under the insurance policy. In 1977, legislators finally saw the incongruousness—Dean Wright called it 'viciousness'[152]—of this limit on recovery, and repealed both section 2(2) and 2(3) of the Ontario Act and the related traffic legislation.[153] All these changes reduced the length of the statute, making it once again comparable in brevity to the Uniform Act.

To keep track of everything and have a reference point for the discussion of what happened next, let's take another side-by-side snapshot of our two Acts. This is set out in Table 3. For the Ontario Act, I am using the version from the 1980 Revised Statutes of Ontario;[154] for the Uniform Act, the 1953 version, still 'in effect' in 1980 in the sense that no changes had been made to it by that time.

Despite the injustices they had caused, the spousal and guest passenger provisions were useful in showing how a statutory immunity fits within a regime based on apportionment and contribution. This came up in *DiCarlo v DiSimone*,[155] a case of first impression under the Workmen's Compensation Act.[156] After a car accident, DiCarlo had sued: (i) DiSimone, a fellow employee and driver of the car in which he was a passenger; (ii) Street Construction, their common employer; and (iii) the Watsons, driver and owner of the other car in the accident. Street Construction got a ruling from the Workmen's Compensation Board

[149] Family Law Reform Act 1975, SO 1975, c 41, s 1.

[150] Ibid, s 3(a).

[151] Ibid, s 7.

[152] See Wright, 'Case and Comment' (n 87) and accompanying text.

[153] The Negligence Amendment Act 1977, SO 1977, c 59, s 1 and The Highway Traffic Amendment Act 1977 (no 3) SO 1977, c 54, s 16(1).

[154] The 1980 version also reflects some changes in drafting conventions, such as revising instances of the future tense ('shall be') to the present ('is' or 'are'). The extent to which such changes were implemented seems somewhat arbitrary: like many statutes, and in contrast to civilian drafting practice, the Act is still not drafted so as to fully read as though it is 'always speaking'. See, eg, D Elliott, 'Using Plain English in Statutes' (1992) 26 *Clarity* 14, 20 (part of *Clarity's* 1992 submission to the Hansard Society Commission on the Legislative Process, the whole submission being available at davidelliott.ca).

[155] *DiCarlo v DiSimone* (1982) 140 DLR (3d) 477, 39 OR (2d) 445 (HCJ).

[156] The Workmen's Compensation Act, RSO 1980, c 539 (now Workplace Safety and Insurance Act 1997, SO 1997, c 16, Sch A).

Table 3: Side-by-Side Comparison of 1980 Ontario Act and 1953 Uniform Act

The Negligence Act, RSO 1980, c 315	**The Uniform Contributory Negligence Act 1935[157]**
1. In this Act, (a) 'action' includes a counterclaim; (b) 'defendant' includes a plaintiff against whom a counterclaim is brought; (c) 'plaintiff' includes a defendant who counterclaims. 2. Where damages have been caused or contributed to by the fault or neglect of two or more persons, the court shall determine the degree in which each of such persons is at fault or negligent, and, where two or more persons are found at fault or negligent, they are jointly and severally liable to the person suffering loss or damage for such fault or negligence, but as between themselves, in the absence of any contract express or implied, each is liable to make contribution and indemnify each other in the degree in which they are respectively found to be at fault or negligent. 3. A tort feasor may recover contribution or indemnity from any other tort feasor who is, or would if sued have been, liable in respect of the damage to any person suffering damage as a result of a tort by settling with the person suffering such damage, and thereafter commencing or continuing action against such other tort feasor, in which event the tort feasor settling the damage shall satisfy the court that the amount of the settlement was reasonable, and in the event that the court finds the amount of the settlement was excessive it may fix the amount at which the claim should have been settled. 4. In any action for damages which is founded upon the fault or negligence of the defendant[,] if fault or negligence is found on the part of the plaintiff which contributed to the damages, the court shall apportion the damages in proportion to the degree of fault or negligence found against the parties respectively.	1. This Act may be cited as The Contributory Negligence Act. 2. (1) Where by the fault of two or more persons damage or loss is caused to one or more of them, the liability to make good the damage or loss is in proportion to the degree in which each person was at fault but if, having regard to all the circumstances of the case, it is not possible to establish different degrees of fault, the liability shall be apportioned equally. (2) Nothing in this section operates so as to render any person liable for any loss or damage to which his fault has not contributed. 3. (1) Where damages have been caused by the fault of two or more persons, the Court shall determine the degree in which each was at fault. (2) Except as provided in sections 4 and 5, where two or more persons are found at fault they are jointly and severally liable to the person suffering the damage or loss, but as between themselves in the absence of any contract express or implied, they shall be liable to make contribution to and indemnify each other in the degree in which they are respectively found to have been at fault. 4. Where no cause of action exists against the owner or driver of a motor vehicle by reason of section … of the … Act, no damages, contribution or indemnity is recoverable from any person for the portion of the damage or loss caused by the fault of such owner or driver and the portion of the damage or loss caused by the fault of such owner or driver shall be determined although such owner or driver is not a party to the action.

(continued)

[157] ULCC 1953, 76–77.

Table 3: ***(Continued)***

The Negligence Act, RSO 1980, c 315	**The Uniform Contributory Negligence Act 1935**
5. If it is not practicable to determine the respective degree of fault or negligence as between any parties to an action, such parties shall be deemed to be equally at fault or negligent. 6. Wherever it appears that any person not already a party to an action is or may be wholly or partly responsible for the damages claimed, such person may be added as a party defendant to the action upon such terms as are considered just or may be made a third party to the action in the manner prescribed by the rules of practice for adding third parties. 7. In any action tried with a jury, the degree of fault or negligence of the respective parties shall be a question of fact for the jury. 8. Where the damages are occasioned by the fault or negligence of more than one party, the court shall have power to direct that the plaintiff shall bear some portion of the costs if the circumstances render this just. 9. Where an action is commenced against a tort feasor or where a tort feasor settles with a person who has suffered damage as a result of a tort, within the period of limitation prescribed for the commencement of actions by any relevant statute, no proceedings for contribution or indemnity against any other tort feasor are defeated by the operation of any statute limiting the time for the commencement of the action against such tort feasor provided, (a) such proceedings are commenced within one year of the date of the judgment in the action or the settlement, as the case may be; and (b) there has been compliance with any statute requiring notice of claim against such tort feasor.	5. In an action founded upon fault and brought for damage or loss resulting from bodily injury to or the death of a married person, where one of the persons found to be at fault is the spouse of the married person, no damages, contribution or indemnity is recoverable for the portion of damage or loss caused by the fault of such spouse, and the portion of the damage or loss caused by the fault of such spouse shall be determined although the spouse is not a party to the action. 6. In every action the amount of damage or loss, the fault, if any, and the degrees of fault are questions of fact. 7. Whenever it appears that person not already a party to an action is or may be wholly or partly responsible for the damages claimed, such person may be added as a party defendant or may be made a third party to the action upon such terms as may be deemed just. 8. Where the damages are occasioned by the fault of more than one party, the court has power to direct that the plaintiff shall bear some portion of the costs if the circumstances render this just. 9. This Act shall be so interpreted and construed as to effect its general purpose of making uniform the law of those provinces that enact it.

that the accident had occurred in the course of employment and thus fell under the Board's compensation scheme rather than the jurisdiction of the courts. And so on a motion, the action was dismissed as against DiSimone and Street Construction. But DiCarlo also asked for another question to be decided, that being whether he could recover from the Watsons 'any of [his] damages in excess of the degree of negligence determined against [the Watsons] at trial'.[158] Justice Osler ruled that, having elected to sue the Watsons rather than claim under the statutory compensation regime, DiCarlo could only recover damages against the Watsons that were proportionate to their share of fault, even though the Workmen's Compensation Act also required the court to determine the employer's share of fault. In other words, the system operated just like the spousal and guest passenger provisions. Furthermore, this meant that the Watsons couldn't 'compel the employer to respond to litigation and to an assessment of damages made by a court in the guise of exercising a statutory right to contribution by reason of the Negligence Act', as the employer 'has, in a sense, already answered to the plaintiff for his injuries by virtue of its contribution to the accident and its inclusion as [a scheduled employer]'.[159]

In the same year that Ontario abolished the spousal and guest passenger provisions, change was afoot at the 1975 meeting of the Uniform Law Conference in Halifax. The Alberta Commissioners presented a report based on working papers of the Alberta Institute of Law Research and Reform and the English Law Commission. The first thing the Alberta Commissioners noted was that although the Uniform Act had abolished the common law rule that a *judgment* against one joint tortfeasor discharged another, it was silent on the rule that a *release* of one joint tortfeasor released another. Citing Wright, the Alberta Commissioners found it 'unfortunate, and somewhat strange, that neither the English Act nor the Canadian statutes contain any provision with respect to releases'.[160] The Alberta Commissioners thought it was time to abolish the distinctions between joint and several tortfeasors, and recommended a new Uniform Act that would do this by integrating the provisions in the Tortfeasors Acts and addressing the judgment rule at the same time.[161] It took time for the provinces to respond to this call, and when some of them did, they took a different approach from that suggested at the Conference. In 1984, Ontario enacted section 149 of the Courts of Justice Act 1984,[162] now found in section 139 of the current version of that statute:[163]

> **(1) Joint liability not affected by judgment or release**
> Where two or more persons are jointly liable in respect of the same cause of action, a judgment against or release of one of them does not preclude judgment against any other in the same or a separate proceeding.
>
> **(2) Two proceedings in respect of same damage**
> Where a person who has suffered damage brings two or more proceedings in respect of the damage, the person is not entitled to costs in any of the proceedings, except the first proceeding in which

[158] *DiCarlo v DiSimone* (n 156) DLR 478.
[159] Ibid, DLR 480.
[160] ULCC 1975, 66, citing C Wright, *Cases on Torts*, 4th edn (Toronto, Butterworths, 1967), 390.
[161] Ibid.
[162] Courts of Justice Act, SO 1984, c 11.
[163] Courts of Justice Act, RSO 1990, c C.43.

judgment is obtained, unless the court is of the opinion that there were reasonable grounds for bringing more than one proceeding.

The enactment thus addressed both the judgment and release bars to subsequent proceedings against jointly liable defendants, and did so in a more general way than by amending the apportionment and contribution statutes, which tended to be restricted to tort causes of action. Manitoba, Prince Edward Island and British Columbia took similar approaches.[164] In contrast, when Saskatchewan enacted a similar section, it did so in its apportionment statute,[165] meaning that the effect of the reform was limited to actions in negligence, because of the interpretation given to that statute in Saskatchewan.[166] Importantly, the phrase 'does not preclude' preserved the court's ability to bar a subsequent judgment for other reasons—the most obvious being *res judicata* or abuse of process—so it is as though the phrase reads 'does not, by itself, preclude'.[167]

All of this was salutary, but some problems remain. One is that section 139(1) speaks of joint liability for 'the same cause of action' while section 139(2) speaks of proceedings in respect of 'the damage'. More consistency might have been expected here; the Saskatchewan statute, for example, uses the phrase 'loss or damage' for both provisions.[168] This would seem desirable. One could imagine, for example, the same damage founding a cause of action against one person in negligence and another in nuisance. It is hard to see why the judgment-and-release-bar rules should apply in such a scenario but not when the causes of action are the same.[169] The reform also did not address payment into court by one defendant, which, if accepted by the plaintiff, discharges the others.[170] Such a rule may be fair where the payment is in full satisfaction of the claim, but may not be when it is only in partial satisfaction.[171] The 1984 amendment also did not address another aspect of the common law merger rule; namely, that there can be only a single judgment in respect of damages or debt for which two or more defendants are jointly liable. The inability to sever an award can give rise to issues within a single action, as when one defendant is liable for punitive damages but another is not,[172] or in subsequent actions, as when the defendant in

[164] In Manitoba, The Court of Queen's Bench Act, CCSM c 280, ss 95 and 96, enacted by SM 1988–89, c 4; in Prince Edward Island, Judicature Act, RSPEI 1988, c J-2.1, s 64, enacted by SPEI 2008, c 20, s 64 (the apportionment statute also has a section, predating this one, that addresses only the judgment-bar rule: Contributory Negligence Act, RSPEI 1988, c C-21, s 7). The language of the Ontario, Manitoba and PEI sections is almost identical. In British Columbia, the judgment-and-release-bar rules have been addressed with somewhat different language in the Law and Equity Act, RSBC 1996, ss 53(2) and 53(3), enacted by SBC 1976, c 33, s 94.

[165] The Contributory Negligence Act, RSS 1978, c C-31, s 7.1, enacted by SS 1992, C 24, s 4.

[166] See *Cherneskey v Armadale Publishers* (1974) 53 DLR (3d) 79, [1974] 6 WWR 162 (Sask CA).

[167] Compare Contributory Negligence Act, RSPEI 1988, c C-21, s 7 ('no action … shall be barred by reason only' of a judgment or release).

[168] The Contributory Negligence Act, RSS 1978, c C-31, s 7.1, ss (1) and (2).

[169] See *Cassimjee v Jarrett* (1975) 8 OR (2d) 726, 59 DLR (3d) 174 (HCJ) and *Consultoka Services Inc v Peat Marwick Ltd*, 2000 CarswellOnt 2631, [2000] OJ No 2736 (SCJ).

[170] *Reaney v National Trust Co* [1964] 1 OR 461, 42 DLR (2d) 703 (HCJ); *Cassimjee v Jarrett* (n 169). Fridman suggests that, based on these cases, the rule on accepting a payment into court, unlike the rule on executing a release, might also apply to several, not joint, tortfeasors. GHL Fridman, *The Law of Torts in Canada* (Toronto, Carswell, 2010) 863. However, *Lederer v Dunlop* (1985) 47 CPC 242, 49 OR (2d) 72 (HCJ) says that *Cassimjee v Jarrett* should be confined to cases of joint tortfeasors.

[171] *Lederer v Dunlop* (n 170) (refusing to apply the payment-into-court rule where the claim had not been fully satisfied by the plaintiffs' acceptance of the payment).

[172] See Cheifetz, *Apportionment of Fault in Tort* (n 79) 12–13 and the cases cited therein.

the first action had a defence unavailable to the defendant in the second one (for example, a contractual limit on liability).

The Alberta Commissioners also sought guidance from their fellow Commissioners on a number of issues. Many of these related to contribution, and I will now adopt some further terminology when referring to these issues. I will refer to the person experiencing loss or damage as 'the injured person'. I will also refer to 'concurrent wrongdoers', the term coined by Williams, and sometimes will simply shorten this to 'wrongdoers'. When discussing contribution between or among wrongdoers, I will refer to the one seeking contribution as the 'contribution claimant' and the one from whom contribution is being sought as the 'contribution defendant'. The literature often refers to these parties as D1 and D2 ('D' standing for *defendants*) or T1 and T2 ('T' standing for *tortfeasors*) and to the persons suffering loss or damage as P1 and P2 ('P' standing for *plaintiff*). More recently, W1 and W2 ('W' standing for *wrongdoer*, the more general term) have also appeared on the scene.[173] While convenient shorthand, these terms are not entirely satisfactory for a few reasons. First, as we have already seen, contribution may be sought after settlement, including settlement of a case that never became an action—and thus had no 'plaintiffs' or 'defendants'. Second, if the Act's scope is to extend beyond tort law, it is better to have a term that isn't derived from 'tortfeasors'. Third, the use of acronyms is, for some, too abstract; meaning may be better conveyed by using the actual words. Here, then, were the issues presented at the 1975 meeting, along with some of the context that gave rise to them:

1. Should the law be changed to a regime of several (proportionate) liability instead of joint and several (solidary) liability?[174] This would involve issuing separate judgments, which the Alberta Commissioners thought 'would eliminate the need for any contribution'.[175] This was an overstatement, since the need for contribution after settlement would still exist. Furthermore, it ignored the risk of dry judgments or, rather, implied that it should fall on the injured person. The Alberta Commissioners actually doubted that the current system worked a 'manifest injustice',[176] but sought guidance anyway.
2. Should contribution apply to all torts?[177] In provinces with Tortfeasors Acts, this was already the case. But the Uniform Act spoke of 'fault', and its title, like those of the provincial Acts based on it, had the word 'negligence' in it, which had led some courts to conclude that apportionment and contribution was limited to negligence.
3. Should contribution extend to wrongdoers other than tortfeasors?[178] The English working paper had noted that there was already the potential at common law for contribution among co-contractors, co-sureties and co-trustees. But, curiously, where a person had one contract with, say, an architect and another, with, say, a builder, there could be no contribution at common law where the injured person suffered loss through breach of both contracts. In fact, this sort of scenario was being litigated in several Canadian

[173] See D Cheifetz, 'Silk Purses and Silver Linings: *Waterloo Region District School Board v CRD Engineering Ltd*' (2011) 38 Advocates' Quarterly 391.

[174] ULCC 1975, 67.

[175] Ibid.

[176] Ibid.

[177] Ibid.

[178] Ibid.

courts at the time, with differing conclusions about the role of contribution legislation, especially where the breach of contract might also be a tort.

4. Should contribution extend to co-trustees?[179] The Alberta Commissioners thought that the common law might be adequate but sought guidance.
5. Even if contribution should extend to concurrent wrongdoers other than tortfeasors, what is the appropriate statutory language? The Alberta Commissioners noted that the words 'who is, or would if sued, have been liable' had caused 'endless difficulty'.[180] Along with some English cases under the 1935 Tortfeasors Act,[181] a case fresh in the Commissioners' minds was *Parkland (County of) v Stetar*,[182] a 1974 Supreme Court decision emanating from Alberta. A fatal collision involving two cars, one driven by Stetar and the other by Poirier, occurred at the intersection of two rural roads in Alberta. The Court held that Stetar was 75 per cent at fault for not having yielded the right of way, and said that if Parkland County had to bear any liability, it was 25 per cent at fault for not having maintained a warning sign regarding the intersection. But Poirier hadn't given prior notice of claim as required under municipal legislation, and so lost at trial as against the county. The question then became whether Poirer could recover 100 per cent of the damages from Stetar, even though Stetar was only 75 per cent responsible for the accident.

   The Court noted that Alberta had both a Contributory Negligence Act and a Tortfeasors Act, and that the Contributory Negligence Act declared the joint and several liability of persons at fault and spoke of contribution and indemnity between them, suggesting the possibility of contribution. But Dickson J, writing for the Court, said that the Tortfeasors Act spoke 'more particularly to … the question of recovery as between tort-feasors'[183] and so took precedence over the Contributory Negligence Act. Applying some of the English authorities, the Court held that they did not 'admit of a claim for contribution by one tort-feasor against another when that other has been sued by the injured person and held not liable'.[184] Thus Stetar was not only liable for 100 per cent of the damages, but also precluded from recovering any portion of that from Parkland County. The Alberta Commissioners needed no guidance here—they recommended that this outcome be changed so that a contribution claimant could only be defeated when the contribution defendant had succeeded on the merits, and not because of a pleading, procedural or limitation point.[185]
6. As a result of a 1944 case,[186] Ontario courts had consistently held that damages should be litigated but once; they thus refused claims for contribution where the contribution

[179] Ibid, 68.

[180] Ibid.

[181] *Wimpey (George & Co) Ltd v British Overseas Airways Corp* [1955] AC 169 (HL); *Hart v Hall and Pickles Ltd* [1968] 3 All ER 291 (CA).

[182] *Parkland (County of) v Stetar* [1975] 2 SCR 884. The synopsis that follows is a simplified version of the case, both as to the proceedings and the parties.

[183] Ibid, 898.

[184] Ibid, 896.

[185] ULCC 1975, 69.

[186] *Cohen v S McCord & Co Ltd* [1944] 4 DLR 753, [1944] OR 568 (CA) (*Cohen*). See also *Magee v Canada Coach Lines Ltd* [1946] OWN 73 (Master) aff'd [1946] OWN 76 (HCJ) (in a three-defendant case in which the

claimant could have joined the contribution defendant as a third party in the original action. This stance continued even after the 1948 amendment that contemplated a tortfeasor 'thereafter [that is, after judgment or settlement] commencing or continuing [a contribution] action'. The Alberta Commissioners acknowledged that it is usually best to proceed with all the parties in the original action, but thought there might be exceptions when it would be unfair to exclude subsequent contribution proceedings. The Alberta Commissioners sought guidance for appropriate statutory wording.[187]

7. The Alberta Commissioners also asked when time should begin to run against a contribution claimant. If it starts when the injured person's cause of action arises, the contribution claim will frequently fail because a limitation period will have passed. If it starts when the right to contribution arises (for example, at the time of judgment), the claim is more likely to succeed. The Alberta Commissioners sought guidance.[188]
8. The Alberta Commissioners also sought guidance on whether an exclusion-of-liability clause between the injured person and one of two concurrent wrongdoers should be able to insulate that wrongdoer from contribution. At that time, the trial decision had recently come down in *Dominion Chain Co v Eastern Construction Co*,[189] a defective roofing case from Ontario involving three parties: Dominion, Eastern and Giffels. Dominion had contracted with Eastern to have a roof built and with Giffels to prepare specifications and supervise construction. The contract with Eastern said that on issuance of the engineer's final certificate, Dominion waived all claims against Eastern. The trial judge found that because of Eastern's construction practices in the winter of 1964–65 that involved keeping the building closed up and using artificial heat, there was high humidity and condensation that caused the roof to blister or buckle by 1970. The trial judge found both Giffels and Eastern at fault. But Giffels had approved the roof as satisfactory in the fall of 1965 and Eastern's one-year guarantee had expired in the fall of 1966. The trial judge held that Eastern, though not directly liable to Dominion, was liable to Giffels for contribution in the amount of 75 per cent of the damages awarded to Dominion. The Ontario Court of Appeal was to reverse this holding the following year, a decision that the Supreme Court of Canada would uphold in 1977.[190] Thus Eastern ultimately succeeded. But in the meantime, the case raised significant issues about the Act—including the relationship between section 2 and section 3 and the Act's application to claims that sounded in both contract and tort—that attracted the attention of the Commissioners and others.[191]
9. The Alberta Commissioners noted that Ontario had provided for contribution after settlement by adding section 3, and that Saskatchewan and Nova Scotia had added

plaintiff discontinued as against one of the defendants, *Cohen* applied under protest, with the Master saying that it led to 'a result which was not provided for in drafting and enacting [the *Negligence Act*]' and to 'hardship and injustice' to the two remaining defendants).

[187] ULCC 1975, 69.

[188] Ibid, 70.

[189] *Dominion Chain Co v Eastern Construction Co* (1974) 46 DLR (3d) 28, 3 OR (2d) 481 (HCJ).

[190] *Giffels v Eastern Construction, sub nom Dominion Chain Co v Eastern Construction Co* [1978] 2 SCR 1346, 84 DLR (3d) 344, affirming 12 OR (2d) 201, 68 DLR (3d) 385 (CA).

[191] ULCC 1975, 68–70.

the same language in their legislation.[192] The other provinces, though, lacked such a provision. So did the 1935 Tortfeasors Act, but the English Court of Appeal had read contribution after settlement into it as a matter of practicality in *Stott v West Yorkshire Car Co.*[193] In that case, Stott was injured when the motorcycle he was riding collided with an oncoming bus that had pulled out to avoid a bakery van parked in the road. He sued the bus company, who in turn blamed the van owner as well as Stott himself, for not taking due care. The bus company settled with Stott and then sought contribution against the van owner. The settlement stipulated that the bus company did not admit liability, and the van owner said this disentitled the bus company from claiming contribution. Distinguishing some of the English authorities[194] relied on in *Parkland (County) v Stetar*, Lord Denning thought the meaning of 'liable' in the 1935 Tortfeasors Act varied with the context, and that in the contribution context, it meant that 'a tortfeasor is entitled to recover contribution from another tortfeasor (i) when he has been held liable in judgment; (ii) when he has admitted liability; and (iii) when he has settled the action by agreeing to make payment to the injured person, even though, in making the settlement, he has not admitted liability'.[195] On this test, the bus company was allowed to bring contribution proceedings against the van driver.

The Alberta Commissioners agreed with this, but disagreed with one aspect of the *Stott* case. The Court had said that the van owner could defend the contribution claim on the basis that the bus company was never liable at all, and that the bus company would have to prove that it was. The English Law Commission paper disapproved of such a requirement and the Alberta Commissioners agreed. They thought it was enough for the contribution claimant to have to prove that the settlement was reasonable. In terms of statutory language to give effect to all of this, they preferred section 22(1) of the Irish Civil Liability Act 1961:

> Where the [contribution] claimant has settled with the injured person in such a way as to bar the injured person's claim against the other concurrent wrongdoers, the [contribution] claimant may recover contribution in the same way as if he had suffered judgment for damages, if he satisfies the court that the amount of the settlement was reasonable; and, if the court finds that the amount of the settlement was excessive, it may fix the amount at which the claim should have been settled.

This, in effect, is like section 3 of the Ontario Act, except that it avoids the problematic 'who is, or would if sued have been, liable' wording.[196] The Alberta Commissioners sought guidance but tentatively recommended this language.

10. It can be seen from the opening words of the Irish provision that the remedy it provides is premised on a settlement that bars the plaintiff from suing other concurrent wrongdoers. Different issues arise if the settlement preserves the plaintiff's right to sue others.

[192] See nn 126 and n 127 and accompanying text.

[193] *Stott v West Yorkshire Car Co* [1971] 2 QB 653 (CA).

[194] Above (n 181).

[195] *Stott v West Yorkshire Car Co* (n 193) 656.

[196] In fact, s 22 of the Irish Civil Liability Act 1961 was inspired by the Ontario enactment. See Civil Liability Bill 1960, Explanatory Memorandum, 9 (noting that s 22 was 'based on s 1 of the Ontario Negligence Act, 1948'). I thank Eoin Quill for providing me with a copy of this memorandum, which remains a useful guide to the Irish legislation.

One issue is that the second wrongdoer could turn around and seek contribution from the first one. That is relatively easy to address, though, by drafting the settlement to have the injured person agree to indemnify the first wrongdoer for any amounts required to pay another wrongdoer by way of contribution. Another issue is that if the case goes to trial, the settlement with the first wrongdoer, when added to the judgment with the second one, could result in the injured person getting more or less compensation than his or her actual loss or damage. The result would depend in part on how good a bargain the injured person had been able to make with the first wrongdoer. Williams had thought that the injured person should never recover more than 100 per cent of his or her actual loss or damage, and drafted a provision to achieve this that formed the basis for section 22(2) of the Irish Civil Liability Act 1961. I will not reproduce that provision here in part because its wording is complicated, and in part because it is only one of several possible rules that could be formulated to address the issue, and not the one ultimately chosen under most Canadian law reform initiatives. Suffice it to say that the Alberta Commissioners sought guidance.[197]

11. The Alberta Commissioners noted the Saskatchewan provision that presumptively made costs proportionate to liability. They thought this was reasonable and sought guidance.
12. The Alberta Commissioners then turned to contributory negligence and concluded that the legislation was generally working well, and would work even better if the spousal and guest passenger provisions were repealed across the country.[198] One thing that the Commissioners noted was that 'fault' was generally understood to include vicarious liability, 'but it would be better to say so'.[199] Now this was not quite correct—vicarious liability arises not from fault but out of relationships—and a better way to put it would have been to say that the vicariously liable person is identified with the wrongdoer's fault. Nevertheless, courts were reaching the right results even if the way that the concepts might have been described lacked precision. For example, if an injured person sued a wrongdoer as well as the person vicariously liable for that wrongdoer, and if the injured person was found equally at fault with the wrongdoer, liability would not be apportioned three ways, but 50:50, with the wrongdoer and the vicariously liable person jointly responsible for 50 per cent of the damages.

It took time to consider all the Alberta Commissioners' questions. Assistance came from the Alberta Institute of Law Reform and Research, which, in 1979, produced the first significant reform paper in Canada since the publications that had led to the 1924 statutes.[200] The 1979 Alberta Report included a draft 'Contributory Negligence and Contribution Act' that formed the basis for the report.[201] Each section was presented along with an explanation

[197] ULCC 1975, 72.

[198] ULCC 1975, 74.

[199] ULCC 1975, 73.

[200] Institute of Law Research and Reform, *Contributory Negligence and Concurrent Wrongdoers: Report No 31* (Edmonton, University of Alberta, 1979) (1979 Alberta Report).

[201] The legislation was drafted by David Elliott, former legislative counsel for Alberta (the same David Elliott referred to in n 154).

of its intent and relationship to other key legislation. As the Alberta Commissioners[202] explained, one of the decisions that the Conference had made was to bring legislation dealing with tortfeasors under the umbrella of the Uniform Act and, indeed, to start using the more general term 'concurrent wrongdoers' rather than 'tortfeasors'. This was consistent with the Alberta Commissioners' vision of extending the Uniform Act to include all torts as well as breaches of duty of care arising from contract, which I will discuss below. The amalgamation of apportionment and contribution principles into a single Act was also reflected in the initial title, though other titles were mooted too.[203] The Alberta Commissioners also elevated their concerns about the spousal and guest passenger provisions that still remained in provincial legislation and called again for their abolition, noting that such provisions were stalling the development of a new Uniform Act.[204]

One of the issues that came to the fore in this period was whether contributory fault—the term emerging as a replacement for 'contributory negligence'—could be a defence to an action for breach of contract. Courts varied or equivocated in their willingness to interpret the statute to allow such a remedy. Thus in *Giffels*,[205] Laskin CJC had said that 'it is not necessary in this case to come to a final determination on whether s 2(1) of The Negligence Act is broad enough to embrace contractual liability when other provisions of the Act, like ss 3 and 9, clearly do not'.[206] This is the point adverted to earlier: section 2(1) of the Ontario Act speaks of 'fault or negligence' whereas section 3 refers to 'tortfeasors'. In *Giffels*, the issue was contribution between tortfeasors rather than contributory fault, and while the case was ultimately decided on a different basis, Laskin CJC understandably opined that it was 'difficult to see how a contract basis for contribution can be read into one provision of a statute which has interrelated provisions dominated by a reference to tortfeasors'.[207]

At its 1979 meeting, the Uniform Law Conference of Canada took up this theme. In a note to the contributory fault section, the Alberta Commissioners said:

> We do not think that [contributory fault] should apply to the usual breach of a contractual obligation, but we do think that it can appropriately apply to a claim resulting from a failure to carry out a duty of care under contract. A contributorily negligent bus passenger or patient should not, we think, be able to avoid the consequences of his failure to take care for himself by choosing to sue in contract rather than tort … The defence has expressly or by implication been held available in cases of negligence under contract.[208]

Other Commissioners, though, found the distinction between 'usual breach' of a contract and a 'breach of a duty of care' under the contract either ambiguous or problematic. The Alberta Commissioners went back to the drawing board, enlisting the aid of the Alberta Institute of Law Research and Reform and Professor David Percy of the University of

202 I have so far spoken of the Alberta Commissioners as though they were a constant group. In fact, the group changed composition over time. In the 1975 ULCC proceedings, it comprised Glen Acorn, WF Bowker, LR Meiklejohn and WE Wilson. In the 1979 ULCC proceedings, it comprised E Gamache, WH Hurlburt, Graham Reid and WE Wilson.

203 ULCC 1979, 101 ('The Contributory Fault and Contribution Act' and 'The Apportionment and Contribution Act').

204 ULCC 1979, 97–101.

205 *Giffels* (n 190).

206 Ibid, SCR 1354.

207 Ibid.

208 ULCC 1979, 105–06 (citations omitted).

Alberta. In the reports he was commissioned to write through the Institute and that were presented at the 1982 meeting, Percy concluded that 'it is possible that the introduction of contributory fault [into contract law] might induce courts to apportion the loss between the parties rather than to reach a different result by interpreting the terms of the contract', in turn raising 'the larger issue of the effect of apportionment on general contract theory'.[209] This was neither a ringing endorsement nor a rousing condemnation for extending fault-based apportionment to contract law. After all, apportionment had induced at least some courts to abandon the grail-like search for 'ultimate' or 'sole' cause, with a salutary effect on tort theory. Indeed, it may be no coincidence that shortly after the introduction of apportionment legislation, courts began developing more sophisticated approaches to common law causation, particularly in industrial settings where diseases form over years and are attributable to more than one cause.[210]

Percy was most concerned about extending apportionment to contract cases that didn't involve a breach of a duty of care. In such cases, he thought, 'the determination of relative fault threatens to distort the fundamental nature of contractual liability'.[211] Percy's concern was understandable, especially in relation to warranties intended to create a strict liability regardless of fault, and presumably paid for as such by the warranty recipients. By way of example, Percy cited *Steel Company of Canada Ltd v Willand Management Ltd*,[212] in which a builder was held liable for repair costs due to the failure of a roofing product called 'Curadex', even though the owner was the one who had specified Curadex in the tender documents. The builder had warranted that the building would remain 'weather tight' for five years, which, the Court held, trumped any fault that might have existed on the owner's part for specifying a defective product. Percy worried that in a similar case under an apportionment regime, courts would be inclined to find fault on both sides, but that 'apportionment would be very difficult, because it is almost impossible to compare the culpability of the parties'.[213]

However, the proposed solution—defining fault to include contractual breaches, but only those arising from a duty of care—poses its own difficulties. The Alberta Institute of Law Research and Reform had noted this in commenting on its own draft Act. It gave the example of a contractor failing to use a particular grade of steel, saying this could be characterised as 'either a breach of the term of the contract or a breach of a duty of care'.[214] Curiously, neither report discussed the idea that Percy's problem could be addressed by having the statute let contracting parties exclude or limit apportionment, much as parties routinely exclude or limit liability. Although a draft Act was presented at the 1982 meeting,[215]

[209] ULCC 1982, 155. This is from the second of the two Percy papers annexed to the proceedings. The first, Annex I, is at p 124 and is entitled 'Contribution Claims and Contract Principles'. The second, Annex II, is at p 148 and is entitled 'The Impact of the Contribution Proposals of the Uniform Law Conference on the Common Law of Contract'.

[210] See *Bonnington Castings v Wardlaw* [1956] AC 613 (HL) (setting out a 'material contribution' test where the traditional 'but for' test would have barred workers from succeeding when two sources of silica dust—one 'innocent' and one 'guilty'—contributed to their pneumoconiosis).

[211] ULCC 1982, 158.

[212] *Steel Company of Canada Ltd v Willand Management Ltd* (1966) 58 DLR (2d) 595 (SCC).

[213] ULCC 1982, 159.

[214] 1979 Alberta Report (n 200) 25.

[215] ULCC 1982, 162–65.

the contract issue was divisive enough that further consideration of it was deferred to the 1983 meeting, but being 'disapproved'[216] at that meeting, went back for redrafting.

Finally, in 1984, 60 years after adopting the original Uniform Act, the Conference received and adopted the Uniform Contributory Fault Act. On the issue that had divided the Conference, the Alberta Commissioners prevailed. Fault, originally defined to include 'a breach of contract … giving rise to a right of action for damages'[217] became 'a breach of a duty of care arising from a contract that creates a liability for damages'.[218] As there have been no further amendments to it, the 1984 version of the Uniform Act—the UCFA—continues to the present day, in an English and a French version.[219] Unfortunately, no annotations were prepared for the 1984 Uniform Act, so the intended meaning and purposes of its sections must be gleaned from the Conference proceedings and the annotations to the draft Act in the 1979 Alberta Report, on which it was originally based. This is an unsatisfactory state of affairs for a piece of model legislation that took so many years to produce. I will set out the full text of the Act in the next section, where I will compare it with a subsequent reform initiative and draft legislation of the Ontario Law Reform Commission.

Before leaving this section, though, I should note that this period was also an important one for reform initiatives elsewhere. In keeping with the Anglo-Canadian theme that has dominated the history of much of the reforms in Canada, I will focus on the UK, though there were significant developments elsewhere too.

In 1978, the UK Parliament repealed section 6 of the 1935 Tortfeasors Act and enacted two pieces of legislation that influenced Canadian reforms. The Civil Liability (Contribution) Act 1978[220] abolished a rule in the 1935 Tortfeasors Act that had capped the damages recoverable in subsequent proceedings to the amount 'in which judgment is first given'.[221] The concern that had originally given rise to this cap—that plaintiffs might sue defendants separately and sequentially in the hope of getting higher jury awards on a second round—had largely disappeared, along with the virtual disappearance of the English civil jury trial. The 1978 Act also extended the abolition of the judgment-bar rule, so that judgment against 'any person liable in respect of any debt or damage' would not bar an action against 'any other person who is (apart from any such bar) jointly liable' for the same debt or damage.[222] In other words, the judgment-bar rule (though still not the release-bar rule) was effectively abolished for all causes of action for damages and for debt.

A third reform was to extend to all concurrent wrongdoers the two-year limitation period that had governed contribution claims among concurrent tortfeasors. The problem of ascertaining the appropriate period had been a vexed one, leading to a variety of possible conclusions on how it should be calculated. The decision to have a single, common limitation period brought certainty to the law. The change was originally enacted through Schedule 1 of the 1978 Act, which amended the limitation legislation then in effect.[223] Now found

[216] ULCC 1983, 28. Under the Conference rules, if two or more jurisdictions disapproved of a uniform Act or amendment thereto, the Act or amendment was defeated. Disapprovals had been received from two provinces.

[217] Ibid, 162 (original draft of UCFA, s 1(c)(ii), defining 'fault').

[218] ULCC 1984, 98 (UCFA, s 1, defining 'fault' and 'wrongful act').

[219] ULCC 1984, 98–102 (English) and 103–06 (French).

[220] Civil Liability (Contribution) Act 1978, c 47 (UK).

[221] 1935 Tortfeasors Act (n 111) s 6(b).

[222] Civil Liability (Contribution) Act 1978 (n 220) s 3.

[223] Limitation Act 1963, c 47 (UK) s 4.

in section 10 of the Limitation Act 1980,[224] the two-year limitation period[225] for claiming contribution runs from the date of a civil judgment or arbitration award (without regard to any variation of the judgment or award on appeal)[226] or from the date of settlement.[227]

The 1988 Ontario Law Reform Commission Report and Draft Contribution and Comparative Fault Act

One law reform initiative engenders another, and of all the provinces, Ontario took the keenest interest at this time in reforming large areas of private law. On 23 March 1988, five Commissioners[228] of the Ontario Law Reform Commission transmitted their 289-page *Report on Contribution Among Wrongdoers and Contributory Negligence*[229] to The Honourable Ian Scott, Ontario's Attorney General. The project, directed by Professor John M Evans (subsequently Evans JA of the Federal Court of Appeal), was the most sophisticated law reform initiative in the Commonwealth since Williams's 1951 opus. It recommended repealing the Negligence Act and replacing it with a draft statute appended to the report, the Contribution and Comparative Fault Act.[230] In some respects, the report confirmed, clarified or codified existing law; in other respects, it advocated substantial reform. A glance at the chapter structure of the 1988 OLRC Report gives some idea of its scope:

1. *Introduction.* The Commissioners set out the critical issues and acknowledged the work of others, noting particularly the importance of the 1984 Uniform Act.

2. *Joint and Several Liability.* The Commission reviewed the law on joint wrongdoers—both tortfeasors and contractors—and the judgment-and-release-bar rules. The Commission concluded that section 149 of the Courts of Justice Act, discussed above,[231] should be modified to address certain further unresolved issues and moved into the new statute.

3. *In Solidum Liability.* The Commission considered the work of the Ontario Task Force on Liability Insurance,[232] set up in response to an 'insurance crisis' allegedly caused by

224 Limitation Act 1980, c 58 (UK), s 40(3) and Sch 4 of this Act repealed the relevant sections of the Limitation Act 1963.

225 Ibid, s 1.

226 Ibid, s 3.

227 Ibid, s 4.

228 James Breithaupt, H Allan Leal, Earl Cherniak, Robert Pritchard and Margaret Ross. The Commissioners also acknowledged the contributions of four former Commissioners whose tenure spanned much of the project: Derek Mendes da Costa, Richard Bell, William Poole and Barry Percival.

229 Ontario Law Reform Commission, *Report on Contribution Among Wrongdoers and Contributory Negligence* (Toronto, Ministry of the Attorney General, 1988) (1988 OLRC Report). A digitised version is available at archive.org/details/reportoncontribu00onta.

230 Ibid, 281. The Commissioners explained at p 6 of the report that the statute had been drafted by Arthur N Stone, former Senior Legislative Counsel for Ontario.

231 See above (n 162) and the text that accompanies and follows it.

232 Ontario Ministry of Financial Institutions, *Final Report of the Ontario Task Force on Insurance* (Toronto, Queen's Park, 1986).

this type of liability. The Commission also studied legislation, actual or pending, dealing with the subject in every US state. After commissioning a report that summarised the academic analysis and holding a workshop with academics in March 1987,[233] the Commissioners concluded that they were not persuaded of the arguments for rejecting *in solidum* liability (more generally known as 'joint and several liability', albeit mistakenly, as the Commission explained). The Commission recommended keeping the existing law with one exception: where there are more than two concurrent wrongdoers, and one wrongdoer's share of a judgment is uncollectable, that share should be reallocated among the remaining ones in proportion to their degrees of fault. This would achieve greater fairness among defendants, at least in cases of three or more defendants, than a regime in which one defendant may be left carrying the entire share of the uncollectable amount and left to enforce whatever contribution rights it might still have against the others.[234]

4. *The Nature and Scope of the Right to Contribution.* The Commission set out the restitutionary framework on which the statutory right to contribution is based. It is one of the report's most important chapters. I will return to the restitutionary theme later, when I discuss the principles that should animate any further reform efforts. Among other things, the Commission recommended that a right to contribution should be capable of arising among wrongdoers who cause a single loss, regardless of the nature of the legal obligation that gave rise to their liability.[235] The Commission thought that the proposed new statutory right should supersede other rights to contribution (as distinct from indemnity), unless another statute specifically provided that the contribution provisions of that statute would apply instead.[236]

5. *Settlements and Contribution Claims.* The Commission considered issues relating to contribution claims arising out of settlements, as opposed to judgments. Since such claims usually arise after a settlement has been reached between an injured person and one concurrent wrongdoer, the topic may generally be referred to as 'contribution after settlement'. I have already touched on some of the statutory provisions and case law on this topic, but the field is larger than my discussion would suggest, and I will return to it later. Partial settlements are particularly problematic. The Commission found it 'difficult to produce a rule that will encourage the making of fair and final settlements, ensure that the injured person is fully compensated, but no more, and produce equity among concurrent wrongdoers'.[237]

   The Commission's first recommendation was that 'it should be no defence to the contribution claim that the claimant could never have been successfully sued by the injured person'.[238] This policy was already reflected in section 9 of the Ontario Act, at

[233] 1988 OLRC Report (n 229) 32.

[234] Ibid, 48. The recommendation contemplated that the reallocation of liability would be made without discharging the liability to contribute of the defaulting concurrent wrongdoer.

[235] Ibid, 82.

[236] Ibid, 82–83.

[237] Ibid, 105.

[238] Ibid, 108.

least with respect to limitation periods, and was consistent with how the case law was emerging in both Canada and England. The Commission nevertheless thought that the court should be able to refuse contribution if the contribution claimant settled without believing that he was or might be liable and 'without regard to any legal proceedings that might be instituted against him by the injured person for the claim settled'.[239] The Commission's attempt to craft a rule that balances all the policy concerns was also reflected in two other recommendations. First, if an injured person obtains judgment against a concurrent wrongdoer, the damages should be reduced by the settlement amount already received from another concurrent wrongdoer.[240] Second, where, after a settlement with one concurrent wrongdoer, another concurrent wrongdoer is held liable to the injured person or settles that person's claim for an amount that exceeds the second wrongdoer's proportionate share of liability, he should be entitled to claim contribution from the first wrongdoer for the excess, even though the first wrongdoer has ceased to be liable to the injured person due to the settlement.[241]

These recommendations went against the grain of most other reform proposals, which, in various forms, weighed finality of settlement more heavily than either exactness of compensation or restitution among wrongdoers.[242] I will return to this theme when discussing the most recent Canadian reform proposals.

6. *Defences to Contribution Claims: Liability to the Injured Person.* This chapter examined whether, in separate contribution proceedings, the contribution defendant should be able to assert that the court that found the contribution claimant liable erred either as to liability or quantum of damages. The chapter also considered situations in which the contribution defendant could *never* have been liable for the loss in respect of which the contribution claimant had lost or settled. The Commission recommended that where everything had been litigated in one action, both the contribution claimant and the contribution defendant should be bound by the judgment in that action.[243] It also concluded that where the contribution proceeding was separate, the contribution defendant should not be able to contest the contribution claimant's *liability* except where the judgment in the first case was obtained by collusion or fraud; however, it also concluded that the contribution defendant should be able to contest the *quantum* of damages—subject to the contribution claimant being estopped from arguing that they should have been higher.[244]

   The Commission also recommended that if specific relief had been ordered against the contribution claimant in the first action, the court hearing the contribution claim should be required to place a value on that relief so as to determine the amount recoverable.[245] This was a unique proposal in Canadian reform initiatives, but was consistent with a provision in the Irish statute[246] and with the Commission's recommendation

239 Ibid.
240 Ibid, 109.
241 Ibid.
242 See the discussion, ibid, 106.
243 Ibid, 139.
244 Ibid, 139–40.
245 Ibid, 140.
246 Civil Liability Act 1961, c 41 (Ireland) s 26.

in Chapter 2 that a right to contribution should not depend on the nature of the legal obligation that gave rise to liability in the first place. So, for example, if Starkey had sued Merryweather and Nixan in detinue rather than trover, and if that had resulted in Merryweather having to return the milling equipment to Starkey rather than paying him £840,[247] the court would have had to assess the value of the equipment in the contribution action by Merryweather against Nixan.

The Commission also recommended that the contribution defendant should not have to pay contribution if the injured person could never have been successfully sued by the contribution defendant (for example, because of a contract made before the cause of action arose or because of a statutory immunity); similarly, if the contribution defendant's liability to the injured person was limited, as opposed to being precluded (again, this could arise under a contract or, for example, a statutory cap on recovery), that would operate as a limit to the contribution defendant's liability to contribute.[248]

7. *Defences to Contribution Claims: Subsequent Immunities.* The Commission considered situations in which the contribution defendant was *once* liable to compensate the injured person, but in which subsequent events immunised him from suit. The most common scenario is that of differing limitation periods. For example, in *Paquette v Batchelor*,[249] the plaintiff sued two drivers, Batchelor and Brown, in relation to an accident that occurred at an intersection. The action was commenced just within the one-year limitation period that then prevailed in Ontario's Highway Traffic Act.[250] Batchelor and Brown then brought a third-party proceeding against Constable Polie, who had been directing traffic at the intersection. Polie sought refuge in the six-month limitation period in the Public Authorities Protection Act.[251] Osborne J held that Polie was indeed entitled to rely on the six-month limitation period, but the important question was when it should start running. He held that it should run from when judgment issued against Batchelor and Brown in the main proceedings. This is consistent with the notion that a contribution action is a separate cause of action. Since the contribution claims had, in accordance with typical third-party procedure, been commenced before the judgment was issued against Batchelor and Brown, they were within the shorter limitation period and were entitled to seek contribution from Polie.

The Commission endorsed this line of reasoning and recommended that it should not be open to a contribution defendant to defend on the basis that his liability to the injured person 'had ceased to be enforceable by reason of the failure of the injured person to comply with a procedural requirement, the expiry of a statutory limitation period, dismissal of the injured person's action for delay, or an analogous equitable bar upon a successful suit by the injured person'.[252] The experience with multiple limitation periods and notice periods, such as the one in *Parkland (County) v Stetar*,[253] also led the Commission to wonder if it would make sense to rationalise such legislation, and

[247] See nn 50–54 and accompanying text.
[248] 1988 OLRC Report (n 229) 140.
[249] *Paquette v Batchelor* (1980) 111 DLR (3d) 642, 13 CCLT 237, 28 OR (2d) 590 (HCJ).
[250] RSO 1970, c 202, s 86(1).
[251] RSO 1970, c 374, s 11.
[252] 1988 OLRC Report (n 229)170.
[253] Above (n 182).

the Commission thought that if its recommendations were to be enacted, government officials should 'review the nature and purpose of the statutory notice requirements in order to determine whether they are of overriding importance',[254] and thus ought to apply despite the new proposed Act. The Commission also thought it should not be a defence to a contribution claim to establish that the contributor's liability had ceased because of a settlement with the injured person after the cause of action arose.[255] On the other hand, a contract limiting or excluding liability that had been entered into before the cause of action arose—recall that this was the Giffels scenario[256]—should continue to be a good defence to a contribution claim, as should a non-collusive judgment in the contribution defendant's favour.[257]

8. *Assessment of Contribution.* The Commission dealt with difficult questions relating to the 'contributable sum'—the amount that a contribution defendant is required to pay to a contribution claimant—as well as questions about the persons among whom the contributable sum should be divided. These questions involve both final and partial settlements and successive judgments, as well as the degree to which any legislation should entrust judges with developing the law on a case-by-case basis. The Commission thought that the Negligence Act, which gave the court the power to consider only the comparative fault of wrongdoers when assessing contribution, was too narrow. The Commission found the English approach—a division that is 'just and equitable' having regard to the 'responsibility' of each party—would be more flexible and permit consideration of 'both the causative factor and the fault of the parties'.[258] The Commission also thought that an 'indemnity'—in the sense of 100 per cent contribution—would be more possible under this broader apportionment test, since the court could look not only to the 'fault' of the parties, but rather to their respective degrees of 'responsibility'.[259]

9. *Some Procedural Aspects of Contribution Claims.* The Commission considered the interrelationship of contribution law with procedural law and limitations law. Co-defendants should cross-claim and a defendant wanting to bring a contribution claim against a non-party should normally bring a third-party claim, with some flexibility to depart from this rule where there were jurisdictional or other issues that made it impossible or impracticable to commence third-party proceedings. One of the most important recommendations was in relation to the start time and length of a limitation period for bringing a contribution claim. Surprisingly, neither the Negligence Act nor the Limitations Act[260] specified that. The Commission recommended a two-year period starting from judgment or settlement:

> The limitation period governing the enforcement of the right of contribution among concurrent wrongdoers should be two years. Where the claim is based upon a judgment against the

[254] 1988 OLRC Report (n 229) 170.
[255] Ibid, 171.
[256] Above nn 189–91 and accompanying text.
[257] 1988 OLRC Report (n 229) 170–71.
[258] Ibid, 196.
[259] Ibid, 197.
[260] RSO 1980, c 240.

> [contribution] claimant in favour of the injured party, the period should run from the date of the judgment. Where the claim is based upon a settlement, the period should commence from the date when the settlement was made.[261]

This recommendation reflected what the UK had enacted in 1978, both as to the duration of the limitation period and the timing of its commencement.[262]

10. *Contributory Negligence.* Although this was only one chapter in the report, the Commission made a large number of recommendations. The most important one was to retain the regime of apportioning liability by degrees of fault. Interestingly, the Commission did not adopt the English 'just and equitable' approach here, as it had done with contribution. Following a formula by then well tested in Canada, the Commission thought the court 'should determine the degrees of fault … and should apportion the damages in proportion to the degrees of fault that are so found'.[263] Like the Uniform Law Conference of Canada, the Commission thought that all torts should be subject to apportionment, even though some intentional torts, such as fraud, would rarely attract a successful defence of contributory fault. The Commission deferred its recommendations on actions for wrongful interference with goods—sometimes called the 'chattel torts'—for consideration in its separate project on that topic. The following year, the Commission endorsed the use of apportionment in the field of wrongful interference with goods, subject to some specific features relating to those torts.[264] The Commission also recommended that apportionment apply in the contractual setting, and was willing to go further than the Uniform Act in this regard. For example, apportionment, in addition to applying to a breach of a duty of care arising from a contract that creates a liability in damages, should also apply to a contractual breach that creates a liability for damages for personal injury or property damage. The Commission did not recommend applying apportionment to breaches of fiduciary duty or trust, though, preferring to allow the doctrine to develop under the common law. The Commission suggested a number of other provisions similar to those found in the Uniform Act, including a clause abolishing last clear chance.

Having set out a broad-brush synopsis of the work of both the Uniform Law Conference of Canada and the Ontario Law Reform Commission (OLRC), let us now take a side-by-side look at both model acts. As Table 4 shows, while the OLRC draft Act was influenced by the Uniform Act, it is considerably more detailed—twice the word length of the UCFA and 26 sections long instead of 16. To accommodate both Acts in a single comparative table, I have changed the orientation.

[261] 1988 OLRC Report (n 229) 228.

[262] See nn 223–27 and accompanying text.

[263] 1988 OLRC Report (n 229) 264.

[264] See Ontario Law Reform Commission, *Study Paper on Wrongful Interference With Goods* (Toronto, Ministry of the Attorney General, 1989) c 13 and 170–72. While this was a novel recommendation in much of the common law world, Ireland has long had a provision for conversion: see Civil Liability Act 1961 (n 246) s 34(2)(d).

Table 4: Side-by-Side Comparison of 1984 Uniform Act and 1988 OLRC Draft Act

Uniform Contributory Fault Act 1984[265]	**Contribution Among Wrongdoers and Contributory Negligence Act (Draft), 1988**[266]
1. In this Act, 'concurrent wrongdoers' means (a) two or more persons whose wrongful acts contribute to the same damage suffered by another, and any other person liable for the wrongful act of any of those persons; or (b) a person whose wrongful act causes damage suffered by another and a person liable for the wrongful act; 'damage' includes economic loss; 'fault' means an act or omission that constitutes (a) a tort, (b) a breach of statutory duty that creates a liability for damages, (c) a breach of duty of care arising from a contract that creates a liability for damages, or (d) a failure of a person to take reasonable care of his own person, property or economic interest, whether or not it is intentional. 'release' includes a settlement or any other agreement limiting the liability of a person for damages, either in whole or in part;	1. In this Act, 'concurrent wrongdoer' means one of two or more persons whose wrongful acts contribute to the same damage suffered by one or more persons and includes a person who, without fault, is liable for the wrongful act of another; 'injured person' means a person who suffers damage as a result of an act or omission of a concurrent wrongdoer. COMPARATIVE FAULT 2. (1) Where a person is injured by the wrongful act of one or more persons and the fault of the injured person is found to have contributed to the damage, the court shall determine the degrees of fault of the person or persons and of the injured person that contributed to the damage, and shall apportion the damages in proportion to the degrees of fault that are so found. (2) This section applies where the liability for damages arises from (a) a tort other than conversion, detinue and injury to a reversionary interest;[267] (b) a breach of statutory duty; (c) a breach of duty of care arising from a contract; or (d) a breach of contract that results in personal injury or property damage, whether the tort or breach is intentional or not.

(continued)

[265] 1984 ULCC, 98.
[266] 1988 OLRC Report (n 229) 281.
[267] Following further study, the Commission recommended that apportionment apply to these torts. See above (n 264).

Table 4: ***(Continued)***

Uniform Contributory Fault Act 1984	Contribution Among Wrongdoers and Contributory Negligence Act (Draft), 1988
'wrongful act' means an act or omission that constitutes (a) a tort, (b) a breach of contract or statutory duty that creates a liability for damages, or (c) a failure of a person to take reasonable care of his own person, property or economic interest, whether or not it is intentional[.]	(3) Subsection (1) applies notwithstanding that the person making the claim for damages is not the person suffering the damage.[268] (4) The apportionment of fault under subsection (1) where damage arises under a contract is subject to an agreement, express or implied. (5) The damage referred to in this section includes economic loss. (6) If the degree to which the fault of persons contributes to the damage cannot be determined in relation to each other, those persons shall be deemed to have contributed equally in relation to each other. (7) Nothing in this section derogates from a power a court has to apportion damages apart from this section; but where the power is given by or under another Act, section 23 applies.
GENERAL 2. Her Majesty is bound by this Act. 3. This Act applies where damage is caused or contributed to by the act or omission of a person notwithstanding that another person had the opportunity of avoiding the consequences of that act or omission and failed to do so. 4. In every action, (a) the fault or the wrongful act, if any; (b) the degree to which the fault or wrongful act of a person contributed to damage; and (c) the amount of damages, are questions for the trier of fact.	LIABILITY AND CONTRIBUTION OF CONCURRENT WRONGDOERS 3. (1) Sections 4 to 19 apply where liability for damages or to deliver goods or perform services arises from, (a) a tort; (b) a breach of statutory duty; (c) a breach of contract; (d) a breach of a fiduciary duty, including a breach of trust, except as otherwise specifically provided by the *Trustee Act*;[269] or (e) a breach of any other legal duty. (2) Sections 4 to 6 apply where the liability is for a debt, as specifically provided herein.

(continued)

[268] eg, survivors' claims under fatal accidents legislation.

[269] The Commission's 1984 *Report on the Law of Trusts* contained a revised draft Trustee Act that had provisions dealing with contribution among trustees.

Table 4: ***(Continued)***

Uniform Contributory Fault Act 1984	**Contribution Among Wrongdoers and Contributory Negligence Act (Draft), 1988**
CONTRIBUTORY FAULT 5. (1) Where the fault of two or more persons contributes to damage suffered by one or more of them, the liability for damages of a person whose fault contributed to the damage is reduced by an amount of the damages proportionate to the degree to which the fault of the person suffering the damage contributed to the damage. (2) Where a person, other than a person referred to in subsection (1), makes a claim arising from the damage suffered by a person referred to in subsection (1), the liability for damages of a person whose fault contributed to the damage is reduced by an amount of the damages proportionate to the degree to which the fault of the person who suffered the damage from which the claim arose contributed to the damage. (3) If the degrees to which the fault of persons contributed to damage cannot be determined in relation to each other, those persons shall be deemed to have contributed equally in relation to each other.	CONCURRENT LIABILITY 4. (1) Each concurrent wrongdoer or debtor is liable for the damage or debt that would be assessed if the concurrent wrongdoer or debtor were the only person who is liable to the injured person or creditor. (2) The total amount recoverable by an injured person or creditor shall not exceed the amount of that person's damage or debt. 5. (1) A judgment against one concurrent wrongdoer or debtor does not preclude judgment against another concurrent wrongdoer or debtor in the same or a separate proceeding. (2) Where a person brings separate proceedings against two or more concurrent wrongdoers or debtors, the person is not entitled to costs in a proceeding other than the one in which judgment is first given, unless the court is of the opinion that there are reasonable grounds for bringing more than one proceeding. (3) In an action brought by an injured person, the injured person may establish the amount of damages for which a concurrent wrongdoer is liable without regard to the amount of damages awarded to the injured person against another concurrent wrongdor. 6. A release of one concurrent wrongdoer or debtor or the acceptance of an offer of settlement does not preclude judgment against another concurrent wrongdoer or debtor, unless the release or settlement expressly so provides, or in the case of a debt, prejudices the rights of another debtor who is liable for the same debt.

(continued)

Table 4: *(Continued)*

Uniform Contributory Fault Act 1984	Contribution Among Wrongdoers and Contributory Negligence Act (Draft), 1988
CONCURRENT WRONGDOERS 6. The liability for damages is joint and several. 7. Subject to sections 8 to 14, a concurrent wrongdoer is entitled to contribution from the other concurrent wrongdoers. 8. (1) The amount of contribution to which a concurrent wrongdoer is entitled from another concurrent wrongdoer is that amount of the total liability for damages of all concurrent wrongdoers that is proportionate to the degree to which the wrongful act of the other concurrent wrongdoer contributed to the damage. (2) If the degrees to which the wrongful acts of persons contributed to damage cannot be determined in relation to each other, those persons shall be deemed to have contributed equally in relation to each other. 9. Where the court is satisfied that the contribution of a concurrent wrongdoer cannot be collected, the court may, on or after giving judgment for contribution, make an order that it considers necessary to apportion the contribution that cannot be collected among the other concurrent wrongdoers, proportionate to the degrees to which their wrongful acts contributed to the damage. 10. No person is entitled to contribution under this Act from a person who is entitled to be indemnified by him for the damages for which the contribution is sought.	CONTRIBUTION 7. (1) A concurrent wrongdoer is entitled to claim contribution from other concurrent wrongdoers whether or not his or her conduct is intentional or of a criminal nature or whether or not the damages awarded are punitive. (2) A concurrent wrongdoer who is entitled to contribution from another concurrent wrongdoer is subrogated to the rights of the injured person against the other concurrent wrongdoer for the purpose of recovering the contribution to which he or she is entitled. (3) Nothing in this Act affects any express or implied contractual or any other right to indemnity, or any express or implied contractual provision respecting contribution, and in particular, no person is entitled to contribution from a person who is entitled to be indemnified, by the claimant, for the damages for which the contribution is sought. 8. (1) A judgment in favour of the injured person against a concurrent wrongdoer is, for the purpose of claiming contribution from another concurrent wrongdoer who was not a party in the action or was not joined as a third party [,] conclusive as to the liability of the concurrent wrongdoer but not as to the assessment of the damage, except that the sum to which the concurrent wrongdoer may be required to contribute shall not be an amount greater than the amount determined by the judgment.

(continued)

Table 4: ***(Continued)***

Uniform Contributory Fault Act 1984	**Contribution Among Wrongdoers and Contributory Negligence Act (Draft), 1988**
11. Where a concurrent wrongdoer is exempt from liability for damages under the (*Workers' Compensation Act*), the liability for damages of the concurrent wrongdoers who are not exempt is reduced by an amount of the damages proportionate to the degree to which the wrongful acts of the concurrent wrongdoers who are exempt contributed to the damage, and there shall be no contribution between those concurrent wrongdoers who are exempt and those who are not exempt. *(Note: Any other statute that exempts a concurrent wrongdoer from liability for damages can also be inserted.)* 12. (1) This section applies where a person suffering damage enters into a release with a concurrent wrongdoer, whether before or after the damage is suffered. (2) Where the person suffering the damage does not release all concurrent wrongdoers, the liability for damages of those concurrent wrongdoers who are not released is reduced by an amount of the damages proportionate to the degree to which the wrongful acts of the concurrent wrongdoers who are released contributed to the damage, and there shall be no contribution between those concurrent wrongdoers who are released and those who are not released.	(2) Where the injured person has obtained judgment against two or more concurrent wrongdoers in separate proceedings and the damage of the injured person has been assessed differently, in a claim for contribution by one of them from another of them the court shall determine the sum to which the parties to the claim shall contribute. 9. (1) The amount of contribution recoverable by one concurrent wrongdoer from another is the amount that is found by the court to be just and equitable having regard to the degree of responsibility of each concurrent wrongdoer for the damage of the injured person. (2) The degree of responsibility found by a court under subsection (1) may include any degree of responsibility, including responsibility for none or all of the damage. (3) If the degree of responsibility of a concurrent wrongdoer cannot be determined in relation to another concurrent wrongdoer, they shall be deemed to be equally responsible. (4) A concurrent wrongdoer whose liability for damages is less than that of another concurrent wrongdoer because of, (a) the contributory fault of the injured person; (b) a contract made with the injured person before the cause of action arose; (c) a statute; or (d) any other reason, is not liable to pay by way of contribution a sum that exceeds the amount of his or her liability to the injured person.

(continued)

Table 4: ***(Continued)***

Uniform Contributory Fault Act 1984	Contribution Among Wrongdoers and Contributory Negligence Act (Draft), 1988
(3) Where all concurrent wrongdoers are released, a person who gives consideration for the release, whether he is a concurrent wrongdoer or not, is entitled to contribution in accordance with this Act from any other concurrent wrongdoer based on the lesser of (a) the value of the consideration actually given for the release; and (b) the value of the consideration that in all the circumstances it would have been reasonable to give for the release. 13. In proceedings against a person for contribution under this Act, the fact that the person has been held not liable for damages in an action brought by or on behalf of the person who suffered the damage is conclusive proof in favour of the person from whom contribution is sought as to any issue that has been determined on its merit in the action. 14. Unless the person suffering the damage has been fully compensated or the court otherwise orders, a concurrent wrongdoer shall not issue execution on a judgment for contribution from another concurrent wrongdoer until (a) he satisfies that amount of the total damages that is proportionate to the degree to which his wrongful act contributed to the damage; and (b) the court makes provision for the payment into court of the proceeds of the execution to the credit of those persons that the court may order.	(5) Where the liability of a concurrent wrongdoer to the injured person is reduced as set out in subsection (4), the reduced liability does not affect the amount of contribution payable except as provided by subsection (4). (6) Where there are three or more concurrent wrongdoers and one cannot pay his or her due share of the liability because of insolvency or for any other reason, that share shall be allocated to the other concurrent wrongdoers proportionately to the degrees in which they are found responsible, without discharging the liability of the defaulting concurrent wrongdoer to contribute. (7) The delivery of goods or performance of a service by a concurrent wrongdoer in satisfying his or her liability to the injured person shall be included in a claim for contribution, and the value shall be fixed by the court for the purpose. 10. (1) Where a concurrent wrongdoer makes a settlement with the injured person that does not discharge the liability of another concurrent wrongdoer, the sum to which they may be required to contribute is the value of the consideration given for the settlement that is established by the concurrent wrongdoer who settled to have been reasonable in all the circumstances.

(continued)

Table 4: ***(Continued)***

Uniform Contributory Fault Act 1984	Contribution Among Wrongdoers and Contributory Negligence Act (Draft), 1988
15. An action against one or more concurrent wrongdoers is not barred by (a) a release of any other concurrent wrongdoer; or (b) a judgment against any other concurrent wrongdoer, and may be continued notwithstanding the release or judgment. 16. (1) Where a judgment determines the total liability for damages of concurrent wrongdoers in an action against one or more of them, the person suffering the damage is not entitled to have the total liability determined in a higher amount by a judgment in the same or any other action against any other concurrent wrongdoer. (2) Except in an action first taken against a concurrent wrongdoer, the persons suffering damage is [*sic*] not entitled to costs in an action taken against any other concurrent wrongdoer unless the court is of the opinion that there were reasonable grounds for bringing more than one action.	(2) Where the court is satisfied that the amount of consideration given for a settlement referred to in subsection (1) was not reasonable in all the circumstances, the court may fix the value of a reasonable consideration for the purposes of contribution. (3) Where, in a case referred to in subsection (1), the injured person obtains judgment against a concurrent wrongdoer who claims contribution from the concurrent wrongdoer who settled, the sum to which they may be required to contribute is the amount of the injured person's damages as determined by the court determining the claim for contribution. (4) Where, in a case referred to in subsection (1), proceedings are instituted against a concurrent wrongdoer to which the concurrent wrongdoer who settled is joined as a third party, the sum to which they may be required to contribute is the amount of their common liability for the damage as determined in those proceedings. 11. (1) Where a concurrent wrongdoer makes a settlement with the injured person that discharges the liability of another concurrent wrongdoer, the sum to which they may be required to contribute is the value of the consideration given for the settlement that is established by the concurrent wrongdoer who settled to have been reasonable in all the circumstances. (2) Where the court is satisfied that the amount of consideration given for a settlement referred to in subsection (1) was not reasonable in all the circumstances the court may fix the value of a reasonable consideration for the purposes of contribution.

(continued)

Table 4: ***(Continued)***

Uniform Contributory Fault Act 1984	Contribution Among Wrongdoers and Contributory Negligence Act (Draft), 1988
	12. In a proceeding to determine contribution between concurrent wrongdoers, the court shall disregard the existence of concurrent wrongdoers who are not parties to the proceeding. 13. (1) A concurrent wrongdoer shall not execute an order for contribution against another concurrent wrongdoer until the wrongdoer claiming contribution has paid to the injured person more than his or her share of the liability or until the contributing wrongdoer can no longer be sued successfully by the injured person. (2) Where the judgment of the injured person is not satisfied, any amount paid under the order shall be paid into court toward satisfaction of the judgment. DEFENCES 14. (1) It is a defence to a claim for contribution that, (a) the person against whom the claim is made could not at any time be held liable to the injured person for the damage; (b) the person against whom the claim is made has ceased to be liable to the injured person by virtue of the expiration of a limitation period contained in a contract between them that was entered into before the injured person's cause of action arose; or (c) the person from whom contribution is claimed has been held not liable on the merits in an action by the injured person.

(continued)

Table 4: *(Continued)*

Uniform Contributory Fault Act 1984	**Contribution Among Wrongdoers and Contributory Negligence Act (Draft), 1988**
	15. A concurrent wrongdoer may recover contribution from another concurrent wrongdoer even though the person against whom the claim is made has ceased to be liable to the injured person because of, (a) the expiration of a statutory limitation period, or the existence of an equitable defence based on delay; (b) the dismissal of an action by the injured person for the delay; (c) the failure of the injured person to comply with a procedural requirement; or (d) a settlement with or a release or waiver by the injured person after the injured person's cause of action arose, whether the person against whom the claim for contribution is made ceased to be liable to the injured person before or after the time when the claimant's right to contribution arose, determined in the same manner as set out in section 18. SETTLEMENTS 16. The damages awarded to an injured person against a concurrent wrongdoer shall be reduced by the amount of consideration received under a settlement with another person against whom the injured person has made a claim for the same loss. 17. (1) A concurrent wrongdoer who has made a settlement with the injured person, including a settlement that is approved by a court or is the subject of a judgment obtained by consent, may institute or continue proceedings for contribution from another concurrent wrongdoer, if the settlement provides for the discharge or reduction of the liability of the other concurrent wrongdoer to the injured person.

(continued)

Table 4: ***(Continued)***

Uniform Contributory Fault Act 1984	**Contribution Among Wrongdoers and Contributory Negligence Act (Draft), 1988**
	(2) Subsection (1) applies even though the person who is claiming contribution can be shown to have been not liable to the injured person, but the court may, in its discretion, refuse to order contribution if the person claiming contribution made the settlement without believing that he or she was or might be liable and without regard to any legal proceedings that might be instituted against him or her by the injured person for the claim settled.
	LIMITATIONS
	18. (1) A proceeding to claim contribution between wrongdoers must be commenced within two years after the right to contribution arose. (2) Where the claim to contribution is based on a settlement, the right to contribution shall be deemed to arise when the settlement is made. (3) Where the claim to contribution is based on a judgment, the right to contribution shall be deemed to arise when the judgment is given.
	PROCEDURE
	19. (1) A claim for contribution between parties to a proceeding commenced by an injured person must be made by crossclaim in accordance with the Rules of Civil Procedure. (2) A claim for contribution against a concurrent wrongdoer who is not a party to a proceeding commenced by an injured person must be by third party claim in accordance with the Rules of Civil Procedure.

(continued)

Table 4: *(Continued)*

Uniform Contributory Fault Act 1984	**Contribution Among Wrongdoers and Contributory Negligence Act (Draft), 1988**
	(3) A concurrent wrongdoer who has been held liable to an injured person may institute a separate proceeding to claim contribution from another concurrent wrongdoer only if the court is satisfied that it was impossible to proceed by crossclaim or impossible or impracticable to proceed by third party claim. GENERAL 20. This Act binds the Crown. 21. This Act applies where the damage is caused or contributed to by the act or omission of a person notwithstanding that another person had the opportunity of avoiding the consequences of the act or omission and failed to do so. 22. A question of the degree of fault or responsibility that contributed to the damage is a question for the trier of fact. 23. (1) This Act has primacy over any other Act that provides for the same subject matter, unless the other Act specifically provides that it is to apply notwithstanding this Act. (2) This Act is subject to the Workers' Compensation Act and section 34(1) of the Trustee Act. 24. The Negligence Act, being chapter 315 of the Revised Statutes of Ontario, 1980 and section 149 of the Courts of Justice Act 1984, being chapter 11, are repealed. 25. This Act comes into force on a day to be named by proclamation of the Lieutenant Governor. 26. The short title of this Act is the Contribution and Comparative Fault Act, 19—.

What was the response to this monumental labour on the part of the Uniform Law Conference of Canada and the Ontario Law Reform Commission? If the public record is any guide, it was a striking indifference. It does not appear that any legislation based on either model statute was ever introduced. In the case of the Uniform Contributory Fault Act, the Conference must bear some contributory fault. Some of the Act's language was highly technical and grammatically challenging, and, as I have noted, there were no annotations or examples[270] to explain the provisions. Also, once the Conference adopted the Act, it abandoned any sort of watching brief. This is because the ULCC follows the take-up of the current version of its model Acts, but not of the previous versions. There has been no take-up, so there is virtually nothing in the Conference's subsequent reports about the UCFA. But these factors have less force when it comes to the OLRC's proposed Contribution and Contributory Fault Act. For one thing, even though the OLRC act is longer and is based on the UCFA, its language is more streamlined and accessible. Where it is longer, it is so because it needs to be; otherwise not. Compare the basic sections on contributory (comparative) fault:

Table 5: Comparison of UCLA and ORLC Definitions on Contributory Fault

1984 Uniform Act, Section 5:	1988 OLRC Draft Act, Section 2:
(1) Where the fault of two or more persons contributes to damage suffered by one or more of them, the liability for damages of a person whose fault contributed to the damage is reduced by an amount of the damages proportionate to the degree to which the fault of the person suffering the damage contributed to the damage. (2) Where a person, other than a person referred to in subsection (1), makes a claim arising from the damage suffered by a person referred to in subsection (1), the liability for damages of a person whose fault contributed to the damage is reduced by an amount of the damages proportionate to the degree to which the fault of the person who suffered the damage from which the claim arose contributed to the damage. (3) If the degrees to which the fault of persons contributed to damage cannot be determined in relation to each other, those persons shall be deemed to have contributed equally in relation to each other.	(1) Where a person is injured by the wrongful act of one or more persons and the fault of the injured person is found to have contributed to the damage, the court shall determine the degrees of fault of the person or persons and of the injured person that contributed to the damage, and shall apportion the damages in proportion to the degrees of fault that are so found. ... (6) If the degree to which the fault of persons contributes to the damage cannot be determined in relation to each other, those persons shall be deemed to have contributed equally in relation to each other.

While OLRC section 2(1) is not without its drafting problems,[271] it is markedly more readable than the labyrinthine language of UCFA section 5(2). And though there is no annotated version, the 1988 OLRC Report provided footnotes throughout to the draft Act. So it is possible to 'reverse-engineer' the 1988 draft to create an annotated version. Indeed,

[270] On the benefits of including examples in legislation, see Elliott (n 154).

[271] eg, the phrase 'and the fault of the injured person is found to have contributed to the damage' suggests that the section only applies when the plaintiff is also at fault. Of course, apportionment applies even when the plaintiff is without fault. Also, the section uses the phrase 'wrongful act', yet the definition of 'injured person' in s 1 uses the phrase 'act or omission'. A start at further improving s 2(1) of the OLRC draft might be:

the project that I suggest at the end of this paper—a new model Apportionment of Liability Act based on the best aspects of all Canadian reform efforts to date—would do just that. Second, the OLRC was working under a specific mandate to reform interrelated areas of the law, one aspect of which was contributory fault and contribution among wrongdoers. The Commission identified 'substantial defects' in the 'limited, and ambiguous, scope of the Negligence Act',[272] and enlisted the Government's most senior legislative draftsman to correct them.[273] It is hard to believe that all of this would have taken place without a legislative vision. However, the vision likely went into abeyance when the government changed in 1990,[274] in the manner of the out-with-the-old-and-in-with-the-new cycle that has always plagued long-term reform initiatives.

The Revised 1990 Ontario Act

While no amendments to the Ontario Act followed from the 1988 OLRC Report, Ontario's statutes were revised in 1990, including minor changes made under powers delegated to its Chief Legislative Counsel.[275] Thus, the definitions of 'action', 'defendant' and 'plaintiff' that

> (1) Where a person is injured by the wrongful act or omission of one or more persons, the court must determine the degrees of fault of all persons contributing to the damage and apportion liability for damages according to those degrees of fault.

This could be followed by two examples, one showing how the section would work when the injured person is not at fault, and one showing how it would work when the injured person is at fault. Alternatively, if it were thought necessary, a sentence could be added to explain that the injured person is included in the calculation.

Note that, for the purposes of this example, I am accepting the use of the words 'person' and 'persons' instead of 'party' and 'parties'. This in itself is problematic, as it suggests that the court might be required to apportion fault to missing wrongdoers, in turn leading to the prospect that a portion of the plaintiff's loss could never be recovered as against those wrongdoers—a result that itself seems wrong. See Lewis N Klar, 'Contributory Negligence and Contribution Between Tortfeasors' in L Klar (ed), *Studies in Canadian Tort Law* (Toronto, Butterworths, 1977) 145, 157, where Klar criticises *Houle v British Columbia Hydro and Power Authority* (1972) 29 DLR (3d) 510 (BCSC) (jury assigned 10 % of blame to defendant and 15% to one of two plaintiffs, the remaining 75% to nobody). The effect, Klar notes, is to place 75% of liability for the damages on innocent parties. See also *Wells v McBrine* (1988) 33 BCLR (2d) 86 (CA), 47 CCLT 94, [1989] 2 WWR 695, 54 DLR (4th) 708, leave to appeal to SCC ref'd (1989) 36 BCLR (2d) xxxvii (Esson JA doubting whether *Houle* was correctly decided if, in effect, the jury had simply refused to assign the remaining 75%, but concluding in the case before him that a group of 'troublemakers' described in the pleadings, though not named as parties, could be assigned 40% of the blame). However, the decision turned on the fact that by the time *Wells v McBrine* was decided, the Court had started interpreting the BC statute as converting joint and several liability into several liability when there was contributory negligence: see *Leischner v West Kootenay Power & Light Co* [1986] 3 WWR 97 (BCCA). In *Martin v Listowel Memorial Hospital* (2000) 192 DLR (4th) 250, 48 CPC (4th) 195, 51 OR (3d) 384 (CA), the Ontario Court of Appeal emphatically denied that such an approach was proper in Ontario. It concluded at para 8 that in an apportionment under s 1 of the Negligence Act, 'joint and several liability to the plaintiff can and will attach only to a party defendant, although others who may also have been at fault could potentially have been found jointly and severally liable had they been sued by the plaintiff'. In Alberta, courts have followed *Martin v Listowel Memorial Hospital*, not *Wells v McBrine*: see *Hartum v Sitko*, 2004 ABQB 854, 43 Alta LR (4th) 333, 366 AR 75, [2005] 9 WWR 531, paras 38–42.

[272] 1988 OLRC Report (n 229) 1.

[273] See n 230.

[274] David Peterson's Liberal Government was voted out in favour of Bob Rae's New Democratic Party. The 35th Parliament ran from 6 September 1990 to 28 April 1995. With the possible exception of a brief fling with the United Farmers Party in the early 1920s, this was the only period in Ontario's history in which it was governed by a left-of-centre party.

[275] See now, Legislation Act 2006, SO 2006, c 21, Sch F, Pt V.

had long been in section 1 of the Ontario Act were deleted, these terms being more than adequately defined in the revised Courts of Justice Act.[276] However, what may be a minor issue to some can be major to others. The result of this change was to again renumber the Ontario Act, so that the all-important sections 2 to 5 became sections 1 to 4, and the original section 8, which had become section 9 in a previous revision, returned to becoming section 8—for a while. There is no substantive fuss in all of this, and there is something to be said for occasionally cleaning house. But it makes researching and referring to the legislation over time a nightmarish task.[277] As it turns out, section 8 was repealed 12 years later, in the last amendment to the Ontario Act. This was a repeal of some consequence, to which I turn next.

The Limitations Act 2002 and Repeal of the 1948 Amendment to the Ontario Act

As my synopsis of the 1988 OLRC Report indicates, the Ontario Law Reform Commission (since superseded by the Law Commission of Ontario)[278] had examined issues relating to limitation periods and contribution law in chapters 7 and 9 of the 1988 OLRC Report.[279] And though the subject of limitation periods typically 'does not excite a great deal of attention from legislators',[280] it *was* on the Government's reform agenda after the 1990 election, as it had been off and on since the mid-1960s.[281] In 1991, a 'Limitations Act Consultation Group' appointed by former Attorney General Ian Scott reported to his successor in the new

[276] Courts of Justice Act, RSO 1990, c C.43, s 1 (defining 'action' to mean a civil proceeding 'that is not an application and includes a proceeding commenced by claim, statement of claim, notice of action, counterclaim, crossclaim, third or subsequent party claim, or divorce petition or counterpetition' and defining 'plaintiff' and 'defendant' to mean a person who commences an action or a person against whom an action is commenced).

[277] There are at least two common legislative techniques for addressing the numbering problem. When a section is repealed, the word 'Repealed' is inserted after the number, with a citation to the repealing statute. When a section is added between two other sections, decimal numbering will be used. So, for example, if two new sections are inserted between sections 3 and 4 of an Act, they will be numbered s 3.1 and s 3.2. The Income Tax Act, RSC, 1985, c 1 (5th Supp) has taken this to a high art, and there is an apocryphal story that if there were ever an attempt at cleaning up the numbering in a revised statute, income tax lawyers would be unable to cope and would have to take up some other line of work.

[278] See the non-ironically titled Good Government Act 2009, SO 2009, c 33, s 53 (repealing the Ontario Law Reform Commission Act, RSO 1990, c 24) and Law Commission of Ontario, www.lco-cdo.org/en/strategic-plan-2008-2012-highlights (noting that LCO was 'launched' 7 September 2007, though with nary a word about its illustrious predecessor).

[279] 1988 OLRC Report (n 229) 144–71, 217–23, 228.

[280] G Mew, 'Limitations Act 2002: A Huge Reform of Existing Law', www.practicepro.ca/practice/Limitations_Act.asp. Prior to his appointment as a judge of the Ontario Superior Court of Justice on 20 December 2013, Mew was a leading lawyer, mediator and arbitrator and authority on limitations law. I am indebted to his summary of Ontario's pre-2002 attempts at reforming limitations law, parts of which I have adopted in this paragraph.

[281] See *Report of the Ontario Law Reform Commission on Limitation of Actions* (Toronto, Department of the Attorney General, 1969); digitised version at ia600702.us.archive.org/31/items/reportoflimitation00onta/reportoflimitation00onta.pdf., 7, the Commission said that to the ordinary citizen, Ontario's limitation laws were 'beyond comprehension'. In 1977, the Attorney General released a discussion paper comprising a draft Bill and brief commentary that reflected the recommendations of the Commission, with some modifications based on reforms introduced in British Columbia. Discussion continued until Bill 160 was introduced in 1983, but by 1985 there was a change of government and other priorities intervened.

government, Howard Hampton.[282] The following year, on 25 November 1992, Hampton introduced Bill 99,[283] based on the Consultation Group's report. It would have substantially reformed the law, but died after first reading. The legislative agenda proceeded apace, unencumbered by limitations law; the government changed again; then in 2000, the new Attorney General, Jim Flaherty,[284] introduced Bill 163.[285] After the 2001 prorogation of the legislature, Attorney General David Young reintroduced it as Bill 10,[286] and it passed first reading on 25 April 2001. The legal community provided suggestions for improving it, some of which were integrated into the Bill. But nothing happened until November 2002, 'when with little fanfare and no real opportunity for the profession to make further comments',[287] the legislation appeared for the final time as the Limitations Act 2002, a schedule to Bill 213, the Justice Statute Law Amendment Act.[288] It passed without debate and came into effect on 1 January 2004. And so a modern Ontario limitations law was born.

Or was it? In some respects, yes. Section 4 created a basic two-year limitation period, running from the day a claim is or ought to have been discovered (section 5). It replaced the general limitation periods in the previous Limitation Act, as well as many of the nasty (or nice, depending on your perspective) limitation periods scattered in other statutes, like the three-month period for claims against municipalities for non-repair of roads or the one-year period for claims against health professionals (section 25).[289] And it provided an ultimate limitation period of 15 years for most causes of action, promoting finality in litigation (section 15). This simplification was welcome. But according to commercial litigator John Chapman, while Ontario had been 'trying half-heartedly' to reform its statutes over three decades, 'the law in courts and other jurisdictions itself was rapidly evolving',[290] and reforms that might have been germane in the 1960s were not necessarily so in light of intervening judge-made law. Moreover, by Chapman's account, the statute was 'maddeningly imprecise' and its implications, even in 'garden variety situations',[291] had not been thought through, leading to what he thought would likely be 'a large and accelerating volume of case law'.[292] Chapman's prediction, made in 2008, seems to have been borne out; there are already over a thousand decisions on the 2002 statute, and no sign of a plateau yet.[293]

A small but difficult part of the case law is on contribution. The Limitations Act 2002 did a few things affecting contribution law, the most important of which was to enact a specific

[282] Limitations Act Consultation Group, *Recommendations for a New Limitations Act: Report of the Limitations Act Consultation Group* (Toronto, Ministry of the Attorney General, 1991).

[283] Bill 99, An Act to Revise the Limitations Act, 2nd Sess, 35th Leg, Ontario, 1992.

[284] Later, MP and Canada's Finance Minister. Flaherty died in April 2014: *Wikipedia*, *sv* 'Jim Flaherty', en.wikipedia.org/wiki/Jim_Flaherty. Flaherty's stint as Ontario's Attorney General was brief, lasting from 17 June 1999 to 7 February 2001: 'Jim Flaherty, MPP', www.ontla.on.ca/web/members/members_detail.do?locale=en&ID=35.

[285] Bill 163, An Act to revise the Limitations Act, 1st Sess, 37th Leg, Ontario, 2000.

[286] Bill 10, An Act to revise the Limitations Act, 2nd Sess, 37th Leg, Ontario, 2000.

[287] Mew (n 280).

[288] Limitations Act 2002, SO 2002, c 24, Sch B.

[289] ss 25–49 set out the very extensive list of repealed or amended limitation provisions in other statutes.

[290] J Chapman, 'Eight (Unanswered) Questions on the New Limitations Act' (2008) 34 *Advocates' Quarterly* 285, 291.

[291] Ibid, 285.

[292] Ibid, 289.

[293] Chapman provided a LexisNexis search to corroborate his claim. Updating it on Westlaw, I got these results (year: *number of cases*): 2004: *13*; 2005: *32*; 2006: *40*; 2007: *60*; 2008: *89*; 2009: *127*; 2010: *139*; 2011: *183*; 2012: *176*; 2013: *207*.

period governing contribution proceedings (in section 18) and to repeal section 8 of the Negligence Act (in section 25).

Section 18 read, and still reads, as follows:

> 18(1) Contribution and indemnity
>
> For the purposes of subsection 5(2) [the date that one is presumed to have discovered the basis for a claim] and section 15 [the ultimate 15-year limitation period], in the case of a claim by one alleged wrongdoer against another for contribution and indemnity, the day on which the first alleged wrongdoer was served with the claim in respect of which contribution and indemnity is sought shall be deemed to be the day the act or omission on which that alleged wrongdoer's claim is based took place.
>
> 18(2) Application
>
> Subsection (1) applies whether the right to contribution and indemnity arises in respect of a tort or otherwise.

Coupled with section 4, the basic two-year limitation period,[294] this meant that the time for the first wrongdoer (now the contribution claimant) to claim contribution against the second wrongdoer (now the contribution defendant) would be two years from the plaintiff serving the first wrongdoer with the statement of claim. In one aspect, this was like the 1978 English reform that I mentioned earlier.[295] That was the notion of enacting a single limitation period that would clearly apply to contribution claims, not restricted to tort causes of action. But in two other aspects, section 18 differed from both the English reform and the 1988 OLRC Act.

First, those enactments, actual and model, covered settlements, whether the injured person had sued or not, and section 18 was silent on settlements. Presumably, settlements that take place without an action ever being commenced—a common occurrence—are covered by section 5, which declares several ways in which one can 'discover' the existence of a claim. Some of these justify Chapman's 'maddeningly imprecise' label, such as section 5(1)(a)(iv), which starts the two-year clock running from the day 'that, having regard to the nature of the injury, loss or damage, a proceeding would be an appropriate means to seek to remedy it'. Generally, the common sense inference, and one that would be consistent with the Negligence Act, is that a wrongdoer 'discovers' the existence of a contribution claim against another wrongdoer at the time of settling with the injured person.[296]

[294] s 4 reads: 'Unless this Act provides otherwise, a proceeding shall not be commenced in respect of a claim after the second anniversary of the day on which the claim was discovered'. The word 'claim' is defined in s 1 as 'a claim to remedy an injury, loss or damage that occurred as a result of an act or omission'. To learn what 'discovered' means, the starting point would be s 5, which is a *pièce de résistance* that I will not attempt to reproduce here.

[295] See nn 224–27 and accompanying text.

[296] See *Canada Building Materials Co v Osler Paving & Construction Ltd* (Trustee of) sub nom *St Mary's Cement Inc v Osler Paving & Construction Ltd* (2009) 80 CLR (3d) 295, 95 OR (3d) 448 (SCJ Master) para 28. The case deals with the transitional provisions under the Limitations Act 2002. Master Dash applies, but factually distinguishes, a Court of Appeal decision on those provisions decided three weeks prior: *Placzek v Green*, 2009 ONCA 83, 69 CPC (6th) 42, 307 DLR (4th) 441. The Court in *Placzek v Green* concluded at paras 41–42 that the words 'act or omission' in s 5(1)(a)(iii) of the Limitations Act 2002 should, for contribution claims, be construed to mean the contribution defendant's failure to discharge his or her fair share of an injured person's claim before the contribution claimant's liability for a disproportionate share of the injured person's damages has crystallised. This interpretation stems from the restitutionary nature of contribution claims. I have used the word 'generally' at the beginning of the sentence accompanying this footnote because the idea that one 'discovers' a contribution claim at the time of settling isn't iron-clad. Recall *Marschler v G Masser's Garage* (n 123) where the driver's insurer, having

Section 18 overrides this for settlements following service of a statement of claim by deeming the service date to be the 'discovery' date for starting the contribution limitation period. But not for settlements in which no statement of claim is served. For this, one has to turn to section 5, and one may ask why that should be necessary when there is a section entitled 'Contribution and indemnity'.

Second, the 1978 English reform and 1988 OLRC reform had said that the two years would run from the date of judgment or settlement,[297] not from the date of being served with the statement of claim. The difference is dramatic. As Chapman explained, for defendants, the new provisions meant that 'effort must be made up front to identify all persons against whom there may be a contribution claim'.[298] As practitioners know, this can be challenging to do before getting the kind of information that comes from the discovery process, especially in complex litigation. By that time, a limitation period running from the date of service of claim may have expired, and the contribution claimant would have to try to argue under section 5 that the later discovery should override the deeming effect of section 18. Far from promoting certainty, this could promote uncertainty. Section 18 also seemed to be inconsistent with the restitutionary principle on which the statutory right to seek contribution is based—generally, it is understood to arise when a wrongdoer has settled with, or been held liable to, the injured person. At the time of service of the statement of claim, neither of those things will have happened in the ordinary case.

Regarding the repeal of section 8 (formerly section 9), let us first recall how it read. For convenience, I reproduce it again here:

> Where an action is commenced against a tort feasor or where a tort feasor settles with a person who has suffered damage as a result of a tort, within the period of limitation prescribed for the commencement of actions by any relevant statute, no proceedings for contribution or indemnity against any other tort feasor are defeated by the operation of any statute limiting the time for the commencement of the action against such tort feasor provided,
>
> (a) such proceedings are commenced within one year of the date of the judgment in the action or the settlement, as the case may be; and
>
> (b) there has been compliance with any statute requiring notice of claim against such tort feasor.

As explained earlier, the circumstance addressed by this section was one in which a plaintiff sues or settles with one tortfeasor when the plaintiff's limitation period for suing another has expired. The section gave the first tortfeasor a year from the settlement or judgment to bring contribution proceedings against the otherwise protected second tortfeasor, so as not to make contribution dependent on the plaintiff's whim in deciding when to bring an action. This is *not* equivalent to saying that section 8 had previously enacted a one-year limitation period for bringing contribution proceedings. Yet it appears that some courts and some commentators, including the Limitations Act Consultation Group, had interpreted it in just that manner. David Cheifetz, a long-time analyst of the law of contribution

settled with the plaintiff without an action having been commenced, discovered on further investigation that the mechanic was at fault and brought a successful subrogated contribution claim.

[297] See s 18 of the OLRC Act 1984, above Table 4.

[298] Chapman (n 290) 290.

and contributory fault, has explained this in depth, and I cannot do better than reproduce his analysis here, which also includes an excerpt from the Limitations Act Consultation Group's report:

> It appears that the consultation group's belief was that the significant aspect of s 8 was that, because it provided a limitation period for the contribution claim that did not start to run until W1 [the first wrongdoer] was held liable or settled, and because it permitted W1 to wait too long a time to wait to commence the contribution claim, the ability of the (*sic*) W2 [the second wrongdoer] to defend would be unduly prejudiced.
>
>> The difficulty with the present law is that the first wrongdoer can wait to commence legal proceedings against the second wrongdoer until long after the limitation period between the second wrongdoer and the plaintiff has expired, even though the first wrongdoer's claim is based on the second wrongdoer's liability to the plaintiff. If the second wrongdoer has been sued by the plaintiff in a timely manner, the second wrongdoer may have been able to defeat the plaintiff's claim. But, years later, the second wrongdoer may have lost his or her evidence or the plaintiff may no longer exist.
>>
>> The Ontario Law Reform Commission recently examined the law relating to contribution among wrongdoers and recommended that there be no changes to the basic principles of contribution. In the context of their particular study they did not recommend major reforms of the limitations provisions. Nevertheless, in the context of a comprehensive review of limitations policy, especially with emphasis upon the discovery principle, it does not seem unfair to encourage the first wrongdoer to commence proceedings for contribution as soon as possible. Thus in these proposals, it is recommended that time against the first wrongdoer begin to run not when he or she is found liable to the plaintiff, but as soon as the plaintiff serves him or her with the original claim. It is at that point that the first wrongdoer is on notice to consider what other wrongdoers may be liable.
>>
>> By moving the limitation starting point of the first wrongdoer's contribution claim from the date of judgment up to the date of the plaintiff's claim, the limitation policy shortens the second wrongdoer's exposure to potential liability and increases the second wrongdoer's ability to defend the claim.
>
> In short, the focus of the contribution portion of the report is on the complications created by the possibility that the contribution claim may be made in an action litigated separately and after the action in which P's claim against W1 is tried.
>
> My impression is that no member of the consultation group had any special expertise in contribution jurisprudence. Perhaps there was some consultation with someone who had that expertise. If so, the report did not say. Remarkably, the report does not mention, at all, that s 8, where it applied, prevented the contribution defendant from defeating the contribution claim on the basis that the contribution defendant was no longer liable to the injured person because the limitation period for the injured person's action against the contribution defendant had expired. The text of the report implies that the consultation group thought that s 8 was somehow inconsistent with 'discoverability-based' limitations of action legislation because it allowed the contribution claim to be commenced after the contribution claimant was held liable to the injured person, or settled with the injured person.
>
> There were some things that were clear enough by 1991, even in Ontario contribution jurisprudence. Section 8 did not establish the limitation period for either the commencement or the duration of Negligence Act contribution claims. The section was a saving provision for the contribution claimant. Where it applied, s 8 extended the limitation period otherwise applicable to the

> contribution claim by one year from either the date of the injured person's judgment against the contribution claimant, or the date of the settlement between the injured person and the contribution claimant.[299]

As might be expected, the confusion that had infiltrated the Limitations Act 2002 also infiltrated the jurisprudence. Yet courts have a way of reaching the right results even when working with problematic material—and even if the ways of getting there create other problems in the law. I say this despite the long and unsatisfactory history of the common law contributory negligence rule, no-contribution-among-tortfeasors rule, and judgment-and-release-bar rules discussed in this chapter. This, in effect, is what Cheifetz has concluded in relation to the problem that was formerly addressed by section 8 of the Negligence Act—the problem of an injured person suing one of two wrongdoers within the applicable limitation period for *that* wrongdoer but after the expiry of the applicable limitation period for the *other* wrongdoer. Such was the problem in *Waterloo Region District School Board v CRD Engineering Ltd*,[300] the case on which Cheifetz was commenting in the above analysis.

The essential facts of this multiparty case were as follows. In 2002, a severe storm blew down the walls of a school gymnasium being built for the Waterloo school board. The engineering firm on the job was Truax Engineering Ltd. At that time, the Professional Engineering Act had a 12-month limitation period for bringing an action for damages arising from the provision of engineering services. By the time the school board commenced an action, that period had long passed, so the board didn't sue Truax, but named as parties the general contractor, CRD Construction Ltd, the architect, JL Cortes Architect Corporation, and some others. I will call these parties 'CRD'. After being sued, CRD cross-claimed against Truax within the two-year limitation period, seeking contribution and indemnity. Truax moved for dismissal of the action and the contribution claims against it. The motions judge refused the motion, as did a five-judge panel of the Court of Appeal. Truax became liable to have to pay contribution to CRD even though the school board couldn't sue Truax directly. Cheifetz says this was the right result as a matter of contribution law. In other words, nothing in the Limitations Act 2002 suggested that CRD's contribution rights became unenforceable just because the limitation period for the school board's action against Truax had expired before CRD commenced contribution proceedings.

However, Truax had also made arguments about section 8 of the Negligence Act. It had argued that section 8 was enacted in 1948 to address the state of the law, which it said was that contribution and indemnity could only be claimed against a concurrent tortfeasor who, at the time of the claim, could have been liable to the plaintiff; that the language of section 18 of the Limitations Act 2002 didn't have the same effect and, therefore, whether deliberately or inadvertently, the legislature had removed the effect of section 8, making the law on the issue what it was pre-1948.[301] This was an ingenious argument,[302] and the Court of Appeal spent quite a bit of time on it; indeed, the case starts out with an analysis

[299] Cheifetz, 'Silk Purses and Silver Linings' (n 173) 450–52. The double-indented portion is an excerpt from the Limitations Act Consultation Group (n 282) 42–43.

[300] *Waterloo Region District School Board v CRD Construction Ltd*, 2010 ONCA 838, 327 DLR (4th) 611, 103 OR (3d) 81.

[301] Ibid, para 3.

[302] Though one that ignores the provision, analogues of which can be found across the country, that the 'repeal, revocation or amendment of an Act or regulation does not imply anything about the previous state of the law', Legislation Act 2006 (n 275) s 56, cited in Cheifetz, 'Silk Purses and Silver Linings' (n 173) 453.

of the Negligence Act and the history of section 8 in particular. The Court concluded that the Limitations Act 2002 'effectively replaces s 8 of the Negligence Act with a new two-year limitation period, but with the same legal effect'.[303] Cheifetz says this is wrong, for a host of interconnected reasons. I will not go into all of them here, but the key one is that the Court presumed 'that the Legislature did not intend to change "the s 8 regime" in enacting the Limitations Act 2002 and repealing s 8 other than in relation to the commencement and duration of the contribution limitation period'.[304] This stance, says Cheifetz, 'repeats the too-common mistake of conflating the separate issues of the duration of the contribution limitation period with the issue of whether still-existing potential liability on the part of W2 to P is a prerequisite for contribution'.[305] The court should first decide,

> without regard to the limitation of actions legislation, what the substantive law requirements are for the cause of action for contribution under the Negligence Act, or otherwise. Then and only then would the court need to look at the limitations of action legislation to see if it mandates that W1 could not claim contribution from W2 if P's limitation period against W2 had expired before W1 commences the contribution claim.[306]

If Cheifetz were asked to put it in idiomatic terms, he might say that 'the limitations tail shouldn't wag the contribution dog'. And though disagreeing with the Court's reasoning, he takes comfort that the result 'is the right result'.[307]

Evidently, the interaction of contribution law with limitations law is complex, and will likely be a work in progress for some time to come.[308] As with other aspects of the Act, the jurisprudence should be developed, not only in accordance with precedent, but also with the principles that animate it. I turn to that in the next section. In the meantime, though, let's have a last look at the Ontario Act. Table 6 shows it with the 1990 renumbering and after the repeal of section 8 came into effect at the beginning of 2004. As there have been no further changes since then, this is also how the Act appears today—after all its many contortions, the shortest it has looked since the early 1930s.

A Matter of Principle(s)

In this section, I discuss five principles that animate the legislation on concurrent fault. It may seem strange to have delayed the discussion of principles until this point. But the fact is that some of these principles have only emerged over time, as courts and law reformers have reflected on the purposes to accord to the legislation. A statute originally enacted chiefly to overcome the contributory negligence rule and the no-contribution-among-tortfeasors

[303] *Waterloo* (n 300), para 4.
[304] Cheifetz, 'Silk Purses and Silver Linings' (n 173) 454.
[305] Ibid, 454–55.
[306] Ibid, 456–57.
[307] Ibid, 515.
[308] The issues discussed in this section are especially relevant to Saskatchewan, where, on 1 May 2005, The Limitations Act, SS 2004, c L-16.1 was proclaimed. It followed the same procedure as Ontario: enacting a section dealing with contribution and indemnity (s 14, identically worded to s 18 of Ontario's Limitations Act 2002) and repealing s 10 of The Contributory Negligence Act, RSS 1978, c C-31 (identical to s 8 of Ontario's Negligence Act). Unlike in Ontario, though, there has so far been very little litigation associated with the transition.

Table 6: The Consolidated Ontario Act, c 2014

1.	Where damages have been caused or contributed to by the fault or neglect of two or more persons, the court shall determine the degree in which each of such persons is at fault or negligent, and, where two or more persons are found at fault or negligent, they are jointly and severally liable to the person suffering loss or damage for such fault or negligence, but as between themselves, in the absence of any contract express or implied, each is liable to make contribution and indemnify each other in the degree in which they are respectively found to be at fault or negligent.
2.	A tort feasor may recover contribution or indemnity from any other tort feasor who is, or would if sued have been, liable in respect of the damage to any person suffering damage as a result of a tort by settling with the person suffering such damage, and thereafter commencing or continuing action against such other tort feasor, in which event the tort feasor settling the damage shall satisfy the court that the amount of the settlement was reasonable, and in the event that the court finds the amount of the settlement was excessive it may fix the amount at which the claim should have been settled.
3.	In any action for damages which is founded upon the fault or negligence of the defendant[,] if fault or negligence is found on the part of the plaintiff which contributed to the damages, the court shall apportion the damages in proportion to the degree of fault or negligence found against the parties respectively.
4.	If it is not practicable to determine the respective degree of fault or negligence as between any parties to an action, such parties shall be deemed to be equally at fault or negligent.
5.	Wherever it appears that any person not already a party to an action is or may be wholly or partly responsible for the damages claimed, such person may be added as a party defendant to the action upon such terms as are considered just or may be made a third party to the action in the manner prescribed by the rules of practice for adding third parties.
6.	In any action tried with a jury, the degree of fault or negligence of the respective parties shall be a question of fact for the jury.
7.	Where the damages are occasioned by the fault or negligence of more than one party, the court shall have power to direct that the plaintiff shall bear some portion of the costs if the circumstances render this just.

rule has, over time, increasingly had to serve other interests. Some of the principles are long-standing, but have changed in relative importance over time and will likely change in importance again. All of them are key to the civil litigation process and therefore key to the way the legislation works. And so any question of further law reform must also engage with these principles. I will refer to them as the *compensation principle*, the *apportionment principle*, the *finality principle*, the *settlement principle*, and the *restitutionary principle*.

The *compensation principle* denotes the idea that the basic purpose of the law of civil obligations, and of tort law especially, is to compensate persons for legal wrongs done to them. Of course, the law of civil obligations serves other important purposes, including prevention of harm, deterrence and upholding of rights. But most cases that engage the legislation are brought with the paramount purpose of obtaining compensation for actual or perceived wrongs.

The *apportionment principle* reflects the notion that when more than one person causes or contributes to compensable damage or loss, liability for it should be shared by those who caused or contributed to it, including the person who suffered the loss. Stated so broadly, the principle is quite fluid and capable of modification. It includes, for example, the notion that liability might be apportioned equally, as it once was in English admiralty law, and as it is under all the statutes when it is impossible to attribute degrees of concurrent fault. It also includes the notion that apportionment might be limited, negated or qualified in some way. Examples include the provisions that once attributed a driver's negligence to a guest passenger and a spouse's negligence to the injured spouse. The UK legislation provides another example when it envisions the court as 'having regard' to a plaintiff's own negligence when reducing damages, phrasing that confers a discretion absent from the Ontario Act and other Canadian statutes, which typically state that the court 'shall' apportion damages according to fault or negligence. Another example, prevalent in many US jurisdictions and now codified in a model Act,[309] is the concept that a plaintiff whose fault exceeds the combined fault of the other concurrent wrongdoers should recover no damages at all. No Canadian jurisdiction takes such an approach, but it is useful to remember that a strict apportionment of liability by degrees of fault is only one possibility among many.

The *finality principle* seeks to avoid a multiplicity of proceedings. The law of *res judicata* and issue estoppel, for example, are based chiefly on this principle. The finality principle also informs provisions like section 5 of the Ontario Act, which appears designed to encourage, wherever possible, the determination of all relevant issues relating to liability in one proceeding.

The *settlement principle* favours settling disputes over litigating them. While the principle has always operated,[310] it has taken on greater prominence with the advent of interest-based negotiation,[311] settlement advocacy,[312] mandatory mediation,[313] and court rules that encourage early and reasonable settlement offers, with adverse cost consequences for failure to accept them.[314]

The *restitutionary principle* is central to contribution among wrongdoers. It is based on avoiding unjust enrichment. The Ontario Law Reform Commission was the chief proponent of this principle, characterising it as an 'overarching' theme that 'compels the non-paying concurrent wrongdoer to pay for the benefit he received as a result of the full or partial satisfaction of the injured person's judgment by another concurrent wrongdoer'.[315] The Ontario Court of Appeal has endorsed the restitutionary principle in a number of decisions.[316] The principle is closely connected to joint and several liability—and again,

309 National Conference of Commissioners on Uniform State Laws (2002–03), Uniform Apportionment of Tort Responsibility Act (UATRA) s 3. This Act is the successor to the Uniform Comparative Fault Act. See also n 347.

310 While authority should not be necessary for the long-standing policy in favour of settlement, it can be found, eg, in *Kelvin Energy Ltd v Lee* [1992] 3 SCR 235, 259, quoting with approval the decision of Callaghan ACJHC in *Sparling v Southam Inc* (1988) 41 BLR 22 (Ont HC) 28; *Radhakrishnan v University of Calgary Faculty Assn* (2002) 215 DLR (4th) 624 (Alta CA); and *Jameson v Central Electricity Generating Board* [1999] 1 All ER 193 (HL). See also Confucius, *Analects*, Book 12, c 500 BC ('I can try a lawsuit as well as other men, but the most important thing is to prevent lawsuits').

311 See R Fisher, W Ury and B Patton, *Getting to Yes: Negotiating Agreement Without Giving In*, 3rd edn (New York, Penguin Books, 2011).

312 See J Macfarlane, The New Lawyer: How Settlement Is Transforming the Practice of Law (Vancouver, UBC Press, 2008).

313 See, eg, Rules of Civil Procedure, RRO 1990, Reg 194, r 49.

314 Ibid, r 24.1.

315 1988 OLRC Report (n 229) 1.

316 See especially *Ukrainian (Fort William) Credit Union Ltd (In Liquidation) v Nesbitt, Burns Ltd* (1997) 152 DLR (4th) 640 (Ont CA), leave to appeal granted (1998) 111 OAC 198 (SCC), declared moot (1999) 161 OAC 199 (SCC) paras 21–23.

other approaches are possible here. Over the years, there have been periodic lobbying efforts to convert from a joint-and-several liability regime to a several-only (also called proportionate) liability regime, based on concerns raised by certain defendants, such as municipalities, about being held responsible for other defendants' shares of liability. These efforts have made some inroads, particularly in the US.[317] However, Canadian law reform work has generally favoured retention of joint and several liability,[318] with the result that the restitutionary principle is alive and well in Canada.

As might be expected, these principles are not always in harmony with one another, and what has made the life of the legislation interesting is the conflicts that arise between the principles and the ways in which courts and legislatures reconcile them or decide that one principle trumps another. Thus, the apportionment principle comes to the plaintiff's aid by repealing the common law contributory negligence rule, but also operates to reduce recovery; on its face, that conflicts with the compensation principle. The conflict is reconciled by apportioning liability according to fault: plaintiffs get full compensation awards except for the portions that can be attributed to their own fault. This works well enough for most cases, though 'fault' is a slippery concept and one that is problematic when it comes to strict-liability wrongs and vicarious liability. It requires attenuation to be workable; indeed, it may even require rethinking aspects of traditional tort doctrine. A good example of the need to accommodate or reconcile principles is that of partial settlement. That is the subject of a recent reform proposal out of British Columbia, which I turn to next.

The British Columbia Law Institute Proposal on Contribution After Settlement

In a multiparty case, some defendants typically want to settle early, and hope to get more favourable terms for doing so. But suppose there is then a trial in which the plaintiff succeeds against some or all of the remaining non-settling defendants. The non-settling defendants who pay the judgment may be able to seek contribution from the settling defendants, vaporising any advantage that those defendants may have gained from settling early. Conversely, certain types of agreements that the plaintiff might enter into with the settling defendants may effectively remove the non-settling defendants' contribution rights.

[317] See UATRA (n 309) s 6 (setting out a several-liability-only regime, with exceptions for intentional wrongdoing and statutorily enacted joint-and-several regimes in specific areas, such as environmental law). The UATRA is model legislation, not actually enacted in any state. For the UATRA text, see uniformlaws.org/Act.aspx?title=Apportionment%20of%20Tort%20Responsibility%20Act. The Uniform Law Commission was formerly called the National Conference of Commissioners on Uniform State Laws.

[318] One of the few exceptions is the federal corporations legislation, modified in 2001 to include a limited form of proportionate liability with respect to the provision of financial information. See Canada Business Corporations Act, RSC 1985, c C-44, Pt XIX.1 (ss 237.1–237.9). However, when the Law Commission of Ontario was asked to consider a similar step for Ontario's corporations legislation, it rejected the idea: Law Commission of Ontario, *Joint and Several Liability Under the Ontario Business Corporations Act: Final Report* (Toronto, LCO-CDO, 2011), www.lco-cdo.org/en/joint-several-liability-final-report (2011 OLC Report). In Canadian maritime law, when the fault or neglect of two or more ships causes loss to one or more of those ships, to their cargo, to other property on board, or to earnings, liability is not joint and several; for other types of loss (eg, personal injury), it is: Marine Liability Act, SC 2001, c 6, Pt 2 (ss 15–22); see particularly s 17.

Any attempt to address these problems engages, implicitly or explicitly, all five of the principles, leading to conflict among at least some of them. Judges and lawyers have developed methods to address this, but the conflict is still being worked out and is the subject of a 2013 British Columbia reform proposal.

The British Columbia Law Institute (BCLI), in its *Report on Contribution after Settlement under the Negligence Act*,[319] explained that its project was concerned with the relatively narrow (though not uncommon) issue of partial settlement, more or less as I have just outlined it. In fact, the issue is narrower or less common in British Columbia than elsewhere, because the Court of Appeal has interpreted its Negligence Act so as to convert joint and several liability into several or proportionate liability if the plaintiff is at all contributorily negligent.[320] Under such a regime, which is atypical for most of the rest of Canada, each defendant is only responsible for his or her share of liability when the plaintiff is also at fault. Thus in setting up its analysis, the BCLI assumed a scenario in which there is no fault or negligence on the part of the injured person. This leaves intact the normal rule of joint and several liability, as well as the reform issues that arise out of partial settlements. In Ontario and other provinces, the issues examined by the BCLI would arise even in scenarios where the plaintiff contributed to his or her own loss. The BCLI saw four key issues. It set them out at the beginning of the report, along with a summary of how it thought they should be resolved:[321]

1. Should the Negligence Act be amended to address partial settlements? The BCLI noted that parties to settlement agreements had, in response to case law, come up with ways to try to protect settling defendants from subsequent contribution claims. But the BCLI thought that amending the statute would provide greater certainty and promote early settlement of complex litigation, 'which would benefit litigants and the broader society'.[322]
2. What should be the content of any amendment? Drawing on the work done for the 1984 Uniform Act and the 1988 OLRC draft Act, the BCLI examined four potential rules. It recommended a rule that would reduce the plaintiff's claim 'by an amount proportionate to the degree to which the settling defendant or defendants are found to be at fault for the damage or loss',[323] along with a rule that says a settling defendant is not subject to a contribution claim from a non-settling defendant.
3. What effect should any recommendations have on the basic rule of joint and several liability? Party attempts to craft 'proportionate share settlement' agreements had been 'dogged by uncertainty'[324] over whether they converted joint and several liability into several liability. The BCLI concluded that the amendments should make clear that its proposed legislation would not have this effect.

[319] British Columbia Law Institute, *Report on Contribution after Settlement under the Negligence Act* (Vancouver, BCLI, December 2013) (2013 BC Final Report), www.bcli.org/publication/report-on-contribution-after-settlement-under-the-negligence-act.
[320] *Leischner v West Kootenay Power & Light Co* (n 271).
[321] 2013 BC Final Report (n 319) xii–xiii.
[322] Ibid, xii.
[323] Ibid.
[324] Ibid.

4. If a settling defendant pays more than a court ultimately determines to be its share of the fault, should the settling defendant have a contribution claim against a non-settling defendant? The common law generally says 'yes', but under the proposals recommended by the BCLI for the second issue, this would lead to imbalance between the two types of defendants. To ensure 'balance and reciprocity',[325] the BCLI recommended reversal of this common law rule.

Reaching these recommendations involved a consultation process that took place after a widely circulated consultation report.[326] After consultation was complete, the BCLI in the final report first outlined the general law on concurrent fault as well as specific case developments in British Columbia. It then considered various private types of agreements designed to address the issues.

In the first type of agreement, already alluded to, the plaintiff provides a covenant not to sue, along with an indemnity requiring the plaintiff to repay, 'dollar for dollar',[327] any amount that the settling defendant might ultimately have to contribute to a non-settling defendant. The second type of agreement goes by the umbrella term 'proportionate share settlement agreements'.[328] There are several variations, named after the cases under which they developed—*Mary Carter* agreements, *Pierringer* agreements and *BC Ferry* agreements[329]—but they all work in different ways to try to cap the settling defendant's share of liability. An example is the *Pierringer* agreement endorsed by the Supreme Court of Canada in a lawsuit over paint that allegedly failed to prevent corrosion of gas processing facilities.[330] The plaintiff settled with some parties, agreeing to amend its statement of claim against the non-settling defendants to pursue them only for their share of liability; the settling defendants in turn agreed to turn over to the plaintiffs all relevant evidence in their possession to be discoverable by the non-settling defendants.[331] The plaintiff also agreed that at the end of the trial, once liability had been determined, it would disclose the settlement amounts to the trial judge; thus if the non-settling defendants could establish a right to set-off, their liability would be adjusted downwards if necessary, to avoid overcompensating the plaintiff.[332] The Court not only accepted the virtues of this type of agreement, but accepted the plaintiff's argument that the non-settling defendants were not entitled to know in advance the amounts for which the plaintiff settled, as those amounts were protected by settlement privilege.[333] The BCLI also noted that the issues raised by these various approaches raised similar issues to those raised with lapsed limitation periods, statutory immunities and contractual exclusion clauses.[334]

[325] Ibid.

[326] British Columbia Law Institute, *Consultation Paper on Contribution after Settlement under the Negligence Act* (Vancouver, BCLI, March 2013) (2013 BC Consultation Report).

[327] 2013 BC Final Report (n 319) 22.

[328] Ibid.

[329] See ibid, 22–27 for the cases on which these types of agreements are based and an outline of how they work. The *Pierringer* agreement is discussed below.

[330] *Sable Offshore Energy Inc v Ameron International Corp*, 2013 SCC 37, [2013] 2 SCR 623.

[331] Ibid, para 7.

[332] Ibid, para 25.

[333] Ibid, para 30.

[334] 2013 BC Final Report (n 319) 27–28.

The BCLI concluded that 'leaving it to the parties to sort out issues of contribution and indemnity shifts the burden of tailoring the settlement agreement to achieve the desired result on to them'.[335] This generates both additional costs and additional uncertainty, as well as creating potential traps 'that can ensnare even experienced lawyers'.[336] The BCLI noted that respondents to the consultation paper who addressed this issue were 'uniformly in favour of amending the *Negligence Act*'[337] rather than leaving the problems to be dealt with by private agreement in a difficult area of the law.

To address the content of the necessary amendments, the BCLI referred to the 1979 Alberta Report[338] and the 1988 OLRC Report[339] and considered a simplified scenario. Assume that the plaintiff (P) suffers a $100,000 loss in circumstances in which D1 and D2 are eventually found at fault in the ratio 75:25. P settles with one defendant (D1) and releases it from liability. Assume also that the amended legislation bars the non-settling defendant (D2) from claiming contribution against D1. The quid pro quo is that D2's exposure to liability should be reduced to take account of the settlement. But how should that be done? And should it matter if the settlement was, from P's perspective, a poor one or a good one? The BCLI considered four possible rules. P's claim against D2 could be reduced by:

1. The amount P receives from D1.
2. The amount of D1's share of liability to P, as determined in the subsequent trial.
3. The greater of (1) and (2).
4. The lesser of (1) and (2).[340]

The BCLI provided two tables to show how these rules might work in practice. In the first version of the scenario, shown in Table 7, P settles with D1 for $50,000 and pursues D2, the non-settling defendant. In hindsight, the settlement is, from P's perspective, a 'poor' one, in that it is for less than $75,000, the share of D1's liability that would be found at trial. From D1's perspective, though, the settlement is a 'good' one, and results in a premium for early settlement.

Under rule 1, the court takes the settlement into account dollar for dollar when reducing D2's liability. The $100,000 claim is reduced by $50,000, the amount needed to make P whole when added to the $50,000 settlement. In this case, D2 ends up paying more than its $25,000 share of liability—in fact, twice that amount—in order for P to be fully compensated. Under rule 2, the $100,000 claim is reduced by $75,000—D1's share of the liability. D2 thus pays its share: $25,000. But here, P is not fully compensated. Under rule 3, we compare the amount that P received from D1 in settlement ($50,000) with D1's share of the liability as would be found at trial ($75,000), and reduce D2's liability by the greater of those two figures. Here, D2's liability is reduced by $75,000, yielding the same result as rule 2. Under rule 4, we make the same comparison but reduce D2's liability by the lesser of the two figures. This means that D2's liability is reduced by $50,000, yielding the same result as under rule 1.

[335] Ibid, 31.
[336] See, on this point, the remarkable case of *FBI Foods Ltd v Glassner*, 2001 BCSC 1472, 15 CPR (4th) 482; 95 BCLR (3d) 385.
[337] 2013 BC Final Report (n 319) 33.
[338] Above (n 200).
[339] Above (n 229).
[340] 2013 BC Final Report (n 319) 33, citing the 1979 Alberta Report (n 200) 57.

Table 7: Operation of Four Rules for P's Claim Against D2 When P and D1 Settle for $50,000[341]

Rule	P's claim against D2 reduced by:	P's claim against D2 amounts to:	P's total recovery (D1's $50,000 + D2's amount)
1	$50,000	$50,000	$100,000
2	$75,000	$25,000	$75,000
3	$75,000	$25,000	$75,000
4	$50,000	$50,000	$100,000

Let us now turn the tables, so to speak. In the second version of the scenario, shown in Table 8, P settles with D1 for $90,000 and, again, pursues D2, the non-settling defendant. In hindsight, the settlement is, from P's perspective, a 'good' one, in that it is for more than $75,000, the share of D1's liability that would be found at trial.

Table 8: Operation of Four Rules for P's Claim Against D2 When P and D1 Settle for $90,000[342]

Rule	P's claim against D2 reduced by:	P's claim against D2 amounts to:	P's total recovery (D1's $90,000 + D2's amount)
1	$90,000	$10,000	$100,000
2	$75,000	$25,000	$115,000
3	$90,000	$10,000	$100,000
4	$75,000	$25,000	$115,000

Under rule 1, the court takes the settlement into account dollar for dollar when reducing D2's liability. The $100,000 claim is reduced by $10,000, the amount needed to make P whole when added to the $90,000 settlement. In this case, D2 ends up paying less than its $25,000 share of liability—in fact, $15,000 less—so that P won't be overcompensated. Under rule 2, the $100,000 claim is reduced by $75,000, D1's share of the liability. D2 thus pays its share: $25,000. But when the $25,000 is added to the $90,000 settlement, the resulting total of $115,000 means that P is overcompensated. Under rule 3, the claim against D2 is reduced by the greater of the two figures, $90,000, yielding the same result as under rule 1. Under rule 4, the claim is reduced by the lesser of the two figures, $25,000, yielding the same result as under rule 2.

Now let's look at the merits and demerits of each of these rules.

Rule 1 honours the compensation principle; indeed, by its very operation, it follows that principle strictly, regardless of whether P made a 'poor' or a 'good' settlement with D1. But as the BCLI (and others before it) noted, it does so at the cost of potential unfairness to D2. Where P's settlement is a 'poor' one, D2 has to make up the difference between what D1 pays by way of settlement and the amount needed to make P whole. To the extent that D2 ends up paying more than its share of liability—in the first version of the scenario, an extra

[341] 2013 BC Final Report (n 319) 34 (adapted with slight modifications).
[342] Ibid.

$25,000—D1 benefits. Thus under this rule, the compensation principle apparently trumps the restitutionary principle.

The BCLI noted that rule 1 'does not appear to have been tested in practice',[343] though as I will explain in a moment, it had been adopted in theory by the Ontario Law Reform Commission. And even a rule that has no practice equivalents still serves a useful purpose as a comparative benchmark and illustration of the policy choices to be made and their effects.

Rule 2 honours the finality and settlement principles, but in a way that protects D2. It does this when, 'in litigation between P and D2, the court determines whether D2 is liable to P, assesses P's recoverable loss, but gives judgment against D2 only for the amount of P's loss that is proportionate to D2's degree of fault'.[344] Rule 2 therefore also honours the apportionment principle in respect of the judgment against D2. Under this rule, though, D1 pays less than its share of liability ($25,000 less) when P makes a 'poor' settlement. But this benefit to D1 occurs, not at D2's expense, but at P's. Instead of recovering $100,000, P recovers only $75,000 ($50,000 from the settlement with D1 plus $25,000 from the judgment against D2). The principle that has been sacrificed is the compensation principle. But now look at the 'good' settlement scenario. Again, judgment is awarded against D2 for $25,000, the amount of P's loss that is proportionate to D2's fault. But when added to the $90,000 from the settlement with D1, P now recovers $115,000. This detriment to D1 occurs, not because of any benefit to D2, but because P had been able to drive a harder bargain with D1. Again, the principle that has been sacrificed is the compensation principle—this time, in the other direction, towards overcompensation.

Rule 2 effectively converts joint and several liability to proportionate-share liability as between settling and non-settling defendants. Indeed, the BCLI noted that rule 2 'bears more than a passing similarity to the results of a typical *BC Ferry* agreement',[345] which also has this effect. The BCLI also noted that the rule has, with some wording variations, been adopted in both the UCFA[346] and the American Uniform Act.[347] The Ontario Law Reform Commission had concluded that '[t]he advantages of this scheme are manifest'.[348] However, it did not like the fact that the rule

> purchases the benefits of the finality of the settlement between P and D1, and achieves equity between D1 and D2, at the price of derogating from the principle that the purpose of civil litigation is to ensure that the injured person is fully compensated, no more and no less, for the loss that is attributable in law to the wrongful conduct of the defendant.[349]

In other words, for the OLRC, the compensation principle was paramount. For this and other reasons,[350] the OLRC had adopted rule 1 over rule 2.[351]

343 Ibid, 35.
344 Ibid, 36, citing 1988 OLRC Report (n 229) 99.
345 2013 BC Final Report (n 319) 35.
346 See s 12(2) of the OLRC Act 1984, above Table 4.
347 See UATRA (n 309) s 8 (formerly found, with variant wording, in s 6 of the Uniform Comparative Fault Act).
348 1988 OLRC Report (n 229) 100.
349 Ibid, 101.
350 Ibid, 102–03.
351 Ibid, 108–09.

Rule 3 is based on a proposal advanced by Williams[352] and adopted with variant wording in Ireland[353] and Tasmania.[354] Under this rule, D2, the non-settling defendant has no right of contribution against D1, the settling defendant, but D1 may claim contribution from D2. This gives D1 room to settle on generous terms with P, knowing that he can claim contribution for the excess. But the effect of the rule is to prevent the plaintiff from ever recovering more than $100,000—the full legal compensation—at the price of making the plaintiff pay for a poor settlement. This happens because P is identified with D1's fair share of liability. If P underestimates D1's degree of fault or badly needs the money or simply succumbs to settlement exhaustion, P bears the shortfall. But 'this risk is not offset by the possibility that if he settles favourably with D1, he can keep the benefit of a good bargain'.[355] The BCLI concluded that rule 3 respects the concern that some courts have expressed regarding over-compensation,[356] but that it 'may sap P's incentives to enter into a settlement'[357] and has the disadvantage of greater complexity.[358]

Rule 4 is the obverse of rule 3. Here, P benefits from a good settlement with D1 but is not exposed to the downside risk of a poor settlement. Under rule 3, P gets no more than $100,000. Under rule 4, P gets no less than $100,000. This benefit to P is won at the expense of D2, who has cannot seek contribution against D1 for the excess that P has received. The BCLI noted that rule 4 does not appear to have been implemented anywhere, and was complex and unfamiliar.

How did the BCLI reconcile the principles that are so in tension in these rule formulations? As it turns out, the comments it received during the consultation period were 'intensely polarized'[359] between rules 2 and 3. Acknowledging the merits in both sets of views, the BCLI nevertheless recommended rule 2, which would be accompanied by a no-contribution rule. It thought that this option best encourages settlements, is fair to non-settling defendants and is relatively clear.[360] It noted that evaluating a settlement simply by comparing it with the amount that the plaintiff would ultimately receive if the case went to trial 'may not accurately reflect the value of settlement to the parties at the time of the agreement'.[361] This is a crucial insight: especially in the early stages of an action, before parties have incurred large litigation costs, 'may not' could easily be translated as 'will not'. In other words, some of the criticism levelled at rule 2 fails to consider the discount rates that parties apply when comparing a 'bird in the settlement hand' with a 'bird in the trial bush'. Put another way, while it may appear at first glance that the settlement principle is trumping the compensation principle, it is a different story once compensation is adjusted

352 See Williams, Joint Torts and Contributory Negligence (n 129) 152–55.

353 See Civil Liability Act 1961 (n 246) s 17(2).

354 See Wrongs Act 1954, s 3(3).

355 1988 OLRC Report, (n 229) 104. Williams also recognised this problem, *Joint Torts and Contributory Negligence* (n 129) 155.

356 2013 BC Final Report (n 319) 37.

357 Ibid, 38.

358 Ibid. One thing lacking in all of this analysis is empirical research on how the rule actually plays out in Ireland and Tasmania, where it has been adopted. It would be useful to know whether either the asymmetric settlement incentives or the relatively greater complexity of the rule has caused the problems that Canadian commentators suggest it would cause.

359 Ibid.

360 Ibid, 39.

361 Ibid.

for risk. A defendant who is willing to pay a higher settlement amount is more risk-adverse than one who is not willing to pay as much; conversely, a plaintiff who is willing to accept a lower settlement amount is more risk-adverse than one who will only settle for more. When compensation is adjusted for party perception of litigation risk, it is not possible to say, a priori, whether a plaintiff will end up being over-compensated or under-compensated. Under such circumstances, it is better to give parties the chance to make a settlement that makes sense to them. As the BCLI concludes, 'that a plaintiff may be sometimes worse off and sometimes better off under this option does not trump the general value, both to litigants and the broader society, of encouraging settlements of multiparty litigation'.[362] Also, some of the criticism levelled at rule 2 was addressed in the final report by making it clear that under rule 2, neither the settling defendants nor the non-settling defendants would have contribution rights vis-a-vis each other.[363] Implicitly, then, this rule also gives significant weight to the finality principle.

The Manitoba Law Reform Commission Proposal for a New Act

The BCLI should be commended for its work on contribution after settlement and for the draft legislation put forward in its final report. However, the mandate given to the BCLI was a narrow one, which greatly restricted the scope of what it could study and recommend. For example, the BCLI had to take as a given that the least bit of contributory negligence on the part of the plaintiff converts a joint-and-several-liability judgment into a several-liability judgment, even though this is aberrant law throughout the most of the rest of Canada. Across the country, all the legislation is sorely in need of revision or rationalisation, and a holistic approach would be preferable to partial amendments, often done simply by borrowing provisions from one statute and transplanting them into another. For the most part, this is how apportionment and contribution legislation has developed in Canada—the 1984 Uniform Act and the 1988 OLRC draft Act being notable exceptions.

This is where the work of the Manitoba Law Reform Commission comes in. In its 81-page report delivered in late 2013, it calls for a new apportionment statute modelled on the UCFA, 'with modifications as appropriate and required by the Commission's recommendations',[364] of which there are 25. Some of these are idiosyncratic to Manitoba, such as the one that the new statute not address the judgment-and-release-bar rules. But that is because those rules are already abolished for all civil actions by Manitoba's Court of Queen's Bench Act.[365] I will use the 2013 Manitoba Final Report as a launching point for discussing some of what needs to happen next on the reform agenda.

362 Ibid. The BCLI included draft legislation to implement its recommendation at pp 51–53 of the report.

363 Ibid, 52.

364 *Contributory Fault: The Tortfeasors and Contributory Negligence Act* (Winnipeg, Manitoba Law Reform Commission, September 2013) (2013 Manitoba Final Report), www.manitobalawreform.ca/pubs/pdf/128-full_report.pdf, 9.

365 Ibid, 61, recommendation 16, citing the Queen's Bench Act, CCSM c 280, s 95.

First, what of key substantive matters, such as the Act's scope? The Manitoba Commissioners, after surveying domestic and international legislation, law reform reports and judicial decisions across the Commonwealth, made the following recommendations[366] on the scope of its new Act:

1. It should refer to a person's 'fault', not 'negligence', and define 'fault' using the UCFA definition as a model with necessary modifications.[367]
2. It should provide for apportionment of damages for contributory fault in respect of intentional torts, strict-liability torts, torts that are crimes, as well as negligence.[368]
3. It should provide that a person's contributory fault includes fault for which the person is vicariously liable.[369]
4. It should provide for apportionment of damages for contributory fault in respect of any breach of contract that creates a liability for damages.[370]
5. It should *not* provide for apportionment of damages for contributory fault in respect of breaches of fiduciary duty and should stipulate that nothing in the new statute be interpreted as affecting a remedy available in equity.[371]
6. It should *not* provide for apportionment of damages for contributory fault in respect of breaches of statutory duty; also, provincial statutes that create a right for damages should be reviewed for consistency with the recommendations and apportionment principles.[372]

The sources and support for several of these recommendations should be apparent from the discussion in this chapter. However, a few of them bear elaboration.

Regarding intentional torts, the Commission noted that, while courts vary, some have interpreted apportionment statutes to cover intentional wrongdoing, including battery, assault, defamation and fraud. This may require rethinking tort doctrine. Alternatively, apportionment legislation, and its understanding of concepts such as 'fault', may have to be rethought in order to work with causes of action other than negligence. For example, provocation, while not a full defence to the intentional tort of battery, can reduce the damages a defendant must pay to an injured plaintiff. *Ergo*, it can be seen as a type of 'fault' for apportioning liability, achieving the same result it does in traditional doctrine.[373] In an English decision, Smith LJ regretted that because of the statutory definition of 'fault' and its construction by the House of Lords, he couldn't apportion fault in a battery case where the claimant's conduct was provocative, even 'verging on the intimidatory'.[374] Similarly, while courts have generally rejected apportionment of liability in fraud cases—'you shouldn't have trusted me' carries an odious ring—there may be cases in which the all-or-nothing

[366] The Commission's report comprises recommendations for a legislative framework, rather than a model Act.
[367] 2013 Manitoba Final Report (n 364) 33–34 (recommendations 5 and 6).
[368] Ibid, 38–40 (recommendations 7 and 8).
[369] Ibid, 41 (recommendation 9).
[370] Ibid (recommendation 12). This modifies the *UCFA* definition for 'fault', which uses the phrase 'breach of a duty of care arising from a contract'.
[371] Ibid, 44–45 (recommendations 10 and 11).
[372] Ibid, 56 (recommendations 13 and 14). Recommendation 13 modifies the *UCFA* definition for 'fault', which uses the phrase 'breach of a statutory duty that creates a liability for damages'.
[373] Ibid, 34, fn 36 (citing cases going both ways on this interpretation).
[374] Ibid, 37, citing *Cooperative Group v Pritchard* [2011] EWCA Civ 329, para 61.

approach fails to do justice. For example, the defendant may have fraudulently induced the plaintiff to buy defective goods, but the plaintiff has unreasonably used the goods after learning of the fraud and defect.[375] Thus the Manitoba Commissioners concluded, as had the Ontario Commissioners before them, that the apportionment principle should be able to develop beyond its original narrow purpose of overcoming the rule in *Butterfield*. Both Commissions thought that courts were able to make appropriate decisions on the facts of each case, and shouldn't be hampered from doing so by restrictive statutory language.

Regarding strict liability, the Commission noted that courts have held apportionment to be unavailable for torts like conversion, nuisance and liability for wild animals. In the case usually cited for this proposition, *Boma*,[376] Iacobucci J thought it a 'matter of principle that contributory negligence should not be available in the context of a strict liability tort'. Like the *Merryweather* headnote,[377] this may be another example of overstatement. In *Boma*, the plaintiff companies sued under the Bills of Exchange Act[378] for a bank's conversion of their cheques; they succeeded even though the conversion happened largely by their bookkeeper's fraud. The case turns on sections of the Bills of Exchange Act, so it may not stand for as wide a proposition as frequently cited. With respect to the banking context, Iacobucci J cited academic authority to the effect that in cheque conversion cases, 'there are varying degrees of innocence and carelessness on both sides' and that it may be 'more equitable to apportion liability in accordance with the actual facts … than to expect banks to be the insurers of the "true owner" of a cheque whose carelessness has contributed to the conversion'.[379] However, Iacobucci J preferred to 'leave that innovation to Parliament because such a change would be more appropriate for the legislative branch to make'.[380]

In *Cowles v Balac*,[381] the Ontario Court of Appeal considered a rather different instance of strict liability. A couple had visited the African Lion Safari, near Cambridge. There, the animals roam free while the visitors are caged—in their cars. After the couple entered the tiger reserve, tigers attacked their car, and in the confusion, Balac hit the automatic window button. A Siberian tiger named Paca lunged through the window and mauled the couple, causing long-term physical and psychological injuries for both, assessed at $2.5 million. The trial judge held the Safari strictly liable for damage caused by wild animals and appeared to reject the idea that a contributory negligence defence was available. The Safari appealed on several grounds, including the trial judge's decisions to strike a jury based on trial complexity and to bar a defence of contributory negligence. A majority of the Court of Appeal focused on the finding that a 'forceful assault on the vehicle [by a tiger] caused Mr Balac's body to inadvertently come into contact with the window switch resulting in the lowering of the windows … which admitted the tiger into the vehicle'.[382] Given that finding, the majority saw no need to discuss contributory negligence.

[375] Ibid, 37, citing 1988 OLRC Report (n 229) 238.

[376] *Boma Manufacturing Ltd v Canadian Imperial Bank of Commerce* [1996] 3 SCR 727, 140 DLR (4th) 463 (Boma) para 35.

[377] See n 54 and the text accompanying and following it.

[378] Bills of Exchange Act, RSC 1985, c B-4.

[379] *Boma* (n 376) para 33, citing Margaret Ogilvie, *Canadian Banking Law* (Carswell, 1991) 593–94.

[380] *Boma*, ibid, para 35.

[381] *Cowles v Balac* (2006) 42 CCLT (3d) 161, 41 CCLI (4th) 227, 273 DLR (4th) 596, 83 OR (3d) 660 (CA), leave to appeal to SCC ref'd (2007) 233 OAC 399 (note), 367 NR 400 (note), [2006] SCCA No 496.

[382] Ibid, para 101, citing the trial judgment.

Justice Borins, dissenting, noted that six witnesses had given evidence, which, were it presented to a jury, could lead them to conclude that Cowles, the passenger, had rolled down her window to take photos. Justice Borins would have sent the case back for a new trial based on the trial judge having erred in striking the jury. Though not necessary for his decision, he also considered strict liability, noting that it 'is not absolute and that in the appropriate circumstances may give rise to a defence arising from the plaintiff's conduct'.[383] He noted authority for the proposition that defences to liability for damages caused by animals were like those available in another strict-liability tort, the action based on the doctrine in *Rylands v Fletcher*.[384] These include the plaintiff's default, consent, trespass and illegality. Justice Borins distinguished *Boma*, concluding that Iacobucci J 'was not intending to state a general principle [but] was referring to the law of bills of exchange in respect to which Parliament has legislated'.[385] The following excerpt from Borins JA's reasons supports the Commission's recommendation and my contention that apportionment legislation may require us to reconceptualise tort doctrine and vice versa:

> Although it may appear to be doctrinally counterintuitive to apply comparative negligence principles [ie, apportionment] where a defendant's liability is strict and not dependant on negligence, in my view functional and fairness considerations strongly suggest that comparative negligence principles are appropriate where a plaintiff's misconduct or want of care is a contributing factor to his or her damages.[386]

I realise that some may think the Commission's recommendations too radical. To that, I would answer that Saskatchewan has already taken the very route suggested by Borins JA and recommended by the Manitoba Commissioners. With the enactment of The Environmental Management and Protection Act 2002,[387] the question of whether the Act can be adapted to causes of action other than those involving negligence or fault has been answered affirmatively. The statute gives the responsible Minister broad powers concerning environmental enhancement and protection, including the power to bring a civil action for discharge into the environment (section 15), to issue an environmental protection order (section 47(3)), to carry out the order if the person to whom it was issued fails to comply, and to recover the associated costs as a debt due to the Crown (sections 51, 52).[388] In section 15(8), the Act is part of this scheme, modified as necessary:

> For the purposes of apportioning liability on a just basis, and recognizing that liability pursuant to this section or section 51 or 52 is not based on fault or negligence, The Contributory Negligence Act applies, with any necessary modification, to an action commenced pursuant to this section or section 51 or 52.[389]

Thus, while the concepts of fault and negligence may be irrelevant for the purpose of *establishing* liability under the EMPA, the same concepts may be relevant for the purpose of *apportioning* liability (eg, among multiple parties who are or may be liable in respect

383 Ibid, para 205.
384 *Rylands v Fletcher* (1868) LR 3 HL 330 (strict liability for escape of non-natural substances from land).
385 *Cowles* (n 381) para 216.
386 Ibid, para 218.
387 The Environmental Management and Protection Act, 2002, SS 2002, c E-10.21 (EMPA).
388 Ibid, s 15 (added to the statute in 2003). The terms 'discharge' and 'environment' are defined in s 2.
389 Ibid, s 15(8).

of a discharge). 'It must be remembered', Klar exhorts when discussing apportionment statutes, 'that what is being apportioned is *liability* for injuries, the apportionment being made according to relative degrees of fault'.[390] Or, perhaps, according to other factors too, though here I would be inclined to view things differently from the Manitoba Commission. It recommends that apportionment under the new statute 'be based on the relative blameworthiness *and causal relevance* of the person's conduct, as the court finds just and equitable'.[391] (emphasis added) I understand the Commission's laudable purpose here, which is to address the kinds of concerns that have been raised with respect to intentional torts and strict liability. I also understand that the 'just and equitable' phraseology is used in the English legislation, both in the apportionment statute and the contribution statute. Along with the phrase 'responsibility for the damage', which also appears in both statutes, this has been interpreted as allowing for apportionment based on causation; hence the term 'causal relevance'. But the weight of opinion, both academic and jurisprudential, is that this is not the way to do apportionment. Indeed, were we to introduce it, I would be concerned that it could reopen the 'last clear chance' or 'ultimate negligence' doors that law reformers have tried so hard to close.

As usual, for help on this, we can turn to Williams. Here he is, speaking about the English provision for recovering contribution in an amount 'as may be found by the court to be just and equitable having regard to the extent of [the contributor's] responsibility for damage':

> One of the first cases on this provision was *Smith v Bray* (1939), 63 TLR 466, where Hilbery J laid it down that the reference to 'responsibility' meant that damages were to be apportioned on the basis of causation and not on the respective degrees of negligence of the parties. It is submitted, with great respect, that this is making an unnecessary difficulty. 'Responsibility' does not necessarily refer to causation; in the context it refers more naturally to the degree of fault or blame. It means 'fault causally connected with the damage'. As this suggested definition shows, *legal fault implies causation; but the point is that apportionment should not be on the basis of causation (if such a process is logically possible) but should be on the basis of fault.*[392] (emphasis added, footnote omitted)

Williams finds, though, that in practice, 'Hilbery J does not seem to have operated the Act any differently [than other judges], who have not expressed themselves as concurring in his theoretical interpretation, but, on the contrary, have spoken of apportionment in terms of degrees of blame'.[393] Klar thinks the difference in views in this area may be 'no more than semantics' since it is 'not possible to speak of one person's negligence being a greater or lesser cause of another's injury except in terms of it being more or less "blameworthy" in the circumstances'.[394] A little less deferentially than Williams, Klar describes 'degrees of causation' as 'meaningless'.[395]

To like effect is the Ontario Court of Appeal in *Rizzi v Marvos*.[396] In that case, sharp metal sheets fell on a tenant in the storage room of an apartment building, and the trial judge had

[390] Klar (n 271) 157.
[391] 2013 Manitoba Final Report (n 364) 12 (recommendation 2).
[392] Williams, *Joint Torts and Contributory Negligence* (n 129) 157.
[393] Ibid (fn omitted).
[394] Klar (n 271) 156–57, fn 48.
[395] Ibid.
[396] *Rizzi v Marvos*, 2008 ONCA 172, 236 OAC 4.

told the jurors how to apportion fault between plaintiff tenant and defendant landlord. He had said: 'That can go from zero to 100 in each case, and you would decide. You would say that this incident would not have occurred but for, and you would apportion it'.[397] The jury found the plaintiff 75 per cent liable; the landlord, 25 per cent liable. On appeal, Lang and Juriansz JJA held that Ontario's Negligence Act plainly 'requires apportionment based on the "fault or negligence" of each party, rather than on the basis of causation' and that it would be wrong 'to apportion liability on the degree to which the [each party] caused the damages'.[398] However, they thought that in this context, the jury would have taken 'but for' to refer to the parties' negligence and not to injury causation. Laskin JA, in the minority, agreed with apportioning blame rather than cause; though he thought that, in context, the 'but for' instruction was a reversible legal error 'because it likely misled the jury on the proper approach to apportionment'.[399] He would have switched the proportions, holding the landlord 75 per cent liable; the plaintiff 25 per cent liable. I am skipping his detailed reasons for the conclusion on the jury instruction, as the key part of the case for my purpose is the point on which all members of the Court agreed. According to Laskin JA, the point is that 'the principle of apportioning fault on the basis of comparative blameworthiness, not comparative causation, has been approved by this court, by most academics, and by other provincial appellate courts in Canada'.[400]

Vicarious liability is in some ways an even stranger animal than strict liability. Indeed, when an employer is held vicariously liable for an employee's torts or a principal for an agent's transactions, liability is imposed because of the *relationship*, not because of the employer's or principal's fault. There is an analogy here to the spousal and guest passenger provisions, in that the employer is, in a way, identified with the employee; the principal, with the agent. However, something more than relationship is required to found vicarious liability. It has typically been expressed as a requirement that the employee was acting 'in the course of employment' or that the agent was acting 'with actual or apparent authority'. But even such limitations have proved slippery, especially when applied to intentional torts. If a bus driver assaults an unruly passenger, is he doing it in or out of the course of employment?

In *Bazley v Curry*,[401] an influential case both in Canada and abroad, McLachlin J (as she then was) tackled these sorts of questions. Bazley had been under the care of the Children's Foundation, a non-profit organisation that operated residential care facilities for emotionally troubled children between the ages of six and twelve. The Foundation had hired Curry to work in its 'total intervention' programme. The Foundation's employees were to do everything a parent would do, from general supervision to bathing and tucking in at bedtime. Unbeknownst to the Foundation, Curry was a pedophile who ended up abusing children at the facility, including Bazley. He was fired and criminally convicted and died not long after. The Foundation took the position that since it had committed no fault in hiring or supervising Curry, it was not legally responsible for what he had done. The parties

397 Ibid, para 45.
398 Ibid, para 48.
399 Ibid, para 85.
400 Ibid, para 86 (citations omitted).
401 *Bazley v Curry* [1999] 2 SCR 534.

stated a case to determine whether, apart from any case that Bazley might have against the Foundation in negligence, he could maintain a cause of action against the Foundation in vicarious liability for Bazley's intentional sexual abuse.

Both parties agreed that employers are vicariously liable for: (i) acts authorised by the employer; or (ii) unauthorised acts so connected with authorised acts that they may be regarded as modes—albeit improper modes—of doing an authorised act. But they couldn't agree on the application of that test. In particular, the test's second branch was contentious, because the Foundation said that Curry's sexual assaults couldn't be seen as modes of doing authorised tasks. Justice McLachlin said that in many cases, one could characterise a tortious act either as a mode of doing an authorised act or as an independent act altogether. In that case, what is a court to do? The answer, said McLachlin J, is twofold. First, one should see if there are precedents that unambiguously determine on which side of the line the case falls. This can be challenging, because fact patterns are infinitely variable. But it makes sense to follow precedent if possible. If precedents suggest no clear solution, the next step is to determine whether vicarious liability should be imposed 'in light of the broader policy rationales behind strict liability'.[402]

Drawing on Fleming, who thought vicarious liability should be acknowledged as being heavily policy-based rather than proceeding solely from legal premises, McLachlin J saw two key policies: providing a practical remedy and deterring future harm. Both are linked by risk. The employer creates a situation that gives rise to a risk, which, on materialising, causes injury despite the employer's reasonable efforts, and 'it is right and just that the person who creates a risk bear the loss when the risk ripens into harm'.[403] Further, '[b]eyond the narrow band of employer conduct that attracts direct liability in negligence lies a vast area where imaginative and efficient administration and supervision can reduce the risk that the employer has introduced into the community'.[404] At the same time, the risk theme embeds some limits on the expansion of liability. Thus, a wrong that is 'only coincidentally linked to the activity of the employer and duties of the employee cannot justify the imposition of vicarious liability on the employer'; moreover, it 'serves no deterrent purpose, and relegates the employer to the status of an involuntary insurer'.[405] Applying the risk framework, McLachlin J found that the Foundation, through its practices, created and enhanced the risk that led to Curry abusing Bazley. The abuse 'was not a mere accident of time and place, but the product of the special relationship of intimacy and respect' that the Foundation fostered, 'as well as the special opportunities for exploitation of that relationship it furnished'.[406] Hence the Foundation bore the loss.

Bazley v Curry offers a lens for viewing vicarious liability under the Ontario Act and similar legislation in other provinces. Either the Act's requirement of fault needs to be abandoned, or the concept itself needs to be reimagined. Reimagining 'fault' to include an employer's creation and enhancement of risk would be in harmony with *Bazley v Curry* and provide a doctrinal basis for extending the Act's scope to include vicarious liability, even

[402] Ibid, para 15.
[403] Ibid, para 32.
[404] Ibid, para 33.
[405] Ibid, para 36.
[406] Ibid, para 58.

where the underlying tort is an intentional one. That this could be accomplished through judicial innovation is implicit in *Blackwater v Plint*.[407] This was a claim by former students of an Indian residential school in British Columbia, operated by the Government of Canada and the United Church of Canada in the 1940s, 1950s and 1960s. For the sexual assaults that took place at the schools, the trial judge had apportioned vicarious liability 75:25 to Canada and the Church. When the Supreme Court of Canada heard the case in 2005, a key issue was whether unequal apportionment was even possible for vicarious liability, given that it is a form of no-fault liability. The Court, speaking unanimously through McLachlin CJC, first noted that selection of a vicariously liable defendant isn't random, but principled, and that vicarious liability 'is imposed on someone who was in a position to have supervised and thus to have prevented the occurrence of the harm'.[408] From this premise, the Court concluded that the degree of 'fault' may vary with level of supervision, and parties may be more or less vicariously liable depending on their level of supervision and direct contact. The trial judge had found that one of the parties, Canada, had more control or was a more important player than the Church, and it was therefore appropriate for it to have been apportioned a higher share of the vicarious liability. This reasoning is not entirely free of problems, because the more one tries to make out a case of failing to supervise, the more it looks like a case of direct liability in negligence. And since a negligence action may be barred by a limitation period, it may be inappropriate to let a plaintiff do indirectly what could not be done directly. However, keeping in mind the policy exhortations in *Bazley v Curry* and noting that much of the risk analysis in that case could apply to the residential school scenario, the results in the two cases seem congruent.

I have treated this issue at some length to suggest that the Act can be construed to support vicarious liability and its apportionment, mindful that legislative action to update the Act has been notoriously slow in Ontario, as it has in other provinces. But the better solution would be to follow the Manitoba recommendation, and simply enact a definition of 'fault' under the Act that includes fault for which a person is vicariously responsible.

As to breach of fiduciary duty, the Manitoba Commissioners found it 'consistent with principles of fairness to take the fault of the plaintiff into consideration in appropriate cases', but that equitable approaches 'are being applied satisfactorily by the courts, and should be allowed to develop'.[409] This is perhaps an area for further investigation, the main policy concern being here, as elsewhere, that courts 'should strive to treat similar wrongs similarly, regardless of the particular cause or causes of action that may have been pleaded'.[410] If the Manitoba recommendation were to be accepted in a new Ontario statute, one of the issues that would also need to be decided is whether the statute should nevertheless apply to contribution and indemnity proceedings arising out of fiduciary breaches, or if they should continue to be governed solely by judge-made law.

As to breach of statutory duty, the Manitoba Commission recommendation makes sense given that in Canada, there is no stand-alone cause of action for breach of statutory

[407] *Blackwater v Plint* 2005 SCC 58, [2005] 3 SCR 3.

[408] Ibid, para 69, citing DN Husak, 'Varieties of Strict Liability' (1995) 8 *Canadian Journal of Law & Jurisprudence* 189, 215.

[409] 2013 Manitoba Final Report (n 364) 44.

[410] *Hodgkinson v Simms* [1994] 3 SCR 377, 444, 117 DLR (4th) 161.

duty.[411] For the few statutes that create causes of action with rights to damages, such as Saskatchewan's EMPA, which incorporates the Act by reference with necessary modifications,[412] the Manitoba recommendation seems commendable.

Where To From Here?

In tracing an outline of the 90-year history of concurrent fault in Canada, I have focused largely on the two original statutes—the Ontario Act and the Uniform Act—and their repeals, replacements, amendments and judicial development since 1924. Much of what I have said, though, also applies to the other provinces. I have glossed over a great amount of detail, and even so, this has been a very long chapter. Clearly, it is time for a new statute. Moreover, with the combined efforts of the Uniform Law Conference of Canada, the Ontario Law Reform Commission, the British Columbia Law Institute, the Manitoba Law Reform Commission and many others, we have excellent models and analytical frameworks from which to work.

There remains the question of what to call the new statute, should one be developed. The Manitoba Commissioners have suggested the Contributory Fault Act, which has the virtues of removing 'negligence' from the title and being called the same as the UCFA. Again, there is merit in harmonising the law in this area—even harmonising the labels we put on the law. However, I would hark back to Klar's comment about what is actually going in the Act—that what is being apportioned is *liability*, with apportionment being made according to degrees of fault,[413] though under the proposals I have discussed, that may mean some reimagined ideas of 'fault'. Furthermore, when it comes to such things as contribution among wrongdoers and reallocation of uncollectable amounts, the focus is also on *liability*. Indeed, at that point, fault is often either already established through a prior proceeding or presumed for the purpose of settlement, so as to avoid a proceeding. Therefore, why not use a title that reflects this focus? My suggestion, then, would be the Apportionment of Liability Act. It removes 'negligence', which has always suggested a restricted scope to the Act; it removes 'contributory', which is not in the title of the Ontario Act but is in the title of the Uniform Act and the titles of other provincial statutes. That word creates confusion (especially when the same word or its derivatives refers both to 'contributory negligence' and 'contribution towards amounts paid'). And it removes 'fault', even though fault will continue to be a guiding factor in much of the statute's application. The title of the proposed Act says what it does.

This project is long overdue. I call on practitioners, academics and legislators to take up the cause. The Act has had a long and productive life. Long live the new Act!

[411] *R v Saskatchewan Wheat Pool* [1983] 1 SCR 205.

[412] See n 389 and accompanying text.

[413] See n 390 and accompanying text.

11

Individualism and Autonomy in Occupiers' Liability and Compensation Culture

DESMOND RYAN

It is of course understandable that organisations like the Royal Society for the Prevention of Accidents should favour policies which require people to be prevented from taking risks. Their function is to prevent accidents and that is one way of doing so. But they do not have to consider the cost, not only in money but also in deprivation of liberty, which such restrictions entail. The courts will naturally respect the technical expertise of such organisations in drawing attention to what can be done to prevent accidents. But the balance between risk on the one hand and individual autonomy on the other is not a matter of expert opinion. It is a judgment which the courts must make which in England reflects the individualist values of the common law.[1]

Introduction

The above passage, from one of the leading judicial authorities on the subject of occupiers' liability in the common law word, identifies individualism as being at the heart of the common law and therefore an imperative value influencing how the courts will approach occupiers' liability cases. The purpose of this chapter is to interrogate the nature of the individualistic values identified in the above words of Lord Hoffmann—and repeatedly espoused by the courts in occupiers' liability cases since—in order to examine critically why, and to what extent, such values have informed the courts' assessment of liability in the most significant judicial decisions in the past 15 years in English and Irish law. In these decisions, the courts in both jurisdictions have placed express reliance on individualistic values in dealing with occupiers' liability cases.

This chapter is divided into three sections. The first explores in detail the leading United Kingdom decision in this area, that of the House of Lords in *Tomlinson v Congleton Borough Council*,[2] and assesses the implications of this decision on subsequent cases. Using *Tomlinson* as the prism through which the courts' articulation of the individualist philosophy of the

[1] *Tomlinson v Congleton Borough Council* [2003] UKHL 47, [2004] 1 AC 46, [47] (Lord Hoffmann) (*Tomlinson*).
[2] *Tomlinson* (n 1).

common law can be analysed, the section seeks to examine the ways in which individualist values are particularly relevant to the area of occupiers' liability and assesses what reliance on those values can reveal to us about the common law. In doing this, I seek to identify two distinct strands of reasoning discernible in *Tomlinson*. The first is the notion of personal autonomy, respect for which is frequently stated to comprise a manifestation of the individualism of the common law. The second is the related but distinct notion of there being a positive social value inherent in risky activities being pursued, a notion which comes across particularly strongly in the *Tomlinson* decision[3] but which can also be identified in many occupiers' liability cases. But although this latter rationale is frequently cited in the case law, its citation is seldom accompanied by any in-depth analysis or explanation. It therefore merits closer scrutiny.

The second section of the chapter considers the relationship between autonomy and responsibility in occupiers' liability law in Ireland, focusing on the impact in the last 20 years of the major legislative overhaul in this area in Ireland with the introduction of the Occupiers' Liability Act 1995, and evidenced in, inter alia, the approach of the Irish Supreme Court in its leading decision of *Weir-Rodgers v SF Trust Limited*.[4] The Irish Supreme Court in delivering the latter decision specifically invoked the philosophy of *Tomlinson* and this judgment therefore enables further reflection to be offered on how and why the courts have recourse to notions of autonomy and responsibility in occupiers' liability cases.

The third and final section of this chapter concludes that the invocation of autonomy and responsibility arguments in occupiers' liability case law resonates with and contributes to the broader thematic tension increasingly discernible in tort case law since approximately the year 2000 on concerns about the rise of a 'compensation culture', prompted by concerns over the perceived cost (or potential cost) of claims. My argument is that individual autonomy and responsibility arguments are important and legitimate bases on which to confine the scope of liability in occupiers' liability cases, but that there is a tendency to interweave into the analysis of these concepts much looser and broader concerns about the rise of a compensation culture—and in so doing preclude potentially worthy claimants from accessing compensation. It is, therefore, necessary to strive for a clearer demarcation between the treatment in occupiers' liability cases of autonomy and responsibility arguments, on the one hand, and compensation culture concerns, on the other.

Conceptions of Individualism and Autonomy in *Tomlinson*

There can be no question but that individualistic values lie at the heart of the common law—particularly in tort law and property law. The emphasis placed within various tort and property doctrines on values of personal responsibility; the highly individuated nature of private property rights; the common law's long-standing emphasis on freedom of choice and action; causation rules: these and many more elements of private law doctrine unite

[3] See in particular the opinion of Lord Hoffmann in *Tomlinson* (n 1) [34]–[43].
[4] *Weir-Rodgers v SF Trust Limited* [2005] IESC 2, [2005] 1 IR 47.

to produce an intensely individualistic vision of the plaintiff in a tort action. This marked emphasis on individualism in the common law can be contrasted with civilian systems, which are, as Markesinis and Unberath have commented, 'more socially impregnated'.[5]

In the common law system, the law reports are replete with references in tort cases to the 'individualistic philosophy of the common law'.[6] When tort disputes themselves centre on the use of property—as in the context of occupiers' liability cases in which statutory regimes in both English and Irish law place their focus on injuries caused due to the state of the defendant's premises—the potential for this individualistic philosophy to be further intensified is clear. As regards the law of real property, it has recently been said that '[t]he core values realised through legal protection of private ownership are still understood primarily in individualistic terms'.[7] Little wonder, then, that when tort cases involve judicial consideration of personal injuries occasioned by the use of land—the paradigmatic example being occupiers' liability cases—a still greater emphasis is laid upon these individualistic values of the common law. Of all the discrete areas within tort law, it may be that occupiers' liability is one of the most likely contexts in which arguments as to the individualist values of the common law should be brought to the fore. For, given the strong influence on occupiers' liability case law and legislation of concerns about respecting private ownership of land, these cases are particularly suitable vehicles for the courts to have articulated strong individualistic ideologies.

A number of high-profile judicial developments in English and Irish law within the last 15 years indicate that it will be extremely difficult for claimants to argue that occupiers have acted with reckless disregard towards them in circumstances where they deliberately choose to engage in inherently dangerous or risky activities. Two leading English cases provide dramatic evidence of this: *Donoghue v Folkestone Properties*[8] and *Tomlinson v Congleton Borough Council*.[9] It is 'probably fair to say', as Brodie has recently remarked, that *Tomlinson* comprises 'the key case in the law of occupiers' liability'.[10] The decision is particularly significant for the purposes of my analysis in this chapter and it therefore warrants analysis in some detail.

Tomlinson v Congleton Borough Council: The Background

The background to *Tomlinson* is well known. Mr Tomlinson ran into the shallows of a lake and then plunged or dived[11] forwards, breaking his neck on the bed of the lake. The lake was in a country park owned and occupied by a local authority which Mr Tomlinson sued. His claim failed before the trial judge, but was upheld by a majority of the Court of Appeal.[12]

[5] BS Markesinis and H Unberath, *The German Law of Torts: A Comparative Treatise*, 4th edn (Oxford, Hart Publishing, 2002) 90.

[6] For examples from the case law see *McTear v Imperial Tobacco Ltd* [2005] ScotCS CSOH 69, [7.134], and *Flanagan v Houlihan* [2011] IEHC 105, [2011] 3 IR574, [4.3].

[7] R Walsh, 'Stability and Predictability in English Property Law—The Impact of Article 8 of the European Convention on Human Rights Reassessed' (2015) 131 *LQR* 585, 602.

[8] *Donoghue v Folkestone Properties* [2003] EWCA Civ 231, [2003] QB 1008.

[9] *Tomlinson* (n 1).

[10] D Brodie, '*Tomlinson v Congleton* and the Child' [2015] *Reparation Bulletin* 7, 7.

[11] Lord Scott of Foscote was not satisfied that it was correct to describe Mr Tomlinson as having executed a 'dive' in the ordinary sense: (Lord Scott in *Tomlinson* (n 1) [93]).

[12] *Tomlinson v Congleton Borough Council* [2002] EWCA Civ 309, [2003] 2 WLR 1120 (Ward and Sedley LJJ, Longmore LJ dissenting).

In identifying precisely the relevant breach of duty alleged to be owed to Mr Tomlinson, it was contended on his behalf that the Council was 'luring people into a deathtrap'.[13] In the Court of Appeal, Ward LJ said that the water was 'a siren call strong enough to turn stout men's minds'.[14] The local authority appealed successfully to the House of Lords. It was held that the defendants had owed no duty to protect the claimant from dangers inherent in swimming in such circumstances, for example by taking measures to render access to the lake difficult.

It is very important to note that the claimant in *Tomlinson* conceded that the relevant duty owed to him, if any, was that owed to a trespasser under section 1(4) of the Occupiers' Liability Act 1984 (the 1984 Act)—*not* that owed to a lawful visitor pursuant to section 2(2) of the Occupiers' Liability Act 1957 (the 1957 Act). As Lord Hoffmann would note in his opinion, this was, in one sense, 'a rather odd hypothesis',[15] in that the claimant's contention was that he should have been prevented or discouraged from entering the water and thereby turning himself into a trespasser. The case nevertheless proceeded on the basis of this concession,[16] with the claimant contending, inter alia, that the conditions set out in subsection (3) of the 1984 Act were satisfied, and that accordingly the defendant was under a duty under subsection (4) to take reasonable care to see that he did not suffer injury by reason of the danger from diving.

At this juncture it is necessary to recall the wording of section 1 of that Act, the relevant subsections of which provide as follows:

> (3) An occupier of premises owes a duty to another (not being his visitor) in respect of any such risk as is referred to in subsection (1) above if—
>
> (*a*) he is aware of the danger or has reasonable grounds to believe that it exists;
> (*b*) he knows or has reasonable grounds to believe that the other is in the vicinity of the danger concerned or that he may come into the vicinity of the danger (in either case, whether he has lawful authority for being in that vicinity or not); and
> (*c*) the risk is one against which, in all the circumstances of the case, he may reasonably be expected to offer the other some protection.

[13] Ibid, [28].

[14] Ibid, [31].

[15] *Tomlinson* (n 1) [11].

[16] Noting the reservations which had been expressed by both Longmore LJ in the Court of Appeal and by Lord Phillips of Worth Matravers MR (as he then was) in *Donoghue*, Lord Hoffmann nevertheless concluded that the concession was rightly made. He explained (at [13]): 'As a matter of logic, I see the force of these observations. But I have nevertheless come to the conclusion that the concession was rightly made. The duty under the 1984 Act was intended to be a lesser duty, as to both incidence and scope, than the duty to a lawful visitor under the 1957 Act. That was because Parliament recognised that it would often be unduly burdensome to require landowners to take steps to protect the safety of people who came upon their land without invitation or permission. They should not ordinarily be able to force duties upon unwilling hosts. In the application of that principle, I can see no difference between a person who comes upon land without permission and one who, having come with permission, does something which he has not been given permission to do. In both cases, the entrant would be imposing upon the landowner a duty of care which he has not expressly or impliedly accepted. The 1984 Act provides that even in such cases a duty may exist, based simply upon occupation of land and knowledge or foresight that unauthorised persons may come upon the land or authorised persons may use it for unauthorised purposes. But that duty is rarer and different in quality from the duty which arises from express or implied invitation or permission to come upon the land and use it'. Lord Scott, however, continued to have a reservation about the correctness of this concession: see the opinion of Lord Scott in *Tomlinson* (n 1) [85].

> (4) Where, by virtue of this section, an occupier of premises owes a duty to another in respect of such a risk, the duty is to take such care as is reasonable in all the circumstances of the case to see that he does not suffer injury on the premises by reason of the danger concerned.
>
> (5) Any duty owed by virtue of this section in respect of a risk may, in an appropriate case, be discharged by taking such steps as are reasonable in all the circumstances of the case to give warning of the danger concerned or to discourage persons from incurring the risk.
>
> (6) No duty is owed by virtue of this section to any person in respect of risks willingly accepted as his by that person (the question whether a risk was so accepted to be decided on the same principles as in other cases in which one person owes a duty of care to another).

In *Tomlinson*, the claimant argued that the notices erected had been totally ineffectual and therefore it was incumbent upon the defendant to take more drastic measures to prevent people like himself from going into the water.

Running throughout the speeches of the judges in the House of Lords in *Tomlinson* is a strong emphasis on the freedom of choice of the individual and the fact that the claimant was an adult of sound mind choosing to engage in risky activity. This emphasis is expressly marshalled in order to support the conclusion that neither the 1957 nor the 1984 Act applied in *Tomlinson* given the legislative requirement[17] that the danger complained of be due to the state of the premises.[18] Thus, Lord Hoffmann, who delivered the leading speech, states:

> Mr Tomlinson was a person of full capacity who voluntarily and without any pressure or inducement engaged in an activity which had inherent risk. The risk was that he might not execute his dive properly and so sustain injury. Likewise, a person who goes mountaineering incurs the risk that he might stumble or misjudge where to put his weight. In neither case can the risk be attributed to the state of the premises. Otherwise any premises can be said to be dangerous to someone who chooses to use them for some dangerous activity. In the present case, Mr Tomlinson knew the lake well and even if he had not, the judge's finding was that it contained no dangers which one would not have expected. So the only risk arose out of what he chose to do and not out of the state of the premises.[19]

As to the finding made in the Court of Appeal to the effect that the defendant Council had effectively lured people into a deathtrap, Lord Hoffmann rejected such a conclusion as 'gross hyperbole'.[20] Lord Hoffmann drew attention to two factors which militated against the imposition of liability: (1) 'the social value of the activities which were to be prohibited in order to reduce or eliminate the risk';[21] and (2) 'whether people should accept responsibility for the risks they choose to run'.[22] It is necessary to deal with each of these factors in turn in order to explore fully the implications of the approach in *Tomlinson*.

[17] This requirement is mirrored in the Irish legislation discussed below in this chapter: Occupiers' Liability Act 1995, s 1.

[18] *cf* Lord Hutton in *Tomlinson* (n 1) [53].

[19] Ibid, [27].

[20] Ibid.

[21] Ibid, [41].

[22] Ibid.

The Relevance of the Social Value of Activities in the Context of Autonomy Analysis

On the question of the social value of the activities which would have to be prohibited in order to reduce or eliminate the risk, Lord Hoffmann noted that the Court of Appeal had made no reference whatsoever to this point.[23] Lord Hoffmann emphasised the fact that the majority of people who went to the beaches to sunbathe, paddle and play with their children were 'enjoying themselves in a way which gave them pleasure and caused no risk to themselves or anyone else'.[24] He concluded that this 'must be something to be taken into account' in deciding whether it was reasonable to expect the Council to destroy the beaches (a measure which the Council had in contemplation but had not carried out by the time of Mr Tomlinson's accident). It is, with respect, not clear as to what is the nature of the balancing exercise to be engaged in by the courts as between the social value of accessing beaches, on the one hand, and the need to warn against dangers, on the other.

Nor is any guidance given in this part of Lord Hoffmann's judgment as to when a court will be able (or likely) to conclude that a particular activity has an obvious social value. The reference to the beach activity giving the families pleasure and causing no risk to anyone else does not, with respect, provide any real framework for assessing whether or to what extent the probable curtailment of a given activity should influence the courts in declining to impose a duty upon the occupier. It is, moreover, not clear whether the social value is to be identified in the enjoyment or fulfilment being imputed (to continue with Lord Hoffmann's example) to the families, or whether a broader social value is generated to all members of society merely by having the option of engaging in the enjoyable and essentially risk-free activities in question, regardless of whether a given individual takes up that opportunity or not. If the former is what Lord Hoffmann's argument refers to, then it is submitted that it is necessary at the very least to have some sort of criteria by way of guidance as to how that is to be balanced against the individual claimant's interests in a case such as *Tomlinson*. If it is the latter, however, such an understanding of social value would appear to be extremely broad. It is questionable whether the amorphous and abstract possibility of having access to a pleasurable activity which one may have no interest whatsoever in taking up can meaningfully be relied upon so as to justify the non-imposition of a duty to guard against even obvious dangers.

Another construction of Lord Hoffmann's social value analysis also seems possible—that each individual within a community has his or her life enriched and enhanced by the possibility that other persons in the community can engage in enjoyable activities. Such a construction seems, however, highly questionable and it is by no means clear why effectively speculative assumptions about the common good should be identified as a factor militating against the imposition of liability.

In conclusion, then, it may well be the case that 'social value' arguments can, to an extent, legitimately be invoked so as to rule out liability in a case such as *Tomlinson*. The difficulty with the 'social value' strand of Lord Hoffmann's reasoning, however, is that it is not clear what the nature of the social value is, and nor are any criteria provided as to how

[23] Ibid, [42].
[24] Ibid.

such a claimed-for social value can be weighed against an assessment of potential liability in favour of an individual claimant. And while Lord Hoffmann correctly notes that the approach of the Court of Appeal in *Tomlinson* did not make any reference to the social value of the activities under consideration, it could equally be argued that the strong emphasis placed by the majority of the Court of Appeal on the fact-specificity of occupiers' liability cases itself comprises an acknowledgement by the majority of the limited use of social value arguments in cases such as *Tomlinson*.[25]

Free Will

I now turn to the second of Lord Hoffmann's justifications for denying liability in *Tomlinson*. In a key passage of his judgment entitled 'Free Will', Lord Hoffmann said:

> The second consideration, namely the question of whether people should accept responsibility for the risks they choose to run, is the point made by Lord Phillips of Worth Matravers MR in *Donoghue v Folkestone Properties Ltd* and which I said was central to this appeal. Mr Tomlinson was freely and voluntarily undertaking an activity which inherently involved some risk.[26]

The reference to *Donoghue v Folkestone Properties*[27] is, of course, very significant. In *Donoghue* the defendants occupied a harbour which contained horizontal concrete beams used for boat repair purposes. While these beams were visible at low tide, they became submerged at high tide, thus providing a concealed hazard for swimmers. Awareness of the hazard, for the purposes of the 1984 Act, was accepted by the defendants, who conceded that they owed a duty to prevent trespassers, especially children, from swimming in the harbour during the summer; and security guards were employed to discourage such activity. Unfortunately, the claimant, a 30-year-old adult, broke his neck as a result of hitting one of the beams while diving into the harbour at midnight in December. He contended that warning notices should have been provided at the point from which trespassers were known to enter the water. The trial judge found in favour of the claimant, but his judgment was reversed by the Court of Appeal. The defendants could not reasonably have been expected to anticipate midnight swims by trespassing adults in December.

Having referred to *Donoghue* in *Tomlinson*, Lord Hoffmann concluded:

> I think it will be extremely rare for an occupier of land to be under a duty to prevent people from taking risks which are inherent in the activities they freely choose to undertake upon the land. If people want to climb mountains, go hang gliding or swim or dive in ponds or lakes, that is their affair. Of course the landowner may for his own reasons wish to prohibit such activities. He may think that they are a danger or inconvenience to himself or others. Or he may take a paternalist view and prefer people not to undertake risky activities on his land. He is entitled to impose such conditions, as the Council did by prohibiting swimming. But the law does not require him to do so.
>
> …

[25] Above (n 12) (Sedley LJ in *Tomlinson* [42]).

[26] *Tomlinson* (n 1) [44]. Lord Hoffmann contrasted the position of Mr Tomlinson with that of the claimant in *Bolton v Stone* [1951] AC 850, who was innocently standing on the pavement outside her garden gate when she was struck by a cricket ball. He concluded that, 'compared with *Bolton v Stone*, this is an *a fortiori* case'.

[27] *Donoghue* (n 8).

> I think that there is an important question of freedom at stake. It is unjust that the harmless recreation of responsible parents and children with buckets and spades on the beaches should be prohibited in order to comply with what is thought to be a legal duty to safeguard irresponsible visitors against dangers which are perfectly obvious. The fact that such people take no notice of warnings cannot create a duty to take other steps to protect them.[28]

In 'a crucial passage which has proved to be highly influential',[29] Lord Hoffmann articulated the circumstances in which a duty would arise in such a case:

> A duty to protect against obvious risks or self-inflicted harm exists only in cases in which there is no genuine and informed choice, or in the case of employees, or some lack of capacity, such as the inability of children to recognise danger … or the despair of prisoners which may lead them to inflict injury on themselves.[30]

A number of points arise from the above passages. First, Lord Hoffmann identifies an 'important question of freedom' as being at stake. It is not clear, however, whether this important freedom is the freedom to engage in the harmless recreation in the example given by Lord Hoffmann, or whether it is the individual claimant's freedom, acting as an autonomous individual, to engage in risky conduct. Both conceptions of freedom appear to be contemplated in the above passages, but the title of 'Free Will' which introduces this section of the opinion seems to suggest that it is the latter conception of freedom that is in strong focus. If this is so, it seems, with respect, that Lord Hoffmann's example of the parents and children with their buckets and spades does not properly belong in this analysis but ought instead to be viewed as an extension of the analysis which his Lordship provides earlier in his speech on the social value of the conduct in question. This may, with respect, comprise an example of the difficulties for courts in occupiers' liability cases in demarcating adequate boundaries between rationales of individual autonomy, on the one hand, and social value, on the other.

In the same way that Lord Hoffmann's judgment arguably intermingles the boundaries of social value and autonomy analysis, so too can it be argued that Lord Hutton combines arguments as to the inconvenience for defendants of taking certain precautions with an insistence that claimants must display common sense in their actions. The latter reasoning appears to be closely associated with the individualist values set out at length by Lord Hoffmann. It is instructive to consider how Lord Hutton, for his part, arrives at the conclusion that no duty is owed in *Tomlinson*. He does so by reliance on, inter alia, *Stevenson v Glasgow Corporation*[31] and *Hastie v Magistrates of Edinburgh*.[32] In *Stevenson*, Lord M'Laren stated:

> [I]n a town, as well as in the country, there are physical features which may be productive of injury to careless persons or to young children against which it is impossible to guard by protective measures. The situation of a town on the banks of a river is a familiar feature; and whether the stream be sluggish like the Clyde at Glasgow, or swift and variable like the Ness at Inverness, or the Tay at Perth, there is always danger to the individual who may be so unfortunate as to fall into the stream. But in none of these places has it been found necessary to fence the river to prevent children or

[28] *Tomlinson* (n 1) [45]–[46].

[29] Brodie (n 10) 7.

[30] *Tomlinson* (n 1) [46], referring to *British Railways Board v Herrington* [1972] AC 877 and *Reeves v Commissioner of Police of the Metropolis* [2000] 1 AC 360 respectively.

[31] *Stevenson v Glasgow Corporation* 1908 SC 1034.

[32] *Hastie v Magistrates of Edinburgh* 1907 SC 1102.

> careless persons from falling into the water. Now, as the common law is just the formal statement of the results and conclusions of the common sense of mankind, I come without difficulty to the conclusion that precautions which have been rejected by common sense as unnecessary and inconvenient are not required by the law.[33]

In *Tomlinson*, Lord Hutton explained his interpretation of the above passage thus:

> I think that when Lord M'Laren referred to physical features against which 'it is impossible to guard by protective measures' he was not referring to protective measures which it is physically impossible to put in place; rather he had in mind measures which the common sense of mankind indicates as being unnecessary to take.[34]

Lord Hutton concluded of *Stevenson* and *Hastie* that, although they were decided (then) almost a century ago and the judgments 'are couched in old-fashioned language', they were still applicable to *Tomlinson*. Lord Hutton continued:

> I consider that they express a principle which is still valid today, namely, that it is contrary to common sense, and therefore not sound law, to expect an occupier to provide protection against an obvious danger on his land arising from a natural feature such as a lake or a cliff and to impose a duty on him to do so. In my opinion this principle, although not always explicitly stated, underlies the cases relied on by the appellants where it has been held that the occupier is not liable where a person has injured himself or drowned in an inland lake or pool or in the sea or on some natural feature.[35]

It is, with respect, not clear from this passage whether the value of 'common sense' being referred to is one which is drawing from the autonomy-based reasoning of Lord Hoffmann, although they appear to be closely connected. The argument seems to regard the 'common sense' rationale in different ways: first, if a danger is obvious, then it would offend against common sense to impose a duty on an occupier to take precautions; second, that individuals must exercise common sense in approaching obvious dangers. These two accounts of 'common sense' are not, however, necessarily the same. The first emphasises the illogicality of making a defendant pay to avoid obvious risks; the second prays in aid the individualistic nature of the common sense of the particular claimant, with the recognition of the claimant's common sense being an important manifestation of the individualist values of the common law. As will be seen later in this chapter, this particular passage in the judgment of Lord Hutton has been specifically endorsed and applied by the Irish Supreme Court in *Weir-Rodgers*, so I return to this point below.[36]

Returning to the approach of Lord Hoffmann—and as Elvin has pointed out[37]—the approach to free will and autonomy adopted by Lord Hoffmann in *Tomlinson* does not appear entirely consistent with certain other House of Lords decisions, such as, for example, the *Reeves* case which is cited by Lord Hoffmann in the above passage.[38] In *Reeves*, the

[33] *Stevenson* (n 31) 1039.
[34] *Tomlinson* (n 1) [58].
[35] Ibid, [59].
[36] See below, 'Individualism and Autonomy in Occupiers' Liability Case Law in Ireland'.
[37] J Elvin, 'Occupiers' Liability, Free Will, and the Dangers of a "Compensation Culture"' [2004] *Edinburgh Law Review* 127, 129.
[38] *Reeves* (n 30).

House of Lords imposed liability upon the police for the suicide of a prisoner, albeit that it was very clear that he intended to kill himself.[39]

Third, with respect, it is not altogether straightforward to accept an autonomy-based analysis predicated upon the proposition that a duty can be imposed to guard against deliberate self-inflicted injury in the case of all prisoners, on the one hand, but not in the case of claimants in the position of Mr Tomlinson, on the other.[40] Lord Hoffmann's delineation of the duty to protect against obvious risks or self-inflicted harm in the passage referred to immediately above posits an extremely restrictive range of situations in which such a duty would be engaged. The fact this is normatively grounded in an autonomy or 'free will' argument makes it all the more necessary for a normative distinction to be drawn between *Tomlinson* and *Reeves*, but this is not provided in *Tomlinson*. With respect, it seems difficult to avoid the conclusion that the autonomy argument is being deployed in *Tomlinson* as a mechanism of declining to countenance the recognition of a duty which could, admittedly, have many undesirable or awkward social and practical consequences. To use the language of autonomy and free will as the normative explanation for this policy decision, however, is not convincing and indeed does not appear to cohere with cases such as *Reeves*, decided only a few years before *Tomlinson*.

In this regard, it is very significant to note that Lord Hobhouse in *Tomlinson* specifically emphasised the dangers of a compensation culture. It is submitted that, in so doing, Lord Hobhouse was expressly articulating the policy choices which also lie—at least in part—at the root of Lord Hoffmann's autonomy-based reasoning. Lord Hobhouse said:

> [I]t is not, and should never be, the policy of the law to require the protection of the foolhardy or reckless few to deprive, or interfere with, the enjoyment by the remainder of society of the liberties and amenities to which they are rightly entitled. Does the law require that all trees be cut down because some youths may climb them and fall? Does the law require the coast line and other beauty spots to be lined with warning notices? Does the law require that attractive water side picnic spots be destroyed because of a few foolhardy individuals who choose to ignore warning notices and indulge in activities dangerous only to themselves? The answer to all these questions is, of course, no. But this is the road down which your Lordships, like other courts before, have been invited to travel and which the councils in the present case found so inviting. In truth, the arguments for the claimant have involved an attack upon the liberties of the citizen which should not be countenanced. They attack the liberty of the individual to engage in dangerous, but otherwise harmless, pastimes at his own risk and the liberty of citizens as a whole fully to enjoy the variety and quality of the landscape of this country. The pursuit of an unrestrained culture of blame and compensation has many evil consequences and one is certainly the interference with the liberty of the individual.[41]

One of the many striking features of the above passage is the two very different senses in which the value of liberty is used. Emphasis is primarily placed on the liberty of the

[39] A point noted by Elvin (n 37) 129. Elvin cites the characteristically insightful commentary of the late Tony Weir who remarked of *Tomlinson* that 'it is undeniable that [decisions like this diminish] … the responsibility, indeed the autonomy, of the individual' (T Weir, *Tort Law* (Oxford, Clarendon Press, 2002) 6).

[40] This is, as Elvin rightly points out, something that Lord Hoffmann 'did not explain' in *Tomlinson*: Elvin (n 37) 129.

[41] *Tomlinson* (n 1) [81].

individual to engage in risky conduct. It is noteworthy, however, that the language of 'liberty' is also used in defending the rights of all persons 'fully to enjoy the variety and quality of the landscape of the country'. These two varying conceptions of autonomy then appear to be consolidated into the compensation-culture focused conclusion concerning the need to prevent interference with the liberty of the individual.

Another important point to be gleaned from this passage is the strong tone of disenchantment with a perceived compensation culture in Lord Hobhouse's ominous description of 'the road down which [the House of Lords], like other courts before, have been invited to travel'. This conjures up concerns of limitless liability and floodgates but those concerns are not explored with reference to any concrete evidence or arguments. With respect, this is an important dimension of the approach in *Tomlinson* and it is one that suggests that familiar compensation culture concerns, resting on assumptions the validity of which is not explained in the judgments, form an important strand of the ultimate decision in *Tomlinson*. Although this is articulated more clearly by Lord Hobhouse, it is submitted that it is also a very real feature of the reasoning of Lord Hoffmann in *Tomlinson*.

I now wish to consider the influence of *Tomlinson* in Irish law, and will do so chiefly through an analysis of the leading authority of the Irish Supreme Court in this area, which is its decision in *Weir-Rodgers v SF Trust Limited*.[42] In analysing that decision, it is possible to discern the same tensions concerning both autonomy and compensation culture analysis which have been analysed above in the judgments in *Tomlinson*.

Individualism and Autonomy in Occupiers' Liability Case Law in Ireland

The law in Ireland relating to occupiers' liability was radically overhauled by the introduction of the Occupiers' Liability Act 1995 (the 1995 Act). For the purposes of my analysis in this chapter (and indeed for any consideration of the significance of the 1995 Act overall), the most important judgment in the 20 years since the 1995 Act has been in force is the judgment of the Irish Supreme Court in *Weir-Rodgers*.[43] There, the Irish Supreme Court overturned a High Court decision imposing liability on an occupier for failing to impose a warning sign in respect of a danger at a cliff face in Donegal. The judgment represented the first signal at Superior Court level since the coming into force of the 1995 Act of the increased difficulty that entrants who did not enter on to the premises as visitors now face in suing occupiers for injuries sustained due to the state of the premises. The Irish Supreme Court's invocation of the *Tomlinson* reasoning evinces an acute awareness of the potential societal downside of imposing liability on an occupier. Like *Tomlinson*, it is a judgment carrying significant implications for the interrelationship in judicial reasoning in occupiers' liability case law between compensation culture concerns, the individualism of the common law, and the value of autonomy.

[42] *Weir-Rodgers* (n 4).

[43] Ibid.

Background to the Occupiers' Liability Act 1995

It is necessary to provide some brief contextual background to the introduction into Irish law of the 1995 Act.[44] From the perspective of compensation culture concerns and their impact upon this area of tort law, it is relevant to note that the momentum for the enactment of the 1995 Act came, at least in part, from concern amongst the farming community in Ireland about potential liability to persons who suffered injuries on their lands, having entered onto the premises without the permission of the occupier. The courts' sympathy for such entrants had been most evident in cases involving children who were injured under such circumstances. Two leading decisions of the Irish Supreme Court in the 1960s and 1970s—*Purtill v Athlone Urban District Council*[45] and *McNamara v ESB*[46] respectively—effectively sowed the seeds for the clamours for reform which resulted in the 1995 legislation. In *McNamara*, the Irish Supreme Court had held that a trespasser was owed a duty of care in negligence by the occupier. There followed a sustained and highly effective campaign to introduce reforming legislation in this area, which was ultimately to lead to the enactment of the 1995 Act. As McMahon and Binchy comment of the debates leading up to the enactment of that legislation, '[t]he voice of the trespasser, notably the adventurous urban child, was not heard'.[47]

Accordingly, the 1995 Act sought to relieve occupiers of the duty of care in negligence to such entrants, imposing instead the lesser duty not to intentionally injure such persons, nor to act with reckless disregard for them, or their property.[48] The 1995 Act thus marked a watershed in Irish tort law, bringing about sweeping reforms in the area of the duty owed by an occupier to entrants onto his or her premises. In the wake of the 1995 Act, then, a crucial question was whether the onus of establishing reckless disregard would pose a formidable hurdle to plaintiffs, and result in a far greater number of such claims being dismissed. Important guidance on this very issue was provided by the Irish Supreme Court decision in *Weir-Rodgers*. Before turning to analyse the decision, it may be helpful to sketch the background to the Act and to summarise the principal changes which it brought about.

The 1995 Act achieved the reform so strongly desired by its proponents not only through the creation of an entirely new system of classifying persons entering onto a premises, but, more specifically—and indeed more radically—through the considerable reduction of the extent of an occupier's liability towards uninvited entrants. A key feature of the Act was the introduction of the extremely broad 'recreational user' category of entrant in respect of whom, as with trespassers, the occupier essentially owes no greater duty than a duty not to act with reckless disregard. Although the concept is not defined in the legislation, section 4(2) of the Act does set out a list of nine factors which must be taken into account by the court in assessing whether reckless disregard can be attributed to an occupier. These are:

(a) whether the occupier knew or had reasonable grounds for believing that a danger existed on the premises;
(b) whether the occupier knew or had reasonable grounds for believing that the person and, in the case of damage, property of the person, was or was likely to be on the premises;

[44] For comprehensive treatment, see BME McMahon and W Binchy, *Law of Torts*, 4th edn (Dublin, Bloomsbury Professional, 2013) 444–46.
[45] *Purtill v Athlone Urban District Council* [1968] IR 205.
[46] *McNamara v ESB* [1975] IR 1.
[47] McMahon and Binchy, *Law of Torts*, 4th edn (n 44) 444.
[48] s 4(1).

(c) whether the occupier knew or had reasonable grounds for believing that the person or property of the person was in, or was likely to be in, the vicinity of the place where the danger existed;
(d) whether the danger was one against which, in all the circumstances, the occupier might reasonably be expected to provide protection for the person and property of the person;
(e) the burden on the occupier of eliminating the danger or of protecting the person and property of the person from the danger, taking into account the difficulty, expense or impracticability, having regard to the character of the premises and the degree of the danger, of so doing;
(f) the character of the premises including, in relation to premises of such a character as to be likely to be used for recreational activity, the desirability of maintaining the tradition of open access to premises of such a character for such an activity;
(g) the conduct of the person, and the care which he or she may reasonably be expected to take for his or her own safety, while on the premises, having regard to the extent of his or her knowledge thereof;
(h) the nature of any warning given by the occupier or another person of the danger; and
(i) whether or not the person was on the premises in the company of another person and, if so, the extent of the supervision and control the latter person might reasonably be expected to exercise over the other's activities.

As is immediately apparent from the above checklist of factors, it enshrines into the Irish statutory code on occupiers' liability specific 'compensation culture' concerns, particularly in its overt concern about the increased costs to defendants of putting in place preventive measures. Another important point to be made about the above section is that it is not necessarily straightforward to determine whether the above criteria are entirely objective.[49] While the language of reasonableness of belief abounds in this section, so too is it replete with references to what the occupier 'knew' or ought reasonably to have known. It is perhaps significant to note that in another judgment delivered by Geoghegan J in the Irish Supreme Court in the same year as the delivery of *Weir-Rodgers*, Geoghegan J noted that subjectivity and recklessness as concepts may be somewhat 'uneasy bedfellows'.[50] The concept of reckless disregard within the meaning of the 1995 Act was first considered by the Irish Supreme Court in the *Weir-Rodgers* case to which I now turn. As will be seen, the judgment reveals the force and impact of the 'individualistic values' approach in *Tomlinson*—while also raising concerns about the intermingling of this approach with far broader concerns about the compensation culture.

Weir-Rodgers: The Background

The background facts to *Weir-Rodgers* may be briefly stated. The plaintiff had been sitting down with some friends close to the edge of a cliff at Coolmore, Rossnowlagh, Co Donegal, admiring the sunset over the sea. When she stood up she lost her footing and fell down the edge of the cliff, which proved to be far more sheer than she had expected. Due to loose

[49] It has been remarked that the section 'is not easy to interpret': R Byrne and W Binchy, *Annual Review of Irish Law 2013* (Dublin, Round Hall, 2014) 560.
[50] *Kennedy v The Law Society of Ireland* [2005] IESC 23, [2005] 3 IR 228, 261 (Geoghegan J).

materials she was unable to stop herself and ended up in the water, from which she was rescued by her friend. She suffered fractures to her left shoulder, left elbow, left hip and pelvis, injuries to her ankle and foot, as well as other injuries. In the High Court, the plaintiff claimed that the defendant occupier had breached its duty owed to her under section 4 of the 1995 Act. The plaintiff claimed that she was on the defendant's premises as a 'recreational user', within the meaning of section 1(1) of the Act, and alleged that the occupier had been guilty of 'reckless disregard' in two respects. First, it was contended that, in failing to have the area fenced off so as to prevent anyone entering into it, the occupier had acted with reckless disregard. Second, it was argued that the occupier should have erected a warning notice and thus had again acted with reckless disregard in failing to do so.

The trial judge, Butler J, while rejecting the first contention above, upheld the second, stigmatising the defendant's failure to put up a warning notice as amounting to reckless disregard within the meaning of section 4(1) of the Act. Accordingly, Butler J imposed liability and, after making a 25 per cent reduction for contributory negligence, awarded damages. The defendant appealed to the Supreme Court against both the imposition of liability and the apportionment of contributory negligence. For her part, the plaintiff cross-appealed against the finding of contributory negligence and claimed that the assessment of damages was too low.[51]

Judgment in the Irish Supreme Court: Strong Echoes of *Tomlinson*

On the defendant's appeal, a unanimous Supreme Court reversed the High Court, and dismissed the plaintiff's action.[52] Before assessing the importance of the judgment, two preliminary points as to its scope should be made. First, because section 4 of the Act imposes upon the occupier the same duty in respect of recreational users and trespassers, Geoghegan J (Murray CJ and Denham J concurring) chose to analyse that section without 'expressing any view as to whether the respondent was a recreational user within the meaning of the Act or not'.[53] Very significantly, Geoghegan J was of the view that even had the plaintiff been a visitor—thus enjoying a duty of care in negligence—she would still have been unable to recover. This, it is submitted, is telling: in the Court's view the status of the plaintiff on the premises was irrelevant to liability, since even if she had been owed the highest duty (in negligence, as a visitor) she still would have been unsuccessful. It is clear, therefore, that the Court considered the notion of 'reckless disregard' to be very far indeed from having been met in this case, given that even the far more indulgent threshold involved in a duty of care analysis would not have been satisfied.

Second, Geoghegan J declined to express a view as to whether 'reckless disregard' under section 4 posits a subjective element, or whether it is entirely objective.[54] One point that emerges with striking clarity from *Weir-Rodgers*, however, is the Court's emphasis on the position that the 'reckless disregard' test is far more difficult for the trespasser

[51] A Court of Appeal in civil cases was only introduced in Ireland with the enactment of the Court of Appeal Act 2014.

[52] For analysis see R Ryan and D Ryan, 'Trespassers (and Recreational User) Beware: The Supreme Court Decision in *Weir-Rodgers v SF Trust*' (2005) 23 *Irish Law Times* (new series) 59.

[53] *Weir-Rodgers* (n 4) 53.

[54] Ibid, 55.

(or recreational user) to satisfy than the negligence standard. Geoghegan J expressed concern that the High Court judge had not 'addressed himself to this much higher threshold now enacted for a plaintiff trespasser'.[55] Geoghegan J considered the note of caution sounded by McMahon and Binchy in the then current edition of their textbook where, in a passage described by Geoghegan J as being 'astute and prescient',[56] the authors had cautioned that the Act's enumeration of criteria to be considered when addressing the issue of reckless disregard

> might constitute a trap to an unwary judge who could easily seek to apply them without adverting to the fact that, although they are similar to criteria applicable for determining the issue of negligence, they have to be pitched at a level more indulgent to the defendant.[57]

It is clear, then, that *Weir-Rodgers* provides strong judicial insistence on the greater difficulties facing plaintiffs in occupiers' liability cases since the introduction in Ireland of the 1995 Act. Building on this analysis, I now examine the influence of *Tomlinson* on the approach in *Weir-Rodgers*, and the extent to which similarities in reasoning can be discerned between the two judgments.

The Impact of *Tomlinson* on *Weir-Rodgers*

For the purposes of my analysis in this chapter, it is submitted that what is most significant about Geoghegan J's judgment is the reliance placed on the (then very recent) House of Lords decision in *Tomlinson*. Although Geoghegan J conceded that the equivalent English legislation considered in *Tomlinson* was 'of limited assistance' in an Irish context, Geoghegan J was clearly persuaded by the philosophy conveyed by the Law Lords in their speeches. Geoghegan J referred in detail to the approach taken by Lord Hutton, who, as I have analysed above in section one, vigorously defended in *Tomlinson* the position that the law relating to occupiers' liability must be based on common sense, an approach which Geoghegan J declared that he would 'heartily endorse'. Returning to my analysis in section one of Lord Hutton's comments in this regard, it is interesting to note that Geoghegan J states in *Weir-Rodgers* immediately after expressing his agreement with Lord Hutton's approach that '[t]he person sitting down near a cliff must be prepared for oddities in the cliff's structure or in the structure of the ground adjacent to the cliff and *he or she assumes the inherent risks* associated therewith'.[58] The words I have italicised are, with respect, telling, in signalling that Geogeghan J's application of the common sense value appears to be more closely concerned with the individualistic approach as opposed to the alternative interpretation discussed above in the context of Lord Hutton's speech. This again shows the need for a greater demarcation between autonomy and compensation culture rationales in the case law.

On the compensation culture theme permeating these cases, it is submitted that the approach of Geoghegan J in *Weir-Rodgers* reveals strong influences of this theme. It is salutary, for example, to note an observation by Geoghegan J in the course of dismissing the

[55] Ibid, 54.
[56] Ibid, 56.
[57] BME McMahon and W Binchy, *Law of Torts*, 3rd edn (Dublin, Butterworths, 2000) [12.109].
[58] *Weir-Rodgers* (n 4) 58 (italics added).

argument that failing to erect a warning sign constituted reckless disregard. Ruminating on the potentially far-reaching adverse consequences of such a ruling, Geoghegan J felt bound to 'confess that this conjures up in my mind huge areas of coastline right around Ireland fenced against the public and littered with warning notices'.[59] It is submitted that this type of sentiment, stressing as it does the adverse ripple effect which imposing liability in these cases can have, reveals the overlap in *Weir-Rodgers* between autonomy values and compensation culture concerns.

On the centrality of the compensation culture concerns in *Weir-Rodgers*, a number of crucial points emerge from the decision. First, the burden on a trespasser or recreational user in establishing reckless disregard is a high one, and will not be easily discharged. While it is correct to observe, as Quill does, that the case law in Ireland in the 20 years since the enactment of the 1995 Act 'provides little insight'[60] into the interpretation of reckless disregard, it does seem clear that, for the occupier to be deemed guilty of reckless disregard owing to the presence of a danger due to the state of the premises, the plaintiff will need to show that that danger was something quite exceptionally unusual and dangerous. In *Weir-Rodgers*, Geoghegan J stated:

> There could, of course, be something quite exceptionally unusual and dangerous in the state of a particular piece of ground which would impose a duty on the occupier the effect of which would be that if he did not put up a warning notice he would be treated as having reckless disregard. But this is certainly not such a case.[61]

This is indeed a strict interpretation of section 4 of the 1995 Act, and one which illustrates that plaintiffs will have a difficult time of it in attempting to show that a defendant occupier has acted with reckless disregard to them. In this respect, it is submitted that the benchmark selected by Geoghegan J of 'something quite exceptionally unusual and dangerous', affords a hint as to just how formidable a hurdle plaintiffs will hereafter face.

The *ex tempore* judgment of the Irish Supreme Court in *Raleigh v Iarnród Éireann* is a further significant contribution to the case law in this regard.[62] There, a three-judge Supreme Court reversed O'Donovan J,[63] and dismissed the plaintiff's action, in the following circumstances. The plaintiff was hit by a train after he fell asleep beside a railway track on the Clara-Tullamore railway line 'with a feed of alcoholic drink on him' in the early hours of the morning. He and his girlfriend and others had gone to a part of the railway where, the plaintiff claimed, people were accustomed to gather from time to time to socialise and drink. Access was gained by climbing a 4ft 6in high (1.4m) wall and then negotiating a steep bank. Having had some drinks at the entry point, the plaintiff and his companions moved to another location 200 yards away where they had more drink. The plaintiff's friends left and he and his girlfriend stayed, sitting on sleepers with their backs to the railway, and he and his girlfriend fell asleep on the sleepers. The plaintiff was awakened and alerted to the oncoming train because the driver saw him and his girlfriend on the track as the train approached them and the driver sounded the train's horn. The plaintiff pushed his girlfriend out of the way but the train hit his leg, resulting in such severe injuries that it had to be amputated.

[59] Ibid, 53.
[60] E Quill, *Torts in Ireland*, 4th edn (Dublin, Gill and MacMillan, 2014) 159.
[61] *Weir-Rodgers* (n 4) 58.
[62] See M Carolan, '€111,000 Rail Incident Award Overturned' *Irish Times* (1 December 2006).
[63] *Raleigh v Iarnród Éireann* [2003] 12 JIC 1907.

The judgments of both the Irish High Court and the Supreme Court reveal a marked emphasis on individualism and personal autonomy. In light of my earlier analysis of *Tomlinson* in section one, it is interesting to note that the approach of the High Court and the Supreme Court in *Raleigh* were both heavily critical of the actions of the plaintiff and couched such criticism in the language of individual responsibility. Thus, O'Donovan J in the High Court stated:

> I have no doubt at all but that the plaintiff, himself, was largely the author of his own misfortune and, in apportioning blame worthiness I am satisfied that I must visit the plaintiff with a much greater degree of fault than that of the defendants. In this regard, I cannot think of anything more irresponsible than that a grown man would sit on a railway line in the middle of the night with a feed of alcoholic drink in him and I think that the plaintiff's wrongdoing was compounded by the fact that the point at which he chose to sit on the railway line was such that he had very little room to manoeuvre in the event of an emergency because of the existence of adjoining vegetation. Furthermore, apart altogether from the obvious danger, he well knew that he was an unwelcome trespasser.

The strong emphasis here on the irresponsibility of the plaintiff's conduct is particularly striking, and is further echoed in the judgment of the Irish Supreme Court in the same case, where Murray CJ described the plaintiff as 'the author of his own misfortune' and said that the defendant could not be held liable for this tragic accident on grounds that it must be expected to foresee such acts of 'folly' or 'stupidity' by adults who came onto its property. The Supreme Court held that the cause of the accident was not the fact of Mr Raleigh entering onto the railway embankment but the fact that he, having entered, caused the danger to himself by first of all taking drink, then staying in the area for some six hours and falling asleep beside the railway line in such circumstances that he could not avoid the danger of an approaching train when he was woken up by the sound of its horn. It also rejected claims that the company should have erected a palisade fence at the point where Mr Raleigh and others entered onto the embankment.

Thus, it can be seen that, of the two Irish Supreme Court judgments considering the Occupiers' Liability Act 1995 to have been handed down post-*Tomlinson*, the philosophy of that judgment has been clearly in evidence in the approach of the Irish Supreme Court. What does this signify for how the courts are applying autonomy and individualism values to these cases, and how those values interrelate to compensation culture concerns? I turn to address this question in section three below.

The Meaning of the Value of Autonomy in this Context and its Interrelationship with Compensation Culture Concerns

The final section of the chapter explores the notions of autonomy and responsibility both in the leading cases considered in the first two sections, as well as more recent jurisprudence bearing out the application of these principles. This section seeks to evaluate the relationship between individualism and autonomy principles and compensation culture arguments so as to assess the current position in the case law in this area, and consider its future development.

As has been shown in the first two sections of this chapter, an analysis of the occupiers' liability case law in both the United Kingdom and Ireland in the last 15 years reveals a very strong thematic focus being placed on personal responsibility, articulated as an example of the individualistic values of the common law. These judicial decisions have, however, been characterised by a lack of clarity as to what precisely is meant by the value of autonomy. Is it being regarded, in the words of McCormack, as 'a virtue, possessed by those who cultivate a clear understanding of their responsibilities as citizens and in other roles they play, and who exhibit a steady will to fulfil these responsibilities'?[64] Such a definition appears to accord to the individual a very significant degree of contemplation of their duties, which seems very difficult to apply meaningfully to the facts of a case such as *Tomlinson* or *Weir-Rodgers*.

Perhaps a definition that sits more appositely with the case law analysed is that provided in a judgment of the High Court of Australia in which it was stated that: '[E]xpressed in the most general way, the value described as personal autonomy leaves it to the individual to decide whether to engage in conduct that may cause that individual harm'.[65] A difficulty with such a definition, however, is that it provides no clear or cogent basis on which to determine whether a genuine and informed choice can be or has been made by the claimant in an occupier's liability case.

A further difficulty with cases such as *Tomlinson* and *Weir-Rodgers* is that they do not always reveal a consistent approach to the role of personal autonomy in the determination of occupiers' liability cases. A good example of this—as has been highlighted by Mullender[66]—is the unevenness in emphasis on the value of personal autonomy discernible in a comparison of the approaches of the House of Lords and the Court of Appeal in *Tomlinson* itself. Thus, in contrast to the approach of Lord Hoffmann, neither Ward nor Sedley LJJ in the Court of Appeal in *Tomlinson* placed nearly so strong a degree of emphasis on personal autonomy in such cases.[67]

Notwithstanding this unevenness of approach amongst the judges in *Tomlinson* itself, however, more recent case law suggests that the courts in these cases are perhaps now invoking all too readily the individualistic values theme as shorthand for in-depth analysis of the liability considerations in a given case. Consider, for example, the following passage in the 2014 Irish High Court decision in *Deehan v Loughlinstown Inns Ltd t/a The Lough Inn Public House*, in which Barrett J stated:

> [A] person who freely elects to go to a pub, who freely elects to drink alcohol, who freely elects to engage in a party game and who freely elects to jump for a spot prize, can reasonably anticipate that she may fall, cannot reasonably expect that every part of the pub will be proofed so that there can be no injury occasioned if she does fall, and ought not to assume that she will be entitled to compensation when in fact she falls. Bad things can happen to good people and still no compensable event may arise.[68]

[64] N McCormack, 'Taking Responsibility Seriously' [2005] *Edinburgh Law Review* 168, 168.

[65] *Stuart v Kirkland-Veenstra* [2009] HCA 15, [89] (Gummow, Hayne and Heydon JJ) (internal citation omitted).

[66] R Mullender, 'Negligence Law and Blame Culture: A Critical Response to a Possible Problem' (2006) 22 *Journal of Professional Negligence* 2.

[67] See, eg, the judgment of Ward LJ ((n 12) in *Tomlinson* [32]) where he states of the claimant that '[h]e did not freely and voluntarily wish the injury on himself'.

[68] *Deehan v Loughlinstown Inns Ltd t/a The Lough Inn Public House* [2014] IEHC 182, [12].

The above passage is instructive not only because, with respect, it illustrates an extreme invocation of the individualism principle—with it being highly questionable as to whether the repeated recourse to the language of freedom of choice can meaningfully be applied to the factual matrix being considered. Second, it is telling that the above passage shifts very swiftly from a repeated invocation of the individualism principle, on the one hand, to a far broader articulation of compensation culture concerns, as seen in the express reference to managing claimants' expectations about entitlements to compensation.

This raises the question as to whether the individualism principle is being relied upon as a somewhat formulaic incantation leading inevitably to the ventilation of compensation culture concerns. While the two themes potentially have much in common, it is submitted that this trend in the case law—which, as seen in section one above, is also particularly apparent in *Tomlinson*—does create a risk of the intermingling of what are essentially two very different enquiries. Managing claimants' expectations of compensation, and concerns about the costs of damages awards, are matters which ought to be debated clearly and openly—not occluded by the invocation of the individualism principle and autonomy arguments which are then interwoven into these compensation culture concerns. Where such interweaving occurs, as it seems increasingly to do in the case law of the courts in both the United Kingdom and Ireland, the risk is created that worthy claimants may be denied compensation altogether. In order to guard against such a risk, what is needed is greater clarity in the invocation of individualistic and autonomy-based reasoning, when this is employed, and in particular in separating such reasoning out from the judicial articulation of concerns about addressing the compensation culture.

Conclusions

It has been said of the decision in *Tomlinson* that it shows 'a commendable respect for the liberty of the individual'.[69] While this is certainty arguable, this chapter has called for a greater demarcation between the notions of individualism and responsibility as those values have been espoused in occupiers' liability case law, on the one hand, and concerns about the compensation culture, on the other. In analysing the *Tomlinson* and *Weir-Rodgers* decisions, and subsequent case law, the chapter has sought to demonstrate that compensation culture concerns—whether expressly identified, as in the judgment of Lord Hobhouse in *Tomlinson*, or more tacitly acknowledged, as I have argued the judgments of Lords Hoffmann and Hutton in *Tomlinson* and that of Geoghegan J in *Weir-Rodgers* respectively are to be read—have clearly had a very significant influence on the courts' approaches to dismissing claims. There is, I have argued, a danger that the repeated emphasis being laid on free will, liberty and autonomy rationales can give rise to these concepts being invoked in a manner that lacks any clear judicial articulation of the precise values being respected or upheld, and their relationship to compensation culture concerns. This has been seen not only, for example, in what is effectively the unexplained distinguishing of *Reeves* in *Tomlinson*, but also in later jurisprudence in the High Court of Ireland analysed in section three above.

[69] Elvin (n 37) 129.

In conclusion, the last decade or thereabouts has raised important questions as to the rationales influencing the judiciary in occupiers' liability case law. *Tomlinson* and *Weir-Rodgers* were both decided in a period of intense public focus upon concerns about the compensation culture, much of which is dealt with in other chapters within this collection. In Ireland, for example, the Personal Injuries Assessment Board 2003 and the Civil Liability and Courts Act 2004 brought about very significant reforms of the compensation system which must be viewed against the backdrop of concerns about the compensation culture. Against such a backdrop, the potential for interweaving individualism and autonomy values, on the one hand, and compensation culture concerns, on the other, was perhaps all too clear. What is now needed, however, is clarification of the boundary lines between those values and concerns, in the case law of the courts both in the United Kingdom and in Ireland. Future case law will provide that opportunity—will it be grasped?

12

Compensation Culture and Sport[1]

TIM O'CONNOR

Introduction

The relationship of sport and the law has traditionally been not so much at arm's length, but an active hand-off. One early rugby referee is supposed to have said that he only intervened to prevent manslaughter; Bertie Wooster describes a friendly Gloucester derby game of rugby as 'each side is allowed a certain amount of assault and battery and do things to its fellow-man which, if done elsewhere, would result in fourteen days without the option, coupled with some strong remarks from the Bench'.[2]

However, even casual sports fans know that fear of litigation has entered even the sporting arena. It is, indeed, the reason why casual sports fans can no longer enter the sports arena, but are religiously warded off the pitch where previous generations would have invaded it at the final whistle.

One would assume these changes are spurred by a tidal wave of litigation sweeping away the customs, rules and habits of over a century. Yet there appears surprisingly little evidence of this. One must wonder, therefore, if there is a fear on the part of sporting bodies that litigation is more likely than it actually is. If 'compensation culture', defined for the purposes of this chapter as being a state where financial redress will normally be sought for injuries that would formerly have been regarded as mere accidents of life, does not per se exist in sport to a significant degree, the question that must be posed is whether a *wider* societal apprehension of the prevalence of litigation has induced a fear of such litigation in sport; and whether that fear has, in turn, had an effect on sport itself.

In short: has sport been spooked by society to such an extent that the fear of being sued changes the games themselves?

The aim of this chapter, therefore, is to attempt to set out the background position as regards liability for personal injury in sport; to then examine what evidence there is for such litigation in a sporting context; to suggest a possible explanation as to why there seems to be such fear of litigation in sport; to then examine the scrum in rugby as a case study where an excessive fear of litigation has distorted the playing of the game; and to then examine concussion in rugby as an example of how a genuine, under-appreciated risk of litigation may be addressed without affecting a sport.

[1] Some of the ideas in this chapter have been expressed in shorter form in the *Law in Sport Journal* (18 December 2013) and in other short communications.

[2] PG Wodehouse, 'The Ordeal of Young Tuppy' in *Very Good, Jeeves* (Doubleday, New York, 1930).

'Compensation Culture'

Arguably, 'compensation culture' is but a subset of a wider litigiousness in society, an increased likelihood to resort to formal, legally-centred methods of dispute resolution instead of informal, community-centred methods. It is undoubtedly the case that, in that regard, sport has been far from unaffected; arguably, it has not only been as prone as any other area, it has long been one of the worst in this regard. Vicious disputes over disciplinary decisions, suspensions and interpretations of competition rules have long been a feature of sport; one need only think of the America's Cup in sailing, perpetually marred by court cases over the Deed of Gift, of challenges to suspensions in football or rugby, or the Gaelic Athletic Association (GAA), where it reached a pitch that the Dispute Resolution Authority had to be created.

Nor has sport become any less reticent, with the expansion of sporting brawls into the area of EU law on free movement[3] and competition,[4] social media defamation,[5] the supervisory jurisdiction over disciplinary matters and even the use of *Norwich Pharmacal* orders against ticket touts.[6] So far from being scared of the courts, one might observe that historically it has been remarkably hard to keep sportsmen and women out of them.

Yet, it is notable that personal injury litigation has historically not been prone to the same levels of resort to the courts. Therefore, one must distinguish between a *litigious* culture—an accusation one might level at sport in general and Irish sport in particular—and a *compensation* culture. For the purposes of this chapter, while one must be aware of the background litigiousness, it is not in and of itself the compensation culture to be examined in relation to sport; and, therefore, the focus of this chapter must necessarily be on personal injury litigation in a sporting context.

Liability for Personal Injury in Sport

To return to Bertie Wooster, while he correctly identified the nature of rugby, it is a feature of any contact sport that it involves doing things that would lead, anywhere else, to liability in tort. Battery, a free approach to robust physical contact inflicting pain and distress,

[3] Case C-415/93 *Union Royal Belge des Sociétés de Football Association ASBL v Bosman* [1995] ECR I-4921; Case C-438/00 *Deutscher Handballbund eV v Kolpak* [2003] ECR I-4135.

[4] Case C-519/04P *Meca-Medina and Majcen v Commission* (2006) ECR I-6991 and also something noticeably a part of the recent, remarkably ill-tempered, disputes over the future of European rugby.

[5] *Cairns v Modi* [2012] EWCA Civ 1382, [2013] 1 WLR 1015, involving a £90,000 award for libel via *Twitter* and its subsequent fallout of a charge of perjury, see www.stuff.co.nz/sport/cricket/65142459/Chris-Cairns-pleads-not-guilty-to-perjury-charge; www.stuff.co.nz/sport/cricket/70670078/Former-Black-Cap-Chris-Cairns-a-no-show-for-London-perjury-hearing; and www.bbc.com/news/uk-34469658 'Chris Cairns trial: Former cricketer accused of perjury' www.theguardian.com/sport/2015/nov/30/chris-cairns-match-fixing-southwark-crown-court-new-zealand-cricket-acquitted.

[6] The order is named after the seminal case, *Norwich Pharmacal Co v Customs and Excise Commissioners* [1974] AC 133. Most recently discussed in relation to the sale of tickets for the Rugby World Cup in England.

a modicum of defamation and a soupçon of assault; what makes up a good game is, when looked at objectively, an almost unique combination of causes of action.[7] Yet, the courts have cheerfully accepted as a given the robust nature of sport, to the extent that the English courts have held that punching an opponent is so foreseeable a part of the occupation of a professional rugby player that it can incur vicarious liability for his employer.[8]

At common law, a player in a contact sport will not be liable for injury inflicted on another player so long as he is playing within the rules of the game. Foul play can lead to liability, as can reckless play even within the rules of the game in question; however, these are long-settled law, and cannot reasonably be viewed as part of a compensation culture. In respect of referees and/or governing bodies, the cases of *Smoldon*[9] and *Vowles*[10] are of particular interest. Both of these cases involved catastrophic spinal injuries sustained in a scrum. Both cases involved a player who was not well versed in playing in the front row of the scrum—in *Smoldon*, the plaintiff, in *Vowles*, the loose-head prop. In both cases there was a problem with a scrum and as a result the two young men suffered injuries to their spinal cord leading to paralysis. The decisions of the Court of Appeal in both cases throw a substantial amount of light on what exactly is the duty of care owed on the rugby pitch.

In *Smoldon*, the plaintiff was a 17-year-old back-row player who had never played in the front row. After an exceptionally long series of collapsed scrums which was at least partially due to the failure by the referee properly to enforce the laws relating to scrummaging, one scrum collapsed and the plaintiff, playing at hooker, suffered a broken neck. Bingham CJ stated clearly that injury is to be expected on the rugby pitch;[11] the mere fact that injury is to be expected in the normal course of the game, however, does not remove liability for any such injury negligently caused, nor does it remove from a referee the obligation correctly to enforce any law intended to minimise the risk of such an injury. The jurisprudence in relation to liability on the pitch was examined, and the Court held that the threshold for establishing negligence on the part of a referee—and *Smoldon* was the first such case to be dealt with—was contextual:

> The level of care required is that which is appropriate in all the circumstances, and the circumstances are of crucial importance. Full account must be taken of the factual context in which a referee exercises his functions, and he could not be properly held liable for errors of judgment, oversights or lapses of which any referee might be guilty in the context of a fast-moving and vigorous contest. The threshold of liability is a high one. It will not easily be crossed.[12]

The Court (Bingham CJ), after examining the laws of rugby and the directions given to referees by their governing bodies, directly held that one of the duties of a referee 'is to safeguard the safety of the players'. Crucially for the purposes of this discussion it was held

[7] Bingham CJ in *Smoldon v Whitworth & Anor* [1996] EWCA Civ 1225, [1997] ELR 249, 251—'Anyone participating in serious competitive games of rugby football must expect to receive his or her fair share of knocks, bruises, strains, abrasions and minor bony injuries'.

[8] *Gravil v Carroll & Redruth RFC* [2008] EWCA Civ 689, [2008] IRLR 829, [23] (Clarke MR)—'Regrettably the throwing of punches after the whistle could fairly be regarded as an ordinary incident of a rugby match'.

[9] *Smoldon* (n 7).

[10] *Vowles v Evans and the Welsh Rugby Union* [2003] EWCA Civ 318, [2003] 1 WLR 1607, [2002] EWHC 2612.

[11] *Smoldon* (n 7).

[12] Bingham CJ in *Smoldon* (n 7) 256.

that if serious harm was a foreseeable risk which certain laws were aimed at preventing, and if those laws were not enforced and the harm in question did occur, liability would ensue:

> If the second defendant were properly found to be in breach of his duty of care owed to the plaintiff by failing to take appropriate steps to prevent a collapse of the scrum, and if as a result of his failure a scrum did collapse and a player such as the plaintiff thereby suffered spinal injuries of the kind which the rules were designed to prevent, then in our judgment the second defendant would be liable in law for that foreseeable result of his breach of duty, despite the fact that (quantified statistically) it was a result which was very unlikely to eventuate.[13]

The fact that the plaintiff had consented to putting himself at risk of the very thing that had caused his injury was of no matter:

> The plaintiff had of course consented to the ordinary incidents of a game of rugby football of the kind in which he was taking part. Given, however, that the rules were framed for the protection of him and other players in the same position, he cannot possibly be said to have consented to a breach of duty on the part of the official whose duty it was to apply the rules and ensure so far as possible that they were observed.[14]

In *Vowles*, the plaintiff was badly injured in the engagement of the last scrum of a match between two local rivals, Tondu and Llanharan. Unlike the plaintiff in *Smoldon*, he was a hooker, properly trained and experienced as such. However, when a prop on his own side had gone off injured with no replacement available, a back-row forward had gone in as prop, thereby contributing to unstable and unsatisfactory scrums. The referee had not ordered uncontested scrums, as he could and should have done, to minimise the risk of having an untrained player in the front row, even though that untrained player volunteered to play there. Morland J held at first instance that:

> Mr Leighton Williams [for the Defendants] rightly submitted that the referee does not create the risk of injury but in my judgment insofar as he can stop that risk becoming a reality by appropriate application of the laws it is not unreasonable to expect him to do so.[15]

He went on to hold that:

> In my judgment as a matter of policy it is just and reasonable that the law should impose upon an amateur referee of an amateur rugby match a duty of care towards the safety of the players. Such a duty would be breached if the claimant established that the referee failed to take reasonable care for the safety of the players by sensible and appropriate application of the laws of rugby having regard to the context and circumstances of the game. I consider that the imposition of such a duty would be consistent with the spirit of the laws of rugby.[16]

The Court of Appeal agreed with *Smoldon* in stating that even where players voluntarily assumed a risk of such injury, the referee could still be liable for injury sustained as a result of a negligent failure to implement a law intended to protect such a player from a foreseeable risk.[17]

[13] Ibid, 257.

[14] Ibid, 264. This would appear to be the case even where it may be illegal but is ordinarily part of the game—*cf Gravil v Carroll & Redruth RFC* (n 8).

[15] *Vowles* (n 10) [29].

[16] Ibid, [42], relying on *Smoldon* (n 7); [34]–[41] of *Vowles*.

[17] *Vowles* (n 10) [25].

It should be noted that this is a general proposition of the law on the sports field. While it is freely accepted that rugby, as a collision sport, is possessed of risks that many others do not have, it must be accepted that, for example, hurling is hardly a risk-free game either. A referee can be expected to apply rules of the particular game which exist to further player safety, and to face liability if a player is injured as a result of his or her negligent failure so to do.

A failure to take reasonable steps to minimise the risk of the sport in question in the context of the laws of that sport at that time can attract liability. So, in *Watson v British Boxing Board of Control*,[18] where the defendant's failure to provide adequate ringside medical assistance in the aftermath of a notably fierce middleweight world title bout led to Michael Watson suffering brain injury, that failure to take the reasonable steps to make the sport safer within the rules as they stood was held to be a breach of the duty of care. However, a governing body will not be required to make a sport perfectly safe. So, in *Agar v Hyde*,[19] Australian rugby players who had suffered catastrophic neck injuries sued the governing body of rugby, the then International Rugby Football Board (IRFB)[20] for failing to institute rule changes that would, they argued, have made the game safer. They were unsuccessful, in part because of the then unincorporated nature of the IRFB and its then amateur members affecting the duty of care required, but also because a positive requirement to effect rule changes to make a game safer was felt to be a step too far. So, in the judgment of Gleeson CJ:

> Further, from the earliest times, the common law has drawn a distinction between a positive act causing damage and a failure to act which results in damage. The common law does not ordinarily impose a duty on a person to take action where no positive conduct of that person has created a risk of injury to another person. Here the appellants were members of the IRFB, an institution which 'saw itself as the law-giver for the sport of rugby'. *But they have done nothing that increased the risk of harm to either of the respondents.*[21] (emphasis added)

Thus, while personal injury claims are possible in sport, and do happen, they are significantly more difficult to get off the ground than the general run of such cases, both because of the nature of sport, and because of a general sympathy to sport in the courts towards the duties of organisers, especially amateurs who, if they are doing their reasonable best inside the laws or rules of their sport, have a significant chance of avoiding liability. The comment of Longmore LJ in *Sutton v Syston Rugby Football Club*[22] that 'the Court must not be too astute to impose duties of care which would make rugby playing as a whole more subject to interference from the Courts than it should be' may be taken as a fair reflection of the attitude of the courts to more marginal claims in a sporting arena. This has, in turn, received statutory support in Ireland.

[18] *Watson v. British Boxing Board of Control & Anor* [2000] EWCA Civ 2006 [2001] QB 1134

[19] *Agar v Hyde* [2000] HCA 41, 201 CLR 552.

[20] Now the International Rugby Board, the IRB.

[21] *Agar* (n 19) [68]–[69].

[22] *Sutton v Syston Rugby Football Club* [2011] EWCA Civ 1182, [18]. *cf*, as a recent example, *Hall v Thomas & Ors* [2014] EWHC 1625 (QB).

Statutory Changes

A significant, but little remarked, change was enacted in 2011. In the Civil Law (Miscellaneous Provisions) Act 2011, Part 3 changed liability in the arena to a quite astonishing extent. It consists of one section only, amending Part IV of the Civil Liability Act 1961. Under this amendment, a volunteer is defined as a person who does voluntary work—defined in turn as including 'any work or activity carried out for … (c) the purpose of sport or recreation', 'authorised by a volunteer organisation and does so without expectation of payment (other than reasonable reimbursement for expenses) or other reward'. A volunteer organisation is defined as 'any body (whether or not incorporated) that is not formed for profit and that authorises the doing of voluntary work whether or not as the principal purpose of the organisation'. As is apparent from this, almost all sporting bodies are volunteer organisations, and the overwhelming majority of all participants in all sport are volunteers.[23]

The effect of this is set out in section 51E inserted by this Act. Succinctly, but firmly, it places most sporting actions beyond the reach of litigation:

> 51E (1) A volunteer shall not be personally liable in negligence for any act done when carrying out voluntary work.
>
> (2) The protection from personal liability conferred on a volunteer by subsection (1) shall not apply to any act done by the volunteer if
>
> (*a*) the act was done by the volunteer in bad faith or with gross negligence, or
> (*b*) the volunteer knew or ought reasonably to have known that the act was
> (i) outside the scope of the voluntary work authorised by the volunteer organisation concerned, or
> (ii) contrary to the instructions of the volunteer organisation concerned.

Further, it then goes on to provide:

> 51F The protection from personal liability conferred on a good Samaritan by section 51D or a volunteer by section 51E is in addition to any protection from personal liability conferred on the good Samaritan or volunteer by or under any other enactment or rule of law.

The effect is clear. Bar bad faith, gross negligence or wilfully unauthorised activities, a person involved in any work or activity for the purpose of sport—which, under the heading of 'activity', one must assume participating in sporting activity itself is included—will not be liable for negligence. In short, a compensation culture in sport is, in an Irish context, a near impossibility, given the limitations placed on the range of possible actions. Any such action must not only be meritorious; in the context where gross negligence, bad faith, or going off on a frolic of one's own must be pleaded against the defendant, even to be able to plead these would require evidence on which these pleadings could be grounded. It is an enormous defence to sporting bodies against the threat of speculative personal injuries litigation against the actions of their volunteers where, as a matter of course, it is the body whose deeper pockets that plaintiff would seek to make vicariously liable.

[23] eg, in rugby, the highest profile professional sport in the State, there are some 200 professional rugby players employed in the State and Northern Ireland. They constitute less than 1% of the registered adult male rugby-playing population under the jurisdiction of the IRFU, North and South, of 25,000.

The organising bodies themselves are not afforded the protection of a gross-negligence threshold for liability to attach to their actions; but the Act does afford them another shield:

> 51G (1) This section applies to proceedings relating to the liability of a volunteer organisation for negligence arising from activities carried out by or on behalf of the organisation.
>
> (2) In any proceedings to which this section applies, when determining whether the volunteer organisation owed a duty of care to the plaintiff or any other person, a court shall consider whether it would be just and reasonable to find that the organisation owed such a duty having regard to the social utility of the activities concerned.
>
> (3) Nothing in this section shall operate to limit the matters that a court may consider, in proceedings to which this section applies, when determining whether a volunteer organisation owed a duty of care to a plaintiff or other person.

Significantly, this is not limited to voluntary work, but to activities carried out by or on behalf of a volunteer organisation; as activities are not limited in any manner, it would thus include professionals carrying out activities on behalf of a volunteer organisation. Thus, every activity carried out on behalf of a normal sporting governing body is covered by this section.

And, as a result, a new test is added in deciding if a duty of care was owed, that of whether it would be just and reasonable given the social utility of those activities. In the context of the provision of normal, amateur sporting activities, where such are of almost incalculable social utility and reliant on volunteers to exist, this will again weight the scales heavily against not just speculative, but normally meritorious actions, to the point where one would view it as almost requiring an arguable, if not quite prima facie, case to be pleaded rather than merely a stateable one.

Sporting bodies have been afforded defensive armour by this Act not lightly to be pierced. Most darts of a compensation culture aimed at such would merely clatter harmlessly away.[24]

Evidence of a Compensation Culture in Sport

One would assume that where it was felt necessary to legislate to such an extent to protect sport, that there would be weighty evidence of a pressing need for such dramatic protection. Surprisingly, the Explanatory Memorandum to the Bill that became the Act seems to make almost no reference to such in regard to sport—the word 'sport' being mentioned only once.[25]

This becomes less surprising when one looks at the Law Reform Commission Consultation Paper which was the genesis of this Part of the 2011 Act, *Civil Liability of Good Samaritans and Volunteers*.[26] As is clear from the Paper, this arose in the context of fears over potential liability for Good Samaritans intervening in emergencies. The Paper refers

[24] It should be noted that the relatively recent SARAH Act in the UK seems to have very similar provisions (Social Action, Responsibility and Heroism Act 2015, c.3).

[25] www.oireachtas.ie/documents/bills28/bills/2011/2911/B2911s.pdf.

[26] LRC CP 47/ 2007 (hereafter, the Paper). This chapter does not seek to address the recent SARAH Act in the UK, save to note that not only is it seemingly the first example of legislation by acronym, but is an example of the problem in a wider context of an extreme nature, www.publications.parliament.uk/pa/ld201415/ldhansrd/text/150106-0001.htm#15010644000364.

to sporting bodies as volunteer organisations in a list including 'voluntary public hospitals, major sporting organisations (such as the GAA or the Special Olympics), church-based institutions, credit unions, political parties, employer organisations, trade unions, major organisations supporting those with limited intellectual capacity and educational institutions',[27] but is clear that this is merely one, small, category. In the analysis of Volunteer Service Providers in Chapter 3,[28] sport and sporting bodies are not mentioned at all. Significantly, so firmly was this Paper centred on the Good Samaritan provision in which it had its origin and which is also included in Part 3 of the Act, that no sporting body even made submissions on the subject. It seems a fair inference that this is not indicative of a pressing need for protection against a wave of baseless litigation; there is no reference whatsoever to such in the context of sport in the Paper.

The parliamentary debates are somewhat more enlightening, but not noticeably so. The Bill commenced in the Seanad.[29] In the debate there, while considerable reference was made to the Good Samaritan element of Part 2 of the Bill, only one speaker directly raised the point about sporting bodies,[30] and it was answered, in one sentence, that it was understood that sporting bodies were organisations.[31] No reference to a pressing need to fend off a wave of litigation in sport was made at this stage, or the Committee Stage.[32] When it first reached the Dáil, it may fairly be said that sport did not feature as a topic of scrutiny of Part 3 at all.

As to wider evidence—even on which to establish a comparative basis on whether there is an over-eagerness to sue sporting bodies—this is difficult to come by. There are several reasons why this is so. First, the bodies themselves do not appear to keep significant records of the number of times they are sued.[33] Second, other sources of data are fuzzy at best. One may attempt an approximation based on the number of times a given sporting body appears as a defendant in a personal injury list; this is, however, no real indicator as to truly sporting-related cases, as it would include road traffic accidents where the body may be vicariously or personally liable, construction accidents in the building of clubhouses, workplace accidents, and other incidents which are entirely unrelated to the sporting character of the body as opposed to the normal course of life in a litigious country.

Significantly, one reference was made by Senator Jillian van Turnhout:

> I am involved in several voluntary organisations and I have noted an undue expectation of a duty of care. This may arise where, as a result of an accident, a case is brought against an individual or an organisation by a concerned parent. The problem is that the insurance companies will urge organisations to settle before it goes to court, thereby not allowing the courts to intervene as is

[27] Ibid, 1.64, 22.

[28] Ibid, 3.99 ff, 89–106.

[29] www.oireachtas.ie/viewdoc.asp?fn=/documents/bills28/bills/2011/2911/document1.htm.

[30] Senator Michael Mullins: 'I wish to pick up on two points. First, I greatly welcome the proposed Good Samaritan provision and it is right and proper for it to be enshrined in legislation. Will GAA clubs and other sporting organisations be regarded as organisations covered under this Bill?'.

[31] Alan Shatter TD: 'Senator Mullins asked if the legislation will cover GAA clubs. Organisations—which GAA clubs are—engaging in volunteer work are, as I understand, volunteers within the definitional provision in the legislation'.

[32] debates.oireachtas.ie/seanad/2011/07/05/00008.asp.

[33] Private enquiries made of the IRFU. A search of the courts, ie, High Court Search facility as of 31 July 2015 (the end of the legal year) showed only one personal injury case live against the IRFU.

> proposed in this Bill. This results in an increase in insurance costs for the voluntary organisations. I can provide examples of where this has happened.[34]
>
> In that regard, one must turn to the Paper, where it refers to the provisions of the UK Compensation Act: 1.108 The Compensation Act 2006 was enacted as a response to the concern that the UK was succumbing to a 'compensation culture'. *Although this concern was criticised as unfounded, it was acknowledged that the mere perception was having disastrous effects.*[35] The Commission notes that the 2006 Act has been criticised for confusing the situation, by doing no more than restating the current common law approach in the UK, and by introducing the ambiguous term 'desirable activity'[36] (emphasis added).

It would therefore appear that the reason sport and sporting bodies obtained the significant protection of the 2011 Act was on the basis not of data, but of anecdote at best, and that not from the sporting area.[37] If reason there was, it was not that there was a risk of litigation but an unfounded fear of it. So far as one can tell, that fear of litigation is not supported by evidence for it.

Compensation Culture: Is Sport Spooked?

That does not, of course, mean that the fear itself is not real. Unfounded it may be, but it exists generally. And it exists in a sporting context, too.

To take one iconic image of an Irish sporting summer, the invasion of a GAA pitch at the final whistle by the jubilant supporters of a successful county. It is now banned at Croke Park, the GAA's headquarters; supporters are now herded away from pitches on the basis of a fear of the GAA being sued for trip and fall accidents, despite the protection afforded by common law, the 1995 Occupiers' Liability Act and the 2011 Act. Indeed, so firmly has this trope of pitch invasions meaning court cases settled into the national psyche, that the GAA sought legislation to ban pitch invasions even after the existing legislation that afforded it such protection was enacted—and seemingly in ignorance of the 2011 Act.[38] This recently reached a new pitch where it was reported in the media that there were claims taken against

[34] oireachtasdebates.oireachtas.ie/debates%20authoring/debateswebpack.nsf/takes/seanad2011063000008?opendocument.

[35] *cf* the comments of Baroness Ashton introducing the Compensation Bill to the House of Lords that it was at least in part to 'tackle perceptions that can lead to a disproportionate fear of litigation and risk averse behaviour': webarchive.nationalarchives.gov.uk/+/http://www.dca.gov.uk/legist/compensation_wms_lords.pdf. Apparently, one must now legislate for fear of fear itself; one cannot but wonder what FDR would make of it.

[36] Paper, 40.

[37] For an analogous situation in relation to the origins of the Occupiers Liability Act, see 'The Lobby is Marshalled' in BME McMahon and W Binchy, *Law of Torts*, 4th edn (Dublin, Bloomsbury Professional, 2013) 12.61-2, 444–45. *cf* the report of Lord Young of Graffham, *Common Safety, Common Sense*, where the notion of compensation culture was stated as being one 'more of perception than reality', born of the fertile imaginations of the media. Significantly, it notes at p 24 that the Lord Chief Justice had never seen cases of the type that were discussed at length as risks in the Oireachtas debates on the 2011 Act, www.gov.uk/government/uploads/system/uploads/attachment_data/file/60905/402906_CommonSense_acc.pdf.

[38] www.independent.ie/sport/gaelic-football/gaa-to-seek-legislation-to-ban-pitch-invasions-26529540.html; the GAA's report for 2011 refers to the necessity to ban pitch invasions, but makes no reference whatsoever, oblique or direct, to the protections of the 2011 Act, www.gaa.ie/content/documents/publications/annual_reports/2011_GAA_Annual_Report_Congress.pdf.

the GAA over a pitch invasion after the 2013 Munster hurling final at the Gaelic Grounds in Limerick;[39] these reports were rapidly shown to be urban legend,[40] yet not only were these repeated by the Limerick County Secretary as fact, but were included in the annual report of the Limerick County Board and used as evidence of the risks of pitch invasions by the head of the GAA itself.[41] One could hardly wish for a more perfect demonstration of the fear of a compensation culture being on the wing despite not a breath of fact under it.[42]

However, here we see an interesting departure for sport; unfounded fear, repeated often enough, becomes so firmly entrenched in the mind of those engaged in and running that sport as a real threat that no evidence will shift it, with the result that rule changes to important elements of that sport's culture are proposed to deal with this phantom. It is not compensation culture itself; there are no actual compensation claims, or none above the normal incidents of a robust society. It is a *fear* of a perceived wider compensation culture, leading to effects on the sport. As Williams notes:

> The fact that there may be no objective proof that we live in an increasingly 'blame and sue' society is beside the point when an 'urban myth' to the contrary is said to have taken hold. Thus, whatever the actual likelihood of being the target of litigation, many increasingly believe themselves to be at heightened risk of being unfairly sued.[43]

The Availability Heuristic: A Possible Mechanism?

To examine this further, one must suggest a mechanism as to how this happens. This chapter would suggest as such the 'availability heuristic'.[44] The availability heuristic is one of a group of similar cognitive biases (which may conveniently be thought of as rules of thumb for thinking) that lead one incorrectly to calculate the risks involved in a course of action.

In the case of the availability heuristic, it is the process where one assumes that the risk of something which one can readily call to mind, or which one hears about despite it being rare, is significantly higher than is actually the case. For example, one hears about almost every fatal shark attack on a human, so that is perceived as being a real risk; yet one is actually more at risk of death from debris falling from aircraft.[45] So, one high-profile case in exceptional circumstances where a referee is successfully sued can lead to a fear that there is a real risk that *all* referees will be sued. Further, a general *belief* that a course of action will lead to being sued, *even if this is not the case*, can easily be called to mind, and will lead to an overstatement of the probability of being sued. In other words, a *perception* of

[39] www.irishexaminer.com/sport/gaa/personal-injury-claims-after-limerick-pitch-invasion-253261.html.

[40] www.irishexaminer.com/sport/gaa/hurling/no-injury-claims-from-pitch-invasion-255634.html.

[41] www.limerickleader.ie/news/local-news/pitch-invasion-ban-presents-own-risks-1-5820616.

[42] See in this regard the comments of Lord Dyson, reported in J Hyde, 'Compensation Culture is "Media-Created" Myth -Dyson' [2013] *Law Society Gazette*, 25 March (available at www.lawgazette.co.uk/70091.article).

[43] K Williams, 'Politics, the Media and Refining the Notion of Fault: Section 1 of the Compensation Act 2006' [2006] *Journal of Personal Injury Law* 347, 348.

[44] See A Tversky and D Kahneman, 'Availability: A Heuristic for Judging Frequency and Probability' (1973) 5 *Cognitive Psychology* 207; G Gigerenzer and C Engel, *Heuristics and the Law* (Cambridge MA, MIT Press, 2006).

[45] See Tversky and Kahneman (n 44); Gigerenzer and Engel (n 44).

a compensation culture can lead to easily thought of examples where one was sure that a given course would lead to being sued, and steps then being taken to avoid something where the risk was minimal. This, it is suggested, fits perfectly with the analysis noted above from other jurisdictions as to the influence of reporting, in that one report makes it so much easier for so many more to call a reported instance to mind, and thereby overestimate the chances of it occurring in the future.

The perfect example of this is the GAA sued-for-a-pitch-invasion example given above; it never happened, but because the trope that it was bound to happen made it so easy to call to mind the belief that it would happen, those involved appear to have convinced themselves that it did happen because 'everyone knows' this litigation happens. After all, no smoke without fire one tells oneself, and one acts accordingly; even if that smoke turns out to be just hot air. So, GAA fans are now penned in the stands instead of being allowed onto the pitch after a game.

Another example is the perception that playgrounds for children are falling victim to litigation. In *Ahmed (A Minor) v Longford County Council*[46] the Supreme Court dismissed a claim arising out of an accident in a Longford playground. Causation was somewhat unclear, but it was common cause that the seat of the swing from which the infant plaintiff fell, breaking a leg, was 20mm too low. At the initial hearing, de Valera J had held he was "satisfied that the defendants in this case were not negligent, they took all appropriate steps in designing, in manufacturing, if that's the correct word, or having built for them and in subsequently supervising the use of this particular facility. You can't avoid accidents to children, I know this as a fact, it just can't be done".[47]

He further held that he was satisfied that there was no link between the deviation from standards and the accident. Even assuming for the sake of argument that to have a swing that low was negligent, Clarke J in the Supreme Court noted the deviation from standard was small, and that even counsel for the plaintiff accepted that a balance was to be struck between safety and letting children play freely, and further noted that the plaintiff had used the swing in question before, including on the day, going on to hold that

> [i]n those circumstances it necessarily follows that there must have been something different about the way in which he was positioned on the swing when he fell as opposed to all previous occasions (including the earlier part of his use of the swing on the day in question) when no such problem had arisen. The real question on causation which arises is as to whether, as a matter of probability, an extra 4/5 of an inch would have made any difference on the day in question.[48]

The Court was satisfied there was not, and dismissed the appeal. One would suggest that between the initial decision and that of the Supreme Court, one might reasonably view this as evidence not of a successful compensation culture, but an approval of a robust common sense to be applied to the nature of children's play, and indicative of a wider view. Yet that this *is* at the very least arguably the view of the courts is something one will search for in vain in the popular press or public opinion, where the perception remains unshifted.

To move to another example, these misplaced fears arising from perceptions can in fact create just the risks that they are supposed to address.

[46] *Ahmed (A Minor) v Longford County Council* [2014] IESC 46.
[47] Ibid, [2.3], quoted by Clarke J in the Supreme Court.
[48] Ibid, [5.9].

Suing and the Scrum

Rugby, as a collision sport, carries with it the inherent dangers noted in *Smoldon*. Arguably, half the fun of the game is summed up in the line from *Lawrence of Arabia* that the trick isn't that it doesn't hurt, it's not minding that it hurts.[49] One of the consequences of full-bore contact aiming to drive the opposition backwards is not just that it hurts, but that it risks leaving you hurt. Scrummaging, for example, has innate risks implicit when one 900kg group of eight tries to push the other backwards on often wet and muddy ground. Surprisingly, the risks have shifted so that roughly half of all catastrophic injuries now happen in the tackle, instead of the scrum.[50]

That scrum injuries are more likely to go terribly wrong instead of just wrong, means that the scrum has been most targeted by the lawmakers in the game. Well and good; anything that makes for safer scrums while not affecting scrummaging is to be welcomed.[51] To that end, there are rules for under-age players who are still learning the skills of scrummaging, aimed at protecting them while they learn and before they go on to playing the game properly. These under-19 laws restrict the amount a scrum can turn, or the distance it can be pushed, making pushover tries impossible. In effect, a full scrummaging contest is sacrificed for the safety of the inexperienced.[52]

Yet the perception of risk of litigation has led to the introduction of the under-age scrummaging rules for adult players in Ireland. Given just how much this affects the game for forwards—eight of the 15 players in a team—it has, effectively, drastically altered the playing of the game for a majority of adult rugby players in Ireland. When full scrummaging dominance is no longer a game winner, there's no reason to seek to win the game through the scrum, or even pick a player who can give you that dominance. Scrummagers go the way of the battleship; formerly unquestioned, now obsolete. Moreover, since, as was once remarked, 'weight is only of intrinsic value in the design of a steamroller',[53] the notion so valued in rugby that there is a valuable place for the less athletic player is also lost. Because of *Smoldon* and *Whitworth*—two cases hedged with caveats, which stressed that they were exceptional in the circumstances involved—it is easy to call to mind examples of litigation from the scrum, so, the likelihood of that is overstated, and restrictions fundamentally altering a key part of a game are imposed.

[49] Horizon Pictures, 1962. One should note at this juncture that Peter O'Toole was well-known for his love of rugby.

[50] www.bjjprocs.boneandjoint.org.uk/content/94-B/SUPP_XXXIX/250.short; www.rfu.com/managingrugby/firstaid/injuries/~/media/files/2009/firstaid/citg%20report.ashx; www.ncbi.nlm.nih.gov/pmc/articles/PMC2907385/. Even allowing for the caveats of the lower number of scrums suggesting a potentially higher risk, the scrum does not seem to be the most dangerous facet of play—www.ncbi.nlm.nih.gov/pubmed/17513332/. Anecdotally, well-known players such as Tom Croft of England, Joe Ansbro of Scotland, Pat McCabe of Australia have all suffered broken necks in the 2013–14 season in legal tackles; Ansbro and, ultimately, McCabe had to retire as a result.

[51] See, eg, the recent moves to reduce the initial impact as the two scrums come together—the 'hit'—and thereby reduce collapsed scrums, www.irb.com/newsmedia/mediazone/pressrelease/newsid=2068584.html#irb+referees+ready+scrum+trial+debut.

[52] For an example of a graduated, stepping-stone approach, see the South African version at www.sharksmart.co.za/documents/SARUScrumLawModificationsForSAAmateurRugby-2013.pdf.

[53] Attributed to Uffa Fox, the great sailing designer.

Paradoxically, this can be dangerous. Prior to this, an adult player in the second team of a club would have graduated from underage play and have learnt to scrummage fully and safely, capable of playing at the level to which his or her talent could reach. Now, subsequent to this change, an adult player in the second team of a normal junior rugby club will never have scrummaged fully. If his or her club suffers an injury crisis, and he or she is called up to the first team, he or she will be playing full scrummaging rules when he or she is neither trained not experienced in those rules. Here one has an example of how a misguided fear induces a rule change in a sport which turns what would, without that rule change, have been the normal course of sport in a club into a genuinely risky situation, one on all fours with that in *Smoldon*.

Even more astonishingly, as this level of rugby is entirely amateur, it would attract the protection of the 2011 Act. It is unnecessary in terms of protection from litigation, it is unnecessary in terms of player protection as the South African example with its more graduated progression shows, yet the *fear* and the perceptual biases caused by the availability heuristic ensure it stays as it is.

Missing the Open Goal

A worse effect yet is where concerns of safety are used as a reasoning for law changes in a sport when real evidence of risk is absent. One thinks, for example, of a recent controversy in hurling, where efforts to restrict the free-taking style of Cork goalkeeper, Anthony Nash, were made on suggestions that otherwise danger will arise from players wearing helmets being less than 20 metres from a ball struck at high speed; yet the fact is that close-in fielders in cricket, with a similar ball, face balls driven at high speed all the time with minimal incidents of injury.[54] At this juncture, one might wonder if misplaced fears of risk of litigation, and the sporting urge to outlaw what one cannot stop, walk hand-in-hand.

However, there are cases where real risks of personal injury arising from breach of duty arise, and yet do not give rise to waves of compensation cases. This chapter would argue that concussion in rugby is one such example. Rugby, in some regards, is a leader in the field of concussion management. It will not be surprising that it has been New Zealand, and the New Zealand Rugby Union (NZRU) that has been leading the way. The history of pitch-side concussion management by the NZRU dates back to 2001, with the introduction by the NZRU of their RugbySmart concussion management programme, including compulsory education and the use of cards for pitch-side management that are in many regards the forerunner of the modern Pocket SCAT card. It was a notable, and immediate success, so much so that it was rapidly adopted as best practice by the Australian Rugby Union (ARU) in its SmartRugby scheme, the South African Rugby Union in its BokSmart scheme and the English Rugby Football Union (RFU). In all cases, and in a manner deserving of note and praise, the NZRU assisted in setting up the schemes and shared its expertise and resources.

[54] The tragic death of Phillip Hughes, the Australian batsman, occurred when the ball hit below the back of his helmet and was from a ball bowled from the other end of the pitch—20 metres away.

A comprehensive study was conducted in New Zealand to examine the results of this management scheme. New Zealand, by happy coincidence, was the perfect location for this, in that not only has it a very large sample size of rugby players of all ages, it also has its no-fault compensation ACC model. Due to this, the number of days lost from work and the amount of compensation paid to those who had lost time due to concussion and other injuries could accurately be recorded. The results were unequivocal: the concussion management system showed an improvement in the incidence and severity of concussions.[55] It made the game safer for players without affecting the game.

Influenced by this, the second Zurich Consensus (so-called as it is the consensus statement on the subject of the expert conference in Zurich in November 2008) endorsed the approach which led to the Sports Concussion Assessment Tool 2 (SCAT2) and Pocket SCAT2 cards for use in concussion assessment. The governing body of rugby, then the IRB,[56] was represented at the conference by Dr Mick Molloy, Chief Medical Officer of the IRB and former second-row partner for Ireland of Willie John McBride, and the IRB logo appeared on the SCAT2 and Pocket SCAT2 from the start. From this point on in 2008, there was an awareness on the part of the governing body of best practice, and a means whereby the medical care could be provided without unreasonably affecting the sport. It is argued, therefore, that this would attract liability for the failure to implement those policies.

Yet, tragically, rugby did not begin to take active steps to enforce those polices until after concussion had killed a young player, Benjamin Robinson. There were many other high-profile incidents, including French player Morgan Parra being concussed twice in the Rugby World Cup final in 2011; several incidents involving Brian O'Driscoll of Ireland; George Smith of Australia in the Lions series in 2013; and, worst, an incident involving Florian Fritz of Stade Toulousain in 2014. In each of these, a clearly concussed player was returned to play in breach of the regulations of the game made for player safety—which, in the light of *Smoldon* and *Vowles*, one can clearly see would raise issues with regard to liability for professional players, and possibly, it being in breach of the regulations made for player safety, at amateur level in Ireland and many other jurisdictions. Yet, because there have been so few cases taken in respect of concussion injuries in rugby, it has taken these high-profile incidents and litigation in the US in respect of concussion injuries in American Football for the first steps to be taken in respect of enforcement and education of the requirements made for player safety. Concussion education programmes are now being rolled out in all major rugby playing nations; the Fritz incident was the subject of a formal investigation by the French Rugby Federation, reporting to the IRB.

Here, one would argue, is the perfect case where if there were a compensation culture in sport in Ireland, one would have seen a flood of cases already; instead, there has been only one high-profile such case in Ireland, and that an assessment. A real risk, and a real source of potential liability, failed to lead to a wave of litigation because there had not yet been the reporting needed for those in the game to call to mind examples that would allow them to consider concussion a real locus of liability. A lack of fear of a real peril has led to possible damage being caused to players—and possibly to a death.

[55] See S Gianotti and PA Hume, 'Concussion Sideline Management Intervention for Rugby Union Leads to Reduced Concussion Claims' (2007) 22 *Neurorehabilitation* 181.

[56] Now renamed 'World Rugby'.

Conclusion

There are very significant protections for sport against personal injury claims in this jurisdiction; arguably, there are considerably more such than the evidence suggests are needed. There is little evidence of a compensation culture in sport here, or, indeed, elsewhere. Yet a misplaced fear of litigation exists, and, at least at anecdotal level, is a primary driver of rule change and rule enforcement in one of the more innately dangerous major sports. The mechanism by which this happens, relying as it does not on statistical evidence of claims made or risk exposure but on the ease with which incidents can be called to the minds of those in the game, raises a question as to whether legislation can address even the misplaced fears of compensation culture when the changes of the 2011 Act appear to have gone so unremarked. The long, unglamorous grind of education may be of more effect in the long term; in the meantime, sporting bodies might do worse than to hold their nerve against the headline induced jitters.

INDEX

www.ingramcontent.com/pod-product-compliance
Ingram Content Group UK Ltd.
Pitfield, Milton Keynes, MK11 3LW, UK
UKHW051449290926
15471UKWH00008B/1105